RICHARD WAGNER AND HIS WORLD

THE BARD MUSIC FESTIVAL
A list of titles in this series appears at the back of the book.

RICHARD WAGNER
AND HIS WORLD

EDITED BY THOMAS S. GREY

PRINCETON UNIVERSITY PRESS
PRINCETON AND OXFORD

Copyright © 2009 by Princeton University Press

Published by Princeton University Press, 41 William Street,
Princeton, New Jersey 08540
In the United Kingdom: Princeton University Press,
6 Oxford Street, Woodstock, Oxfordshire OX20 1TW

All Rights Reserved

For permissions information, see page xv

Library of Congress Control Number 2009926766

ISBN: 978-0-691-14365-1 (cloth)
ISBN: 978-0-691-14366-8 (paperback)

British Library Cataloging-in-Publication Data is available

This publication has been produced by the Bard College Publications Office:

Ginger Shore, Consultant

Natalie Kelly, Designer

Text edited by Paul De Angelis and Erin Clermont

Music typeset by Don Giller

This publication has been underwritten in part by a grant from
Furthermore: a program of the J. M. Kaplan Fund.

Printed on acid-free paper. ∞

press.princeton.edu

Printed in the United States of America

1 3 5 7 9 10 8 6 4 2

Contents

PART III
TOWARD A MUSIC OF THE FUTURE, 1840–1860

PART IV
WAGNER AND PARIS

PART V
THE BAYREUTH ERA

Contents

Preface and Acknowledgments

It would be difficult to point to another figure in the history of Western music who was as comprehensively involved with the larger "world" about him than Richard Wagner, or whose impact was felt throughout so many varied domains in his lifetime and for long after. Wagner's intensive involvement in the music, the arts, and ideas of his century is witnessed in the famously vast bibliography that has grown up around him, and of course no single volume can hope to encompass the whole range of his musical and cultural legacy. That legacy seems to remain, for the time being, nearly inexhaustible, and Wagner's many-faceted career provides an ideal object for a book series examining composers in the context of their life and times by means of critical essays and annotated historical documents. While the life, in Wagner's case, ends in 1883, his "times" are interpreted more freely in this volume as extending up to or beyond the turn of the twentieth century. As with his Italian counterpart, Giuseppe Verdi, who was born in the same year (1813) and who outlived him by almost twenty years, Wagner's "world" was that of the nineteenth century as a whole. The controversial prestige of Wagner the *Gesamtkünstler* or "total-artist" reached a high-water mark with the founding of the Bayreuth Festival in 1876, which featured the premiere of the most ambitious operatic undertaking of the century, the epic tetralogy *Der Ring des Nibelungen*. With the quasi-sacral "consecration" of this festival endeavor in the premiere of *Parsifal* in 1882, near the end of Wagner's life, the range of his cultural ambition extended even further, and for at least another quarter of a century the momentum of "Wagnerism" as an artistic and ideological phenomenon seemed almost unstoppable. Hence, while the material of the present volume focuses largely on the life, work, and immediate context of the composer himself, it also extends into the early twentieth century and addresses other issues of interpretation, aesthetics, and performance that are not historically delimited.

Since Wagner insisted so volubly on the larger national, indeed worldwide cultural significance of his musical dramas, conceived ultimately as a modern answer to the mythic tragedies of ancient Greece, and since he himself published on almost every conceivable subject, writing about Wagner has often tended to overlook his specifically musical achievements in favor of his broader "messages" and ideas. The present volume attempts to address the whole range of his activities—musical, theatrical, critical, polemical—without, of course, pretending to cover them all equally or fully. Karol Berger's "Note on Tristan's Death-Wish" is the only essay here to address one specific work, though it does address that work as a paradigm, of sorts, of Wagner's musical-dramatic enterprise generally, that is, of Wagner's passionate belief in the "redeeming" power of the musical-dramatic work of art. Lydia Goehr, by contrast, addresses issues pertaining to the entire oeuvre through the contested question of what the works are to be called—operas, music dramas, or something else? The concern of Wagner and his contemporaries for the naming of new genres and practices, as Goehr demonstrates, is reflected in concerns thematized by his own characters such as Lohengrin or Hans Sachs. The essay touching most directly on the actual notes of Wagner's scores does so, appropriately, in a manner mediated by the world around him, specifically, through the numerous arrangements or transcriptions of Wagner's music made by his friend and advocate Franz Liszt, as well as the subtler traces of a musical dialogue one might discern in the compositions of these two friends, especially in the 1850s. These "Elective Affinities" described by Kenneth Hamilton are reflected, too, in the influential essay on Wagner's *Tannhäuser* published by Liszt in the early stages of their friendship, excerpted in Part III of this volume with commentary by David Trippett.

The "combined" or "total artwork" advocated in Wagner's theoretical writings from the time he was conceiving the *Ring* cycle has often been thought of as necessarily the work of single artistic mastermind: poet, composer, designer, director, and conductor all in one. Wagner did participate in most of these roles, if not in all of them equally. At the same time, this unusual degree of "multitasking," as we might put it today, required Wagner to engage in the same collaborative networks as would any opera composer of his day, indeed more intensively so, given the scope of his artistic ambitions. Such interaction of creative and collaborative work is demonstrated in Katherine Syer's study of Wagner as stage-director or *Regisseur* of his own dramas.

The concept of opera as a "stage festival" in the spirit of ancient Greek tragedy invited (or demanded?) a new level of attention or aesthetic participation on the part of the audience; they, too, had a part in this collaboration. Since the early days of opera it had been customary to provide audiences with texts of the libretto (a practice revived only recently in the form of projected supertitles). The system of associative musical themes or motives, or "leitmotifs," made famous by Hans von Wolzogen's musically illustrated handbooks (*Leitfäden*) to the *Ring* cycle and other Wagner operas, initiated a new level in the "aesthetic education" of the opera audience. This process is described in Christian Thorau's essay on these "Guides for Wagnerites," publications that combined the qualities of the traditional hymnal or prayer-book with the modern touristic guidebook.

A notable consequence of Wagner's involvement with the political and social world about him was his long period of exile from the federated German states following his implication in the socialist uprising in Dresden in May 1849. A little over a year later he published his provocative denunciation of "Judaism in Music," initiating the most lasting and controversial aspect of his social-political legacy. Between the time of the first, pseudonymous publication of the "Judaism" article in 1850 and its republication under Wagner's own name in 1869, he had also started to become associated with a new German "national" identity, cultural as well as political. For Wagner, this identity was intimately bound up with personal antagonism toward those "foreign" cultures closest to hand and hence most implicated in the definition of the "German," namely the French and the Jews. The dynamic of a love-hate relationship is evident on all sides of this triangle of Wagner, the French, and the Jews, as illustrated in my essay on Wagner's polemical wartime satire *Eine Kapitulation*, and in Leon Botstein's analysis of German-Jewish musicians in the era of European "Wagnerism."

Wagner's fame in his own day ensured that his career was exceptionally well documented. Indeed, Wagner's sense of his own importance has vouchsafed us an ample documentary record, for example in the form of several autobiographical works, ten volumes of collected writings (not counting posthumously published texts), and a vast quantity of letters (the ongoing critical edition of these has accumulated eighteen substantial volumes and only reached the year 1866, leaving sixteen very busy years yet to fill). Reviews, articles, and monographs on Wagner as composer, theorist, and cultural phenomenon reached legendary proportions even in his lifetime. For all that, there is still much primary material that remains either unpublished, untranslated, or out of print.

The documentary materials collected in Parts II through VI of this volume present a cross section of such sources. Franz Liszt's early and influential appreciation of *Tannhäuser* published in the Parisian *Journal des débats* in 1849, for instance, was the first piece of significant international media acclaim enjoyed by Wagner. In various revisions and translations it became, along with a companion essay on *Lohengrin*, one of the most widely read accounts of the composer in his lifetime. The translation presented here in Part III reached readers in Boston as early as 1853 (although there is no English translation currently in print of either of Liszt's essays). The *Revue wagnérienne* published in Paris between 1885 and 1888 is among the most famous documents of Wagner's European cultural impact, representing his founding role in the aesthetics of French modernism as formulated by the Symbolist school of poets under the influence of

Baudelaire. The three samples offered in Part IV of this volume provide a glimpse of this major document of "Wagnerism" and early literary modernism still unavailable in any complete modern edition either in French or English. Another celebrated Parisian episode in the history of Wagner's career was the abortive production of *Tannhäuser* which he hoped would launch a new phase of his international celebrity in 1861 (it did at least advance the cause of his notoriety). Original documentation of this episode remains scarce, however. The two reviews included here give a taste of the cultural politics and latent national tensions of this critical moment, also the time when Baudelaire encountered Wagner's music.

In the native German sphere of Wagner's activity—places such as Dresden, Leipzig, Vienna, and Bayreuth—his path to fame was smoother, but hardly uncontested. In Part V, the two short *feuilleton* pieces by his most formidable critical opponent, Eduard Hanslick, represent the considerable opposition Wagner's claims to reform the essence of music, drama, and society continued to arouse even after he had established himself as the most visible icon of modern German culture with the first Bayreuth Festivals of 1876 and 1882. These claims go back to his writings from the early years of his political exile in Switzerland, around 1850, but they were also given significant external stimulus when the critic and historian Franz Brendel declared Wagner a lynchpin in a "New German School" of music in his address to the Leipzig Tonkünstler-Versammlung (Musician's Assembly) of 1859—another frequently cited text hitherto unavailable in a complete translation. Brendel's address (Part III) responded to ongoing debates over the concept of a "music of the future," debates that constitute a key episode in the formation of modernist and avant-garde discourses that continued to dominate Western culture for over a century. Johann Christian Lobe's "Letters to a Young Musician about Richard Wagner" from 1854–55 illustrate the attempt of a musically literate critic and pedagogue to negotiate the specific musical and aesthetic challenges of this "new music" in the early years of these debates (also Part III).

Issues in the performance of Wagner's operas are represented in early as well as later stages of his career. Details of his autobiographical claims about the impact of the dramatic singer Wilhelmine Schröder-Devrient on his first ambitions to compose opera are in some crucial respects lacking in documentary support. Original accounts of her included in Part II of this volume allow us, at any rate, to evaluate Wagner's impressions of this influential singer against those of his contemporaries, and indeed against her own biography. At the other end of his life Wagner was at pains to establish "model performances" of his music dramas and even some kind of "school" of Wagnerian singing and acting in Bayreuth. After his death, his indomitable widow Cosima made it her mission to carry on this project, and the documentation of the Festival performances she directed in the later years of the century, reaching into the early years of sound recording, provide an important link between Wagner's own activity as director and producer and the subsequent history of Wagner performance in the twentieth century. The Bayreuth enterprise involved a dedicated school of Wagnerian criticism and interpretation, well represented by the prolific acolyte Hans von Wolzogen ("*Parsifal* Criticism") and it witnessed, too, aspects of the dawning of a new era of cultural media relations, as suggested by the series of "press releases" about the first Festival, also included in Part V.

While Cosima Wagner left a definitive account of Wagner's daily life during his later years in the diaries she kept between 1869 and 1883 (first released for publication in the 1970s), it is interesting to have an outside perspective on the composer's domestic sphere. The selections included in Part II from memoirs by French writer Catulle Mendès and the Wagners' American acquaintance Newell Sill Jenkins confirm the picture of the composer's character and manners we know from his wife, but in a slightly different accent and allowing a different range of observations.

The final group of documents, in Part VI, is drawn directly from Wagner's own (mostly) published writings: short accounts of his own works programmed in concert performances, as well as the works of Beethoven he was most closely associated with as a conductor. While some of these are well known, such as his program for Beethoven's Ninth Symphony or those in which he describes the overtures to *Der fliegende Holländer* and *Tannhäuser*, many others have not been translated before. As a group they offer a valuable glimpse into Wagner's activity as a conductor and as his own concert impresario, and also into fundamental issues of musical style, influence, and interpretation. Furthermore, the inclusion of these assorted "program notes" by Wagner seems like an appropriate tribute to the Bard Music Festival's distinguished legacy in bringing together performance, criticism, and historical scholarship over the past twenty years.

The books of essays and historical documents published annually in conjunction with the Bard Music Festival have tended to expand in size over recent years, and it is perhaps no surprise that the present collection devoted to the subject of Richard Wagner has pushed this length to the limits of the possible. For accommodating this abundance of material and helping see it through to publication on the tight production schedule required by this series I am extremely grateful to Paul De Angelis; his expert advice and tireless assistance throughout the process of compiling, organizing, and editing the contents of this book have been invaluable. Much thanks is also owed to Erin Clermont and Natalie Kelly for their quick and careful assistance in copy-editing, design, and proof stages; to Don Giller for the meticulous setting of musical examples (including some long and fairly complicated ones); and to both Ginger Shore, consultant to the Bard Publications Office, and Irene Zedlacher, executive director of the Bard Music Festival, for the continuing excellence of their oversight of this valuable publication series.

The value of these books depends ultimately, of course, on the contributors of the essays and of the introductions, translations, and annotations of the assorted documentary texts; so I am above all grateful to the many individuals who were willing to contribute and able to meet the tight deadlines imposed. In addition, I would like to thank Stewart Spencer for his advice in the early stages of this project and for providing a copy of a chapter from the privately published memoirs of Newell Sill Jenkins included in Part II. I am very grateful to H. Colin Slim for his kind permission to reproduce in Part II the painting in his possession which he has recently identified as an 1839 portrait of the singer Wilhelmine Schöder-Devrient.

When it turned out that the Wagnerian amplitude of the projected contents of this volume had finally overflowed its permissible bounds, Barry Millington kindly agreed to provide a home in future issues of his recently founded *Wagner Journal* for two substantial items we decided to omit from Part III of the documents section: Franz Liszt's 1851 commentary on *Lohengrin* and a detailed critique and analysis of Wagner's *Faust* Overture by Hans von Bülow. Ilias Chrissochoidis provided impeccable assistance, once more, in correcting proofs and in a variety of bibliographic matters. Finally, I would like to express my personal gratitude to Leon Botstein, founder of the Bard Festival, and to Christopher Gibbs for extending to me the opportunity to participate in this series, one which continues to provide such an outstanding model for the collaborative interaction of musical performance, musical scholarship, and informed spectatorship.

Thomas S. Grey
Portola Valley, CA
April 2009

Permissions

"From Page to Stage: Wagner as *Regisseur*," by Katherine Syer. The following four photographs are used with the permission of the Deutsches Theatermuseum, Munich: Figure 1, Gottfried Semper's model for a Wagner theater in Munich; Figure 2, Anton Fuchs as Klingsor; Figure 5, the opening scene of *Das Rheingold* (1906), in the Prinzregententheater; and Figure 6, Ernst von Possart and others. The page from Anton Seidl's notebook during rehearsals for the *Ring* in 1876 is used with the permission of Columbia University's Rare Book and Manuscript Library.

"The *Revue wagnérienne*: Symbolism, Aestheticism, and Germanophilia": Henri Fantin-Latour's *Siegfried and the Rhine Maidens* is reproduced with the permission of the National Gallery of Canada, Ottawa; Fantin-Latour's *Around the Piano* is reproduced with the permission of the Musée du Jeu du Paume, Paris.

"*Eine Kapitulation*: Aristophanic Opera as Cultural Warfare in 1870," by Thomas S. Grey: Pierre Puvis de Chavannes's *The Balloon: The Besieged City of Paris Entrusts to the Air Her Call to France, 1870* is reproduced with the permission of the Musée d'Orsay, Paris; Narcisse Chaillou's *Skinning a Rat for the Pot: A Rat-Seller in the Siege of Paris, 1870* is used with the permission of the Musée Carnavalet/Roger-Viollet, Paris; Anton von Werner's *Quarters at a Base Outside Paris in 1871* from the Nationalgalerie, Berlin, is used with the permission of the Bildarchiv Preussischer Kulturbesitz/Art Resource, NY.

PART I
ESSAYS

From Page to Stage: Wagner as *Regisseur*

KATHERINE SYER

Nowadays we tend to think of Richard Wagner as an opera composer whose ambitions and versatility extended beyond those of most musicians. From the beginning of his career he assumed the role of his own librettist, and he gradually expanded his sphere of involvement to include virtually all aspects of bringing an opera to the stage. If we focus our attention on the detailed dramatic scenarios he created as the bases for his stage works, we might well consider Wagner as a librettist whose ambitions extended rather unusually to the area of composition. In this light, Wagner could be considered alongside other theater poets who paid close attention to production matters, and often musical issues as well.[1] The work of one such figure, Eugène Scribe, formed the foundation of grand opera as it flourished in Paris in the second quarter of the nineteenth century. Wagner arrived in this operatic epicenter in the fall of 1839 with work on his grand opera *Rienzi* already under way, but his prospects at the Opéra soon waned. The following spring, Wagner sent Scribe a dramatic scenario for a shorter work hoping that the efforts of this famous librettist would help pave his way to success. Scribe did not oblige. Wagner eventually sold the scenario to the Opéra, but not before transforming it into a markedly imaginative libretto for his own use.[2] Wagner's experience of operatic stage production in Paris is reflected in many aspects of the libretto of *Der fliegende Holländer*, the beginning of an artistic vision that would draw him increasingly deeper into the world of stage direction and production.

Opera and Theater in Paris and Wagner's New Path

The two and a half years that Wagner spent in Paris from September 1839 to April 1842 were full of eye- and ear-opening opportunities, despite the many challenges he encountered. From his post as musical director in Riga and work as conductor in a handful of provincial German houses, he had gained in-depth experience with a cross-section of repertoire, including

Auber's influential early grand opera *La muette de Portici*. What he could have only gleaned up until this stage, however, was the extraordinary level of resources that supported opera production in the French capital, together with the intricate production system that was inherent to grand opera. An 1836 performance of Gaspare Spontini's *Fernand Cortez* in Berlin had made a strong impression on him on account of its overall integrity and level of professionalism—Spontini oversaw the production. In Paris, the growing complexities of grand opera and *opéra comique,* with their large moving choruses and elaborate production-specific designs and technical effects, went hand in hand with a process that supported and coordinated the efforts of many specialists. The results were carefully documented so that productions in Paris could serve as models for other performances, the concept of the work now also extending to its realization onstage.[3] The seeds of Wagner's far-reaching and idealistic view of what could be achieved technically in opera took firm root in these years. Cutting-edge technology and high-level illusions were featured above all in popular forms of theater, offering a spectrum of possibilities that fueled Wagner's imagination, especially as he developed the two works that he would produce toward the end of his life in his own theater in Bayreuth: *Der Ring des Nibelungen* and *Parsifal.*[4]

Although Wagner left Paris deeply ambivalent about the operas that thrived there, he soon lamented the means and method of opera production in Paris compared with what he returned to find in Germany, not least the lack of a healthy-size violin section in Dresden as he began rehearsing *Rienzi*: "I sensed a certain poverty in German theatrical efforts, most evident when operas from the Parisian repertory were given. . . . Although I had already felt profound dissatisfaction with this kind of opera during my Paris days, the feelings that had formerly driven me from the German theaters to Paris now came back to me."[5] The ultimately successful premiere of *Rienzi* on October 20, 1842, enabled the premiere of the riskier *Der fliegende Holländer* the following January. Although on a more modest scale, *Der fliegende Holländer* is nevertheless ambitious scenically, involving as it does a regular and a ghostly ship in the framing acts and a closing scene in which the Dutchman and Senta are to be seen rising out of the waves. This final tableau did not feature in Wagner's prose sketches for the opera but emerged as a stage direction in the first version of the full libretto, completed on May 28, 1841.[6] The evolution of this ending takes us to a core of issues that engrossed Wagner as he began to develop the innovative ideas that would lead to the "music drama," including new ideas about acting and stagecraft.

As initially envisioned in prose, Senta leapt into the waves at the end of the opera and disappeared along with the Dutchman and his ship. It is a tragic close, ringing with irony as the Dutchman sets off without recognizing that Senta *is* the extraordinarily faithful woman he has been seeking to redeem him from his cursed existence. She proves true to her oath of fidelity until death in an extreme fashion. In developing his prose material into a libretto Wagner placed additional value on Senta's angelic nature and on her role as redeemer, both ultimately manifested in the final image of her ascent with the Dutchman.[7] In the weeks prior to July 11, 1841, when he began working on the continuous composition sketch, Wagner further developed Senta's character through the addition of stage directions connected to new compositional options. In this phase, his handling of Senta's Act 2 Ballad unlocked the potential of the opera's final tableau, moving beyond tragedy to a celebration of the extraordinary psychological nature of Senta, which first enabled her to commit to being his redemptress.

"Senta's Ballad" is one of several stage songs performed within the opera, none of which unfolds as a discrete musical-dramatic unit; each is broken off, interrupted, and resumed in accordance with varying dramatic contexts. In Act 1, for example, the Steersman's song, anticipating reunion with his sweetheart, breaks off as he is overcome by weariness. When he reawakens many minutes later he resumes singing his song after a substantial contrasting musical-dramatic unit has unfolded—the Dutchman's arrival and monologue. Such strategies are typical of the more realistically shaped and extended musical-dramatic units of grand opera and other repertoire that Wagner knew. Related here, too, is Wagner's practice of composing gesturally or mimetically significant music, whereby stage action and musical gestures are interconnected.[8] More remarkable still is Wagner's recourse to psychological nuances of the dramatic scenario to shape and correlate text, music, gesture, and stagecraft. Each of the opera's acts features a stage song that is sung by characters who are at work (the Steersman sings while on watch) and/or who are doing something physical that dovetails with material in which the legendary and supernatural emerge with substantial expressive power. But the eerie and the uncanny is ultimately only a way station. Each time, mundane realism opens out toward a formal and psychological complexity that outstrips the ways the supernatural functions in the *Schauerromantik* style of Marschner's *Der Vampyr*, for example. The juxtaposition and intermingling of a conventional but finely wrought kind of musical-dramatic realism with a more psychologically driven form is a characteristic of all of Wagner's mature stage works. He unstintingly demanded that things incredible to our rational minds should be acted, designed, and carried out onstage persuasively, expanding the aesthetic horizon.

Against the melodically winsome but mechanical "Spinning Song" of the women's chorus, Senta offers her rendering of the Ballad in a song contest of sorts. Within the Ballad's basic strophic framework of three verses, the description of the legendary Dutchman's terrible plight is contrasted with a refrain questioning the possibility of his redemption. As an advance promotional excerpt written before he had fleshed out the libretto, Wagner's first version of this text ended after the third refrain but did not include Senta's subsequent bold claim to be the Dutchman's redemptress. Weaving the song into the libretto Wagner added stage directions that yielded not merely a solo performance but a more dynamic and interactive one, with the onstage audience of women sympathetically participating in the close of the second refrain. Senta becomes increasingly involved with her performance until, after the third and final refrain and "suddenly carried away in exaltation" ("von plötzlicher Begeisterung hingerissen"), she claims to be the redeeming woman the Dutchman seeks.[9] It is not clear whether at this stage Wagner foresaw this text having any musical relationship to the setting of the Ballad proper. However, shortly before he began composing, he added another stage direction before the third refrain: "Senta pauses, exhausted, while the girls continue to sing quietly."[10] While Senta is outwardly disengaged from the performance, the chorus takes over and quietly sings the final refrain's crucial questions: "Ah, where is she, who can point you to the angel of God? / Where might you find her, she who will remain true to you even unto death?"[11] Senta is reenergized at this point, as per the earlier stage direction, but her offer to save the Dutchman represents both an answer to the questions of the other women as well as her displaced offering of the final refrain in a radically reinterpreted form. In Wagner's musical realization of the Ballad, it is as if Senta is able to command the orchestra to assist in the dramatic rendering of her part; the orchestra collapses into silence with her while the song continues, realistically, with the other women singing a capella. Senta's reengagement and vocal reentry brings the orchestra back into play with a transformation of the refrain's originally gentle woodwind melody and sympathetic questioning tone, extending the framework of the Ballad just as she claims the role of the redeeming woman in an assertive coda. In this process, Wagner found a way to develop material within the Ballad that could come into play in later parts of the drama to underscore not simply Senta's uncommon sympathy for the Dutchman but also her uncommon willingness to be his redemptress or, in more general terms, her exceptional transformational powers. At the same time, Senta became a more psychologically unusual character, demanding more of a singing actress than if Wagner had pursued a simpler teleological path in her performance of the Ballad.

Wagner did not suddenly change Senta's nature. Instead, he sharpened its profile as he aligned it with other parts of the libretto in which she behaves extraordinarily. Later in Act 2, Erik shares with Senta his dream in which he has seen the arrival of the Dutchman. The dialogue with Senta in which he describes this dream triggers her to repeat her assertion to be the Dutchman's redemptress. In his last round of revisions to the libretto before he began composing, Wagner inserted the performance direction "in a muffled voice" ("mit gedämpfter Stimme") so that again Senta's striking response is to material delivered in an understated, hushed manner. As composed, Erik's dream narration is arguably one of the most innovative passages in the score, its more nebulous shape emulating both the narrative's origins in a dream state as well as the process whereby Senta gradually becomes confirmed in her resolution, and hence motivated to reclaim the confident coda with which she had concluded the Ballad. For the published piano reduction, Wagner expanded the stage direction at the onset of Erik's narration to read: "Senta falls exhausted into the chair; at the onset of Erik's narration she sinks as if into a magnetic sleep, so that it seems as if she dreams the dream that is told to her."[12] In clarifying the state Senta is in as she hears Erik's dream and his questions, Wagner drew further attention to the connection with her performance of the Ballad. The reference here to "magnetic sleep" points to the concept of animal magnetism, also known as mesmerism or artificial somnambulism, a stepping-stone in the development of hypnosis and the source of much fascination as well as skepticism.[13] In both cases, Senta passes into a state in which she does not seem to be outwardly conscious, while significant material concerning the Dutchman unfolds and serves as a link to her audacious proclamations.

What is pertinent here is that Wagner explicitly identifies a psychological model that served as a primary creative stimulus in his shaping of Senta's character, her manner of performance, and the experimental musical processes that prepare and illuminate her role as the Dutchman's redemptress. Somnambulism was a popular theme on Parisian stages in the late 1820s, spilling over into French literature through the 1840s.[14] Scribe's own work in this vein includes the libretto for Ferdinand Hérold's 1827 ballet-pantomime *La somnambule*, the precursor to Bellini's 1831 opera *La sonnambula*, which Wagner had conducted. The plot hinges on a private somnambulistic episode of the female protagonist that places her in a potentially compromising situation that is misunderstood; her innocence is only established by a second somnambulistic episode that is observed by the entire community. The somnambulistic experience itself is not explored. It is characteristic of Wagner's radical approach that what Senta psychologically experiences in a profound way is shown as becoming so vital as to challenge our perception of reality. This idea echoes throughout the rest of Wagner's oeuvre, for example, in Tannhäuser's response to the Pilgrims after his miraculous relocation to the Wartburg as well as in his "Rome Narration," in Elsa's vision of Lohengrin, in Mime's "Verfluchtes Licht" soliloquy after the Wanderer's visit in Act 1 of *Siegfried*, in Hagen's twilit dream scene with Alberich and Siegfried's death scene in *Götterdämmerung*, as well as in Amfortas's first lament and Parsifal's response to Kundry's kiss in *Parsifal*. It is a guiding idea for the lovers throughout much of *Tristan und Isolde*. Wagner became acutely aware that such psychologically distinctive characters and their altered states of consciousness were not readily transparent or comprehensible to others, including the singers he required to bring these characters to life onstage. Wagner's many plans for operatic reform in Germany included better dramatic training opportunities for opera singers, and his expectations for his own works were on an altogether different plane from anything he encountered in contemporary theatrical practice.

Dresden and the Staging of the "Romantic Operas"

Dresden afforded Wagner his first opportunities to bring his own operas to the stage in a fully professional context, with substantial resources available for production. Rarely did he know in advance which singers would create his characters onstage. For the role of Senta (as well as Adriano in *Rienzi* and later Venus in *Tannhäuser*), Wagner was able to work with the very singer who created the first strong impact on his notion of the ideal opera performer. Wilhelmine Schröder-Devrient's persuasively acted performances that so impressed Wagner in his youth remained uppermost in his mind when he began creating such atypical operatic characters as Senta.[15] Past her prime by the mid-1840s, Schröder-Devrient was no longer as compelling onstage, especially in the voluptuous role of Venus, yet her critical understanding of Wagner's goals remained acute. She recognized, as Wagner painfully did, too, that Josef Tichatschek was fully capable of singing the role of Tannhäuser but completely unable to understand the character's complexity and the gravity of key moments in the drama.[16] Wagner worked painstakingly with Tichatschek, whom he thought a better Lohengrin than Tannhäuser, but came much closer to his ideal performer only twenty years later with the tenor Ludwig Schnorr von Carolsfeld, who created the role of Tristan (1865). Wagner knew from these early experiences that the roles he was creating would be difficult to cast well, especially dramatically, yet he continued moving ever further in the same direction.

As Kapellmeister in Dresden, Wagner was not only concerned with the creation and production of his own operatic works, but with the theater in general and its ability to produce a range of repertoire. In the heady revolutionary days just before Wagner began his long term of exile outside Germany, he wrote a report proposing a series of reforms intended to improve the level of quality of performances, provide better support for all employees (including theater poets and composers), and reduce less successful activities so that the overall budget was a little tighter and more balanced.[17] Once exiled to Zurich, Wagner focused more exclusively on his own artistic activities, pursuing with renewed energy a revolutionary path. As for the performances of his existing stage works, he was indebted to his friend Franz Liszt for undertaking a revival of *Tannhäuser* (1849) as well as for the premiere of *Lohengrin* (1850) in Weimar. Unable to participate directly in productions of his own works during those years, Wagner wrote two essays concerning *Der fliegende Holländer* and *Tannhäuser* that give us detailed insight into his views about optimal rehearsal conditions and handling of stagecraft and describe how he, as *Regisseur*, would direct singers to interpret their roles in key scenes. Although the term *Regisseur* had been used in spoken theater since the 1770s and the role soon came to involve dimensions that we associate with stage directors today, *Opernregisseure* at this time were far less involved with dramatic interpretation.[18]

Wagner begins the essay "Über die Aufführung des 'Tannhäuser'" (On the production of *Tannhäuser*)[19] by proposing that the current division of labor of stage direction, musical direction, and set design does not support dramatic coordination and that the *Regisseur* should play a larger interpretive as well as mediating role. With more than a little disdain Wagner refers to the "book" usually used by stage directors in their main task of blocking of characters. Production books (*livrets de mise en scène*) had become a specialty in Paris in part due to the practical need to organize the large number of people that move about stage in grand opera and *opéra comique*. The production book for *Le prophète* (1849), for example, is an elaborate, semi-choreographic record including many details about gestures and poses (meant to signal an understanding of characters' emotions or motivations), lighting, and costumes.[20] It does not include a complete libretto nor is there any indication of the stage directions actually published in the score; the manner of cuing when something is to happen involves references to the appropriate fragment of text and occasionally to the beginning or ending of a clear-cut musical section; otherwise there is scant mention of the musical part of the score. In German-speaking regions at this time, the *Regiebuch* or *Dirigirbuch* was more typically a version of the *Souffleurbuch*, the prompter's copy of the libretto, into which similar types of details were written.[21] Wagner asks that the *Regisseur* study the score, in which the relationship between his stage directions and music is clear, while seeking the conductor's assistance. At the same time, he urges the conductor to study the libretto, which would have been the common focus of all involved in rehearsals before preparation of the musicians got under way.

Working at a distance from theaters mounting his operas, Wagner out-lined what he felt needed to happen to avoid pitfalls that he himself had encountered in producing these works and those which he felt were likely to happen if performance and production norms prevailed. As follow-up to his critique that singers are primarily concerned with technical execu-tion and only remotely with the drama, Wagner claimed that his work demands "an approach to performance directly opposite to the usual" ("ein geradesweges umgekehrtes Verfahren als das gewöhnliche für seine Darstellung").[22] Wagner was completely opposed to all routine manners of gesture and blocking not specifically meaningful to what was happening onstage. At the same time he emphasized that he was creating works with uncommon scenarios and characters that involved a special sensitivity in their portrayal. Whereas in production notes he could specify precisely at which beat of a measure the Dutchman should take a further step toward land as he disembarks from his ship, such directions are less of a rigid road map than a way of explaining how a man so weary would disembark so slowly. The simple stage direction in the score for the Dutchman to descend to the stage does not make clear the pacing, nor how he might also be reluc-tant to again search for a faithful wife, something which becomes clearer only in the course of his monologue. A good example of how Wagner's expec-tations might be counterintuitive to contemporary practice or to an interpretation based on the libretto alone is evidenced by the amount of physi-cal restraint he wished the Dutchman to show during much of his monologue; the protagonist is obviously frustrated, which could well encourage a good deal of flailing about onstage. But the Dutchman's frustration is not fresh and he has already reached a stage beyond hopefulness, most originally and effectively conveyed in the hushed otherworldly interior section of his mono-logue concerned with the redemption clause offered him by "God's angel." As he begins another phase on land, he is to convulse at the onset of this mid-dle section and then collapse after the negating climax, before the relentless musical ritornello drags him back into the rendition of his cursed state. His appeal to divine forces is actually an anti-prayer that underscores how he has no faith or desire to participate in the process already under way.[23]

Wagner never imagined that the score could bear the amount of detailed stage directions necessary to convey how a singer or conductor might arrive at a completely satisfactory understanding of text and music and how they should be performed. Interpretation for Wagner was a matter of study and reflection, a process that combined the efforts of many performers of which he, in the role of *Regisseur*, was typically the most lively and committed. Traces of the process of interpretation can be found in the many reports of those with whom he worked and those who observed his working meth-ods, as well as in entries written into rehearsal scores.

Fleeting Dreams in Munich

The records that exist of Wagner in action are remarkable and varied, beginning from the brief time he was active in Munich under the patronage of Ludwig II. A greater reverse of fortunes is scarcely imaginable.[24] After years of working in relative isolation and with limited but frustrating attempts to produce his operas, Wagner was suddenly granted the opportunity to bring several of his works to the stage through the extreme generosity of the freshly crowned young king, while also gaining the support he needed to continue working on his ambitious but still incomplete *Ring* cycle.

Wagner's welcome in Munich was, at best, a deeply divided one, and he swiftly wore it out. But during the time he was active there he was given opportunities that helped crystallize his ideas about preparing and carrying out productions of his works that would spill directly into the realization of his own theater in Bayreuth. His persistent claim to need his own special venue for producing the *Ring* reflects Wagner's belief that no existing theater in Germany had a resident ensemble and orchestra strong enough, or the necessary stagecraft, to cast and perform his post-*Lohengrin* works. *Tristan und Isolde* and *Die Meistersinger* demanded relatively little in the way of extraordinary stage effects, but much in terms of musical preparation. Ludwig soon began exploring the idea of a special theater for the *Ring* in Munich to be designed by Gottfried Semper. Semper eventually produced three different models, trying to cater to both the king's desire for a magnificent theater on the bank of the Isar and to Wagner's more modest wishes. Semper's models feature characteristics that Wagner would take over as he built his own theater in Bayreuth: an amphitheater-like auditorium, double proscenium, and sunken orchestra— all features intended to focus the audience's intentions on the drama onstage.[25] Though Wagner's written report to the king concerning an affiliated national singing school made it clear that he encouraged the training of a pool of talent, he was already committed to preparing his works along the lines of the festival model, drawing the best singers from houses all over Germany.[26]

The first modern style "arts festival" in Munich was a group of spoken theater performances organized a decade before Wagner arrived by Franz Dingelstedt, who had written an essay on the occasion of the Weimar premiere of *Lohengrin* in 1850. It was during his tenure as Intendant of the Munich Hof- und Nationaltheater that Dingelstedt organized his *Gesamtgastspiel* or "collective guest performance," as he called it. Dingelstedt pooled the best actors for a series of model performances of classic German works outside of the regular season in the summer of 1854 (the same summer he had promised to produce Wagner's *Tannhäuser*; that plan was put off until

Figure 1. Gottfried Semper's model for a Wagner theater in Munich.

the following year). For his own series of model productions in 1864–65, Wagner drew upon the orchestra, production staff, and physical resources of the Hoftheater, but he had freedom to choose singers from elsewhere.[27]

For *Holländer* in 1864, Wagner served as *Regisseur* and installed himself as conductor. Generally pleased with the musical results, he nonetheless realized again how difficult it was to bring off the stagecraft side of this work satisfactorily. A far greater and different challenge lay in the premiere of *Tristan und Isolde* on June 10, 1865. Having found in Schnorr von Carolsfeld a singer of rare sensitivity and responsiveness, Wagner committed himself fully to coaching his interpretation of Tristan, as the vocal pedagogue Julius Hey reported:

> Then the imposing figure of Schnorr moved forward into the circle of performers. Curiosity on every face! . . . I could at most describe the impressions that Schnorr's powerful presence, voice, and dramatic presentation made on his colleagues in the course of the rehearsals. For all present, Wagner's rapport with this exemplary singer conveyed a wholesome lesson, providing insight into the meaning of the work itself as well as the nature of its creator in his role of a master of interpretation [*Vortragsmeister*]. More and more, all of those

involved recognized that precisely in this capacity Wagner had extraordinary things to offer. Largely as a result of Wagner's inspiring guidance, the evening's rendition exerted on all such a surprising impact that the composer could justifiably assert that it had exceeded his wildest expectations.[28]

Schnorr's death a few weeks later, on July 21, was a tremendous blow to Wagner, who admired the singer's artistry at length in an essay for the *Neue Zeitschrift für Musik*.[29] Further clouding this great artistic accomplishment was the rapidly escalating political opposition to Wagner's undue influence on the Bavarian king, and the uncomfortable atmosphere resulting from his less than smooth handling of his affair with Cosima (née Liszt), then wife of the conductor of the *Tristan* premiere, Hans von Bülow. Ludwig defended Wagner as much as he felt he could at this time, but he could no longer support him in Munich past the end of the year. Soon Wagner was again in exile, this time in Tribschen, Switzerland, and his involvement in the preparation of the three ensuing Munich premieres—*Die Meistersinger* (1868), *Das Rheingold* (1869), and *Die Walküre* (1870)—dwindled radically. Still, Wagner had formed a network of professional relationships that were to bridge what otherwise might seem a mostly hostile divide between his activities in Munich and Bayreuth.[30] Albeit more coolly than before, Ludwig continued to support Wagner financially as he moved toward realizing his idea of a festival theater in Bayreuth, in Bavaria's northernmost region. Individual artists connected to Wagner's work in Munich also contributed to the new project. Julius Hey, the keen observer of the *Tristan* rehearsals, for example, served as vocal teacher in Bayreuth. Franz Betz, who created the role of Hans Sachs, went on to sing the role of Wotan in the first complete *Ring* cycles. A young Heinrich Vogl (1845–1900) sang Loge both in Munich (where he also sang Siegmund) and Bayreuth, where he also performed in the first revivals of the *Ring* at Bayreuth, in 1896 and 1897, under the direction of the composer's widow Cosima Wagner.

Crucial to the Bayreuth project was the entire technical setup of the theater, an area where Wagner needed to rely most on experts.[31] Ludwig had obliged Wagner by having certain improvements made to the stage of the Munich Hoftheater for the demanding scenic effects in the two individual *Ring* operas produced there. Although the special effects may not have been optimally realized, Wagner recognized that he could work with few better machinists than Carl Brandt as he set out to build his own theater and equip it in the best possible manner. In the area of scenic and costume designs, Wagner usually left the details of execution up to other artists and machinists so long as they were naturalistically rendered and the stagecraft was sophisticated and efficient enough to integrate special illusions relatively seamlessly.[32] He was far less bound up with the growing trend toward historical detail in set and costume design than were many of his contemporaries and successors, including Ludwig and Cosima. This lack of visual fussiness was part of his basic premise that matters of design should not be distracting for their own sake. The goal was always to convey a somewhat dreamlike world.[33] The technical challenges in attaining that dreamlike world were more problematic with the *Ring* than with *Parsifal*, and it is hard to avoid thinking that Wagner's willingness to experiment with new technology might have found better solutions a few years into the future, as developments in electricity and lighting technology enabled new design possibilities and major shifts in production aesthetics.

Figure 2. Wagner directs Franz Betz in the role of Wotan.

Wagner's work at Bayreuth made intense and lasting impressions on everyone with whom he collaborated. Although he himself would not direct revivals of either the *Ring* or *Parsifal*, his conductors, singers, designers, and machinists all played a direct role in the ongoing life of these artworks, in Bayreuth and elsewhere.[34] And of course there was Cosima, the woman who devoted herself with the zeal of a martyr to the success of her husband's enterprises. Starting in 1869, the year before their legal marriage, Cosima began painstakingly recording in her diaries a myriad of details about the creation and production of Wagner's works. Following Wagner's death, a half year after the successful premiere of *Parsifal*, Cosima found ways to resume the festival (not annually at this stage), ardently championing and defending her husband's practices and wishes as she recalled them. She maintained *Parsifal* as the festival's backbone, preserving the 1882 production as long as possible. Wagner himself had seen *Parsifal* as the financial solution to his family's future; he had gone to lengths to exclude it from his arrangement with Ludwig of handing over performance rights to his operas as repayment for debts from the *Ring* premiere. With the Berne Convention for the protection of Literary and Artistic Works of 1886, Cosima was able to prevent other performances of *Parsifal* from taking place in most of Europe during the three decades following Wagner's death. The original production was virtually frozen in time until Siegfried Wagner began to modify the sets in 1911.[35] Cosima's efforts to continue the Bayreuth festival project were nothing short of Herculean, especially as she began adding to Wagner's repertoire operas that had not been previously staged there. However, a balanced appraisal of the singers who worked only with Cosima reveals a rigidity in her approach to gesture as well as vocal declamation that contradicts Wagner's more flexible approach to acting, which, as Patrick Carnegy argues, "should retain, within limits, an essential element of improvisation."[36] Despite her surely good intentions, Cosima's lack of involvement as a singer, pianist, or conductor perhaps prevented her from achieving an even closer relationship to Wagner's own practices as a stage director.

The Bayreuth Festival and Wagner's Early Legacy as *Regisseur*

Wagner was certainly ambitious in regard to stagecraft, but the most important influence he exerted as *Regisseur* was on the musicians he worked with closely in Bayreuth and who embraced the process of dramatic-musical interpretation he espoused. Angelo Neumann—decidedly not an artist, but an ambitious impresario who would take the *Ring* on tours of incredible scope—sensed a seismic change when he attended performances in

Bayreuth in 1876: "To be sure, I had already learned to admire Richard Wagner as a stage director in Vienna, but through the performance of *Rheingold* it became clear to me that new and unprecedented challenges had been posed by the greatest of the world's stage directors [and] that from then on a new epoch of reform was under way."[37]

In addition to the care that Wagner paid to stage design and technology, he took exceptional care with specific roles that were less certain to make their mark on the public. For the role of Siegfried, for example, Wagner chose a singer whose vocal technique was rather immature, as was his acting technique. Capitalizing on the overall naïveté of Georg Unger, Wagner groomed the performer with Julius Hey's assistance in a manner that suited his gradually emerging hero. In the environment of Bayreuth Wagner thrived as "schoolmaster Mime" (Hey's words) in coaching this raw talent:

> This rehearsal of the first act of *Siegfried* was unforgettable! Wagner marked not only Mime's key words, but he sang the part *through the entire act* with full voice!! And *how* he sang his "schoolmaster Mime." Unger's mouthy, colorless singing tormented me, and I listened to it without interest, whereas the master teacher offered an incomparably characteristic expressive rendering (although he did not at all possess a trained voice in the normal sense); he created without caricatured awkward physical gestures [*Gangeln und Gehn*] a character of such sharp, strongly etched depiction, the likes of which one would perhaps never experience on the stage![38]

Unger was not fully adequate in performance in Bayreuth, but Wagner continued to work with him and regarded him as key to future performances of his operas. Several of the singers Wagner coached in Bayreuth already possessed better technique and more effortlessly conquered stages as his acting emissaries: Franz Betz, Karl Hill, Albert Niemann, Amelie Materna, Emil Scaria, Lilli Lehmann, and Marianne Brandt.[39] While the Bayreuth stage remained dark following the financial disaster of the 1876 premiere of the *Ring*, which had been far from satisfactory in terms of stagecraft, many of the original cast participated in the first performances of the complete *Ring* elsewhere, as in Munich in 1878. Several of these singers also participated in the touring production of the *Ring* led through Europe by Neumann in 1882–83.

A subset of Wagner's singers embraced the role of operatic *Regisseur* themselves, emulating their dramatic coach in an era when the title had not yet acquired much meaning beyond someone who controlled onstage traffic. Swedish bass Johannes Elmblad sang in the *Ring* at Bayreuth in 1876 and then again in 1896, as well as in revivals through to 1904, around the time it seems that Cosima became uncomfortable with his competing views on Wagner's intentions about staging.[40] Elmblad sang at the Metropolitan Opera in the 1887–88 season when Anton Seidl was active there. During his return to the Met in 1902–3, he mostly directed Wagner operas and sang his farewell performances as Hunding, in a production he also directed. In 1907 he was responsible for directing some of the performances of the first complete *Ring* in Stockholm. Anton Fuchs, who premiered the role of Klingsor in 1882, directed the hotly debated production of *Parsifal* in 1903 at the Metropolitan in New York (while copyright was in effect elsewhere). Especially with *Parsifal*, a personal link to the premiere production was prized on other stages.

If there is one primary heir to Wagner's legacy as *Regisseur*, that role can only belong to Anton Seidl, the young conductor who became an indispensable member of the theater team as the complete *Ring* came to the stage and a member of the Wagner household until 1878 as the composition of *Parsifal* neared completion. Through years of copying the scores for the *Ring* (and half of *Parsifal*), participating in rehearsals for its premiere, and studying all of his operas with the composer, Seidl became uniquely qualified to take Wagner's place in preparing his operas for the stage. Had the orchestra from Munich not arrived equipped with its resident conductor Hermann Levi in 1882, Wagner would have entrusted Seidl with the premiere of *Parsifal*. There was nobody else as gifted in musical interpretation who understood the intimate relationship between the music and stage as Seidl. Despite Wagner's huge reservations about a revival of *Tristan und Isolde* in Leipzig, given the massive challenges entailed in bringing it to the stage the first time, Seidl had scored a major success with the work. Following a report of the event by Neumann, then Intendant in Leipzig, Wagner replied in a letter dated 16 January 1882 "I also beg you for the sake of the whole, to give him more authority over the scenic disposition than is usually granted to conductors, for herein lies what he has especially learned from me."[41]

Seidl's close identification with the *Ring* in these years was confirmed by the far-ranging tour of Neumann's "Traveling Richard Wagner Theater," during which Seidl conducted nearly 135 *Ring* performances and 58 concerts between September 1, 1882, and June 5, 1883. Seidl took note of all these performances in a small notebook, a study in understatement given the nature of the enterprise:

Friday Sept. 1 early little concert: rehearsal, evening concert 7 o'clock. Succeeds fabulously. The 2nd: first performance of *Rheingold*: aside from a few minor errors, goes well. Performance from 7–9:30. The 3rd: *Walküre*. Much imprecision in the orchestra in the first act; the rest

Figure 3. Anton Fuchs as Klingsor.

of the performance very good. Much enthusiasm from the audience. The 4th: repetition of *Walküre*. Goes very well. 6:30–10:30.[42]

From its first complete performances in a specially built festival theater with an elaborate setup, the *Ring* had become a compact show that traveled by rail to play in many theaters of varying capabilities.[43] For all of Wagner's ambition and vision of how the *Ring* could be produced using elaborate stagecraft, such a tour placed the greatest burden of success on the more fundamental levels of the musical-dramatic rendering. It is worth noting that Seidl was only thirty-two at the time—youth was surely an asset for the troupe's grueling performance schedule (although he was also known for sleeping late). Seidl had arrived in Bayreuth when he was twenty-five. He quickly became aware of the concurrent levels of theatrical activity involved in the enterprise, as evidenced by the notes he took during the *Ring* rehearsals. Upon two pages of the notebook he used during this time we can see entries on the printed staves concerning the transition to scene 3 of *Das Rheingold* as Loge and Wotan descend to Nibelheim in search of Alberich. Seidl notes the emergence of pallid mist (*fahle Nebel*) in conjunction with Loge's query "Was sinnt nun Wotan so wild?" (What wild thoughts are Wotan's?) as well as the *Schwefeldampf* (sulfur vapors) in connection with Loge's call to Wotan to slip with him into the rock's cleft. Stressed on the page's lower lines are the dynamic levels of the dotted rhythmic figure associated here with the anvils, and these performance directions are repeated at the top of the facing page (see Figure 4). Stage directions in the score make clear when Wagner's much-loved steam machines were to come into play, but they lack details about how the machinery would be used to achieve such special effects. The rest of what is written on this page concerns the ways in which Alberich's various disappearances would be handled, specifically the floor traps that would enable him to disappear while concealed by a column of smoke. The trap would take him out of sight completely— "Versenkung ab. (ganz)"—before the mist disappeared and Wotan and

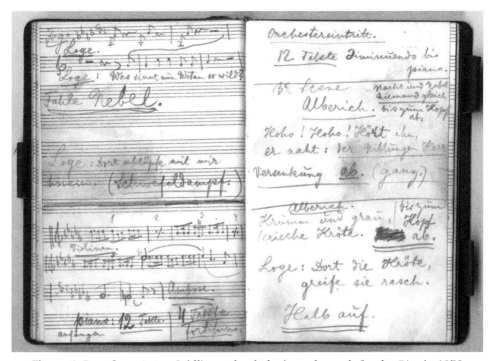

Figure 4. Page from Anton Seidl's notebook during rehearsals for the *Ring* in 1876.

Loge arrived in Nibelheim. Later, when Alberich transforms himself into a toad while wearing the Tarnhelm, the trap would lower him until only his head was above stage ("bis zum Kopf ab") and then raise him halfway up ("Halb auf") when Loge is to seize him by the head. From the onset, Seidl embraced the Wagnerian theatrical world *in toto*.

It is hardly surprising that early in Seidl's treatise "On Conducting," clearly written in homage to the man who groomed his career as a great Wagner interpreter, he recalls a moment before the stage rehearsals for the *Ring* began when Wagner took him and another young colleague behind the scenes. As recalled, Wagner told them that they "must assume responsibility on the stage for everything that has anything to do with the music—that is, you must act as a sort of musical stage manager."[44] From the stages of Europe to New York and the American Eastern seaboard, where Seidl established Wagner's operas as theater, he carried out his work in a wide array of production environments, always ready to support and defend vibrant and sensitive dramatic interpretations.[45]

It is perhaps worthwhile to remind ourselves again of the atypical operatic scenarios that Wagner created and the ease with which they could be misinterpreted onstage. In his defense of the serious dramatic nature of Siegfried's death scene, for example, when the hero relays what he has learned from the Woodbird, Seidl critiqued the practice of adopting "an utterly unnatural comic falsetto tone to make it seem as if a bird's voice might be imitated by a tenor." Instead, Seidl argued for a "Siegfried, who did not twitter the words of the bird to the men, but told them in a simple manner what the bird had sung."[46] Wagner commented upon the unusual paths that many of his idiosyncratic characters follow while coaching Seidl on the first act of *Holländer* in the fall of 1877. Wagner was then working on the first act of his final stage work, *Parsifal*. Cosima Wagner recorded the following: "From *Holländer* to *Parsifal*—how long the path and yet how similar the character!—Following the music, R. talks about the influence of the 'cosmos,' the outside world, on characters who, though basically good, do not perhaps possess the strength to resist it, and who then become quite exceptionally bad, indeed perverse."[47]

Following Wagner's death, Seidl remained a warmly embraced member of the Wagner family. In 1885–86, he began to lead German seasons at the Met. Critical to the success of many of Wagner's operas in this time was Seidl's ability to bring singers who had worked with Wagner and himself in Europe to New York. Seidl also fanned the flames of interest in *Parsifal* in semi-staged performances that deferred to Cosima's wishes. Finally, she offered him the chance to conduct at Bayreuth, for the 100th performance of *Parsifal* in 1897. Seidl died in March of the following year. According to Joseph Horowitz, Seidl was, unlike Wagner, "poised and mysterious, undemonstrative and impassioned, attractive and remote," with the adjectives "magnetic" and "electric" often surfacing in reviews of his performances at the Met.[48] In some ways, Seidl trumped Wagner as the perfect performer. Yet his natural and flexible approach to dramatic pacing owed a great deal to Wagner, and this was perhaps the most challenging idea for Cosima to grasp and maintain.

In the case of *Tristan und Isolde,* for example, Seidl wrote how his primary concern in conducting the passages of Tristan's grave illness in Act 3 was to accommodate the idiosyncracies of a given performance.[49] In stark contrast is the 1936 publication by Anna Bahr-Mildenburg, in which she advances her detailed description of a strict and near continuous mimesis for the principal characters in *Tristan und Isolde.*[50] The extent of movement and degree of histrionics she calls for often work against Wagner's stage directions and practices, yet the account is offered as an authentic staging tradition emanating directly from Wagner. Bahr-Mildenburg sang at Bayreuth from 1897 until 1914, where she studied several roles under Cosima. As Nicholas Baragwanath argues, contemporary accounts of a naturalness and economy of gesture in her performances of Isolde in 1903 in Vienna may reflect the tempering influence of Gustav Mahler, with whom she had worked since 1895.[51] The revolutionary Wagner performances that Mahler began to shape together with the stage designer Alfred Roller from 1903 to 1907 mark the first important break—and a highly successful one—from staging practices at Bayreuth.[52] Utilizing light as a powerful dramatic medium in and of itself, Mahler and Roller moved toward a simpler design aesthetic. Fundamentally important, however, remained musical-dramatic interpretation.

Late in 1903, Cosima faced her greatest contest to date when Heinrich Conried managed to produce *Parsifal* at the Met in New York, free from Berne restrictions. Ernst von Possart, Cosima's rival in producing Wagner's operas in Munich since 1894, supported Carl Lautenschläger's sharing his expertise concerning the original stage machinery of *Parsifal,* and the stage of the Met was renovated so as to meet or exceed the technical capabilities in Bayreuth. Anton Fuchs, of the original *Parsifal* cast, directed the performances and Alfred Hertz conducted. Cosima vowed never to work again with anyone affiliated with this New York production; Hertz never conducted in Germany again. By this time, Fuchs had devoted himself to stage direction. From November 1903 until December 1904 he acted as director for twelve productions at the Met, including a new *Ring* with the conducting split between Felix Mottl, who assisted Richter in Bayreuth for the premiere of the *Ring* and was at this time a guest at the Met, and Hertz, as well as new productions of *Tannhäuser* and *Meistersinger*. Fuchs also directed the 1914 premiere of *Parsifal* at Munich's Prinzregententheater,

Figure 5. The opening scene of *Das Rheingold* (1906) as directed by Anton Fuchs in the Prinzregententheater.

where he had already directed the *Ring* and other Wagner repertoire since the theater opened in 1901.

Fifteen years after Ludwig's death in 1886, his dream of a Wagner theater in Munich was realized with a modified version of Semper's plans. The project to build the Prinzregententheater was spearheaded by Possart, Intendant of the Hoftheater and fittingly, perhaps, one of Germany's greatest actors. Whether in Munich, Vienna, or New York, the intense interest in producing Wagner's most ambitious music dramas, including *Parsifal*, made the opening years of the twentieth century challenging ones for Cosima Wagner, as she attempted to hold on to some unique vestige of Wagner's legacy. Although Anton Seidl had passed from the scene, and only a few singers who had worked directly with Wagner remained active, a generation of expertise with the later stage works continued to bear fruit, nurturing strong production traditions that in a variety of ways endeavored to keep alive Wagner's ideas about dramatic interpretation.

Figure 6. Under the photo sit Ernst von Possart and (to his right) Anton Fuchs. Further to right (seated): conductors Hermann Zumpe, Franz Fischer, and H. Röhr, each of whom would conduct the production of *Götterdämmerung* (playbill hanging in rear) that Anton Fuchs directed and premiered in the 1903 festival. Photo possibly from that year, when Zumpe and Fischer both conducted. Röhr holds in his hand what appears to be the playbill for the world premiere of *Die Feen* that Fischer conducted in Munich in 1888. Seated to Possart's left: the stage machinist Carl Lautenschläger, stage director Jocza Savits, and W. Schneider.

NOTES

1. Although eighteenth- and early nineteenth-century stage direction practices in Italy were mostly uneven, theater poets often played a role in blocking and role preparation. Pietro Metastasio was exceptional in the specificity of the dramatic realizations of his work; to this end he remained involved in the rehearsal process. See Gerardo Guccini's "Directing Opera," in *Opera on Stage*, ed. Lorenzo Bianconi and Giorgio Pestelli, trans. Kate Singleton (Chicago and London, 2002), 125–76, esp. 134–42.

2. On aspects of the work and its genesis, see *Richard Wagner: "Der fliegende Holländer,"* ed. Thomas Grey (Cambridge, 2000). Other early works, especially *Rienzi*, are important in tracing the development of Wagner's mature aesthetic strategies, but the libretto of *Der fliegende Holländer* is especially distinctive.

3. Although H. Robert Cohen has drawn substantial attention to these production books in several publications reaching back to the late 1970s, his assertion that these books documented Parisian premieres for replication elsewhere has been challenged. A more flexible understanding of opera production practices and these important documents emerges in Arne Langer's in-depth study *Der Regisseur und die Aufzeichnungspraxis der Opernregie im 19. Jahrhundert* (Frankfurt am Main, 1997). Arnold Jacobshagen's reassessment

of the dating of production books shows how they reflect different moments in evolving production practices. See his article "Staging at the Opéra-Comique in Nineteenth-century Paris: Auber's *Fra Diavolo* and the *livrets de mise-en-scène,*" *Cambridge Opera Journal* 13/3 (November 2001): 239–60.

4. Patrick Carnegy traces Wagner's evolving ideas about the theater and their impact on his operatic activities in Part 1 of his *Wagner and the Art of the Theatre* (New Haven and London, 2006); see esp. 15–25 for a description of theatrical offerings in Paris. Mathias Spohr broadens the lens beyond technology in his examination of the influence of melodrama, from the period of Wagner's youth through to the popular forms of theater in Paris. See his "Medien, Melodramen und ihr Einfluß auf Richard Wagner," in *Richard Wagner und seine "Lehrmeister,"* ed. Christoph-Hellmut Mahling and Kristina Pfarr (Mainz, 1999), 49–89. Dieter Borchmeyer fascinatingly probes dense literary and theatrical contexts of Wagner's development in *Das Theater Richard Wagners* (Stuttgart, 1982); trans. Stewart Spencer as *Richard Wagner: Theory and Theatre* (Oxford, 1991).

5. Wagner: *My Life,* trans. Andrew Gray (Cambridge, 1983), 226.

6. The texts that were set independently before the libretto was written and the differences between the four versions of the libretto and later published versions are charted in Isolde Vetter's PhD diss. *"Der fliegende Holländer* von Richard Wagner: Entstehung, Bearbeitung, Überlieferung" (Technical University, Berlin, 1982).

7. See Grey's interpretation of the multiple biographical and symbolic implications of these changes in *Richard Wagner: "Der fliegende Holländer,"* 5–17.

8. Carl Dahlhaus explores this dimension of Wagner's music in *Die Bedeutung des Gestischen in Wagners Musikdramen* (Munich, 1970). For an account that considers Wagner's indebtedness to other composers, see Mary Ann Smart, *Mimomania: Music and Gesture in Nineteenth-Century Opera* (Berkeley, 2004), esp. 163–204.

9. David Levin considers Senta's unusual perspective in contrast with that of those around her in "A Picture-Perfect Man? Senta, Absorption, and Wagnerian Theatricality," *Opera Quarterly* 21/3 (Summer 2005): 486–95.

10. "Senta hält vor Erschöpfung an, —die Mädchen singen leise weiter."

11. "Ach! wo weilt sie, die dir Gottes Engel einst könne zeigen? / Wo triffst du sie, die bis in den Tod dein bliebe treueigen?"

12. "Senta setzt sich erschöpft in den Lehnstuhl nieder; bei dem Beginn von Eriks Erzählung versinkt sie wie in magnetischen Schlaf, so daß es scheint, als träume sie den von ihm erzählten Traum ebenfalls."

13. For a survey of animal magnetism in Wagner's time and in literature, see Reinhold Brinkmann, *"Sentas* Traumerzählung," in *Die Programmhefte der Bayreuther Festspiele* (1984) 1:1–17. Brinkmann is skeptical of Wagner's actual knowledge of the practice/phenomenon and regards the allusion as fashionable among Romantics but as ultimately unhealthy. Of the many other artistic figures also interested in animal magnetism, E. T. A. Hoffmann must be counted as an especially strong influence on Wagner during this time. As with *Der fliegende Holländer*, somnambulists and magnetic states in his literary works serve as thematic material that impacts the shape of the narrative. If we accept the premise of her somnambulistic tendencies, which is not a popular modern critical approach, Senta does not have access to her brazen ecstatic outbursts, which she contradicts when she is in a normal state of consciousness. Carolyn Abbate reads Senta's inconsistencies as "hysteria and spiritual chaos" in "Erik's Dream and Tannhäuser's Journey," in *Reading Opera*, ed. Arthur Groos and Roger Parker (Princeton, 1988), 139. Rarely noted is that Senta's strange psychological behavior ceases when she actually meets the Dutchman.

14. Sarah Hibberd carefully distinguishes somnambulism from madness in French stage works of the late 1820s and illuminates the rich web of musical allusions that Hérold employed in conjunction with Thérèse's somnambulistic tendencies. See her article "'Dormez donc, mes chers amours': Hérold's *La Somnambule* (1827) and dream phenomena on the Parisian lyric stage," *Cambridge Opera Journal*, 16/2 (July 2004): 107–32.

15. Wagner's own accounts of his early experiences of Schröder-Devrient in perform-ance have often been questioned for their accuracy. The fact remains that he was deeply impressed by the conviction of her performances, which superseded the limitations of her vocal gifts. On Schröder-Devrient's career and her influence on Wagner, see Part II of this volume.

16. Ernest Newman, *The Life of Richard Wagner* (New York, 1933), 1:397.

17. "Entwurf zur Organisation eines Deutschen National-Theaters für das Königreich Sachsen." in Richard Wagner, *Gesammelte Schriften und Dichtungen* (henceforth *GSD*), 10 vols. (Leipzig, 1887–1911), 2:233–73.

18. For a detailed history of the evolution of the *Regisseur,* see Langer, *Der Regisseur und die Aufzeichnungspraxis.*

19. Wagner, *GSD,* 5:123–59; here, 124–30.

20. A facsimile of this production book is published in H. Robert Cohen and Marie-Odile Gigou's *The Original Staging Manuals for Twelve Parisian Operatic Premières* (New York, 1990), 151–82.

21. Langer, *Der Regisseur und die Aufzeichnungspraxis,* 157.

22. Wagner, *GSD,* 5:127.

23. The dramaturgy of this monologue is closely connected to "Senta's Ballad," at some moments in markedly inverse ways. The Dutchman has no interest in seeking a redeeming wife and possibly implicating someone further in his curse—a benevolence that he expresses when he sets off to sea, leaving Senta on land.

24. During the years preceding his time at Munich, he was only able to be involved directly in two projects. Lavish sets, excellent stage coordination and choral singing, and some fine performances by the soloists could not outweigh the scandalous divided recep-tion and personal financial disaster of *Tannhäuser* in Paris in 1861. Vienna turned out to be another dead end when orchestral rehearsals for *Tristan und Isolde* were abandoned in 1863.

25. These plans for a festival theater and the eventually completed theater in Bayreuth are comprehensively covered in Heinrich Habel's *Festspielhaus und Wahnfried* (Munich, 1985). A recent dual-language (German-English) publication concentrating on the Bayreuth Festspielhaus is *Das Richard Wagner Festspielhaus Bayreuth/The Richard Wagner Festival Theatre Bayreuth,* ed. Markus Kiesel (Cologne, 2007).

26. "Bericht an Seine Majestät den König Ludwig II. von Bayern über eine in München zu errichtende deutsche Musikschule," *GSD,* 8:174. For a comprehensive discussion of the plans for a special theater in Munich and Wagner's eventual Festspielhaus in Bayreuth, see Heinrich Habel's *Festspielhaus und Wahnfried: Geplante und aufgeführte Bauten Richard Wagners* (Munich, 1985).

27. Detta and Michael Petzet offer a detailed account of the model productions of Wagner's works financed by Ludwig in Munich (through to *Rienzi* in 1871) and those mounted by Wagner in Bayreuth in their *Die Richard Wagner Bühne König Ludwigs II* (Munich, 1970).

28. Julius Hey, *Richard Wagner als Vortragsmeister* (Leipzig, 1911), 82.

29. The essay, titled "Meine Erinnerungen an Ludwig Schnorr von Carolsfeld," was published on June 5 and 12, 1868, and is included in *GSD,* 8:177–94.

30. The background of festival performances in Munich and the strong commit-ment to performing Wagner's works past Ludwig's death is covered in Jürgen Schläder and Robert Braunmüller, *Tradition mit Zukunft: 100 Jahre Prinzregententheater München* (Feldkirchen bei München, 1996), esp. 9–20.

31. The most detailed account of this dimension of the theater is Carl-Friedrich Baumann, *Bühnentechnik im Festspielhaus Bayreuth* (Munich, 1980).

32. Still a landmark in the study of the production history of Wagner's operas is Oswald Georg Bauer's *Richard Wagner: Die Bühnenwerke von der Uraufführung bis heute* (Frankfurt/Berlin/Vienna, 1982), trans. Stewart Spencer as *Richard Wagner: The Stage Designs and Productions from the Premières to the Present* (New York, 1983). For a more analytical and up-to-date perspective, see Mike Ashman, "Wagner on Stage: Aesthetic, Dramaturgical,

and Social Considerations," in *The Cambridge Companion to Wagner*, ed. Thomas S. Grey (New York, 2008), 246–75.

33. Oswald Georg Bauer, "Die Entwicklung des Bayreuther Inszenierungsstils 1876–1979," in *Wagner-Interpretationen, Beiträge zur Aufführungspraxis 5*, ed. Roswitha Vera Karpf (Munich and Salzburg, 1982), 116.

34. In addition to considering the reports of production team members such as Richard Fricke, Heinrich Porges, and Julius Kniese, Martina Srocke also closely considers the entries made by many hands in rehearsal scores in her *Richard Wagner als Regisseur* (Munich and Salzburg, 1988). Fricke's diaries have been translated by George Fricke and published as *Wagner in Rehearsal 1875–76: The Diaries of Richard Fricke*, ed. James Deaville and Evan Baker (New York, 1998), originally published as *Bayreuth vor dreissig Jahren* (Dresden, 1906). They have also been translated by Stewart Spencer as "Wagner in 1876," in *Wagner Journal* 11 (1990): 93–109, 134–50; and *Wagner Journal* 12 (1991): 25–44. For other accounts of the 1876 rehearsals, see *Carl Emil Doepler: A Memoir of Bayreuth 1876*, ed. Peter Cook (London, 1979); and Heinrich Porges, *Wagner Rehearsing the Ring*, trans. R. Jacobs (Cambridge and New York, 1983).

35. For a more detailed discussion of the early production history of *Parsifal* through to the end of World War I, in Bayreuth and elsewhere, see my "*Parsifal* on Stage," in *A Companion to Wagner's "Parsifal,"* ed. William Kinderman and Katherine R. Syer (Rochester, N.Y., 2005), 277–99.

36. Carnegy, *Wagner and the Art of the Theatre*, 93.

37. Angelo Neumann, *Erinnerungen an Richard Wagner* (Leipzig, 1907), 20.

38. Hey, *Richard Wagner als Vortragsmeister*, 110.

39. On the legacy of Wagner's first Bayreuth festival and some of the singers he trained, see the accounts of the 1886 and subsequent festivals in Part V of this volume.

40. The most detailed information about Elmblad's extended Wagner activities is found in Stefen Johansson, "Wagners Ring på Kungliga Operan: Regi och framförande-traditioner under ett sekel," in *Operavärldar Från Monteverdi till Gershwin*, ed. Torsten Pettersson (Stockholm, 2006), 219–46.

41. Neumann, *Erinnerungen an Richard Wagner*, 216.

42. "Freitag am 1sten Sept. früh kleine Concert: probe, Abends 7 Uhr Concert. Prachtvoll gelungen. Am 2ten: erste Aufführung von Rheingold; bis auf einige leichte Versehen gut gegangen. Aufführung von 7–1/2 10. Am 3ten: Walküre. Zum ersten Akt viele Ungenauigkeiten vom Orchester vorgekommen; sonstige Leistung sehr gut. Enthusiasmus im Publikum sehr gross. Am 4ten: Wiederholung der Walküre. Sehr gut gegangen. Von 1/2 7–1/2 11."

43. For a vivid account of Neumann's enterprise and a comprehensive account of the part of the tour that unfolded in Italy just weeks after Wagner's death, see John W. Barker, *Wagner and Venice* (Rochester, 2008), 176–240.

44. Henry T. Finck, *Anton Seidl: A Memorial by his Friends* (New York, 1899), 217.

45. Joseph Horowitz charts Seidl's American career in detail in his *Wagner Nights: An American History* (Berkeley/Los Angeles/London, 1994).

46. Finck, *Anton Seidl*, 211–12.

47. *Cosima Wagner's Diaries*, ed. Martin Gregor-Dellin and Dietrich Mack, trans. Geoffrey Skelton (New York, 1978, 1980), 1:990.

48. Joseph Horowitz, "Anton Seidl and America's Wagner Cult," in *Wagner in Performance*, ed. Barry Millington and Stewart Spencer (New Haven and London, 1992), 171.

49. Finck, *Anton Seidl*, 235.

50. Anna Bahr-Mildenburg, *Tristan und Isolde: Darstellung des Werkes aus dem Geiste der Dichtung und Musik* (Leipzig/Vienna, 1936).

51. "Anna Bahr-Mildenburg, Gesture, and the Bayreuth Style," *Musical Times* 148 (Winter 2007): 65.

52. Mahler's move to New York in 1907 was launched with revivals of the pivotal *Tristan* production.

Wagner and Liszt: Elective Affinities

KENNETH HAMILTON

In biographies of Wagner and Liszt the figure of the other always looms large, whether as supported or supporter, borrower or lender, unlikely son-in-law or reluctant father-in-law. At the first Bayreuth Festival Wagner effusively claimed that "not a note" of his music would have been known were it not for the faith of his friend, while in an apocryphal version of Liszt's death the ailing maestro expires with the word "Tristan!" on his lips.[1] Their destinies had been closely entwined since the late 1840s, when Wagner was enduring one of the deepest of his self-inflicted sloughs of despair, and Liszt was distancing himself from the profession of piano virtuoso that had made him famous. The latter's full assumption in 1848 of the post of Kapellmeister in Weimar heralded an attempt to center the avant-garde of European music in the small but distinguished German town to supplement the literary luster it had acquired in the days of Goethe.[2] In the process, Liszt desperately desired to shift his own artistic persona from pianist to composer, from the ephemeral triumphs of the concert stage to the more lasting laurels of the creative artist. On Wagner's part the needs were more pressingly practical. Exiled from Germany on account of his role in the abortive Dresden uprising of May 1849, he needed money and the means to promote his operas in the native land from which he was now outlawed. Liszt came to the rescue on both fronts.

The traditional view of the situation is that Wagner exploited Liszt—both financially and artistically—and that Liszt allowed himself to be exploited. The traditional view is correct. I do not intend to undertake some perversely implausible "reinterpretation" of the material elements of the Liszt-Wagner interchange, or to claim in twisted tenure-seeking fashion that we have in fact misunderstood the matter—that Wagner was all along the unsung Good Samaritan of the story. Rather, I hope to illuminate some sidelined aspects of the artistic entwining of Wagner and Liszt: the decisive impact that Wagner's works and theories had on Liszt's compositional direction, and the complexities of Wagner's reaction to Liszt's radically evolving musical style. These areas saw a more subtle exchange than the standard story of the grasping, greedy Wagner, and the long-suffering Liszt would allow. Along the way, I shall chart the most convincing chronicle we have of Liszt's creative response to Wagner: his transcriptions from Wagner's operas. They constitute striking evidence of the increasingly divergent musical paths trod by both composers in the latter half of their careers.

Wagner and the Death of Liszt's *Sardanapale*

The desire for success as a composer rather than as a pianist, more particularly as an opera composer, is a recurrent theme of Liszt's correspondence in the 1840s. By that time he had finally established himself as the foremost pianist in Europe, a reputation bolstered by a long series of concert tours that garnered unequaled acclaim and unrivaled amounts of money. But though Liszt basked happily in the adulation of the concert-going public, he was well aware that his fame as a virtuoso had always eclipsed his reputation as a creative artist. In a less than wholly enthusiastic review of the *Douze grandes études* (1837–38), Robert Schumann claimed that Liszt had concentrated on pianism at the expense of his compositional skills and prophesied pessimistically that this neglect would be evident even in his ripest works. It was now, in other words, too late for Liszt to escape his fate. Like an adult struggling to learn a second language, he would never achieve the accent-free fluency of a child mastering a mother tongue.[3]

But try to escape it he did, and with great energy. From the mid-1840s his hopes for a dramatic breakthrough centered on *Sardanapale*, an opera after Byron. The Italian libretto had been cobbled together by an anonymous associate of Liszt's friend and occasionally more-than-friend, Princess Cristina Belgiojoso, luckily a native speaker of a language Liszt understood less than fluently.[4] The reason for the choice of Italian was simple. By at least early 1846, and probably even at the time *Sardanapale* was first conceived, Liszt nurtured hopes of succeeding Donizetti in the prestigious post of court Kapellmeister in Vienna, a much more attractive appointment than the one he would eventually take up in Weimar. He naturally realized that if he wanted to replace a prolific Italian opera composer like Donizetti, experience in composing at least one Italian opera was essential. Liszt seems first to have tested his capabilities in setting shorter Italian texts with the composition of three *Petrarch Sonnets* for piano and voice, along with "very free transcriptions of them for piano, in the style of nocturnes!" Their success promised much. He proudly told his former partner Marie d'Agoult, "I regard them as having turned out singularly well and more finished in form than any of the things I have published."[5]

The biggest problem for Liszt in his desire to succeed Donizetti in Vienna was not simply lack of operatic experience—it was that there was still no official vacancy. Donizetti had indeed been taken seriously ill with tertiary syphilis, but he was still clinging to both his job and his life. And Donizetti, like the proverbial melody, lingered on, steadfastly resisting the grim reaper until 1848. This was too late for Liszt—he was already in the process of settling down in Weimar. He had with him the libretto of *Sardanapale*, although not a note of the score had been written.

After four years of wrangling over changes to the text, Liszt appears finally to have started to sketch the *Sardanapale* music in the middle of 1849. He wrote to his amanuensis Joachim Raff in August of that year expressing confidence that the opera would be swiftly finished by the winter.[6] But by 1850 he was still optimistically plowing away at it, telling his old Parisian friend and onetime biographer Joseph d'Ortigue: "I am applying myself well to *Sardanapale* (Italian text, in three acts), which ought to be completed by the end of the year, and in the intervals, I am achieving some of the symphonic works of which I am undertaking a certain series that can only be ready in its entirety in two or three years."[7]

In January 1851 he informed Wagner that the opera would be fully finished by spring 1852, to be produced in Paris or London.[8] But after this, *Sardanapale* suddenly vanishes from his correspondence. The triumph he had sought for so long was not to be. Instead, the symphonic works he had been writing "in the intervals" between bouts with *Sardanapale* became the main focus of his Weimar years, along with piano pieces and, eventually, religious choral music. What happened?

If we are seeking candidates to charge as accomplices to the death of Liszt's *Sardanapale*, along with what must ultimately have been the composer's lack of confidence in his own developing score, two fairly formidable suspects stand in the dock, arms folded defiantly and casting glances of mutual contempt at each other: Liszt's new partner, the Princess Wittgenstein, and Richard Wagner. But firstly, there is some evidence that the death was as much assisted suicide as murder, evidence compellingly constituted by the libretto. What remains of it seems stilted, wooden, and remarkably old-fashioned. Many passages might not be out of place in a text by Metastasio from the previous century. As Liszt got down to serious work on the music, he must surely have become more and more painfully aware of its drastic shortcomings, and possibly also of his own lack of experience as an opera composer. Moreover, the concluding pyrotechnic conflagration of Sardanapale's funeral pyre—one of the things that first attracted Liszt to the subject—might suddenly have appeared too clichéd just after the similar final scene Meyerbeer's *Le prophète* (1849). It was, of course, also an upcoming special feature of Wagner's *Siegfrieds Tod* libretto (soon to be *Götterdämmerung*).

Liszt's involvement with opera production in the Weimar theater surely gave him firsthand insights into the dramatic dangers of a limping libretto and of the harm an old-style operatic catastrophe would do to his refashioned reputation as a leading composer. He had certainly not yet proved himself in other major genres—the *Beethoven* Cantata of 1845 had scarcely made an impact, and his symphonic works were still far from polished. How would his persistent portrayal of himself as the standard-bearer of the musical avant-garde in Germany sit with the setting of a surprisingly dilapidated Italian opera text, especially now that hopes to succeed Donizetti in Vienna had long evaporated?

It seems likely that Princess Wittgenstein was distinctly lukewarm about *Sardanapale*. The opera was, after all, closely connected to Liszt's intimate friendship with Princess Belgiojoso, a dangerously seductive "other woman," and what's more, another woman of just the type that Liszt tended to go for—titled, talented, and married to someone else. Princess Wittgenstein seems therefore to have directed her indefatigable energies into steering her companion toward symphonic and choral composition. (Only later would she become an operatic muse—not to Liszt but to Berlioz, whose *Les Troyens* was completed with her insistent encouragement between 1856 and 1858.)

And finally, there was Wagner.

Liszt's early activities as an opera conductor in Weimar were heavily slanted toward Wagner's works. He did not only support Wagner on his home ground, he helped to negotiate performances in theaters with which he had little direct connection. He also wrote about Wagner's achievements in enthusiastic detail, even if his extensive articles were penned with the too unrestrained help of Princess Wittgenstein. Liszt being Liszt, he naturally made piano transcriptions from the operas. These were not for his own concert use, like most of his previous transcriptions, but intended primarily to publicize their source material. In sum, he admired Wagner's creative endeavors with unqualified enthusiasm and devoted himself wholeheartedly to their support.

It is not surprising that in January 1851, while rejecting Wagner's insistently well-meaning if typically tactless offer to provide a German opera libretto for him on *Wieland der Schmied*, Liszt made clear a strong reluctance to compete directly on Wagner's turf. He was still clinging to his hopes for *Sardanapale*, because an Italian opera would necessarily be judged by rather different standards:

However great the temptation even for me to forge your Wieland, I can nevertheless not budge from my firm decision *never ever* to compose a German opera. — I don't feel any vocation for it, and I'm quite lacking in the patience to struggle with the conditions in German theaters. Altogether it's much more suitable and more comfortable for me to risk my first dramatic work on the Italian stage (which will probably take place early next year—'52—in Paris or London) and, in the event that things don't go badly for me, to stick with the *Southerners* [*Welschen*]—Germany [*Germanien*] is your possession, and you its honor.[9]

Just after signing this letter, Liszt added a significant P.S.: "Are you already far advanced with your book on opera? I'm eagerly looking forward to it . . ." The book referred to was of course the soon to be celebrated *Opera and Drama*. Wagner wrote back the following month to say that although no publisher was yet in sight, his "very powerful" polemic was indeed finished.[10] Liszt was delighted, largely because he had hopes of finally understanding from *Opera and Drama* what on earth Wagner had been waffling about regarding opera reform. He admitted he had hardly understood a word of its prolix predecessor, *Art and Revolution*.

But Wagner had never been one to leave an awkward issue diplomatically alone, and characteristically returned to the attack over Liszt's own opera plans. From his Zurich exile it must certainly have struck him as strange that Liszt should complain about the difficulty of getting operas produced in German theaters when he himself was the resident conductor in one of them. Not only would any Liszt opera be automatically produced in Weimar under the loving direction of the composer, but there was naturally the expectation that writing operas for the court theater was the sort of thing a Kapellmeister ought to be doing. *König Alfred*, an opera by Liszt's pupil Joachim Raff, had just been premiered with some success in Weimar,[11] and Wagner—no doubt with the best of intentions—continued to browbeat his hapless supporter:

Raff's opera pleased me uncommonly, very nice! But further, to say it directly: *you must do the same*. Write an opera for Weimar—I beg you. Write it for the resources that are available there, and should be improved, ennobled, and expanded through your work. Don't on my account give up your plans for the Southerners (you can also achieve something famous and flourishing in that area, I know!) but stay also with the things nearest to you, on what is now your home ground. . . . Don't bother yourself for the moment worrying about the usual conditions in German theaters; you don't need them to achieve something both beautiful and useful. To say it openly, what would you want to gain *just now, at the height of your present powers*, from the southerners apart from an increase in your fame? Good! But will that make you happy? *You?* Not any more, surely! . . . Do something for *your* Weimar![12]

Wagner had, for once, a point. There was now a growing psychological block with Liszt about German opera, which would soon seemingly extend itself to all opera. All the more ironic that Liszt's most ambitious effort as a child prodigy in Paris had indeed been an opera. *Don Sanche ou le château d'amour* (1825) was a slender one-acter completed with the help of his then composition teacher Ferdinand Paer, but it had nevertheless reached the stage of the most prestigious opera house in Europe in an era when more promising pieces like Berlioz's *Les francs-juges* were being roundly rejected. The situation was not dissimilar from that of Mendelssohn, who like Liszt had little problem composing operas as an adolescent, but always found a good reason not to complete one as an adult. On his death in 1847, Mendelssohn's long-heralded "Lorelei" was in a fragmentary state akin to Liszt's *Sardanapale*, though it is impossible to say if it would have been finished had he lived longer.[13] Liszt, for his part, found himself in a particularly embarrassing position. He was the Kapellmeister of a small German court, a regular conductor of other people's operas and a would-be "great composer." But he himself could only point to a half-sketched opera on an old-fashioned text that had initially been intended for performance in the Italian theater in Vienna, or in Italy itself. The specter of Wagner's pioneering dramas would hover balefully over anything he did in Germany—partly because of his own selfless success in promoting them. Now even students like Raff had stolen the march on him.

The final nail in the coffin of *Sardanapale* could well have been the dauntingly vast Wagnerian polemic on the future of opera that Liszt was so masochistically eager to peruse. *Opera and Drama* was not published in complete form until 1852, but in 1851 Liszt read some advance extracts that appeared as articles in the *Deutsche Monatsschrift*.[14] However difficult Liszt found it to comprehend the convolutions of Wagner's prose, it must have become quickly clear to him just how little an antiquated Italian offering like *Sardanapale* would fit in with Wagner's notions of the artwork of the future. Liszt, usually only too keen to be at the cutting edge of the avant-garde, suddenly found himself potentially to be yesterday's man.

And so Liszt's grand designs for an operatic hit met their end, not with some great theatrical triumph or disaster, but by slinking silently into the wings, unfinished and unsung. The symphonic works that he had been writing "in the intervals" while composing the opera now took center stage.[15] By 1854 he had even found a new and exciting name for them—"symphonic poem," rather than the boring "concert-overture," as most had been called up to that point. Wagner may have played a role here as well. In a letter to Liszt of 1852, he referred to his *Faust* Overture as a *Tongedicht* (tone poem).[16] One wonders whether this might have had any influence on Liszt's otherwise unexplained change of nomenclature?

Whatever the origin of the name, a symphonic poem's "poetic idea" would allegedly inspire the music in the same way as Wagner's "dramatic idea" would be the breath of life for the opera of the future. With the sketches for *Sardanapale* consigned to a drawer in Weimar, Liszt would now set to work solving what he called the "symphonic problem" presented to him in Germany. After having spent the best part of a decade dealing with this to his own satisfaction (if not that of his very vocal detractors), he boldly announced in 1862 that he was now ready to tackle "the oratorio problem."[17] Dramatic symphony and dramatic oratorio—orchestral and choral counterparts of Wagner's music-dramas—would form the core of Liszt's ambitions for the most fruitful compositional phase of his life. Opera on the stage would be left to Wagner, but there was always opera on the piano.

Wagner/Liszt

A profusion of Wagner opera transcriptions flowed from Liszt's pen.[18] But should not the absence of the above-mentioned "dramatic idea"— supposedly so essential to the comprehension of the music—render them unviable from the start, at least in Wagner's own terms? How can the transcription of an operatic extract hope to work when there can be no "dramatic kernel," or at least none immediately present to the listeners? When, to use Wagner's gloriously galumphing phrase coined in the 1872 essay "Über die Benennung 'Musikdrama,'" no "ersichtlich gewordene Thaten der Musik" (deeds of music made visible) were there at all? Like so many of Wagner's all too tiresome problems, this one was self-inflicted.

Writing about the first six of Liszt's symphonic poems in 1857, Wagner could not resist a little sideways swipe at Berlioz concerning this issue. He lamented that in the love scene (Adagio) of the "dramatic symphony" *Roméo et Juliette* the listener "loses the thread" because the music follows the dramatic course of the scene rather than unfolding according to the "logically clear development of specific [musical] motives." Berlioz and Shakespeare may have had a certain narrative in mind, but the auditors could not be expected to appreciate this. They ineffectually had to "hold on to scenic motives that weren't immediately before the eye."[19]

Ironically, Berlioz himself shared similar concerns, at least for the "Scene at the Tomb" from the same symphony. He advised in the score that this movement should always be omitted in public performance, "unless played to a select audience familiar in every respect with the fifth act of Shakespeare's tragedy as conceived and represented by Garrick, and endowed with a highly poetic mind." So, unless you know exactly what goes on in the fifth act of *Romeo and Juliet* (with the *dénouement de Garrick*, of course) you have little hope of understanding Berlioz's Tomb Scene. The staged narrative is the key to the music.[20] Similarly, Wagner was insistent that his own scores were only fully intelligible as part of an operatic production. In 1879 he explained the issue at (for once) reasonable length in "On the Application of Music to the Drama," where the illustrative example was taken from *Lohengrin*:

> The motive the composer of *Lohengrin* allots as the closing phrase of a first arioso to his *Elsa* . . . consists almost solely of a tissue of remote harmonic progressions; in the Andante of a Symphony, we will say, it would strike us as far-fetched and highly unintelligible; here it does not seem strained, but quite arising of itself. . . . This has its grounds, however, in the scenic action. *Elsa* has slowly approached, in gentle grief, with timid down-bent head; one glance at her transfigured eye informs us what is in her soul.[21]

This was hardly a new idea in 1879. It had formed a central thread of Wagner's operatic thinking at least since *Opera and Drama* of 1852. He continued to harp on the topic so insistently that his views were soon common knowledge.

But if the stage setting was so essential for understanding Wagner's music, where did that leave piano transcriptions, or the concert performance of excerpts from his dramas? Not only did Wagner often conduct the latter, he also wrote concert endings for those that would have trailed off a little too indeterminately in their original incarnation. The point was not lost on a skeptical Eduard Hanslick when he reviewed an 1862 Wagner concert in Vienna. This consisted of extracts from the yet uncompleted *Ring* cycle and *Die Meistersinger*. Here Berlioz's hope that "a select audience" would rely on their memory of a previously staged performance could hardly apply, even if Wagner did provide program notes in an attempt to contextualize the music. With more amusement than malice, Hanslick commented:

> It seems noteworthy to us that Wagner can so blithely program such a potpourri from his works—the content of which the public is scarcely even superficially acquainted with—out of context and without the support of scenery. Has Wagner not said countless times that in opera the music is nothing in itself, can be nothing, but on the contrary gets its meaning only in association with the entire action, text, acting and scenery? . . . The author of *Opera and Drama* . . . has indisputably been untrue to himself. Still, it doesn't occur to us to blame him for it. An artistic disposition has other requirements than consistency.[22]

The crowning contradiction concerns the most frequently played type of Wagner opera excerpt—in those days piano transcriptions or, as specifically concerns us here, Liszt's piano transcriptions. It may have been coincidence that the passage from *Lohengrin* that Wagner claimed would be unintelligible without the scenic action had furnished the material for one of Liszt's first Wagner arrangements, *Elsas Traum*, nearly thirty years before—arrangements undertaken with the enthusiastic blessing of Wagner himself. Liszt sometimes included the words in the scores of his transcriptions, but surely this could scarcely compensate for the keenly felt absence of Elsa's "timid, down-bent head." Moreover, the early arrangements were effectively collaborative artistic ventures between Wagner and Liszt, although the publicity benefit was, as ever, mostly on Wagner's side. At no point in the process did Wagner mention any weighty aesthetic objections to transcribed extracts from his opera; nor did he insist that they only be played as accompaniment to a salon staging of the scenes in question, the mistress of the house doing her best to imitate Elsa's coy glances during crucial modulations. On the contrary, he seemed overjoyed that Liszt had devoted himself to the pianistic promotion of his operas. Hanslick was right: for Wagner publicity was more important than probity.

For his part, Liszt later claimed the transcriptions were merely "modest propaganda on the inadequate piano for the sublime genius of Wagner," but the surviving manuscripts and later revisions show that he took great care in working out the details.[23] Even a seemingly simple thing like constructing a few preludial bars to "Isolde's *Liebestod*" was approached with unusual imagination.[24] He made no fewer than three attempts to find something suitable, starting with the rather too subtle connective tissue that appears in the operatic score, and then replacing it with the theme sung to the words "Liebe, heiligste Liebe" in Act 2. Finally, he hit on a reworked version of the latter as the final formula:

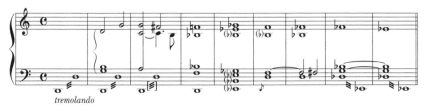

Example 1a. First deleted draft of Wagner/Liszt, "Isolde's *Liebestod*," introduction (Weimar MS. U32).

Example 1b. Second deleted draft of Wagner/Liszt, "Isolde's *Liebestod*," introduction (Weimar MS. U32).

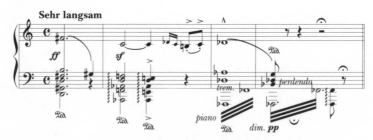

Example 1c. Published version of Wagner/Liszt, "Isolde's *Liebestod*," introduction.

The passages above are clear evidence of Liszt's improvisatory approach —we can almost hear him trying out the variants on the piano as we read the manuscript. Liszt's initial engagement with Wagner's music apparently also involved improvisation, at first on excerpts from *Rienzi* during his concert tours of the 1840s (although his only published fantasy on that opera dates from much later).[25] With the exception of the *Ring*, from which only *Das Rheingold* was represented, Liszt's transcriptions eventually traversed every one of Wagner's mature works.

Naturally the first transcriptions to appear in print were connected with Liszt's Weimar performances of Wagner's *Tannhäuser* (1849) and *Lohengrin* (1850). It was in fact those performances that fostered the close friendship between the two composers. They constitute the most numerous group among the Wagner transcriptions (three excerpts from *Tannhäuser* and four from *Lohengrin*) and fall into two distinct classes: works designed for the parlor pianist versus those only playable by top-class virtuosi.[26]

From the first, however, even the former category was not intended to result in routine arrangement, but something "after Liszt's unique manner" —hardly a surprise, given that Liszt usually found it difficult to leave well enough alone.[27] It is all the more remarkable, then, that he sometimes did attain that level of renunciation when dealing with Wagner's works. In the "Overture to *Tannhäuser*," for instance, he produced a remarkably faithful yet pianistic arrangement. His solution to the problem of the climax of the Pilgrims' Chorus was so striking in its treatment of the three distinct textural levels of the score that it was transferred over to one of his own original works for piano, the rather unimaginatively named *Grosses Konzert-Solo*, a preliminary study for the much better-known Sonata in B Minor.[28] Here was an example of Wagner influencing Liszt, rather than the other way around, even if through the indirect medium of Liszt's own transcription.

Example 2. Wagner/Liszt, *Tannhäuser* Overture, mm. 38–41.

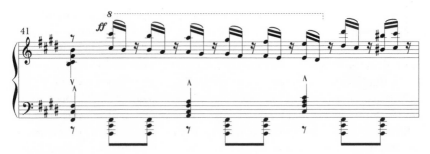

Example 2 continued

Example 3. Liszt, *Grosses Konzert-Solo*, mm. 235–38.

Liszt regularly consulted Wagner in his Zurich exile over questions ranging from titles for his arrangements to the structural details of their layout.
On the former issue the usually so verbally incontinent Wagner had little
to say, on one occasion responding to Liszt's request for suitable titles
with the distinctly dull suggestion: "Two pieces from *Tannhäuser* and
Lohengrin."[29] On the latter point things were different. The formal scheme
of Liszt's arrangement of the Act 3 prelude and "Bridal Chorus" from
Lohengrin—two statements of the main material of the prelude framing a
treatment of the chorus "Treulich geführt" ("Here Comes the Bride" to
English speakers)—was devised by Wagner for his Zurich concerts of May
1853 and quickly taken over by Liszt for his transcription.

If the whole concept of transcribing operatic excerpts was acceptably
Wagnerian—at least when it suited Wagner himself—then there was relatively little that could have disturbed him in the slick artistic working out
of the early Liszt arrangements. Liszt did admittedly add his own short chromatic coda to the "Song to the Evening Star" from *Tannhäuser* (Example 4),

Example 4. Wagner/Liszt, "Song to the Evening Star," from *Tannhäuser*, mm. 104–15.

and dared to vary part of the "Entry of the Guests" from the same opera with the sort of flippant virtuoso figuration Wagner despised. Most piquantly, he produced an amusingly inappropriate Italianate ending for Lohengrin's "Reprimand to Elsa" (the arioso, "Atmest du nicht mit mir die süssen Düfte?") which sounds momentarily as if it might suddenly break into "Santa Lucia" (Example 5):

Example 5. Wagner/Liszt, "Lohengrin's Reprimand to Elsa," mm. 58–63.

Liszt began to plow his own furrow more obviously toward the end of the 1850s. The "Fantasy on Themes from *Rienzi*" of 1859 is less of a transcription and more of an original work. Unusually for an opera fantasy, it is organized in sonata form, with the "second subject" (Rienzi's battle cry, "Santo spirito, cavaliere") in Liszt's favorite major-third relation to the tonic—a feature of many of his symphonic poems.[30] Liszt had a special reason for writing such an elaborate fantasy—an unexpected throwback to the more extended arrangements of his earlier years. Wagner had just been offered the prospect of a production at the Opéra in Paris, and planned to put on *Tannhäuser*. Liszt, however, was insistent that *Rienzi* was best suited to the tastes of the French public. He hoped that presenting Wagner with an advance piece of pianistic publicity would persuade him to take his advice. But Wagner would not budge. The well-known tale of the catastrophic Paris *Tannhäuser* tells us who was right.

Two subsequent excerpts from *Der fliegende Holländer* ("Spinning Chorus" and "Senta's Ballad") return to the more modest format of Liszt's later transcriptions. They are not so much structurally as harmonically divergent

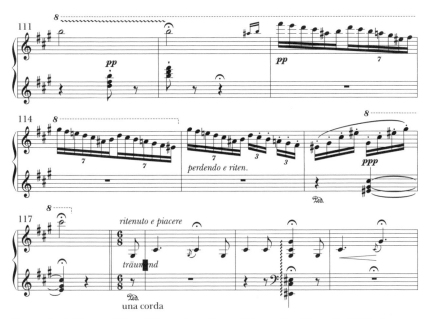

Example 6. Wagner/Liszt, "Spinning Chorus" from *Der fliegende Holländer*, mm. 111–20.

from Wagner's original, with the inclusion of languid Lisztian chromaticism quite alien to the world of the early operas.

If Isolde's *Liebestod* is devoid of any additions after its new introduction, "Am stillen Herd" from *Die Meistersinger* shows the opposite approach. A floridly chromatic improvisation on the theme, it showcases a sequential development of motives extended even beyond that found in the opera. The Russian composer Alexander Borodin had personally heard Liszt experimenting in this style around the same period: "[Liszt] improvised new arrangements like Balakirev, sometimes altering the bass, sometimes the treble notes. By degrees there flowed from this improvisation one of those marvelous transcriptions in which the arrangement for piano surpasses that of the composition itself."[31]

Had Wagner believed he had been "surpassed," these later Liszt transcriptions would not have found much favor at Wahnfried. Yet Liszt played the *Tristan* and *Meistersinger* extracts to an enraptured Cosima in 1872, and occasionally extemporized other excerpts, such as "O sink hernieder Nacht der Liebe" from *Tristan*, before the master himself.[32]

But toward the middle of the 1870s, a gradually deepening artistic gulf between Liszt and Wagner began to manifest itself in the transcriptions. This did not affect Liszt's unbounded admiration for Wagner's music, but it did affect Wagner's opinion of Liszt's. Some aesthetic aspects of the last Wagner arrangements constitute not just extempore extensions and embellishments of their source material but downright distortions. The beginnings of this can be seen in a third, radically revised version of the "Entry of the Guests" from *Tannhäuser,* made specifically at the request of Breitkopf & Härtel in 1876. Breitkopf, the publisher of Liszt's 1853 and 1874 versions, had unexpectedly and preposterously been threatened with legal action by C. F. Meser, the original publisher of the *Tannhäuser* score. The latter alleged that Liszt's transcriptions were so close to the vocal score as to constitute infringement of their copyright.

It must have been the first time that Liszt had been accused of undue fidelity in any walk of life, and he responded by casting aside all restraint in what at times constitutes a free fantasia rather than a transcription. The piece starts perfectly soberly with Wagner's unadulterated introduction before the main theme suddenly turns up in the wrong key (D major instead of B major). Liszt then spends a wittily wandering page trying to get to the right one, producing what is effectively a development section before we have even heard the theme in the tonic. If one already knows Wagner's march the effect raises a smile; if not, it can only seem utterly puzzling—exactly the sort of eccentricity without dramatic justification that Wagner so often railed against. He laid down the law a few years later: "Properly speaking, we cannot conceive of a chief motive of a symphonic movement as a piece of eccentric modulation, especially if it is to present itself in . . . a bewildering dress at its first appearance."[33] This arrangement remained unpublished in Liszt's lifetime, and Wagner was probably never aware of its existence. The threat of legal action having presumably receded, it languished in Leipzig until 2002, when it was unearthed by the indefatigable editors of the New Liszt Edition.[34]

On the other hand, the even more outrageous Wagner/Liszt "Grail March from *Parsifal*" (1882) did reach the press the following year and was honored with a public premiere by none other than Liszt's brilliant pupil Eugen d'Albert. This is indeed a peculiar piece—dragging *Parsifal* into the fragmentary, depressively willful world of Liszt's late music. The themes are routinely "downsized"—broken up and repeated in circling sequences that never seem to have any particular tonal goal in view and rarely reach anything more than a halfhearted cadence. Wagner's mysticism becomes Liszt's pessimism.

It all sounds like a twisted parody of *Parsifal* rather than a transcription from it, as if Liszt is trying to remember the music but can't quite figure out how it goes. And Wagner's reaction? Surely this was one of the compositions he referred to in 1882 as evidence of Liszt's "budding insanity."[35] The insanity reached full bloom soon afterward in *Am Grabe Richard Wagners*

Example 7. Wagner/Liszt, "Grail March" from *Parsifal*, mm. 1–21.

(At the grave of Richard Wagner), where further intensification of the tendencies shown in the "Grail March" reduce the entire piece to a disjointed, nostalgic sketch. Both works constitute a jarring compositional comment on the source material. Certainly not a condemnation—for their author remained the most steadfast of Wagner enthusiasts—but an unsettling reflection of Liszt's own personal disillusion and disappointment.[36]

Liszt/Wagner

And what of Wagner's reaction to Liszt's original music—before and after the "insanity" had taken its toll? Although the influence of Liszt on Wagner has been acknowledged as important by numerous writers, Wagner's remarks on Liszt have mostly been ignored, as indeed has his influence on Liszt's oeuvre. This is all the more strange in that Liszt's encomiums for Wagner's creative genius are cited *ad nauseum*, in fulfillment of his role in reception history as John the Baptist to Wagner's Messiah. But Wagner's own viewpoint is of compelling interest. He was better acquainted with Liszt's output than most contemporary musicians, and brought to it a critical faculty capable of genuine insights when it was not being diverted by rants against Judaism, Catholicism, or theater directors. Wagner's "borrowings" from Liszt's music, too, are a type of criticism—a compelling musical commentary obscured neither by his bigotry nor his prose style. But as we shall see, ascertaining what these borrowings might actually constitute is hardly simple. Even what seems at first to be outright theft is sometimes only evidence of a striking artistic affinity.

Wagner's opinion of Liszt's music was as inconsistent as Liszt's music itself was. Evaluating Wagner's views is all the more delicate because most of his casual comments have come down to us through the agency of his second wife, Cosima, either in her own voluminous diaries or in *Mein Leben*, the autobiography dictated to her. Cosima, as Liszt's daughter, was hardly a neutral interlocutor. Although Wagner seemed to be happy enough both to praise and criticize her father's music in her presence, we might suspect that the frequent indignation expressed over the baleful influence of his companion Princess Wittgenstein (who had replaced Cosima's mother, the Countess d'Agoult, in Liszt's affections) may easily have been intensified in this context.

When Liszt and Wagner first forged an artistic alliance in the late 1840s Liszt was by far the more famous musician, but Wagner was already the more successful composer. As we have seen, Liszt's eventual concentration on orchestral and choral music was decisively influenced by potential competition with Wagner, whereas Wagner's initially grudging admission that after getting to know Liszt's music he had become "ein ganz anderer Kerl als Harmoniker" (a completely different chap as a harmonist) is a standard line in the history books.[37] In his old age, Wagner was more relaxed about things, reminding Liszt in 1878 that he had "stolen" much from the symphonic poems, joshingly calling them "un repaire des voleurs," (a den of thieves).[38] He had more chance than most to borrow ideas from Liszt's music. The first set of six symphonic poems was published in 1856; the next six, with the *Dante* and *Faust* Symphonies, did not appear in print until a few years after. But Wagner had already been introduced to earlier versions of many of these works in 1853 when Liszt was his guest in Zurich. The laconic entry in Wagner's "Brown Book" diary was only: "Liszt's visit. Poetry. Symphonies."[39] Yet Wagner reminisced in his autobiography that he was given an extensive *grand tour* at the piano of Liszt's latest music, likely including drafts of several symphonic poems (not just the first six) and certainly including sketches for the *Faust* Symphony.[40] In a subsequent visit in 1856 Liszt brought with him a revised version of *Faust* and a draft of the *Dante* Symphony. The ensuing discussion is also detailed in Wagner's *My Life*.[41] So, although Wagner's essay (or "open letter") from 1857 "On Franz Liszt's Symphonic Poems" is ostensibly a reaction to the final publication of some of the symphonic poems, he had been acquainted with the pieces in manuscript for some years. He had even heard Liszt conduct *Orpheus* and *Les preludes* in 1856 at a music festival in St. Gallen in which both composers participated.

One can rarely say for sure what constitutes direct theft from Liszt's "den of thieves," but the sheer number of possible cases is significant. The melody used for Sieglinde's feverish nightmare in Act 2 of *Die Walküre* perhaps recalls the initial impact of Liszt playing through the *Faust* sketches to Wagner in 1853 (compare Examples 8a and 8b, on the following page).

Equally striking is the suggestive opening of Liszt's wonderful song "Lorelei" (published 1856). It is so astonishingly similar to the start of *Tristan und Isolde* (begun December 1856) that the resemblance has drawn a bewildered gasp of recognition from at least one concert audience (Examples 9a and 9b).[42]

We might further speculate that the unusually consistent focus on the diminished seventh chord in the "Inferno" of the *Dante* Symphony inspired Wagner's reliance on another, less strident seventh harmony—the famous "Tristan chord"—at significant points in his opera. This approach gives both works a distinct harmonic flavor, even if many critics have found the taste of the latter more palatable than the former. It has also been argued, intriguingly, that the open-ended harmonic and melodic construction of *Orpheus* was not without influence on the "endless melody" of *Tristan und Isolde*.[43]

On a more specific level, the bluff Kurwenal motive in the same opera sounds uncannily like a tune in Liszt's largely forgotten *Beethoven* Cantata of 1845, while the theme for the "Wanderer" in *Siegfried* seems partly to have been inspired by a passage from *Orpheus*. Moreover, if *Tristan* begins with a salute to "Lorelei," then the opera ends with an ecstatic climax distinctly recalling that of Liszt's *Bénédiction de Dieu dans la solitude*, one of his favorite party pieces when playing the piano for friends (Examples 10a and 10b).[44]

Example 8a. Liszt, *Faust* Symphony, first movement, mm. 1–7 (piano solo arrangement by August Stradal).

Example 8b. Wagner, *Die Walküre*, Act 2, "Kehrte der Vater nun heim!"

Example 9a. Liszt, "Die Lorelei," mm. 1–10.

Example 9b. Wagner, *Tristan und Isolde*, Prelude, mm. 1–7.

Example 10a. Liszt, *Bénédiction de Dieu dans la solitude*, mm. 294–301.

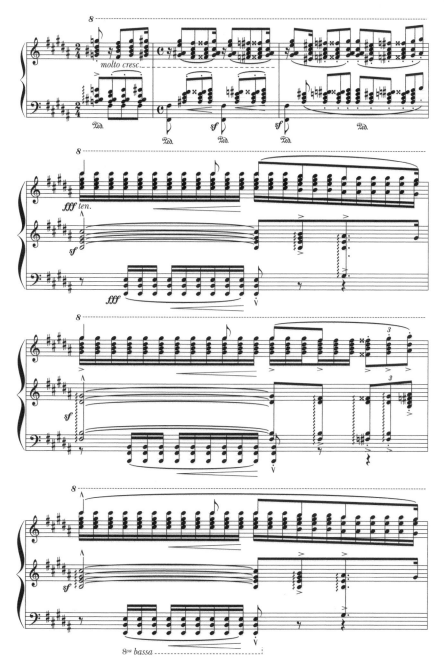

Example 10b. Wagner, *Tristan und Isolde*, Act 3, "Transfiguration" ("In des Welt-Atems wehendem All"), arr. Liszt.

But before we decide that the issue of Wagner's artistic indebtedness to Liszt is an open-and-shut case—convincingly proven and brazenly admitted by the debtor himself—we should take a look at some contradictory evidence that certainly complicates matters. Particularly thought-provoking is the issue of the twin *Fausts*: Wagner's *Faust* Overture and Liszt's much more ambitious *Faust* Symphony. A glance at the opening of the Overture (Example 11) immediately reveals a remarkable similarity to the second theme (with the falling seventh) of the Symphony (Example 8a).

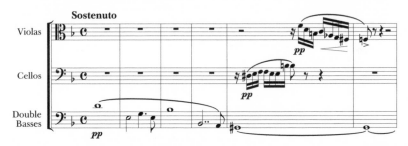

Example 11. Wagner, *Eine Faust-Ouvertüre*, mm. 1–6.

Is this yet another example of Wagner pillaging Liszt's music? It would be easy to assume so, especially as the initially pensive atmosphere of both pieces is also virtually identical. But the chronology simply does not work. The first version of Wagner's overture was written in 1840, and the initial sketches of Liszt's Symphony seem to date from the middle of that decade.[45] Could Liszt, then, have borrowed from Wagner? This too is unlikely, for Liszt did not get to know the overture until 1849, well after his first *Faust* sketches, when he requested a score from its composer with a view to performing the piece in Weimar.[46] Liszt later told his student August Göllerich, "Wagner and I adopted the same theme for *Faust* before we even knew each other—I give you my word on this."[47] The melody with the falling seventh soon became one of Liszt's favorite thematic shapes—variations of it appear in the *Grosses Konzert-Solo* (1849) as well as the later Sonata in B Minor. And we should not forget the additional influence of Berlioz (its dedicatee) on the *Faust* Symphony, which adds to an already tangled web. The beginning of the "Mephistopheles" movement is so close to the opening of the last movement of the *Symphonie fantastique* that Liszt must have intended it either as a friendly gesture of homage or a brazen plagiarism.

The explanation for all this is simply a certain affinity of musical styles between Liszt and Wagner. Both composers were, after all, quite capable of independent musical invention.[48] This artistic intertwining becomes the more remarkable when we consider that in the 1840s Liszt already appears to have intended his *Faust* Symphony to comprise at least a "Faust" and a "Gretchen" movement, while Wagner's *Faust* Overture was originally planned as the first movement, titled "Faust in Einsamkeit" (Lonely Faust), of a *Faust* Symphony of his own.[49] The second movement of this was going to be—yes—"Gretchen." Liszt, however, did not learn of Wagner's abortive *Faust* Symphony scheme until late 1852, when Wagner mentioned it in a letter.[50] If this were not enough, a revised version of Wagner's *Faust* Overture was completed in 1854–55 at Liszt's prompting, and very much with Liszt's detailed advice in mind.[51] Finally, the piano score of the Overture was arranged by none other than Liszt's pupil, soon to be son-in-law, and eventually former son-in-law (owing to Wagner's celebrated intervention): Hans von Bülow. A cozy compositional coterie indeed.

It can sometimes be difficult to say who the borrower and who the lender really is in this tangled musical web. To take another instance, Liszt's song "Ich möchte hingehen" has often been pointed to as yet another prefiguring, like "Lorelei," of the opening of *Tristan und Isolde*. In this case even the "Tristan chord" itself appears. But as with the *Faust* Overture, chronology throws a spanner in the works. The anticipation of *Tristan* turns out to be a quote from it—Liszt added the relevant bar after he got to know Act 1 of the opera.[52] And even when a direct Wagner borrowing seems fairly likely, as in the *Orpheus-Siegfried* similarities, Liszt's ideas tend to be treated with a new sophistication in Wagner's hands.[53] The latter's version of the *Orpheus* passage is less four-square, less repetitive, more contrapuntal (Liszt's elegant melodic melisma appears to have been transformed into Wagner's inner part writing in the second bar). We note a striving after a longer line, and a greater richness of texture. Now, it is quite true that complexity is not always more satisfying than simplicity (otherwise Reger and Sorabji would be among the twentieth century's most lauded composers), but Wagner seems to know where to stop—how to keep on the right side of satiety.

Many other fascinating instances of this type of transformed borrowing could be cited, capped with one specific resemblance admitted by Wagner himself—that of the opening theme of *Parsifal*'s Act 1 prelude to the "Excelsior" prelude of Liszt's cantata *The Bells of Strasbourg Cathedral*.[54] The copious use of bells in Liszt's cantata certainly inspired a similar sound-world in *Parsifal*. Cosima even noted that in 1879, when drafting the Act 1 "Grail March" (probably the transformation music and its continuation), Wagner refreshed his memory of Liszt's score "to make sure that he has not committed a *plagiarism*" (*CWD*, 28 December 1877). Or too much of a plagiarism, at any rate. Both pieces are pervaded by thematic fragments based on familiar patterns of bell chimes, even if Wagner's tintinnabulations were ultimately different in outline and much lower in pitch than Liszt's.

But let us return for a moment to the famous borrowed theme:

Example 12a. Liszt, *Excelsior,* mm. 1–8.

Example 12b. Wagner, *Parsifal*, Act 1, Prelude, mm. 1–6.

Liszt's music seems like a mere skeleton of Wagner's, for the latter spins out melodic lines of vastly greater length and subtlety. Yet however short-breathed and sketchy Liszt's phrases are here, they obviously contain the germ of the *Parsifal* idea. We might also ask if the opening of "Purgatio" from the *Dante* Symphony had a further influence on Wagner's continuation. Liszt presents his material in the symphony just as Wagner was later to do in the opera, in separate, transposed blocks, each ending with ethereally arpeggiated chords floating like the perfume of incense up into the higher reaches of the orchestra.[55] Again, Wagner does something more with the material. The Liszt version is beautiful but static—a very pretty picture in which nothing much is actually going on.[56] Wagner's harmony has, on the contrary, both variety and forward motion. With the transposition to C minor, the music unexpectedly takes on a newly piercing poignancy, suggesting a film narrative rather than a photo.

Thus it is especially ironic that it should have been Liszt's transcription from *Parsifal* that most jarringly illustrated just how far his own musical world had moved from Wagner's by the early 1880s—a divergent path that was trod further in the poignantly brief *Am Grabe Richard Wagners*. This nostalgic eulogy for Wagner incarnates the interaction between the two men both in the music and in Liszt's written preface to the score: "Wagner once reminded me of the similarity between his *Parsifal* motive and a theme in my previously written 'Excelsior' (the Introduction to the *Bells of Strasbourg*). May this resemblance be enshrined here. He has fulfilled all that is great and noble in the art of the present day." The composer of *Parsifal* would probably have hated the bizarrely meandering melodic distortions in this shadowy sketch. It twists the theme back into an exhausted echo of Liszt's cantata, then stumbles fitfully heavenward, blindly searching for the "grail motive" that opened *Lohengrin*.[57] Failing, it descends exhausted to more earthbound regions with a gentle chiming of *Parsifal* bells. But Wagner was now in no position to complain.

Example 13. Liszt, *Am Grabe Richard Wagners*, mm. 1–24; continued on next page.

Example 13. Liszt, *Am Grabe Richard Wagners,* mm. 25 – conclusion.

Wagner on Liszt

Naturally enough, Wagner's celebratory "open letter" to a pointlessly mysterious *MW* (Marie Wittgenstein, Princess Carolyne's daughter) "On Franz Liszt's Symphonic Poems" (1857) mentions nothing of any musical borrowings.[58] Such admissions were not for public consumption. Indeed, the essay is couched in unusually vague terms, even taking into consideration Wagner's typically tortuous writing style. His private evaluation of Liszt's music was more direct, more mixed and frequently more thought-provoking. Nevertheless, one thing that shines through the pretentious fog of Wagner's prose is his enormous admiration for Liszt's artistic personality. Like Hanslick, he was never in doubt that Liszt was a "great man." His enthusiastic response to Liszt's Sonata in B Minor was effectively based on this—that the music reflected the personality of its creator—"Dearest Franz, you were suddenly with me!"[59] Later on, Liszt's artistic personality seemed to be shaped by forms other than the sonata—but always with the obligatory "apotheosis." Privately, Wagner waxed poetic to Cosima:

> Your father's life course is stated for me in the "variation." One has before one nothing except the theme, repeated ever anew, but always somewhat altered, adorned, decorated, in different clothes, now virtuoso, now diplomat, now martial, now spiritual, always amiable, always himself, at bottom incomparable and for that reason presented to the world only in variation form; personality ever to the fore, noticeable above all, always so placed that the latter is shown to advantage, as under a prism—ever unique, repeatedly astonishing, but always the same, and—following each variation, it goes without saying, applause. Then comes the peroration, the apotheosis—the coda of the variations.[60]

Whatever the success of individual Liszt pieces, then, they luckily partook of the fascination of Liszt's personality. "It is all interesting, even when it is insignificant," Wagner declared (*CWD*, 30 November 1872). Nevertheless, his fascination with Liszt's compositions was tempered by intermittent reservations. One of his bugbears was Liszt's fondness for clamorous conclusions—what Wagner described as his *Apotheosen-Marotte* or "apotheosis obsession," a feature of *Les preludes* and *Tasso: Lamento e trionfo* among many other works (*CWD*, 2 August 1869).

Accordingly, Wagner preferred the slightly more restrained orchestral ending of the *Faust* Symphony without the chorus, and had little time for the alternate fortissimo peroration of the *Dante* Symphony.[61] Wagner's shadow fell over the latter work particularly strongly (he was to be its dedicatee). Liszt's original plan had been to compose a three-movement symphony, *Inferno-Purgatorio-Paradiso*, following the ground plan of Dante's *Divine Comedy*. The last movement was to include a chorus. But Wagner argued him out of this—he felt that the *Paradiso* part of Dante's poem was by far the weakest section. It certainly wasn't Wagner's idea of a good time: after the trials of Hell and Purgatory, Dante's Paradise turns out to involve endless discussions of theology (whereas Wagner's favorite pink silk underwear is nowhere even mentioned). An effective representation of Paradise in music, Wagner insisted, was impossible, and he counseled Liszt to abandon plans for an elaborate choral finale.[62] His advice was followed. As published, the symphony includes only movements depicting hell and purgatory, the latter finishing with a fairly short choral passage intoning the *Magnificat*. But Liszt still provided alternate endings in the score of the Symphony—the one fading away mystically, the other concluding clamorously—an apotheosis yet again.

The inclusion of these histrionic farewells, Wagner had no doubt, was due to the malign influence of the Princess Wittgenstein. She "understood only the crudest effects."[63] As early as 1849, before he had heard a note of Liszt's orchestral music, Wagner had inveighed against the "brainless herd of imitators" of Beethoven's C-Minor Symphony. Their music charted a clichéd course from misery in the minor key to martial triumphs in the major.[64] Liszt may not have been brainless, but he was certainly fond of swaggering codas. He even added an "apotheosis" to *Die Ideale* when one was, regrettably, not to be found in the source poem by Schiller. It is not surprising that out of all Liszt's compositions, Wagner reserved "a special place of honor" for the delicate and restrained symphonic poem *Orpheus*, although he could not deny the "great drive" of *Mazeppa*, even if it did end with a bang (his admiration for *Mazeppa* is enshrined in the wonderful "Ride of the Valkyries").[65] Unfortunately, many of Liszt's other orchestral works also feature the hysterical endings Wagner hated, and Princess Wittgenstein certainly cannot be blamed for them all. *Tasso: Lamento e trionfo* is even in C minor/major, marred by a load of "triangles, gong-strokes and rattling of chains"—this from the man who wrote for sixteen anvils in *Das Rheingold*.[66]

Noticeably, an "apotheosis obsession" is not mentioned in Wagner's essay on Liszt's symphonic poems, despite it being a prominent trait of five out of the six pieces under discussion. But in the context of his apologia, Wagner does not hesitate to catalog other common contemporary criticisms of Liszt's music: its rambling "formlessness" and eccentric harmonic effects, typically viewed as the result of a misguided attempt by a great performer also to be a great composer. He certainly chooses a surprisingly roundabout way of rebutting these criticisms. To claim, as he does, that Liszt's piano playing constitutes "genuine production, rather than just reproduction," is rather beside the point, since the inspiration of the playing was never an issue, only the compositions. Moreover, Wagner's assertion that Liszt's music has a "form" derived from the "poetic idea" remains nothing more than an assertion. Although he condemns Beethoven for writing a too-conventional recapitulation in the third *Leonore* Overture, and criticizes Berlioz for "losing the thread" in the Adagio movement from *Roméo et Juliette*, he never seems to want to go into details about exactly how Liszt does things better. Perhaps he is referring to the much freer treatment of recapitulation in *Tasso* and *Orpheus*, but if he is, why does he not simply say so? Wagner does at least directly rebut complaints about Liszt's willful treatment of harmony, and openly praises the "pregnancy of the themes."[67]

In private, Wagner's evaluation of Liszt was at times more directly critical, but at least less opaque. He lauded the *Faust* Symphony, especially the "masterly conception of the *Mephisto* movement" (*CWD*, 23 May 1882), and admired the "musical scene painting" of the *Dante* Symphony (*CWD*, 27 August 1878), even if it required listeners to know too much about Dante's poem for easy accessibility (*CWD*, 22 September 1880). Anyway, the *Dante* Symphony was just too Catholic for Wagner's taste, as indeed was *Christus*, where "the resources of a great and noble art" were used to "imitate the wailing of priests" (*CWD*, 7 June 1872). Almost needless to say, the fanatical Catholicism of Princess Wittgenstein was blamed for this, too. When the Wagners attended a Weimar performance of *Christus*, conducted by the composer, their reaction ranged from "ravishment to immense indignation," although the conducting was pronounced to be excellent. Liszt was, alas, "the last great victim of this Latin-Roman world" (*CWD*, 29 May 1873). A performance of *Christus* with full orchestral and choral complement at least allowed it a fair hearing. On receiving the vocal score of the oratorio, Wagner had stumbled through it on the piano, criticizing along the way the clumsy choral writing (*CWD*, 7 June 1872). The clumsiness, however, may have lain elsewhere. When Liszt played over the score, it suddenly sounded much better. Cosima ingenuously remarked, "It certainly seemed very different under his fingers" (*CWD*, 16 October 1872).

However tendentious Wagner's evaluation of *Christus*—later he would speak more highly of it when it gave him a corresponding chance to condemn Brahms's *Triumphlied* (*CWD*, 8 August 1874)—he unerringly identified one significant feature of Liszt's musical makeup that is underrated today, namely his fondness for French grand opera. The oratorio was indeed, as Wagner asserted, "thoroughly un-German" in its blend of "Old Church style" with echoes of Meyerbeer and Halévy, whose operas had "a decisive influence" on Liszt in his youth (*CWD*, 9 June 1872). (Undeniably, they had just as strong an effect on Wagner.) Even today, many find the stylistically

Catholic cosmopolitanism of Liszt's music difficult to swallow, and although Wagner himself did not make the connection, French grand opera likely shared some responsibility for Liszt's apotheosis obsession. The more pompous passages of *Les preludes* could easily be inserted into the "Blessing of the Daggers" scene of *Les Huguenots* and hardly an eyebrow would be raised.

Eclecticism and extroverted conclusions were simply part of Liszt's middle-period musical style, whether one warmed to it or not. But technical failings were quite another matter. Wagner could not ignore the odd lapses in concentration that marred even fine works such as the *Faust* Symphony. Here he was surprised to find scrappy inner-part writing, in contrast to his own care over such things.[68] Liszt thought no one bothered listening to the inner voices, claimed Wagner. He might also have pointed out that Liszt's music generally shies away from contrapuntal complexity—the melodies are memorable, the harmonies often novel, but the texture tends to be "tune with accompaniment" (see discussion of *Orpheus/Siegfried* above), even in supposedly fugal passages. Moreover, a startling unevenness, as Wagner noted, is disconcertingly evident not only within but between pieces. A Liszt rhapsody might be "original . . . and reflect [the composer's] individuality" (*CWD*, 10 October 1882)—the "great personality" once more makes its bow—whereas the symphonic poem *Hamlet* gave Wagner the impression of "a disheveled tomcat lying there before him."[69] The revised *Beethoven* Cantata of 1870 was supposedly even worse—impossible to appreciate owing to the text, its treatment, and indeed the entire genre to which it belonged. Worst of all, the main theme of the *Eroica* Symphony was sung! (*CWD*, 30 June 1870)

The most trenchant criticism reported in Cosima's diaries, however, was reserved for Liszt's late music. Admittedly, Wagner still seemed to be able to enjoy *Les jeux d'eaux à la Villa d'Este* and *Aux cyprès de la Villa d'Este* from the third *Année de pelerinage*.[70] He was also mightily amused at the sudden moderation of Liszt's technical demands. "Now I too am a Liszt pianist!" he proclaimed, gleefully pointing out a resemblance between the main tune of *Zum Andenken Petöfys* and Brünnhilde's "War es so niedrig" from *Walküre*, Act 3 (*CWD*, 8 July 1879). But the Second *Mephisto* Waltz of 1881 was resolutely trashed (a "dismal production," *CWD*, 2 March 1882), as was the *Christmas Tree* Suite.[71] One evening he announced ("sharply, and in much detail") that Liszt's latest efforts were "completely meaningless" (*CWD*, 28 November 1882). Cosima made a mental note to consider writing to her father, in the hope that Wagner's verdict might bring him to his senses, as it were. Yet her husband had not quite exhausted his interest in the topic. The next night he pursued his quarry further, unleashing a frothing tirade of abuse against Liszt's recent music.[72] The Wagner children seem to have found his choice of words a bit too near the bone.

They were, after all, also Liszt's grandchildren, and Daniela was no doubt proud to be the dedicatee of the condemned *Christmas Tree* Suite.[73] Part of the relevant passage in Cosima's diary was energetically obliterated. Enough remains to read the words *keimender Wahnsinn* (sprouting insanity) and a final verdict: "It is impossible to develop a taste for these dissonances."

Was it Liszt's transcription of the "Grail March" from *Parsifal* that broke the camel's back? It certainly could also have been a number of other radical experiments, like the bizarre *Csardas macabre*, whose manuscript bears the inscription "May one write or listen to such a thing?" But *Parsifal* lay closer to Wagner's heart. He might have been able to endure "without comment" the bleak fragmentation creeping into Liszt's original music, but not when the style was applied to his own operas. Wagner's music had retained the long lines, the generous elaboration that Liszt's only sporadically attained and had now completely abandoned. Perhaps Liszt's futuristic fragments arose as much from failing powers of concentration as from disappointment with life, but whatever their catalyst, they were utterly alien to Wagner's musical aesthetic. Cosima was taken aback by the intensity of her husband's tirade, remaining "silent, sad," uncertain how to reply. But she could have said that Liszt's creative approach had remained consistent. The new music was as expressive of his current personality as the confident cosmopolitanism of his Weimar years had been. It was simply now the music of a different man—a man who had suffered one setback too many. Liszt's grand apotheosis obsession had finally burned itself out, but Wagner was still living through his own personal apotheosis. The years of artistic affinity had passed.

NOTES

1. There are many eyewitness accounts of Wagner's tribute to Liszt at the 1876 Bayreuth Festival; see, for example, Berthold Kellermann, *Erinnerungen: Ein Künstlerleben* (Zurich, 1932), 193–95. For Liszt's last days and the "Tristan!" story, see Alan Walker, *The Death of Franz Liszt: Based on the Unpublished Diary of his Pupil Lina Schmalhausen* (Ithaca, N.Y., 2002), 3. Wagner once remarked to Cosima that had it not been for her father, his works would possibly be "moldering beside Reissiger and his *Schiffbruch der Medusa*," referring to one of the largely still-born operatic efforts of his former Dresden colleague Karl Gottlieb Reissiger. *Cosima Wagner's Diaries*, ed. Martin Gregor-Dellin and Dietrich Mack, trans. Geoffrey Skelton, 2 vols. (New York and London, 1978, 1980), 2:42 (entry of 16 March 1878). Subsequent references to the *Diaries* in the main text and endnotes are given as *CWD*, with the date of entry.

2. Liszt had officially been Kapellmeister im außerordentlichen Dienst (Kapellmeister Extraordinary) since 1842, but this committed him to spend only three months a year in the small German town of Weimar. Before 1848 he rarely got around to fulfilling even this less than onerous attendance requirement.

3. Robert Schumann, *Music and Musicians*, trans. F. R. Ritter (London, 1878), 1:351. Ironically, some critics could have made the same complaint about Schumann—who started as a composer much later than Liszt—and indeed some did. Such an evaluation lies at the heart of Hans von Bülow's description of Schumann as a "sentimental" composer— one who actively struggled in his mature years for compositional mastery—as opposed to the "naïve," precociously talented Mendelssohn. Bülow was evidently adopting Schiller's famous distinction between "naïve" and "sentimental" poetry.

4. For a full account, see Kenneth Hamilton, "Not with a Bang but a Whimper: The Death of Liszt's *Sardanapale*," *Cambridge Opera Journal* 8/1 (1996): 45–58.

5. Adrian Williams, *Franz Liszt: Selected Letters* (Oxford, 1998), 238. It has been customary for scholars to claim that the *Petrarch Sonnets* were first written in 1838–39. See, for example, Humphrey Searle, *The Music of Liszt* (New York, 1966), 31. In this letter of 1846, however, Liszt acknowledges them as brand-new works. According to Rena Mueller ("The Lieder of Liszt," in *The Cambridge Companion to the Lied,* ed. James Parsons [Cambridge, 2004], 170–1) the melodies (without words) first appear in a sketchbook around 1843–44.

6. La Mara, ed., *Franz Liszts Briefe*, 8 vols. (Leipzig, 1893–1905), 1:287.

7. Ibid., 8:62

8. Hanjo Kesting, ed., *Franz Liszt-Richard Wagner Briefwechsel* (Frankfurt am Main, 1988), 162.

9. Ibid., 161–62. (All translations of the Liszt-Wagner correspondence are mine.) *Welsch* is the word that Hans Sachs notoriously uses toward the end of Wagner's *Die Meistersinger* with reference to the foreign (implicitly Franco-Italian) artistic influences threatening German culture.

10. Ibid., 163.

11. The appearance of Raff's opera was accompanied by the obligatory Liszt transcriptions for piano—in this case the Andante Finale and March. The former is an attractive and perhaps unjustly forgotten piece, which obviously owes a lot to Liszt's own "Cantique d'amour" from *Harmonies poetiques et réligieuses*. The latter piece is, alas, justly forgotten.

12. Kesting, *Liszt-Wagner Briefwechsel*, 180.

13. See Monika Hennemann, "Mendelssohn's Dramatic Compositions: From *Liederspiel* to *Lorelei*," in *The Cambridge Companion to Mendelssohn*, ed. Peter Mercer Taylor (Cambridge, 2004), 206–32.

14. Kesting, *Liszt-Wagner Briefwechsel*, 187. The *Deutsche Monatsschrift* extracts were slightly revised by Wagner, and therefore the text differs somewhat from that of *Oper und Drama*.

15. Liszt toyed with a handful of other operatic plans in later years, but none of them came anywhere near fruition.

16. Kesting, *Liszt-Wagner Briefwechsel*, 248.

17. Letter from Liszt to Franz Brendel, 8 November 1862, in La Mara, *Letters of Franz Liszt*, trans. Constance Bache (London, 1894), 2:33. One can't help feeling that Liszt's routine tendency to "problematize" things would have ensured him a solid career in twentieth-century musicology.

18. Liszt's opera transcriptions were published under a profusion of titles: the *Tannhäuser* Overture, for example, was a "Concert Paraphrase," and most other pieces appeared as "arrangements" (*Bearbeitungen*). For *Rienzi* Liszt produced a "fantasy piece" (*Fantasiestück*).

19. "Über Franz Liszts Symphonischen Dichtungen" (1857), in Richard Wagner, *Gesammelte Schriften und Dichtungen* (henceforth *GSD*), 10 vols. (Leipzig, 1887–1911), 5:193–94.

20. David Garrick's eighteenth-century performing text of *Romeo and Juliet* was still as commonly performed in the early nineteenth century as it is ignored in ours. It was

accordingly the Garrick reworking that Berlioz first saw on stage. The difference in quality between Garrick's and Shakespeare's versification would hardly have been evident to anyone with as little knowledge of English as Berlioz.

21. Translated from "Über die Anwendung der Musik auf das Drama" (1879) by William Ashton Ellis, in *Richard Wagner's Prose Works*, 8 vols. (London, 1895–99), 6:189–90.

22. Eduard Hanslick, *Aus dem Tagebuch eines Rezensenten*, ed. Peter Wapnewski (Kassel, 1989), 13 (my translation).

23. Letter of 23 November 1876 to Breitkopf & Härtel, in La Mara, *Letters of Franz Liszt*, 2:307. Several of the early transcriptions from *Tannhäuser* and *Lohengrin* were subsequently revised (sometimes more than once), resulting in a sequence of published editions with minor pianistic differences.

24. For the practice of piano preluding in the nineteenth century, see Kenneth Hamilton, *After the Golden Age: Romantic Pianism and Modern Performance* (New York, 2008), 101–38. The manuscript of Liszt's transcription of "Isolde's *Liebestod*" partially survives in the Goethe-und Schiller-Archiv, Weimar (MS. U32). It was Liszt, incidentally, who was largely responsible for the subsequently familiar attribution of this name (*Liebestod*) to the final episode of the opera, which Wagner had referred to as Isolde's *Verklärung* ("Transfiguration"). He himself applied the term "love death" (*Liebestod*) to the Act 1 Prelude.

25. Richard Wagner, *My Life*, trans. Andrew Gray and Mary Whittal (Cambridge, 1983), 270. Liszt's published "Fantasy on Themes from *Rienzi*," S.439, dates from 1859.

26. For the amateur: Wolfram's "Song to the Evening Star," or "O, du mein holder Abendstern," from *Tannhäuser*; "Elsa's Dream," "Elsa's Procession to the Minster," and "Lohengrin's Reprimand to Elsa," from *Lohengrin*. For the virtuoso: *Tannhäuser* Overture and "Entry of the Guests at the Wartburg"; Act 3 Prelude and "Bridal Chorus" from *Lohengrin*.

27. Liszt's letter of 26 February 1849 and Wagner's of 1 March 1849 in Kesting, *Liszt-Wagner Briefwechsel*.

28. Listening to a performance of Liszt's arrangement of the overture, Wagner admitted to having been influenced by some figuration in the first movement of Berlioz's *Harold in Italy* (*CWD*, 14 January 1882).

29. Kesting, *Liszt-Wagner Briefwechsel*, 274.

30. There are also hints of sonata form in Liszt's juvenile Impromptu on Themes of Rossini and Spontini, and in his much later arrangement of the Waltz from Gounod's *Faust*.

31. A. Habets, *Borodin and Liszt* (London, 1895), 141.

32. *CWD*, 20 October 1872. Cosima refers to "the A-flat music from *Tristan*," which surely means "O sink hernieder." Liszt, of course, never published a transcription of this section.

33. From "On the Application of Music to the Drama," in Ellis, *Richard Wagner's Prose Works*, 6:189.

34. New Liszt Edition, series 2, vol. 10 (Budapest, 2002), ed. László Martos and Imre Sulyok. The manuscript of Liszt's additions is presently housed in the Sächsische Staatsarchiv in Leipzig.

35. "Today he begins to talk about my father again, very blunt in his truthfulness; he describes his new works as 'budding insanity' and finds it impossible to develop a taste for their dissonances" (*CWD*, 29 November 1882). The editors note that "about twelve words" in the latter part of the sentence were obliterated in the manuscript of the diaries.

36. The only hint I can find of criticism of Wagner's later music by Liszt is in the Russian composer (and member of the so-called *Kuchka*) Cesar Cui's reminiscences of a chat with Liszt: "Later, over tea I told him what I thought of Wagner, the falseness of his system, the insignificant role he assigns to the voice, the melodic poverty resulting from his monotonous reiteration of themes, and so on. The Baroness [von Meyendorff] listened with horror, Liszt—with a slight smile. "Il y a du vrai dans ce que vous dites là, mais, je vous en supplie, n'allez pas le répéter à Bayreuth!" (There's some truth in what you say, but I

beg you, don't go around Bayreuth repeating it!) Vladimir Stasov, *Liszt, Schumann and Berlioz in Russia* (St Petersburg, 1896), in *Vladimir Stasov: Selected Essays on Music*, trans. F. Jonas (New York, 1968), 183.

37. Richard Pohl's "indiscreet" article mentioning Liszt's harmonic influence on Wagner appeared in the *Neue Zeitschrift für Musik* in four installments, from 17 to 19 August 1859, at the height of the critical debates over the so-called music of the future. The article is reprinted in Richard Pohl, *Richard Wagner: Studien und Kritiken* (Leipzig, 1883). For Wagner's reaction (in a letter to Hans von Bülow), see *Richard Wagner: Sämtliche Briefe*, ed. Martin Dürrer (Wiesbaden, 1999), 11:282.

38. *CWD*, 27, 29 August 1878. Wagner's expression seems rather ill-chosen here—after all, he is the one admitting stealing from Liszt, so the symphonic poems are more a target for thieves than a den of them. But one cannot really expect constant vigilance over linguistic accuracy in casual conversation.

39. Joachim Bergfeld, ed., *The Diary of Richard Wagner, 1865–1882: The Brown Book*, trans. George Bird (London, 1980), 102–3.

40. Wagner, *My Life*, 495.

41. Ibid., 537–38.

42. At the Bard College *Liszt and His World* Festival in 2006. Not surprisingly, "Lorelei" was one of Wagner's favorite Liszt pieces (see, for just one example, *CWD*, 30 November 1872).

43. See Rainer Kleinertz, "Liszt, Wagner, and Unfolding Form," in *Franz Liszt and His World*, ed. Christopher Gibbs and Dana Gooley (Princeton, N.J., 2006), 231–54.

44. With a preceding page of surging harmonic sequences possibly inspired by, of all things, "Padre, tu piange?" from Bellini's *Norma*. But then, Wagner was a big Bellini fan before he transformed himself into the savior of German opera.

45. Goethe- und Schiller-Archiv, Weimar, MS. N4, a sketchbook from the mid-1840s. An undated separate page of sketches (probably from later in the decade) is the first to show the opening of the symphony in a form that we can recognize as similar to the final version, with the juxtaposition of the two principal themes. See Laszlo Somfai, "Die Musikalische Gestaltwandlungen der 'Faust-Symphonie' von Liszt," in *Studia Musicologica* 2 (1962): 87–137, esp. 100 and 113.

46. Kesting, *Liszt-Wagner Briefwechsel*, 60. Of course, if the page mentioned in above n. 45 turns out to date from after Liszt got to know the *Faust* Overture, the issue of a direct influence from Wagner may have to be nuanced yet again. The situation is somewhat complicated here by Wagner's misdating of his 30 January 1849 letter to Liszt assenting to the dispatch of the *Faust* Overture score. As is so easy to do early in a new year, he absent-mindedly scribbled "1848." Both the context and the subsequent course of the correspondence make it clear that 1849 is correct, an interpretation usually adopted by modern editors of Wagner's letters.

47. August Göllerich, *Franz Liszt* (Berlin, 1908), 172.

48. The search for borrowings can easily reach obsessive levels, as if music were written on the basis of Tom Lehrer's song "I Got It From Agnes . . ." ("And just because we really care / Whatever we get, we share!").

49. See Somfai, "Die musikalische Gestaltwandlungen der 'Faust-Symphonie' von Liszt," 100. Although in the initial (1840s) sketches for the *Faust* Symphony the first movement is fairly thoroughly drafted, Liszt had devised little more than a melody for "Gretchen." The final "Mephistopheles" movement is notable by its complete absence, although it seems probable that Liszt intended even at this point to complete the work with this.

50. Kesting, *Liszt-Wagner Briefwechsel*, 248.

51. The fascinating exchange of views over the revision of the *Faust* Overture will be found in ibid., 241, 248, 254, and 398. Liszt suggested, among other things, a revision of the orchestration—especially the use of the brass section, which he found too overpowering—and an expansion of the second-subject group, including the addition of a new, tender,

Gretchen-like theme. Wagner followed most of this advice, reworking the orchestration and lengthening the second key area. He did not, however, add the recommended new theme, on the grounds that this would effectively force him to write an entirely new piece.

52. One can trace the thread of inspiration beyond "Lorelei," *Tristan* and "Ich möchte hingehen," to end up at Liszt's late *Aux cyprès de la Villa d'Este* no. 2, in which a variant of the "Lorelei"/*Tristan* opening phrase again raises its familiar head.

53. One might, however, wish to nuance Charles Rosen's verdict that the resemblance between the openings of "Lorelei" and *Tristan* "is not entirely to Liszt's credit, as Wagner's reworking is both more interesting and more powerful." Rosen, *The Romantic Generation* (Cambridge, Mass., 1995), 475. Rosen's view is partly based on what he considers (correctly, in my opinion) to be Liszt's routine overuse of harmonies based on the chord of the diminished seventh. Wagner's rewriting of the "Lorelei" opening is indeed more novel harmonically, but Liszt's employment of the hollow-sounding, directionless diminished seventh is perfectly suited to the mood (puzzlement, rather than yearning) of the words he intends to illustrate ("Ich weiß nicht, was soll's bedeuten"). This is immediately obvious if we try recomposing Liszt's introduction using Wagner's harmonies.

54. For the full story, see the account by Liszt's student and amanuensis August Göllerich in his *Franz Liszt*, 22–23. (Liszt pointed out that he did not invent the Excelsior melody— it was based on a Catholic Church chant.) One might also speculate that the "dragging" motive of Amfortas in *Parsifal* was influenced by the opening of Liszt's *Vallée d'Obermann*, or even Wotan's "spear" motive in the *Ring* by the similarly commanding descending-scale theme in Liszt's B-minor Sonata. The prelude to Act 1 of *Die Walküre*, too, unfolds in a surprisingly static, Lisztian fashion—what Gerald Abraham (*One Hundred Years of Music* [London, 1974], 40–41) memorably called Liszt's "wallpaper-pattern" style of construction—and the sinuous chromaticism of Brünnhilde's "Magic Sleep" in Act 3 of the same opera strongly recalls Mephistopheles' final disappearance in the third movement of the *Faust* Symphony.

55. This cyclopean style of construction is probably partly inspired by the opening of Beethoven's Ninth Symphony, and perhaps also by the development section in the first movement of his Sixth. Liszt had another go at rewriting the beginning of Beethoven's Ninth in the *Kyrie* of his *Gran Mass*.

56. We know from Liszt's associate Richard Pohl what this picture is actually intended to be. In a (gushingly sycophantic) "Einleitung zu Liszts *Dante*-Symphonie" (printed by Breitkopf & Härtel as the preface to August Stradal's piano solo transcription of the score) we are told that it illustrates the passage in Dante's poem where the travelers emerge from hell, enchanted by the sight of the rising sun from their gently undulating boat.

57. *Am Grabe Richard Wagners* exists in two versions: for piano and for string quartet and harp. The *Lohengrin* allusion—a reminiscence of the high string sonorities at the start of the opera—naturally appears more immediate in the string/harp scoring. Liszt also wrote a short funereal piece in memory of Wagner titled *RW-Venezia*, and a reworked version of his *La lugubre gondola* (the first sketch of which was written during a stay with the Wagners in Venice, shortly before Wagner's death) was published in the year of Liszt's death with a title page depicting Wagner's grave. Liszt had come to consider the piece as a musical prophecy of Wagner's demise.

58. Wagner, *GSD*, 5:182–98. The original, rather different manuscript version of this "open letter" can be found in Wagner, *Sämtliche Briefe*, 8:265–81. None of these differences, however, significantly affect the broad thrust of the argument.

59. Kesting, *Liszt-Wagner Briefwechsel*, 417.

60. Bergfeld, ed., *The Diary of Richard Wagner*, 72 (entry of 10 September 1865, addressed to Cosima).

61. Wagner, *My Life*, 537–38. The *Faust* Symphony originally ended with a fairly short orchestral coda. Later Liszt had the idea of appending a setting for solo tenor and male voices of the Chorus Mysticus from *Faust,* Part II. Wagner's memory was at fault when he

implied in *My Life* that the orchestral ending faded away quietly ("ended delicately and sweetly with a last, utterly compelling reminiscence of Gretchen, without any attempt to arouse attention forcibly"). *Pace* Wagner, it, too, forms a loud, grandiloquent close, but certainly one less hyperbolic than the choral version.

62. Wagner and Liszt's discussion of the form of the *Dante* Symphony can be found in Kesting, *Liszt-Wagner Briefwechsel*, 423, 425–27, 431, 436.

63. *CWD*, 2 August 1869. See also *CWD*, 21 August 1881, where Wagner laments that he and Liszt "have become strangers to each other through 'bad influences.' As far as the *Dante* Symphony is concerned, Liszt seems eventually to have come over to Wagner's view of the alternate endings. In his transcription of the symphony for piano solo, Liszt's pupil August Stradal added a footnote to the effect that in his last years the composer personally told him the "fading out, floating away conclusion was the only proper one" whereas the "pompous second ending was no longer valid."

64. "The Art Work of the Future," in Ellis, *Richard Wagner's Prose Works*, 1:123.

65. See Wagner, *My Life*, 537. Wagner also spoke highly of *Orpheus* in correspondence to Otto Wesendonck (*Sämtliche Briefe*, 8:211–12) and Hans von Bülow (*Sämtliche Briefe*, 8:204). Although Liszt never attempted a piano transcription of Wagner's "Ride of the Valkyries," his pupil Carl Tausig tackled it—not entirely successfully, it must be said—as did Louis Brassin.

66. *CWD*, 2 August 1869. See also *CWD* entry for 28 November 1879, where *Tasso* is additionally criticized, with some justification, for "the long drawn-out lament at the beginning."

67. Wagner extolled in private, too, what he later called "die Drastik" (the vividness) of Liszt's themes—with particular reference to the song "Lorelei." *CWD*, 30 November 1872 and 21 October 1878.

68. *CWD*, 9 June 1872. Wagner also remarked that Liszt and von Bülow completed things quickly, whereas he was cursed with the tendency to work hard and more thoroughly at them (*CWD*, 13 November 1874).

69. *CWD*, 1 May 1879. "Musicians should not concern themselves with things that have nothing to do with them," Wagner went on to say. "Hamlet offers nothing to musicians."

70. *CWD*, 10 April 1878. The main theme of the second *Aux cyprès* piece nostalgically refers both to Liszt's "Lorelei" and to Wagner's *Tristan* (see n. 52).

71. *CWD*, 2 December 1882. Wagner grumbled that any comment he was likely to make on it "would be cruel."

72. *CWD*, 29 November 1882; see n. 35 above.

73. Daniela was the daughter of Hans von Bülow, although she had been brought up as part of the Wagner family.

From Opera to Music Drama:

Nominal Loss, Titular Gain

LYDIA GOEHR

Name: *Musikdrama* abominable (according to Richard Wagner)

If Wagner continues to be the name for the *ruin of music*, as
Bernini for the ruin of sculpture, he is not its cause.

—Friedrich Nietzsche

I

A recent contribution to Wagner scholarship is a *New Grove Guide* titled
Wagner and His Operas.[1] In each chapter devoted to the individual works,
the author, Barry Millington, opens with a descriptive name, given in
German, with mention thereafter of the work's number of acts. Usually
that number is three, although there are some exceptions, as the following chronological list makes explicit. Millington designates *Die Feen*, first,
as a *grosse romantische Oper* (grand romantic opera); second, *Das Liebesverbot
oder die Novize von Palermo* as a *grosse komische Oper* (grand comic opera) in
2 acts; and, third, *Rienzi, der Letzte der Tribunen* as a *grosse tragische Oper*
(grand tragic opera) in five acts. After this, *Der fliegende Holländer* is introduced as a *romantische Oper*, *Tannhäuser* as a *grosse romantische Oper*, and
Lohengrin also as a *romantische Oper*. *Tristan und Isolde* follows as a *Handlung*
(action, implicitly "dramatic action"), after which comes *Der Ring des
Niebelungen* as a *Bühnenfestspiel* (stage-festival-play), of which *Das Rheingold*
is the Prologue (*Vorabend*) in four scenes, *Die Walküre* the first day, *Siegfried*
the second, and *Götterdämmerung* the third, in three acts with a Prologue.
Parsifal, a *Bühnenweihfestspiel* (stage-consecration-festival-play) concludes
the oeuvre.

So far, no surprises. However, one opera is made into an exception.
Millington withholds from *Die Meistersinger von Nürnberg* Wagner's own

designation—*Komische Oper in 3 Akten*—and calls it instead, in English, a music drama. Why single out *Meistersinger* in this way? The answer is not clear; maybe the exception is made unwittingly. Still, something interesting can be made out of it. Had Millington introduced *Meistersinger* with the German term *Musikdrama,* he might have led readers to believe something false, that this work alone is a music drama or that Wagner assigned to this work this particular description, which he did not. Millington does not make this mistake. Designating *Die Meistersinger* as a music drama, in English, he seems to treat the descriptive name generically, as though *Meistersinger* were just one of Wagner's many music dramas, of which *Holländer* is sometimes claimed chronologically to be the first and *Parsifal* the last.

But if Millington uses the term "music drama" generically, why does he title his book with the other generic name, *Wagner and His Operas,* and not *Wagner and His Music Dramas*?[2] It would not have been controversial to do the latter. Quite the reverse: it would have continued a well-established tradition within Wagner reception, according to which Wagner's mature works are all named music dramas—and this despite Wagner's sometimes vigorous objections to doing so.

This essay concerns the difference it makes, if it makes a difference, to speak of Wagner's works either as music dramas or as operas. It assumes this concern as part of a larger interest in the practice of naming or titling works of art. The general literature on titles awarded or denied artworks is remarkably sparse, which is surprising given the significance that even the briefest inquiry will show acts of naming or titling to have.[3] Of course, titling and naming are not the same acts, although we will find them here inextricably connected. In what follows I argue that a significant part of the tension regarding naming and titling, as it manifests itself in Wagner's oeuvre, turns on a move Wagner encouraged, to cease thinking about names and titles as merely descriptive or classificatory and to start thinking about them as pointing toward an *unnameable* ideal. Given his outlook, what he produced were *operas* aspiring toward an *ideal* of a form of art that was preferably left unnamed (*namenlos*), though if the ideal had to be named, then the term *Musikdrama* probably served him better than any other he considered.

Wagner's argument bears on how one thinks about the concept of a genre under early Romantic-idealist conditions of modernity and on how one identifies, individuates, and interprets his works. Although he produced several operas, the *Musikdrama* remained for him a singular ideal or Idea, though this was not to pronounce the Idea either fixed or determinate. The point was to leave the Idea underdetermined by conceptual articulation and thus sufficiently open for each opera to approximate it *differently* and in its own *exemplary* way.

Wagner suggested this argument in several of his essays and most explicitly when he described his operas as moving toward music drama, where, however, music drama was now the end toward which *all* opera ought to aspire. Nowhere did he treat the argument more evidently than in one of the most polemical pieces he ever wrote, "Über die Benennung 'Musikdrama.'" The title is usually translated into English as "On the Name 'Music Drama,'" missing much of what is actively involved in *giving something a name*.[4] Behind Wagner's polemics was a serious theme: naming or titling a work is just as serious a baptismal act as naming a person. In his piece, Wagner addressed the compromises implicit in the act of naming his works with a general or generic descriptive term. He did this to support a critical strategy characteristic in nineteenth-century German aesthetic theory bearing on the thesis of *exemplarity*. To name an Idea too academically risks closing off productive possibilities in the works themselves. As long as the Idea is not so named, the focus remains on the works as self-standing exemplars. The more a name fixes the Idea, the more the works resist being named, even if, in this resistance, each work strives to define the Idea by *its* name alone. In this sense, an exemplary work *entitles* itself to the Idea.

Accompanying Wagner's aesthetic argument of exemplarity was, however, a grand conceit. Although he did all he could to prevent his works from being fixed by a generic name, especially when that name was awarded by his critics, he also did all he could to affix his own name—and his name *alone*—to the future of art. He desired that his name would come to stand for an entire age in the history of German culture as Goethe's name did before him (the *Goethezeit* naming the era of Weimar Classicism). The more he regarded his name as having found its place, the more he turned to the names "Bayreuth" and "Germany" to fix them, too. On one occasion, in a piece on "Das Bühnenfestspielhaus zu Bayreuth," he contrasted eighteenth-century court culture with nineteenth-century bourgeois culture—or, more specifically, an extraordinarily spirited performance of Beethoven's Ninth, performed by German musicians and singers, with the earlier spiritually impoverished offerings of Italian opera and French comedy—only to declare:

> Without any resistance, I was granted the opportunity to give this meaning to our introductory festival. And for all who celebrated with us, the name *Bayreuth*, which now carried this meaning, became a dear memory, an encouraging notion, a meaningful motto.
>
> And such a motto is needed to sustain us in the daily fight against the intrusive demonstrations of the profoundly alienated spirit that shows itself now in the German nation. (*GSD*, 9:333–34)

Wagner's obsession with naming and titling sustained a lifelong and highly charged confrontation between aesthetic resistance and cultural-political arrogance. For there to be a new concept of art there had to be a new institution of opera and a new country. The confrontation did not lead to what Wagner wanted. It led far more to "Wagnerism" than to a *Wagnerzeit*. No one commented more immediately or with more passion on the missed opportunity than Nietzsche. When he proclaimed that "Wagner *sums up* modernity," he added: "It doesn't help, one must first be a Wagnerian."[5]

Nietzsche was no less fascinated than Wagner with acts of naming. That Nietzsche never employed the term "music drama" in his text on the birth of Wagnerian opera out of the ancient spirit of Greek tragedy (*The Birth of Tragedy*, 1872) is a fact one should not ignore.[6] When, in "The Greek Music Drama," another essay of the same period (1869–70), Nietzsche employed the term with a distinct titular pride, Wagner strongly objected.[7] As Cosima Wagner recorded, "In the evening Prof. N. reads us a lecture on the Greek music drama ["Das griechische Musikdrama"], a title for which R. pulls him up, explaining the reason for his disapproval."[8] Unfortunately, Cosima didn't spell out exactly *why* Wagner objected on this night of June 11, 1870, but given Wagner's own essay ("Über die Benennung 'Musikdrama'"), written in October 1872, one sees that the issue was and remained for him, as for Nietzsche, an urgent one.

Wagner's argument for and against the name "music drama" is traceable throughout his writings. Let us focus on one of the first observations from his piece "Über die Benennung," namely, on the "astounding" works of Aeschylus, which, Wagner wrote, the Athenians "named not dramas, but left with the holy names of their origin: 'tragedies.'" Apparently the Greeks were content to have no generic name for their unprecedented works and to leave them "nameless" (*namenlos*). Everything, however, began to go wrong when the great and powerful critics began to insist on fixing the canonic works of opera and drama according to "abstract ideas" (*Begriffe*), when they began to celebrate the word as absolute or the generic name for *its* sake alone. Recall, Wagner continued, the "good Polonius" who edified everyone with an "elegant list" of names in *Hamlet* or the Italians who "topped up" their works with the generic name *dramma per musica*.[9] After which Wagner listed all the empty, *nichtssagenden* (literally, "nothing-saying"), generic names imposed on the musical world: "music drama," "opera," "opus," and "work." And yet, despite all this *namenlos Unsinniges* (nameless nonsense), the aim behind these acts of naming was to capture something *unnennbar Tiefsinniges* (unnameably profound) (*GSD*, 9:305–6). Why this sudden turn in an otherwise damning criticism? Likely because Wagner wanted to remind his readers that it is one thing to grant the deep value of an artist *searching* for a name, and another to complain of the burdens or restrictions that result once it has been found.

There was an extraordinary synchronicity of language and terms between Wagner's and Nietzsche's criticisms, raising questions of who was influencing whom. Thus, Nietzsche also opened his lecture on "The Greek Music Drama" with the issue of names.

> In our theater of today, one finds not only memories and echoes of the *dramatic arts of Greece*: no, their fundamental forms also stem from the *Hellenic* soil, either in *natural* development or because of *artificial* borrowing. Only the *names* have often changed and shifted, just as the medieval music still really possessed the Greek scales as well as the names for these, except that, for example, what the Greeks called "*Locrian*" was renamed "*Doric*" as a church mode. Similar confusions present themselves regarding the terminology associated with drama: what the Athenians understood by "tragedy," we have at best subsumed under the notion of "grand opera": or at least this is what Voltaire did in a letter he wrote to Cardinal Quirini. (*KSA*, 1:517)

Like Wagner, Nietzsche also traced the "genealogical affinity" between the ancients and moderns, to claim:

> What we call opera today is a caricature of the antique music drama. It developed solely out of a direct aping of antiquity according to an abstract theory and without the unconscious influence of a natural drive. As a result, it is an artificially generated *homunculus*, an angry goblin in the development of our modern music. (*KSA*, 1:518)

Nietzsche's lecture was a *tour de force*, as Wagner well recognized. Nevertheless, what Nietzsche most wanted to tell Wagner, Wagner least wanted to hear. "The Greek music drama," Nietzsche concluded,

> had for the entire ancient art a free sort of drapery: everything unfree, everything isolated in the individual arts was surmounted. In the sacrificial festivals, beautiful as well as daring hymns were sung. Commitment but also grace, diversity but also unity, different arts at the peak of their activity, but still *one* work of art—this was the ancient music drama. But whenever someone is reminded of all this when looking at contemporary reforms of art, they will have to conclude that the artwork of the future is less a shining image than a deception. What we expect from the future was already once a reality—that existed in the past, one thousand years ago. (*KSA*, 1:531)

Nietzsche, I suggest, preserved this conclusion in the first fifteen original sections of his *Birth of Tragedy*, yet compromised the conclusion in the sections he subsequently wrote on the birth of Wagnerian opera. Here he changed the thought that there could be nothing genuinely new for the modern art of the future to do. However, the change was rendered most subtle the moment Nietzsche decided not to use the term "music drama" as a designation for Wagner's works. This way he complied with both Wagner's demand that the term not be used and Wagner's conviction that Wagner alone could do something new (a conviction Nietzsche more elaborately supported in the fourth of his "untimely meditations," that of 1875–76, "Richard Wagner in Bayreuth").[10] Nevertheless, Nietzsche left it ingeniously ambiguous as to whether the "new" that Wagner would do would now necessarily be a discontinuation of what the Greeks once did under a rubric or name Nietzsche determined no longer to speak.

If there were tensions in Nietzsche's argument, there were tensions equally in Wagner's. Although Wagner wanted to show his aesthetic commitment to protecting his works from an overly subsuming generic articulation, he frequently argued from a position of resentment. For example, he wrote that he would rather leave his acts of art unnamed to protect them from those critics he didn't regard as his "friends" or, more provocatively, to protect his acts of art from an opera world that was unable to produce them as anything but "operas." Consider the conclusion of his essay "Über die Benennung":

Since my poor labors [*Arbeiten*], given their great dissimilarity to *Don Juan*, were not even allowed to pass as *operas*, I was unhappily obliged to hand them over to the theaters without any designation of their genre at all. By this means, I believed I could survive so long as I had anything to do with theaters that understandably knew nothing other than opera, and hence, even if one were to offer these theaters a *music drama*, they would have made an *opera* out of it. In order to emerge from this confusion successfully, I hit upon the idea of the stage-festival-play [*Bühnenfestspiel*], which I hope now to bring about with the help of my friends in Bayreuth. This designation came to me from the nature of my enterprise; I already knew of singing festivals, gymnastic events, etc., and I was well able to imagine a theater festival in which the stage and that which happens on it—which we sensibly term "a play" [*ein Spiel*]—would clearly be the main thing. If those who attend my stage-festival-plays preserve some memory of the event, they will easily think of a proper name for that which I now propose to offer to my friends as an unnamed deed of art.[11]

However bitter at times the expression, it would be wrong to conclude that names or titles signified for Wagner only loss. Indeed, there was profound purpose in his having so long sought the right name or best designation for his works, even if ultimately he was tempted to refuse the name as inadequate the moment it was made explicit or public. Likewise, in the reception of Wagner's oeuvre there has been considerable purpose in becoming similarly preoccupied with names, especially when the point has been to determine which of Wagner's works stands, for good or bad, as music drama's best exemplar. Does the best exemplar lie in the more suggestive and youthful first, *Der fliegende Holländer*, or in the mature and culminating last, *Parsifal*? Or perhaps it lies in one of the operas—*Tristan, Meistersinger*, or *The Ring*—produced in the middle of his creative life? Much is gained in posing this interpretative question.

In constructing my own argument, I follow neither Wagner nor his critics in trying to determine the correct or authoritative description of his artistic labors. I aim only to render transparent something that was profoundly at stake in the many Wagnerian acts of naming and titling both within the works and of the works. Here I am influenced by an argument Adorno once offered in notes he collected under the title *Titel*. In one of these notes, he remarked that the "and" in the title that joins Tristan to Isolde and she to him (which is also an "and" taken by the characters themselves in the lines they sing), resembles, "in gothic print, . . . a black flag flying from the bow of a sailing ship."[12] For Adorno, the conjunctive "and" sealed the fate of the lovers, just as, following Walter Benjamin, a person's name seals his fate, which is a thought originating in the Book of Genesis. Pursuing this argument further, the titular "and" is increasingly given the power to remove from both Tristan *and* Isolde their ability to remain differentiated from each other, rendering them nameless as they themselves sing "ohne Nennen, ohne Trennen, neu Erkennen" (without naming, without dividing, new perceiving). Allegorically, the opera's title seals the fate of a modernity that is content to move toward an emptying out of both name and title, rendering each a slogan or caption, because any is now exchangeable for any other: Tristan becomes Isolde, Isolde Tristan. Or, if the title is not completely emptied out, then, at the other extreme, it becomes overloaded with conceptual meaning, as though the title was meant now wholly to determine the work's meaning: sucking all enigmatic content out of it, denying to the work its aesthetic life. A title, Adorno argued, serves a work best when it remains elusive, suggestive, and nonconceptual, when it refuses to give away the work's secret, when it renders the actual experiencing of the work necessary. A title that assumes all the power for itself ultimately forbids entry into the work—and the work dies. What Adorno argued of titles, he argued of all aesthetic principles or "prescripts" (*ästhetische Präskripte*).[13]

Wagner also recommended this sort of resistance when it came to naming the future genre or kind of art his works should point toward. Against this background, what explanation should now be given of his decision to title so many of his works with men's names corresponding to characters who might have brought about far less destruction in their worlds had they themselves remained nameless? Lohengrin, Siegfried, Parsifal: is it their namelessness or their naming that marks the redemptive possibility in the works? When Siegfried, for example, asks where he comes from, he discovers that his origin is also the source of his name. The moment he sings out his name, the "wild one"—Fafner—meets his death.

The answer to the question of redemptive possibility isn't obvious. What is at stake in naming Wagner's works "music dramas" or in speaking a man's name? Given the intricate relationship that Wagner developed between name and title, why is it that, in the one "exceptional" opera in which Wagner focused on presenting an explicit philosophical argument regarding the thesis of exemplarity, he chose a title that pointed not to a man's name at all, but to a group—*Die Meistersinger.* This title refers to a community in which the formal pomp and ceremony associated with its singing shows itself perfectly when master Fritz Kothner dutifully sings out the names of the other masters in roll call.

II

Although Millington describes *Meistersinger* as a music drama, he stresses its comic nature. Describing it first as "a comic appendage to *Tannhäuser*" and later as the "only comedy among Wagner's mature works," he emphasizes how much this work is "a rich, perceptive music drama widely admired for its warm humanity." Only "by some," he then adds almost dismissively, is it regarded "with suspicion . . . for its dark underside," as though, now in my terms, the dark underside contradicted rather than sustained its comic character.[14]

I suggest that whatever talent for comedy Wagner had was an unfortunate one for making manifest the cruelty made possible by comedy: the barbarism of humiliation, the satire of didacticism, the polemic of bitter reflection. If *Meistersinger* paints a picture of "warm humanity," it does so at the expense of those characters who fail to contribute to its warm tones. The mastersinger Sixtus Beckmesser is coldly dismissed with no acknowledgment from the final warm tableau after he has been made to stand abstractly for the "*Beckmesserei*" of his times. The name that makes of him a mastersinger is denied him in an act of dehumanizing humiliation. To deny a man his name or to assign him a generic name is to deny him his personhood. In Wagner's philosophy of history, a warm humanity is not one that exists in the present, but, having existed in the past, might exist again in the future if only the present would rid itself of the coldness Wagner claimed to find in the stifling pedantry of the culture.

The argument here tracks Adorno's. In a chapter he titled "Musikdrama" in his monograph on Wagner, Adorno concluded that when Wagner gave music the Schopenhauerian task "to *warm up* the alienated and reified relations of men to make it *sound* as if men were still human," he simultaneously displayed his hostility toward a consciousness that had become technological and his favor toward that which remained unconscious. For Adorno, Wagner's hostility marked no less than "the a priori of the music drama," signifying as it did a refusal to try to save enlightenment reason from its decline. When Wagner gave up on reason and entered the realm of unconsciousness and myth, the catastrophic fate was sealed not only of art but also of enlightenment as a whole.[15] In my terms, when namelessness is used to sustain mythic construction instead of aesthetic resistance, the name—here, *Musikdrama*—should now be explicitly named or rendered explicit if the naming exposes the dehumanizing work Wagner's operas ended up performing.

For Wagner, the move toward the music drama was a move of musical form, aesthetic concept, and sociopolitical life. The move has been described as away from opera toward the symphony, from Rossini toward Beethoven, or from Italy and France toward Germany. Or, away from the externally operatic toward the internally symphonic, away from patchwork construction toward wholeness, away from fragmentation toward unity, or away from the hollowness of absolute or formally constrained music toward the reuniting of the sister arts of sound, word, image, and gesture. Moving away from what then dominated in culture and society toward a better future also required, in this historicizing scheme of things, a moving back or, more accurately, a rebirth of something lost. For Wagner, as for the young but only sometimes compliant Nietzsche, it was the muse-inspired spirit of music or musicality that had to be reborn from the womb of the world, a spirit once present in the tragic music dramas of the ancient Greeks. On what did this rebirth depend? On determining the correct form for an artwork, one most fitting the condition and needs of the modern age. "We must seize the day," Wagner insisted, "and seek to develop its forms in new and solid ways" (*GSD*, 12:4).

In my reading, *Meistersinger* presents an explicit argument for the future terms of Wagnerian art. Whereas for Millington the opera is "a comic appendage of *Tannhäuser*," for me it is also an intentionally produced or highly reflective analogue to *Tristan und Isolde*, a sustained, almost six-hour argument offered in archaic operatic form in support of a vision of the future form of art. Even more broadly, *Meistersinger* offers an argument designed to award Wagner, as composer, a true freedom from the community he desired but which he also refused to be a part of. To what end is this true freedom? So that he could compose an opera in a form that rejected the operatic form of his day, to show his contemporaries—by example—to what they should also aspire. To compose this way, in freedom or by retrieving a freedom repressed by the community, was to give back to that community something that both Wagner and Nietzsche thought it had lost.

I shall not repeat what I have written elsewhere regarding the relationship of *Meistersinger* to *Tristan* or the role the concept of musicality (*das Musikalische*) had in the modern rebirth of opera as *Musikdrama*.[16] Nevertheless, I do want to stress that the move toward *Musikdrama* was made by Romantic and idealist aesthetic theorists and composers in France, Italy, Germany, and elsewhere before Wagner made the move, as Wagner acknowledged. I emphasize this point because Adorno seemed more or less to be denying it in the opening sentences of his chapter on music drama: "Even though [Wagner's] intention was to obliterate the frontiers separating the individual arts in the name of an all-pervasive infinity and even though the experience of synaesthesia is one of the corner-stones of Romanticism, [his] *Gesamtkunstwerk* is actually unrelated to the Romantic theories of fifty years earlier."[17]

Adorno argued from a double perspective: first, from the Wagnerian perspective of the mid- to late-nineteenth century, and, second, from his own perspective fifty years after Wagner's death, when, as he argued, the rational planning, the emptying out of aesthetic substance, and the movement toward totality in Wagner's self-described phantasmagoric production of the *Gesamtkunstwerk* had become most explicit. In my view, however, it should remain more open than it does for Adorno whether what one claims of the *Gesamtkunstwerk* is automatically to be claimed of the *Musikdrama*, as though one could simply glide from one name to the other quid pro quo because they now connoted the same thing. Indeed, one might argue that the *Musikdrama* continued the early Romantic project, while the *Gesamtkunstwerk* did not. Or that, when the *Musikdrama* transformed itself into a *Gesamtkunstwerk*, the former was deprived of any freedom it once promised. Nothing is stable here. Depending on what content one attaches to the different names, the claim might be reversed: that the *Gesamtkunstwerk* continued to hold out more promise than the *Musikdrama*.

To make the instability more evident, note that it is quite misleading to speak of the move *toward* music drama as a move *away from* opera, as though it were not Wagner's point to *continue* the production of opera under the *condition* of *Musikdrama*. When Wagner pronounced that he was no longer composing opera (which he did many times), his insistence should be read rhetorically as, "I'm not composing what others are currently composing under the rubric of opera, but what I produce are operas nonetheless." So read, Millington might after all be justified in titling his book *Wagner and His Operas*, especially if what his title expresses is some resistance to Wagner's own often exaggerated claims.

III

Millington is only one of many Wagner scholars to have devoted attention to the right naming or correct describing of Wagner's works. However, critics have rarely treated the matter of naming or titling explicitly; more often they have engaged in further and sometimes quite authoritative acts of naming. Contrast Millington's list of names with another list, offered by Werner Breig, extrapolated from the authoritative *Wagner-Handbook* in a chapter titled in translation "The Musical Works" and in the original "Wagners kompositorisches Werk."[18] Even if the aim of the chapter title is somehow to avoid the conflict between opera and music drama, the reference to musical works or to compositional process (as suggested by the German) only creates other conflicts bearing on the work concept, as we shall see more explicitly below in presenting Carl Dahlhaus's view.

In Breig's list, *Die Feen* is named, in historical context, a "three-act Romantic opera," citing Wagner's own claim, "I set [my opera libretto] according to my impressions of Beethoven, Weber and Marschner." *Das Liebesverbot* is then described as a work modeled more after French and Italian opera than after German Romantic opera, and *Rienzi* subsequently a "grand tragic opera" after Auber's *La muette de Portici* of 1828. In discussing *Rienzi*, Breig quotes Wagner's declaration, here taken from his 1851 essay *A Communication to My Friends* (so titled to exclude his enemies): "'Grand opera,' with all its scenic and musical splendor, its richness of effects, its large-scale musical passion, stood before me, and my artistic ambition was not merely to imitate it, but with unbridled extravagance to surpass all its previous manifestations."[19] Breig next describes *Der fliegende Holländer* as Wagner's "first fully valid work" and, quoting Wagner again, as marking a breakthrough to his "true style," moving away from the "species of Romantic opera" and toward "a true musical drama." Breig notes Wagner's albeit tentative suggestion written in a letter to Ferdinand Heine, April 1842, that with *Holländer* he perhaps founded a new genre, or at least that with its rejection of broken, modern patchwork construction this new work was meant to be "very unlike what we now understand by the term 'opera.'"[20] After this, Breig seems more or less to brand all the works that follow *Holländer* as music dramas, although he continues to employ

Wagner's alternate descriptions. *Siegfried's Tod* is thus described as a "grand heroic opera" until it became part of a music drama, in which Siegfried thrived for quite a while unnamed. However, Breig notes, the *Ring* cycle might also have been named a "word-music drama." Breig further cites Wagner's *Communication*:

[Whoever looks forward to the Nibelungen *opus*] with the expectation of experiencing something similar to *opera* is completely mistaken. I no longer write operas: since I do not wish to invent an arbitrary term for this *work*, I am calling it a *drama*, because this describes most clearly the viewpoint from which my work must be received.[21]

Parsifal, finally, is described by Breig as "Wagner's sole music drama (if we discount the four-voice setting of the motive 'Durch Mitleid wissend' for four squires in Act 1) which is completely without ensemble singing."[22]

To further understand Breig's approach to music drama, consider what he writes while discussing *Tristan*'s relationship to *Meistersinger*, just having quoted Wagner's remark from a letter to Mathilde Wesendonck from 1860 that "in a certain very deep sense that only the World-Spirit can understand, I can now only repeat myself in new works: I can reveal no new essence of my nature [*Wesenhaftigkeit*]." Breig comments: "Even in view of his later works, Wagner never retracted these astonishing words; in fact he even repeated them in March 1879, when the draft of *Parsifal* was nearly complete." To support the thought, Breig then quotes from Cosima's diary Wagner's apparent conviction that after *Tristan* he "produced nothing new [*nichts Neues*]," whereupon Cosima reminded her husband of all that was new from a "technical point of view" in *Meistersinger*, *Siegfried*, and *Götterdämmerung*. Putting technical matters aside, all that Wagner meant (in Cosima's view) was that after *Tristan* "there had been no need for him to write a single note more: he could have just said 'Do it as I do'" [*Macht mir's nach*], bidding others to follow him as he had followed the truth *opened* up to him by *Tristan* (even if, Wagner added, only the "World-Spirit" could fully *understand* that truth).[23]

By quoting Cosima, Breig arguably obscured the far more intimate point of Wagner's earlier comment to Mathilde. If, according to the "World-Spirit," works after *Tristan* could only ever be repetitions of what had already been achieved, then plausibly it was *Tristan* even more, say, than *Parsifal* that most deserved the honor of being named *the* music drama. That Wagner never called *Tristan* a music drama does little to halt the realization of the World-Spirit or, better, the expression of the World Will. For in Schopenhauerian matters of Will, such expression requires no name, no conscious understanding, only the closest possible musical approximation to that *a priori* or unconscious something (to which Adorno referred), experienced at a complete remove from representation (*Vorstellung*). In these terms, namelessness certainly suits an opera that strives to shed itself of any daytime semblance of individuation or reason, as when during the night Tristan melts into Isolde and Isolde melts equally into him.

Du Isolde,	You Isolde,
Tristan ich,	Tristan I,
nicht mehr Tristan,	no longer Tristan,
nicht Isolde;	no longer Isolde;
ohne Nennen . . .	without names . . .

Yet this is the exact proposition that Adorno subjected to critique. For the metaphysical namelessness that promised so much freedom marked, in his view, the beginning of another kind of namelessness, according to which, increasingly under the conditions of late modernity, names that once named were turned into empty slogans of the culture industry. Still, it is important to recognize here that the emptiness that resulted from the sloganizing of names was actually more a reorganization of meaning by which the very term "meaning" lost its former honorific connotation. When Isolde relinquished herself to Tristan, as he to her, it was his name and not hers that remained to serve as the singular title of their work. But was this to his or to her or ultimately to the listener's or to culture's advantage? The answer pulls in two directions. The more the reference to Isolde's name is withheld, the more the audience forgets what her voice once stood for—namely, sirenic music. In this forgetfulness, all that is heard are Tristan's solo words. Yet the more Isolde's name and voice are shielded from the appropriating tactics of the culture industry, the more chance *her* work has to hold on to its aesthetic or musical meaning, if only as residue, for those who have ears still open enough to hear it. Here, in the fragile space between the memory of meaning and the amnesia that comes with the culture industry's reorganization of meaning, Adorno situated a redemptive gesture of hope.

Consider Adorno's further claim that when Samuel Beckett titled his work *L'innommable*, he did this not so much to comment upon art's modernist movement into abstraction or untitling as to point to art's passage toward death. In this thought, nameability goes hand in hand with the idea that art is still possible and unnameability with the idea it is not. In other words, the idea that something is still *nameable* suggests that acts of *Benennung* are still part of a living, productive activity, though, dialectically, nameability preserves the possibility of art because something in art remains unnamed—"das Mehr." After everything is named or titled, art reaches its end or its death and only cold repetition is possible. There is nothing further to be named and nothing exemplary further to be shown, because all has *already* been named. "Can literary works that can no longer be called anything still exist?" Adorno asked, and answered: "One of Beckett's titles *L'innommable*, *The Unnameable*, not only fits its subject matter but also embodies the truth about the namelessness of contemporary literature. Not a word in it has any value now if it does not say the unsayable, the fact that it does not leave itself unsaid."[24] Everything in this thinking turns on what happens to names when they become empty words.

Another way to make the point is to render explicit a distinction between names and titles that Adorno leaves implicit. The distinction draws on a theological argument for the *Bilderverbot*, which could also be called the *Namensverbot*. The beginnings of the distinction are suggested in the sixth paragraph of Benjamin's essay on technological reproducibility in a passing remark in a discussion of Atget's photographs and the new picture magazines, in which "for the first time, captions become obligatory. And it is clear, that they have a character altogether different from the titles of paintings."[25] Where once titles had the power of names and kept the language attached to things, so now titles, under modern conditions of disassociation, have been turned into empty or interchangeable inscriptions. Adorno concurred: the more names "concede to communication," the less they serve as names: "Material with the dignity of a name no longer exists."[26]

Let us return now to *Meistersinger*, where it is argued that after the lesson of art has been learned—as it is learned in Walther's "morning dream interpretation" song—repetition does not necessarily preclude further technical development or even a different sort of culmination, as Cosima suggested. That something can come after the lesson is learned is demonstrated by what was named, *not in the opera itself*, but soon after by Wagner and contemporary critics, as the "Prize Song" (*Preislied*).[27] Even if, following Wagner's own anxiety, Walther's "Prize Song" no longer expresses the freedom of his second dream song or the naturalness of the song with which he first goes to trial, the last song does confer public honor and reward on this songwriter. Nevertheless, whereas Cosima seemed content with the argument of public recognition, the troubled ending of the opera suggests more ambiguity the moment it leaves open the question whether Walther, as Wagner, will ever again produce or need to produce anything new once the "Prize Song" has been sung. When master Pogner proposes to confer the title of master on Walther, the young singer resists: "Not *master*, no! I'll seek my bliss without that," after which Sachs sings his most famous speech, here interpreted as attempting to convince Walther not to throw out the baby (the song) with the bathwater (the potentially corrupting baptismal act of being named *master*).[28]

Wagner gave the title *Die Meistersinger* to this work, although there were earlier versions, such as Albert Lortzing's of 1840 (after Johann Ludwig Franz Deinhardstein's play), that went by the name of *Hans Sachs*. In the earliest drafts, Wagner referred to *Die Meistersinger* and only later added the city of belonging: *von Nürnberg*. This meant that he never considered awarding the opera with the name of a man, be it Walther or Hans, just as he never considered naming *Tristan und Isolde* after King Marke, or even Melot, despite the latter's explicit assertion that it was he alone who had protected the King's name from shame.

Generally in Wagner's operas names are often spoken of in relation to the honor or disgrace that attaches to them. So much turns on the dramatic, cultural, and political significance of knowing a name, withholding a name, learning one's name, naming a name, protecting a name, and living up to one's name. Consider Magdalene's opening explanation to Walther: "No one yet knows the bridegroom's name, until the masters' court names him tomorrow." Or David's "St. John's Day" song performed for Sachs about the "woman from far-off Nuremberg" who had her little son baptized *Johannes* in the river Jordan (by none other than John himself), only to discover that back home on the Pegnitz he was just plain *Hans*. Or Lohengrin's refusal to speak his name as the condition for fulfilling his roles as husband to Elsa von Brabant and overall protector of the culture—*der Schützer von Brabant*. Intent on destroying Lohengrin, Ortrud is both first and last to recognize that his mythic or magical power, which is to say, his persuasiveness over the people of Brabant, lies in his refusal to make his name known, which is also connected (as in *Siegfried*) to his demand that no one ask where he comes from.

Wagner's acts of naming play into the crucial transition he urged on the path to music drama, from *history to myth*, a transition that began in his historical opera *Rienzi* but was made quite explicit in *Fliegende Holländer*, which some deem his first music drama. Senta's leap to her death tracks or mirrors the living death of the forever-unnamed Dutchman, and might well be read as the first of several failures for the women in Wagner's works to release the men from their namelessness by denying them their mythic status. Having failed to do this, they then turn back, as it were, to express their own fidelity to the myth. When the woman of all women, Kundry, openly names Parsifal "the foolish one," she expresses no doubt where his "blessedness" will lead. Similarly, Wagner expressed no doubt where his name would lead so long as he remained the protector of German culture. However, my point is both Kundry and Wagner *could* have expressed doubt.

Maurice Merleau-Ponty once used "Cezanne's Doubt" as a title for a marvelous essay.[29] I would like to borrow the title and suggest that "Wagner's

Doubt" would have been an excellent title for the book Adorno actually titled *Versuch über Wagner*, although *Versuch* is also a term that perfectly precludes certainty. Adorno's actual title and my own suggested title both thus serve to remind readers of Adorno's doubt that Wagner was to be dismissed outright through vigorous critique. In fact, Adorno shared the conviction with Nietzsche, captured in the second epigraph of this essay, that however much one holds "Wagner" responsible for opera's decline, Richard Wagner or, even better, his works cannot and should not alone be held responsible. To mark him as solely responsible is to inflate his status, whereas the aim of critique is to deflate it. Even in the most damning critique there is always something still being sought after, something that remains in the works of value for Nietzsche, and of resistance for Adorno, a resistance even to the most pervasive Wagnerism of their times. To speak of *Wagner's Doubt* is to do a little justice to this deflationary aim.

IV

Carl Dahlhaus titled his classic book of 1971 *Richard Wagners Musikdramen* (*Richard Wagner's Music Dramas*). In his preface, he justified himself thus: "Wagner rejected the expression 'music drama,' which he interpreted as meaning 'drama for music.' It has nevertheless taken root, since his own expressions—'artwork of the future,' 'word-note-drama' (or 'drama of words-and-music'), 'action,' 'festival drama'—are impracticable as titles for a genre."[30] Interestingly, in this list of names, Dahlhaus omitted *Gesamtkunstwerk*, leaving it uncertain as to whether it also counted for him as an "impracticable" term. More intriguing, his remark prompts one to ask why, if he dismissed names on the grounds of practicality, he did not then resort to the most practical term already available: "opera." Had Dahlhaus pursued this route, he would have joined forces not only with Millington after him but Ernest Newman before him. That he did not join these forces prompts one to wonder whether there has been an attitudinal difference between German and English Wagner scholars, and whether the difference, if there is one, has demonstrated a greater or lesser deference to the Master. Unfortunately, pursuing this compelling thread takes us too far afield.

Consider, instead, the issue at stake in individuating a genre, and whether the quarrel between opera and music drama, taken as a quarrel characteristic of modernity, demonstrates the failure to determine the right name for "a new genre." Was Wagner's aim to exemplify "a new genre"? Surely sometimes it was, but how then should this aim be interpreted? How, for example, was the new genre meant to relate to the old one? Did the birth or rebirth of modern opera suggest the creation of something new in kind or a radical change only in what already existed? Wagner wrote confidently against his critics about this in the opening of the essay on the naming of opera as music drama:

> More and more often these days we read of a "music drama" and of how, for example, in Berlin, there is a society that aims to help the music drama on its way—without, however, our being able to form an accurate idea of what is meant. I certainly have reason to suppose that this term was invented for the sake of honoring my later dramatic works with a distinctive classification. But the less I have felt disposed to accept it, the more I have perceived an inclination in other quarters to use this name "music drama" to designate a new art-genre which, it would seem, was bound to evolve in answer to the temper and tendencies of the day, even without my intervention, and is now readily available to anyone, as a cozy nest to hatch one's musical eggs in.[31]

If the question of genre is difficult, so is the question regarding the status of Wagner's works the moment Dahlhaus named them "musical works of art." A year before writing his book on Wagner's music dramas, Dahlhaus edited an essay collection titled *Das Drama Richard Wagners als musikalisches Kunstwerk*.[32] The purpose of this collection, he wrote, was to explore facets of musical form and structure in Wagner's oeuvre taken as a whole. But what are the consequences of interpreting Wagner's dramas under the rubric of musical works of art? Doesn't this rubric risk reducing drama to what is exhausted by the music itself, thereby denying to the drama the representational part of the deed (*Tat*) made either visible by images or conceptual by words? And doesn't Dahlhaus's title imply exactly what Wagner most denied, that the term *musikalisch* be treated merely as an adjective or appendage to what already exists substantially as either "the drama" or, in this case, "a work of art"? On this matter, Wagner wrote again at some length:

> I cannot indulge in the flattering view, that things are so pleasantly situated; and the less, as I don't know how to read the title "Musik-drama." When we unite two substantives to form one word, with any understanding of the spirit of our language, by the first we always signify in some sort of way the object of the second; so that "Zukunfts-musik," though invented in derision of me, had its sense as "music for the future." —But "Musikdrama" similarly interpreted as "drama for the object of music" would have no sense at all, were it not point-

blank the old familiar libretto, which at any rate was a drama expressly constructed for music. . . .

Upon closer inspection, however, we find that the solecism here consists in the now favorite conversion of an adjectival predicate into a substantival prefix: one had begun by saying "musical drama." Yet it perhaps was not solely that evil habit that brought about the abbreviation "Musikdrama," but also a hazy feeling that no drama could possibly be "musical" like an instrument or (in rare enough events) a prima donna. A "musical drama," taken strictly, would be a drama that made music itself, or was good for making music with, or even that understood music, somewhat as our musical reporters [do].[33]

Dahlhaus did not pursue the consequences of speaking of Wagner's dramas as musical works of art beyond saying that the contributors to his volume were concerned with form and structure. However, he did remark insightfully on Wagner's preoccupation with naming and the mythologizing that accompanied it:

The first principle that provokes the suspicion of historians is Wagner's inclination to mythologize his own work, which was meant to be neither opera nor music drama, nor any particular, delimited genre at all that might tolerate others alongside it, but rather was supposed to represent the perfection of both history and drama and thus was removed from any classification that would have limited it: the difficulty of designation was a consequence of the all-inclusive claim.[34]

Given this remark, I suggest interpreting Dahlhaus's treatment of Wagner's operas as "musical works of art" as a deliberate strike against the mythologizing of Wagner and in favor of treating Richard Wagner as a composer of musical form and structure. Put this way, the aim was to deflate not the metaphysical or dramatic meaning implicit in Wagner's most musical works but the mythologizing trajectory of Wagner reception that had dominated up to Dahlhaus's day (and arguably still does). Dahlhaus fully understood what he was doing when he spoke of matters of genre. Whether or not Wagner was creating a new genre or continuing an old one, Dahlhaus aimed overall to deflate Wagner's conceit precisely by fitting Wagner's works into more established musical categories. In this matter, Dahlhaus assumed a more sober approach than Adorno, who, as I note below, posed the question as part of a much more highly charged negative dialectic: whether the category of genre had retained any classificatory power at all under the destabilized conditions of late modernity.

V

Dieter Borchmeyer opened the twelfth chapter of his study *Richard Wagner: Theory and Theatre* by quoting from the 26th part (*Stück*) of Lessing's *Hamburgische Dramaturgie*.[35] He did this to introduce a claim that influenced both Wagner and Nietzsche regarding the birth of Wagnerian opera out of the spirit of ancient Greek tragedy. The claim regarded the modernization and replacement of the ancient chorus by the modern symphony orchestra, such that music was awarded not only a purely expressive role but also a reflective or commenting role. Music, accordingly, was no longer simply *applied* to the word-image-drama as accompaniment or as adjective (where the word *applied* plays off Wagner's essay title, "Über die Anwendung der Musik auf das Drama" (1879), *GSD,* 9:324–42); music, rather, won its substantive claim to stand not just as equal with but now ahead of all other terms: hence, *music* drama.

Borchmeyer made it quite clear that Wagner knew Part 26 of Lessing's text. If Wagner knew this part, he likely knew other parts. My final argument takes us to Part 21, in which Lessing introduced a topic that found little echo in the reception of German literature—as far as I can tell— until Adorno drew upon it to open his essay on titles, an essay he in fact subtitled "Paraphrasen zu Lessing."

In Part 21, Lessing asked after the purpose of a title, rejecting immediately the idea that it should serve as "ein Küchenzettel"—a cooking recipe, which is more or less what Nietzsche suggested when he used the term "formula" and when Adorno wrote of an "aesthetic prescript." Lessing wrote: "The less a title divulges the content, the better it is."[36] Adorno picked up on this thought immediately in his own "notes," remarking that when Lessing saw a certain mindlessness (*Stumpfsinn*) in a "conceptual title" (*begrifflicher Titel*), he in fact was expressing his aversion to the Baroque. With Lessing, Adorno then noted the absurdity, even the misguided humor (*Witz*) of naming works after the drama's chief personage. Lessing asked: "What sort of ownership is granted a poet who titles his work after a certain character?"[37] To which Adorno answered: Perversely, what the poet gains is exactly what he probably doesn't intend, to strip the character of his heroic demeanor to make of him a living person (*eine leibhafte Person*).[38] For Adorno, there was a fundamental failure in the use of proper names as titles when they created the fiction or false promise of a personal or live presence. In my view, however, this use has also a potential dialectic reversal the moment the mythic status associated with the proper name is deflated; when, in the end, a man's name just refers to a man. Adorno used his dialectical argument to show the contemporary insecurity of the very category of the genre. Genre, he argued, is most appealed to in modern times, when it is least apparent that any generic borders still hold. I use my dialectical argument to suggest that appealing to proper names says as least as much about Wagner's quest for purity and honor as it does about his tendency to "go Baroque" or to try to stabilize a genre that would have a far better chance of surviving were the Wagnerism of the times actually destabilized.

Lessing argued against the gross proliferation of descriptive titles and subtitles since these had come to dominate the theater pieces of his day. Wagner almost entirely dispensed with the convention of the subtitle. Recently I came across a commentator congratulating Wagner for having had the good taste not to subtitle *Tannhäuser* with something like *Or, His Journey Home*, as if the commentator had forgotten the already-given subtitle *Und der Sängerkrieg auf Wartburg* (And the singers' contest at Wartburg). *Rienzi* also has a subtitle, *Der letzte der Tribunen* (The last of the tribunes), but the other works do not and if they do, mostly they are descriptions of what kind of work it is and how many acts it has. To "Breitkopf & Härtel, Leipzig," Wagner thus wrote: "Esteemed Sirs! You have requested a title for the piano-vocal score, and here it is: Lohengrin, Romantic Opera, in three acts, by Richard Wagner" (*GSD*, 4:148).

I began my essay with these sorts of descriptions of Wagner's operas. So this is where I end, noting, finally, how the genre designations that Wagner gave to his individual works managed to attain at least the authority of a subtitle. Name and description: each is rendered unique for each of Wagner's works, as though each opera, as I claimed at the start, were in its own exemplary way aspiring to the unnameable idea of what, if it must be named, is best named *Musikdrama*. Comic opera, romantic opera, *Handlung*, *Bühnenfestspiel*, or *Bühnenweihfestspiel*: all these singular descriptions making their way, like the singular names of exemplary men, toward what, given the force of logic, can only end up being subsumed by a general name.

Lessing wrote: "Earlier, writers gave to their comedies seldom more than meaningless titles."[39] Adorno concluded his own essay on titles by isolating part of a sentence from Part 17 of Lessing's treatise, in which Adorno said he found a "secret and melancholy pathos." Lessing's words read: "The title is truly a nothing [*Kleinigkeit*]. . . . What is easier to change than a title?"[40] Wagner, as we have seen, sought no *Kleinigkeit* and thus no insignificant title. Far more, he sought a true metaphysical namelessness for works he mostly titled with men's names. Given Lessing and Adorno on the one hand, and Wagner on the other, we are given a glimpse, as we have been given a glimpse here, of the many deflationary and inflationary tactics that have accompanied the long history of titles. These are tactics that have also served to make this history most significant—because in matters so small (*klein*) as how one titles one's work, often the most is learned.

NOTES

All translations in this essay are my own unless stated otherwise. The present essay was first published in German in *Wagner und Nietzsche, Kultur-Werk-Wirkung: Ein Handbuch,* ed. Stefan Loren Sorgner, H. James Birx, and Nikolaus Knoepffler (Reinbek bei Hamburg, 2008). I thank the editors for permission to reuse the essay here. Thanks also to Andreas Dorschel, Susan Gillespie, Thomas Grey, Robert Hullot-Kentor, Craig Knobles, Ernst Osterkamp, Christian Thorau, David Sidorsky, Hans Vaget, and Ståle Wikshåland for their insights and expertise.

1. Both epigraphs are drawn from Friedrich Nietzsche, *Sämtliche Werke—Kritische Studienausgabe in 15 Bänden* (henceforth *KSA*), ed. Giorgio Colli and Mazzino Montinari (Munich and New York, 1967), vol. 7, *Nachgelassene Fragmente*, 79; and "Der Fall Wagner," 6:46. The author of *The New Grove Guide to Wagner and His Operas* is Barry Millington (Oxford, 2006).

2. For the sake of the argument, I have to ignore the fact that Millington's book belongs to an Oxford series of which *X and His Operas* is the generic title.

3. For a witty essay with overlapping concerns, see Ludwig Kusche, "Von der Magie des Operntitels," in *Der nachdenkliche Musikant: Eigenwillige Beiträge zur Musikgeschichte* (Munich, 1964), 78–98. I am grateful to Thomas Schmidt-Beste for pointing out this essay to me. Kusche's essay pays attention specifically to the difference between opera and film titles, the author's point being that what has worked for opera has not necessarily worked for film, and vice versa.

4. Richard Wagner, "Über die Benennung 'Musikdrama,'" *Gesammelte Schriften und Dichtungen* (henceforth *GSD*), 10 vols. (Leipzig, 1887–1911), 9:302–7. See also William Ashton Ellis, trans., "On the Name 'Musikdrama,'" in *Richard Wagner's Prose Works* (London, 1896; repr. Lincoln, Neb., 1994), 5:299–304.

5. Nietzsche, "Der Fall Wagner," *KSA,* 6:12.

6. Nietzsche, *Die Geburt der Tragödie, KSA,* 1:9–156.

7. Nietzsche, "Das griechische Musikdrama," *KSA,* 1:515–32.

8. Cosima Wagner, *Cosima Wagner's Diaries: An Abridgement,* ed. and trans. Geoffrey Skelton (New Haven, 1977), 62.

9. By mentioning Polonius, Wagner was referring to that character's speech from *Hamlet,* Act 2: "The best actors in the world, either for tragedy, comedy, history, pastoral, pastoral-comical, historical-pastoral, tragical-historical, tragical-comical-historical-pastoral, scene individable, or poem unlimited: Seneca cannot be too heavy, nor Plautus too light, for the law of writ and the liberty: these are the only men."

10. Nietzsche, "Richard Wagner in Bayreuth," *Unzeitgemäße Betrachtungen* 4, *KSA,* 1:429–510.

11. Wagner, *GSD,* 9:307; trans. amended from Ellis, *Wagner's Prose Works,* 5:304.

12. Theodor Wiesengrund Adorno, "Titel," *Noten zur Literatur,* in *Gesammelte Schriften* (henceforth *AGS*), 20 vols. (Frankfurt am Main, 1974), 11:325–34 (quotation, 327); "Titles," *Notes to Literature* 2, trans. Shierry Weber Nicholson (New York, 1992), 3–11 (amended quotation, 5).

13. Adorno, "Titel," 327.

14. Millington, *Wagner and His Operas,* 85 and 94.

15. Adorno, *Versuch über Wagner, AGS,* 13:95; trans. amended from Rodney Livingstone, *In Search of Wagner* (London, 2005), 89.

16. Lydia Goehr, *The Quest for Voice: On Music, Politics, and the Limits of Philosophy* (Oxford, 1998); and "The 'Ode to Joy': Music and Musicality in Tragic Culture," in *Elective Affinities: Musical Essays on the History of Aesthetic Theory* (New York, 2008), 45–78.

17. Adorno, *In Search of Wagner,* 86.

18. Werner Breig, "The Musical Works," in *Wagner Handbook*, ed. Ulrich Müller and Peter Wapnewski, and trans. John Deathridge (Cambridge, Mass., 1992), 397–482.

19. Ibid, 405–8 (page range covers all quotations contained in this paragraph).

20. Ibid., 414–17 (translation amended).

21. Ibid., 349–40.

22. Ibid., 475.

23. Ibid., 467.

24. Adorno, *AGS*, 11:326; and "Titles," 4 (translation amended).

25. Walter Benjamin, "The Work of Art in the Age of Its Technological Reproducibility," *Selected Writings* 1938–1940, vol. 4, ed. Michael Jennings (Cambridge, Mass., 2003), 251–83 (quotation, 258).

26. Adorno, *AGS*, 11:325; and "Titles," 4.

27. How Wagner's "songs," such as Walther's "Prize Song" or "Senta's Ballad," attain their names is a topic that deserves independent inquiry. Recall here, however, the young David's explanation to Walther von Stolzing that, concerning the songs sung by masters: "Those are just the names: now learn to sing them/just as the Masters have ordained them!"

28. I have written more on Walther's refusal in "The Dangers of Satisfaction: On Songs, Rehearsals, and Repetition in Wagner's *Die Meistersinger*," in *Wagner's "Meistersinger": Performance, History, Representation*, ed. Nicholas Vazsonyi (Rochester, N.Y., 2003), 565–70.

29. Maurice Merleau-Ponty, "Cezanne's Doubt," in *Sense and Non-Sense*, trans. Hubert L. Dreyfus and Patricia Allen Dreyfus (Evanston, Ill., 1964), 9–25.

30. Carl Dahlhaus, *Richard Wagners Musikdramen* (Stuttgart, 1996); *Richard Wagner's Music Dramas*, trans. Mary Whittall (Cambridge, 1979), 4.

31. Wagner, *GSD*, 9:302; translation amended from Ellis, *Wagner's Prose Works*, 5:299.

32. Carl Dahlhaus, ed., *Das Drama Richard Wagners als musikalisches Kunstwerk* (Regensburg, 1970). For further pertinent discussion of genre matters in Wagner, see Thomas Grey, "Opera and Music Drama," *The Cambridge History of Nineteenth-Century Music*, ed. Jim Samson (Cambridge, 2002), 371–423, and Grey, "Richard Wagner and the Legacy of French Grand Opera," *The Cambridge Companion to Grand Opera*, ed. David Charlton (Cambridge, 2003), 321–43.

33. Wagner, *GSD*, 9:302–3; Ellis, *Wagner's Prose Works*, 5:299–300.

34. Dahlhaus, *Das Drama Richard Wagners*, 7–8.

35. Dieter Borchmeyer, *Richard Wagner: Theory and Theatre* (Oxford, 1991), 161.

36. G. E. Lessing, *Hamburgische Dramaturgie*, in *Werke*, ed. Karl Eibl and Herbert G. Göpfert (Munich, 1973), 4:229–720, 326.

37. Ibid., 327.

38. Adorno, "Titles," 3.

39. Lessing, *Hamburgische Dramaturgie*, 326.

40. Ibid.

Eine Kapitulation: Aristophanic Operetta as Cultural Warfare in 1870

THOMAS S. GREY

Composers who distrusted and shunned each other in the light of day often come together in secret: Wagner and Offenbach in the crimson salon of a God-forsaken love.
> — Theodor Adorno, *Quasi una fantasia*

If one understands by artistic genius the greatest freedom under the law, divine frivolity, facility in the hardest things, then Offenbach has even more right to the name "genius" than Wagner. . . . But perhaps one might understand something else by the word genius.
> — Friedrich Nietzsche, *The Will to Power*

Everything that recalls the modern immorality of Parisian life, everything that might encourage its cultivation in our land we will seek to destroy. . . . Offenbach out of Germany!
> — Alfred Dörffel, "Aus neuester Zeit"
> (*Musikalisches Wochenblatt*, 23 September 1870)

I

In the seclusion of his Swiss villa Tribschen on the shores of Lake Lucerne, Richard Wagner enjoyed the Franco-Prussian War immensely. Of course, the war against France aroused patriotic, not to say chauvinistic enthusiasm in Germans of all stripes, Brahms no less than the young Friedrich Nietzsche, for instance. Especially following the strategic defeats of the French at Sedan, Strasbourg, and Metz in the late summer and autumn of 1870, German support for the war was vigorous and nearly universal. For Wagner, however, it was a personal as well as a national affair: the

Prussian-led campaign against the French Second Empire was nothing less than a vindication of the deprivations and humiliations inflicted on him by a heartless and soulless Paris during his failed attempt to achieve international recognition there in 1839–42, the Parisian *Tannhäuser* fiasco of 1861, and several brief, equally troubled encounters in between. If the protracted siege of Paris following the military defeat at Sedan was for Bismarck a political tactic to force diplomatic cooperation from the unstable government replacing Louis Napoleon (Napoleon III), a tactic which he to some extent regretted, Wagner experienced the siege as an act of personal vengeance conveniently staged for him by the armies of the federated German states. He was also very willing to take spiritual credit for the success of the German armies. When his infant son Siegfried was christened on September 4, 1870 (the day on which a provisional republican "Government of National Defense" was declared after the fall of Sedan and the capture of the emperor), Wagner declared proudly, "I am bad for the Napoleons! When I was six months old there was the Battle of Leipzig, and now Fidi is hacking up the whole of France."[1]

Cosima Wagner's diaries provide a running commentary on the entire course of the conflict, from July 1870 to the final capitulation of Paris in late January 1871. They also provide the background to a small literary *jeu d'esprit* (or *mauvais esprit*) that occupied Wagner briefly toward the end of the fall, when the Germans continued to fight the armies of the new French government and to maintain their strategic blockade of the French capital. As a diversion from work on *Siegfried* and the tone poem *Siegfried Idyll* (being written secretly as a birthday surprise for Cosima), he drafted a topical and tasteless farce on the wartime dilemma of the French titled *Eine Kapitulation* and designated "ein Lustspiel in antiker Manier" (a comedy in the manner of the ancients). The inspiration for this piece of self-entertainment was a celebrated episode that occurred a month after the founding of the provisional government, when the charismatic one-eyed republican leader Léon Gambetta—at first appointed Minister of the Interior, afterward of Defense—journeyed by hot-air balloon from a beleaguered Paris to the vicinity of Tours in order to energize political and military support and to establish an alternative provincial seat for the new government.[2] (This adventurous mode of air transport, along with the extensive use of carrier pigeons, became an emblematic image of the siege, as shown in the 1870 painting by Puvis de Chavannes, *The Balloon: The Besieged City of Paris Entrusts to the Air Her Call to France*, reproduced as Figure 1.)[3] A few weeks after Gambetta's balloon voyage Wagner commented: "The French government in balloons would be a subject for an Aristophanic comedy; a government like that, up in the air in both senses, would provide a writer of comedy with some splendid ideas" (*CWD*, 6 November 1870).[4]

Figure 1. Pierre Puvis de Chavannes, *The Balloon: The Besieged City of Paris Entrusts to the Air Her Call to France,* 1870. Oil on canvas (Paris, Musée d'Orsay).

The remark suggests that Wagner had in mind Aristophanes' political satire, *Birds*, in which two disgruntled Athenians, Euelpides and Peisetairos, join forces with assorted avians to establish a rebel utopia, "Cloudcuckooland" (*Nephelokokkugia*), suspended in the air between the domain of humans on earth and the gods above. And indeed, between the time of Gambetta's balloon flight and this inspiration, a month later, for a modern satire in the "manner of the ancients," Richard and Cosima had been reading Aristophanes' *Knights* and *Peace* (though apparently not *Birds*, just now).[5] The previous February they had read together *Frogs*, *Wasps*, and *Acharnians*.[6] Early in 1874, following an evening of Buddhist studies, Richard began to read *Lysistrata* to his wife ("Great fun," she remarks), but cut it short two days later: "There is too much licentiousness, in which women can take no part" (*CWD*, 26, 28 January 1874; not a surprising verdict, but more than a little ironic in view of the women's role in *Lysistrata*!) Whatever elements of these comedies Wagner may have drawn on for his own modern political satire (details from *Frogs* and *Peace* also provide lively models), the aptness of the Aristophanic oeuvre as a whole to Wagner's purposes is clear enough: the pervasive role of topical political references, pointed and often coarse cultural satire, and a background of military conflict in the protracted wars between Athens and Sparta. A trait preserved in Aristophanes from a more primitive, "non-literary" tradition of comedy, as Kenneth McLeish notes, can be seen in "numerous short interludes which lampoon known individuals, picking on eccentric character traits and demolishing by ridicule."[7] Later references in Cosima's diaries to Aristophanes also suggest Wagner found particular inspiration in the poet's uninhibited *naming* of his targets (his unceasing stream of invective against the demagogic Athenian leader Cleon, for example), in addition to his ludicrously fantastical-satirical scenarios.

During the October 1870 readings that led to the *Kapitulation* project, Wagner remarked "how naïve and full of genius" the Greek comic poet was—not so much as a poet, he adds, but as "a dramatist, and above all a musician" (*CWD*, 18 October 1870). Naturally, the master of the music drama was well attuned to the role of music in Greek comedy, no less than in tragedy. The role of the chorus, dance, and the variety of meter and verse (or whatever he gleaned from the translations he read, presumably those of Gustav Droysen) must have commanded his attention during his readings of Aristophanes, first in the 1840s and now during this wartime intermission to his completion of the *Ring of the Nibelung* cycle. His own political farce about the French war was thus also conceived as a *musical* comedy. And as Wagner reasonably deduced, the most suggestive modern analogue to the "musical" satire of Aristophanes was the *opéra bouffe* or "operetta" of Jacques Offenbach, that guiding spirit of Second Empire giddiness. Another German-Jewish expatriate in Paris, Max Nordau (later famous as the diagnostician of fin-de-siècle cultural "degeneration") specifically dubbed Offenbach "the Parisian Aristophanes," the title of an essay on the cultural phenomenon of Second Empire operetta written in the 1870s.[8] This contemporary model is made explicit in the concluding episode of *Eine Kapitulation*, where Offenbach himself emerges from beneath the stage (the "Underworld," as it were), playing one of his tunes on the *cornet à pistons*. While Victor Hugo, here transformed into the "Genius of France," floats above the stage in Gambetta's balloon, Offenbach leads the whole cast in a series of cotillion dances, concluding with a galop meant to evoke, no doubt, the "Galop infernal" of *Orphée aux enfers*—that is, the famous "cancan" that became the essential signature of Offenbach and the operetta, rather like the "Ride of the Valkyries" became that of Wagner and the music drama.

Offenbach's operettas were widely perceived as the very embodiment of the Second Empire's pleasures and vices—the frivolous irresponsibility and political cynicism that brought France low, as was often claimed at the time.[9] The modern operetta would thus seem a natural vehicle for Wagner's satirical celebration of the regime's collapse (even if his central characters are drawn from the government of the nascent Third Republic). But the initial point of reference remains Aristophanes and the Greek theater, as the opening stage directions already make clear:

> The proscenium, as far as the middle of the stage, represents the square before the [Paris] Hôtel de Ville and is used in the course of the piece in the manner of the "orchestra" of the ancients; in the center, in place of the *Thymele*[10] is the altar of the Republic, adorned with Phrygian cap and *fasces*. . . . The classical stairs on each side of the stage lead to the raised portion in the rear, representing the balcony of the Hôtel de Ville; behind it the towers of Notre Dame and the Panthéon are visible.[11]

Wagner indicates that the "altar" should resemble a modern prompter's box, and should also provide a practicable mode of entrance and exit. The pointed references to the disposition of the classical theater—"orchestra" or dancing platform for the chorus, the altar, the *skene* or stage building behind the orchestra, the lateral stairs or walkways (*parodoi*, referred to here as the *antike Treppe*)—are all offered as further proof of the author's credentials for emulating the "manner of the ancients," the *antike Manier*.[12] (Perhaps, too, classical erudition is meant to justify a joke that even Wagner sensed was in questionable taste.)

The cast of this Aristophanic operetta includes contemporary personages (for example, the foreign minister and vice president of the new republic, Jules Favre, Léon Gambetta, Victor Hugo, the photographer Nadar, and Émile Perrin, director of the Opéra) as well as representative "comic" types (Alsatians and Lotharingians speaking in dialect). These figures are deployed in a whimsically parodic and improvisational scenario after the manner of Aristophanes, without any of the linear narrative or comic imbroglio typical of modern operetta. Still, the superimposition of some elements from Parisian operetta onto the classical template was easily effected: noisy marching songs, giddy dances, familiar tunes in the *vaudeville* tradition of popular allusion, and a steady stream of choral intrusions evoke the kinetic energy of modern operetta and of classical "Old Comedy" alike.

Wagner himself scarcely deserves credit for discovering the affinity of the modern *opéra bouffe* with Old Comedy, since two of Offenbach's signal successes, *Orphée aux enfers* and *La belle Hélène*, treat the gods and heroes of Greek antiquity in a mockingly irreverent manner distinctly reminiscent of Aristophanes, updated to allude to the *vie parisienne* of the mid-nineteenth century. Max Nordau, as noted above, wrote appreciatively about Offenbach as "The Parisian Aristophanes." In that essay, written apropos of an 1876 revival of *La belle Hélène*, Nordau also mounts an interesting argument that it is the "philosophical" contribution of Offenbach *as a musician* that earns him this title. Offenbach, he says, is altogether a perfect product of his times, a *representative man* ("as the English express it so nicely").

> The intellectual currents and perspectives of our times are alive in him, and he gives an entirely original expression to them. The secret of his success is that he thinks in a modern way, that his talent beats with the very pulse of our century. Here is the explanation for the fact that a poor German Jew could arrive in Paris, unknown and without recommendations, and yet, after a brief period of struggle for survival, could so soon establish himself among the first rank of international celebrities.[13]

No doubt Wagner was keenly aware of this. Like that other German Jew of his generation, Giacomo Meyerbeer, Offenbach had made a fabulous success precisely where Wagner had failed. Unlike Meyerbeer, he did so without the advantages of money, education, or connections. He flourished, as Nordau suggests, not simply because of his native musical talent, but because of an uncanny ability to take the cultural "pulse" of this modern metropolis. Other composers of the "light genre" boasted similar melodic gifts: Johann Strauss Jr., Franz von Suppé, Charles Lecocq. They befriended the popular muse quite as fully as did Offenbach, but for the most part their musical comedies have not attained the immortality of Offenbach's, Nordau remarks. For *they* are, in the end,

> nothing more than composers; Offenbach, on the other hand, is a composer and a philosopher. He is a true innovator; he has extended the realm of music, introducing polemics into the field of music. He is the creator of a satirical music. The melodies of other operetta composers are pleasantly harmless, while Offenbach's are pointed, and have someone or something as their target. Offenbach is one of the chief challengers in a struggle against authority and tradition; he is the champion of those who would fight against received opinion. With a merciless hand he has torn away the halo from the head of Greek mythology, exposing its figures to the mockery of the world.[14]

Besides skewering the pious worshipers at the altar of "classical" learning (the culture of the Gymnasium and the University) through his parody of the cardboard heroes of classical mythology, Offenbach set his sights on the modern "idols" of royalty and the military in what Nordau calls his *Tendenzoperetten* (topical operettas) such as *Barbe-bleu, La grand-duchesse de Gerolstein, La Perichole*, or *Madame l'archiduc*. Obviously, the libretti of Henri Meilhac and Ludovic Halévy are a crucial ingredient of Offenbach's musical satires, but the texts alone would not qualify the operettas for the Aristophanic prize, as Nordau sees it. He reads this "philosophical" element in the cultural-critical character of Offenbach's scores from the vantage point of post–Second Empire Paris. But it seems that the great musical "philosopher" of the century, Wagner, already appreciated something of this critical potency at the outbreak of the French-German war. He intimated, it seems, a distinctively urban and even political modernity in Offenbach that challenged the anti-modern mythologizing of his own music dramas and their effort to fight the commodification of culture (an urban and Jewish phenomenon, as Wagner saw it) with an aesthetic "truth" he wanted to regard as timeless and priceless.

II

Eine Kapitulation is among the least noticed of Wagner's published works —deservedly so, perhaps. It can be seen as a companion piece of sorts to the (nowadays) much more frequently cited essay "Judaism in Music." That formal denunciation of "public enemy no. 1," the Jews, was published pseudonymously in 1850, at a time when Wagner was not yet much a name to conjure with, but later reissued under Wagner's name in 1869, when he

was very much one. Soon after, the war of 1870 prompted this less formal, more playful, but similarly vicious attack on "public enemy no. 2," the
French. Subsequent history has given much greater urgency to the issue
of Wagner's outspoken anti-Semitism, and his fulminations against
the French have paled in significance. Today Wagner's anti-French invective
seems scarcely more relevant than his rantings against the Jesuits, or for
that matter, the Prussian "Junkers." Throughout the later nineteenth
century, however, the anti-French rhetoric figured more prominently in
Wagner's controversial status than did his denunciation of the Jews. And
in the last months of 1870 it was the besieged Parisians who were suffering under the scourge of German "barbarity," as it was styled in the French
press, as well as some foreign papers sympathetic to the French cause. Such
sympathy had been scarce at the outbreak of the war in August, since the
French were at least nominally the aggressors and Napoleon III's political reputation was reaching a low ebb, both abroad and at home. But by
November 1870 the Prussian siege had begun to reduce much of the Parisian
population to near-starvation, while dwindling supplies of fuel began to
reduce grand parks such as the Bois de Boulogne to mere deserts.

The attempt to carry on the gastronomic traditions of the French capital under siege conditions captured the collective imagination. "The
emergence of horse, dog, cat, and rat as part of the Parisian diet became
a staple of conversation," as Rupert Christiansen notes, and menus featuring these new ingredients dressed up in elegant culinary preparations
became emblematic of the privations suffered during the siege as well as
during the political chaos of the Paris Commune the following spring.
(Figure 2 reproduces a painting by Narcisse Chaillou commemorating this
topical feature of Parisian life during the siege: a young butcher's appren-
tice prepares to apply his skills to a freshly caught rat against a trompe-l'oeil
background of posted bills advertising political plays and pamphlets,
household necessaries, and, in front, an almanac for the new year with a
feature on "cooking in the time of siege.") Wagner was not alone in his
fascination with the role of the rat on the Parisian menus, but his whimsical deployment of it in the scenario of *Eine Kapitulation* has seemed to most
observers a lapse of taste and judgment not readily excused by either the
conventions of Aristophanic comedy (whatever allowances it made for crude
and earthy humor) or by the vehemence of the composer's political and
cultural opinions. (Perhaps, though, Wagner did exercise some element
of self-restraint in refraining from giving his comedy the very plausibly
Aristophanic title *Rats*.)

Aside from these cultural and ethical factors, the specifically "Aristophanic"
manner of *Eine Kapitulation* also accounts for its obscurity. Scholars have
worked hard over the centuries to illuminate the whole range of poetic

idiom and cultural reference to mythical, literary, political, military, and civic personalities embedded in the plays of Aristophanes. The figures who populate Wagner's comedy are scarcely remote, by comparison. They were the stuff of daily headlines in the international press some 140 years ago

Figure 2. Narcisse Chaillou, *Skinning a Rat for the Pot: A Rat-Seller in the Siege of Paris,* 1870. Oil on canvas (Paris, Musée Carnavalet/Roger-Viollet).

(indeed, *Eine Kapitulation* is a kind of "CNN operetta" of 1870, a political comedy skit with certain pretensions to learning in the tradition of university theatricals of earlier eras—similar to what Nordau called the *Tendenzoperetten* of Offenbach). Yet the daily news of a century ago is also a kind of ancient history, which may also have contributed to the general neglect of Wagner's questionable "comedy" and its politics.

One justification for my dragging this nearly (and perhaps best) forgotten "jest" briefly back into the light could be its value as evidence of Wagner's creative reception of Aristophanes—a potentially interesting footnote, at least, to the more familiar pedigree of the Wagnerian *Gesamtkunstwerk* in the tragic drama of the ancient Greeks. *Eine Kapitulation* is of potential historical interest, too, as a document of Wagner's and Germany's attitude toward the French at this critical juncture of modern European history. (The French-German conflict of 1870 might be regarded as something like the *Rheingold* to the *Götterdämmerung* of European warfare some seventy years later.) Just as Bismarck felt he needed a war against France to consolidate support for the unification of the German states under a Prussian leadership, Wagner perhaps considered a war on French culture (or rather, *civilisation*) valuable in cultivating the ground for a musical-dramatic festival that would serve as a unifying "cult" of true German art; within half a year he and Cosima were investigating Bayreuth as a venue for the great national rite that would be consummated by the premiere of the *Ring* cycle. (Coincidentally, Wagner was received by Bismarck in Berlin later on the same trip in the spring of 1871; but the hope that Bismarck and the Kaiser would patronize Wagner's grand enterprise in the name of the new Reich would be repeatedly disappointed.) Finally, this wartime *pièce de circonstance* is a unique document of Wagner's in some ways surprising response to Jacques Offenbach, a German Jew who—like Meyerbeer or Heine—forsook the *Vaterland* to become the toast of Paris, and whose steady stream of operettas from the 1850s and '60s suggest a swarm of satyr-plays to the "trilogy" of Meyerbeer's grand operas (*Robert le diable, Les Huguenots, Le prophète*) that continued to dominate the international repertoire through those decades. Where Meyerbeer was to Wagner an antagonizing rival and even an operatic father figure of sorts who had to be slain twice over (as a "father" and as a Jew), Offenbach operated in a sphere wholly unconnected to him. *Eine Kapitulation* makes fun of Offenbach as the "bandmaster" of a decadent, culturally bankrupt regime. But in an odd way it also represents a latent desire to *compete* with Offenbach: at the very moment he is styling himself the high priest of German culture, Wagner succumbs here to a passing temptation to address the modern, urban *Volk* with a political-satirical operetta: "classical" in form but in the absolutely "modern" style of the Variétés, the Gaîté, and the Bouffes-Parisiens. (As we will see, Wagner was for a time quite earnest about getting his comedy composed and staged, if not necessarily by himself or under his own supervision.) Rather than slaying Offenbach, Wagner imagined *becoming* him, if only for a day, and in semi-respectable classical disguise.

Couching his anti-French "operetta" in the guise of an early classical comedy not only provided an aura of intellectual, scholarly (German) respectability to the enterprise; it also excused, in a way, the unsavory, distinctly *un*respectable character of the humor. The so-called Old Comedy of Aristophanes enjoyed a kind of carnivalesque dispensation to ridicule contemporary personalities with relative impunity, and even to indulge in scurrilous, obscene jesting that would never be tolerated as part of normal public discourse. The obscenity and satirical unrestraint of Old Comedy are comprehended under the term *aischrologia*, or "speaking what is shameful," as Stephen Halliwell remarks. The genre "incorporated an extreme but temporary escape from the norms of shame and inhibition which were otherwise a vital force" in Athenian society.[15] Something of this carnivalesque dispensation applied also to the works of Offenbach and his long-term collaborators Henri Meilhac and Ludovic Halévy. With a candor transgressing the bounds of what would be acceptable in the "legitimate" theater or in a newspaper editorial, these musical revues and farces skewered the pretenses of Second Empire Parisian society (or for that matter the foibles of German *Kleinstaaterei* and Prussian militarism, in a work like the *Grand Duchess of Gerolstein*). For Wagner, Offenbach's infectious frivolity presented at once the perfect target and the perfect vehicle for his own scurrilous satire on the French enemy. In parodying the "Mozart of the Champs-Elysées," Wagner supposed he could have his fashionable Parisian *gâteau* and eat it, too. Indeed, in emulating the giddy frivolity and nonsense of the modern operetta in his neoclassical musical farce, Wagner was not so much attacking Offenbach as "consuming" him, cannibalizing an alien musical-theatrical genre in a gesture of covert cultural imperialism.[16] Just as the end of the Franco-Prussian War would see the crown of empire and military dominance usurped from France by the new German nation (declared at Versailles in January 1871), Wagner briefly imagined conquering the Parisian operetta and transplanting it to the popular stages of the new Reich for the purposes of satirizing the defeated Empire.

III

True to its Aristophanic models, Wagner's satirical skit is built around a loose tissue of topical allusion and whimsical (even crude) imaginative conceit, difficult to reduce to a cogent narrative core. Roughly summarized, it goes something like this. Victor Hugo returns from his nineteen-year exile to a newly republican Paris, under siege by the Prussian army.[17] (Hugo sneaks in through the sewers, famously explored in the climactic sequence of *Les misérables*.) He observes the dilemmas and divisions of the provisional (National Defense) government, and is at the same time courted by a nebulous, underground socialist faction, headed by Gustave Flourens. A debate over whether the new state should banish religion in favor of an official atheistic policy is resolved through the decision of opera director Émile Perrin to promote opera and ballet to the status of official national "cult." French opera, and above all ballet, Perrin argues, will serve to rally the support of all Europe—even the Germans cannot resist. The photographer Nadar makes a startling and uncanny appearance; his photographer's hood is inflated to serve as a balloon. The republican leader Léon Gambetta volunteers to join Nadar in an aeronautical expedition to collect the dispersed personnel of the opera and ballet from the provinces and the eastern front. While these two hover in their hot air balloon above the stage, the underground socialist faction (identified as "the Blacks" rather than the Reds) tries to seize control of the government, led by the communard Flourens.[18] A chorus of human-sized rats emerges from below, which Flourens and his followers try in vain to catch and slaughter. Gambetta returns, full of promises but empty-handed. He commands the people not to slaughter the rats for food, however, as they hold the secret to the ultimate victory of France and the new regime. Jacques Offenbach appears (also from below stage), playing a *cornet à pistons* and conducting the chorus and assembled cast in a series of cotillion dances. Under the influence of his music, the rats are transformed into a female *corps de ballet* "in the lightest of opera costumes." Victor Hugo returns *ex machina* as "the Genius of France," in the balloon vacated by Gambetta. While Hugo delivers a valedictory recitative and aria, the rest (including an international delegation of diplomats) dance a vigorous and awkward cancan. Hugo is "transfigured by the light of a Bengal fire."

Wagner's knowledge of Aristophanes and the Greek Old Comedy seems to have been limited to his own occasional readings. He first encountered the poet in the course of his intensive study of the classics during his later years in Dresden. In the summer of 1847, as he recalls in *Mein Leben*, he would slip off to a secluded, shady corner of the gardens behind the Marcolini Palais, "where I would read, to my boundless delight, the plays of Aristophanes . . . having been introduced by *The Birds* to the world of this ribald darling of the Graces, as he boldly called himself."[19] Otherwise, we only know about his (sometimes expurgated) readings for Cosima in 1870 and occasionally again in later years.[20] It is not surprising that his informal attempt at a "comedy in the manner of the ancients" reflects the structure and detail of Aristophanic comedy only loosely, at best. All the same, it is perfectly possible to identify the model.

The expository *prologos* in Old Comedy may take various forms. Among the earlier plays of Aristophanes a solo character is sometimes found reflecting on a scene just "uncovered" by the break of day: Dicaeopolis brooding before the still-closed gates of the Athenian assembly in *Acharnians*, or Strepsiades in *Clouds* waking up just before dawn to survey the signs of extravagance and waste in his household, prompting him to learn the art of sophistry from his neighbor Socrates so he might argue his way out of his debts. The playwright is also fond of injecting a bit of earthy, scatological humor near the beginning of the *prologos*: the care and maintenance of Trygaios's giant dung-beetle in *Peace*, for example. Wagner combines both elements at the beginning of *Eine Kapitulation*, when Victor Hugo emerges from the depths of the Parisian sewers through the altar-cum-prompter's box to find himself at the place de Grève, the site of the city hall. In an extended opening monologue he reflects on the adventurous route of his return, and how it may furnish him—celebrated for his prolific output in poetry as well as prose—with the stuff for untold volumes yet to come. (The extensive bawdy humor in the Greek comedies finds no place here, however, beyond the "lightly clad ballerinas" into which the chorus of rats is transformed.)

It is not clear if Wagner understood the convention of the *parodos*—the official introduction of the Chorus, following the *prologos* or exposition of the principal characters and their concerns—in which the Chorus generally engages with the cause of the comic protagonist, either pro or contra. Aware perhaps of the way the Chorus in Aristophanes might change voice or identity (especially later, in the *parabasis*), Wagner deploys his Chorus in multiple roles, even somewhat indiscriminately.[21] Right after Hugo's opening monologue we hear indeterminate "voices" from below. Soon after that, a "Chorus of the National Guard" marches on singing (and subsequently high-kicking), well before it is entrusted with any form of more substantial dramatic address.

Though structurally premature, according to the pattern of Old Comedy, this Chorus of the National Guard embodies an attempt to wed the manner of Aristophanes to that of Offenbach. In anatomizing the word *Republik* the Chorus generates a kind of musico-poetic nonsense reminiscent at once of the croaking in Aristophanes' *Frogs* ("Breke-ke-kex koax koax") as well as the playful rhythmic deconstruction of text that was a specialty of Offenbach. Compare the text of Wagner's republican Chorus, for instance, with a well-known example of Offenbach's musical wordplay in the "Marche et couplets des rois" from Act 1 of *La belle Hélène*:

CHORUS OF NATIONAL GUARD:	MÉNÉLAS:
Republik! Republik!	Je suis l'*epoux* de la reine
Republik blik blik!	*-poux* de la reine, *-poux* de la reine,
Repubel Repubel	le roi Ménélas, le Mé- le Ménélas.
Repubel blik blik! (usw.)	
Repubel pubel ... pupubel ...	
Replik! (usw.)	
(*Eine Kapitulation, GSD*, 9:7)	(*La belle Hélène*, Act 1)

Following the Offenbachian model, Wagner has tried—somewhat labo-riously—to tease out punning syllables from this syllabic deconstruction of the word *Republik*: "blik" to suggest *Blick!* (Look!); "pubel" to suggest, perhaps, the French *poubelle* (trash can). He tries this and similar effects elsewhere: isolating the last syllable of *Gouvernement*—"*ment, ment!*"—to suggest a conjugation of the verb *mentir* (to lie); punning between German and French (the Chorus hails the aerial departure of Gambetta and Nadar: "Fahr wohl, und *vole au vent! Gouvernement! Gouvernement! Vol-au-vent! Vol-au-vent!*"); or simply inventing "froggy" sounds (or is it the crowing of the Gallic cock?) to celebrate the arrival of Offenbach as national band-master: "Krak! Krak! Krakerakrak! / Das ist ja der Jack von Offenback!"[22]

The closest Wagner comes to providing a proper *parodos*, the formal introduction of the Chorus, occurs with the presentation of the republican government, seated on the balcony of the Hôtel de Ville, which occupies the position of the classical *skene*. In response to Victor Hugo's inquir-ies about the state of the city hall and government, the Chorus calls forth the members of the new regime, to vigorous "military" rhythms and gestures:

Regierung, Regierung!	O Government, where are you
Wo steckst du?	hiding?
Die Feinde dahin, wann	Our foes now, why aren't you
streckst du?	fighting?
Wo träumen die Jules?	Where dream all those Juleses?
Was treibt der Gambetta?	What's up with Gambetta?
Mach' ich ihm Beine	Let's get his feet moving
zur kriegerischen *Stretta*?	to a military *stretta*.

(*Eine Kapitulation, GSD*, 9:13)

Another formal articulation of this juncture is the sudden disappearance of Hugo from the scene, a Looney Tunes variation on the end of Don Juan: "The Chorus grabs Hugo by the head, while his feet are being pulled from below; his figure becomes elastically elongated"; voices from below sum-mon him again, as his head snaps back to join the rest of him below stage.

Though brief, the choral sequence here fulfills the common function of the *parodos* by underlining the fundamental situation of the comedy (here, the instability of the new government) in verse, music, and dance, while also setting up the confrontation or debate at its center.[23]

This central debate, or *agon*, duly follows: the discussion between the "three Juleses" regarding an official religious (or anti-religious) policy for the new regime. (Later, there is a larger confrontation between the underground socialists and the moderate republicans aboveground.) The decision in favor of reestablishing opera—or more particularly, ballet—as a national "religion" with international and commercial appeal resolves the *agon* and at the same time establishes a further central characteristic of the Old Comedy, a fantastical quest or some other quixotic scheme, loosely directing the remainder of the plot. In *Frogs,* Dionysus journeys to Hades to bring back the "good old boys" of Tragedy, Aeschylus and Euripides; in *Birds,* the two Athenian men join forces with another species to establish a new utopian republic of the air; in *Lysistrata*, the women occupy the Acropolis in their antiwar protest and temporarily seize sexual as well as political control from the Athenian men; in *Peace,* Trygaios flies to Mount Olympus and back on a beetle, likewise with the aim of ending the protracted war with Sparta. In *Eine Kapitulation*, Wagner reimagines Gambetta's escape to Tours by hot-air balloon as a recruiting expedition for the Parisian opera and ballet. Like Trygaios's beetle-borne flight to Olympus, Gambetta's balloon journey is intended as a means of concluding hostilities, in this case by garnering international support for the Opéra and its indispensable *corps de ballet*. (Unlike Aristophanes, whose comedies repeatedly protest ill-conceived Athenian military campaigns, Wagner himself remained hawkish to the end, waxing indignant at the Prussians' hesitation to conclude the siege of Paris with a large-scale bombardment.)

Perhaps the most distinctive formal sequence of Old Comedy is the *parabasis*, in which the Chorus addresses the audience at some length on the subject of the play or otherwise editorializes—typically exhorting the judges to award the playwright first prize in the competition (the "Lenaea" or the "City Dionysia"). At first glance a *parabasis* seems to be entirely lacking in *Eine Kapitulation*. Wagner was of course always willing to blow his own horn; but then, he was not actually competing with anyone (except perhaps Offenbach, in an imaginary way). On closer consideration, however, he *has* preserved something of the *parabasis* function, if we view it as being transferred from the Chorus to the role of Gambetta in his balloon. The term *parabasis* indicates, literally, a "stepping aside" on the part of the Chorus from its dramatic role to assume the poet's voice or some neutral voice, rather like the Chorus of Greek tragedy. Here, it is Gambetta's balloon, the central prop of the piece, that almost literally breaks through the theatrical "fourth wall": Wagner instructs that it should float out beyond the Chorus (and "Orchestra" stage space) "as far as possible into the audience" (*GSD,* 9:26). With the aid of Nadar's opera glasses, Gambetta surveys the audience and announces that throughout Europe, Germany very much included, everyone is eager to return to the theaters of Paris. Wagner explicitly addresses his imagined *German* audience through Gambetta here: the main point of his satire, he insisted, was to castigate his own countrymen for surrendering so readily to the lure of Paris fashions, above all Parisian music and theater. (As Gambetta surveys the continental landscape from on high and catalogues the peoples longing to return to their accustomed Parisian diversions, the Chorus asks, "And what about the Germans?" "They sit there peaceably among the rest," replies Gambetta; "they have capitulated, and are blissful at the prospect of returning to our theaters!")[24] Perpetuating this bit of (characteristically Aristophanic) meta-theatrical comedy, Gambetta and Nadar steer their airship into the wings in search of *artistes* as well as costumes to refurbish the Paris stage.[25]

From the perspective of later Latin and modern European comedy, with its traditional emphasis on the construction and resolution of intrigue, the conclusion (or *exodos*) of the Old Comedy can seem a bit slapdash. Wagner's *Kapitulation* follows suit. Both of them naturally turn to theater's originary ingredients, song and dance, to effect comic closure. As the Parisians are about to attack and consume the rats that have swarmed up from the prompter's box, Gambetta halts them, anticipating their transformation into the redemptive *corps de ballet.* "Just as the tumult reaches its frenzied peak, the sound of a cornet playing an Offenbach melody is heard from the prompter's box" and the composer's torso emerges, Erda-like, from the subterranean depths to celebrate the mock victory of Parisian light entertainment. The concluding *galop général* led by Offenbach suggests the *cordax* of Old Comedy, a riotous comic dance sometimes concluding the play, "associated with lewdness and drunkenness." This piece of high-spirited entertainment would round out the performance, willy-nilly, with the rhetoric of sheer physical exuberance, something like the "jig" that traditionally ushered out any performance, either comic or serious, in the Elizabethan theater. Aristophanes had actually claimed to purge comedy of this particular pandering to common tastes; but at the end of *Wasps* he recalls it parodistically, bringing on the "three sons of Carcinus" (a rival comic playwright), to execute a coarse, athletic high-kicking dance, itself suggesting a sort of classical cancan.

Although the apotheosized Victor Hugo occupies the flying machine in the closing scene (as the "Genius of France"), it is really Offenbach who figures as the piece's parodic deus ex machina when he pops up from the same altar-cum-prompter's box whence Hugo had emerged at the beginning, ready to save the day with his music. Jules Ferry hails him as France's "secret weapon." Offenbach's cornet has been mistaken by Flourens and his insurrectionary followers for the advancing Prussian army, and they accuse the Republicans of having capitulated to the enemy. But Ferry corrects them:

FERRY:
False claim! No capitulation! We bring you the most international individual of the world, who will secure for us the intervention of all European powers. The city that has this man within its walls is forever invincible, and has the whole world as its friend! Do you recognize this man of wonders, Orpheus from the Underworld, the venerable rat-catcher of Hamelin?[26]

Through the figures of Hugo and Offenbach, Wagner weds the idioms of mock exalted hymn and frenzied Dionysian dance to conclude his comedy in appropriately "classical" fashion. Both Hugo and Offenbach exalt the Parisian pleasures that Wagner means to denounce as exemplifying the moral and aesthetic decadence of modern France, admonishing the Germans to desist from their mad infatuation with such frivolities. The Germans, Wagner implies, must resist the blandishments that Hugo offers them in the form of an enemy ruse:

HUGO:

Als Feinde nicht nehmt ihr Paris,	As foes you'll never take Paris,
doch schenken wir's euch als *amis*.	But as friends, we offer it *gratis*.
Was klopft ihr am Fort?	Why knock at our forts?
Wir öffnen das Tor,	We'll open the doors,
was ihr alle begehrt,	and whatever you wish
's ist hier euch beschert:	is entirely yours:
Cafés, Restaurants,	*cafés, restaurants,*
dîners den *Gourmands;*	*dîners* for *gourmands;*
Garde Mobile	both the *Garde Mobile*
und *Bal Mabile*	and the *Bal Mabile;*[27]
Mystères de Paris	those *Mystères de Paris*
und *poudre de riz,*	and that *poudre de riz,*
Chignons und Pomaden,	*chignons* and pomades,
Theater, Promenaden,	theater, promenades,
Cirque, Hippodrôme,	circus, hippodrome,
la colonne de Vendôme;	the *Colonne de Vendôme;*
concert populaire, —	popular concerts, —
was wollt ihr noch mehr?	what more can you ask?

(*Eine Kapitulation, GSD,* 9:40)

Hugo goes on to point out how Parisian opera has made German culture palatable to the rest of the world, citing the examples of *Guillame Tell*, *Don Carlos*, *Faust*, and *Mignon*. "So kommt und laßt euch frisieren, parfümieren, zivilisieren!" he exhorts in aptly Frenchified German (Come have yourselves coiffed, perfumed, and civilized!).[28] The message, Wagner assumed, was perfectly clear. Celebrate with me the *Untergang* of Paris and all it represents, but for heaven's sake don't then continue to ape Parisian fashions, importing Parisian entertainments back into Germany and further risking the decline of our own culture.

IV

If *Eine Kapitulation* approximates the model of Aristophanic comedy rather loosely, it is even further from providing a practical libretto in terms of the contemporary operetta, a "book" with "lyrics" viable for composition and staging. Apart from Wagner's obvious lack of experience in either genre (ancient comedy or modern operetta), and quite apart from the fundamentally questionable nature of the material, the practical problem is precisely the admixture of these two very different models. For a viable operetta there are too few proper song or ensemble texts; notably missing are any of the *couplets* that were the essence of *opéra bouffe*. The Chorus, on the other hand, is deployed with indiscriminate frequency, presumably under the influence of Greek comedy; its many brief interjections would defy any normative compositional practice of Wagner's day, whether in opera, operetta, or even his own "music drama." Otherwise, the more concrete musical points of reference in the text derive, as we could expect, from the operetta: strongly rhythmic rhyming lines, abundant cues for marching and dancing, as well as generally frenetic stage business and a large dose of fantastic spectacle in the manner of popular pantomimes and melodramas (though not without some resonance with the fantastical scenarios and occasional stage effects that made the comedies of Aristophanes popular with his audiences).

Despite the implausible nature of the text as an actual libretto, however, Wagner at first fully intended to have his comedy set to music and performed at the same German theaters that were currently featuring the newly popular Parisian and Viennese operetta.[29] If he had no particular compunction about associating his name with the text, he nonetheless would not compromise himself to the extent of composing music in the requisite style.[30] That task fell to Hans Richter, future conductor of the first Bayreuth festival and then living with the Wagners at Tribschen as a combination house musician and *au pair*. (His fondness for joking and playing with the children, in addition to his versatile musical talents, suggested him as a good candidate for the job.) But the project withered quickly on the vine. A week after Wagner finished the text, Richter began composing (November 21, 1870). A week after that, Wagner sent off a copy of the text to Franz Betz (the first Hans Sachs and Wotan, then resident in Berlin) suggesting he peddle it to the "minor" metropolitan theaters—most likely he had in mind the Friedrich-Wilhelmstädtisches Theater, which had come to specialize in productions of Offenbach's operettas, along with the "Krollsches Etablissement" and the Viktoria Theater. On December 16, Richter previewed his music to the Tribschen household. He "admits to us," Cosima noted that evening, "that he would find it embarrassing to put his name to it." The following day "Betz returns *Die Kapitulation*; the theaters are frightened of the production costs" (apparently Betz's face-saving excuse).[31] "R. is basically glad, for the situation in Paris has changed, the mood is no longer the same." For weeks the besieged Parisians had been freezing and starving, reduced to eating not only most of the city's horses but even their own pets, in addition to the much reported rats. Even Wagner had to admit that his little satire might not be appreciated quite as he had hoped.

What had he hoped, then? *Eine Kapitulation* began as a private diversion, not unlike the *Siegfried Idyll* he was simultaneously composing in secret to celebrate Cosima's birthday that Christmas. But Wagner was always able to convince himself that his views on any subject were of ultimate value to society. When he eventually published the text in the ninth volume of his collected works (first edition, 1873), he prefaced it with a somewhat shame-faced apologia.[32] The French themselves had been "performing" their envisioned defeat of Germany for public entertainment before the outbreak of the war, he claimed.[33] The Germans, for their part, had been satirizing the subsequent French military defeats in popular theater and cabaret. Here, he explains, he saw an opportunity of reforming the taste of "our so-called *Volkstheater*, which has heretofore been limited to poor imitations of Parisian entertainments."[34] Wagner recalls, too, in this preface the relief of a "young friend" (i.e., Hans Richter) when his anonymously submitted text had been rejected for production, "since he confessed he would have found it impossible to put together the necessary music *à la* Offenbach; from which we both concluded that all things require a certain genius of one kind or another, and this was one kind we readily conceded to Herr Offenbach himself." In this minimally self-effacing way Wagner concedes a small "capitulation" on his own part, before going on to underline his alleged principal aim: to castigate his countrymen in their excessive cultivation of French fashions and music.

Wagner's brief (editorial) "capitulation" in this foreword to the published text suggests a grudging admiration for the "peculiar genius" of Offenbach. And whether his satire was principally aimed at the decadent frivolity of the French or at the Germans who imitated them, music *à la* Offenbach was deemed the appropriate vehicle for this "Lustspiel in antiker Manier" that attempted to revive the comic art of Aristophanes, genuinely admired by Wagner, in a modern style and context. There is a further confluence of his views on the Greek comedian and the German-Jewish-Parisian musician. Both at the time of his first reading of Aristophanes in the late 1840s and again at the time of the Franco-Prussian war, Wagner hailed the Old Comedy as a laughingly critical, self-aware embrace of Athenian "decline" toward the end of the fifth century BCE. It seems that he perceived something similar in the operettas of Offenbach: a popular art merrily conniving at the perceived decline of French political and cultural hegemony in Europe. Under these circumstances, operetta would be one product of modern Parisian culture Wagner was willing to embrace.

It is difficult to say how much of Offenbach's music Wagner had actually heard. Obviously, it does not figure prominently in the repertoire of Bayreuth *Hausmusik*. (Richter's halfhearted tryout for *Eine Kapitulation* was probably the closest approach to it there.) It would not be unreasonable to speculate on a sort of prurient curiosity on Wagner's part toward Parisian operetta, but it would have to remain speculation. To judge from Wagner's few recorded remarks about Offenbach, and from the composer's cameo role in *Eine Kapitulation*, Wagner seems to have regarded him principally as a composer of *dance* music—instinctively responding, perhaps, to that compulsive sense of rhythm and "the body" in Offenbach's idiom that, as Nietzsche was to complain, became increasingly absent from Wagner's own music.[35] And of course, then as now, Offenbach was associated in the popular imagination with the cancan, a dance of somewhat obscure origins that acquired iconic status as the music of uninhibited Parisian debauchery once it became identified with the riotous "Galop infernal" of *Orphée aux enfers*. Even if Wagner never intended to put himself forward publicly as a composer of operetta, we would be justified in speculating on the intriguing question of what sort of music Wagner "heard" in writing the text of *Eine Kapitulation*, especially in view of the authentic Wagnerian dogma that the composer generally anticipated important details of musical composition in drafting and versifying the texts of his operas.

To judge from the "lyrics" of *Eine Kapitulation*, as distinct from the prose dialogue, Wagner seems to have been particularly attracted to the rhythmic-musical wordplay of his model, as suggested earlier. Offenbach's librettists, Meilhac and Halévy, were ingenious in devising material for such effects.

A classic example is the opening chorus of *La vie parisienne* (1864), one of the most frequently performed of their works by 1870, in which the chorus of railway employees simply rattles off, to the inexorable rhythm of a modern locomotive, the names of all the stops on the "Western line" between Paris, St.-Mâlo, and Brest. An extreme case is the "Alphabet Sextet" from the postwar operetta *Madame l'archiduc* (1874), where two comic servants mistake the conspiratorial code "S-A-D-E" ("Supprimer Archi- Duc Ernest" or "Down with Archduke Ernest") for an alphabet song they recall imperfectly from their school days, such that the characters end up spewing out a chaotic string of letters resembling modern-day computer programming. Elsewhere, as paradigmatically in the "Marche et couplets des rois" introducing the Greek kings in Act 1 of *La belle Hélène*, it is Offenbach's musical setting that teases out latent rhythmic and verbal jests, puns, or simply amusing nonsense. Agamemnon, for example, announces himself, "Le roi barbu qui s'avance, c'est Agamemnon," and then renders his royal beard ("Le roi barbu") a silly, meaningless expletive by isolating the syllable -*bu* ("-*bu* qui s'avance, -*bu* qui s'avance"), echoing the comical march rhythms of the kings who have preceded him. Or, to cite one last example, in the "Rondeau des maris récalcitrants" that concludes Act 2 of *La Périchole*, Don Andrès leads the chorus in anatomizing the syllables "ré-cal-ci-trants" as he admonishes the uncooperative husband of La Périchole, Piquillo, whom he has cruelly duped. Each syllable of the offending word (recalcitrant) is accompanied by a vigorous musical kick:

Conduisez-le, bons courtisans,	Lead him, my good courtiers,
Et que cet exemple serve,	where he may set an example:
Dans le cachot qu'on reserve	to that dungeon we reserve
Aux maris *ré-*	for husbands re-
Aux maris *cal-*	for husbands cal-
Aux maris *ci-*	for husbands ci-
Aux maris *trants* . . .	for husbands -trant . . .
Aux maris récalcitrants.	for husbands recalcitrant.

Wagner attempts something of this sort a number of times with his "Greek" chorus. In the following, for example, he tries to pun the name of the director of the Opéra, Perrin, with the *perron* or balcony of the Hôtel de Ville (represented by the upper portion of the *skene*), incorporating a gratuitous, though rhythmical, reference to the troublesome cousin of Napoleon III, Prince Joseph-Charles-Paul (Napoléon-Jérôme), whose nickname "Plon-Plon" is matched up to the repeated final syllable of the doggerel-verse refrain word, *Mirliton*:

Seht, Bürger, Perrin	Behold there, Perrin
steigt auf den *Perron:*	ascends the *perron:*
Perron, Perrin,	Perrin, *perron,*
Mirliton—ton—ton!	*Mirliton—ton—ton!*
Den möchten wir statt aller	That's who we want, no more
Plon-plon-plon!	*Plon-plon-plon!*[36]

Toward the climax of his musical skit, Wagner has the "subterranean chorus" of underground socialist agitators marching to the old revolutionary anthem "Ça ira." In this rendition, the demotic chanting and drumming shakes off the final syllable of "aristocrats" and transforms it into a new battle cry of "Rats, Rats!" (equating the two "underground" populations of wartime Paris while also capitalizing on the opportunity to invoke once again this signature feature of Paris under siege):

Pumperumpum! Pumpum!	Pumperumpum! Pumpum!
Ratterah!	Ratterah!
Ça ira, Ça ira, Ça ira!	*Ça ira, Ça ira, Ça ira!*
Aristocrats!—Crats! Crats!	*Aristocrats!—Crats! Crats!*
Courage! En avant! Rats! Rats!	*Courage! En avant! Rats! Rats!*
Ihr Ratten! Ihr Ratten!	On rats! On rats!
Pumpum ratterah!	Pumpum ratterah!*[37]

Surely Wagner was tapping out reminiscences of Offenbach in the back of his mind as he wrote this.

On the other hand, as mentioned before, his text pays scarcely any attention to the most basic unit of the operetta: the *couplet.* The sole example of the latter is embedded in Victor Hugo's valedictory *scena,* the first strophe beginning "Die Barbaren zogen über den Rhein — / *Mirliton! Mirliton! Tontaine!*" followed by the appropriate choral refrain ("Dansons! Chantons!) and a second strophe ("Nun zogen wir selber über den Rhein — / *Mirliton! Mirliton! Tontaine!*").[38] Hugo prefaces his *couplets* with a parodic allusion to the apotheosis of Goethe's *Faust,* by which Wagner mocks the French poet's literary ambitions in contrast to the imputed triviality of the culture he celebrates.

HUGO:	
(rezitativisch, zu einer goldenen	*(in the manner of recitative, to a golden*
Lyra, welche er spielt)	*lyre, which he plays himself)*
Alles Geschichtliche	All that's historical
ist nur ein — *trait:*	is merely — *trait*

das rein Gedichtliche
mach' ich zum — *fait*.

(*Melodisch*)
Als echtes *Génie de la France*
verlier' ich nie *contenance*;
victoire, gloire
ich immer mir wahre!
civilisation,
pommade, savon,
die sind meine Haupt-*passion.*
Chantez, dansez,
allez aux soupers
Je veux qu'en France on s'amuse,
und verlange von niemand
    Excuse."

the purely poetical
I've turned into — *fait*.

(*Melodically*)
As the genuine "Genius of France"
I never will lose counte*nance*;
victory, glory!
so runs my story!
civilisation,
pommade, savon,
these are my principal *passion.*
Chantez, dansez
allez aux soupers
Je veux qu'en France on s'amuse,
and require of no one *excuse.*

OFFENBACH:
(*kommandierend*)
Chaîne des Dames!

(*calling the dance*):
Chaîne des Dames!

CHORUS: *Dansons! Chantons!* (etc.)

HUGO [*Couplets*, first strophe]:
Die Barbaren zogen über den
    Rhein
Mirliton! Mirliton! Tontaine!—
Wir steckten sie alle nach Metz
    hinein—
so gesteckt vom Marschall
    Bazaine!
Mirliton! Plon! plon!
In der Schlacht bei *Sedon*
da schlug sie der grimmige
    MacMahon!
Doch die ganze Armee
General *Troché*—
Troché—Trochu,
Laladrons, Ledru—
der steckte sie ein in die
    Forts von Paris.

The Barbarians have crossed over
    the Rhine
Mirliton! Mirliton! Tontaine!—
We captured them all there at
    Metz, just fine,
with the help of our Marshal
    Bazaine.
Mirliton! Plon! plon!
As we fought at *Sedon* [Sedan]
they were beat by the terrible
    MacMahon![39]
The entire *armée*
under General *Troché*—[40]
Troché—Trochu,
Laladrons, Ledru—
he hid them all safe in the forts of
    Paris.

Im Jahre *mille-huit-cent-soixante* *-dix*	In the year *mille-huit-cent-soixante- dix*
da ist geschehen all dies!—	so it was, if you please!—
Als echtes *Génie de la France* (usw.)	As the genuine "Genius of France" (etc.)

OFFENBACH:
Chassé croissé!   *Chassé croissé!*

CHORUS:
Dansons! Chantons! (usw.)   *Dansons! Chantons!* (etc.)

HUGO [*Couplets*, second strophe]:

Nun zogen wir selber über den Rhein—	Now we ourselves had crossed the Rhine—
Mirliton! Mirliton! Tontaine!—	*Mirliton! Mirliton! Tontaine!*—
Wir nahmen das ganze Deutschland ein,	We pushed back and back the German line,
à la tête Mahon und *Bazaine*—	at the fore [Mac]Mahon and Bazaine.
Schnettertin tin! tin!	*Schnettertin tin! tin!*
Mayence und *Berlin*	*Mayence*[41] and *Berlin*
von Donau und Spree bis zum *Rhin*.	from the Danube and Spree to the *Rhin*.
General *Monsieur*	General *Monsieur*
auf Wilhelmshöh'—	up at Wilhelmshöh'—[42]
Tropfrau! Tropmann	Tropfrau, Tropmann
Tratratan! Tantan!	*Tratratan! Tantan*
Über die dreimalhundert- tausend Mann!	Three times a hundred thousand men!
Im Jahre *mille-huit-cent-soixante- dix* (usw.)	In the year *mille-huit-cent-soixante- dix* (etc.)

OFFENBACH: *En avant deux!*   *En avant deux!*

CHORUS: *Dansons! Chantons!* (usw.)   *Dansons! Chantons!* (etc.)

Even the *couplets* shown here are preoccupied mainly with rhythmic-syllabic nonsense: folklike refrains such as "Mirliton! Tontaine!" and more attempted wordplay, or rather name-play, alluding, for example (and with no particular rhyme or reason), to the military governor of Paris, General

Louis-Jules Trochu, or to the notorious serial murderer Jean-Baptiste Troppmann, "whose bestial crime," Siegfried Krakauer notes, "was regarded by the revolutionaries as a symptom of the moral degeneration caused by the Empire."[43] The whole passage, incidentally, is accompanied by "Offenbach" playing his *cornet à pistons*. The verbal-rhythmic frivolity or nonsense is meant to underscore here the literal "non-sense" of the rest of the text in these strophes, which fantasizes French victory precisely at the key sites of signal French defeats of the past months (Sedan and Metz).

In nearly all of these examples Wagner seems to be invoking a genre of rhythmic march-song he would have known well from pre-Offenbach *opéras comiques* by Auber or Donizetti, among others: the *rataplan*. The prototype is to be found in the duet in Donizetti's *La fille du régiment*, "Au bruit de la guerre j'ai reçu le jour," whose *rataplan* refrain expressly imitates the sound of drums to which "militaire Marie" grew up as the regimental mascot (see Example 1). The repetitions and fragmentations of the word *Republik* in the Chorus of the National Guard at the opening of *Eine Kapitulation* ("Republik! Republik! Republik blik blik!") are undoubtedly meant to echo this modern comic opera staple. (In fact, the closest Wagner got to composing any of this text is the notation of a repeated rhythm of two eighth notes plus a quarter note—followed by isolated eighth notes,

Example 1. Gaetano Donizetti, *La fille du régiment*, Act 1, "*Rataplan*" chorus, mm. 12–37.

presumably followed by rests, for "blik blik!"—which he entered above these lines in a prose draft for his *Kapitulation* project from mid-November 1870: precisely the traditional *rataplan* rhythm.)[44]

Closer in the background of Wagner's wartime satire is Offenbach's *Grande-duchesse de Gerolstein*. Premiered during the 1867 Paris World's Fair, the piece turned into something of a topical *Zeitoperette* with the outbreak

Example 1 continued

Example 1 continued

of the Franco-Prussian War three years later. The none-too-delicate Grand Duchess with her pronounced fetish for the military ("Ah que j'aime les militaires!") seems to embody the very spirit of Prussia as it appeared to the outside world in these years, while the inept bumbling of her officers (no less than her own shameless favoritism for the handsome foot soldier Fritz) might have suggested all too neatly the conditions that led to rapid defeat of the French armies in August of 1870. At least for its first act, the *Grande-duchesse* is a veritable medley of *rataplan*-style songs and choruses. It is tempting to fit some of Wagner's texts to Offenbach's tunes—indeed, Hans Richter might easily have spared himself some effort by resorting to this military operetta by the *maître* himself. The mock-military *couplets* of Général Boum from the opening scene, "A cheval sur la discipline," sport a refrain almost tailor-made for Wagner's chorus of insurrectionary rats: "Et pif, paf, pouf, et tara papa poum!" (Example 2 suggests a simple contrafactum or re-texting to this effect.) The assorted French refrain words sprinkled throughout Victor Hugo's own mock-military *couplets* at the end of *Eine Kapitulation* ("Mirliton! Tontaine!" or "Mirliton! Plon! Plon!") inhabit more or less the same musical position and idiom as, say, the "ta ta, ta ta, rantaplan rantaplan" choral interjections to the Grand Duchess's "Chanson militaire" (Act 1, no. 4).[45] And even a presumably more lyrical number, such as the culminating "aria" in which Hugo delivers the moral (?) of the piece, fits without much strain to the concluding sections of the duet (Act 1, no. 2) introducing the *ingénu* protagonists of Offenbach's operetta (with Hugo's "als Feinde nicht nehmt ihr Paris" replacing Wanda's line "Et si pour toi perdant la tête," and so on to the end of the number).

Wagner himself, as we have seen, thought better of trying to compose in imitation of Offenbach. But one prominent critic, Eduard Hanslick, sug-

Example 2. Offenbach, *La grande-duchesse de Gerolstein,* Act 1, Introduction:
Couplets of General Boum ("Et pif paf pouf "), refrain with contrafactum from
Wagner, *Eine Kapitulation.*

gested he might have learned something from the exercise—for example,
from Offenbach's canny sense of rhythm. (Nietzsche, although entirely
under the spell of *Tristan und Isolde* at this particular moment, would later
come to agree wholeheartedly.) "I'm sure if you gave ten German composers the line 'Ah que j'aime les militaires!' to set," Hanslick speculated,
"at least nine of them would scan it uniformly in four trochaic feet; while

scarcely one would come up with such a lively, piquant rhythmic setting as Offenbach did." With regard to his other great strength, his innate musical sense of theatrical effect, Offenbach can only be compared with Wagner. "Indeed," Hanslick continues, "when I consider how Wagner so often forgot all sense of proportion in his later works, I have to concede the more acute sense of theater to Offenbach."[46]

V

The hypothetical success or failure, in stylistic terms, of Wagner's attempts either to revive the comedy of Aristophanes or to emulate the *opéra bouffe* of Offenbach might seem supremely beside the point, if that point is the one usually made about *Eine Kapitulation*, which is that it exemplifies all the worst features of Wagner's many-faceted character: tasteless and callous humor, egregious cultural chauvinism, poor judgment, and a complete inability to exercise self-restraint or appropriate self-censorship. Without meaning to defend him against any of those charges, I believe that his essay in Aristophanic satire, however marginal, can provide an interesting window on the composer's psychology and on the national conflicts of 1870, in which he participated so vigorously, if vicariously. Wagner's sense of personal victimhood vis-à-vis the French remains the key to his response to the war, and there is no doubt that it was a profoundly exaggerated, even irrational, one. Nonetheless, he knew his "enemy" a great deal better than many flag-waving and saber-rattling German artists or writers of the day. Musical representations of awakening German national feeling normally involved heavy doses of counterpoint, chorale, turgidly serious (and perhaps "descriptively" bellicose) development, and general bombast—whether practiced at the level of Joachim Raff's *Vaterland* Symphony (premiered in 1863) or, with more finesse, in Brahms's neo-Handelian *Triumphlied*, expressly composed to celebrate the German victory over the French in 1870. Wagner practiced this genre, too (at least for a fee), in the *Kaisermarsch* composed to honor the proclamation of the Prussian king as Emperor Wilhelm I of Germany early in 1871. (Anton von Werner's 1894 painting *Quarters at a Base Outside Paris in 1871,* in which uniformed Prussian officers in muddy boots lounge about a requisitioned salon entertaining themselves and their French hosts with good German lieder, has often been cited as an image of German *Kultur* imposing its allegedly inward spiritual values in this aggressive vein; see Figure 3.) But among his fellow Germans only Wagner, it is safe to say, would have contemplated a satire of the French on their own cultural ground, by adapting French operetta (however ineptly) to Aristophanic comedy.

Figure 3. Anton von Werner, *Quarters at a Base Outside Paris in 1871,* 1894. Oil on canvas (Berlin, Nationalgalerie).

As mentioned, he saw Aristophanes as greeting the decline of the Athenian golden age with a knowing smile, a philosophical resignation grounded in comic awareness. While Wagner took a more personal, more malicious pleasure in what he regarded as the decline of France in 1870, he also believed he was taking a broadly "philosophical" view—mocking not just the French defeat but also the perennial German "surrender" to French culture. At least, this is the gist of Wagner's defense of his comedy, as we have seen. Just as Prussia and the other German states rallied against French political hegemony, Wagner rallied his followers against French cultural hegemony. The German Empire was born from the downfall of the French Second Empire; the Wagnerian cultural imperium soon to be founded in Bayreuth was likewise nourished in the atmosphere of German triumphalism of 1871. If *Eine Kapitulation* might at first seem like an inconsequential bad joke, it could also suggest that Wagner had at least some fleeting insight into the emergent power of an urban popular culture, the power of a completely non-Wagnerian music as parody and entertainment, epitomized in the Parisian operettas of Offenbach.

"Operetta is the vital theatrical question of our time," a concerned provincial critic stated in the *Schlesische Volkszeitung* of 10 September 1878. "Just as the materialistic tendencies of our day have engendered it and encouraged it to thrive," he continues, operetta in turn "has provided abundant nourishment to every impure and deplorable seed in the hearts of our contemporaries." (Earlier in the same article, the writer expresses similar opprobrium toward the "sensual and salacious content" of Wagner's own operas—"all of which are more or less concerned with the relation of woman to man.") This provincial prudery is mocked by a more sophisticated Berlin critic, Robert Musiol, who quotes the Silesian journalist ("some sage village pastor or schoolmaster") at length in his own reflections "On the Question of Wagner, Opera, and Operetta."[47] Yet while Musiol shares his provincial colleague's low opinion of the aesthetic and moral value of the modern operetta, on the whole, he is equally cognizant of the potential significance of the genre, the potential influence of an emergent popular culture on the modern urban masses. "The messiah of the operetta is still to come."[48] For a brief moment, Wagner toyed with that idea, too.

In retrospect, the Franco-Prussian War can be seen as a dress rehearsal for the First World War, or rather a curtain raiser, though one that failed to alert Europe to the catastrophic dimensions, and consequences, of the "main act" to follow—*Untergang* on a scale that would scarcely inspire laughter. If Wagner had been a better reader of Aristophanes (the anti-war message, for instance), or had paid closer attention to Offenbach, he might have produced a rather different, perhaps more successful comedy.[49] A postscript to Cosima's diaries, entered by Daniela von Bülow, tells us that on February 12, 1883, the day before his death, Wagner had "asked Mama's opinion on whether he should retain *Die Kapitulation* in the second edition of his works, since it had been received so stupidly even in Germany, and by no means understood by his friends, either."[50] In the case of his little "Aristophanic" musical comedy, he understood that he had to admit defeat. The tragedy is that he never really understood why.

NOTES

1. *Cosima Wagner's Diaries*, 2 vols., ed. Martin Gregor-Dellin and Dietrich Mack, trans. Geoffrey Skelton (New York, 1978, 1980), 1:266; entry of 4 September 1870. (Subsequent citations to this edition are given in the text and notes as *CWD* with date of entry only.) Compare also Wagner's ebullient response to the fall of Orléans to Bavarian troops a month later: "That we should live to see this, the humiliation of the French nation! And on top of that a wife and a son—is it not a dream?" *CWD,* 14 October 1870.

2. On Léon Gambetta and his celebrated balloon journey across enemy lines from Paris to Tours, see also Rupert Christiansen, *Paris Babylon: The Story of the Paris Commune* (New York, 1994), 194–95, as well as the biography by Daniel Amson, *Gambetta ou le rêve brisé* (Paris, 1994), chap. 24, 192–200. Gambetta's airship, named the *Armand-Barbès*, departed from the Place Saint-Pierre in Montmartre in the company of a second one named the *George-Sand*, at 11:30 a.m. on October 7, 1870, and arrived in the vicinity of Tours only after several close encounters with Prussian artillery.

3. The famous photographer Nadar, who is given a leading role in Wagner's comedy, painted a portrait of Gambetta's own airship, the *Armand-Barbès*, together with its companion, the *George-Sand*. This 1870 painting, housed at the Musée de l'Air et de l'Espace in Le Bourget, France, is reproduced in John Milner, *Art, War and Revolution in France 1870–1871* (New Haven and London, 2000), 82. The volume is a rich repository of visual documentation of the Franco-Prussian War, the siege, and the Paris Commune.

4. Wagner, who had already commented on Aristophanes' resignedly comic perspective on the "decline" of Athenian political power (and culture) in *Art and Revolution* (1849), could have observed some parallels to the French situation in 1870–71 and the Athenian defeats and "capitulation" to Sparta and Persia in 405–4 BCE. On the latter, see, for example, Alan H. Sommerstein's introduction to *Lysistrata and Other Plays* (London and New York, 1973; 2nd ed., 2002), xvi–xvii. Cosima recorded Wagner's later remarks on Aristophanes as an observer and critic of Athenian political decline (*CWD,* 1 March 1877): "in the evening we read *Peace* to the end, . . . —it is enough to numb us with its genius: the Athenians went laughing to their downfall"; and 4 April 1877, regarding *Plutus.*

5. We know from *Mein Leben* that Wagner had read *Birds* upon first encountering the plays of Aristophanes in 1847.

6. See *CWD*, entries of 4, 5, 6, 22, and 23 February 1870. This interest in Aristophanes seems to have been suggested by a letter from Cosima's half sister, Claire Charnacé, mentioned on 17 November 1869.

7. Kenneth McLeish, *The Theatre of Aristophanes* (New York, 1980), 52.

8. The essay appears in the collection *Aus dem wahren Milliardenlande: Pariser Studien und Bilder,* 2 vols. (Leipzig, 1878), and is reprinted with commentary in Friedrich Chrysander, "Max Nordau über Offenbach und die Operette," in the *Allgemeine musikalische Zeitung* 16 (4, 11 May 1881): cols. 279–86, 295–302. "Offenbach strikes me as being the Aristophanes of our times," writes Nordau. "He shares with his Athenian predecessor the same high spirits, biting wit, fecundity, and the same superior *Weltanschauung*. But like Aristophanes, he does not write for children, and the charge of immorality that has been leveled against him by school headmasters can be quite simply answered by pointing out that satire is intended for mature minds, and that the inmates of boys' and girls' schools are better off reading their exciting stories of Indians in the Wild West than attending a performance of *La belle Hélène*" (cols. 282–83).

9. Queen Victoria's daughter, the Crown Princess Victoria of Prussia, expressed this view (shared by many outside of France), writing to her mother a few days after the defeat at Sedan and the fall of Louis Napoleon: "May we all learn what frivolity, conceit, and immorality lead to!" "Gay and charming Paris!" she continues in the same didactic mode.

"What mischief that very court, that still more attractive Paris, has done to English society, to the stage and to literature! It would be well if they would pause and think that immoderate frivolity and luxury depraves and ruins and ultimately leads to a national misfortune. Our poverty, our dull towns, our plodding, hardworking *serious life* has made us strong and determined; is wholesome for us." Letter of 6 September 1870, cited in Christiansen, *Paris Babylon*, 162. Though writing from Germany, indeed as a member of the Prussian royal family, the Crown Princess seems to be speaking here for and about the English.

10. The altar of Dionysus, which stood in the center of the dancing floor or "orchestra" of the Theater of Dionysus, on the slope of the Acropolis in Athens.

11. The Hôtel de Ville did not have a balcony in 1870. Nonetheless, Wagner's image of the Hôtel de Ville missing its upper stories forecasts, unwittingly, the fate of the building at the end of the Paris Commune some months later (May 1871), when, along with the Tuileries Palace and numerous other public buildings, it was gutted by fire.

12. Chapter 3, "The Theater of Dionysos" (38–49), in McLeish, *The Theatre of Aristophanes*, gives a detailed description of what is known about the theatrical space in which the comedies of Aristophanes were performed in Athens as well as what can be speculatively reconstructed. Wagner clearly took both a scholarly and practical interest in the design of the ancient Greek theater; his plans for the auditorium of the Bayreuth theater, begun shortly afterward, would adapt the classical amphitheater seating to the modern, indoor proscenium stage.

13. Nordau, "Der Pariser Aristophanes," in Chrysander, "Max Nordau über Offenbach und die Operette," col. 281.

14. Ibid.

15. Stephen Halliwell, introduction to Aristophanes, *Birds, Lysistrata, Assembly-Women, Wealth*, trans. Stephen Halliwell (Oxford, 1997), xix.

16. The issue of food assumed both practical and symbolic dimensions in the Prussian siege of Paris; the public fascination with Parisian responses to dwindling food supplies (alluded to in the role of the Parisian "rats" in *Eine Kapitulation*) reflects what might be viewed as a form of gastronomic warfare, considered especially apt for this particular campaign.

17. Victor Hugo returned to Paris after his extended self-exile on September 5, 1870, the day after the fall of the imperial government. After the 1848 Revolution Victor Hugo had been elected a member of the Corps Législatif and supported Louis-Napoleon in his initial bid for the presidency of a French republic. Hugo opposed, however, Louis-Napoleon's 1851 coup d'état and the establishment of the Second Empire, after which he fled to Brussels and then spent most of the intervening years in exile on the Channel islands of Jersey and Guernsey until the fall of Napoleon's government at the end of 1870. He briefly served as a deputy in the new National Assembly in 1871 and published an extended series of verses on the experience of the siege and the Paris Commune (*L'année terrible*, 1872).

18. The "flamboyant and buccaneering Gustave Flourens," as Rupert Christiansen calls him (he had previously fought with the Greeks against the Ottoman Turks in Crete), led an attempted coup, together with fellow communist insurrectionary Auguste Blanqui, against the Government of National Defense at the Hôtel de Ville on October 31, 1870, just one week before Wagner came up with the idea for his comedy. Flourens and his associates formed a "Committee on Public Safety," echoing the name of Robespierre's notorious revolutionary body during the Terror. The group was disbanded before the night was out, following extensive vandalism and consumption of large quantities of food and wine. General Trochu and Jules Ferry were briefly imprisoned in the city hall, but were freed by members of the National Guard with whom they subsequently reentered the building through various subterranean passages to reclaim control of their government. "Then, like the finale of one of Offenbach's operettas," Christiansen remarks, "the 3 a.m. exodus from the Hôtel de Ville brought the government leaders to the portals arm-in-arm with the communards" (*Paris Babylon*, 207, citing also a contemporary account from the *Illustrated*

London News). The episode is equally suggestive of elements in Wagner's "operetta," and most likely the mêlée at the climax of *Eine Kapitulation* alludes to it.

19. *My Life*, trans. Andrew Gray (Cambridge, U.K., 1983), 343.

20. After beginning *Lysistrata* in January 1874, they read *Plutus* (*Wealth*) and reread *Peace* in 1877 (4 April, 1 March), and returned to parts of *Frogs* in 1878 (6 October) and 1881 (11 April). As mentioned in note 3 above, the 1877 readings elicited remarks on Aristophanes as a "laughing" and "sublime" reflection of Athens and the Greeks at the moment of decline.

21. This may also be a function of the fact that he never got to the point of composing or producing the piece and thus was not forced to work out practical dramaturgical issues.

22. See *Eine Kapitulation*, in Richard Wagner, *Gesammelte Schriften und Dichtungen*, 10 vols. (Leipzig, 1887–1911), 9:13, 23, and 35–36 (henceforth *GSD* in both text and notes). In the second instance Wagner puns on the imperative "Vole au vent!" (Fly with the wind) and the familiar French term for a puff-pastry shell (vol-au-vent), anticipating further gastronomic "jokes" that make light of the famous famine visited on Paris by the German siege in the last month of the war.

23. Stephen Halliwell's description of the treatment of the chorus in the *parodos* (its "movements are always choreographed to represent a particular kind of action, condition, or mood" characteristic of the group represented) would apply to the first appearance of the Chorus in *Eine Kapitulation* as members of the National Guard, vigorously marching and singing. See Halliwell introduction, *Birds, Lysistrata, Assembly-Women, Wealth*, xxxiii.

24. *Eine Kapitulation*, *GSD*, 9:27.

25. As Wagner would have been aware, the comedies of Aristophanes frequently involved such "meta-theatrical" play with the boundaries of stage, audience, and theatrical illusion, most obviously in the generic institution of the *parabasis* (the direct choral address to the audience), but also in the form of self-conscious allusions to the technology of the stage, such as the *skene* itself or the crane used to lift actors on and off it. On this dimension of Old Comedy, see Niall W. Slater, *Spectator Politics: Metatheatre and Performance in Aristophanes* (Philadelphia, 2002).

26. "Falsche Anklage! — Nichts kapituliert! — Wir bringen euch das internationalste Individuum der Welt, das uns die Intervention von ganz Europa zusichert! Wer ihn in seinen Mauern hat, ist ewig unbesieglich und hat die ganze Welt zum Freund! — Erkennt ihr ihn, den Wundermann, den Orpheus aus der Unterwelt, den ehrwürdigen Rattenfänger von Hameln?" *Eine Kapitulation*, *GSD*, 9:35.

27. The Garde Mobile—the mobile guard, a military unit—hardly belongs in this list, but here, as earlier in the play, Wagner is drawn to pun on the term in connection with the popular ballroom dance establishment, the Bal Mabile.

28. *Eine Kapitulation*, *GSD*, 9:40–41.

29. Probably the Friedrich-Wilhelmstädtisches Theater or the Viktoria-Theater. See Ruth Freydank, *Theater in Berlin: Von den Anfängen bis 1945* (Berlin, 1988), 245–323. The index of opera and musical theater performances in the *Neue Berliner Musik-Zeitung* 23 (1869) lists about twice as many performances and/or individual productions of Offenbach works than for any other theatrical composer. Most of the titles listed were presented at the Friedrich-Wilhelmstädtisches Theater.

30. The text had initially been submitted anonymously, via Hans Betz, to "the larger of the Berlin *Vorstadttheater*" (minor or suburban theaters), as Wagner noted in the preface to the published edition (*GDS*, 9:5). Although it is not possible to say for sure whether he would have had the "book" attributed to him had it come to a performance, he did include this text in the first edition of his collected writings, which he already began to prepare for publication in 1872.

31. Prior to that, Richter had tried to offer excuses of his own: "He declares that the reason Betz does not reply to him is undoubtedly that he thinks Richter needs money and has therefore started to compose!" *CWD*, 16 December 1870.

32. See *CWD* entry from 24 June 1873 with reference to the preface and plans to publish the text of *Eine Kapitulation,* called in the diaries either *Die Kapitulation* or *Nicht kapituliert;* the latter version presumably referring to Ferry's speech upon the providential arrival of Offenbach. Cosima quotes Wagner's own sense of his questionable judgment in printing this text, as in his decision to republish "Judaism in Music" several years earlier: "He says he must always be doing things of which I cannot entirely approve, yet . . . I never reproach him."

33. *GSD,* 9:3. Wagner doesn't specify examples or sources. It would be conceivable to read Offenbach's 1867 operetta *La grande-duchesse de Gerolstein* in this light were it to have been revived in the summer of 1870. More likely he is alluding to some explicitly topical popular entertainments he may have read about in the newspapers.

34. "During the siege of Paris by the German army toward the end of the year 1870 I learned that the wit of German theatrical writers was being channeled into the exploitation of our enemy's discomfiture for the popular stage. I could see nothing offensive in this, considering that the Parisians themselves had already been performing our supposedly inevitable defeat for their own entertainment before the outset of the military campaign; and I even entertained the hope that some clever minds might succeed in producing an original popular treatment of such material, whereas up to now our so-called popular theaters [*Volkstheater*], down to its lowest dregs, had proven unable to raise itself above poor imitations of Parisian fare" (*GSD,* 9:3). Wagner omitted to mention, not surprisingly, how precisely around this time parodies of his own operas were becoming a staple of these same urban popular theaters, very likely including music borrowed from the more popular pieces of Offenbach. For extensive documentation of theatrical parodies of Wagner's operas, see Andrea Schneider, *Die parodierten Musikdramen Richard Wagners: Geschichte und Dokumentation Wagnerscher Opernparodien im deutschsprachigen Raum von der Mitte des 19. Jahrhunderts bis zum Ende des ersten Weltkrieges* (Anif-Salzburg, 1996).

35. This view of Offenbach as fundamentally a composer of "dance music" would correspond to Wagner's response to the "quintessentially French" quality of dance-based rhythmicality he had admired in Auber's music back in the 1830s, if not something he was prepared to emulate in his own works, at least not after the "youthful indiscretion" of *Das Liebesverbot.*

36. *GSD,* 9:17.

37. *GSD,* 9:28

38. There is an additional textual reference to the form, if not an example of it per se, toward the end of the text, where the Chorus sings: "Wir wollen Ballett und kleine Soupers, / und dazu republikanische Kraftcouplets!" (We want the ballet and little *soupers,* and with them republican power-*couplets!*) (*GSD,* 9:37). In the culinary (or anti-culinary) context of Wagner's satirizing of the Parisian famine, the prefix *Kraft* (power) seems also to be meant as a pun on its role as a prefix in the term for meat-broth or bouillon (*Kraftbrühe*).

39. MacMahon and Bazaine: French generals who suffered strategic defeats in the first month of the war.

40. General Louis-Jules Trochu was appointed military governor in Paris and head of the Government of National Defense, following the collapse of the Empire on September 4, 1870.

41. French name for Mainz.

42. Alluding to the temporary confinement of Napoléon III at Wilhelmshöhe, by Kassel.

43. Siegfried Krakauer, *Jacques Offenbach and the Paris of His Time,* trans. Gwenda David and Eric Mosbacher (New York, 2002), 336.

44. This draft is transcribed in *The Diary of Richard Wagner: The Brown Book, 1865–1882,* ed. Joachim Bergfeld and trans. George Bird (Cambridge, 1980), 181–85. For the passage in question, see 182: "Chorus of the National Guard marches on, headed by band: singing in 6/8 march time. 'Only the Republic: Republic for ever; Republic–blic–blic: Rerepubul–pub–pubbulreplic!' etc. They dance around the altar to the Republic gestur-

ing as in the cancan (muskets in their arms, bear-skin caps on their heads). Hugo sobs with bliss and emotion."

45. A further possible example, but not explicitly in the *rataplan* genre, would be the entrance of Offenbach: "Krak! Krak! Krakerakrak! Das ist ja der Jack von Offenback!" (*GSD*, 9:35–36).

46. Eduard Hanslick, *Aus meinem Leben* (Berlin, 1894), 2:83–84.

47. R. Musiol, "Zur Wagner-, Opern- und Operettenfrage," *Allgemeine Deutsche Musik-Zeitung* 5/38 (20 September 1878): 317–19.

48. Ibid., 318. "Perhaps some combination of the old Hiller-Dittersdorf-Kauer type of Singspiel—which itself cannot offer much satisfaction any longer, however 'pure' and classic it may be—with the Lorzting-Nicolai style of operetta [*sic*], along with *couplet*-based farces and Offenbachiads might yield a work corresponding to the modern spirit and its requirements. But this is a theoretical speculation, with no practical value."

49. Alan H. Sommerstein claims that it would be "an egregious error to regard Aristophanes as a pacifist" (introduction to *Lysistrata and Other Plays*, xx). It is not entirely clear why this should be the case, even if we need to regard ancient Athenian attitudes for and against war in historical context. Allowing for ample room in the overall debate over the political agendas (or lack of such) of Aristophanes and the genre Old Comedy, it is impossible to see how plays like *Peace* or *Lysistrata* could actually be construed as pro-war or anti-pacifist.

50. *CWD*, 2:1010, undated entry, after 13 February 1883.

A Note on Tristan's Death Wish

KAROL BERGER

I

Tristan und Isolde, a story of love's consummation in a transfiguring death, raises two obvious questions. Is death as inevitable an issue of love as this opera suggests? And what exactly is the sense of the "transfiguration" at the end, how does it differ from death *tout court*? The first of these questions is answered within the opera; the second is not, and hence is more challenging. The final orchestral cadence, by providing the ubiquitous Tristan chord for the first and only time with a tonic resolution (but one a whole tone higher than what had been implied throughout the opera, B major rather than A minor), assures us that the "transfiguration" hinted at in the accompanying stage direction does indeed take place, but it does not explain what the precise content of that transfiguration might be. By leaving us without a clear answer, Wagner forces us to come up with something on our own.

The two questions are related and troubling: they go to the heart of the unease with which the work leaves us. No matter how highly we value Wagner's artistic (musical and dramatic) achievement in *Tristan und Isolde* (and it would not be easy to overestimate that), it is hard not to entertain some doubts about the ultimate significance of the work. After a performance of any of Wagner's music dramas, one leaves the theater exhausted and full of the highest admiration, but also with a more or less distinct undertone of resistance. A serious consideration of a music drama should account for both the admiration and the resistance, and indeed, from Nietzsche on, the most interesting Wagner critics attempted to account for both.

In *Tristan*'s case, the source of the resistance is easy to identify (although it is surprising how rarely it gets explicitly acknowledged—perhaps precisely because it is so obvious): the protagonists of this story are in love with death. Death is not something they accept as a necessary evil, a high price worth paying for their ecstasy; rather, it is a good worth longing for in its own right, the desired outcome and fulfillment of their passion. Mindful of the Fascist cult of death and of its roots in Romanticism, mindful of how the wish to escape the terrestrial reality, which is the essence of Romanticism, fed the Fascist wish to invent a new aestheticized politics-beyond-the-everyday-politics, we cannot be wholly indifferent to the veritable orgy of necrophilia unleashed in *Tristan*—even if we remember, as we should, that the opera is concerned exclusively with the private sphere.[1] The orgasmic "jauchzenden Eil" (scream-ing-with-joy haste; Act 3, 1278–79) with which Tristan tears the dressing from his wound and greets the free flow of his blood just before he dies—"Ahoy, my blood! Flow now cheerfully!" ("Heia, mein Blut! Lustig nun fließe!;" Act 3, 1267–70)—leaves even the unsqueamish disturbed and ill at ease.[2]

To be sure, it is not simply death the two lovers seek: they wish to die together, in each other's arms. The easiest way to assuage our doubts about the opera's infatuation with death would be to see death in *Tristan* as nothing more than a time-honored metaphor of erotic fulfillment and to see the opera as a whole as a dramatization of a particularly drawn-out and satisfying sexual encounter. But the temptation should be resisted. It is not that death in *Tristan* does not function as a stand-in for erotic fulfillment—it does, of course. But to reduce the issue to no more than that would be to trivialize it beyond recognition. It is not difficult to see where the triv-ialization lies in this case: it consists in the depriving of sex of its metaphysical dimension which, quite evidently, mattered to Wagner.

To recapitulate, then: the intertwining of love and death is the central issue this opera raises. To understand *Tristan* is to understand this inter-twining. And though death does stand for erotic fulfillment, it cannot be wholly reduced to it. We need to go deeper.

Wagner himself spelled out his intention for what he hoped to achieve in *Tristan und Isolde* with unusual clarity. It was "to erect a . . . monument to this most beautiful of all dreams"—the "true happiness of love," which he has never known in real life—"a monument in which this love will be properly sated from beginning to end," as he wrote to Liszt in December 1854—that is, after he first conceived the work in the fall of 1854, but long before he began the prose draft (August 1857) or composition (October of the same year).[3] "Dream" is the key word here. Erotic love, whose monument the opera was to become, was not love as it exists among us humans, even at its best tran-sient, intermittent, and shot through with disappointments and compromises exacted from it by our finitude and by the social world, the world of Day, that we cannot completely escape. It was not love as it is, but as it should be, purified of all accidental imperfections, love as an ideal, a "dream." The aim of the opera was to capture what was essential about love. (An examina-tion of love in the light of Day, love suitable for the finite and social beings that we are, was to be undertaken in *Die Meistersinger*.)

The opposition that governs the two lovers' self-understanding in the love duet of Act 2 ("O sink' hernieder, Nacht der Liebe," 1117–1631) and beyond is that of existing in a world split into two metaphysically distinct levels—in their language, Day and Night. Day is the realm of conscious-ness, that is, of separation between subject and object, between the I and the World with its multiple phenomena, and this unbridgeable separa-tion necessarily breeds unappeasable desire. Night is the realm of oblivion where the separation between subject and object, between the I and the World, is canceled, where the multiplicity of phenomena turns out to be illusory, where all is one, where the desire born of separation is appeased. Since what love aims at is, precisely, the appeasement of desire and the can-cellation of any separation between subject and object, clearly what the lovers wish for, in their duet and beyond, must be to leave the world of Day behind and merge together into the Night.

But, of course, the wish to escape Day and merge into Night implies death: it is the logic of love that, since it aims at obliterating the distance between subject and object, if pursued with sufficiently radical single-mindedness and exclusivity, if "properly sated from beginning to end," has to issue in obliv-ion and death. The upshot of the lovers' colloquy in the love duet is that their common death would not be in alliance with Day, it would not interfere with their love and bring it to an end; on the contrary, it would, in alliance with Night, remove all obstacles to their complete and permanent union. It would be hard to maintain that the logic of the argument is entirely faultless, but for the lovers it is strong enough to allow them to talk themselves (or, to be precise, to allow Tristan to talk Isolde) into what an unsentimental observer can only call a suicide pact. In the second cantabile of the duet Tristan spells out the conclusion toward which their argument was driving them, and Isolde obediently repeats after him, "We would die so as to live only for love—unseparated, forever endlessly united, without waking, without fearing, namelessly enveloped in love, given completely to one another!" ("So stürben wir, um ungetrennt, ewig einig ohne End', ohn' Erwachen, ohn' Erbangen, namenlos in Lieb' umfangen, ganz uns selbst gegeben, der Liebe nur zu leben!"; Act 2, 1377–1424). The form of the cantabile, with its seem-ingly redundant, almost exact repetition of the same words and music (exceedingly rare in late Wagner), brings to mind a solemn oath-taking, with one party reciting the text of the oath first and then both parties repeating it. What began in the first cantabile as a love duet ("O sink' hernieder"; Act 2, 1117–1210) is transformed by the second cantabile section into a death, or love-death, duet. Where death is a synonym of Night, a "night of love" (*Nacht der Liebe* or *Liebesnacht*) is bound to be transmuted into a "love-death," or literally, a "death of love" (*Liebestod*).

In short, as Tristan and Wagner both thought (there is no need to dis-tinguish the two in this case), death clearly belongs to the essence of love; it is its proper goal, its consummation. Erotic love begins with two distinct separate persons, each reciprocally the subject and object of the desire to become one with the other, to cancel the separation. Hence it is bound to end—if pursued radically enough to its logical conclusion, and if successful—with precisely this: the annulment of the distinction between the subject and object, the merger and disappearance of the two separate persons. Thus death is the appropriate name for the ultimate destination of the erotic desire. More positively, one might also talk of a complete and permanent union of two individuals, without forgetting, however, that death of the individuals is what such a union implies.

This seems to be the strongest case one can make in defense of the intertwining of love and death in the opera. But death remains death, even when it is dressed up in fancy philosophical vocabulary. From the standpoint of Day, "Frau Minne" (the tutelary goddess of love) is to be feared and avoided, or at least civilized, but surely not worshipped unconditionally—unless one can give some concrete positive sense to the final "transfiguration," unless, that is, one can show that the lovers not only die but are also transfigured, and can explain what the value of such a transfiguration might be.

In other words, to be transfigured is to be raised to a different, higher ontological plane, to transcend existence as it is here and now, and the erotic desire is precisely a desire of transcendence. The separation of subject and object, the subject's lack of immediate access to object, is what defines human finitude. To overcome the separation of subject and object is to go beyond the limitations of human condition, to leave behind the finitude of Day for the infinity of Night. No less than Plato in the *Symposium*, Wagner understood that Eros drives us on to transcend our limits, to reach outside the confines of self and nature, to raise ourselves from our transient and conditioned state toward the permanent and unconditioned realm beyond.

It is on purpose that I invoke the *Symposium* here. On April 9, 1870, Cosima noted in her diary: "R. places this work [*Symposium*] above everything else: '. . . what would the world know of redeeming beauty without Plato?'" She further quoted Richard as saying: "'I, too, thought today of *Tristan* and the *Symposium*. In *Tristan* it is also Eros who holds sway, and what in the one is philosophy is music in the other.'"[4] Ultimately, it is this Platonic view of Eros as driving us to transcendence that lies behind the intertwining of love and death and needs to be confronted in any interpretation of *Tristan und Isolde*. The desire for transcendence, if satisfied, has to end in self-annihilation. What is its point, then? Does it have a point? Or is it rather—as Nietzsche and his numerous successors, Dewey and Heidegger, Rorty and Derrida, in their various idioms urged—merely a self-destructive temptation to be avoided at all costs, a siren song that accompanied European philosophical and religious tradition for a few millennia bringing us nothing but grief, a song we should finally stop listening to and leave behind?

A quick clarification is in order here: even if we answered this last question in the affirmative, this would not count against Wagner's opera. Wagner can be, and has been, accused of many sins, but moralism is not one of them. His aim in *Tristan und Isolde* was surely not to teach us how we should live, but, as he suggested, to erect a monument to a particularly glorious and terrifying divinity; and this aim he did accomplish brilliantly. Success in cases like this one is measured by the truthfulness and depth of the portrayal, and Wagner's picture of love is both true and probing. Eros, on his account, inspires and deserves worship as a giver of ecstatic bliss; equally, he inspires and deserves fear as a bringer of most terrible suffering and destruction. When Isolde apostrophizes Frau Minne in an aria-like culmination at the end of the first scene of Act 2 (370–471), what she finds important about this "administrator of the world's becoming" ("des Weltwerdens Walterin"; Act 2, 386–88) is that "life and death, which she weaves out of bliss and sorrow, are subordinated to her . . ." ("Leben und Tod sind untertan ihr, die sie webt aus Lust und Leid . . ."; Act 2, 389–97).

But, in any case, it is not clear that our question *will* be answered in the affirmative. The simplest, and only preliminary, answer might take a clue from Isolde's words: Frau Minne dispenses both bliss and sorrow, brings ecstasy that takes us beyond our narrow everyday limits as well as suffering and annihilation. Each one of us will have to calculate the benefits and risks individually, but Isolde's and Tristan's heroic choice to worship at Frau Minne's altar (assuming that one has a choice in such matters) might be taken to be the less craven, more admirable one.

An answer of this sort, however, while an acceptable first step and correct as far as it goes, is insufficient; it does not go to the heart of the matter. For both Plato and Wagner, more was at stake in the erotic drive to transcendence than the decision whether to take life-threatening risks for the sake of life-transforming ecstatic experiences. The question raised by them both is, rather, whether the pursuit of transcendence is the pursuit of a chimera that brings us nothing worthwhile, a bargain whereby we stop paying attention to the only existence we have in order to chase an empty dream.

II

Now, in a certain sense of the term, transcendence is something we could not avoid even if we wanted to. We may, and should, be wary of the Platonic, or Christian, or Kantian dualisms, of the splitting of reality into two distinct levels, the realms of appearance and truth, of human earthly temporal mutability and divine heavenly eternal permanence, of the phenomenal and noumenal—the former invariably mediated and contingent, the latter available immediately if at all and unconditional, the rock-bottom foundation of all there is. Much intellectual effort of the modern era (Spinoza, Hegel, Nietzsche and the pragmatic tradition he inaugurated) has gone into the overcoming of such dualisms, into providing a monist vision of reality. But even the most hardnosed monists, convinced that the realm of appearance is all there is (and hence that calling it "appearance" does not make much sense), cannot avoid going beyond the world immediately at hand. Unlike other earthly creatures, humans do not live in the present moment alone; rather, in addition to experiencing the world in the present, they also recollect it in the past and anticipate it in the future. Even a most rigorous monist could not limit himself to the present only; our world is necessarily split between the actually experienced present and the imagined past and future. It is in this modest sense that transcendence, going beyond the actually experienced present, is something inevitable. Since, to use a Hegelian idiom, we humans must supplement the dumb nature with the self-conscious spirit, we cannot but confront the actual with the imagined.

But normally, when we talk of transcendence, we have in mind something stronger than that, something that requires a full-blown dualist worldview: the transcendent realm in this stronger sense is the realm not only beyond here and now, but one representing a completely distinct ontological level. In this sense it is not so much the realm of personal imagination, remembrance and expectation, as it is one of abiding truth beyond the changeable appearances, the unconditional foundation of everything.

Both kinds of transcendence have a similar point: their job is to provide a standard against which the real can be evaluated. This is obviously the case with the strong transcendence. The value of items in the realm of appearances, or in the earthly city, is measured by their proximity or distance from their models in the realm of ideas, or in the heavenly city. But it is also the case with the weaker form of transcendence. Our ability to imagine the future is particularly relevant here. It implies that we have available to us not only the world as it is and was, but also the world as it might or should be. We do not just confront the actual with the imagined, we confront what is with what should be. Moreover, we evaluate and judge what is in the light of what should be. This is how real things, persons, events acquire sense and value for us. "Transcendence" in the most general sense is the name for our best and most comprehensive vision of what should be and how it relates to what is. If the pursuit of transcendence is to have any value for us, is to be more than a pursuit of a chimera, it is in this general, comprehensive sense of the idea that we should look for this value.

What, then, is the content of the transcendence our lovers pursue and attain at the Transfiguration?

It would be hard not to notice that the protagonists speak the dualist language. We have seen that their fundamental outlook is articulated in terms of the opposition between Day and Night, between the surface realm of illusion and the deep realm of truth. The world of Day is the normal world they share with all of their contemporaries, the social world of separate individuals relating to one another through a system of traditional feudal rights and obligations—the "custom" (*Sitte*) that is the initial subject of Isolde's and Tristan's conversation when they finally face each other in Act 1 (Tristan, "Sitte lehrt, wo ich gelebt," 1378ff). The world of Night is one whose very existence is not suspected by most of their fellows, even by such socially exalted personages as King Marke, not to mention Kurwenal or the Shepherd. When Marke inquires after the deepest causes of his nephew's actions, Tristan tells him: "O King, . . . what you would know, that you can never learn" ("O König, . . . was du frägst, das kannst du nie erfahren"; Act 2, 1893–1904). And Kurwenal tells the Shepherd, when the latter asks what is wrong with their lord: "Do not ask, since you can never know" (or "learn") ("Laß die Frage: du kannst's doch nie erfahren"; Act 3, 128–31); but it is doubtful that Kurwenal himself knows much more. It is the world beyond, preceding and succeeding all individuality, and hence one in which traditional rights and obligations are irrelevant. Most important, Day, we have seen, is where consciousness reigns and hence where subject and object, the I and the multiple phenomena of the World, are separate; thus it is also where unappeasable desire can arise. Night is where oblivion reigns, and hence where the separation between subject and object is canceled, where the very multiplicity of phenomena turns out to be illusory; thus it is also where the desire born of separation can be appeased.

The Schopenhauerian origin of this outlook is obvious, well documented, much discussed, and undeniable. But precisely because the outlook of the protagonists (and of Wagner, at this point) is Schopenhauerian, its ostensibly dualist structure may not matter all that much. (It is not even clear that Schopenhauer himself should be considered a dualist: he rather talks as if the realm of Representation and that of Will were two different perspectives on the same worldly reality—the world is Representation when it appears to us; in itself it is Will.) The realm of Night as the protagonists conceive it, like the realm of Schopenhauer's Will, is certainly neither the domain ruled by God, nor even one ruled by Reason. For Isolde of the Transfiguration it is "the blowing all of the world-breath" in which she asks "to drown, to be absorbed, unconscious . . ."—the realm where all consciousness ceases ("[in] des Welt-Atems wehendem All, — ertrinken, versinken, — unbewußt"; Act 3, 1680–89). For Tristan of the first monologue in Act 3 it is the domain of "divinely eternal, primordial oblivion"("göttlich ew'ges Urvergessen"; 319–22)—again the realm where all consciousness ceases, the kingdom of non-being, of nothingness, whence one emerges at birth and with which one will merge again when one dies.

However, whether All or Nothing, it is clear that Night cannot provide us with a standard against which the real could be evaluated, that it is not where we shall find models against which the multiple phenomena in the realm of Day could be measured. The world of Tristan and Isolde is closer to that of Schopenhauer and Darwin than to that of Rousseau, Kant, and Hegel, let alone to the world of Paul, Augustine, and Luther. Neither God nor an autonomous, self-legislating Reason underwrites the meaningfulness of the opera's universe—in fact, it is hard to see this universe as intrinsically meaningful at all. The vision of fulfillment the lovers aim at has obviously nothing in common with the modern desire to live within bounds drawn by their own autonomously self-legislating Reason; but neither has it anything in common with the Christian desire to be reconciled and united with the loving Creator. Human existence, as they see it, comes from nowhere and goes nowhere. Since neither God nor Reason will be found there, not even the most intimate acquaintance with Night will tell us anything about what "should be." But, if this is the case, can Tristan's desire to go back to the realm of Night and Isolde's wish to follow him there be at all justified? Enthusiasm for death can be justified only when death is the door through which one escapes a deficient reality to enter a better world, or when it offers the only available respite from a wholly insufferable existence. These conditions do not seem to obtain here: Tristan and Isolde are not (nor are we) led to believe that in their final Night they will be vouchsafed a beatific vision of one sort or another—all they and we can expect is eternal unconsciousness and oblivion; and one can imagine a fate much worse than Isolde's at King Marke's court, even if "unloved," she must "see the most glorious man always nearby" ("Ungeminnt den hehrsten Mann stets mir nah zu sehen—!"; Act 1, 961–73).

Briefly put: Eros drives our lovers to transcendence, makes them leave the finitude of Daily existence and enter the infinite Night; but the Night offers them Nothing. Unless one is able to take the thoroughgoing Schopenhauerian pessimism seriously, unless one truly believes that nothing is better than something, one's doubts about the ultimate significance of Wagner's work seem to be confirmed at this point: the opera appears to be no more than yet another Romantic glorification of the nihilistic death wish—entrancing and sublime, to be sure, but all the more pernicious for its sublimity.

III

And yet, both the protagonists and we experience the ending of *Tristan und Isolde* as a success, not as a failure. Now, they may be mistaken about this, they may take a failure for a success, but we cannot be: Wagner's resolution of the *Tristan*-chord at the end is calculated, we have seen, to make sure that we understand the ending not as a mere cessation but as a triumph, that we believe in the final transfiguration. Is this sense of final triumph simply a lie, a mendacious consolation proffered by skillfully deployed cadential resources of tonal harmony?

One might argue at this point that this, after all, is a story of a couple that in the end triumphs rather than fails: in the second cantabile of the love duet the lovers solemnly undertake to "die so as to live only for love— . . . forever endlessly united" and, though unable to fulfill this oath then and there, they do fulfill it in the end. In this one crucial respect Wagner and his protagonists part company with Schopenhauer: the lovers' trajectory does not aim at resignation—they want their love perfectly and completely fulfilled, not abandoned. And what is more, they succeed: their project ends in triumph, not failure. Here Wagner's heroes might be seen to anticipate early Nietzsche, accepting Schopenhauer's premises (the world is at bottom nothing but pointless striving that produces incessant oscillation between the torments of desire and the boredom of satiety), but rejecting his conclusions (that the wise will opt for resignation as the only sensible attitude to existence).

But to this argument a skeptic will respond: yes, they do manage to die at the end, but surely not to "die so as to live . . . forever endlessly united." The realm they enter at the end, the realm of Night, is where all individuality and all consciousness ceases. This is not the kind of place in which the idea of living forever endlessly united, in the posthumous manner of, say, Paolo and Francesca, makes any sense. The dissolution of all particularity in the Night's solvent makes nonsense of any notion of unity of particulars. If Tristan and Isolde think they triumph at the end, they are deluded.

There is only one way, it seems to me, that we can take our unmistakable final sense of triumphant success rather than tragic failure seriously, in spite of the natural skepticism aroused by the fact that what we see as the curtain goes down contradicts what the orchestra is telling us. What we see are two dead bodies on top of each other instead of the apotheosis that opera since Monteverdi's *L'Orfeo* has accustomed us to expect, that Isolde imagines, and that the orchestra hints at. From now on, after the opera's ending, we can tell ourselves, Tristan and Isolde will "live only for love— . . . forever endlessly united" in our memory, in cultural memory, transfigured (not for nothing did Wagner call the final tableau a Transfiguration and directed that we see Isolde "as if transfigured") into protagonists of an endlessly repeated myth of a love that trumps all competing considerations. The complaint that they will not literally live so, permanently and perfectly united, will be seen to lose much of its force once we reflect that finite beings like ourselves cannot really know or imagine what it would mean for such a union to be literally permanent and perfect; we can see such things only through a glass, darkly, if at all. Nevertheless, the complaint is well taken: for the lovers themselves, their project ends in failure. But not for us. Tristan and Isolde's permanent and perfect union as uniquely single-minded lovers in a myth that our culture endlessly recycles, not least in Wagner's own telling, is the only form of such a union we can truly imagine and understand.

And this is also, it seems to me, the only way one can make sense of the protagonists' eagerness for death. Their dying together is the prerequisite for their transformation into figures of myth. As long as they live, their story is not completed and hence not ready to be told. Perhaps more important, as long as they live they are subject to the usual earthly contingencies and accidents that stand in the way of any permanent and perfect union and may at any moment spoil their story: aging, disease, the unexpected withdrawal of the passionate tide in which they drown now—the list is endless. As long as they live, their story cannot be "a monument in which this love will be properly sated from beginning to end."

Without the aesthetic transfiguration of their lives into a story, their existence would have to be considered a tragic mistake and failure. With that aesthetic transfiguration, it still remains a failure for them, but not for us. The transfiguration leaves *them* empty-handed: the content of the transcendence they attain turns out to be Nothing (or, what amounts to the same thing, All). But it does not leave *us* empty-handed: we are left with "a monument to this most beautiful of all dreams," a vision of love at its most radical and uncompromising and hence necessarily tragic. The lovers' transfiguration into a myth does take place, and although it is of no use to them, it is of use to us. They may be under the impression that they sacrifice themselves on the altar of Love; in fact, they sacrifice themselves on the altar of Art.

NOTES

1. George L. Mosse, *The Fascist Revolution: Toward a General Theory of Fascism* (New York, 1999).

2. Citations of text and musical passages are indicated by act and measure number (within acts) throughout. The measure numbers in Act 1 include the Prelude.

3. Richard Wagner, letter to Franz Liszt in Weimar, Zurich, 16 (?) December 1854, in Wagner, *Selected Letters*, trans. and ed. Stewart Spencer and Barry Millington (New York, 1988), 323.

4. Cosima Wagner, *Diaries*, ed. Martin Gregor-Dellin and Dietrich Mack, trans. Geoffrey Skelton (New York and London, 1978–80), 1:208.

Guides for Wagnerites: Leitmotifs and Wagnerian Listening

CHRISTIAN THORAU

It is July 1876, in Bayreuth. In the weeks preceding the premiere of Wagner's long-awaited "stage festival drama," Hans von Wolzogen publishes a one-hundred-page booklet titled *Thematischer Leitfaden durch die Musik zu Richard Wagners Festspiel "Der Ring des Nibelungen"* (Thematic guide through the music to Richard Wagner's festival drama *The Ring of the Nibelung*; see Figure 1). Together with an introduction to the mythological plot, this *Leitfaden* offers a detailed musical analysis of the entire work. By naming, systematizing, and interpreting all of the principal musical motives of Wagner's score, Wolzogen weaves a "leading thread" through the fourteen-hour cycle of music dramas. His text inaugurates a new method of analyzing Wagner's works that would remain the dominant musical-critical approach to this oeuvre up to World War I. By 1910, when nearly all major German opera houses had embraced Wagner's *Ring* as part of their regular repertoire, 160,000 copies of Wolzogen's *Thematischer Leitfaden* had been sold. By the turn of the century, at the peak of the era of European "Wagnerism," Wolzogen's 1876 thematic guide had become arguably the most successful musical analysis ever published to date.

The impact of Wolzogen's thematic guide was broad and lasting, likewise the spate of imitative publications it triggered. Since then, labeling, learning, and discussing leitmotifs has been taken for granted as the main approach to understanding and appreciating Wagner's works. Orienting listening by means of named motives was an attempt to domesticate a new kind of opera, one that at first had been rejected by the majority of bourgeois listeners, especially by the traditionally and academically educated middle class or *Bildungsbürger*. As we know, the project of bourgeois appropriation was tremendously successful in the case of Wagner's initially challenging music dramas. In this process, Wagner's technique of organizing the structure of music drama by means of a network of dramatically

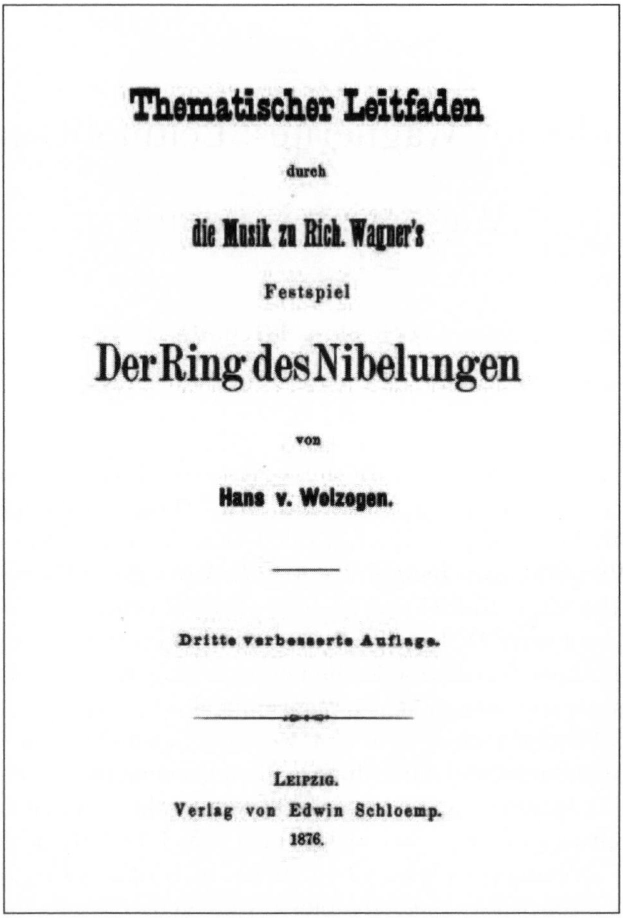
Thematischer Leitfaden

durch

die Musik zu Rich. Wagner's

Festspiel

Der Ring des Nibelungen

von

Hans v. Wolzogen.

Dritte verbesserte Auflage.

Leipzig.

Verlag von Edwin Schloemp.

1876.

Figure 1. Hans von Wolzogen, *Thematischer Leitfaden durch die Musik zu Richard Wagners Festspiel "Der Ring des Nibelungen"* (Leipzig, 1876), frontispiece.

associative motives also became a preparatory and instructional technique for conveying the structure and content of a work to its audience, of organizing the listener's experience. As distinct from the compositional technique *per se*, we might use the phrase "leitmotivic reception" to describe the way Wagner's musical dramas were approached by means of the category of leitmotif (as well as through the categorization of leitmotifs). In this essay I will show that Wagnerian leitmotivic reception was a central factor in making the musical motives a trademark of Wagner's music, and why one can say in retrospect that the labeled, interpreted, and canonized leitmotifs have proven to be a powerful marketing strategy for Wagnerians. I will argue that leitmotivic reception can be seen as a cultural phenomenon: a central symptom of the *embourgeoisement* of Wagner's music, and at the same time a central means of achieving that.

Leitmotifs of Ambivalence

Since the premiere of the *Ring* in 1876, Wagner's compositional technique has been an object of fierce polemics as well as lasting fascination. One theme of critical reaction goes back to Eduard Hanslick's derogatory remark that the heroes of Wagner's operas are all equipped with a "rich musical wardrobe" in the orchestra, while their voices on the stage remain mostly denuded of proper "melody."[1] This criticism was taken up again, eventually intensified in Stravinsky's verdict on the "monumental absurdity which consists of bestowing on every accessory, as well as on every feeling and every character of the lyrical drama, a sort of checkroom number called a 'Leitmotiv.'"[2] The intellectual fascination commanded by the technique, on the other hand, leads from true Wagnerian enthusiasm like that of Christian von Ehrenfels (the father of the Gestalt theory of psychology), to Claude Lévi-Strauss's idea that Wagner's compositions constitute, in themselves, a kind of "structural analysis" of myth, an analysis carried out in and through music.[3]

The full spectrum of views regarding Wagner's leitmotif technique can be appreciated through an understanding of the ambivalence that has characterized the compositional means itself, its critical reception, and the ways that listeners have applied it to their experience of the music dramas. The history of leitmotif is thus shot through with internal contradictions (often critically productive ones), which themselves form something like (one is tempted to say) a principal leitmotif of that history.

Work and Commentary

Leitmotivic reception is in a sense paradigmatic of a basic problem faced by reception theory in general: how can we assess the interaction between effects determined by the work as such, and the work's reception as shaped by the audience? Where do the implications of the composed structure end and the explicatory role of the listener begin?

The case of the *Ring* and its *Leitfaden* was a first in music history in terms of a work and published commentary. Although there had been many forms of explanatory writings on music in the nineteenth century, never had the premiere of a work coincided with the publication of such a detailed commentary intended to accompany the visual and oral perception of it. Indeed, Wolzogen's text with its commentary and musical examples appeared four weeks *before* the first note of Wagner's gigantic work had been heard in the Bayreuth festival theater.[4] The fact that this *Leitfaden* was presented in advance of the festival by a well-known Wagnerian made it appear to be an officially sanctioned guide, written on behalf of the festival's "author" himself, Richard Wagner. One could even say that the *Ring* (like *Parsifal* after it) never had a chance for a pure "first hearing"; before it was born, it had already been analyzed (see Figure 2).

The near simultaneity of work and commentary was the precondition for a process fundamental to Wagnerian musical listening. In the following years, Wolzogen's method remained tightly associated with the work itself, in fact it became virtually merged with the work by means of the leitmotif tables that came to be attached to librettos or were printed at the front of piano-vocal scores. The fact that Wolzogen's extensive verbal commentary disappeared in the process of its being condensed into leitmotif tables (and with it, the awareness that Wolzogen's analysis had been a secondary, interpretive product) was the crucial technical step for the leitmotif to become the trademark of Wagner's music.

Emotion and Intellect

Although there is no question that Wolzogen's commentary blended with the work, the question whether this listening according to verbally or conceptually identified leitmotifs was a true "Wagnerian" way or ran counter to Wagner's own intentions is more complicated. Wagner never commissioned guidebooks providing such semantic definition, nor did he encourage their use. The composer tolerated Wolzogen's efforts but never really welcomed them. The ambivalence generated by Wolzogen's commentary in critical responses to the *Ring* premiere is certainly one of the reasons why no support for the *Leitfaden* is to be found in Wagner's letters to Wolzogen. There is only one private utterance that shows Wagner's candid opinion about the practice of publishing names for the leitmotifs. When in 1881 Wagner received the first four-hand piano score of the *Ring*, which was provided with Wolzogen's leitmotif names written right into the music (see Figure 3), Cosima noted:

> Unfortunately in this edition there are many hints like *Wanderlust-Motiv*, *Unheils-Motiv* etc. R. says: "In the end the people believe that such nonsense happens by my suggestion!"[5]

Verzeichniss der Motive.

I. Rheingold.

1. Motiv des Urelementes.
2. M. der Rheintöchter.
3. Frohnmotiv.
4. M. der Drohung.
5. Rheingoldfanfare.
6. Rheingoldsang. (3.)
7. Rheingoldmotiv. (3.)
8. Ringmotiv.
9. Entsagungsmotiv.
10. Walhallthema. (8.)
11. Vertragsmotiv. (3. 9.)
12. M. der Liebesfesselung.
13. Freiamotiv. (1.)
14. Fluchtmotiv. (3.)
15. Riesenmotiv.
16. Runenphrase.
17. M.d.Riesenvertrages.(11.)
18. M. d.Jugendäpfel.(2.9 10.)
19. Dämmermotiv. (9. 18.)
20. M. Loge's.
21. M. des Feuerzaubers. (3. 20.)
22. Schmiedemotiv.(4.7.15.)
23. Tarnhelmzauber. (3.21.)
24. AlberichsHerrscherruf (3. 7. 22. 26.)
25. M. d. Sinnens. (16.)
26. M. des aufsteigenden Hortes. (24.)
27. M. des Nibelungen- triumphs. (10. 20. 26.)
28. Drachenmotiv.
29. M. des Fluches.
30. M. der Weltvernich- tungsarbeit.
31. M. der Nornen. (1. 13.)
32. M. d. Götterdämmerung. (9.)
33. M. d. Gewitterzaubers.
34. M. d. Regenbogens.
35. Schwertmotiv. (5. 29.)

II. Walküre.

36. M. d. Siegmund. (11.)
37. M. d. Mitleids. (9.)
38. Liebesmotiv.
39. Wälsungenmotiv. (37.)
40. Heroenthema. (10. 35.)
41. Hundingsmotiv. (4.15.22.)
42. Siegesruf der Wälsungen. (35. 40.)
43. M. der Ahnung. (10.)
44. Liebesweben in der Natur. (38.)
45. Walkürenmotiv.
46. Unmuthsmotiv.(9.11.36.)
47. M.d.Götternoth.(31.32.)
48. Nibelungensegen.(10.5.)
49. M.d.Verfolgung.(32.47.)
50a. M.d.Schicksalskunde.

— 124 —

50b. Sterbegesang. (50a. 31.)
51. Schwertwartfanfare. (35. 53.)
52. Reitmotiv. (45.)
53. Siegfriedmotiv.(29.35.51.)
54a. Waldknabenruf.(52.53.)
54b. Siegfrieds Heroen- thema. (54a.)
55a. Wotans Strafgebot. (46.)
55b. Rechtfertigungsgesang. (11. 55a.)
56. Schlummermotiv. (11. 36.)
57. Scheidegesang.

III. Siegfried.

58a. M. der Lebenslust.(44.)
58b. Liebesmelodie. (14.)
59. M. der Fahrtenlust.
60. Wotans Wanderschritt.
61. M. d. Göttermacht. (47.)
62. Kriechmotiv.
63. Nothungphrase. (35.)
64. M. d. Gelingens.
65. Fafnermotiv. (15.)
66. M. des Rachewahns. (46. 55a.)
67. Vogelsang. (2. 18. 45. 56.)
68a. Beutemotiv. (64.)
68b. Gibichungenmotiv. (31. 68a.)
69. M. d. Liebeslust resp. Verwirrung. (39. 36.)
70. M.d.Welterbschaft. (8. 59b.)
71. M. d. Vaterfreude.
72. M. d. Weltbegrüssung.
73. M. d. Liebesgrusses. (38. 14.)
74. M.d.Liebesentzückens.
75. Friedensmelodie. (90.)
76. M. Siegfrieds des Welten- hortes.
77. M.d.Liebesentschlusses.

IV. Götterdämmerung.

78. Brünnhildenmotiv.(73)
79. M. der Heldenliebe. (69b. 76.)
80. Hagens Motiv. (70.)
   a. Gibichungen-Besitz.
   b. Liebesschlinge.
   c. Gunth. Freundschaft.
   d. Gutrunes Gruss.
   e. Gutrunes Liebe.
81. M.d.Zaubertruges.(48.)
82. M. des Sühnerechtes. (11. 32.)
83. M. des Mordwerkes. (68b. 66.)
84. M. d. Lustigkeit Hagens. (20. 80 +.)
85. Hochzeitruf. (80d.)
86. Schwurmotiv. (29.)
87. M. d. Rachebundes. (3. 65. 66.)
88. Nixenjauchzer. (6.)
89. M. d. Nixenspottes. (6. 4.)
90. M. d. Liebeserlösung. (50b. 75.)

Figure 2. Wolzogen, catalog of motives (1876), 123–24.

It must have bothered Wagner a great deal to see the image of his music shaped by a conceptual apparatus issued side by side with his work. He was very sensitive about the descriptive layer that the motivic labels added to the music, giving an appearance of fixed meanings attached to his musical material. Such a blending of work and commentary was not at all Wagner's idea of how he wished to have the content of his music communicated to listeners. He realized that putting labels in the score was an infringement on the work, a new level of verbalization that risked the distortion or falsification of the reception process. These labels were "nonsense" in terms of Wagner's idea of *Gefühlsverstehen*—of understanding "through feeling," an idea of perception that (compared with the emerging reality of "leitmotif reception") must be called idealistic, if not utopian. Wagner's ideal was a mode of aesthetic perception in which conceptual, rational comprehension is resolved in favor of an understanding at an emotional level. Wagner's theory of art is pervaded by the idea that in drama the crucial part of the intellect, the "poetic intent" (*dichterische Absicht*, that is, the word, idea, or conceptual content of the poetry) "is lifted into utmost imperceptibility, by its entire realization."[6] A whole chapter of the second part of *Opera and Drama* is devoted to the relation of intellect (*Verstand*) to emotion (*Gefühl*). Emotional understanding is viewed as making the rational sensuously perceptible, intelligible. This is what legitimizes the drama (the "total work of art")

> for the very reason that, through employment of every artistic expressional faculty of man, the poet's aim (*Absicht*) is in Drama the most completely carried from the Understanding to the Feeling—to wit, is artistically imparted to the Feeling's most directly receptive organs, the senses.[7]

The ambivalence of the recurring "melodic moments" is aggravated, since Wagner regards the motives as the core of what he coined the "emotionalizing of the intellect" (*Gefühlswerdung des Verstandes*).[8] What the composer had in mind for this layer was, precisely, an unconscious or at least pre-conceptual mode of perception. The musical *motives* are supposed to transfer the dramatic *motives* (or *motifs*) of the plot into the nonverbal artistic expression of the music. The semantic referential dimension of the motives, its function of reminiscence and anticipation, should not rise into awareness as a conceptual definiteness (*Bestimmtheit*) but should remain part of the total effect, where that which is shown is understood in a holistic, integrated manner as being the instinctively right thing, the motivated and the motivating at the same time. In no sense was the listener or spectator meant to go back to the "poetic intent" to arrive once more at the rational level.

Yet this was exactly what the *Leitfaden* booklets propagated by providing the verbal labels as an aid for understanding. They took literally Wagner's notion of "melodic moments" (motives) as *Gefühlswegweiser* (signposts for the emotions) and erected them as labels all over the work.[9] No wonder Wagner lost his patience when he first saw Wolzogen's posts in the musical text. The complex and transformed nature of the "poetic intent" was not only betrayed by being turned into an "utmost perceptibility" through the names, but also trivialized by the tautology many names produce in relation to the scene (for example, the Siegfried motive accompanying Siegfried's entry).

Apparently Wagner misjudged the semiotic effect and intellectual potential of leitmotifs with regard to the process of reception. In Wagner's own wording from *Opera and Drama* describing the listener's role, the "melodic moments," meant as "signposts for the emotions," make the recipients "constant fellow-knowers of the profoundest secret of the poet's Aim, the immediate partners in its realisement [*Verwirklichung*]."[10] The small but essential difference between Wagner's reception theory and the practice of later "Wagnerians" lies in the semantic-musical conceptualization encouraged by the guidebooks, which fosters a listener who is in command of a conscious verbalized knowledge that seems to transfer the profoundest secrets of the poetic intent to the referential level of linguistic meanings. But since the listener who sees through the composer's motivic technique into the poetic intent becomes an initiate who is no longer the immediate but the *mediated* partner in the "realisement," or realization, Wagner's original intention is turned on its head: a means to motivate emotional understanding becomes a means to rationalize this very process.

Reduction vs. Stimulation

A third-level ambivalence generated by leitmotivic reception is semiotic. The names as hermeneutical instruments illustrate paradigmatically how closely paired are reduction and a stimulation of listening options when music is verbalized. Wagner disapproved of the labels in the piano score because he rejected a semantic fixing, which guides the listener by reducing his or her scope of understanding. In terms of reception, however, adding this denotative layer of signs was both functional and, historically, very successful.

Undoubtedly, compressing the music to a handful of named motives (Wolzogen's successors were more effective in reducing the number of designated motives) provided orientation. New listeners facing the sensuous abundance of Wagner's musical dramas, while at the same time

Figure 3. Richard Wagner, *Götterdämmerung*, piano score for four hands, arranged by Albert Heintz (Mainz, 1881), 17. The leitmotifs indicated parenthetically on this page of the piano score are named, respectively: Alberich's motive of doom, Young Siegfried motive, Renunciato motive, and Fate-question motive.

experiencing the loss of traditional operatic forms, could get their bearings from musical phrases repeated in the same or similar forms throughout the work. The names tied firmly to the phrases suggest that what sounds the same also means the same. The correlation of label and sound produces conceptually identifiable units that make the music appear structured and meaningful. Such units give the listener the impression of understanding the combined levels of discourse (musical, poetic-dramatic), and a feeling of certainty in the face of so much novelty.

At the same time, the names become the precondition for penetrating the music; they serve as a stimulus to processing an unfamiliar style, despite the possible "reduction" or narrowing of the semantic field. The correlation of musical motives with concepts, names, or verbal labels in general brings the motives in line with words and their functions. Unsurprisingly, such labeled music fits into classical concepts of the linguistic sign. The name explicates and selects references interpolated from the interplay of music, text, and scene. By fixing a reference, the label enables meaning as a product of interpretation. It makes the music compatible with all varieties of conceptual hermeneutical discourses. The so-called sword motive refers to Siegmund's weapon; by extension, it might also signify (for example) physical strength, freedom, or heroism, depending on the musical-dramatic context. Securing reference in this way produces discursive meaning (even if Wagner rejected it as "nonsense"). Transforming musical motives into signs with reference and meaning was the precondition of the "Wagnerian analytic industry of considerable proportions" that emerged after the premiere of the *Ring* and Wolzogen's first guidebook. The continued use of these verbal tags, as Carolyn Abbate and Roger Parker have written, "even if only as a convenience," underlines "all the referential connotations of the motives, whether self-evident or ridiculous and whether or not we ourselves believe in them."[11] However, the power of this semiotic transformation aroused Wagner's suspicions.

The ambivalence of the semiotic process stems from the mixture of verbal and nonverbal elements of the leitmotif. The potential structural and metaphorical features a motive presents sensuously (that is, exemplifies) are reduced, selected, and narrowed by the denoting name.[12] Without this fixation the motives are semantically open, floating, referentially flexible, and unstable signs that adapt to the corresponding dramatic context. Only a correlated object or content turns them into graspable musical metaphors. The semiotic construct closes, the reference is stable, the floating semantics freeze. Adorno spoke of the "congealed meaning" (*geronnene Bedeutung*) transmitted by the leitmotifs as signs.[13] Looking at the long tradition of teaching and discussing the semantics of the leitmotifs, it becomes clear that such congealed units of music are rather a function of the discourse they enable than of the live performance one follows. Only references with some stability are objects to argue about, only selection of meaning makes competing exegesis possible. In this sense, the labeled, interpreted, and canonized leitmotifs of Wagner's musical dramas are constructs of reception. The advantages of this reduction—the prospect of semantic certainty and discursivity—is one secret of the leitmotif's success story.

Embourgeoisement: The Cicerone Syndrome

The formation of leitmotivic names in the closing decades of the nineteenth century, together with explanations of the drama's content and biographical information about the artist's life and the making of the work, can be regarded as an unmistakable symptom of the bourgeois appropriation of his music. The integration of Wagner's works into the middle-class canon of high art toward the end of the century owed not a little to this form of "reception knowledge" for Wagner listeners. Yet the Wagnerians were not the first in this field. Models for a reception knowledge had already been developed in the visual arts and in the travel business. In 1855 Jakob Burckhardt published his *Der Cicerone: Eine Anleitung zum Genuss der Kunstwerke Italiens*, appearing in English under the title *The Cicerone, an art guide to painting in Italy. For the use of travel.*[14] Burckhardt's *Cicerone* became a reference work in bourgeois homes and a must-have for every educated middle-class traveler through Italy. The travel book was one of the first genres to generate an interpretative knowledge about art that became part of a social habitus and a cultural norm. The cognitive and intellectual demands attached by bourgeois culture to the reception of art are exemplarily manifested in the historical, biographical, interpretive, and evaluative knowledge compiled and created in this guidebook.

The most widely read travel books that preceded Burckhardt were those published by Karl Baedeker starting in the 1830s with guidebooks to Germany, Holland, and Belgium. During the following decades *Baedeker* became a synonym for travel guides (as did *Cicerone* for art guides); Baedeker extended its program all over Europe and exists as a publishing company to the present day. It was this model that Hanslick invoked when commenting on Wolzogen's brochure during the festival of 1876. Writing from Bayreuth, he poked fun at the *Leitfaden,* which he called "a musical 'Baedeker' that no decent tourist here dares leave home without."[15] Hanslick took precise aim at the motivation behind this explanatory literature. He sensed clearly that the phenomenon was still fairly foreign to the musical field. In 1856 George Grove had started to provide commentary program notes for the Crystal Palace concerts in London. Hermann Kretzschmar cited Grove's guides as a model for the explanatory movement that swept German musical culture three decades later, starting with the first edition of his own *Führer durch den Konzertsaal* in 1887.[16] In the meantime, Wolzogen's *Leitfaden* and the succeeding brochures by other authors could have been an inspiring model for the young critic Kretzschmar, who sent enthusiastic reviews from the Bayreuth premiere of 1876. It seems that the educational ambition of the Wagnerians acted as a catalyst for and a driving force of the explanatory movement.[17] At least in the field of opera, their untiring missionary spirit created something new that could be called the Cicerone syndrome. The promotional material for the sale of these guides suggested that the libretto, as the traditional preparation instrument, would no longer suffice; listeners would be robbed of the full enjoyment of the performance should they fail to purchase a knowledgeable guidebook.

When *Das Rheingold* and *Die Walküre* were performed for the first time in Cologne in 1878 a local bookstore advertised the libretti of the works together with the "best commentaries" of Wolzogen and others, stating that prior study of this material is "strongly recommended" ("Das vorherige Studium ist dringend zu empfehlen").[18] Going out to a Wagner performance became an educational tour, and one did not set out without a Cicerone.

George Bernard Shaw's brochure *The Perfect Wagnerite* from 1898 echoed Hanslick's "decent tourist" in satirizing the Cicerone syndrome: it had already become the duty of an immaculate Wagnerian to read or at least own a guidebook. Establishing such a reception norm produced a growing demand for brochures. Thus a competitive market emerged. In 1896, when the second Bayreuth production of the *Ring* was premiered, Wolzogen's own publisher promoted the *Leitfaden* not only with the notorious statement "For all visitors of Richard Wagner's dramas the following guidebooks are indispensable" but also with the warning, "Look carefully for the names of the authors and of the publisher, since many low-quality imitations have occurred."[19] Between 1876 and 1914 more than fifty booklets with motivically illustrated commentary on individual Wagner works were published in Germany. In the year 1910 alone, for example, one had the choice of more than a dozen guidebooks covering all of Wagner's works in addition to Wolzogen's classic brochures. The *Leitfaden* literature was a product of the spreading Wagner fever, but the genre of illustrated commentaries also boosted Wagnerism.

With greatly varying degrees of quality all of these brochures and books tried to promulgate at least the pretension of a "demanding" way of listening by suggesting that musical knowledge—whether historical, biographical, structural, or semantic—is an obligation of the listening experience. Around 1900 the Wagnerian Cicerones had been joined by many similar brochures in the concert business. The Meisterführer series (Berlin and

Vienna, 1907–22) embodied the final *embourgeoisement* of Wagner's works through their canonization into classical pieces. All Wagner works since *Rienzi* were included in four out of the fifteen booklets in this series, and the *Ring* appeared twice in two different guides (due to the fusion of two publishers), framed by Beethoven's nine symphonies and Mozart's "master operas."

Wolzogen's model—once an innovative attempt to convey an unknown and difficult work to the audience—was gradually absorbed into a widespread culture of musical guides that explained the great works of the great masters, a practice that rapidly became institutionalized and is still familiar in the form of program notes.

Leitmotifs and Social Distinction

"Leitmotivic reception" on the new, Wagnerian model provides a perfect example of the social and communicative functions that musical knowledge assumed in middle-class musical culture. The knowledge of fixed names, meanings, and interpretations enabled an access to the music that differentiated the more knowledgeable listener from the less knowledgeable. Musical semantics served as a language by which one could join an exclusive discourse. Wolzogen's semanticizing method, originally meant to be a missionary aid for an unprepared audience, became an instrument of social distinction. "We often just look for entertainment and distraction," says one of the Wagner Cicerones in his introduction, "where our imagination should be vividly stimulated and our full attention gripped, where not empty pleasure but noble enjoyment is prepared for us."[20]

Authors of such Wagnerian guides were convinced that they supported a self-education that ennobled the aesthetic experience. The strong semantic "surplus value" of the leitmotifs was played off against a hedonistic way of traditional opera listening, against a reception that concentrated on grand singers and grandiose melodies but did not care much about the drama. The listener who was able to distinguish the motives and their semantics was undoubtedly one who was occupied with the drama and its structure (whether in a shallow or a deeper way). Anyone well versed in the vocabulary of the leitmotif could feel himself the better and worthier opera aficionado.

In creating this hierarchy, the guidebook authors were perfect disciples of their master, though in a manner Wagner never proposed. In his writings he had always called for a new and different audience, free from bourgeois listening habits. Wagner was convinced that naïve, unspoiled listeners were the only audience appropriate for his works. He had learned that *Bildung* or *Gebildetheit*—in the negative sense as a conglomeration of prejudices and fixed expectations—had often been a hurdle in the appreciation of his art. But at the same time he was aware of how utopian the idea of an innocent listener was: "I request nothing more from the audience than healthy senses and a human heart. That sounds little, but is just so much that the whole world would have to be turned around and around before this could be achieved," he wrote to Liszt after the *Lohengrin* premiere in 1850.[21] Nearly thirty years later, he had not changed his position substantially. In his 1878 article "Publikum und Popularität" (The public and popularity), he differentiated between a "noble popularity" emerging from an "extreme purity in the communication [*Verkehr*] between the work of art and its audience" on the one hand, and the popularity of an average, misguided middle-class audience on the other, an audience unable to rise above mediocrity.[22] He never considered that it might be the traditionally educated middle class itself that—by establishing a listening code through musical knowledge—was going to define an adequately prepared Wagnerian audience. In this sense the labeled, interpreted, and canonized leitmotifs have proven to be a powerful marketing strategy in building a community of Wagnerian listeners.

Popularizing Leitmotifs

In the process of its *embourgeoisement*, the leitmotif underwent an astounding revaluation. Since the time of *Tannhäuser*, a great part of the audience considered that the compositional means that had enabled Wagner to create more and more through-composed operas (which for him represented musical progress) entailed a genuine loss. In his long essay on *Lohengrin*, Franz Liszt pointed out to his readers that the innovation in Wagner's blending of music, poetry, and stage was precisely the exclusion of passages or melodies that could be taken out of their context and be treated as individual set pieces—a practice that contrasted dramatically with what listeners were used to.[23] In his 1846 *Tannhäuser* review young Eduard Hanslick, who at that time was not yet an anti-Wagnerian, put it more drastically: "The general audience . . . does not like music from whose first performance it cannot take home, humming all the way, some eight-bar march melodies that can be immediately reconstructed at the piano."[24] The musical dramas after *Tristan*, with their radicalized compositional structure, increased these strong feelings of confusion. Wagner's music was perceived by conservative critics as being without melody, structure, or orientation. This impression of musical formlessness came to be one of the central topoi of Wagner critiques.[25] The untiring educational work of Wagnerians managed to convert these prejudices into a preliminary reception knowledge supporting and benefiting the understanding of Wagner's works. The leitmotifs were successfully promoted as a substitute for the lost opera melody and turned more and more into the kind of musical object that Hanslick had seen as missing for the average audience.

On the one hand, the formal grasp that Wagner's music had originally denied was meticulously compensated for by making the labeled motives part of an obligatory reception knowledge that increased understanding on the basic structural level of orchestral melody. On the other hand, some guides simply aligned the leitmotifs with the so-called opera melodies. These "inferior imitators," against whom Wolzogen's publisher had warned in 1896, tried to remove the new demand on listening established with the *Leitfaden* by avoiding the kind of motivic scholasticism Wolzogen had offered with his demanding but not very readable analysis, one that originally included an exegesis of every individual motive. The musical analysis evaporated into names and numbers, and was integrated into a synopsis of the plot. Some brochures were essentially "lite" versions of Wolzogen's *Leitfaden*. To a simple synopsis they would add, in the manner of illustrations, "the principal motives and the most beautiful pearls of music."[26] These guides avoided almost entirely any hints at motivic relationships, reminiscences, or anticipations. The functional difference between a leitmotif in a work of Wagner and a traditional aria melody was completely flattened out. The trademark "leitmotif," which since Wolzogen had stood for a different, more demanding and semantically charged listening, devolved to the level of an almost meaningless label.

A part of this leveling was aimed at educated listeners in command of piano playing, for whom Wagner's works were now prepared in the same way as traditional operas. In 1910 an illustrated series of opera albums was launched under the programmatic title *Musik für Alle* (see Figure 4). These integrated Wagner's musical dramas into the general opera repertoire by reducing them to handy dimensions. A "Reader's Digest" arrangement let a whole act shrink to three pages, the music being transposed into more comfortable keys (for example, the beginning of *Rheingold* in D major), and set in an easy-to-play piano score. The albums included a synopsis, together with information about the history of the work. No analysis or exegesis clouded the user's musical enjoyment; leitmotifs were pointed out by name in the printed score.

Finally, in 1920, the sum of all guides for Wagnerites came out: *The Book of Motives*, compiled by Lothar Windsperger (see Figure 5). It represents the peak and end of the leitmotivic hypostatization of Wagner's music. With its 491 motives listed in the order of their occurrence, this two-volume issue represents the synthesis of all other tables from librettos, piano scores, and guidebooks. From *Rienzi* to *Parsifal*, all thematic phrases are lumped together by the labeling of their dramatic meaning. Every aria theme of *Rienzi*, for example, receives leitmotivic status ("Gebet-Motiv," "Jubel-Motiv," etc.). Part of an ad for this volume reads: "The book [is] a chain of pearls strung together, representing an indispensable guide and an inexhaustible source of

Figure 4. *Musik für Alle. Richard Wagner: Walküre.* This cover of the popular Music for Everyone series (vol. 10, no. 112), which appeared in 1921, shows Martha Leffler-Burkhard as Brünnhilde.

pleasure."[27] In this way Wagner's music eventually assumed the very handiness that enables one to "take it home, humming." The presentation is a result of a logical development: once the leitmotif names had found their way into the piano score, the score could be excerpted with reference to those names. The *Book of Motives* is a curiosity available up to the present day from Wagner's original publisher, Schott. It is still shaping the ambivalent field of work and commentary in which the Wagnerian guides operate in a paradoxical yet pragmatic way. Since Wolzogen's *Leitfaden*, leitmotivic analysis has been identified with Wagner's compositions themselves. That its title page presents the book as *Richard Wagner: Das Buch der Motive* does not lack irony: the reception practice derived from a specific compositional technique acquired here almost the status of a work unto itself.

Figure 5. Lothar Windsperger, (Mainz, 1920), vol. 1, cover.

NOTES

The essay is based on my full-length study *Semantisierte Sinnlichkeit: Rezeption und Zeichenstruktur der Leitmotivtechnik Richard Wagners* (Stuttgart, 2003).

1. Susanna Großmann-Vendrey, *Bayreuth in der deutschen Presse: Beiträge zur Rezeptionsgeschichte Richard Wagners und seiner Festspiele*, 3 vols. (Regensburg, 1977–83), 1:175.

2. Igor Stravinsky, *Poetics of Music in the Form of Six Lessons* (Cambridge, Mass., 1970), 101.

3. See Christian von Ehrenfels, *Richard Wagner und seine Apostaten: Ein Beitrag zur Jahrhundertfeier* (Vienna and Leipzig, 1913), 18–22; Claude Lévi-Strauss, *The Raw and the Cooked: Introduction to a Science of Mythology: I* (New York and Evanston, Ill., 1970), 14–30; Carl Dahlhaus, "Analyse des Mythos: Claude Lévi-Strauss und 'Der Ring des Nibelungen,'" in *Klassische und romantische Musikästhetik* (Laaber, 1988), 458–67.

4. Wolzogen was neither the inventor of the term *Leitmotiv* nor the first to employ detailed motive analyses to Wagner's music. He was preceded by the work of Gottlieb Federlein, who had already published analyses of *Rheingold* and *Walküre* in the *Musikalische Wochenblatt* in 1871 and 1872. Thomas Grey discovered that the term *Leitmotiv* can be traced back to 1860. See Thomas S. Grey, "'. . . wie ein rother Faden': On the origins of 'leitmotif' as critical construct and musical practice," in *Music Theory in the Age of Romanticism*, ed. Ian Bent (Cambridge and New York, 1996), 187–210; Thorau, *Semantisierte Sinnlichkeit*, 106–16.

5. 1 August 1881: "Ich spiele mit Lusch 4händig aus der Götterdämmerung. R. sagt, es freue ihn das Werk. Leider kommen in dieser Ausgabe lauter Andeutungen wie Wanderlust-Motiv, Unheils-Motiv etc. [vor]. R. sagt, am Ende glauben die Leute, daß solcher Unsinn auf meine Anregung geschieht!" ("I play excerpts from Götterdämmerung, arranged for piano duet, with Loldi. R. says he is pleased with the work. Unfortunately in this edition there are a lot of markings such as 'wanderlust motive,' 'disaster motive,' etc. R. says, 'And perhaps people will think all this nonsense is done at my request!'"). Cosima Wagner, *Die Tagebücher*, vol. 2 (1878–1883), ed. Martin Gregor-Dellin (Munich and Zurich, 1976), 772; *Cosima Wagner's Diaries*, trans. Geoffrey Skelton (New York, 1980), 2:697.

6. Richard Wagner, *Opera and Drama*, trans. William Ashton Ellis, *Richard Wagner's Prose Works*, vol. 2 (London, 1893, repr. 1995), 208. Wagner uses the Hegelian "aufgehoben," which means uplifted and preserved by being transformed into another state: "durch ihre vollständige Verwirklichung zur vollsten Unmerklichkeit aufgehoben wird." Richard Wagner, *Oper und Drama*, ed. Klaus Kropfinger (Stuttgart, 1984), 215. On "poetic intent," see Frank Glass, *The Fertilizing Seed: Wagner's Concept of the Poetic Intent* (Ann Arbor, 1983), 4.

7. Wagner, *Opera and Drama*, 208. In German: "weil in ihm durch Verwendung aller künstlerischen Ausdrucksfähigkeiten des Menschen die Absicht des Dichters am vollständigsten aus dem Verstande an das Gefühl, nämlich künstlerisch an die unmittelbarsten Empfängnisorgane des Gefühles, die Sinne, mitgeteilt wird." *Oper und Drama*, 215.

8. In part 3 of *Oper und Drama* Wagner mostly uses "melodische Momente" to characterize the musical motives in contrast to the dramatic motives. The term *Leitmotiv* did not occur until 1860; see note 4.

9. W. A. Ellis translates *Gefühlswegweiser* as "guides-to-Feeling"; see Wagner, *Opera and Drama*, 346.

10. Ibid. The small shift toward the metaphor of guiding in W. A. Ellis's translation is significant: "At their [the guides-to-Feeling's] hand we become the constant fellow-knowers of the profoundest secret of the poet's Aim, the immediate partners in its realisement." Wagner uses a less concrete formulation by using the concept of becoming (*werden*) together

with the preposition *an*: "An ihnen werden wir zu steten Mitwissern des tiefsten Geheimnisses der dichterischen Absicht, zu unmittelbaren Teilnehmern an dessen Verwirklichung." Wagner, *Oper und Drama*, 360.

11. Carolyn Abbate and Roger Parker, "Introduction: On Analyzing Opera," in *Analyzing Opera: Verdi and Wagner*, ed. Carolyn Abbate and Roger Parker (Berkeley and Los Angeles, 1989), 7.

12. See my semiotic approach in *Semantisierte Sinnlichkeit*, chap. 3.

13. Theodor W. Adorno, *Versuch über Wagner,* in *Gesammelte Schriften* (Frankfurt am Main, 1971), 13:42. See also Adorno, *In Search of Wagner,* trans. Rodney Livingston (London, 1981), 45.

14. London, 1873.

15. Großmann-Vendrey, *Bayreuth in der deutschen Presse*, 1:174.

16. Hermann Kretzschmar, *Gesammelte Aufsätze* (Leipzig, 1910), 1:270.

17. See Leon Botstein, "Listening Through Reading: Musical Literacy and the Concert Audience," in *19th-Century Music* 16 (1992): 129–45; and Thorau, "Die Hörer und ihr Cicerone: Werkerläuterungen in der bürgerlichen Musikrezeption," in *Musik—Bildung— Textualität* (Erlangen, 2007), 207–20.

18. See my *Semantisierte Sinnlichkeit*, 159.

19. Advertisement in the appendix of the 1896 edition of Wolzogen's *Thematischer Leitfaden*.

20. Hermann von der Pfordten, *Handlung und Dichtung der Bühnenwerke Richard Wagners nach ihren Grundlagen in Sage und Geschichte dargestellt* (Berlin, 1890), 2.

21. Letter to Franz Liszt, 2 October 1850, in Richard Wagner, *Sämtliche Briefe* (Leipzig, 1967–), 3:431–32: "Nichts weiter fordere ich vom publikum als gesunde sinne und ein menschliches herz. Das klingt wenig und ist doch eben so viel, dass die ganze welt erst um und um gedreht werden müßte, um es zu stande zu bringen."

22. Richard Wagner, "Publikum und Popularität," in *Gesammelte Schriften und Dichtungen* (Leipzig, 1873), 10:61–90; quote, 61.

23. Franz Liszt, *Sämtliche Schriften* (Wiesbaden, 1989), 4:85.

24. Quoted in Helmut Kirchmeyer, *Situationsgeschichte der Musikkritik und des musikalischen Pressewesens in Deutschland*, IV. Teil: *Das zeitgenössische Wagner-Bild* (Regensburg, 1968), 4/3:180: "Das große Publikum . . . mag keine Musik, aus der man sich nicht aus der ersten Aufführung gleich einige achttaktige Marschmelodien summend nach Hause tragen kann, um sie daselbst unverzüglich dem Fortepiano beizubringen."

25. See Thomas S. Grey, *Wagner's Musical Prose: Texts and Contexts* (Cambridge, 1995), 242–56; and Thorau, *Semantisierte Sinnlichkeit*, 59–79.

26. Walther Wossidlo, *Wie verstehen wir Richard Wagners Nibelungen? Populärer Führer durch Poesie u. Musik* (Berlin, 1895), 2.

27. Advertisement in the appendix of the 1920 edition.

German Jews and Wagner

LEON BOTSTEIN

The Wagner Ban in Israel

In his lectures on Richard Wagner at the University of Vienna held during the 1903–4 academic year, the music historian Guido Adler felt obliged to confront the claims in Wagner's notorious essay "Das Judentum in der Musik" (Judaism in Music). He characterized them as reprehensible political commonplaces, part of a social tirade unbecoming a great artist. Adler and his audience were keenly aware of the electoral successes of Vienna's charismatic Christian Socialist mayor, Karl Lueger, who during the 1890s had deftly exploited a potent populist and political anti-Semitism in the city.[1] Adler, who was born a Jew, conceded that the sort of political platitudes Wagner used could inspire modernity's sheep-like masses. But he added no further comments, closing with this thought: "I would prefer to leave to others to speculate on any further conclusions. On such questions, the sort of irritability that, unfortunately, is so morbidly aroused must not play a role, but rather open, brave opposition, calm debate, and thoughtful consideration of all points of dispute. Let us place our confidence in the judgment of history. That judgment, however, must not be based on false 'foundations' derived from false premises that lead to monstrous conclusions."[2]

The judgment of history about Wagner's anti-Semitism and whether its influence, particularly on Germans and Hitler, contributed significantly to Nazi Germany's "monstrous conclusions"[3] remains open to much ongoing debate.[4] The well-publicized ban on Wagner performances in Israel continues to focus our attention on Wagner's role in modern European history and the historical significance of his anti-Semitism.[5] When David Stern was appointed director of the Israel Opera in 2008, he indicated that he would honor the Wagner ban as long as Holocaust survivors remained alive, out of respect for their feelings.[6] His decision reflects a prevailing consensus, not only in Israel, that Wagner was a key inspiration for modern German anti-Semitism, that he influenced Hitler, and that enthusiasm for Wagner helped justify the death camps for those Germans who created them, as well as for those who stood by in silent agreement. This belief persists whether or not one believes that links between Wagner's anti-Semitism and Nazi ideology can be read outside of Wagner's prose and conversations, and are located, tacitly and overtly, in the music, texts, and plots of the operas and music dramas.[7]

Disagreement over the appropriateness of the ban derives only partially from disagreement over the historical claim that Wagner was a decisive influence on the Nazis and the German embrace of Nazism. Wagner died in 1883, long before there were Nazis and even before Hitler was born. The historical debate has therefore centered on the originality and influence of his anti-Semitism. How unusual and persuasive was Wagner in the admittedly highly anti-Semitic context of late nineteenth-century Europe, in which anti-Semitism had long been a historical reality? Does anti-Semitism, cloaked in the seductive beauties of Wagner's works, emerge as symbol and allegory? If so, was it recognized as such in the past and is it still perceptible on the stage and audible in the music? If anti-Semitism is understood as an essential component of the drama and the musical fabric, then the historical debate shifts from Wagner the personality and ideologue to the character and impact of Wagner's art.

Wagner's anti-Semitism first became the subject of heated controversy in 1869 when the composer republished his already notorious "Judentum" essay under his own name, in a slightly revised form with an appendix. The debate regarding its significance and influence has continued with intensity since 1933. Yet despite extensive work on Wagner's influence in Wilhelmine Germany, on Hitler, and on twentieth-century German anti-Semitism, there has been comparatively little investigation on how Jews in German-speaking Europe reacted and responded before World War II to Wagner the anti-Semite, or even how they reacted (as Jews) to Wagner the writer and composer.

Wagner's unparalleled success not only in Germany but throughout Europe and North America from the mid-1870s on, and his popularity among Jews, particularly after 1870, forced German-speaking Jews to confront fundamental issues of their self-image and status in civil society beyond the confines of legal emancipation.[8] Wagner was more than a composer who claimed for himself the mantle of Beethoven in the history of music. Wagner became a potent cultural force and symbol after the unification of Germany, when the success of Jews in integrating and assimilating into German society and culture became increasingly palpable and visible.[9] Not surprisingly, the confrontation with Wagner and Wagnerism among Jews coincided with revivals in Jewish nationalism (including Herzl's Zionist project), the acceleration of a Jewish identification with "Germanness," and the deepening of the pre-1848 Jewish embrace of the ideal of a transnational aristocracy of culture that transcended politics and religion.[10]

Since after 1870 political anti-Semitism became associated with Wagner, and since Wagner and his followers were viewed in liberal circles as "arousing" the "morbid irritability" of the day that anti-Semitism represented, educated Jews could not easily avoid Wagner. One of Wagner's signal achievements was his success in generating a self-serving but persuasive and widespread account of music history. The character of Jewish responses to Wagner, both adoring and critical, helped lend twentieth-century modernism its character, particularly modernism's construct of language and form. Indeed, the reaction against Wagner, in part fueled by the need to counter the aesthetic underpinnings of Wagner's astonishing popularity (and therefore indirectly his ideas, anti-Semitism among them) helped spur a fin-de-siècle "rediscovery" of Mozart and a subsequent renaissance of interest in Offenbach.[11] Only after 1945 did Wagner's role as an anti-Semite inspire an attempt to reconsider the way the modern history of music since Bach is understood.[12] Unfortunately, this post–World War II revisionism resulted in only halting and marginally successful reevaluations of the achievements of the primary victims of Wagner's version of history and anti-Semitic polemics, Mendelssohn and Meyerbeer.[13]

The most powerful argument against Israel's ban, however, invokes none of these issues about cultural reception. Rather it concerns the merit, efficacy, and unintended consequences of official or consensual censorship. By implicitly asserting Wagner's historical responsibility, the ban tacitly avoids confronting two common underlying assumptions: that the Germans under the Nazis were alone responsible for the Holocaust and that the Nazis represented the culmination of a unique, continuous historical trajectory of anti-Semitism in German-speaking Europe in which Wagner played a crucial part.[14] But if one questions the historical assumptions linking Wagner and the Holocaust, arguments against the ban assume a different aspect. By endorsing the assignment of historical responsibility for the extermination of European Jewry, even symbolically, to Wagner, the ban may have the effect of falsifying history.[15] The consequence for current and future generations in Israel is disastrous, for the real causes of the Holocaust become obscured, distorted, and replaced by a facile, convenient, and misleading formula. Any distraction of attention from the historical circumstances that actually made the death camps and *Einsatzgruppen* possible and astonishingly efficient is dangerous. Genuine respect for the survivors might then argue against a ban on Wagner, even if the survivors themselves, for a complex of understandable reasons, viscerally accept the validity of the Wagner-Hitler equation.

Wagner attained a significant Jewish public from the start of his career. Banning Wagner shields Israelis from the historical record of the response among Jews to Wagner, in his lifetime and after. What were the ways in which Wagner influenced not only German and European Christians but also Jews in Germany? This aspect of Jewish history, suppressed and disfigured by the ban, demands recovery. In the process of recovery, affirmative and not defensive reasons to produce, play, and listen to Wagner, in Israel as well as elsewhere, can emerge that do not require a rationalization of the historical record and do not tacitly apologize for the monstrous consequences undeniably present in all forms of nineteenth-century European anti-Semitism.[16]

Responding to Wagner: 1870–1900

There were three distinct eras of debate between supporters and critics of Wagner in German-speaking Europe between 1870 and 1945. In each era Wagner's anti-Semitism played a crucial role. The first of these controversies erupted soon after 1870, in the wake of Wagner's 1869 republication of "Judaism in Music," the German victory (over France) in 1870, German unification, and the 1870 Viennese premiere of *Die Meistersinger*. A public exchange between Wagnerians and anti-Wagnerians continued throughout the decade (which witnessed the opening of Bayreuth) and continued until shortly after Wagner's death in 1883. The second era began at the turn of the century and culminated in 1913, when Bayreuth's right to continue its exclusive hold on *Parsifal* was openly contested. Unauthorized performances in New York, Amsterdam, and Monte Carlo became a subject of controversy.[17] That debate revealed a fin-de-siècle generational divide. The young reacted against the Wagnerian enthusiasm of the 1870s, both in art and politics. It was in this era of reaction that Guido Adler gave the lectures cited at the beginning of this essay. The third era of intense controversy lies beyond the scope of this essay and has been the one most closely scrutinized by modern scholarship. It began in the late 1920s and accompanied the rise of Hitler and the establishment and defeat of Nazi Germany.[18]

The Viennese premiere of Wagner's *Die Meistersinger* took place on February 27, 1870. In 1871, in the wake of the opera's success, Peter Cornelius published an essay in the Viennese *Deutsche Zeitung*, "Deutsche Kunst und Richard Wagner," arguing on behalf of a pan-German campaign for the support of Bayreuth. With *Die Meistersinger,* maintained Cornelius, Wagner had realized his destiny and historical mission, filling a long-standing vacuum by providing the German people with a contemporary artistic and communal expression of the modern German spirit. Having experienced the power of *Die Meistersinger* firsthand, the time had finally come for the Viennese to embrace the creation of Bayreuth.[19] Only two years earlier Wagner had republished "Judaism in Music" under his own name, with an appendix excoriating a Jewish conspiracy against him. Did Cornelius's call for a populist embrace of a Wagnerian "Germanness" include German Jews in Vienna or anywhere else?

Few Jews were regular readers of the pan-German and frequently anti-Semitic *Deutsche Zeitung*, but in 1870 Vienna had more than its fair share of Jewish Wagner devotees. The premiere of *Die Meistersinger* made this abundantly clear. Daniel Spitzer (1835–93), the great Jewish Viennese satirist (who himself briefly wrote for the *Deutsche Zeitung*), described the premiere. A conflict broke out between supporters and detractors. The performance took place, as Spitzer's review acknowledged, in front of an audience that knew Wagner held a Jewish clique responsible for hindering his career. The irony, Spitzer observed, was that among those in the audience shouting on behalf of *Die Meistersinger*, the quintessential articulation of German national pride, there appeared to be a large number of unmistakably Jewish Viennese opera lovers. As Spitzer put it, coyly referencing Wagner's essay, "One could not succeed in getting beyond the verbal insults during the performance, where, as expected, the Wagnerians often lost all sense of proportion, so that a perfectly decent derisive whisper of 'Mendelssohn' was followed by an even more crude insult of 'Meyerbeer' being thrown in one's face. The confessional character of this musical war ultimately receded, so that one could see Christian–musical Germans hissing, and in contrast, possessors of noses bent heavily by the burden of Semitism applauding."[20]

The most vocal skeptics and critics at the premiere turned out to be non-Jews, well informed and articulate connoisseurs who took exception to Wagner's form of theater, poetry, and music. One such critic was Ludwig Speidel (1830–1906), who noted with considerable amazement that "Wagner treats the Hebrews like mangy dogs and in return they follow with tails between their legs and lick his hands with pleasure. They are deaf to the gentle alluring calls of Mendelssohn and the sharp whistling of Meyerbeer. Certainly these paradoxical phenomena belong to the amazing effects that derive from Wagner's personality."[21]

The reaction of Viennese Jews to Wagner's music was not exceptional in German-speaking Europe, despite the composer's public standing as a committed anti-Semite. At the conclusion of the first production of the *Ring* at Bayreuth in 1876, George Davidsohn, critic of the *Berlin Börsen-Courier* and head of the Berlin Wagner Society, stood up and delivered an off-the-cuff public encomium to Wagner, precipitating ovations that forced the composer to the stage to address the audience.[22] Davidsohn (1835–97) was Jewish.[23] Again, Spitzer was there: "The house was full . . . and even the prosperous Wagner-Semite from Berlin was not missing, who, despite the attacks by the music monopolies against their Jewish competitors, could be found in the prominent presence of the happy Master, whose long

Talmud-Sniffing nose reveals clear signs of an earlier racial affinity. It is said that Wagner fears most of all the discovery of his own Jewish ancestry and dislikes when he sees his name shortened to R. Wagner because he fears it could be read as easily to mean 'Rabbi Wagner.'"[24]

By the 1870s three facts seemed clear: Wagner was an outspoken anti-Semite, his art was inextricably bound up with a new German self-definition, and German Jews were among the most enthusiastic consumers of Wagner's work. Writing in response to Cornelius's essay on "Richard Wagner and German Art" in 1871, Speidel, despite deep misgivings about Wagner's aesthetics and morals, conceded that one could not argue with success: "The German people see in Wagner's operas its contemporary musical ideals realized, and whoever wishes to take that from them—assuming that were even possible—would be taking a piece of soul from the bodies of these people. If art, above all music . . . belongs even a tiny bit to the substance of Germanness, Wagner's substance cannot be separated any longer from the essence of the German . . . against my own feelings . . . the conclusion is inescapable: The substance of Richard Wagner can no longer be separated from the substance of the German."[25]

In light of the Germans being defined in Wagnerian terms and therefore connected in substance to Wagner's construct of anti-Semitism, how could German Jews embrace Wagner so enthusiastically?

The implausibility and irony of a Jewish enthusiasm for Wagner did not escape Wagnerians, anti-Wagnerians, or anti-Semites. In the humor magazine *Wiener Luft* (associated with *Figaro*, the publication with which Spitzer first gained his reputation as a satirist), the texts and cartoons from the 1870s show both a persistent exploitation of popular anti-Semitism and a thoroughgoing skepticism about Wagner—his delusions of grandeur, the bizarre character of the content of the *Ring* with its dragons and giants, and the excessive cost of the spectacle. Wagner's own hypocritical attitude to money, power, fame, and Jews is underscored in a cartoon from the spring of 1877, when *Die Walküre* was premiered in Vienna (see Figure 1). Jews are depicted, gathered outside the Opera House. Some well-heeled types are in the background. A sign indicating the sale at wildly high prices for the performance is placed above a set of shabby Jews in the foreground hocking tickets, seeking to make a profit. The phrase "The Temple of Art" is placed on the Opera House above an idealized caricature of Wagner looking shocked and angry. The caption reads "Richard Wagner: 'It appears to me that it is high time that I chase these buyers and sellers from the Temple of Art.'"[26]

In a caustic review of the 1877 performance, Spitzer shredded *Walküre*'s poetic language, the story's pretensions, and any claim to dramatic tension or symbolic meaning. Spitzer took aim once again at the Jewish enthusi-

Figure 1. An 1877 cartoon of a hypocritical Wagner eying Jewish scalpers with disapproval.

asm for Wagner. Poking fun at Siegmund's Act 1 declaration of various incognitos he must refuse (Friedmund, Frohwalt) or accept (Wehwalt), Spitzer suggested three more modern equivalents in use in Vienna that would sound even more apt: Friedmann, Fröhlich, and Wehle—all familiar Viennese Jewish last names.[27]

Non-Jewish observers, particularly Wagnerians, may have marveled at the Jewish embrace of Wagner, but at the same time they used Wagner's anti-Semitism to explain away criticism of the master of Bayreuth, as he himself had tried to do. If critics (often identified falsely as Jews) were opposed to Wagner, it was merely on account of Wagner's politics, not his art, they claimed. Yet as Wagner's popularity grew throughout Europe (particularly in Vienna after Wagner's triumphant appearance there as a conductor in 1875), there was increasing enthusiasm for his music among Jews.

The Jews' marked overcoming of hesitancy and skepticism was subject to scathing contempt: conversion to Wagnerism seemed as pathetic an attempt to erase the indelibility of one's identity as a Jew by conversion to Christianity.[28] It was as if Jews, by becoming ardent Wagnerians, were intent on disproving Wagner's assertion of their essential lack of artistic feeling, their incapacity to recognize and experience the aesthetic. Yet by their actions they actually underscored among anti-Semites Wagner's explicit fear of a "Jewish" skill at mimicry and imitation, as well as an alleged "Jewish" instinct for mere fashion. The Jewish Wagnerian became the ideal type of the insecure parvenu seeking to camouflage his essential vulgarity by proclaiming himself in the forefront of a new and fashionable artistic movement.

Once again, the *Wiener Luft* weighed in. On the occasion of the 1879 Viennese premiere of *Götterdämmerung*, the front page of the November issue sported a cartoon showing three small caricatures of Jewish men (see Figure 2). Two, on ladders, are placing a wreath on an outsized bust of Wagner while the third reads an address to the Master. The caption: "Even the most embittered of Anti-Wagnerians permit Richard Wagner to call himself a genius after the performance of *Götterdämmerung*."[29] Now that it was socially acceptable, joining the Wagner cult would redeem the Jewish capacity for aesthetic judgment. The parvenu Jew, metaphorically speaking, jumped on the bandwagon in a desperate but useless attempt to disguise his true and ultimately unalterable character.

The Jews were trapped. The judgment of serious critics of Wagner (Spitzer, for example) was impugned because their attitudes were ascribed to defensiveness, a desire for revenge, and a philistine but characteristically Jewish adherence to established and conventional norms of judgment.[30] Given Wagner's views and the attitudes of the most enthusiastic of his anti-Semitic followers, particularly those closely associated with Bayreuth, Jewish Wagnerians were either viewed with bemusement or held in contempt for their evident self-loathing. The contempt on the part of Wagner and his circle was so acute that they exploited without apology the enthusiasm of their Jewish followers near and far.[31] Wagner's inner circle knew they had little choice. As early as the 1850s, Hans von Bülow acknowledged, with considerable regret, the importance of the Jewish urban middle class as a crucial audience for music and theater, and therefore an important source of patronage for artists and institutions, including Wagner. By the 1870s the visible significance of the Jewish audience was widely recognized (Figure 3).[32]

Spitzer was among the most eloquent Jewish cultural critics to espouse a normative anti-Wagnerian view of art, in which language and music were distinct and independent, albeit related, entities. Spitzer was born into a Jewish Moravian family; his father founded a printing firm that produced high-quality art reproductions. Unlike many of his fellow intellectuals, Spitzer remained Jewish. His wit and satire took no prisoners; even to Jews he was merciless. Against anti-Semites he used his unabashed willingness to identify with the masses of poor, uneducated, and unassimilated Jews of Vienna. From his grandmother he learned Yiddish, which he later used to satirize Jews in *Figaro* under the sarcastic pseudonym Itzig Kneipeles. His friendship with Brahms led to the rumor, he joked, that Brahms, too, might be a Jew.

Selbst die verbissensten Anti-Wagnerianer erlauben jetzt dem Richard Wagner nach der Aufführung der „Götterdämmerung", sich ein Genie nennen zu dürfen.

Figure 2. An 1879 cartoon of Jews paying tribute to the mighty Wagner.

Yet Spitzer was entirely acculturated, inactive in the Jewish community, and as best one can make out, a skeptical agnostic, if not an atheist.[33] He acquired a strong, classical, Gymnasium education and a law degree. Like Eduard Hanslick, Spitzer's idealized construct of the German was located in the literature of Weimar Classicism (Goethe and Schiller) and in music from the era of Mozart and Beethoven. As his love of Greco–Roman culture and *Tristram Shandy* suggests, there was little in Wagner to attract Spitzer. For him, music was an autonomous art, distinct from poetry and

Figure 3. An 1874 Viennese caricature of Jewish patrons at the opera.

prose. The bombast of Wagner's musical and linguistic rhetoric made the Master an easy prey—as did his endless alliteration and faux archaism, and his penchant for rhetorical questions. Commenting on lines sung by Gutrune in Act 1 of *Götterdämmerung*, Spitzer singled out the "entirely meaningless" words *tapfen* and *ergannt* he saw in the 1876 publication of the libretto as probable printing errors rather than bizarre versions of the familiar words *tapfer* and *erkannt*. Despite desperate efforts of fanatical orthodox Wagnerians to justify this odd language at any cost, might these not be merely overlooked printing errors? If so, Spitzer mused, might one not be compelled to regard "half" of the poetic text to be the work of a poor copy editor rather than that of Wagner?[34]

Spitzer demolished the ethical and symbolic content of both the *Ring* and *Tristan*.[35] About *Walküre*, Spitzer argued that "the action on the stage inspires our disgust, the recitatives are without character, and the crippled verses (that ought have first been admitted to an orthopedic hospital) offend our ears, and the orchestra bores us with long-winded identifying explanations of the plot and the words."[36] Language, in the end, revealed the pretentious vacuity of Wagner. Spitzer opened his *Walküre* review with a nearly untranslatable parody using the letter *W*: "Weh, wie wenig Wonne ward mir wanderndem Wiener Spazierwalt [*sic*] durch Wagner's '*Walküre*'!"[37] This, my dear unlucky new high German reader, is the famous now long dead alliteration that the Master has brought back from the grave where it has rested for a thousand years. In these deadly mechanical rhymes his talkative gods and heroes hold their endless conversations. After one has listened for a while one begins to hear these ghostly rhymes clatter as if bones of the dead were banging against one another. But these heroes are, despite their shriveled language, not the old German heroes who sang together brandishing shields and swords but . . . [represent rather] the triumph of merely boring parliamentary habits."

In Spitzer's view, Wagner's pseudo-archaic recasting of myth revealed the worst of modernity. Wagner's ambition to herald the future, to critique a corrupt civilization, and to offer an idealized universal worldview resulted in precisely the opposite: a spectacle of contemporary moral and ethical self-deception and confusion. The telling symptom was Wagner's own invention, the synthesis of bad language and ugly music. "No melody disturbs the elevated monotony of this work of music," Spitzer concluded.

As if to cast further doubt on Wagner as a serious and revolutionary thinker, Spitzer highlighted Wagner's prowess in publicity, money raising, and self-advertisement. These unmasked Wagner's grandiose ambitions as egregious examples of crass contemporary commercialism. Wagner's musical theater, despite its claim to endless melody, seemed purely about mere spectacle and effect, a cheapening of musical, literary, and philosophical traditions.[38] After seeing the last part of the *Ring*, Spitzer concluded that "with *Götterdämmerung* one finally has survived the *Ring of the Nibelung*, this tiresome Edda travesty in which the devoted listener is presented not with a meaningful epic, but manipulated illusions; instead of something wonderful, something contradictory; instead of power, vulgarity; instead of magical sounds, incomprehensible gibberish; and instead of the naïve, the philosophy of Schopenhauer"—a claim that Spitzer went on to demolish in an effort to rescue Schopenhauer from Wagner's cheap version.[39]

At the crux of the debate about Wagner during the 1870s were questions that would resurface in every subsequent controversy. Why was Wagner so fashionable? What did Wagner mean to communicate in music and poetry? Were the roots of his success his greatness as a musician (and poet) or the consequence of debased cultural trends and fashions manipulated to generate a delusional escape from reality that facilitated an alluring reductive nationalism, replete with anti-Semitism? From the 1870s on, responses to these questions were incongruous and contradictory. Those who were Jews or viewed as Jews within German-speaking Europe knew that Wagner, the anti-Semite, had become the symbolic representative of a modern German civilization. Some, like Spitzer, attacked Wagner for undercutting noble Enlightenment standards of German culture and true learning— *Bildung*—the arenas of achievement Jews used to establish their place in the non-Jewish mainstream of society. Others embraced Wagner as the very epitome of modern culture and progress, as modernity's most powerful expressive voice, its equivalent of Shakespeare, Goethe, and Beethoven.

Responding to Wagner: The Turn of the Century

Guido Adler was a loyal subject of the Habsburg monarchy in the manner best articulated by his better-known younger contemporaries, the writers Franz Werfel (1890–1945) and Joseph Roth (1894–1939), who, like Adler, were of Jewish birth.[40] Culturally, Adler was a German chauvinist. But he was also an optimist who believed in the power of culture, reason, and high art to engender tolerance, as well as ethical and political progress. A close friend of Gustav Mahler and one of the founders of modern musicology, he argued that despite Wagner's biography, political views, and anti-Semitic writings and pronouncements, the artistry and evocation of the "purely human" in his music would triumph in the course of time. The emotions Wagner's work evoked might be unusually powerful, sensual, and irrational, but they sparked a catharsis in which the aesthetic power and beauty of the music cleansed the irrational (e.g., anti-Semitism) and "transfigured and ennobled" the listener. This, for Adler, was precisely the consequence of encountering the great works of art that had passed the test of time.[41]

Adler's 1903–4 lectures on the twentieth anniversary of the composer's death were designed to rescue Wagner's legacy from the radical nationalist and racialist orthodoxies energetically propagated by Wagner's epigones at Bayreuth, including Cosima Wagner, whose anti-Semitism had become more virulent and essentializing in the twenty years since her husband's death.[42] History became the instrument by which Adler sought to counter any continuing radical political appropriation of Wagner. Wagner was no longer relevant to politics, only to art. Adler distanced Wagner from the contemporary by elevating his status and rendering his artistic achievement as the only subject worthy of analysis: "Today the struggle over Wagner's art is over; the art has won. We no longer have to speak for it, much less against it. We only have to speak about it."[43]

A retrospective reading of German history that reverses history by starting with the Holocaust has shaped our judgments about the past.[44] This is particularly evident in recent scholarship on Wagner's polemical writings and anti-Semitism.[45] From this perspective, Adler's optimism in 1903 and 1904 regarding Wagner's future reputation, reception, and influence seems starkly naïve. It reads, in retrospect, like a caricature of a familiar self-delusion all too prevalent among highly acculturated intellectuals of Jewish origin in German-speaking Europe at the turn of the century.

Inherent in the historical critique of Adler's outlook is a contradiction. On the one hand, Adler, lulled into complacency by his own success, failed to see the proverbial handwriting on the wall: the pernicious influence Wagner would continue to have on politics and culture. Assessing Adler in this way assumes a trajectory that connects Wagner to Hitler and the "Final Solution" and assigns a key causal role to art and culture in shaping political realities. Another interpretation, which Adler's case supports, is to acknowledge the weakness of culture in history. Cultural achievement and refinement, even when acknowledged by official status and public recognition, were inadequate social protections against radical, racialist, anti-Semitic politics, even for exceptional Jews like Adler. Jews in post-1870 Germany and the Habsburg monarchy (and later, interwar Austria) who relied on culture and learning as routes to stable social integration and assimilation were shocked by the events of 1933 and the Anschluss of 1938. But despite the ubiquity of anti-Semitism around him, Adler, like so many of his distinguished Jewish contemporaries, sensed no fundamental instability for Jews, in part because he had no doubt about the significance of culture both in history and in contemporary society. Precisely for that reason he felt compelled to attempt a major revisionist interpretation of Wagner. The debate over Wagner's legacy seemed an important public issue.

One needs to differentiate to whom the label "Jew" in the polemics beginning in the 1870s actually referred. Adler and his older colleague Eduard Hanslick (1825–1904), for example, no longer considered themselves Jews and were not officially part of the Jewish community.[46] However, a racial definition of Jewishness was based on descent and lineage. It rendered being Jewish indelible and impervious to conversion. The political and cultural currency of this view owed a considerable debt to Wagner.[47] In late nineteenth-century Vienna, Adler and Hanslick were not legally Jews, but socially, except in refined liberal circles, they were dismissed as Jews, baptism notwithstanding.[48] Adler, who converted for practical reasons, never denied his social status as a Jew. However, being a rationalist and a devotee of science, he rejected all religion.[49] He opened his memoirs by offering the reader a statement he had penned in 1928 regarding his "religion": "Awe for God, respect for all faiths insofar as they reflect moral laws and ethical norms, love of one's neighbor, love of nature, the cherishing of every nation . . . in the criticism of every national sense of superiority . . . in the prizing of all work on behalf of mankind, as well as art and science."[50] No credo could have been more redolent of a tolerant, enlightened, liberal cosmopolitanism.[51]

Hanslick went well beyond Adler's admirable and ardent humanism.[52] From the point of view of a Holocaust-inspired teleology, his path is instructive about the limits of assimilation. His mother had been Jewish, but she converted at the time of her marriage and raised her son as a Catholic. Therefore Wagner's suggestion that Hanslick was Jewish was simply false.[53] But for Wagner and a large segment of contemporary anti-Semitic ideologues, being Jewish was not a matter of confession and religion, but one of race. If the noble and humanistic sentiments Adler located as the essence of Wagner's artistic achievement were to triumph, that victory depended on how successfully one could counter Wagner's own racialist polemics.

Adler sought to inspire a radical shift in the interpretation of Wagner by minimizing Wagner's historical originality. After placing him within a tradition of musical drama that dated back to the Renaissance, Adler explored Wagner's debt to Romanticism. Most radically, given his regard for Mahler's collaborations with Alfred Roller at the Vienna Court Opera, Adler called for a break from orthodoxies of interpretation and for a constant renewal in staging, so that the works might speak powerfully, as art alone, to new eras.[54] With Mahler and Roller's pioneering Viennese productions in mind, Adler called for a philosophically based symbolic revisionism in the way Wagner's work was presented on stage, subordinating its naturalistic and narrative surface.[55] Adler rejected Wagner's normative view that music was inevitably tied to speech. For Wagner, music represented at one and the same time the origin of language and its historical fulfillment. Hence the integration of music with ordinary language became a historical imperative. Adler's critique appropriated an earlier anti-Wagnerian argument about the unique character and autonomy of music vis-à-vis language. Adler's historical method, unlike Wagner's, eschewed obvious historical teleology. In explicitly anti-Wagnerian aesthetic terms, and despite the Master's intentions, Wagner's music, for Adler, was great.

By rendering Wagner not a contemporary phenomenon but a historical one, Adler stripped the political writings of all but biographical significance. They were, he argued, flawed by their lack of clarity and by historical errors. As Adler saw it, Wagner had achieved canonic status only as a composer, not as a thinker or even an innovator. In the canon he was one among many equals. The *Ring*, Adler argued, could not be viewed as literature. Only in combination with music could it be construed as comparable to literary drama. And Adler, deftly through deflection, rejected the idea that one might read contemporary political anti-Semitic stereotypes into the *Ring*. Adler explicitly argued that the centrality of gold and the obsession with the power of money that Wagner placed in the foreground had their root in ancient Nordic and German sources, in pagan mythic traditions (where there was no awareness of Jews and Judaism) in which money was defined as the ultimate source of evil. The overarching message of the *Ring* was not even radical or national. It was at once bourgeois and universal: the exclusive power of love between a man and a woman (e.g.,

Siegfried and Brünnhilde) to triumph over the pain and suffering of life. Wagner's meaning was philosophical, not political. Adler denied Wagner the prophetic status he had so assiduously cultivated during his lifetime.[56]

As Adler's strategy revealed, by 1900 Jewish Wagnerians like Adler, inspired by the experience of Wagner's music in the theater, struggled to circumvent the political implications of Wagner's ideas, particularly anti-Semitism. This is powerfully and poignantly revealed in the experience of the young Ernest Bloch. Born in 1880 in Geneva, Bloch studied composition in Frankfurt and Munich between 1896 and 1903. He became an enthusiastic Wagnerian, spellbound particularly by *Siegfried, Götterdämmerung,* and *Die Meistersinger.* Wagner's music communicated the idealized essence of love and human solidarity. The impact was more than vague and general: Wagner helped define the meaning of intimacy. Writing to his fiancé in 1903 after hearing *Götterdämmerung*, Bloch confessed that the "least significant note of that immense genius, Wagner, can better serve to reconcile us than all the phrases . . . but shall I let it . . . ?"[57] Writing to her eight years later from Berlin, Bloch lamented, "I regret that you are not here . . . and now I have the ardent desire to listen once again to Wagner with you, in this country."[58]

A seminal confrontation with Wagner occurred in the years between 1911 and 1916, when Bloch decided to embark on works known as the "Jewish Cycle," including three Psalm settings (1912–14), the *Israel* Symphony (1912–16), the *Three Jewish Poems* (1913), and last, *Schelomo*, the Hebrew Rhapsody for cello and orchestra (1915–16). He was inspired by encounters with the journalist Robert Godet (1866–1950), Debussy's friend and the translator of *Boris Godunov*, with whom he corresponded about anti-Semitism, and by his reading of H. S. Chamberlain's notoriously anti-Semitic *The Foundations of the Nineteenth Century* (1899). Godet led Bloch to rethink his relationship to his Jewish identity and his allegiances as a composer. For Bloch, Wagner demonstrated that, in order to communicate universality, composers needed to sense membership in a particular national community. In 1911, Bloch studied in close detail the score of a work dear to his heart, *Siegfried*, finding it once again utterly beautiful, admirable, and grand. In the process Bloch resolved to assert his solidarity with the Jewish nation through music. Writing to his close friend Edmond Fleg (a Jew and the librettist of Bloch's 1910 opera *Macbeth*), Bloch confessed that while listening to *Die Meistersinger* in Germany he felt closer to humanity—the same feeling he had when he played Bach and Beethoven. When Hans Sachs addressed the crowd in the third act, Bloch sensed Sachs was speaking to him as well.

But Bloch admitted to Fleg that "we are not French . . . we are also neither German, that is true, but our profound Jewish sensibility is closer to the complete realization of humanity which is German music than to the pretty musical contours of French music."[59] Writing in 1911 to a new-found friend, the Italian composer Ildebrando Pizzetti, Bloch reiterated that he had nothing in common with "French garb" but "contrary to Wagner, who said to the Jews 'Cease being Jews, in order to become fully human with us,' I think, I believe, I am convinced that it is only by becoming once again fully Jewish that the Jews will become fully human."[60] Wagner's explicit anti-Semitism and his conception of music's place in the formation of community led Bloch to reinvent himself as the modern artistic voice of the Jewish people so that Wagner might be proven wrong.[61]

For Jewish Wagnerians, the will to come to terms with the seeming irreconcilability between Wagner's art and his politics did not end with the rise of Hitler. Consider two anecdotes from the early 1940s. In 1940, a thirty-four-year-old Leipzig Jew, without Gymnasium or university education, boarded with his wife and two small boys a train to Genoa, from which they would sail to America. He refused to spend a long layover in Nuremberg, owing to its identification with the Nazi Party. Instead, he arranged a trip to Bayreuth so that he and his family could fulfill a dream: to see the Festspielhaus and Wahnfried. The second anecdote comes from a Jewish woman from Berlin who remembers her "Wagnerian" conversion in 1936, at the age of ten, when she heard Furtwängler conduct the overture to *Tannhäuser*. After coming to America, she recalled, "When in 1944 I put on a recording of Wagner, another immigrant yelled at me 'You have been Nazified!' The next day I played Wagner's music again, but as a Jew."[62]

Aesthetics, Politics, and Anti-Semitism

Bloch grew up in a non-Jewish neighborhood, but in a marginally observant home. His rediscovery of a Jewish national identity through Wagner is reminiscent of a far more significant journey taken nearly twenty years earlier by another highly acculturated Jew: Theodor Herzl (1860–1904).[63] Within the spectrum of responses to Wagner among German-speaking Jews, none is more startling than Herzl's enthusiasm for Wagner. As a student, Herzl witnessed the controversies of the 1870s and early 1880s. He reacted against Hermann Bahr's anti-Semitic speech on behalf of one of the university's *Burschenschaften* at the March 5, 1883, commemoration of Wagner's death.[64] Later, as a successful writer and editor in Vienna he experienced, like Adler, the centrality of anti-Semitism as a political and social force. Nonetheless, he fantasized in his early thirties that the solution might be a mass conversion of the Jews in Vienna's cathedral, the Stephansdom.

Along with Adler, Mahler, and others of his generation, the young Herzl acquired a taste for the Wagnerian experience. The aspiring writer succumbed to Wagner's success in drawing listeners into an intense, constructed world that seemed pregnant with meaning. The attachment endured beyond his youth. He confessed in his 1898 autobiographical fragment that during a crucial period of his life, while in Paris covering the Dreyfus trial, "I worked daily on [*The Jewish State*] until I was exhausted. My only recreation in the evening consisted of listening to Wagner's music, particularly *Tannhäuser*, an opera I heard as often as it was playing. Only on those evenings when there was no opera did I sense doubt about the rightness of my thoughts."[65] Herzl's 1895 diary recounts his return from a *Tannhäuser* performance, whereupon he sketched a vision of the future Jewish state where the masses would react, like the elite of the Paris Opera, "seated for hours, close together, motionless, uncomfortable," for the sake of "imponderables—just for sounds, for music and pictures!"[66]

The Wagnerian spectacle of music and drama and the community that formed around it within the theater helped inspire Herzl's Zionism and his utopian vision of the future Jewish nation. The affinity with the Wagnerian ideal bolstered his self-confidence, his self-image as a leader capable of heroic sacrifice. Vivid and personalized fantasy, whether escapist or political, seems to have enveloped spectators of Herzl's generation who became enamored of Wagner. Born 1860, the same year as Mahler, Herzl came of age in full recognition of the centrality of Wagner in European arts and culture, particularly in Germany. For his parents' generation, who witnessed the rapid expansion of the composer's popularity, Wagner represented radical aesthetic modernity. To Herzl's generation, particularly to its Jews, Wagner was an overwhelmingly dominant cultural and political phenomenon that somehow had to be contended with.[67]

Herzl and his contemporaries recognized in Wagner a unique medium of communication that used word, sound, and sight—a musical drama—to reach a massive public for art and culture, well beyond the more limited public sphere that dominated high culture in the early and mid-nineteenth century. Before Wagner, a sustained tradition of connoisseurship had prevailed, that of the *Liebhaber und Kenner*, dating back to the era of Goethe and Beethoven. After 1815, aristocrats and an elite middle class allied to maintain an aristocratic cultural tradition as patrons, amateurs, and audience. Beethoven's sponsors in the last years of his life reflected this combination, as did the support base for Vienna's post-Napoleonic Society of the Friends of Music. This alliance was still intact when Brahms sought and got his first job in 1857 in Detmold. This exclusive, cultured class thought of music as a participatory art form, similar to but different from literature. Both music and literature required complex cognitive and physical attainments (reading, writing, singing, playing), and in both arenas amateurism was widespread as a mark of distinction.

From the 1830s on, the public for art and culture expanded and by 1860 had developed beyond the type of audience with which Mendelssohn and Schumann had made their reputations. Liszt and Paganini were the first to capture a new broad-based, middle-class public, using the theater of virtuosity and cult of personality as tools. But it was Wagner who reached the enlarged nineteenth-century public through radical innovations in the shape and character of the musical experience. He extended the theatricalization of music explicit in instrumental virtuosity and grand opera by placing drama, defined in terms of ordinary language narrative, at the core of his compositional criteria for melody and harmony. He crafted an expressive musical rhetoric and controlled musical time in ways that aligned the musical experience for the listener with expectations derived from new habits of reading associated with mid-nineteenth-century narrative in fiction and drama, notably the works of Balzac, Stendhal, and Sand, and later, Flaubert and Tolstoy. Their German counterparts were Wilhelm Raabe, Theodor Storm, Gottfried Keller, and Theodor Fontane.

The parallel between Wagner's innovations for the opera stage and the nineteenth-century novel is instructive. In the epistolary novel and other prose fiction forms of the eighteenth century, events in the plot are not overtly reconciled with an awareness of the temporal presence of a narrator or with the reader's self-conscious sense of his or her own time spent reading. Three active dimensions of time provide for a delimited and distanced illusion of realism. The essential artificiality of writing and narration as an object of contemplation is not camouflaged. Spitzer's favorite novel, *Tristram Shandy*, is a famously extreme case. The nineteenth-century novel, however, sought to unify the three temporal elements into a single, continuous illusion of elapsed time in which both the reader and the narrator disappear under the weight of an illusory recalibration of real-time experience directed at the reader. When compared with eighteenth-century fiction, the nineteenth-century novel was far less philosophically self-conscious and made fewer demands on the reader: plot was manipulated to overwhelm any awareness of form, artifice, illusion, irony, and self-referential cues.

Like plot in the nineteenth-century novel, Wagner used music as the instrument of drama in direct opposition to the traditions of grand opera and so-called number opera. Wagner sought to cast a spell over his listeners that hid the artificiality of the stage and induced the listener to submit to a magical mythic realism.[68] Even the role of music as defining the perception of time remained mysterious and overpowering, emanating continuously from the hidden orchestra at Bayreuth. Wagner wished to generate, partly through the extended duration of his works, an integrated psychological experience in which individuals lost self-awareness and were drawn into believing in the emotional and philosophical authenticity of extreme fantasy represented on the stage.[69] Wagner collapsed the ironic distance between spectator and spectacle and thereby defined the terms of the modern theater in a manner that has remained valid for the commercial cinema of the late twentieth and early twenty-first centuries.

Wagner's aesthetic nemesis, Meyerbeer, on the other hand, refused to draw the audience into a coherent illusion of realism.[70] He remained attached to an eighteenth-century construct of art as a mirror of sensibilities. Psychologically plausible and affecting moments of action were generated and then disrupted by Meyerbeer. The artificial scaffolding of spectacle remained fully visible and audible to the spectator. The listener was at once touched by the story, inspired by a nascent political message, enchanted by the music, yet reminded of a received tradition of opera and therefore thrilled at the novel theatrical devices and the star singers. Meyerbeer's grandeur was evidently theatrical. Grand opera became a form in which irony and commentary accompanied representation, narration, and aesthetic pleasure. The listener remained conscious of his own time and place as well as his role as observer witnessing an intentionally inconsistent sequence of disparate theatrical segments. The scaffolding of the theater always remained visible, lending performers parallel identities as functional characters and real personalities.

Franz Rosenzweig (1886–1929), the great German Jewish philosopher, argued in 1921 that the route that both literary and musical art took to enter the community in modernity required the transformation of the aesthetic into theater in the Wagnerian sense (even for poetry). For Rosenzweig, normative aesthetic values in works of art were accessible ultimately only to an elite. For art to reach a mass audience, these aesthetic values had to be transfigured into a seductive theatrical experience. In modernity, aesthetic purity had to be sacrificed on behalf of theatrical illusionism. All art needed to become Wagnerian: "The real drama is the drama of the book. For the aesthete it may seem a crime that it should become theatrical. Yet it is a crime for which Shakespeare is inexplicably forgiven, but Schiller and Wagner are much blamed, although surely the time will come (as it has already for Schiller) when Wagner will no longer be criticized for having written theatrically for the theater." For Rosenzweig, dangerous as theatricalization might be to aesthetic value per se, Wagner's work achieved legitimacy as "pure art."

Wagner, like Shakespeare and Schiller, managed to preserve a valid aesthetic dimension despite his radical use of music as a theatrical framing device of communication with a large public. But the Wagnerian subordination of the purely aesthetic to the theatrical in modernity carried with it the danger of the corruption and debasement of the aesthetic experience of form and drama. In contrast to the demands Beethoven's music asked of listeners, those who listened to Wagner no longer needed the capacity to recognize and follow aesthetic categories such as musical structure. Nonetheless, Rosenzweig defended Wagner's art (just as Adler had) even if it "cannot wholly rid itself of the influence of the assembled masses." In the theater, particularly in Wagner, an "ideal" world of the work fights for itself in the engagement with the "real" world of the assembled public.[71]

By the early 1920s, Rosenzweig's assembled public—to which Herzl belonged and which he hoped, during the 1890s, would characterize the future Jewish state—represented not only a significant segment of the politically enfranchised literate population but also a considerably less musically trained public, despite the impressive spread of a passive piano-based species of musical literacy. Its "engagement," as critics like Hanslick, Speidel, and Spitzer had argued half a century earlier, was no longer with musical culture per se (constituent elements of musical form in, for example, Bach, Mozart, or Schubert—Rosenzweig's "pure art" and the "ideal" world of the work itself) but with the embrace of spectacle and narrative as persuasive, perhaps even escapist surrogates for the real.[72]

George Bernard Shaw identified the source of Wagner's late nineteenth-century success with a markedly expanded audience in his 1898 *The Perfect Wagnerite*. He addressed "those modest citizens who may suppose themselves to be disqualified from enjoying *The Ring* by their technical ignorance of music. They may dismiss all such misgivings speedily and confidently. If the sound of music has any power to move them, they will find that Wagner exacts nothing further. There is not a single bar of 'classical music' in *The Ring*. . . . If Wagner were to turn aside from his straightforward dramatic purpose to propitiate the professors with correct exercises in sonata form, his music would be at once unintelligible to the unsophisticated spectator, upon whom the familiar and dreaded 'classical' sensation would descend like the influenza. . . . The unskilled, untaught musician may approach Wagner boldly; for there is no possibility of a misunderstanding between them. . . . It is the adept musician of the old school who has everything to unlearn."[73]

Wagner reception in German-speaking Europe, particularly among Jews, was decidedly ambivalent about the radical accessibility of music as art that Shaw welcomed. Indeed, political and aesthetic considerations in rejecting or embracing Wagner's "democratizing" innovations were inseparable at the fin de siècle. Wagner's success in reaching a mass audience and generating a sense of collective euphoria through fantasy cloaked in the artifice of realism inspired Herzl with the possibility of generating a new political community. Socialist critic and Wagner admirer David Josef Bach (1874–1947), writing in Vienna's *Arbeiter Zeitung* in 1913, argued reluctantly against maintaining Bayreuth's hold over *Parsifal* precisely because of the imperative to realize Wagner's accessibility to a wider audience. Yet his contemporary, friend, and fellow Jew Arnold Schoenberg was more skeptical about Wagner's populist achievement.

Schoenberg sought to understand Wagner's extraordinary capacity to reach the historically new and wider public in terms of compositional strategy. Wagner's "evolution of harmony expanded into a revolution of form" and represented an "accommodation" to "popular demands."[74] The subordination of musical gestures to the task of expressing the so-called extramusical provided the public with a basis for intelligibility, a narrative equivalent located in an effective system of musical representation. As Schoenberg noted, he learned from Wagner three things: (1) the possibility of using themes as expressive, narrative vehicles; (2) the expansion of harmonic relationships; and (3) the use of motives and themes, primarily with repetition, so that in an enlarged harmonic landscape, dissonance could be incorporated and transcended.[75]

The endless melody, the repetition of motives, the shifting colors without harmonic closure through the extension of tonality, and the use of identifying signifiers attached to melodic fragments allowed Wagner to generate temporal continuity and to use music to frame a seamless story line with clarity that ensured easy comprehension and emotional engagement despite an enlarged harmonic palette. Novelty in harmonic logic and sonority became allied with populism, marginalizing the specialized learning, skills, and awareness of form required for the appreciation of music from the Classical period. Basic to Wagner's intention was the rejection of the claim that music had an inherent logic separate from words and images. Accessibility through music depended on appropriating the linguistic and the visual into music. This integration was accomplished by Wagner's virtuosity in using sound and color, rendering the façade and surface decoration of musical sound the overwhelming factor.[76] By utilizing repetition to generate recognition of motives and musical rhetorical gestures, the link between musical events and ideas on the one hand, and narrative moments, on the other, was effectively communicated.[77]

The democratization of music, the extension of an elite eighteenth-century aristocratic tradition of music connoisseurship to the middle classes of the late nineteenth century, was viewed much more negatively by those for whom culture (*Bildung*) represented a prized possession whose value required that it be a hard-won mark of distinction. The accusation that Wagner represented a watering down of aesthetic standards became a clarion call among anti-Wagnerians like Spitzer and entered the nineteenth-century discourse of cultural decline that flourished throughout the second half of the nineteenth century. Jews, for whom culture and learning had been successful meritocratic routes to integration since the late eighteenth century, worried about the loss of the exclusivity of their achievement of discernment as well as the cultural and political consequences of a debasement in taste and judgment.[78]

This discourse helped frame the fin-de-siècle debate over Wagner. Herzl, Bloch, and David Josef Bach admired Wagner's capacity to enlarge the audience for culture and thereby place culture in the service of generating community as a species of democratization consistent, for example, with socialism and nationalism. But other Jewish intellectuals were skeptics who warned of the consequences.[79] First among equals in this respect was Max Nordau (Simon Maximilian Suedfeld, 1849–1923), who would help found the World Zionist Organization and vigorously defend the importance of Offenbach, a cause he shared with one of his most vociferous critics, Karl Kraus.[80]

In his first book, *The Conventional Lies of Our Civilization*, published in 1883, Nordau called for a new politics of freedom, where heart and brain, the spiritual and the sensual, could find common ground in a new humanist credo. Wagnerian in its vision and scope, but philosophically inclined toward the Enlightenment, the book was banned in Nordau's native Habsburg Empire. But Nordau turned away from this initial proto-Wagnerian impulse in his most famous work, *Degeneration* (1892), in which Wagner plays a crucial negative role alongside Ibsen and Nietzsche. The decorative, seductive surface allure of Wagner, the musical qualities Schoenberg identified as the substance of the Wagnerian narrative and which had contributed to Wagner's wide popularity, led to the danger of widespread moral, civic, and physical deterioration. Wagner was guilty of Nordau's pet sins: egomania and the manipulation of the mystic and the symbolic. Wagner was dangerous because his obscurantism was popular and had so many imitators.

In the fin-de-siècle debate, as Nordau's 1892 attack on Wagner suggests, not all Wagnerians were nationalists, and not all anti-Wagnerians were dreamers on behalf of universalist utopias. Nordau never lost his own intuitive penchant for Wagnerian grandiosity in the language and scale of his ideas. In 1897, the anti-Wagnerian Nordau joined in earnest the Wagnerian Herzl and the Zionist movement.

Those opposed to Wagner could also be radical cultural nationalists. Within his vigorous and harshly chauvinist argument on behalf of German music, the virulent cultural nationalist Heinrich Schenker (1867–1935) accused Wagner of having been unable to compose in the tradition of Beethoven. Schenker took his cue from Spitzer but extended Spitzer's argument about Wagnerian language into an extreme critique of Wagner's compositional practice. Wagner had devised unacceptable shortcuts in the use of musical materials through the creation of the "so-called music drama." His innovations may have been idiosyncratic, but they were crude simplifications of a great artistic tradition. Wagner could not stand the "fiendishly difficult" task of real composing. If composers and listeners enamored of Wagner, "roll about . . . [in] something that can no longer be called the basic material of the musical art," argued Schenker, "then, as I said, Richard Wagner alone bears the blame for having demobilized, as it were, their musical nerves."[81]

Schenker remained an observant Jew who was active in Vienna's Jewish community.[82] He was a lifelong defender of Brahms as the last great master. The procedures represented by the apex of the Classical tradition, in which music was considered autonomous and possessed of its own self-referential logic, divorced from visual associations and expressive linguistic meanings, were normative. This meant that Wagner's musical practice embodied a corrupt cultural representation of the German, an intolerable alternative construct of Germanness. Like Spitzer and Hanslick before him, Schenker's admiring vision of German superiority harked back to an earlier era, that of Goethe and Beethoven.

Schenker's views were not unique. Arthur Schnitzler (1862–1931), a non-observant Viennese Jew, also distanced himself from Wagner and Wagnerism. As Marc Weiner has argued, Schnitzler views Wagner critically in his great 1908 novel *Der Weg ins Freie*, both for Wagner's role in politics (particularly anti-Semitism) and the subordination of musical aesthetics to the demands of theater, narrative, and ideology. Schnitzler agreed that Wagner called for a new kind of listening, a debased perception of the musical experience that inspired either a senseless modernism or a kitsch sentimentalism. The one character who hears music properly, in the sense Schenker defined it (better than the contemporary mass audience), is not the novel's aristocratic protagonist, Georg von Wergethin, but his friend, a Jew, Leo Galowski.[83]

In 1900, Max Graf (1873–1958), a twenty-six-year-old Jewish critic, dedicated a book to Mahler titled *Wagner Probleme*. Graf took a psychological route in his argument against Wagner.[84] He used Wagner's flawed personality to generate an aesthetic critique in which Wagner was invidiously compared with Beethoven. Despite his greatness, Wagner fell short. He lacked character, the sustained aesthetic and creative energy, and the consistency characteristic of Beethoven, Goethe, and, of all people, Bismarck. Graf rejected the cultural and racial idealization of the German encouraged by Wagner in favor of the more limited political definition represented by Bismarck's Prussian-based achievement.

Wagner's nature was too "elemental," Graf wrote. His art was shaped by radical extremes and lacked a firm center and foundation. In Wagner there was a consistent cry "for redemption" as opposed to a "blessing of life," the proper purpose of art.[85] Wagner's inner unconscious life was one of contradictory impulses characteristic of an "unstable conflicted" personality.[86] Graf asked whether a new generation wishing to embrace beauty and positive energy should take as a model Wagner's "affecting cry of need," mirroring a "bewildered and longing soul" in search of death and redemption. Would not Beethoven, who, according to Graf, ended his life with "a hymn to joy," be more appropriate? Graf concluded, "Is the art of Richard Wagner more than the work of an artistic genius, is it really the work of a new culture? Is it more than the work of a representative of modern society and culture who suffered from it and remained unfulfilled and still longing, and who with great effort transcended his historical context just enough to gather around him other longing and unfulfilled spirits? Does it do more than lead us out from modern civilization; does it really have enough power to gather new forces and unite them?"[87] Graf's answer was clearly no, echoing the responses of Schoenberg and Schenker.

These sentiments led to a search for new non-Wagnerian approaches to musical form and content. Schenker and Schoenberg may have agreed on the character of Wagner's revolution in musical composition. Since they diverged on how deleterious it was, they developed different definitions about what a restoration of pre-Wagnerian musical standards would sound like. Schoenberg (Graf's exact contemporary and a figure Graf championed) saw the next step as a progressive historical extension, building on Wagner's achievement through the work of a key intermediary figure, Mahler. Schenker's views were more reactionary, restorative, and conservative. He rejected Mahler, whose interpretations of Beethoven and compositions he regarded as too influenced by Wagner's superimposition of narrative meaning onto music and Wagner's emphasis on sonorities and melodic contours. Wagner's anti-Semitism was not an overt cause for the skepticism of Schenker and Graf. The same can be said for Schoenberg, who never doubted Wagner's achievement as a composer. Rather, he took a line more akin to that of Adler, and placed Wagner alongside Beethoven and Brahms as representative of a musical tradition that demanded a novel response by a new generation. For all three figures one can speculate that their identity as Jews played a role, but in an indirect manner. All three figures sought to reassert or reclaim an aesthetic tradition that predated the advent of modern nationalist and racialist politics.

In 1937 Schoenberg recalled the genesis of his 1906 *Kammersymphonie*, op. 9. He thought he had found an alternative, "a way . . . out of the perplexities in which we young composers had been involved through the harmonic, formal, orchestral and emotional innovations of Richard Wagner. I believed I had found ways of building and carrying out understandable, characteristic, original and expressive themes and melodies, in spite of the enriched harmony that we had inherited from Wagner."[88] The key idea was to sustain comprehensibility but to reject repetition and scale, thereby returning in a starkly contemporary manner to a mode of composition more characteristic of Beethoven and Brahms. Indeed Brahms, Wagner's antipode, became for the fin-de-siècle anti-Wagnerians not only emblematic of an older refined culture in opposition to Wagnerian extravagance and vulgarity, but also the source of a new, progressive modernism.

There was little doubt that Wagner had developed in music a compelling equivalent of the nineteenth-century novel in scope, length, and depth, constructed by a musical prose that exhilarated and captivated the audience in a nearly hypnotic and dangerous manner.[89] The nearly irrational allure of Wagner's music to the German public during *Gründerzeit*, from the 1870s until the outbreak of World War I, confirmed to both sides of the fin-de-siècle debate the extent to which Wagner had realized Schopenhauer's view of the Will and music's unique role as the direct expression and not mere representation of the Will—despite the philosopher's own misgivings about Wagner. But this extreme popularity also generated misgivings, fear, and caution regarding Wagner's influence, particularly among Jews.

In 1913, the fin-de-siècle polemical debate reached an apogee, including an aggressive Wagnerian retort to the composer's new critics. German-speaking Jews were prominent on both sides. Emil Ludwig, the wildly successful popular writer, gave his 1913 anti-Wagner book the title *Wagner oder die Entzauberten* (Wagner, or the disenchanted), using a word that suggested the necessity of reversing the effects of Wagner's magic. Ludwig sought to highlight the contrast between reason and the irrationality and illusionism generated by the embrace of Wagner.[90] For Ludwig, a spell had to be broken in politics and culture if Adler's "monstrous conclusions" were to be avoided. Only *Tristan* eluded Ludwig's criticism. The danger to culture rested not in the "people" but in the "spiritual bourgeoisie" who had been seduced by Wagner, a stratum between the connoisseurs and the modern masses. Ludwig contested the 1871 claims of Cornelius. Wagner had not reached Germany's "people." He merely persuaded an expanded but still elite taste-making "public." Ludwig rendered Wagner the object of the very criticism that the Master himself had directed at a Jewish elite in 1869.[91]

Following Nietzsche's anti-Wagnerian writings, Ludwig accused Wagner of being merely an "actor" who succeeded only with a like-minded public enamored of spectacle. To have persuaded the "Germans" as a whole nation, Wagner needed to have been an authentic poet, dramatist, or a musician, a proponent of absolute music." Ludwig's position resembled Graf's and Schoenberg's. Wagner's failure created an opportunity for contemporary culture. Ludwig's prescription came closer to Schenker's.[92] The solution lay in a return to Mozart: "Mozart will 'redeem' us who are young from Wagner," Ludwig wrote, thereby relegating Wagner to a historical monstrosity akin to Bernini. The task for modernity was to restore clarity and lightness to art and culture.[93]

Two critics, both Jews, challenged Ludwig: Paul Stefan and Kurt Singer.[94] Stefan's 1914 *Die Feindschaft gegen Wagner* argued directly not only against Ludwig but the entire history of anti-Wagnerian criticism, from that of Wagner's early career through to Nietzsche and Ludwig. Stefan, following Adler, rejected the relevance of any criticism of Wagner's personality or writings. However, he took a more classic Wagnerian line by blaming mere journalists for defaming the Master. Stefan, who ridiculed Ludwig's appeal to Mozart, turned the tables on the critics. At the center of the younger generation's doubts about Wagner was the composer's courageous unwillingness to hide behind anachronistic and normative notions of artistic beauty and health (absolute music) in the face of the complexity and contradictions of modernity. Wagner's inspiration stemmed from his recognition of the unique character of modernity. Modernity, for Stefan, was not comforting, logical, or beautiful.[95] Hence he celebrated Mahler as a true contemporary voice, one clearly indebted to Wagner.

Singer took a similar pro-Wagner line in a set of essays from 1913, *Richard Wagner: Blätter zur Erkenntnis seiner Kunst und seine Werke*. Singer weighed in on the *Parsifal* controversy, for which he suggested a compromise that would cede control of performance standards to Bayreuth but open the possibility for performances elsewhere. Singer felt compelled to use his "expertise, experience and good will" to reassert the "ethical, artistic and poetic foundation of the Wagnerian work of art." The "endless feeling" that emerges from late Beethoven is the same as that which *Parsifal* generates: a humbling sense of insignificance as if one were near the presence of God. For Singer, Wagner's works had the power to form a community out of the aggregate of alienated individuals in modern society by inducing a shared sense of recalibrated time as well as a sense of fantasy. They did this by using an extension of sound that was simple to follow precisely because musical elements were linked to a non-musical narrative and symbolism. The parallelism between music and ideas was a virtue. The music and its many moods could be followed easily by listeners without requiring them to follow musical logic per se (e.g., the transformation of themes). Singer, like his contemporary Paul Bekker, understood Beethoven, particularly late Beethoven, in this distinctly Wagnerian manner, as music that argued through instrumental music ideas and sensibilities, and that these rendered possible the formation of communities of shared sentiment.[96]

What emerges from Singer's defense of Wagner is a common thread linking turn-of-the-century Jewish Wagnerians with Jewish critics of Wagner. Wagner's success in captivating the public and its imagination impressed both sides, primarily with regard to the importance of building communities in modernity—both spiritual and political ones. The fear of fragmentation and alienation that accompanied the nineteenth-century urbanization of Europe and its industrialization was that human beings would find themselves isolated, exploited, and without a spiritual center, particularly in a world dominated by a mix of rationalism, competition, and skepticism. The acculturated Jew, a new arrival as a social, economic, and political actor in public life, became at one and the same time the emblem of the perils of contemporary existence and identified as a primary cause of modernity's ills. It is not surprising, then, that a nearly romantic attraction to the idea of community was a common element in the Jewish response to Wagner, both pro and contra. The Jew was, after all, the ultimate pariah who sought entrance as an outsider into a community imagined as authentic. Insofar as culture was a route to that membership, music, whose life took place both in private and public spaces, became a central arena of Jewish ambition. The attraction to musical culture in the fin de siècle was precisely its post-Wagnerian prestige as a powerful element of the formation of community, even the new national community of Jews envisioned by Zionism.

Singer predicted that in a hundred years Wagner would be regarded alongside Leonardo, Raphael, Bach, Beethoven, Goethe, and Schiller as the source of a "healthy culture of the spirit."[97] The figure of Siegfried represented the integrity of the artistic idea, the breaking of the limits of mortality, the spirit of the divine, and the mirror of the essentially human. Singer was an unapologetic enthusiast of the ethical value of Wagner for a new generation. Wagner's positive influence over the modern mass public would become increasingly visible with the passage of time. Singer hoped to encourage the direct study of Wagner's works so that his greatness and centrality to the formation of cultural values could be appreciated.[98]

Perhaps the most eloquent account of the issues at stake in the fin-de-siècle debate over Wagner's potential relevance to a new generation and a new era of artists and listeners was that of Egon Friedell. The son of a Jewish manufacturer, Friedell (1878–1939), born Friedmann, worked as cabaret artist, actor, and writer.[99] As a student in the late 1890s, he, like Schoenberg, converted to Lutheranism. He was best known as the director of the theater cabaret *Die Fledermaus* (for which the designer Josef Hoffmann designed furniture). Yet Friedell was admired as both a satirical and serious writer on history and culture, and as a translator.

In the late 1920s Friedell began his most enduring work, a three-part *Cultural History of Modernity* completed in 1931, in which he devotes space to Wagner. Having witnessed the fin-de-siècle controversies, he revealed a distanced skepticism toward Wagner and a resistance to his charms characteristic of his generation, but without losing sight of Wagner's genius. Following Adler and Graf, Friedell viewed Wagner as no longer contemporary or relevant. He should be understood primarily (as Ludwig did) as a "baroque" artist from the past, a master of effects (here Friedell followed Nietzsche), and therefore principally a theatrical genius. In Wagner's art one could actually witness the "fall of a bourgeois worldview" precisely on account of Wagner's brilliant manipulation of bourgeois taste. Wagner, concluded Friedell, "suggests the recollection of [baroque] culture not only through the pomp and aplomb of his prolix persuasions and his yen for the mystical . . . but also by his sensual will toward the spiritual . . . his cramped and yet delightful artificiality, but most of all through his refined mixture of eroticism and asceticism, of the ardor for love with the yearning for death. His is a sultry metaphysics, that in a particular way . . . is anti-Christian and frivolous. . . . The secret of life is revealed as biological, in a word: understood as Darwinian. . . . The 'music drama' is the spellbinding funeral march, the extravagant burial service at the grave of the nineteenth century, and of modernity in general."[100] Friedell's observation coincides with the critique by many of his contemporaries of the eclectic historicist character of nineteenth-century art and architecture, perhaps best exemplified by the elaborate and decorative costumed parade involving 14,000 participants engineered and organized in 1879 by the Viennese artist Hans Makart (Wagner's favorite painter) to celebrate the silver wedding anniversary of the Emperor Franz Joseph II.

Friedell understood Wagner's achievement, albeit more charitably, in much the same way Spitzer and Ludwig had. Writing after the catastrophe of World War I, Friedell concluded that Wagner created a new audience and thereby broadened an ultimately eclectic and insufficient set of values characteristic of pre–World War I bourgeois culture. That culture's pomposity revealed an absence of humor, self-critical satire, simplicity, and clarity, qualities the contemporary world required from music and literature. Wagner represented a dead end, a mannerism from the past. An ambivalent mix of regret, pessimism, and hope concerning the role of art and culture characterized Friedell's magnum opus. He committed suicide on March 16, 1938, shortly after the Anschluss, jumping from his window to his death while the SS below were arriving to arrest him.

The Aftermath of Controversy: Weininger and Kraus

Paul Stefan's pro-Wagner tract cited slyly, in passing, perhaps the most widely read fin-de-siècle Jewish voice on the subject of Wagner, one for whom the Jewish question was central: the elusive and influential Otto Weininger (1880–1903). Weininger not only built an original theory on the basis of Wagner's anti-Semitic arguments, he also internalized them. He committed suicide in 1903, at the age of twenty-three.[101]

Weininger used Wagner's writings and works to generate a theory of sexuality in which the Jew was the feminine and the Aryan the masculine. Weininger's 1903 *Sex and Character*, reprinted many times after his death, had a profound impact on the likes of Ludwig Wittgenstein, Schoenberg, Freud, and Karl Kraus. Weininger viewed the world through the prism of fertile dualities: male versus female, character versus form, talent versus genius, erotic versus aesthetic. For him, Wagner represented the highest aesthetic achievement in history. *Parsifal* was the greatest of his works (and Kundry was perhaps the most perfect representation of a woman in art).[102] Weininger concluded, "What I seriously wish to try to show— not because everything that Wagner created seems extraordinary—is that the Wagnerian invention [*Dichtung*], on account of the profundity of its conception, is the greatest invention in the world."[103] Stefan had cited Weininger to counter facile attempts to dismiss Wagner purely on account of his anti-Semitism. Stefan suggested quite the opposite. Citing Weininger, Stefan hinted that Wagner's arguments in "Judaism in Music" were creditable and worthy of careful consideration.

Weininger's most powerful duality pitted the Jew against the Aryan, whose modern form was the Aryan Christian. Weininger read Wagner closely. He was inspired by the way in which Wagner interpreted Jewish assimilation into non-Jewish culture. Wagner pilloried the Jewish capacity for imitation and mimicry, the Jewish talent for calculation, abstraction and business, and the Jewish skill in manipulating systems, notably commerce (capitalism) and the press. The Jew attacked most vigorously by Wagner was not the ancient Jew, represented in modernity by observant pious adherents to religious traditions and who lived in ghettos, but the modernizing Jew, the outwardly successful and assimilated urban Jew: the Mendelssohns, the Meyerbeers, the journalists and critics, the businessmen, doctors, lawyers, and scientists.

Wagner perceived Jewish traits as complementing the absence of genuine creativity among Jews. This represented a fundamental character flaw, an ethical lapse, and a complete absence of spirituality. Weininger took Wagner's characterization of the Jew and went further to transform it into a widespread category and phenomenon, a symptom of the bankruptcy of the conceits of modernity, science, and progress. Judaism for Weininger was no longer, as it was for Wagner, "a race, nor a people, nor a recognized creed." It was a tendency of the mind, "a platonic idea," and an analytical construct. It described a psychological "constitution that was, tragically, 'a possibility for all mankind.'" Judaism in Weininger's version became separated from the Jews themselves and the logic of race, even though Jews in modernity were still the best at expressing the traits of Judaism. Judaism had become a universal danger in modern culture and society. There were in contemporary culture "Aryans who are more Jewish than Jews and real Jews who are more Aryan than certain Aryans."[104]

For Weininger, the Jew and Judaism were feminine, as opposed to the Aryan masculine, of which Siegfried was the ideal. Jews had little sense of property, despite the avarice associated with them by anti-Semites. They had little regard for nature. Therefore they were more likely to be communists, whereas Aryans were inclined to socialism, in which a sense of property was preserved. Likewise politics, in the sense of citizenship in the state, was as foreign to the Jew as it was to women, rendering Zionism an "impractical ideal." The Jew was wanting in personality and a free ego. Jews exhibited no capacity or respect for individuality, even though they craved titles and the appearance of distinction. Greatness was absent among Jews just as was any capacity to distinguish between good and evil. Consequently the extremes of existence could not be attained, neither asceticism nor its polar opposite, sexual potency and passion. What Jews were good at were appearances in sexual matters and therefore matchmaking and marriage.

In line with Weininger's celebration of individuality, he claimed that each Jew had to struggle separately to overcome Jewishness. All Jews, he argued, actually recognize their inferiority. Therefore they unconsciously respect the Aryan more than themselves. Unlike race theorists, however, Weininger believed that if a Jew became a genuine Aryan Christian, he deserved to be regarded as such. But conversion would be difficult, because the Jew is immune from mysticism and all that is transcendental and spiritual. Not surprisingly, then, Weininger shared Wagner's notion that the Jew was resistant to all art. The Jew's skill in chemistry, for example, was uninspired, mechanical, and too tied to the empirical and material aspect. Even Spinoza, whom Weininger considered the greatest Jew of modern times, failed to grasp the inner depths of nature and human life. Because Jews were without extremes of good or evil they rarely exhibited either genius or extreme stupidity. They were like humorless Englishmen (again following Wagner). The modern assimilated Jew was secular and irreligious because the cultured modern Jew hid behind a rational skepticism. "The Jew believes nothing," Weininger wrote, "and takes nothing truly in earnest."

But even skepticism was held in suspicion by Jews, since, for Weininger, the Jew was overcome with self-doubt that masks itself in the contemplation of pseudo-philosophical opposites that cancel each other out. For Jews everything was instrumental and temporary. There were no absolutes. The Jew could therefore approach art and love only with superficiality and sentimentality. In modern times, Judaism had lost its ancient potential to produce greatness, men like Samson and Joshua. Jesus was Weininger's greatest Jew in all of history because he overcame Judaism. Here again,

Wagner's ideas came into play, particularly the closing thought of Wagner's notorious essay, which exhorted the Jews to "overcome" being Jews, or perhaps even, as some have suggested, ceasing to be. For Weininger, Judaism's only hope was that a genuinely spiritual religion would, once again, spring from and transform it.[105]

Weininger framed a comprehensive critique of contemporary civilization by using the category of Judaism: the problem of the day was that "Judaism is the spirit of modern life" and "the most evil of all things."[106] Modernity had become both Jewish and feminine and therefore a "decision must be made between Judaism and Christianity, between business and culture, between male and female, between the race and the individual, between unworthiness and worth, between the earthly and the noble life, between negation and the divine . . . there is no middle way."[107]

The core of what Weininger took from Wagner was the insight that the Jew seemed to represent the appearance of historical progress, but actually exemplified the hollowing out by modernity of all that is human. All appearances of progress in external culture, mores and education, prosperity, and health were deceptions. The key to the spiritual vacuum of modernity could be found in the triumph of the assimilated Jew as the model of the civilized person. He appeared cultured, responsible, and learned. Yet his achievements were merely technical deracinated trivializations and debasements of genuine human capacity, notably in art and religion. The language of the Jew gave away the lie. The prose of modern journalism, its manner of judgment, was neither profound nor genuine when compared to authentic poetry and true philosophical idealism.

Wagner's search for redemption through the feminine and his Schopenhauer-like pessimism were reevaluated by Weininger as the need for the masculine artist (e.g., Wagner) to generate, through art, the religious experience to redeem mankind from the Jewish and the feminine. Weininger's project had little to do with German chauvinism, racism, and cultural populism. It rejected any progressive historicist teleology and, as in Nietzsche's pro-Wagner *Birth of Tragedy*, proposed a fundamental re-creation of a glorious distant past in modernity, through the development of new modes of aesthetic experience.

Weininger understood that Wagner's anti-Semitism and nationalism, his capacity to give the "German nation the highest means of expression," revealed that Wagner himself had not been free of "an accretion of Jewishness." This was even audible in the music. In Weininger's view, rabid, non-Jewish anti-Semites could be among the most egregious representatives of Judaism, and therefore Jews. Being anti-Semitic per se was not enough. After all, there were Jewish anti-Semites who despite self-hatred could not shed their fundamental Jewishness. They remained, like

Weininger himself, individuals who were uncertain about their worth, unsure that they could lose the very qualities they reviled.

The task of the artist, writer, and thinker was to further the de-Judaization of culture. This included transcending Wagner's own limitations. *Parsifal* represented a parable of purification for Weininger consonant with Wagner's call at the end of "Judaism in Music" for Jews to "go under," to vanish as a people and a culture. It was Weininger's sense of his own inability to do so that led him to take his life in the very house where that truly masculine Aryan artist, Beethoven, had died. Hitler knew of Weininger's suicide. But according to Hans Pfitzner, himself an anti-Semite and early follower of Hitler and the Nazis, Hitler did not grasp the first thing about Weininger's ideas. Instead he simply lamented that the rest of Jewry did not voluntarily follow Weininger's path to self-annihilation.[108]

Weininger's notion that Judaism represented not a race but a cultural phenomenon that plagued modernity appealed to Karl Kraus, Vienna's greatest twentieth-century satirist and critic. Kraus focused his attention on the fundamental instrument of human expression—language—which he believed held the key to combating the ills Weininger elaborated. Kraus carried on where Spitzer, a generation earlier, had left off, writing primarily polemics beginning in the late 1890s and ending in the mid-1930s. Kraus has often been characterized as the quintessential self-hating Jew, but defined in a manner evocative of Weininger's construct of Judaism.[109] His lifelong attack on the hypocrisies of the modern cultural establishment, notably journalism, routinely saw Jews as the prime suspects. Kraus viewed Jews more in Weininger's sense than Wagner's, but unlike Weininger, Kraus believed in a writer's capacity to fight the cultural corruption around him. Inspired less by philosophy and more by poetry and humor, Kraus drew inspiration from a wide field: Goethe, Johann Nestroy, Oscar Wilde, and Frank Wedekind.

Kraus kept a considerable distance from music, confessing a lack of competence. He admired Weininger, but Kraus treated Wagner with restrained respect, primarily on account of Wagner's critique of modern journalism. Kraus defended Wagner from the fashionable and vacuous interpretations he found in the writings of men such as Graf, Ludwig, and Stefan. Although he shared Wagner's contempt for modern journalism and the commercialization of culture, his closest affinity with respect to language was with writers like Spitzer for whom honesty and clarity were linked to beauty. Like Spitzer, Kraus was allergic to Wagnerian language and rhetoric, and suspicious of myth, sentimentalism, and the absence of irony and humor.[110]

Kraus's concern, like Spitzer's, was the disfigurement and corruption of language. For him, language was the mother of thought. It was an ethical instrument. Like Schenker, he was suspicious of the impact of the successful spread of literacy, an ostensible sign of progress that had become a nemesis. Wagner's capacity to use music reductively to seduce and manipulate a public had its parallel in the impact of journalism. Journalism destroyed language's capacity to speak clearly, to tell the truth, to embody beauty and goodness. Instead, it spun illusions about life that citizens, readers, and even politicians— tragically—sought to realize.

Modern journalism's triumph justified Wagner's and Weininger's notion of modernity as quintessentially Jewish. Journalism manipulated the sense of the real and the possible through language. As a result, modern readers acted in a manner conditioned by journalism's distortion and disfigurement. The most significant proof of this, for Kraus, was World War I.

To rescue ethics and genuine beauty therefore demanded a war on the modern use of language. Like Schenker and Schoenberg, Kraus called for the use of language to demonstrate a commitment to truth and beauty reminiscent of a pre-modern, pre-Romantic world. Consequently the modern, assimilated, successful, and cultured Jew—Kraus's bête noir—remained emblematic of the enemy. Kraus pilloried Wagnerian and anti-Wagnerian participants alike in the controversies of the past, including Ludwig and Stefan, for their rhetoric and logic. Yet he praised others from both sides of the argument, such as the anti-Wagnerians Speidel and Hanslick, and pro-Wagnerians like Robert Hirschfeld, the Viennese critic (whose father was a rabbi), for the clarity of their prose, and their ethical respect for language.

Perhaps Kraus suspected that in the end Wagner may have been, in Weininger's sense, a representative of the modern Jew, in his poetics, his humorlessness, his poetry, and his philosophical claims. As many anti-Wagnerians during the 1870s realized, Wagner was the most brilliant exploiter of the modern commerce of culture that Kraus despised. After all, Wagner had depended in crucial ways on his network of patronage societies, the Bayreuth scheme, and his own uncanny capacity to manipulate the patrons and press. He was his own publicist. Rather than challenge Wagner, whose greatness he acknowledged, Kraus turned, with self-conscious irony, to champion Wagner's polar opposite and his nemesis: Offenbach, a Jew.[111]

Offenbach became Kraus's obsession. In the decade between 1926 and 1936 Kraus gave one-man public readings of Offenbach, performances with musical accompaniment. Nothing could have been less Wagnerian— or more anti-Wagnerian. There were no sets or scenery. The only Wagnerian element was the partial hiding of the piano. Kraus, seated at a table, sang and enacted the Offenbach texts in translation replete with his own emendations. Offenbach, not Wagner, was adequate to challenge modernity's ills in part because Offenbach, rather than Wagner, decoded the hypocrisy of modern urban life.

Offenbach, not Wagner, truly integrated words and music. Offenbach, not Wagner, revealed with affection and insight the human condition, pointing a way out for modernity. Offenbach, like Meyerbeer, reveled in the transparency of the theatrical in a manner that did not distort the temporal reality of the listener but celebrated the engaging spectacle on stage. The tension between the two realms allowed for irony, humor, and self-criticism. Offenbach forced the listener to think, not to lose himself.

The lightness, beauty, clarity of language, thought, and grace of Offenbach represented qualities also valued by those who called for a Mozart revival and a retreat from the Wagnerian, a return to the Classicism of the late eighteenth and early nineteenth centuries. Offenbach displayed humor and irony about the human condition entirely absent from Wagner. As Ludwig Wittgenstein, who admired Kraus (and Weininger) observed, the irony in Wagner, as in *Die Meistersinger*, paled when compared to that in the first movement of Beethoven's Ninth Symphony. Reversing Weininger's assessment, Wittgenstein argued that Wagner displayed not genius, but mere skill.[112]

Wagner's lack of humor, irony, or economy of expression also contrasted with the qualities of Kraus's heroes Nestroy and Spitzer.[113] Like Weininger, Kraus's ire was directed not at Jews as a race but at modern Jews who represented the worst crime of contemporary culture, the concealment of ethical and political evil under the guise of learning, culture, and eloquence cast in pseudo-educated prose. The generational confrontation with Wagner and Wagnerism that Kraus observed (he was, for example, not a Mahler enthusiast) led him to Offenbach and a philosophical view of language use through which art and ethics could further the cause of truth. The erotic and the feminine in Offenbach became objects of delight, just as the heroism and violence in Wagner were pilloried. Last but not least were the facts that Offenbach, although a convert, never shied away from his status as a Jew, while Wagner had become a European standard bearer of anti-Semitism.

Reengaging Wagner

The years that witnessed Kraus's death and Hitler's rise to power brought two distinct phases of an intense controversy over Wagner to a close. A brief torrent of commentary followed in 1933, including the writings of Theodor Adorno and Ernst Bloch, but primarily in response to Thomas Mann. In the postwar period Ludwig Marcuse and Hans Gál reaffirmed Wagner's centrality to a critical self-awareness among German Jews.[114] In the unprecedented and desperate context surrounding World War II, Wagner's works and his anti-Semitism remained a prism through which the terms of Jewish identity, beyond issues of assimilation and integration, were framed and contested. The nexus of art, politics, culture, and ethics remained central, and Wagner was at the core of that nexus. Through Wagner, Jewish anti-Wagnerian critics located a difficulty and a source of hope for modernity: the redemption of language. The Jewish Wagnerians took from Wagner a vision of a renewed national community. Both sides sought an exit from the perils of corruption and violence.

The confrontation with Wagner forced a reconsideration of the way *Bildung* and *Kultur*, highly prized signs of acculturation, were construed after the mid-nineteenth century, particularly by those Jews who sought to integrate into European society. A friend of Kraus, Peter Altenberg (1859–1919), a notorious vagabond writer and aphorist who was born a Jew (as Richard Englander), penned the following vignette in 1917 about his room in the Hotel am Graben, where he lived: "The walls were totally covered with photos . . . Franz Schubert and Hugo Wolf, Beethoven and Tolstoy, Richard Wagner and Goethe."[115] Altenberg's sequence was ironic. Only in one case was chronology reversed in Altenberg's description of the pictures: Goethe came after Wagner.

Wagner was juxtaposed with Goethe: not placed alongside other composers but placed in relationship to the most iconic, enduring, and versatile figure in German culture. But the last word might perhaps have been better left with Goethe. Yet Altenberg relegated both to mere images, shadow presences over life. Reflecting on Wagner's overbearing cultural influence before World War I, Altenberg's wall of photos offers a graceful but admiring snapshot of the place many hoped Wagner would take in German-speaking Europe between 1918 and 1933. Wagner's role in defining the shape of art and culture would no longer remain actual, only historic. Even as history, Wagner would not overpower the influence of that arch anti-Romantic, Goethe. In music Wagner, the master of the grandiose, would take merely an equal place alongside two local Viennese masters of song and the miniature: Schubert and Wolf. But events, particularly the rise of Nazism, brought Wagner back onto center stage.

Altenberg's reduction of Wagner to a mere photograph is a better representation of the situation at the beginning of the twenty-first century. Wagner's popularity and allure remain undiminished, helped in part by the technology of subtitles. But it reflects a sentimentalized enthusiasm that lacks a critical edge informed by history. Outside of Israel and perhaps Germany, Wagner may have receded into history at last. But his work should not be permitted to settle into mere museum entertainment. Wagner needs to be produced in Israel, in Europe, and in North America to illuminate by evocation the complex reactions Wagner can and did arouse.

In 1921 Franz Rosenzweig articulated a challenge facing productions of Wagner, not only potential performances in Israel, but elsewhere in the world, one that remains unanswered by any ban. Rosenzweig argued that art "becomes a reality only when it educates humans to become observers, thereby creating a lasting public. It is not Bayreuth that attests to the enduring relevance of Wagner and his work, but rather the fact that the names Elsa and Eva became fashionable and that the idea of the female as a redeemer strongly colored the character of male eroticism in Germany for decades. Once having attained a public, art cannot be banned from the world; as long as just the work or the artist is at stake, then art lives a rather precarious life from one day to the next."[116] In the case of Wagner, more than the artist or the work has always been at stake: direct encounters with the way his art educates are required to understand his role in history.

For Israel, a comprehensive encounter with Wagner's music and drama, tempered by critical debate and historical candor, could be realized. Instead of the ban, Wagner productions could be mounted in Israel that are historically informed and self-aware, that take Wagner's anti-Semitism into account, and that acknowledge the history of Wagner reception in which rabid anti-Semitic ideology and stereotypes were explicitly validated before and after the Nazi seizure of power in 1933.[117] Consider an integrated cycle, starting with *Rienzi*, in which works by Wagner would be juxtaposed with revivals of Meyerbeer, Halévy, and other Wagner contemporaries, competitors, and followers. Some of the more extravagant Wagnerian claims to originality would be exposed. The contemporary audience would face its own susceptibility to Wagnerian theater. If Wagner is a dangerous force, the audience, particularly in Israel, needs to examine how his innovations work and why they have left a permanent mark on contemporary cinema, television, and political propaganda (the docudrama and miniseries, both part fiction and part fact).

Furthermore, practically all twentieth-century composers have conceded (with the possible exception of Stravinsky) the wealth of imagination and beauty self-evident in Wagner's music, despite all ideology and crass abuse. But to those who may not be persuaded by this argument, there remains the imperative to tell the truth. The Jewish engagement with Wagner and its influence on political anti-Semitism, modern Zionism, and Jewish history, including the post–World War I rediscovery of premodern traditions of Jewish life, needs to be remembered.[118] Only an active and critical encounter with Wagner as composer and dramatist can clarify his place in modern European Jewish history, in the history of anti-Semitism, and in the Nazi era. Israel must restore Wagner to the stage for the sake of the survivors, so that the causes of the Holocaust can be better understood and contemporary Israel can flourish in ways that shed any residual internalization of the deceptions and conceits of Wagner and pre-1933 German culture and society.

NOTES

1. On the historical context of populist anti-Semitism, see John W. Boyer, *Political Radicalism in Late Imperial Vienna: Origins of the Christian Social Movement, 1848–1897* (Chicago, 1981); and *Culture and Political Crisis in Vienna: Christian Socialism in Power, 1897–1918* (Chicago, 1995). On Adler's direct contact with Lueger, see Volker Kalisch, *Entwurf einer Wissenschaft von der Musik: Guido Adler* (Baden Baden, 1988), 20–23.

2. Guido Adler, *Richard Wagner* (Leipzig, 1904), 189–90. See the fine discussion of Adler and Wagner's anti-Semitism in Kevin C. Karnes, *Music, Criticism and the Challenge of History* (New York, 2008), 184–85. An enthusiastic Wagnerian of Jewish descent, Adler was a founding member of the Academic Wagner Society in Vienna in the 1870s, and in 1876 and 1882 he visited Bayreuth, where he met Wagner. Adler was Eduard Hanslick's successor at the University of Vienna and founder of the Musical Historical Institute. Adler died in Vienna in 1941, in isolation, having been stripped of his status and possessions by the Austrian Nazis in control of both the University and the Society of the Friends of Music. See Guido Adler, *Wollen und Wirken: Aus dem Leben eines Musikhistorikers* (Vienna and Leipzig, 1935), 1–18; and Leon Botstein, "Music and Its Public" (PhD diss., Harvard University, 1985).

3. When translated into English, Adler's word for conclusion, *Schlussfolgerung*, may appear suggestive of later Nazi rhetoric, the "Final Solution" to the Jewish question, but Adler's usage derives from eighteenth-century philosophical language. See the entries on "Schluszfolge" and "Schluszfolgerung" in Jacob and Wilhelm Grimm, *Deutsches Wörterbuch* (Leipzig, 1899; repr. Munich, 1999), 15:871.

4. Curiously, there is little critical discussion of the influence of Wagner's subtle and pointed anti-Semitic claims beyond German-speaking Europe, for instance in the case of France's Vincent D'Indy.

5. The most comprehensive discussion of this ban, the debates in Israel, its contradictions vis-à-vis the performance and reception of actual collaborators with the Nazi regime (e.g., Strauss and Orff), and its place in the history of Israeli politics—notably the desire to sustain the memory of the Holocaust—is Na'ama Sheffi's *The Ring of Myths: The Israelis, Wagner and the Nazis* (Brighton, U.K., 2000).

6. David is the son of Isaac Stern, who, after Leonard Bernstein, was the crucial force in employing culture to sustain American Jewish support for Israel in the decade after 1948. See Haggai Hitron, "Israeli Opera to Uphold Wagner Boycott Over Link to Nazis," *Haaretz*, 17 December 2008. See also Leon Botstein, "If Not Wagner, Then Who?" *Haaretz*, 23 January 2009.

7. See Thomas S. Grey, "The Jewish Question," in *The Cambridge Companion to Wagner*, ed. Thomas S. Grey (New York, 2008), 203–18. Also Dieter Borchmeyer, "Renaissance und Instrumentalisierung des Mythos," in *Richard Wagner im dritten Reich: Ein Schloss Elmau-Symposion*, ed. Saul Friedländer and Jörn Rüsen (Munich, 2000); Dieter Borchmeyer, trans. Stewart Spencer, *Richard Wagner: Theory and Theatre* (Oxford, 1991); Hans Mayer, Heinz-Klaus Metzger, and Rainer Riehn, "Diskussion über Recht, Unrecht und Alternativen," 54–78, and other essays in *Wie antisemitisch darf ein Künstler sein?* ed. Heinz-Klaus Metzger and Rainer Riehn, Muzik-Konzepte 5 (Munich, 1981); Hartmut Zelinsky, *Sieg oder Untergang: Kaiser Wilhelm II, die Werk-Idee Richard Wagners und der "Weltkampf"* (Munich, 1990); Hartmut Zelinsky, *Richard Wagner: Ein deutsches Thema* (Vienna, 1983); Joachim Köhler, *Wagner's Hitler: The Prophet and His Disciple* (Malden, Mass., 2000); Marc A. Weiner, *Richard Wagner and the Anti-Semitic Imagination* (Lincoln, Neb., 1995); and Paul Lawrence Rose, *Wagner: Race and Revolution* (New Haven, 1992).

8. See, for example, David Clay Large, William Weber, and Anne Dzamba Sessa, *Wagnerism in European Culture and Politics* (Ithaca, N.Y., 1984), and Rosamund Bartlett, *Wagner and Russia* (New York, 1995). Wagner's anti-Semitism reached America in the form

of an article called "The Work and Mission of My Life" published in *North American Review* 129/273 (1879): 107–24, warning America of the poisonous influence of Jews. Published under Wagner's name, it was actually written by Hans von Wolzogen.

9. Consider Heinrich Mann's satirical use of Wagner in *Der Untertan*, his great novel about German society in the age of Wilhelm II.

10. See the fine discussion on Wagner and responses from within Jewish communal life in Philip V. Bohlman, *Jewish Music and Modernity* (New York, 2008), 189–98.

11. Karl Kraus, for instance, championed Offenbach in early twentieth-century Vienna (discussed later in this essay). Regarding Mozart, see Leon Botstein, "The Fin-de-Siècle Mozart Revival," in *On Mozart*, ed. James M. Morris (New York, 1994), 204–26.

12. The key focus of Wagner's rewriting of music history was the place of Beethoven. See Klaus Kropfinger, *Wagner and Beethoven: Richard Wagner's Reception of Beethoven* (New York, 1991).

13. Regarding Meyerbeer, Max Brod, writing in 1964 on the hundredth anniversary of the composer's death, acknowledged Wagner's pivotal role in damaging Meyerbeer's reputation. Yet Brod, following the same logic Adler used, confessed, "Wagner's anti-Semitism was qualified. . . . I shall disregard the sordid business of his controversial writings on questions of race, because, as I have said before I am not interested in Wagner the journalist. In gratitude for his music I wish to see only the artist in him." Brod, Kafka's friend and a writer himself, was well known for his music criticism and his championing of Janáček in Prague. Brod immigrated to Palestine in the 1930s, was crucial in the formation of Israel's cultural infrastructure, and wrote the first book on music in Israel. See Max Brod, "Some Comments on the Relationship Between Wagner and Meyerbeer," in *Leo Baeck Institute Yearbook* (London, 1964), 9:202–5.

14. These issues were thoroughly aired in the scholarly debate over Daniel Goldhagen's *Hitler's Willing Executioners: Ordinary Germans and the Holocaust* (New York, 1996), itself a response to Christopher Browning's book *Ordinary Men: Reserve Police Battalion 101 and the Final Solution in Poland* (New York, 1992). See, for example, Robert Shandley and Jeremiah Riemer, eds., *Unwilling Germans? The Goldhagen Debate* (Minneapolis, 1998); Geoff Eley, ed., *The Goldhagen Effect: History, Memory, Nazism—Facing The German Past* (Ann Arbor, Mich., 2000); and Dominick LaCapra, "Perpetrators and Victims: The Goldhagen Debate and Beyond," chap. 4 of his *Writing History, Writing Trauma* (Baltimore, 2001), 114–40.

15. On Wagner's role in the history of modern anti-Semitism, see Jacob Katz, *The Darker Side of Genius: Richard Wagner's Anti-Semitism* (Hanover, N.H., 1986); as well as his *From Prejudice to Destruction: Anti-Semitism, 1700–1933* (Cambridge, 1980). On Wagner and the Nazis, see the excellent essay collection *Richard Wagner im dritten Reich*, particularly Reinhold Brinkmann, "Wagners Aktualität für den Nationalsozialismus: Fragmente einer Bestandsaufnahme," 109–41, which provides a provocative contrary view on the Nazi attitude toward *Parsifal*.

16. See Hannah Arendt, "Anti-Semitism," Part One of *The Origins of Totalitarianism* (New York, 2004).

17. Because an unauthorized performance of *Parsifal* had already taken place in New York in 1903, the exclusivity debate concerned only Europe. See the review "Parsifal in New York" by Stephan Zweig (not the famous Stefan Zweig), reprinted in Zelinsky, *Richard Wagner: Ein deutsches Thema*, 121. See also the ironic account and dismissive judgment of *Parsifal* as a work of art written by the distinguished and popular German Jewish writer Leon Feuchtwanger (author of *Jud Süss*) following the Monte Carlo performance, in Susanna Großmann-Vendrey, *Bayreuth in der deutsche Presse, 1908–1944*, Dokumentenband 3 (Regensburg, 1983), 121–22.

18. Highpoints of this debate were the controversy over Thomas Mann's anti-Wagner essay and the 1937 publication of parts of what would later become Theodor W. Adorno's *Versuch über Wagner* (1952). Four chapters of that book had appeared in the *Zeitschrift für*

Sozialforschung. For an English translation of *Versuch über Wagner*, see *In Search of Wagner*, trans. Rodney Livingstone (London, 1981). See also Leon Botstein, "Wagner and Our Century," in *Music at the Turn of the Century: A 19th-Century Music Reader*, ed. Joseph Kerman (Berkeley, 1990), 169–80.

19. Peter Cornelius, *Literarische Werke: Aufsätze über Musik und Kunst* (Leipzig, 1904), 193–200.

20. Daniel Spitzer, *Wiener Spaziergänge* (Vienna and Leipzig, 1879), 2:107. The fact that the Wagner ban in Israel began in 1938 when the Palestine Philharmonic, in the wake of Kristallnacht, canceled a performance of the Prelude to *Die Meistersinger* heightens the irony in Spitzer's observations. Spitzer seems to have sensed the possibility that a work the Jewish audience once enthusiastically embraced might become the symbol of the worst incarnation of anti-Semitism. There was also, it is true, some degree of protest surrounding the premiere in Vienna, centered on the assumption that Beckmesser's serenade was written to "mock Jews and their music." See Thomas S. Grey, "Masters and Their Critics: Wagner, Hanslick and Beckmesser," in *Wagner's "Meistersinger": Performance, History, Representation*, ed. Nicholas Vazsonyi (Rochester, N.Y., 2003), 184–85.

21. In Großmann-Vendrey, *Bayreuth in der deutschen Presse*, Dokumentenband 1, 20. See also Nike Wagner, *Wagner Theater* (Frankfurt am Main and Leipzig, 1998). Speidel was referring to the stark contradiction between the continuing enthusiasm for Wagner's works among educated Jews in light of the recent 1869 republication of "Judaism in Music" and the "outing" of Wagner's radical anti-Semitism. Spitzer's account is in *Wiener Spaziergänge* 2:105–8. See the extensive account of the Vienna premiere in Max Morold, *Wagners Kampf und Sieg dargestellt in seinen Beziehungen zu Wien* (Zurich, Leipzig, and Vienna, 1930), 2:73–75. On Speidel, see Ludwig Hevesi, *Ludwig Speidel* (Berlin, 1910).

22. Großmann-Vendrey, *Bayreuth in der deutschen Presse*, Dokumentenband 1, 230.

23. Theo Stengel and Herbert Gerigk, *Lexicon der Juden in der Musik* (Berlin, 1941), 53. It was to Davidsohn that Hans von Bülow in 1884 defended his support for anti-Semitic legislation, including finding ways to restrict the flow of Jews from the East to stem the tide of "uncivilized" Jews, an objective to which Bülow believed Davidsohn (and other Europeanized Jews) would be sympathic. Bülow cited Levi and other colleagues of Jewish birth who also feared the degrading of language and culture by a population he thought dangerous. See Bülow, *Briefe und Schriften*, ed. Marie von Bülow (Leipzig, 1896–1908), 6:253–54.

24. Spitzer, *Wiener Spaziergänge*, 3:351. Spitzer pursued this satirical goading of Wagner as the Jew par excellence in his 1879 account of the opening scene of *Götterdämmerung*. Spitzer observed that the seemingly endless posing of questions that are answered in turn by questions are "one of the little Jewish traits of the Rabbi of Bayreuth, or as one calls him in the German translation, of the 'Master,'" in Spitzer, *Wiener Spaziergänge*, 5:60. The suspicion of Wagner's supposed Jewish ancestry has a long history, particularly its use to explain Wagner's anti-Semitism. It has its source not only in Nietzsche but also in Ludwig Speidel, who, writing for the *Fremdenblatt* from the same 1876 Bayreuth event as Spitzer, remarked on Wagner's having been born in the Jewish quarter of Leipzig. See Großmann-Vendrey, *Bayreuth in der deutschen Presse*, Dokumentenband 1, 225–26.

25. Großmann-Vendrey, *Bayreuth in der deutschen Presse*, Dokumentenband 1, 22–23.

26. *Wiener Luft*, no. 11 (1877): 3.

27. Spitzer, *Wiener Spaziergänge*, 4:84. Peter Wehle, for example, was the name of two well-known Jewish Viennese cabaret artists (father and son).

28. For the demography and rates of conversion in Vienna in this period, see Marsha L. Rozenblit, *Reconstructing a National Identity: The Jews of Habsburg Austria During World War I* (New York, 2001). See also Robert S. Wistrich, *The Jews in the Age of Franz Joseph* (New York, 1989).

29. *Wiener Luft*, no. 9 (1879): 1.

30. This continues to be the case. Susanna Großmann-Vendrey, for example, mistakenly claims that Paul Lindau (1839–1919), a prominent anti-Wagnerian and friend

of Spitzer who incurred the contempt of Richard and Cosima, was a Jew. He was a Protestant. She misreads one entry in Cosima's diary. See Großmann-Vendrey, *Bayreuth in der deutschen Presse*, Dokumentenband 1, 50. Among those who distanced themselves only partially from Wagner, and whose more restrained mix of admiration and criticism was ascribed to Jewishness, was Heinrich Ehrlich (1822–99), the pianist, critic, and composer. Ibid., 145–50. Despite the surface appeal of the parvenu argument, there is historical merit in ascribing quite conservative tastes to the Jewish audience on account of the insecurity of judgment created by the novelty of assimilation, its precariousness, its evident value, and the need to use taste as a valorization of acceptability outside the Jewish community. See Leon Botstein, "Sozialgeschichte und die Politik des Ästhetischen: Juden und Musik in Wien 1870–1938," in *Quasi una fantasia: Juden und die Musikstadt Wien*, ed. Leon Botstein and Werner Hanak (Vienna, 2003), 43–64. Jews during the early twentieth century could be regarded as prototypical examples of the construct of regressive hearing and fetishism in taste that Theodor Adorno advanced in the 1930s. They may have resisted Wagner in the first instance, but did succumb when a taste for his music was no longer a risk that could jeopardize the utility of acquired musical culture in the process of social integration.

31. I refer here to Wagner's indispensable Jewish colleagues—Hermann Levi, Angelo Neumann, Heinrich Porges, Carl Tausig, and Joseph Rubinstein. Rubinstein committed suicide after Wagner's death (see Rosamund Bartlett, *Wagner and Russia* [Cambridge, 1995], 45–46). Wagner recognized that the use of the Munich Opera Orchestra was contingent (owing to Ludwig II's personal views) on distancing himself from publicly endorsing anti-Semitic political initiatives.

32. Bülow remarked on the prominence of Jews in the Dresden audience for music in the 1850s. Writing to Hans von Wolzogen in 1880, Bülow noted that the Jews were the most committed and generous public for concerts, a group on whom the non-Jewish public depended, including even Wagner. In 1850 he revealed to his father that he had misplaced, along with his passport, his copy of Wagner's essay on the Jews, which indicates that Wagner attempted to conceal his authorship only halfheartedly. See Hans von Bülow, *Briefe*, 1:274, 426; and 6:30; Wagner resisted signing the 1879 petition seeking to revoke civil rights for Jews for fear of losing support from Jewish patrons and colleagues and displeasing Ludwig II, who (like Franz Joseph) viewed Jews dynastically as loyal subjects worthy of equal rights, as he explicitly explained to Wagner. Hitler disliked Siegfried Wagner, Richard's son, because he was seen as currying favor with Jewish patrons in order to keep Bayreuth alive. The caricature of Jewish women at the opera appeared in *Wiener Luft*, no, 2, 1876.

33. On Spitzer, who published the notorious letters between Wagner and a Viennese "Putzmacherin" in 1877 (reissued in 1906), see Ernest Newman, *The Life of Richard Wagner* (London, 1976), 3:567; these letters revealed Wagner's taste for silks and such luxuries. See the appreciation of Spitzer by Paul Lindau, *Nur Errinerungen* (Stuttgart and Berlin, 1919), 2:315–23; and Max Kalbeck's biographical sketch in Daniel Spitzer, *Letzte Wiener Spaziergänge* (Vienna, 1894), vii–xlv; and *Österreichisches Biographisches Lexikon, 1815–1950*, ed. Peter Csendes, Leo Santifaller, and Eva Obermayer-Marnach (Vienna, 1994), 37–38.

34. Spitzer, *Wiener Spaziergänge*, 5:65–66.

35. Ibid., 6:140.

36. Ibid., 4:82.

37. An English version of the opening lines might be "Woe, wandering Vienna's woodlands, walking, whilst Wagner's 'Walküre' wonderment little whelmed me over." Ibid., 4:80. I thank Thomas Grey for encouraging me to emulate Spitzer's parody.

38. Ibid., 5:200–206; and 6:79–80. The parallels between Spitzer's critique and Nietzsche's important, well-known, and influential volte-face on Wagner deserve closer scrutiny.

39. Ibid. Brünnhilde becomes in Spitzer's satire a confused and talkative associate professor (Privatdozentin) who has gotten her Schopenhauer wrong.

40. See Franz Werfel, *Twilight of a World*, trans. H. T. Lowe-Porter (New York, 1937).

As for Roth, the locus classicus is Roth's *Radetzkymarsch* (1932). See also Claudio Magris's *Weit von wo? Verlorene Welt des Ostjudentums* (Vienna, 1974).

41. Adler, *Wagner*, 350–51. Adler was a charter member of the first Vienna Academic Wagner Society, which admitted Jews.

42. The sources for this claim are, of course, the diaries of Cosima Wagner. But one should also consult Carl Glasenapp and Heinrich von Stein's remarkable *Wagner-Lexicon* (Stuttgart, 1883), an alphabetical compendium by subject matter of Wagner's opinions in his own words. Intended as a seventieth birthday gift, it came out after his death. The explicit entries on Jews and Wagner's writings on Jews are useful and revealing. Furthermore, Adler, lecturing in 1903–4, knew that a new Wagner Society had been founded in Vienna in the 1890s that restricted membership to non-Jews. Bruckner was an honorary sponsor of this initiative, which signaled the radicalization of anti-Semitism as a political phenomenon. See Margaret Notley, "Bruckner and Viennese Wagnerism," in *Bruckner Studies*, ed. Timothy L. Jackson (New Haven, 2007), 54–71. On the contrast between Wagner's attitudes in 1876 and in 1882, the year of the *Parsifal* premiere, see the account by the Jewish feuilleton editor of the *Wiener Zeitung*, Josef Oppenheim, in Susanna Großmann-Vendrey, *Bayreuth in der deutschen Presse*, Dokumentenband 1, 226–27.

43. Adler, *Wagner*, 1.

44. A provocative revisionist account of the historical meaning of Wagner's anti-Semitism and its relationship to Nazism and its consequences exonerates Wagner's anti-Semitism through a method that purports that this issue has been treated too much in retrospect. See Dieter David Scholz, *Richard Wagners Antisemitismus, Jahrhundertgenie im Zwielicht: Eine Korrektur* (Berlin, 2000).

45. See Rose, *Wagner: Race and Revolution*; and the writings of Hartmut Zelinsky, particularly the compendium *Richard Wagner: Ein deutsches Thema*; Joachim Köhler, *Richard Wagner: The Last of the Titans* (New Haven, 2004); Köhler, *Wagner's Hitler: The Prophet and His Disciple*; and Ulrich Drüner, *Schöpfer und Zerstörer: Richard Wagner als Künstler* (Cologne, 2003).

46. On the structure of Vienna's Jewish community, see Wistrich, *The Jews in the Age of Franz Joseph*. Hanslick may have been sensitive to allegations regarding his Jewish parentage, but that did not prevent him from writing encomiums on Salomon Sulzer, the Viennese cantor, after going to the main Viennese synagogue to hear him lead the liturgy, as a Christian, not an apostate Jew. Hanslick may have been a Catholic, but he and his parents' home supported a rationalist non-doctrinaire attitude toward religion. See Eduard Hanslick, *Aus meinem Leben* (1894; Kassel, 1987), 9; and "Salomon Sulzer," in *Aus dem Konzertsaal* (Vienna, 1870), 400–404.

47. See the discussion on Wagner and Gobineau and issues of race in "Strange Love, Or, How We Learned to Stop Worrying and Love *Parsifal*," chapter 13 of John Deathridge's *Wagner: Beyond Good and Evil* (Berkeley and Los Angeles, 2008), especially 165, 166–69, 175–77.

48. See Theodor Gompertz, *Ein Gelehrtenlegen im Bürgentum der Franz-Josefs-Zeit: Auswahl seiner Briefe und Aufzeichnungen, 1869–1912*, ed. Robert A. Kann (Vienna, 1974). The Hanslick case is but one example of the failure to erase Jewish identity through conversion and the consequent denial of status as Christian in the public mind. Consider the examples of Hugo von Hofmannsthal and Ludwig Wittgenstein, where conversion went back beyond the parental generation.

49. See Kalisch, *Entwurf einer Wissenschaft von der Musik*, 18–47.

50. Adler, *Wollen und Wirken*, 1.

51. The allure of "Weltbürgertum" lasted well into the twentieth century among German-speaking Jewry. A case in point was Stefan Zweig, whose autobiography, a lament at the passing of this ideal, was severely criticized by Hannah Arendt when it first appeared. See Stefan Zweig, *Die Welt von Gestern: Erinnerungen eines Europäers* (Frankfurt am Main,

1944); and Arendt, "Stefan Zweig: Jews in the World of Yesterday," in *The Jewish Writings*, ed. Jerome Kohn and Ron H. Feldman (New York, 2008), 317–28. On Zweig, see Leon Botstein's Introduction, in Stefan Zweig, *Jewish Legends*, trans. Eden and Cedar Paul (New York, 1987), vii–xxxviii; as well as his "Stefan Zweig and the Illusion of the Jewish European," in *Stefan Zweig: The World of Yesterday's Humanist Today*, ed. Marion Sonnenfeld (Albany, N.Y., 1981), 82–100. Cosmopolitanism has remained a key insult for anti-Semites, suggesting the absence of a spiritual tie to land. It suggested the idea of rootlessness, a view Wagner made even more popular.

52. Hanslick's criticism of Wagner has been the object of extensive commentary. See Grey, "Masters and Their Critics," 165–89; David B. Dennis, "'The Most German of All German Operas': *Die Meistersinger* Through the Lens of the Third Reich," 98–119; and Hans Rudolf Vaget, "'Du warst mein Feind von je': The Beckmesser Controversy Revisited," 190–208, in Vazsonyi, *Wagner's "Meistersinger": Performance, History, Representation*.

53. Hanslick, *Aus meinem Leben*, 7–14. See also the discussion of Hanslick's view of Wagner's suggestion of him as a Jew in the context of the Hanslick-Beckmesser parallel by Grey, "Masters and Their Critics," in ibid. Hanslick characterized the claim as comparable to forced circumcision as a criminal act. Hanslick was eager to let the readers know that unlike "true" Jewish men he had not been circumcised (since his mother converted before his birth), a sign of how touchy this subject was. See Hanslick's review of Wagner's 1869 essay, 232–38, and Ludwig Philippsohn, "Unsere neuesten Gegner," 252–63, both in *Richard Wagners "Das Judentum in der Musik": Eine kritische Dokumentation als Beitrag zur Geschichte des Antisemitismus*, ed. Jens Malte Fischer (Frankfurt, 2000), 256; and Adler, *Wagner*, 188. The discussion of "Jewish" elements in Beckmesser's music was linked to the idea that Hanslick was, racially, a "Jew."

54. Adler bemoaned the fact that "already today the mannerist efforts in Wagnerian style have become a heavy burden. . . . The view of Wagner as monumental that reigns in our time should not, in the name of the master, be allowed to render the work stale. . . . The good 'old' ways must be respected but not retard the inherently progressive character of art. . . . The effective power of a work of art is weakened by rendering it an inert monument unto itself." Adler, *Wagner*, 336.

55. Adler, *Wagner*, 195–98. On the Mahler–Roller collaboration, see Manfred Wagner, *Alfred Roller in seiner Zeit* (Salzburg, 1996); Franz Willnauer, *Gustav Mahler und die Wiener Oper*, 2nd ed. (Vienna, 1993); and Henry-Louis de la Grange, *Gustav Mahler*, vol. 2, *Vienna: The Years of Challenge, 1897–1904* (New York, 1995).

56. Adler, *Wagner*, 159–64. Wagner's views on language and music can be found in *Gesammelte Schriften und Dichtungen* (Leipzig, 1907), 4:115–22 and 208–22; and 7:149–50.

57. Ernest Bloch, *Sa vie et sa pensée*, vol. 1, *Les années de galères, 1880–1916*, ed. Joseph Lewinski and Emmanuelle Dijon (Geneva, 1998), 60–66, 245.

58. Ibid., 1:537. It is interesting that Bloch, in attempting to translate Wagnerism into music with the intent of expressing Jewish national identity as an assimilated Jew, chose to idealize expressive gestures associated with Eastern European Jewry, not his own milieu. Bloch's musical works appropriated an apparently authentic liturgical sentiment of suffering and intense inner feeling linked to being Jewish. This idealized distillation of Jewishness did not derive from Bloch's own personal experience and did not reflect the kind of close ethnographic study that Bartók and Kodály engaged in to locate what they thought was an unromanticized, Hungarian rural folk tradition. Apart from the lushness of orchestral color, Bloch took from the Wagnerian example a leitmotivic sensibility where fragments and gestures become emblems of meaning. They become integrated into recitation, orchestral interludes, and lyrical singing, creating a continuous narrative structure. This is particularly true for *Schelomo*.

59. For the letters to Fleg of 11 March and 17 April 1911, see ibid., 1:536–37. Chamberlain was Wagner's son-in-law.

60. For the letter to Pizzetti of 13 October 1911, see ibid., 1:549.

61. See Klára Móricz, "Sensuous Pagans and Righteous Jews: Changing Concepts of Jewish Identity in Ernest Bloch's *Jézabel* and *Schelomo*," *JAMS* 45/3 (Fall 2001): 439–91.

62. The first anecdote concerns Hertz Ketzlach, father of David Kettler, the eminent political scientist, from whom I got the story. The second is from a letter to the author dated 12 November 2008 from Charlotte Hahn Arner, in which she recounts her experience.

63. The households in which Bloch and Herzl grew up shared social and economic characteristics except for the important fact that Herzl's Budapest and Vienna both had large Jewish populations. By the age of thirteen both men had been given perfunctory religious training and had gone through an obligatory bar mitzvah. On Herzl, see Ernst Pawel, *The Labyrinth of Exile: A Life of Theodor Herzl* (New York, 1989).

64. Bahr later reversed himself and became outspoken against anti-Semitism, despite a relapse later in life during his marriage with Anna Mildenburg.

65. Theodor Herzl, *Briefe und Tagebücher*, vol. 2, *Zionistisches Tagebuch, 1895–1899*, ed. Johannes Wachten and Chaya Harel (Vienna and Berlin, 1983), 776. In 1898 Herzl ordered the "Fantasie" from *Tannhäuser* to be played at the Second Zionist Congress in Basel; see Pawel, *The Labyrinth of Exile*, 360. I thank Stuart Schoffman for alerting me to this fact as well as to the thought-provoking analysis of Herzl's relationship with *Tannhäuser* in Daniel Boyarin's *Unheroic Conduct: The Rise of Heterosexuality and the Invention of the Jewish Man* (Berkeley, 1997), 73ff.

66. Ibid., 69. The significance of Herzl's attachment to *Tannhäuser* rests most likely in his identification with the protagonist. The opera stresses redemption and miracle, acknowledging the superiority of chivalrous and spiritual love to sensual desire and fulfillment. With that recognition a process of suffering and struggle commences. The rediscovery of one's identity as Jew—in Herzl's case—becomes analogous to Tannhäuser's rejection of Venus, which in the analogy becomes the rejection of the dreams of emancipation and liberal illusions of equal citizenship and assimilation for Jews within European nations. But Tannhäuser, when he reappears at the Wartburg, cannot fully banish Venus. So, too, it was with Herzl, who himself could not entirely shed the prejudices and apparatus of acculturation. Furthermore, *Tannhäuser*, in its reception history, was the least problematic of the Wagner operas. The text derived from Heine. Despite the overt Christian aspect, like *Lohengrin*, the text posed far less difficulty than would those of the *Ring*, *Meistersinger*, or *Parsifal*, and the music and musical dramatic structure were less demanding than in, for example, *Tristan*. As to *Lohengrin*, the appeal to the Jewish audience may have rested in the heroic potential of someone whose background and name are not to be revealed, signaling that the act of triumphant intervention on behalf of the nation and society alone—for an outsider—could be possible. The power of the deed would be the only true criterion of value. After all, Elsa's failure to trust is what is at fault, not the deeds of Lohengrin. One might therefore speculate that the Jewish audience could have sensed that the opera argued on behalf of extraordinary achievements even by a Jew, generating a personal fantasy that romance and achievement should be accepted and valued no matter the background of the individual hero.

67. Consider the famous quip of Walther Rathenau, Germany's most prominent acculturated Jew, a public figure, businessman, and writer who would be assassinated by right-wing agitators in 1922. In 1918 he observed that it was hard to conceive "how much under the spell of Richard Wagner the prior generation had fallen," in Walter Rathenau, *An Deutschlands Jugend* (Berlin, 1918), 83.

68. Wagner's realization of a dramatic form that sought to integrate music, the poetic, narration, and action, left one element entirely underdeveloped: the visual. Wagner's weakness, both in theory and practice, was his consideration of the visual arts. His preferred painter, Hans Makart, and the scene painting he endorsed at the 1876 Bayreuth *Ring*, betray an extremely conventional preference for historical painting and undifferentiated genre realism. Whatever one's tastes, there was an undeniable originality in Wagner, beyond

music, in thought and poetry. But there was nothing of the sort in his visual imagination, which is why the later reforms of Appia and Roller were so welcome. They sought to provide a missing link of innovation.

69. See the commentary on the Wagnerian influence in Wilhelmine Germany cast in terms of the life and career of Ernst Bassermann (1854–1917) in Lothar Gall, *Bürgertum in Deutschland* (Munich, 1989), 419–20.

70. On Meyerbeer, see Jürgen Schläder, "Giacomo Meyerbeer, Komponist–Jude–Europäer," 11–23; and Mathias Spohr, "Meyerbeer contra Wagner," 65–79, both in *Giacomo Meyerbeer: Komponist–Jude–Europäer*, Mimundus 10 (Vienna, 1998); Arnold Jacobshagen und Milan Pospíšil, eds., *Meyerbeer und die Opéra comique* (Laaber, 2004); Julius Kapp, *Meyerbeer* (Berlin, 1924); Sieghart Döhring und Jürgen Schläder, eds., *Giacomo Meyerbeer— Musik als Welterfahrung: Eine Festschrift* (Munich, 1995); Reiner Zimmermann, *Giacomo Meyerbeer: Eine Biographie nach Dokumenten* (Berlin, 1998); Heinz und Gudrun Becker, *Giacomo Meyerbeer: Ein Leben in Briefen* (Wilhelmshaven, 1983).

71. Franz Rosenzweig, *Der Stern der Erlösung* (Frankfurt, 1988), 272.

72. See the sympathetic but complementary argument concerning the sources of Wagner's success that stresses the Wagnerian use of sonority in Heinrich Besseler, *Das musikalische Hören der Neuzeit* (Berlin, 1959), 71–74.

73. Bernard Shaw, *The Perfect Wagnerite: A Commentary on the Ring of the Niblungs* (London, 1898), 3–4.

74. Arnold Schoenberg, *Style and Idea*, ed. Leonard Stein, trans. Leo Black (Berkeley, 1984), 129.

75. Josef Rufer, *Das Werk Arnold Schoenbergs* (Basel, London, and New York, 1959), 139.

76. This is reminiscent of the fin-de-siècle critique of historicism (and indirectly Wagner) in the architecture of Adolf Loos, whose *Ornament and Crime* appeared in 1908. On the relationship between Loos and Schoenberg, see Leon Botstein, "Music and the Critique of Culture: Arnold Schoenberg, Heinrich Schenker, and the Emergence of Modernism in Fin-de-Siècle Vienna," in *Constructive Dissonance: Arnold Schoenberg and Transformations of Twentieth-Century Culture*, ed. Juliane Brand and Christopher Hailey (Berkeley, 1997), 3–22. See Leon Botstein, "Egon Schiele and Arnold Schönberg: The Cultural Politics of Aesthetic Innovation in Vienna, 1890–1918," in *Egon Schiele: Art, Sexuality, and Viennese Modernism*, ed. Patrick Werkner (Palo Alto, Calif., 1994), 101–18; and Botstein, "Arnold Schoenberg: Language, Modernism and Jewish Identity" in *Austrians and Jews in the Twentieth Century*, ed. Robert S. Wistrich (New York, 1992), 162–83. For a somewhat different account of the Loos-Schoenberg parallel, see Holly Watkins, "Schoenberg's Interior Designs," *Journal of the American Musicological Society* 61/1 (Spring 2009): 123–206.

77. Schoenberg observed that Wagner, by appending narratives retrospectively to Beethoven, had finally succeeded in making Beethoven's instrumental music widely appreciated.

78. See Leon Botstein, *Judentum und Modernität: Essays zur Rolle der Juden in der Deutschen und Österreichischen Kultur, 1848–1938* (Vienna, 1991); Carl Dahlhaus, "Das deutsche Bildungsbürgertum und die Musik," in *Bildungsbürgertum im 19. Jahrhundert*, ed. Reinhart Koselleck (Stuttgart, 1990), 2:220–36. For a context for this discussion, the shift in cultural politics in Germany after 1900, see Konrad H. Jarausch, "Die Krise des deutschen Bildungsbürgertum im ersten Drittel des 20. Jahrhunderts," in *Bildungsbürgertum im 19. Jahrhundert*, ed. Jurgen Kocka (Stuttgart, 1989), 4:180–205.

79. Wagner's capacity to extend culture to the larger public constitutes one of the reasons Schoenberg sided with David Josef Bach and others against extending Bayreuth's monopoly on *Parsifal*. See Schoenberg's 1912 "Parsifal and Copyright," in Arnold Schoenberg, *Style and Idea*, 491ff.

80. See Edward Timms, *Karl Kraus: Apocalyptic Satirist*, vol. 1, *Culture and Catastrophe in Habsburg Vienna* (New Haven, 1986), 103. On Nordau, see Michael Stanislawski, *Zionism*

and the Fin de Siècle: Cosmopolitanism and Nationalism from Nordau to Jabotinsky (Berkeley, 2001); Christoph Schulte, *Psychopathologie des Fin de Siècle: Der Kulturkritiker, Arzt und Zionist Max Nordau* (Frankfurt am Main, 1997); and Melanie Murphy, *Max Nordau's Fin-de-Siècle Romance of Race* (New York, 2007).

81. Heinrich Schenker, *Der Tonwille: Pamphlets in Witness of the Immutable Laws of Music* (New York, 2004), 1:23–24.

82. On Schenker, see Leon Botstein, "Schenker the Regressive: Observations on the Historical Schenker," *Musical Quarterly* 86/2 (Summer 2002): 239–47; Leon Botstein, "Gedanken zu Heinrich Schenkers jüdischer Identität," in *Rebell und Visionär: Heinrich Schenker in Wien*, ed. Evelyn Fink-Mennel (Vienna, 2003), 11–17; and Nicholas Cook, *The Schenker Project: Culture, Race, and Music Theory in Fin-de-Siècle Vienna* (New York, 2007).

83. See Marc A. Weiner, *Arthur Schnitzler and the Crisis of Musical Culture* (Heidelberg, 1986), 114–17, 126–62.

84. See Max Graf, *Wagner-Probleme, und andere Studien* (Vienna, 1900); *Die innere Werkstatt des Musikers* (Stuttgart, 1910); and *Richard Wagner im 'Fliegenden Holländer': Ein Beitrag zur Psychologie des künstlerischen Schaffens"* (Leipzig, 1911); and *Composer and Critic: Two Hundred Years of Musical Criticism* (New York, 1946).

85. Graf, *Wagner-Probleme*, 40.

86. Ibid., 50.

87. Ibid., 71.

88. Schoenberg, *Style and Idea*, 49.

89. Among the many who have made this point was Ludwig Wittgenstein. In 1941 he observed that "Wagner's motifs might be called musical prose sentences. . . . Wagnerian drama . . . is not drama so much as an assemblage of situations strung together as though on a thread . . . cleverly spun and not inspired as the motifs and situations are." See Wittgenstein, *Culture and Value*, ed. G. H. von Wright and Heikki Nyman, trans. Peter Winch (Chicago, 1980), 41.

90. Emil Ludwig (Emil Cohn) (1881–1948) was best known for popular biographies. He was the German equivalent of the Austrian Stefan Zweig. He converted in 1902, before writing *Wagner oder Die Entzauberten* (Berlin, 1913). But when Walther Rathenau was assassinated in 1922, Ludwig reclaimed his Jewish identity. His sojourn in this regard is somewhat parallel to Schoenberg's. Schoenberg converted as a young man only to reconvert in 1933.

91. Ludwig, *Wagner*, 285–86.

92. Ibid., 293.

93. Ibid., 315–16.

94. Paul Stefan (1879–1943), a critic who studied with Schoenberg, helped found the Vienna Ansorge Verein, and wrote extensively on behalf of Mahler, including a polemic decrying Mahler's departure from Vienna in 1907. He edited the *Musikblätter des Anbruchs* and also wrote popular biographies of Oskar Fried, Bruno Walter, and Arturo Toscanini. He emigrated to the United States in 1938. Kurt Singer represents the most complex case among Wagner's Jewish critics. Born in 1885, he died in Teresienstadt in 1944. He was an eminent neurologist and prolific writer on music. His father was a rabbi. He settled in Berlin, studied music and medicine, and in 1913 founded a doctors' chorus. He combined his interests and wrote on the ailments of musicians. He ultimately rose to sufficient prominence to become Intendant at the Berlin-Charlottenburg Opera in 1931. His most remarkable role in history was as the organizer and driving force of the Jüdischer Kulturbund, the organization established by the Nazis after 1933 in order to provide a segregated cultural forum for Jews. He went to the United States in 1938 to explore ways to help the Kulturbund, perhaps to arrange for a collective emigration. But after Kristallnacht, Singer inexplicably, voluntarily, returned to Germany. The Kulturbund was dissolved in 1941. Singer himself and his role after 1933 have remained enigmatic, elusive, and controversial subjects. The entire Kulturbund idea itself was fraught with obvious difficulties.

Was Singer in some unwitting manner perhaps a collaborator, deluded by authority and station, and therefore blinded, resulting in an influence that supported false hopes and militated against emigration? The intense defense of Wagner in 1913 is perhaps a clue. There seemed little contradiction to Singer between his status as Jew and as a German, even to the end.

95. Paul Stefan, *Die Feindschaft gegen Wagner* (Regensburg, 1914), 16, 21, 60–61, 78, 80–81.

96. See Paul Bekker, *Beethoven* (Berlin, 1911). Also Leon Botstein, "The Search for Meaning in Beethoven: Popularity, Intimacy, and Politics in Historical Perspective," in *Beethoven and His World*, ed. Scott G. Burnham and Michael P. Steinberg (Princeton, 2000), 332–66.

97. Singer's invocation of the image of health reflected a long tradition in Wagner criticism, pro and con. Wagnerians saw a restoration of health, while anti-Wagnerians like Nordau saw disease. For an inspired extension of this use of medical metaphors in describing the culture of the German nation—a practice that was especially characteristic of Nazi ideology—into post-1945 German culture, see Jennifer M. Kapczynski, *The German Patient: Crisis and Recovery in Postwar Culture* (Ann Arbor, Mich., 2008).

98. Kurt Singer, *Richard Wagner* (Berlin, 1913), 8–9, 45, 66, 107, 112–13, 118–19.

99. On Friedell, see *Österreichisches Biographisches Lexikon, 1815–1950*, 362; Felix Czeike, *Historisches Lexikon Wien* (Vienna, 1997), 2:403–4; and *The Vienna Coffeehouse Wits*, ed. and trans. Harold B. Segel (Lafayette, Ind., 1993), esp. 176–77 and 193–99.

100. Egon Friedell, *Kulturgeschichte der Neuzeit* (Munich, 1931), 3:372–73.

101. On Weininger, see Chandak Sengoopta, *Otto Weininger: Sex, Science, and Self in Imperial Vienna* (Chicago, 2000); Nancy Harrowitz and Barbara Hyams, eds., *Jews and Gender: Responses to Otto Weininger* (Philadelphia, 1995); David G. Stern and Béla Szabados, eds., *Wittgenstein Reads Weininger* (New York, 2004); and Jacques Le Rider, *Der Fall Otto Weininger* (Vienna, 1985).

102. Otto Weininger, *Sex and Character* (New York, 2003), 310. Deathridge's "Strange Love" chapter in *Wagner: Beyond Good and Evil*, 159–77, offers a brilliant and provocative reading of *Parsifal* in the context of Wagner's anti-Semitism and contact with Gobineau. Also see Nike Wagner, "Kulturphantasmen: *Parsifal*, Weininger, Wien um 1900," in *Wagner Theater*, 190–211.

103. Otto Weininger, *Über die letzten Dinge* (Munich, 1980), 96.

104. Weininger, *Sex and Character*, 303–5.

105. This summary closely follows the sequence in "Judaism," chap. 8 of Weininger's *Sex and Character*.

106. Weininger, *Über die letzten Dinge*, 190.

107. Ibid., 330.

108. Hartmut Zelinsky, "Der Dirigent Hermann Levi: Anmerkungen zur verdrängten Geschichte des jüdischen Wagnerianers," in *Geschichte und Kultur der Juden in Bayern: Aufsätze* (Munich, 1988), 425.

109. On Kraus, see Timms, *Karl Kraus: Apocalyptic Satirist*, 1:237–49; also, see vol. 2, *The Post-War Crisis and the Rise of the Swastika* (New Haven, 2005), esp. 420–26. See also the provocative, brilliant, and original interpretation of Kraus and his project by Paul Reitter, *The Anti-Journalist: Karl Kraus and Jewish Self-Fashioning in Fin-de-Siècle Europe* (Chicago, 2008). Kraus defended Mahler vigorously against Philistine critics, but, following Robert Hirschfeld, displayed no particular enthusiasm for his music or conducting.

110. For a sample of Kraus's views on Wagner, see *Die Fackel*, May 1899, 2–3; November 1902, 1–13, and March 1904, 1–13 (these two concern the anti-Wagnerian critic and writer Max Kalbeck); and December 1906, 18–21. On Spitzer and Wagner, see also June 1913, 14–17.

111. See Georg Knepler, *Karl Kraus liest Offenbach* (Vienna, 1984); Timms, *Karl Kraus*, 2:433–40; Karl Kraus, "Offenbach-Renaissance," *Die Fackel* 33/29, April 1927–January 1928 (Munich, 1972), 38–48; Jean-Claude Yon, *Jacques Offenbach* (Paris, 2000); and James Harding, *Jacques Offenbach: A Biography* (London, 1980). Kraus, it should be noted, did not share

Weininger's view of Jews being bereft of humor. Kraus was an admirer of Spitzer's, a figure who played no intellectual role in Weininger's intellectual development.

112. See Wittgenstein, *Culture and Value*; Leon Botstein, "Freud and Wittgenstein: Language and Human Nature," *Psychoanalytic Psychology* 24/4 (2007): 603–22; and Rudolf Koder, *Wittgenstein und die Musik: Briefwechsel Ludwig Wittgenstein* (Innsbruck, 2000).

113. For Kraus's views on Spitzer, see Timms, *Karl Kraus*, 1:34–35. For Kraus's views on Nestroy, see his *Nestroy und die Nachwelt* (Vienna, 1912). Nestroy participated in several Viennese premieres of Offenbach: see Hans Kristeller, *Der Aufstieg des Kölners Jacques Offenbach: Ein Musikerleben in Bildern* (Berlin, 1931). It should be noted that Kraus, in contrast to the Wagnerian Shaw, admired Oscar Wilde.

114. The most prominent of these writings was Mann's essay "The Sorrows and Grandeur of Richard Wagner," published in 1933. This publication, in Mann's own view, marked the beginning of his physical and cultural exile from Germany. The essay was virulently attacked by the Nazis and their sympathizers. Mann took up the matter again in a letter published in the New York–based German émigré periodical *Aufbau* (responding to a letter from Walter von Molo), titled "Why I Am Not Returning to Germany." Reinhard Mehring has written about the letter in an unpublished article, "'In einem Brief nach Deutschland wollte allerlei untergebracht sein.' Thomas Manns Antwort auf Walter von Molo." I would like to thank David Kettler for bringing this article to my attention. See also Hans Gál, *Richard Wagner: Versuch einer Würdigung* (Frankfurt, 1982); and Ludwig Marcuse, *Richard Wagner: Ein denkwürdiges Leben* (Zurich, 1973).

115. Peter Altenberg, *Vita Ipsa* (Berlin, 1919), 61.

116. Rosenzweig, *Der Stern der Erlösung*, 272. Rosenzweig indirectly referred to Weininger's interpretation of Wagner's conception of the nature of the Jews when he described the influence Wagner had on German views of the feminine and the erotic.

117. See Helmuth Weinland, "Wagner zwischen Hegel und Hitler," in *Zwischen Beethoven und Schönberg*, Musik-Konzepte 59 (Munich, 1988), 3–30, esp. 29.

118. This refers to the work of Arnold Zweig, Joseph Roth, and Martin Buber. All of them turned toward Eastern Europe after 1918 in search of authentic Jewish life for nourishment as a repudiation of the cultural norms of assimilated Jewry in Wilhelmine Germany, including a shared obsession with Wagner.

PART II

BIOGRAPHICAL CONTEXTS

Wilhelmine Schröder-Devrient and

Wagner's Dresden

CLAIRE VON GLÜMER, HENRY CHORLEY
TRANSLATED, INTRODUCED, AND ANNOTATED
BY THOMAS S. GREY

Throughout his life Richard Wagner consistently attributed a decisive influence on his career as a "musical dramatist" to the early example of operatic performances by Wilhelmine Schröder-Devrient. The daughter of an accomplished operatic baritone, Friedrich Schröder, and his wife, Sophie (née Bürger), perhaps the most celebrated German actress of her day, Wilhelmine was trained from earliest childhood in all aspects of the theater: ballet, pantomime, and acting as well as singing. She was catapulted to fame in November 1822 when, not quite eighteen, she electrified Viennese audiences as the heroine in a revival of the revised *Fidelio*, a production at least partly overseen by Beethoven himself. She went on to specialize in this and a few other carefully chosen roles: the simple, pure, and sentimental young maiden as Emmeline in Weigl's *Schweizerfamilie* and Agathe in Weber's *Der Freischütz*; the noble Greek priestess of Diana in Gluck's *Iphigenia in Tauris* (*Iphigénie en Tauride*); the passionate, reckless, love-torn youth in the trouser role of Bellini's Romeo (*I Capuleti e i Montecchi*), a model for Adriano in Wagner's *Rienzi*, which she would create in 1842; and such sorely tried noble heroines as Julia in Spontini's *La vestale*, the title figure in Weber's *Euryanthe*, Desdemona in Rossini's *Otello*, and Donna Anna in *Don Giovanni*.[1] (Figure 1 reproduces an 1839 portrait recently identified by H. Colin Slim as Schröder-Devrient, here holding a scrolled sheet of music manuscript containing the incipit, in German translation, of the aria "O malheureuse Iphigénie" from C. W. Gluck's *Iphigénie en Tauride*.)[2] Hallmarks of her performances included a thrilling sense of identification with character and situation, the ability to act persuasively in song as well as speech, grandeur and nobility of bearing (or naïve simplicity, where the role demanded it), and a gift for both dramatic and musical timing.

Figure 1. Wilhelmine Schröder-Devrient. Portrait by Joseph Weber, 1839 (oil on canvas, 30 x 25 1/16 in.; Berkeley, California, private collection).

The specific quality of her singing voice was a topic of continual debate throughout her career and subsequently. The general picture that emerges is a voice less than perfectly trained or controlled, but guided by strong musical instincts and, above all, by a highly developed sense of theater. It is characteristic that Ludwig Rellstab's early appreciation of her career identifies as one of her most moving achievements her silent pantomime as she searches for her husband among the prisoners momentarily released into the daylight in the Act 1 finale of *Fidelio*. Citing the musician Bernhard Klein, Rellstab remarks on the way her "silent play of gestures . . . joined itself so flexibly to the music" such that it became "a kind of mute obbligato instrument, performing its own melody, fitting with the whole and yet separate from it."[3] Similarly, in her own account of her debut in the role (as transmitted by Claire von Glümer), the deaf composer is won over by a performance he witnesses more as a dramatic dumb-show than as opera, since he is essentially unable to hear her voice.

Wagner's recollections of Schröder-Devrient's influence on his youthful self are somewhat less consistent in the matter of chronology and repertoire. In his autobiography *Mein Leben* Wagner suggested, without giving precise dates, that he experienced the crucial operatic epiphany of his youth sometime in 1829. The Italian company of Dresden (members of the court opera) had been giving performances in Leipzig, he recalls, enthralling local audiences, himself included, when his attention was suddenly attracted by another guest appearance from Dresden, Wilhelmine Schröder-Devrient, "who then stood at the pinnacle of her career, young, beautiful and ardent as no woman I have since seen on the stage. She appeared in *Fidelio*." "When I look back across my entire life," Wagner continues, "I find no event to place beside this in the impression it produced upon me. . . . After the opera was over I dashed to the home of one of my friends to write a short letter in which I told her succinctly that my life had henceforth found its meaning, and that if ever she should hear my name favorably mentioned in the world of art, she should remember that she had on this evening made of me that which I now vowed to become."[4] He further claims that the singer was able to recite this hyperbolic fan letter to him verbatim when he befriended her upon his return to Dresden in 1842.

Unfortunately, neither this impassioned note nor any other evidence survives to document this legendary performance or Wagner's experience of it. Wagner's earliest autobiographical text, a "sketch" of his early career up to 1842, is suspiciously silent about this event, though it does explicitly mention an 1834 "guest appearance" in Leipzig, as Romeo in Bellini's *Capuleti*—a performance for which there is external corroboration, unlike the 1829

Leipzig *Fidelio*.[5] In the creative autobiography embedded in the 1852 *Communication to My Friends* (a text very little concerned with detailed facts or dates, it must be said) Wagner again mentions a decisive "guest appearance on the Leipzig stage" which, in context, can only refer to Schröder-Devrient's Romeo of March 1834, since he has been speaking of the sources of his "Young German" phase (Heinse's novel *Ardinghello* and the popular French and Italian operatic repertoire of the early 1830s) that shaped the conception of his second opera, *Das Liebesverbot*, between 1834 and its completion in 1836.[6] It seems clear enough, then, that Wagner certainly *did* hear the singer in Bellini's opera in 1834 when both the work and the performance caused him to reevaluate the new Italian bel canto in view of its effective approach to operatic composition, dramaturgy, and singing. "Even the most distant encounter with this extraordinary woman," he commented in the *Communication*, "had a positively electrifying effect on me; for long afterward, even up to the present day, I could hear and feel her presence whenever I was animated with the impulse to artistic creation."[7]

Whether he also saw her famous *Fidelio*, which she reprised in Leipzig in 1834, we cannot be sure. He did in any case have ample opportunity to become well acquainted with the dramatic singer he now admired so much, starting one year later when she agreed to perform several roles with his fledgling company in Magdeburg—Desdemona in Rossini's *Otello* as well as Bellini's Romeo—and above all when he returned to Dresden in 1842, where Schröder-Devrient remained engaged as a singer until 1847. (Like Wagner, she was an active participant in the socialist agitations of May 1849 in Dresden, and likewise had to flee the city.) In Dresden Wagner was able to coach her in creating the roles of Adriano in *Rienzi*, Senta in *Der fliegende Holländer*, and Venus in *Tannhäuser*—all of them roles conceived to some degree with her in mind. Although she was already in vocal decline after 1840, these collaborations cemented the composer's lifelong admiration of Schröder-Devrient's achievements as a singing actress who aspired to a kind of proto-method acting approach of total identification with the parts she played.[8]

In an 1872 essay "On Actors and Singers" Wagner celebrated this quality as *Selbstentäußerung*, a "renunciation of the self" that allows the actor to inhabit a fictional-dramatic persona without the slightest inhibition or distraction. He cites the career of Ludwig Devrient (1784–1832), founder of the theatrical dynasty into which Wilhelmine Schröder married, as a paradigm of this capacity. This sense of emotional conviction conveyed by the elder Devrient was unprecedented on the German stage: the ability of inspiring Hamlet's rhetorical question in admiration of the player-king: "What's Hecuba to him?"[9] Devrient's sometime daughter-in-law transplanted this capacity to the operatic stage like none other, Wagner claims. In her case, Wagner also relates this "renunciation" to what he calls the "liberating consciousness of play," the "terrifying" but at the same time dramatically enabling consciousness that the actor is momentarily trading his own personality or being for that of a fictional creation. "Through the example of this extraordinary woman I became acquainted in a truly astounding manner with the redemptive transference of consciousness, while lost in the most complete self-renunciation, to the sudden interior awareness of the play that had taken hold of it."[10] In this essay, as elsewhere, Wagner's praise for the histrionic "truth" of Schröder-Devrient's performances resonates with his own ongoing polemics against the operatic tradition and its cult of beautiful singing as the ultimate good. The debate as to whether highly trained operatic singing was a prerequisite of a higher species of "dramatic" Wagnerian singing, or simply an obstacle to achieving it, remained a vexed one throughout the early generations of Wagner's Bayreuth festival. (See, for instance, the reviews of festivals from 1886 to 1904 included in Part V of this volume.)

The two authors whose works are excerpted here represent contrasting views of Wilhelmine Schröder-Devrient's operatic achievement. Claire von Glümer, her first biographer, was a fan and true believer, like Wagner. Henry Chorley (1808–72), a respected London music critic, represents a more objective, more skeptical, sometimes even hostile viewpoint.

Glümer's adoring, sentimental, and rather selective account of her life and career has at least the advantage of deriving to some extent directly from Schröder-Devrient, whose friendship she cultivated during the singer's final years.[11] They were first briefly introduced in Frankfurt in 1849, two years after her retirement from the stage. Later, in Dresden, Glümer and her female companion Auguste Scheibe became intimates of Schröder-Devrient during the last two years of her life (1858–60); Glümer was charged with working up her scattered notes, letters, and diaries into a biography, which appeared in 1862.[12]

By the time Wagner had the opportunity to cast Schröder-Devrient in his own operas at Dresden, between 1842 and 1845, he, too, had some misgivings about the actual lyrical capacity of the voice. Later, however, he dismissed such scruples in favor of the larger significance of the theatrical personality, which remained a model for what he believed could be the future of a genuinely dramatic school of singing. It always distressed him, he claimed, to have to answer the question of whether she had a truly "good voice," to be forced to compare this "great tragedienne" with the "female castrati" (!) of the modern opera house. If anyone were to put that question to him now, he wrote in the 1872 essay "On Actors and Singers," he would be inclined to reply:

"No! She had no 'voice' at all; and yet she knew how to work her breath so beautifully and to project with it such a truly feminine soul that one ceased to think anymore about singing or voices at all! Furthermore, she was able to suggest to a composer how he ought to write something worthy to be 'sung' by such a woman." . . .

My entire understanding of the actor's mimetic art I owe to this great woman, a lesson that allows me to view truthfulness as the essential foundation of that art.[13]

Schröder-Devrient embodied, then, the valorization of dramatic "truth" over mere vocal agility and beauty of sound, and in that sense she also embodied the entire aesthetic value system of the Wagnerian music drama that continued to be so vigorously debated throughout the composer's lifetime.

Perhaps it is not surprising that in constructing his official life, posthumously published as *Mein Leben*, Wagner preferred to identify his original musical-dramatic "epiphany" with Wilhelmine Schröder-Devrient's signature role of Leonora/Fidelio. Whether or not this was really the role in which he first heard her (and the evidence suggests that it was not), he could easily have heard or read accounts of her interpretation, accounts that invariably point to her famous transgression from song to passionate speech at the climactic moment of Fidelio's self-revelation as Florestan's ever-faithful wife Leonora (yet another sense of *Selbstentäußerung?*) when she cries out to the villain Pizarro, "Tödt' erst sein *Weib*!" (First kill his *wife*!). This transgression into speech epitomized the challenge to operatic values expressed by Schröder-Devrient's whole theatrical profile: the sacrifice of vocal beauty for dramatic truth in the aim of complete, uncompromising identification with character and situation. Claire von Glümer's description of how this interpretation was coined no doubt corresponds to something like what Wagner might have heard from the singer directly, either when they first became acquainted in 1835 or when he was in regular contact with her in Dresden in the 1840s. Since we may never know for sure what Wagner did hear of this role (or when), Glümer's "authentic" account can at least suggest to us what he imagined, which was based as well on those performances we know he *did* hear, starting from the 1834 *Capuleti*. Glümer's account of this other key role, likewise presented in terms of the singer's own recollections, further reinforces the concept of the singing actor's complete, almost trance-like identification with her role.

Henry Chorley, who wrote for the weekly journal *The Athenaeum*, heard most of the leading Italian and French operatic singers of the fertile era from the 1830s through the 1850s. Against this international standard he judges Schröder-Devrient as something of an interesting aberration, characteristic of certain German ideals that were, of course, assiduously cultivated by Wagner in distinction to Italian or French ideals of bel canto vocal virtuosity. For his part, Chorley remained a devotee of the latter school and fundamentally resistant to the early works of Wagner. Apart from Mendelssohn, whose cult in Victorian England he did much to foster, Chorley was critical of most German Romantic music, despite several extended musical tours of Germany and Austria between 1839 and 1846.[14]

Henry Chorley's picture of Dresden and its operatic establishment is included in the first volume of his collection *Modern German Music* ("Glimpses at Dresden in 1839–40"), and is drawn from his earlier travelogue, *Music and Manners in France and Germany*.[15] It describes the place very much as Wagner would have found it upon returning home in 1842 after his various misadventures in northern Germany, East Prussia, and Paris over the previous decade. The chapter also includes an extended description— not included here—of Weber's *Euryanthe* performed at Dresden in 1839 with favorable accounts of Schröder-Devrient in the title role and the tenor Josef Tichatschek (later Wagner's first Rienzi and Tannhäuser) as Adolar.[16] The second excerpt supplements those personal observations of Dresden with other experiences of Schröder-Devrient and of Wagner's earlier operas, primarily *Tannhäuser*. Like other early critics of that work represented in the present volume, Chorley's response is a mixture of admiration and revulsion, conceding the unusual talent and imagination of the composer but regretting much about the willful, unconventional manner in which it is manifested in the opera as he hears it.

Footnotes reproduced on the page are from the original document. All endnotes are the translator's.

CLAIRE VON GLÜMER
Recollections of Wilhelmine Schröder-Devrient
Leipzig, 1862

Already during her father's lifetime Wilhelmine and her sister retired from the ballet.[17] Now she began to make good her heretofore scanty education, while also preparing herself for more serious theatrical endeavors under the instruction of her talented mother.[18] For the academic side of her education her half brother Wilhelm Smets, the only son of Sophie Schröder's first marriage, took enthusiastic charge. He had come to Vienna as a house-tutor and was fondly reunited there with his mother and the oldest of his sisters, having lived six years apart from them and just now recognizing his sister's unusual gifts.

In 1819 the fifteen-year-old Wilhelmine made her theatrical debut. With growing success she appeared as Aricie in *Phèdre*, Melitta in *Sappho*, Luise in *Kabale und Liebe*, Beatrice in *The Bride of Messina*, Ophelia in *Hamlet*.[19] And at the same time her musical gifts were becoming equally apparent: her voice developed in strength and beauty of tone, she received instruction from Madame Grünbaum and from Josef Mozatti, and not more than a year had passed before she was able to yield to the irresistible urge to exchange the spoken drama for opera.

First she appeared as Pamina in *The Magic Flute*—this was on January 20, 1821. The *Allgemeine musikalische Zeitung* wrote about this, in the somewhat affected style of those days:

> Demoiselle Schröder realized a perfect picture of the most delicate femininity. As long as this character, so faintly depicted by the poet, has been represented on our stages in similarly vague outlines, perhaps no theatrical mime has come closer to drawing out the ideal-poetic side from the prosaic libretto than this pupil of a mother who herself has reached the highest stages of mastery in her craft; and this offers a rare demonstration of how infinitely such common dialogue can be elevated by means of sense, nature, and feeling.[20]

And this Pamina, whose first performance set an example for all interpreters of the role of Pamina, was all of sixteen years old!

Wilhelmine pursued with great diligence the path on which she had embarked so successfully. As early as March of the same year she performed Emmeline in *Die Schweizerfamilie*,[21] the next month Maria in Grétry's *Barbe-Bleu*,[22] and then when Weber's *Freischütz* had its Viennese premiere, the part of Agathe was entrusted to our youthful artist.

On March 7, 1822, *Der Freischütz*, which had put all of Vienna into a frenzy, was given a second time, now as a benefit for Wilhelmine. The house was packed, and the level of enthusiasm—even for the enthusiastic Viennese—was unprecedented. Weber conducted the opera himself, and the high spirits of his admirers made it almost impossible for the performance to go on. As Agathe, Wilhelmine shared in the evening's triumph. She was exactly the blond, pure, gentle maiden the composer and the poet had dreamed of—a simple, modest child all a-quiver with her dreams, lost in reverie, yet finding in love and faith the strength to overcome all the powers of hell.

As evidence of how much a child she really was at that time, Wilhelmine recounts how when Weber came the next morning to congratulate her, she was lying outstretched on the floor, engrossed in setting up toy soldiers with her younger siblings.

In Dresden, too, where Wilhelmine accompanied her famous mother in the summer of 1822, her beauty as well as her talent aroused much admiration; but that which was to make her one of the greatest dramatic singers of all times, the irresistible magic and power of her genius, truly revealed itself only when she returned to Vienna and sang in *Fidelio*.

For some time the opera had been out of the repertoire, since no singer adequate to the leading role was to be found. Then a revival was proposed for November 1822 to celebrate the name day of the Empress, the demanding role of Fidelio being assigned to the seventeen-year-old Wilhelmine.

When Beethoven learned of this he was said to have expressed his considerable dissatisfaction that this exalted figure should be entrusted to "such a child." But so it was decided. Sophie Schröder taught her daughter the role as best she could and the work went into rehearsal.[23]

Beethoven insisted on conducting the performances himself, and he did indeed wield the baton in the dress rehearsal. Wilhelmine had never set eyes on him before. She was sore afraid when she beheld the master (whose ears were by then closed to all sound) gesticulating wildly, his hair in wild abandon, his features distorted and his eyes alight with an uncanny glare. If the music was to be played *piano* he nearly crept beneath the music stand, for the *forte* he sprung up, emitting the most extraordinary sounds. The orchestra and the singers fell into confusion, and after the rehearsal the music director Umlauf had the sorry task of informing the composer that it would be impossible to charge him with conducting the opera.

So it was that, on the evening of the first performance, he sat directly behind the conductor, entirely wrapped in his overcoat, so that only his glowering eyes could be seen. Wilhelmine was afraid of these eyes, and became quite terrified. But no sooner had she spoken her first lines than she felt herself suffused with wonderful energy. Beethoven and the whole public disappeared from her view—any sense of laborious, piecemeal study fell away. She herself was now Leonora, she lived and suffered through every scene.

Up to the scene in the dungeon she remained filled with this illusion, but then her energy began to fail. She knew that she lacked the means to carry out what must next be represented onstage. This growing unease found expression in her bearing, her features, her movements—and yet all of this was so apt to the situation that it made the most compelling impression on the audience. The assembled public sat there in breathless silence—which can affect the dramatic artist just as powerfully as the loudest applause.

Leonora summons her courage and flings herself between her husband and the dagger of the murderer. The dreaded moment has arrived, and she is seized with sheer despair; more shouting than singing, she emits the heartrending line:

Tödt' erst sein Weib!	First kill his wife!

Pizarro tries again to thrust her back, but she then draws the pistol from her blouse and aims it at the murderer. He falls back, while she remains motionless, still threatening him. And now the trumpets announce the rescue, and she relaxes the tension she has so long maintained. No sooner had she managed to force the criminal to the exit, holding the pistol in her outstretched hand, than she let drop the weapon—by now she was deathly tired from this terrible strain, her knees shaking; she leaned back and put her hands to her forehead, involuntarily emitting that famous, unmusical cry which later interpreters of the role have sought to emulate, with such poor results. With Wilhelmine this was truly a cry of distress, searing the listener's heart. Only when, in response to Florestan's outburst:

Mein Weib, was hast du um mich geduldet!	My wife, what you have suffered on my account!

she fell into her husband's arms, declaring, half sobbing and half triumphant:

Nichts, nichts, nichts!	Nothing, nothing, nothing!

only then did the magic spell, which had held every heart in thrall, finally yield. A storm of applause broke out that would not stop. The artist had discovered her Fidelio, and however much and however earnestly she continued to work on this role, its fundamental outlines remained the same.

Beethoven, too, recognized Wilhelmine as his true Leonora. He was not able to hear the actual sound of her voice, but the spirit of her singing was revealed to him in every trait of her face, radiant with inspiration, and in the glowing vitality of her whole appearance. After the performance he went to her. His eyes, otherwise so fierce, were now smiling at her; he patted her cheeks, thanked her for her Fidelio, and promised to compose a new opera for her. Unfortunately, it was never to happen.

The next year the young artist had the opportunity of performing the difficult role of Fidelio under the direction of Carl Maria von Weber. On April 2, 1823, the maestro wrote to Böttiger: "I cannot give *Fidelio* until I have the little Schröder girl here."[24] She soon arrived in Dresden and after eight rehearsals made her debut there in the role. After the performance of April 29 Weber wrote in his diary: "Minna was outstanding, and was justly applauded." . . .

About the role of Romeo [in Bellini's *I Capuleti e i Montecchi*] she wrote to Emmy la Grua, who, like many others, had sought her advice and instruction:

The greatest difficulty posed by this role is the fact that it was written for a woman.[25] The artist is thus faced with the terribly difficult task of forgetting her own sex and representing in her bearing, movement, and stance a fiery youth, suffused with the glow of his first love. Nothing must betray her sex if the whole situation is not to devolve into absurdity. She must walk, stand, and kneel down like a man; she must draw her dagger and prepare for combat like a practiced fighter; and above all there must be no feminine traces in her costume: no delicate locks, no corseted feet, no elegant waistline. No less important is the proper manner of taking on and off hats or gloves.

Wilhelmine Schröder-Devrient knew how to combine all these details into a living whole. From the first entrance of Romeo, where he appears at the head of his warriors with proud step and head defiantly aloft, offering terms of peace to the Capulets, to the last cry of his death struggle, his final sinking down upon Juliet's bier, she knew how to portray the proud patrician son and the young enamored hero in every glance, every movement of the lips or hands, translating Shakespeare's figure back into the Bellini opera. . . .

[Wilhelmine Schröder-Devrient] told us repeatedly how Romeo, afterward one of her favorite roles, had first been "revealed" to her. *I Capuleti e i Montecchi* was given in Dresden first by the Italian opera troupe, and Signora Schiafetti sang the part of Romeo. Returning from an extended holiday Wilhelmine saw one performance of the opera, but she found neither the awkward libretto nor the shallow music any more to her taste than did the rest of the audience. Then suddenly she received a copy of the part with the direction that she was to learn it within eight days so as to take over from the ailing Signora Schiafetti. Wilhelmine was horrified at this demand. It seemed to her an impossibility to learn this extensive role in such a short time, and in a foreign language as well. All the same, she went to work and succeeded in memorizing the music by the given deadline. Yet the figure she was to represent remained alien to her, she could not warm to it; she felt unsure, convinced that she would not be able to accomplish much while in this mood. "This feeling of constraint vanished as soon as I found myself in costume," she said,

but now, instead, I found myself seized with a sort of giddiness. When the final curtain descended I had no idea of what or how I had sung and acted. The public showered me with applause, but I could not say why. It was like a dream. Instead of changing my clothes, as I normally would, I merely asked for my coat; I went home and threw myself on the sofa, still in the costume of Romeo, and with my hands behind my head I stared at the ceiling, eyes wide open, until five o'clock in the morning.

During this time the opera was running through my head, scene by scene. When at dawn I stood up from my resting place I had absorbed the role into the very core of my being, and ever since I have sung it with great enthusiasm.

The artist was nearly always so fully immersed in her task while performing that everything around her was similarly enlivened and spiritualized. Asked once how they perceived the scenery while they were performing on stage, the singers Jenny Lind, Henriette Sontag, and Wilhelmine Schröder-Devrient gave answers entirely characteristic for each of them. Jenny Lind said: "For me, the scenery does not exist; I have no idea what it is there for. I enter, and have no further thoughts than that I am singing, that I must sing." Henriette Sontag responded: "While engaged in my work I always regard the scenic decorations for what they are, but I am always at pains to use them for my own artistic ends, to whatever extent this is possible. I think and feel my way into the scene to the point where it can inspire me, but never to the point of forgetting what is before me." Wilhelmine Schröder-Devrient answered: "Of course, it is all just so much stuff and rubbish to me, but it must also become for me what I wish it to be. It must be imbued with spirit, so that it seems truly to live. Soon again, it will be just bare rubbish, but at the moment, the trees seem truly to rustle, the flowers to breathe, the fountains to purl, the stars to shine, the storm to flash and rage. Whoever cannot see these things this way will himself never be able to flash or rage."

If the too frequent repetition of an opera resulted in the loss of this illusion, then she had to put aside the role, even if one of her favorites. It was a mystery to her how French actors could play the same role a hundred times on end, always exactly the same and with the same success. When once she had to perform in *Fidelio* in London eight times in a row, she had to put it aside afterward for some time; her diary attests to the fact that this occurred in other instances as well. Once, following a performance of *Fidelio*, she writes:

Today I could not get the gears of my feelings properly going; these seemed to grind and rattle most disconcertingly amid Beethoven's divine harmonies. Our dreadful, drafty temple of the muses* (if only hell would send a fire to destroy it!) caused my whole body to shiver with the bitter cold, and the physical cold transferred itself to the soul, which today seemed to me a veritable icicle, from which the heavenly tones of the Master could thaw but a few, isolated drops.[26] One's enthusiasm cannot always be raised up to the proper pitch. Today I simply lacked moral strength, nor is it easy to draw one's warmth from the feeble souls of the public; no matter how hard one strikes, no sparks are to be had from that quarter.

HENRY CHORLEY
Glimpses at Dresden in 1839–40,
with matter concerning a later period

Chapter 1. The Opera and its Envrions—1839.
(London, 1854)

Thirteen years ago, the railroad travelling of Germany had features which were all its own. In England, the tendency, from the first, was to whirl "the human parcel" from place to place along with an irresistible rapidity entirely precluding the possibility of thought, or conversation, or enjoyment; and to make of the journey a disagreeable, bewildering dream, compounded of several blasts of the shrill steam-whistle—a few tunnels—a few broken clamours, timid or troublesome, of passengers on their entrance and exit—perhaps a few broken limbs—the best part of which is its close. . . . But betwixt Leipsic [*sic*] and Dresden was to be seen, in 1839–40, a national propensity in its ripest development; —I mean the disposition of the best-hearted hosts, and soundest instrumentalists of Europe, to stop on every possible occasion—"*etwas zu essen.*"[27]

I cannot describe how whimsically this wonderful appetite struck me on my journeys to Dresden in 1839. The train I used started from Leipsic an hour after the early dinner; when the copious repast might surely, one would have thought, have sufficed for a part, at least, of the afternoon. No such thing. At every one of the six or eight stations between the two towns—fruit, cakes, cups of broth, glasses of brandy, squares of sodden pastry with plums imbedded therein, biscuits, sandwiches, plums, pears, and other garden *et cetera*, were proffered to the caravan, from baskets of hawkers, and in the station-houses. Nor were they proffered in vain: old and young, women and

* The old theater in Dresden.

men—already provided, in nine cases out of ten, with a travelling provision against famine—partook of them with a zeal and an intrepidity which, every time I witnessed it, recalled to me *Petruchio's* disdainful exclamation—

"Nothing but sit and sit, and eat and eat!"[28]

Comfortable in beguiling the way as were these interludes, such are not precisely the best imaginable preparations for Dresden. The Saxon capital, both on first sight and on a subsequent visit, has impressed me with a peculiar feeling of its elegance which is not to be described without the entertainer of it being considered Della Cruscan[29] and fantastic—at least not in work-a-day prose.

On the Bruhl Terrace,
October, 1840

THERE hangs a tranquil and peculiar spell
   O'er dome, and ample bridge, and rapid stream,
   And dim fantastic palace, where the gleam
Of ghostly shapes, methinks, would glimmer well
At dead midnight. Autumn should ever dwell,
   Rich, fading town, with thee! Here I could dream
   Whole days away o'er some sweet solemn theme
Of mystic Fancy, careless how the bell
   Of noisy life importunately tolled
Its children to their tasks. Ay, and such hours,
By some esteemed more worthless than the flowers
   Which drop in silence ere their bells unfold,
Show not our heaviest debt for wasted powers,
   On Truth's eternal chronicle enrolled!

Even the excitements of the far-famed gallery,[30] with its *Madonna del Sisto*, its Reading Magdalen, and its *Christo della Moneta*, —where I lingered for two hours every morning, till eye and mind could receive no more, —could not neutralize the agreeable and soothing impression which the stately Saxon city produced on my mind. Of the ways of its people I know nothing beyond the universal report, which apportions to it a cheerful and cultivated society of refined intelligences. But I have never stayed in a town in which the idea of complete insulation brought with it so little of dreariness—where so many thoughts, and feelings, and fancies, seemed to rise up as companions. I can picture to myself no better residence for any one occupied in the absorbing task of imaginative creation; and, to push speculation one point further, I never passed the door of the house of Herr Tieck,[31] who then lived in the Altmarkt, without feeling as if a certain harmony existed between his fantastic and spiritual tales, and the city of his adoption. This perhaps may be fond trifling; but the musical pleasures of Dresden, in 1839–40, were solid and real—marked with "a white stone" in the calendar of my experiences. —There, on my visit in 1839, I first made acquaintance with the "Euryanthe" of Weber. . . .

The environs of Dresden are beautiful: the suburban houses show more marks of a refined taste in floriculture than I have elsewhere seen in Germany. The road rises gently; and the city, seen as I then beheld it, —with the mist of early day wreathing the beehive-like dome of Our Lady's Church[32] and the spires round it, and the Elbe below and behind the bridge lying under a mantle of deep empurpled shadow, —makes as fair a town-picture as one of those splendid clusters of Italian architecture which Gaspar Poussin loved to build in his landscapes.[33] Advancing further, the banks of the Elbe are striped and dotted with vineyards, among which the rough road winds; almost every half mile curving so as to pass through or escape some of the clean red-roofed *witz*-es (*witz* being as favourite a termination to the names of villages near Dresden as *rode* is in the Harz) which, half composed of garden-houses, half of cottages, are as tempting nooks as poet or musician could retreat to for summer residence.[34] Tottering over the road, like the last tower of a brokendown fortress, and clinging to the wall which keeps the soil up to the roots of the vines, a tiny closet is shown, where Schiller wrote his "Don Carlos." Another little mansion—but a modest one even for a house in a German *weinberg*[35]—saw the birth of Weber's "Oberon." This last is about half-way betwixt the beautiful city and that wild and elvish district, where gigantic rocks, of every menacing and capricious form, strangely overlean the Elbe,[36] and seem to tell of some such miracle performed in the days of "the good people" as was wrought by him who

. . . . "cleft Eildon hills in three."[37]

I gazed wistfully at the cabinets where the poet and musician had carried on their alchemy; but more, I confess, to possess myself of a distinct impression of their aspect, than with that intense enthusiasm which some enjoy on all due occasions: —happy in having feelings like chimes, which cannot fail to answer to the touch, whatever be the mood of the moment, or whosoever hand it be that puts down the key. —Yet it was impossible, even for my slow self, not to be alive to the influences which such a picturesquely placed habitation might have exercised over one whom I have always fancied to have been largely acted upon by the sights and sounds of Nature. —In another point of view, however, on regarding them from a distance, the environs of Dresden seem to me less friendly to the genius of Weber. Not far from this summer residence of his is Pillnitz—the country palace of the Kings of Saxony. I only looked towards it that morning as towards a building of the heaviest possible architecture; the work of some German Vanbrugh.[38] Had I known as much as I have since done, it might not have been the least suggestive station of my Elbe pilgrimage in 1839.

In that dull and grand-looking mansion was preserved, in the composer's time, and, for aught I know, exists to this day, a rag of feudalism, to speak metaphorically, —one of the old condescensions of Royalty, by which the earthenware was allowed to approach the porcelain of society, and Cloth of Frieze to become acquainted with the splendours of Cloth of Gold. The rulers of Saxony dined in public, and dined at two o'clock. More than one friend has graphically described to me the primitive and old-world figures that feasted the eyes of those admitted to the balcony, where common men might learn what and how their rulers eat. There came homely old princes, with white hair, and breeches which never knew what braces meant; —a watch in each fob (in the exploded *macaroni* fashion), and long, long *queues*, those simplest of all symbols of etiquette. There might be seen stately and substantial ladies, decorated in all the German *grandezza* which so amused Bettina when Goethe's mother dressed herself to receive Madame de Staël.[39] There might be smelt the miscellaneously arranged odours of things savoury and things sweet which distinguish a German dinner. There might be heard (O shame to a music-loving family like the Royalties of Saxony!), among the noises of knives and forks and the bustling of perspiring servitors, the tinkle of a pianoforte, or the screech of an Italian air, sung by some well-worn *cantatrice*, who had been lured from the macaroni and *polenta* of her own land to become a fixture at the court of Saxony.[40] And those who looked to see who the pianist might be (compelled, poor soul! to wear a full court dress for the occasion) must have turned away, wondering at the odd forms taken by the much-vaunted patronage of Music in Germany, —especially if they were gifted with the spirit of prophecy, and had already picked up the conviction that a new and brilliant genius was abroad in the person of Carl Maria von Weber!

I confess, whenever I reflect upon such an appropriation of the services of Genius as this—when I think of the *"Concert-Stück"* disturbed by the stirring of a salad, or of the exquisite *Sonata* in A flat, Op. 39, passing unheard in the midst of the discussion of those mighty puddings in which a German cook excels—the corruption of Radicalism rises strong within me. I verily believe, that had I known the nature of the duty which the position of Weber at Dresden demanded from him, while I was in the full glow of enthusiasm consequent on the enjoyment of "Euryanthe," I must have shaken the dust of Pillnitz from my feet, with something of a bitter and disdainful feeling, —instead of turning round and admiring the fine but heavy group which it made when seen in conjunction with two embrowned chestnut trees, ere a sudden bend in the road to Löhmen hid it from my sight.

HENRY CHORLEY
Glimpses at Dresden in 1839–40, with matter concerning a later period

Chapter 3. The Opera from 1840 to 1848.
(London, 1854)

In the interval betwixt the years 1840 and 1848, the losses of the Dresden Opera were heavier than its gains. The great actress [Wilhelmine Schröder-Devrient] who threw all her strength and emotion into Weber's Shakspearian [*sic*] opera, ceased to appear on the stage;[41] and the creative efforts made in the theatre, did not bring to light a new genius so much as a new element of decay and destruction for music.

The decline of Madame Schröder Devrient was more rapid than it should have been in a singer who is some years younger than the century. —But, in truth, a singer the lady never was, though she promised to become one in the early days when she appeared as *Pamina* in "Die Zauberflöte" at Vienna.[42] Her voice, since I have known it, was capable of conveying poignant or tender expression, but was harsh, and torn—not so inflexible as incorrect. —It is a mistake to fancy that the German *prime donne* decline to attempt making an effect with executive brilliancy; they are as prodigal of *roulades* and shakes as the rest of the sisterhood—giving, however, the attempt in place of the reality; and only when their incompetency is made evident by comparison, falling back on that classical defence which sounds so well, costs so little, and has deceived so many, —"*What would you have? I am a German singer.*" —Madame Schröder Devrient resolved to be *par excellence* "the German dramatic singer." Earnest and intense as was her possession of the parts she attempted, her desire of presenting herself was little less vehement. —There is no possibility of an opera being performed by a company, each of whom should be as resolute as she was never to rest, never for an instant to allow the spectator to forget his presence. She cared not whether she broke the flow of the composition, by some cry hardly on any note, or in any scale—by even *speaking* some word, for which she would not trouble herself to study the right musical emphasis or inflexion—provided, only, she succeeded in continuing to arrest the attention. Hence, in part, arose her extraordinary success in

"Fidelio." That opera contains, virtually, only one acting character, — and with her it rests to intimate the thrilling secret of the whole story, to develope [*sic*] this link by link, in presence of the public, and to give the drama the importance of terror, suspense, and rapture when the spell is broken, by exhibiting the agony and the struggle of which she is the incessant victim. If the devotion, the disguise, and the hope of *Leonora*, the wife, were not for ever before us, the interest of the prison-opera would flag and wane into a cheerless and incurable melancholy. This Madame Schröder Devrient took care that it should never do. From her first entry upon the stage, it might be seen that there was a purpose at her heart, which could make the weak strong, and the timid brave; quickening every sense, nerving every fibre, arming its possessor with disguise against curiosity, with persuasion more powerful than any obstacle, with expedients equal to every emergency. Though in what may be called the culminating point of the drama—the grave-digging scene in the vault—Malibran[43] was the more fearful of the two, by her intense southern fervour, which blazed the brighter for its having been so forcibly constrained, —as regards the entire treatment of the part, Madame Schröder Devrient had the advantage. There was a life's love in the intense and trembling eagerness with which she passed in review the prisoners, when they were allowed to come forth into the air—for *he* might be among them! There was something subduing in the look of speechless affection with which she at last undid the chains of the beloved one, saved by her love—the mere remembrance of which makes the heart throb, and the eyes fill. —In "Norma," and "La Sonnambula," Madame Schröder Devrient failed, owing to her deficiency in vocal accomplishment. In the former, too, she too freely indulged in the tendency of the Germans to attitudinize, when a queen or a priestess is the personage to be enacted. —I thought her *Valentine*, in "Les Huguenots," too much of a virago. There was not a touch of the French noble's daughter in her demeanour; she was the impetuous, angry, persecuted woman, whose hour of virgin elegance and virgin reserve had long been over. — But in another less popular work, the impression left by her on me was deep. This was in M. Chélard's "Macbeth;" an opera which, in spite of the preposterous arrangement of the *libretto*, and of some music little less preposterous in its difficulty (considering it as calculated for German songstresses), contains some good points—some fine concerted pieces.[44] None of these, however, dwell in my memory so vividly as the demeanour of the *Lady Macbeth*. One could not look at her without at once recollecting the ideal which Mrs. Siddons is reported to have conceived of this "grand, fiendish" character (to use her own epithets).[45] "She had an idea," says Mrs. Jameson, "that *Lady Macbeth* must, from her Celtic origin, have been a small, fair, blue-eyed woman. Bonduca, Fredegonde, Brunehault,

and other Amazons of the Gothic ages, were of this complexion." Save in
stature, the great German operatic actress (daughter by the way to the great
Lady Macbeth of Germany, "*die grosse* Schröder")[46] gave full justification
to this fancy. With an alluring and dignified grace of manner was combined an aspect of evil—a sinister, far-reaching expression in her eyes, all
the more terrible for their being at variance with those hues and contours which we have been used to associate with innocence and the tender
affections. That which makes the flesh creep, in the name of "the *White
Devil*,"* spoke in every line of Madame Schröder Devrient's face—in her
honeyed and humble smile, as she welcomed the doomed King; in the mixture of ferocity and blandishment thrown by her into the scene of the
murder; in the ghastly soliloquy of the soul that waked when the body
was asleep. When I think of Pasta, as *Medea*,[47] watching the bridal train
pass by her, with her scarlet mantle gathered round her, the figure of
Madame Schröder Devrient's *Lady Macbeth*, too, rises, as one of those visions
concerning which young men are apt to rave and old men to dote. Apart
from its musical interest, the stage has had few more striking personations.

But, except in the right of this inborn, inbred genius, the German and
the Italian artist can hardly be mentioned on the same page. What Pasta
would be, in spite of her uneven, rebellious, uncertain voice—a most magnificent singer—Madame Schröder Devrient did not care to be; though
Nature, I have been assured, by those who heard her sing when a girl, had
blessed her with a fresh, delicious *soprano* voice. In this respect, she is but
one among the hundreds who have suffered from the ignorance and
folly of German connoisseurship—from the obstinacy of national antipathy, which, so soon as Germany began to imagine the possibility of possessing
an opera of its own, made it penal to sing with grace, taste, and vocal self-
command; because such were the characteristics of the Italian method.
—Had she been trained under a wiser dispensation, Madame Schröder
Devrient might have been singing by the side of Madame Sontag at this
very day; and, when she retired, might have left behind her the character of a great dramatic vocalist, instead of the fame of a powerful actress
who appeared in some German operas.

The Opera House at Dresden, during the years preceding the Revolution
of 1848, also witnessed the production of certain musical dramas, by one
who has since made some noise in the world, and who is likely to make

---

* When Nature can be *contradicted* by the might of power and passion within the frame,
the effect is always more fearful than when she co-operates with sinister deeds and emotions by sinister preparations. Thus, there are few personations that I have heard so often
referred to for their terrible fascination as the *Lucrezia Borgia* of Madame Ungher; —an
undersized, colourless woman, without any extraordinary beauty, nobility, or wicked-
ness of countenance.

more—noise, strictly speaking, —not music. I mean Herr Wagner, whose "Rienzi" had already been given in Dresden at the time of my second visit thither, and who was named as *kapellmeister* by the King of Saxony under conditions of almost friendly generosity. In 1840, Herr Wagner was not openly revolutionary; being in composition apparently an imitator of the least amiable peculiarities of Herr Meyerbeer, and showing, it may be apprehended, few signs of that spirit, which, in later times—those of the German riots of 1848—sent him out upon a barricade with the purpose of discrowning the very King whose bread he had been eating.* "Rienzi" was pronounced to be dull, overcharged, and very long. It was endured as a work belonging to Dresden, as other operatic pieces of dullness in other German capitals have been, but, I believe, followed the common lot of local successes, and never travelled far beyond the barriers of the Saxon capital.

It would seem as if the favour with which this "Rienzi" was received, and the position in which its composer was placed, ripened to fever heat that desire to distinguish himself in progress by destruction, which passes for a generous ambition with persons imperfectly organized or crookedly cultivated. But earlier than this, a prophet, an innovator, a celebrity, Herr Wagner had resolved to be; and—weak in musical gifts—he appears to have entered on his quest of greatness by a profound contempt of all other musical celebrities. The confessions which he has recently published,[48] reveal an amount of arrogant and irritable disdain for all opera composers save himself, happily rare in the annals of artistic self-assertion. —His point of departure was to be the union of poetry and music. Operas were to be made of an exquisite completeness, in which both arts were to find the very fullest expression; and since *librettists*, however ingenious, are not always the best of poets, Herr Wagner (wisely enough) resolved to be his own *librettist*.

In this capacity he has proved himself to be strong and felicitous as an inventor, though less excellent as a lyrist, than his self-commendation would have us believe. The wild sea-tale of "The Flying Dutchman" was a happy choice for his second opera, in one desiring to please by legendary interest, grown weary of grand historical pictures in which there is no history;

---

* In justification of the censure conveyed in the above phrase, the English reader must be reminded that many of the musical appointments about German theatres are direct court appointments; and that unhappily for both the aristocratic and the popular side of the question, the courts of Germany do not yet represent the people. The *maestro* was presented by the King to his people of Dresden rather than forced by the people of Dresden upon their King. "But Wagner meant well," said an earnest and thorough-going defender of the composer with whom I was discussing the baseness and disloyalty (in the large sense) of his political courses; "he meant well, I assure you. He was really very fond of his King. He would have made him President of the Republic!"

or of comic intrigues of "cloak and sword," in which there is more intrigue than comedy, and more "cloak and sword" (or costume) than either! —This second opera was completed, —words and music, —while Herr Wagner was resident in Paris; and was offered by him to the managers of the *Grand Opera* there. —They were wise: —recognized the strange, supernatural capability of the drama, but were repelled by the extravagance and crudity of the music. Accordingly they rejected the score, and purchased the poem. —They were less wise, however, in entrusting the latter to be set by their worthy chorus-master, M. Dietsch, since he succeeded in producing music less acceptable than even the original composition by Herr Wagner might have been —and thus killed the story.

Herr Wagner's "Fliegende Holländer" was produced complete at Dresden; and there, in spite of direct royal patronage, in spite of a certain novelty of style, in spite of the acceptance of "Rienzi," and the vogue brought to every theatre by fitting up a genius of its own, the opera, I am assured, failed on its representation. Such immediate failure we know to be no criterion of ultimate success, or intrinsic merit; but it seems to me explained, since I have perused the music.[49] A spinning song and chorus is to be remembered as pleasing, characteristic; a wild sea-tune, too, as being audaciously broken in rhythm, and built on a phrase of the most desperate platitude; but the rest of the work produced on me merely an impression of grim violence and dreary vagueness, which, till then at least, had never been produced in such a fullness of ugliness by the music of a clever man.

Next in order came Herr Wagner's "Tannhaüser" [*sic*].[50] This opera was given for the first time at Dresden in the year 1845, with Madame Schröder Devrient, Mademoiselle Wagner,[51] and Herr Tichatschek[52] in the principal characters; and at Dresden excited the highest temporary enthusiasm on its production. Though the rapture was, at that period, communicated to no other German theatre, considering the events which have followed the rehabilitation of the opera by Dr. Liszt at Weimar, —it is a work to be spoken of in some detail, as the latest appearance in composition previous to 1848, that may make some figure in the annals of German opera. . . .[53]

Meagre as is the above sketch, it will be seen from it that "Tannhaüser" has no common opera book; and that with such a theme, a picture of romantic and elevated beauty might have been wrought by a hand worthy to treat it. If ever subject was musical this is—simple, suggestive, rich in colour, rich in contrast, rich in poetry. —But how am I to speak of the manner in which the musician has set his own drama? I shall hardly be able to represent my impressions without appearing to those, who have not suffered under this extraordinary opera, in the light of one indulging in hyperbole and caricature; for, in truth, I have never been so blanked, pained, wearied,* *insulted* even (the word is not too strong), by a work of pretension as by this same "Tannhaüser." I could not have conceived it possible that any clever person could deliberately produce what seems to me so false, paradoxical, and at such fierce variance with true artistic feeling, on system, before I sat through the opera, and read the "Hallelujah" vented by its maker in homage to his new revelations, which he has been tempted by his own vanity and by the injudicious praise of others, to put forth.

The first general idea derived from Herr Wagner's music to this romantic story, was its entire discordance with its subject. For how could be imagined [any] tale which gave wider scope for melody? —melody sacred in the pilgrims' canticle—melody voluptuous in the court of *Dame Venus*— melody chivalresque in the minstrel contest. In accordance with this spirit a large part of the *libretto* is written in tolerable rhymed verse. Yet it may be asserted, that no opera existed before "Tannhaüser,"—since the cradle-days of Opera—so totally barren of rhythmical melody; the two subjects on which the overture is based being absolutely the only two *motivi* deserving the name from beginning to end of the drama. Now, wherefore (on system or no system), if the pilgrims were allowed a tune, the minstrels were to be denied one, it would puzzle Herr Wagner to tell. What is more noticeable, one of the two said melodies, the pilgrims' hymn, is as utterly clear of the character of a canticle as the *notturno* in Mendelssohn's "Midsummer Night's Dream" music, being a tuneable and graceful strain, but in no respect, either as regards intrinsic character or established form, religious. It would seem as if chance had determined the proceedings of a musician more poor in melodic inspiration than any predecessor or contemporary; that when a tune had presented itself, he used it without caring for its fitness—that when tunes would not come, he forced his way along by a recitative as uncouth and tasteless as it is ambitious,—and as if his system had come upon him as an after-thought, by way of apology for himself, and depreciation of his betters. —To return,—in the magic cave, so harsh, shrill, crackling, and grotesque are the sounds of chorus and dance which surround *Dame Venus*, as to spirit up associations anything rather than voluptuous or fascinating—strange whimsies of skeleton dances in the air, with their distant (but not dulcet) sound of lean bones rattling.

---

* It is fair to state, that though Herr Wagner, by the production of the opera in question, had taken his place as one of the composers of young Germany, some years before the Revolution of 1848 (his "Tannhaüser" thus legitimately coming within the range of this work)—my own acquaintance with its music on the stage is of more recent date. Hence, I have not been called upon to mitigate my impressions under the idea which should never be lost sight of, that distance may lend exasperation to the temper, as well as enchantment to the view. —1853.

—Then the minstrel contest, instead of its offering a flow of song, growing deeper, wider, more musical, and more impassioned, as enthusiasm kindles enthusiasm in the strife, is but a heavy preachment of several men, set to meagre and formless harp accompaniment. A wearisome straining after literal, verbal expression in music (which, however plausible, is utterly false as a principle if it is perpetually employed) is maintained throughout this work, till the ear no longer retains the power of being moved; and by the time that the great scene of the third act was reached—that in which *Tannhaüser* narrates his pilgrimage to Rome to his brethren in song—my attention, wearied by unfulfilled expectation, and abused by one discordant scene after another, refused any longer to follow a work in which every sensation of pleasure, and every principle of beauty, were so ceaselessly outraged. I remember the howling, whining, bawling of Herr Tichatschek (to sing, or vocally to declaim this scene is impossible) accompanied with and disturbed by an orchestra, infuriate where it was not confused, but all idea of art or poetical sensation is gone. What the new thing may be which Herr Wagner has put in its place, let others dispute and decide—it has, at all events, no affinity with that which the masters of the musical stage have done before him.

But allowing this opera to be accepted as a symphony,* accompanied by scenery, bearing part in a drama intoned rather than sung, I cannot fin[d] its symphonic or orchestral portion much more admirable than the wild and over-wrought recitative, which it is to check, support, and alternate. "Fidelio" may, in some respect, be called a symphonic opera also, inasmuch as there, too, the instrumental part is more interesting than the vocal portion of the work; but who that knows "Fidelio" does not know it by the wonderful variety and spirit of Beethoven's orchestral devices? Or, to take a newer instance, on a first hearing of Herr Meyerbeer's operas, the ear, if it can receive nothing else, is cognizant of new and peculiar sonorities. I remember, as if it was only yesterday, the delicious impression first produced on me in 1836, by the scoring of the first and second acts of "Les Huguenots"; in such scenes as the one where *Raoul* is among the gallants peeping through the window at *Valentine*; or, in the interlude of the second act preluding the grand *aria* of *Marguerite de Valois*. No such felicities did my ears derive

---

* Thus must Herr Wagner's operas be accepted, if the composer's thought and purpose are to be met sympathetically, and if his choir of admirers are to be believed. I was speaking to one of them of the utter ruin which must overtake vocal art, if composers followed in the wake of their idol, and, for the sake of the orchestra, like him utterly debased and barbarized the *cantilena* under pretext of truth in declamation. "In six years more," said I, "if this system be accepted, you will not have an artist left capable of singing an air by Handel or Mozart." "Well, what matter," was the quiet answer; "there has been enough of singing."

from "Tannhäuser." To me the instrumentation of that opera is singularly unpleasant—as too preposterous to be overlooked, too untrue to its own conditions to be accepted as a charming monster after its kind. From the pianoforte arrangement of the overture (in which, as I have said, the only two *motivi* deserving the name have been wrought), I had expected striking effects of *crescendo*, *brio*, and, if a noisy orchestra, a rich one also. —The reverse is my impression. The sound is strident, ill-balanced, and wanting body. An awkward treatment of what may be called the tenor part of his band, leaves Herr Wagner often with only a heavy bass to support a squeaking treble poised high aloft. He seems to be fond of dividing his violins, as Weber and Mendelssohn did before him; but neither of these masters of the orchestra considered that by such division alone richness of tone was ensured. Such a full, brilliant, well-nourished sound (to adopt the French phrase), as we find in Mendelssohn's *tenor* orchestra, even when his theme was the wildest—as in his "Hebriden" overture, his "A minor symphony," his "Walpurgis Chorus"—is no where [*sic*] managed by Herr Wagner.[54] There is a brilliant violin figure at the close of the "Tannhaüser" overture, —more than once used by Cherubini, —which was intended to work up the composition with amazing fire. This, however, is so stifled by the disproportioned weight of the brass instruments that deliver the pilgrim tune in contrary *tempo*, as merely to produce that impression of strain which accompanies zeal without result—how different from the brilliancy which Cherubini and Weber could get in similar situations, by means of one half the difficulty, when they tried for a like effect! Throughout the opera, in short, beyond a whimsical distribution of instruments, such as a group of flutes above the tenor voice,* or some lean stringed sound to harass, not support the bass, —I recollect nothing either effective or agreeable—but grim noise, or shrill noise, and abundance of what a wit with so happy a disrespect designated "broken crockery" effects—things easy enough to be produced by those whose audacity is equal to their eccentricity.

Of the fate of "Tannhaüser," at Dresden, on its first production, I have already spoken. It was not till the Revolution of 1848 came, that Dr. Liszt began to interest himself for the composer, and devoted all his generous heart, soul, and spirit (all his ingenuity of enthusiastic paradox, and sophistry of brilliant wit, it must be added), to the production and recommendation of Herr Wagner's music; neither was it, till the composer had made

* Here, again, I am well aware that I may have my own example of Meyerbeer cited against me, if only on account of the octave flute and bassoon in the "Pif, paf!" of "Les Huguenots," which gave occasion to Rossini's sarcastic compliment on that air, as "*musique champetre.*" But *baroque* as this combination may be considered, and unquestionably is *baroque*—the effect is wanting. In the more recent opera by him—"Lohengrin"—there are some brilliant orchestral pages.

himself a martyr, been brought out of prison (as it were), and defended as such, that Herr Wagner bethought himself of his system; to make room for which, he has modestly vituperated and condemned all former opera writers, as weak creatures who weakly conformed to the modes of the hour in which they wrote.

With the rehabilitation in question, however, and its possible influences on German music, I have happily here no concern, still less with Herr Wagner's self-glorification and destruction of old idols. But though I am exempted, by the nature of my task, from examining the old pretexts which in the case of Herr Wagner take the form of new paradoxes, a general remark on the subject must still be offered.

The cardinal fault in the new manner of composition (or decomposition) which has produced fruits so little satisfactory, may not solely arise from Herr Wagner's perversity and poverty in special gifts combined. It may be a necessary consequence of the times we are living in, and of the ferment which is brewing around us. Being progressive, we are also expected to be universal. History must now be as amusing as a romance —romance must be as profound as a history. Poetry must run into the loops and knots and ties of didactic prose; prose must borrow all the garnitures of poetry. We have pictures painted, the subject and scope of which are not to be understood till we have read the book which describes them. We have books written which are not to be endured until they have been informed with a meaning, by aid of "pleasant pictures." So, in Music, the symphony, besides being a good symphony, must now express the anguish of the age, or of some age past. There must be story, inner meaning, mystical significance—intellectual tendency. To what interpretations of Beethoven's quartetts [*sic*] and sonatas have we not been exposed! Then, the opera must be a great poem—picture, drama, and symphony in one. —This extension of desire (not to call it a misuse of imagination) may be lamented, but it cannot be helped. The waters are out—there is no calling them back. But, for the present, unless creative invention should develope [*sic*] itself in some form totally unexpected, such an increased and multiplied variety of requisitions is a hindrance rather than a help to the artist. If one ingredient [should] elude his management, the composite work loses all symmetry, proportion, and power to charm sound taste. It is his comprehension of this difficult truth, and conformity to its conditions, which distinguish M. Meyerbeer, and which will so long maintain his grand operas on the stage. It is some sense of its force, and more unexpressed consciousness of his own incompleteness, which have driven Herr Wagner to the strange lengths of his unmusical proceedings, and which have tempted him, because he is unequal to the strain laid upon him, to break in pieces all the ancient and beloved things which have been worshipped, in place of adding to their number. That his countrymen, for the sake of some unmusical merits in his opera-books, are all, or any of them, willing to stand by and see the special graces of musical drama utterly tumbled into chaos, as so much obsolete rubbish, is a sight suggesting other considerations—suggestions of a disorganization, if not disease, of artistic taste, which is not cheering. For the present, there seems not much chance of the ferment working itself clear; but it is, perhaps, better for the sake of Music, that it should at once boil, and bubble, and overflow the caldron, than struggle darkly beneath the surface, in a state of morbid compression, as was the case before the year 1848. The open proclamation of anarchy is less to be mistrusted than the discontents and plottings of secret conspiracy.

NOTES

1. Ludwig Rellstab, in an early essay on the singer's career, mentions in addition to these roles Rezia in Weber's *Oberon*; the Jewess Rebecca in Marschner's *Ivanhoe* opera, *Templer und Jüdin*; and the bride in Ferdinand Ries's now forgotten operatic melodrama, *Die Räuberbraut*. Rellstab, "Wilhelmine Schröder-Devrient," originally published in vol. 1 of the *Neue Zeitschrift für Musik* (1834); and reprinted with an afterword in vol. 9 of his *Gesammelte Schriften*, 2nd ed. (Leipzig, 1860), 367–415 (here, 383).

2. H. Colin Slim, "Joseph Weber's Diva, *pinxit 1839*: Visual, Musical, Societal Considerations," *Music in Art: International Journal for Music Iconography* 31:1–2 (Spring–Fall 2006): 5–50. The portrait depicts the singer at precisely the time Henry Chorley encountered her in Dresden (see the following document in this section). She sang the role of Iphigenia under Wagner in Dresden in 1845.

3. Rellstab, "Wilhelmine Schröder-Devrient," 388.

4. Wagner, *My Life*, trans. Andrew Gray (Cambridge, 1983), 37. The discrepancies between Wagner's official autobiography and his earlier accounts of the singer were noted by John Deathridge in his contribution to *The New Grove Wagner* (New York, 1984). Deathridge analyzes the role of revision and fabrication in Wagner's construction of his life experiences, more generally, in "Wagner Lives: Issues in Autobiography," in *The Cambridge Companion to Wagner*, ed. Thomas S. Grey (Cambridge, 2008), 3–17.

5. See "Richard Wagner: Autobiographical Sketch (to 1842)," trans. Thomas Grey, *The Wagner Journal* 2/1 (March 2008): 49; *Gesammelte Schriften und Dichtungen* (Leipzig, 1887–1911), 1:9 (henceforth *GSD*).

6. See Wagner, *Eine Mitteilung an meine Freunde*, *GSD*, 4:254. Schröder-Devrient also sang in *Fidelio* and Rossini's *Otello* during the 1834 guest performances in Leipzig.

7. Ibid.

8. For first hand anecdotes of Wagner's collaboration with Schröder-Devrient in these operas, see *My Life*, 226–27, 239–43, 285–87, and 304–5.

9. Wagner, "Über Schauspieler und Sänger," *GSD*, 9:218.

10. Ibid., 219. The somewhat convoluted original text reads: "Durch diese wunderbare Frau ist mir der rettende Zurücktritt des in vollster Selbstentäußerung verlorenen Bewußtseins in das plötzliche Innewerden des Spieles, in welchem sie begriffen war, in

wahrhaft überraschender Weise bekannt geworden. " The word *Entäusserung* (renunciation), can also mean "realization" in a philosophical context, and it seems likely that Wagner is drawing to some extent on both seemingly contradictory meanings: a "renunciation" of the phenomenal self for the purpose of "realizing" the virtual self of the dramatic role.

11. Alfred von Wolzogen, author of another early biography (and father of the prolific Wagnerian acolyte, Hans von Wolzogen) cautioned that even those materials left to Glümer by Schröder-Devrient after her death were "not always reliable and tended to mix fact and fiction [*Dichtung und Wahrheit*] in a rather palpable manner." Wolzogen evaluates this and the various biographical essays and tributes that had appeared during the singer's lifetime in the introduction to his biographical study, *Wilhelmine Schröder-Devrient: ein Beitrag zur Geschichte des musikalischen Dramas* (Leipzig, 1863), 1–6, here 3.

12. Claire von Glümer, *Erinnerungen an Wilhelmine Schröder-Devrient* (Leipzig, 1862; 3rd ed., 1904), 7–9. The original of the translated sections presented here can be found on 19–24, 56–57, and 57–60.

13. Wagner, "Über Schauspieler und Sänger," *GSD*, 9:221.

14. These detailed musical travelogues are modeled on those of Charles Burney from the eighteenth century. *Modern German Music* (1854) reproduces much of the earlier volume, *Music and Manners in France and Germany* (1841).

15. Henry Chorley, *Modern German Music: Recollections and Criticism*, 2 vols. (London, 1854). Excerpts from chap. 1 are taken from 1:291–96 and 314–19; excerpts from chap. 3, 1:342–52 and 360–71. The account of the Dresden opera during Wagner's tenure as Kapellmeister in chap. 3 was added in 1854 to the material from *Music and Manners in France and Germany*.

16. Chorley was surprised to find Schröder-Devrient "singing the terribly difficult music of the part with a force and freshness . . . totally impossible to account for," quite apart from the accustomed "power and pathos" of her acting style. He suspected it might have had to do with the advantage given her by the unusually low tuning of the Dresden orchestra under Karl Gottlieb Reissiger. *Modern German Music*, 1:298–99.

17. Wilhelmine's father, the baritone Friedrich Schröder, died in Karlsbad on July 18, 1818, when she was fourteen years old.

18. Wilhelmine's mother was a celebrated stage actress, Sophie Schröder (1781–1868). From 1798 she was engaged at the Burgtheater in Vienna. Her roles in plays by Shakespeare, Racine, Schiller and the like established her as the leading tragedienne of the German stage in the early decades of the nineteenth century.

19. The plays in question are by, respectively, Racine, Grillparzer, Schiller (*Kabale und Liebe* and *Die Braut von Messina*), and Shakespeare.

20. "Nachrichten. Wien. Uebersicht des Monats Januar. Hofoper. " *Allgemeine musikalische Zeitung* 29:9 (28 February 1821): col. 145.

21. *Die Schweizerfamilie* (The Swiss family), Singspiel by Joseph Weigl (1766–1846), first performed in Vienna in 1809.

22. *Raoul Barbe-bleu* (Raoul Bluebeard), *opéra comique* by André Grétry, first performed at the Comédie-Italienne in Paris on the eve of the Revolution, March 2, 1789. As with a number of popular *opéras comiques* from the 1780s through the 1820s, a translation entered the German repertoire as a Singspiel.

23. The first part of the account of the *Fidelio* rehearsals is based on that contributed by Schröder-Devrient to Gustav Schilling's *Beethoven-Album, ein Gedenkbuch dankbarer Liebe und Verehrung für den grössen Todten* (Stuttgart, 1846); translated in *Beethoven: Impressions by his Contemporaries*, ed. O. G. Sonneck (New York, 1926; repr. 1967), 129–32. The description of her performance is not included in that source.

24. Carl August Böttiger (1760–1835), museum director and drama critic in Dresden, earlier a headmaster of the Weimar Gymnasium, a literary colleague of Goethe and Schiller, and an editor of the *Teutsche Merkur*.

25. Bellini composed the part of Romeo as a mezzo-soprano trouser role, first performed by Giuditta Grisi (Venice, Teatro la Fenice, March 11, 1830).

26. The frigid "old theater" mentioned here, also known as the "Moretti" theater, was replaced by Gottfried Semper's first Dresden opera house in 1841.

27. That is, "to have something to eat, to snack."

28. Shakespeare, *The Taming of the Shrew,* 5.2.12.

29. The "Della Cruscan" circle involved a circle of British poets active in Italy in the 1780s (founded by Robert Merry and including Hester Thrale Piozzi) who rallied around the name of a Florentine academy of the late Renaissance, the Accademia della Crusca, which aimed to cultivate a purified poetic Italian. The pre-Romantic movement became a byword for poetic preciosity and stylized sentiment.

30. The Dresden picture gallery (*Gemäldegalerie*) had been celebrated since the eighteenth century, when the Saxon Electors August II and III started collecting, above all, Italian masters of the Renaissance and Baroque.

31. Ludwig Tieck (1773–1853), a leading figure of German literary Romanticism, settled in Dresden in 1801 and was still residing there when Wagner returned in 1842. Like Hoffmann, he was also an influential writer on musical aesthetics.

32. The Frauenkirche.

33. Gaspard Poussin (1615–75) was the brother-in-law of the more famous Nicolas Poussin. He specialized in landscapes of the Italian countryside, particularly the Roman *campagna*.

34. Among these *witz*-es were Blasewitz and Loschwitz, towns across the Elbe to the north where Wagner spent time in the summer during his Dresden years.

35. Vineyard or wine-growing district.

36. The so-called Sächsische Schweiz or "Saxon Switzerland" between Saxony and Bohemia.

37. Sir Walter Scott, "The Lay of the Last Minstrel," Canto 2, stanza 13. The line refers to the medieval theologian, scholar, and astrologer Michael Scot (Scotus) and the powers attributed him to alter the landscape with a spell: "And, warrior, I could say to thee / The words that cleft Eildon hills in three, / And bridled the Tweed with a curb of stone."

38. Sir John Vanbrugh (1664–1726), British architect of stately homes of massive, imposing symmetry such as Castle Howard in Yorkshire and Blenheim Palace in Oxfordshire. Chorley's remark ("Had I known as much as have since done") evidently alludes to the political insurrection of 1849 in Dresden, the cause of Wagner's dozen years of exile from Saxony and the other German states.

39. Anne-Louise-Germaine Necker, Baroness of Staël-Holstein (1766–1816), a notable French woman of letters, of German extraction. Bettina von Arnim (née Brentano, 1785–1859) became famous for her enthusiastic correspondence with and memoirs of both Goethe and Beethoven.

40. A footnote in the original is omitted here, quoting at length Charles Burney's description of an episode that illustrates the condescension of eighteenth-century royalty to their musicians.

41. In a section of chapter 1, "The Opera and its Environs," not included in the foregoing excerpt, Chorley described in some detail Weber's opera *Euryanthe* as he heard it performed in Dresden with Schröder-Devrient singing the role of the heroine. Chorley likens the plot to that of Shakespeare's *Cymbeline*.

42. Her first operatic role, performed in January 1821 (see Claire von Glümer excerpt above).

43. Maria Malibran (1808–36), daughter of the Spanish composer, singer, and vocal pedagogue Manuel Garcia (1775–1832) and sister of the equally (though later) celebrated mezzo-soprano Pauline Viardot-Garcia (1821–1910). Malibran began her career in London in 1825 and performed both there and in Italy during the remaining decade

of her career. The role of Fidelio, which she sang at Covent Garden (in English) was a rare exception to her predominantly Italian repertoire. Ludwig Rellstab, in his 1834 essay on Schröder-Devrient's career, considers the Munich-born soprano Anna (Nanette) Schechner (1806–60) as the principal point of comparison in this role (*Gesammelte Schriften*, 9:383–91). Schechner had retired from the stage due to vocal deterioration by 1835. Among German opera singers in general, the soprano Henriette Sontag (1806–54) was considered by most critics and audiences as the major competitor, vocally more proficient in terms of tone quality and agility.

44. Chorley refers to the opera *Macbeth* by Hippolyte-André-Baptiste Chélard (1789–1861), French-born composer who moved to Germany after 1830, first to Munich, and was later appointed Kapellmeister in Weimar (1840), where he remained through Liszt's time. His *Macbeth* premiered in Paris in 1827, but only met with some success when a revised version was produced in Munich during the following two years. Composed in the neoclassical vein of the *tragédies lyriques* of Cherubini (*Medée*) or Spontini (*La vestale*), it remained in the German repertoire into the 1830s.

45. Sarah Siddons (1755–1831), the leading tragic actress of the British stage in the later eighteenth century. Lady Macbeth was her most famous role.

46. Sophie Schröder, Wilhelmine's mother.

47. Giuditta Pasta (1797–1865). The role in question is the lead of Giovanni Simone Mayr's *Medea in Corinto* (1813), not Cherubini's opera.

48. The *Mitteilung an meine Freunde* (*Communication to My Friends*), published in 1852 as a preface to the librettos of the three operas after *Rienzi*, and as an epilogue, of sorts, to the three increasingly lengthy essays or treatises on music, the arts, and operatic reform written between 1849 and 1851 (the "Zurich" writings).

49. *Der fliegende Holländer* was not performed in London until 1870 (at the Drury Lane Theatre in an Italian translation), the first of Wagner's operas to be produced there.

50. Chorley's misplaced umlaut in the title of *Tannhäuser* was probably carried over from Liszt's (French-language) brochure on this opera and *Lohengrin*. Liszt insisted on the misspelling, claiming that it gave French readers a better idea of how the name ought to be pronounced. (See the introduction to excerpts from Liszt's essays included in this volume.)

51. Johanna Wagner (1826–94), the adoptive daughter of Wagner's older brother Albert. She became one of the leading German opera singers of the 1840s and 1850s, also in French and Italian repertoire.

52. Joseph Aloys Tichatschek (1807–86) was the principal tenor at Dresden during Wagner's time there, having debuted in 1837. The role of Rienzi was one of his signal successes and he helped to define the Wagnerian Heldentenor as a vocal *Fach*.

53. Chorley's detailed account of the *Tannhäuser* libretto (352–60) is omitted here.

54. References are to Mendelssohn's concert overture *The Hebrides* (*Fingal's Cave*), op. 26 (1830–32); the Symphony no. 3 in A Minor ("Scottish"), op. 56 (1842); and the cantata-style setting of Goethe's *Die erste Walpurgisnacht*, op. 60 (1832, rev. 1842). By "tenor" Chorley seems to refer to the handling of inner voices generally in the orchestration, perhaps with particular reference to second violin and viola parts, cellos (when divided or in higher registers), middle-range woodwinds (clarinets, bassoons, French horns), etc.

Catulle Mendès Visits Tribschen

CATULLE MENDÈS
TRANSLATED, INTRODUCED, AND ANNOTATED
BY THOMAS S. GREY

Although the hard-fought production of *Tannhäuser* in Paris in 1861 was a notorious fiasco,[1] Wagner's presence in Paris at this fertile moment in French cultural history captured the attention of several notable literary figures, above all Charles Baudelaire, whose essay "Wagner and *Tannhäuser* in Paris" (*Révue européenne*, 1 April 1861) proved to be the cornerstone of an illustrious Wagnerian legacy among French poets of the pioneering generation of modernism. The Symbolist movement, led by Stéphane Mallarmé, is often traced back to Baudelaire's essay.[2] Of the same generation as Mallarmé and Paul Verlaine was the poet, playwright, and novelist Catulle Mendès (1841–1909), initially the most devoted of the French literary Wagnerians. In the year of the Paris *Tannhäuser,* then twenty-year-old Mendès founded the literary journal *La revue fantaisiste*, which published works by Baudelaire as well as Villiers de L'Isle-Adam, who would accompany Mendès on his pilgrimage to Wagner's Swiss retreat at Tribschen near Lucerne in 1869. As editor of *Le Parnasse contemporain* (1866–76) Villiers de L'Isle-Adam oversaw the formation of a Parnassian movement, subsequently overshadowed by the more radical avant-gardism of the Symbolists.[3] The Parnassians represented a modern strain of neoclassical formalism and shared with Symbolists, Decadents, and other aestheticist movements toward the end of the century an underlying philosophy of *l'art pour l'art* (art for art's sake), explaining their shared fascination with the phenomenon of Wagner and his theories of a "total work of art."

In 1866 Mendès married the daughter of Théophile Gautier, Judith, who also stopped at Tribschen with her husband in the summer of 1869. The fact that Mendès's short memoir of the visit, published as an introduction to his 1886 monograph on Wagner's oeuvre, suppresses any mention of her name may have to do with the fact of their separation not long afterward (she later married the novelist Pierre Loti); this gesture of discretion might also reflect the husband's awareness that Judith had gone on to conduct a brief affair with the aging composer, with whom she remained on friendly terms to the end of his life. The outbreak of hostilities between France and Germany the following summer (1870) interrupted the budding friendship of the Mendès couple with Wagner, and as Catulle suggests in his memoir of Tribschen, it would take some years for the wound of Wagner's vitriolic anti-French chauvinism to heal. The novel Mendès published in 1880, *Le roi vièrge* (The virgin king), parodies the psychological dependency of the Bavarian king Ludwig II (here styled as King Frederick of Thuringia) on a private aesthetic cult of Wagnerian mythology. Despite the initial fallout from the Franco-Prussian War, both he and Judith continued to spread the gospel of Wagnerism in France, Judith in several personal memoirs as well as a full-length study, *Richard Wagner et son oeuvre poétique depuis Rienzi jusqu'à Parisfal* (Paris, 1882) and Catulle in contributions to the *Revue wagnérienne* (which were reprinted in *Richard Wagner,* his 1886 monograph from which the following text has been taken).[4] His later work as a librettist for post-Wagnerian French composers such as Chabrier, Massenet, and the young Debussy can be seen as a continuation of his early devotion to the Wagnerian idea and its propagation in France.

CATULLE MENDÈS

Personal Recollections: At Tribschen
(Paris, 1886)

It should not be without interest if I were to give some details on the most curious and rather unfamiliar personality of the man of genius who is now no more. It was above all at Lucerne that I had the opportunity of intimate visits with him. Already in Paris, if I remember correctly, I had occasion to see him at his quarters in the Rue d'Aumale with regard to the *Revue fantaisiste*.[5] But that would have been shortly before the first performance of *Tannhäuser* at the Opéra, and at that point he had been driven to the utmost degree of nervous exasperation by a thousand annoyances and *misérabilités* (as he used to put it). He was like an angry cat, his back up and his claws out. It was not a well-chosen moment to establish relations with him, besides which my very young age then was an obstacle to any real familiarity. But some years later a somewhat less irritable if not exactly calm Richard Wagner (for calm he never was!) was living in peaceful solitude more favorable to creative productivity near Lucerne, at Tribschen,[6] with the woman who was to become his wife. When the train pulled up at the station my heart was beating rapidly, and I believe I can say that my traveling companion, Villiers de L'Isle-Adam, was no less moved.

For all that, we were no strangers to Wagner; and given that he knew how we were fighting passionately toward the triumph of his ideas and his oeuvre, we had reason to hope for a cordial reception and, before long, a sense of mutual sympathy. No sooner had we stepped off the train than we saw a large straw hat; under it a pale face looked very quickly to the right and the left, as if in search of something.

It was he. Intimidated as we were, we observed him without daring to approach.

He was small, thin, and tightly wrapped in a frock coat with maroon brocade. His whole slender but certainly quite robust body seemed a bundle of energy, while the tension of waiting had apparently produced the almost convulsive trembling of a woman suffering from "nerves." Still, his face retained a magnificent expression of hauteur as well as serenity. His mouth—the lips very thin and pale, almost invisible—was twisted into a bitter smile; beneath the hat, somewhat cast back, his large, pure, well-formed brow surrounded by very fine hair, already graying and thinning, exhibited a stable, peaceful character due, I suppose, to the influence of some immense idea. In the ingenuous transparency of his eyes—eyes like those of a young child or a virgin—there was all the beautiful candor of an unspoiled dream.

As soon as he saw us Richard Wagner trembled from head to toe like the high string of a violin suddenly struck *pizzicato*; he threw his hat into the air with wild cries of welcome: almost dancing for joy he leapt upon us, grabbing us by the arm and the neck. Quite moved—nearly knocked down, for that matter—we were swept up in a torrent of words and gestures, suddenly finding ourselves in the carriage that was to take us to the home of the master. For many years I felt compelled to suppress the memories of several weeks spent entirely in that hospitable domicile, thanks to that odious brochure; but I have explained why I now feel I have the right to revive them.[7]

The next morning, after a hurried breakfast, we left our hotel, the object of much curiosity on account of our visit to Richard Wagner. I recall even now a rather amusing incident from that moment. Each time we descended the staircase together with the young woman whom we had the honor of accompanying on this trip, the servants came running, lining the hall and bowing low to the ground. The owner himself escorted us to our carriage with an air of deep respect, once even insisting on kissing our hands quite vehemently. What on earth could have earned us such signs of respect? Consider that we were lodged quite simply in three small rooms on the fifth floor of the Hôtel du Lac, and that our attire was only moderately sumptuous, at best. Yet in town as well we were met with salutes, whispered exchanges, groups of bared heads. Better still, as we took the boat across the lake to Tribschen, other boats full of English visitors followed us as far as the promontory on which the Wagner villa was situated, where the English waited until evening with incredible patience. All this obsequious attention finally began rather to annoy us, and we said straight out to the hotel owner that we only wanted to be treated like the ordinary tourists we really were. Adopting a knowing air, that wise gentleman turned to me, saying: "Sir, we will do whatever is required by your Majesty, and if that means respecting your incognito, we shall certainly do that." My majesty? You can imagine how we were ready to explode with laughter. The fact was, our arrival in Lucerne coincided with an announcement in the papers regarding the imminent arrival of the King of Bavaria, so that I had been taken for King Ludwig and Villiers de L'Isle-Adam for the Prince Taxis.[8] As for our other young traveling companion, it was firmly believed that she was none other than Mme. Patti, come to Lucerne to study an operatic role with Richard Wagner, and it was in hope of hearing her sing that the English group had spent the day waiting in their boat next to the promontory of Tribschen.[9] It required infinite pains to disabuse the good people at the hotel and to convince them not to render us any further royal honors.

At Wagner's house the days passed in the most charming fashion. Hardly would we enter the garden than our arrival was greeted by the barking of an enormous black dog, accompanied by children's laughter from the steps, while at the window the poet-musician would shake his black velvet beret in a signal of welcome.[10] On more than one occasion our morning visit caught him in that odd costume that legend has often since attributed to him: dressing gown and slippers of gold satin, brocaded with pearl-colored flowers (for he had a passionate love of luminous fabrics, spreading out like flames or spilling out in splendid waves).[11] Velvets and silks were in abundance in the salon and in his study, freely dispersed in swelling heaps or torrential trains in no particular relation to the furnishings—simply for the sake of their beauty and to enchant the poet with their glorious warmth.

The midday meal was always served at precisely two o'clock, and prior to that conversation would be struck up in the large, light salon where four large windows let in the air of the hills and the moist countryside. Sometimes we would be sitting at this point, but never him! No, I cannot recall seeing him seated even once, except at the piano or at table. Coming and going through the large room, moving this chair or that, searching his pockets for a misplaced snuffbox or his eyeglasses (sometimes they had become hung up on the pendants of the chandeliers, but never in any case on his nose), grasping the velvet beret that hung down over his left eye like a black cockscomb, rubbing it between his clenched fists, then thrusting into his waistcoat only to take it out again and replace it on his head—all the while talking, talking, talking! Often he spoke of Paris. He had not *yet* become so unfair toward our country. He loved this city where he had suffered and hoped; with the warmth and anxiety of an exile he asked after the neighborhoods where he had lived, which might have been much changed under the recent construction projects. I saw his eyes well up with tears when he recalled a house at the corner of this or that street which he now learned had been demolished.[12] Then, too, he would let fly with great outbursts: sublime metaphors, puns, barbarities—an incessant stream of observations, flowing in fits and starts, alternately proud, tender, violent, or comical. Now smiling ear to ear, now turning emotional to the point of tears, now working himself up into a prophetic frenzy, all sorts of topics found their way into his extraordinary flights of improvisation: the dramas he still dreamed of writing, *Parsifal*, the King of Bavaria ("not a *méchant garcon*," he told us),[13] the tricks played on him by Jewish music directors, the subscribers who hissed at *Tannhäuser*, Mme. de Metternich,[14] Rossini (the most "voluptuously" endowed of musicians), a reply he had in mind to send to the *Augsburg Allgemeine Zeitung*, the theater he would build one day on a hill outside of a town and to which people would come from all over the world, Sebastian Bach, Monsieur Auber who had been very kind to him,[15] his idea for a comedy titled *Luther's Wedding*.[16] And then dozens of anecdotes: stories of his political involvements in Dresden, the happy dreams and escapades of his childhood, looking out from the last row of the orchestra stalls to see the great Weber conducting, Mme. Schröder-Devrient (the dearest, most significant memory of all, "that admirable, dear, dear woman!" he added with a sigh), the death of Schnorr, creator of the role of Tristan.[17] And when he uttered the name "Tristan!" it was with a tremendous exaltation of his whole being directed toward a febrile eternity of love-in-death, suggesting the conception of a frenetic void! We, however, who were overwhelmed and dazed by all this, laughed and cried along with him, sharing his ecstasies, seeing his visions; we felt like a cloud of dust stirred up by a storm, but also illuminated by his imperious discourse, frightful and delightful at once.

NOTES

1. See the reviews of this production in Part IV of this volume, "Wagner in Paris."

2. On this legacy, see Steven Huebner's introduction to the excerpts from the *Revue wagnérienne* in Part IV.

3. Jean-Marie-Mathias-Philippe-Auguste, comte de Villiers de L'Isle-Adam (1838–89) was later more closely affiliated with the Symbolists than Mendès. His prose works explore spiritualist, uncanny, and "fantastic" motifs; an overtly Wagnerian symbolist drama, *Axël*, written in 1886 during the brief run of the *Revue wagnérienne*, evokes Mallarmé's ideal of a psychological "theater of the mind" as well as a Wagnerian love-death for Axël and his beloved ideal, Sara.

4. Catulle Mendès, *Richard Wagner* (Paris, 1886), 5–17. In addition to the memoirs of Tribschen, Mendès includes in the monograph an "epistle to the King of Thuringia" (alluding to his fictionalized account of King Ludwig II of Bavaria in the 1880 novel *Le roi vièrge*), an essay on the "Wagnerian theory" of musical drama (reprinted from the *Revue wagnérienne*), individual essays on each of Wagner's operas from *Der fliegende Holländer* on, and a dialogue between "an old Wagnerian and a young Prix-de-Rome fellow," also reprinted from the *Revue*.

5. Wagner and his wife, Minna, took lodgings at 3 rue d'Aumale in October 1860. The *Revue fantaisiste* was founded by Mendès in 1861 with the help of Théophile Gautier.

6. Mendès spells the name Triebchen.

7. Mendès's explanation as to why he feels entitled now to ignore "that odious brochure" (an allusion to Wagner's famously offensive satirical "operetta" text, *Eine Kapitulation*, discussed at length in my essay in Part I of this volume) is contained in the *avant-propos* to his book. (As the son of a banker of Portuguese-Jewish descent, Mendès might equally well have taken offense at the 1869 republication of "Judaism in Music" in brochure form.) In the *avant-propos* he quotes some lines he had published in 1880 lamenting the anti-French satire in Wagner's libretto, then appends some further text written in 1883, soon after Wagner's death: "Once the tomb is closed, we have the right, even the duty to choose among our memories. Yes, we cannot help but remember that the incomparable poet-musician was also the wretch who saw fit to insult our national defeat as well as our national glories. For my part, I no longer think of how I had to scorn and hate him. I see him again as I once knew him, before those terrible times, in the days of unrestricted enthusiasm" (vi–vii).

8. Prince Paul Maximilian Lamoral von Thurn und Taxis (1843–79), of the Bavarian noble family Thurn und Taxis, was an adjutant to the young Ludwig II.

9. As mentioned in the introduction, the discreetly unnamed "other" traveling companion was the author's wife (and daughter of Théophile Gautier), Judith Gautier-Mendès (1845–1917), with whom Wagner became smitten and conducted a transient affair in later years. The internationally celebrated soprano Adelina Patti (1843–1919) was at the height of her fame in the 1860s.

10. The dog was Wagner's Newfoundland, Russ (acquired in memory of Robber, the Newfoundland he and Minna Wagner had lost in Paris after the dog had accompanied them in all the trials and privations of their voyage to Paris in 1839). The children, at this point, were Hans von Bülow's daughters Daniela and Blandine, as well as the two fathered by Wagner out of wedlock, Isolde and Eva. Wagner's one son, Siegfried, had been born in early June, just a month before this visit.

11. Wagner's fondness for delicate silks, satins, and furs to wear about the house, a fetish that sometimes bordered on transvestism, became notorious with the (obviously unauthorized) publication of *Briefe Richard Wagners an eine Putzmacherin*, his correspondence with a high-class Viennese seamstress, Bertha Goldwag. The serialized publication of the

letters was the brainchild of the anti-Wagnerian Viennese satirist Daniel Spitzer and appeared in the *Neue freie Presse* in 1877.

12. Wagner had spent his longest time in Paris in 1839–42, visited it again periodically between 1849 and 1850, and during the *Tannhäuser* "campaign" of 1860–61 signed a three-year lease for an apartment at 16 rue Newton, near the Étoile, only to discover that it was about to fall victim to the grand construction schemes of Baron Georges-Eugène Haussmann. The large-scale urban renewal program of Haussmann began in 1852, but the bulk of the new construction (and removal of older quarters) took place in the 1860s and after.

13. Mendès quotes Wagner's French here—*méchant garçon* (bad boy). It is unclear whether Wagner is defending Ludwig against imputations of homosexuality, already familiar by this time, or just joking in a more general way.

14. Pauline von Metternich (1836–1921), wife of the Habsburg ambassador to Paris, Prince Richard Metternich, had notably intervened on Wagner's behalf to obtain an imperial decree for the performance of *Tannhäuser* in Paris in 1861.

15. D.-F.-E. Auber (1782–1871), composer of the grand opera *La muette de Portici* and *Fra Diavolo*, among dozens of other *opéras comiques*. Wagner wrote an obituary essay on the composer, "Reminiscences of Auber," in 1871.

16. Wagner had drafted some plans for a comedy on the subject of "Luther's wedding" the previous summer at Tribschen, possibly intended as either a prose play or a libretto.

17. On the impact of Wilhelmine Schröder-Devrient on the young Wagner, see the first document in this section. Ludwig Schnorr von Carolsfeld (1836–65) was the son of the painter Julius Schnorr von Carolsfeld and became a devoted interpreter of Wagnerian heroes, including the first Tristan, until his death a few weeks after the premiere of that opera on June 10, 1865.

Recollections of Villa Wahnfried from Wagner's American Dentist

NEWELL SILL JENKINS
INTRODUCED AND ANNOTATED BY THOMAS S. GREY

Toward the end of his life Wagner frequently entertained the fantasy of moving himself, his family, and his whole artistic enterprise to America. The principal motive was financial. Continually harassed and depressed by the debts incurred through the Bayreuth festival of 1876, which of course had entailed the construction of an entire custom-designed theater, Wagner imagined that the New World of infinite enterprise and commerce might easily take up the reins of patronage that had slackened in the hands of Ludwig II, and which Bismarck and the Kaiser had disdained to take over in the name of the German nation. "Despair over Germany" is a recurrent refrain of Wagner's from 1877 onward. The emigration fantasy also had an ideological side, fueled by the composer's notions of cultural and racial "regeneration," vaguely articulated in various essays written in conjunction with his final music drama, *Parsifal*. Hardy, right-thinking, hardworking German émigrés, unspoiled by modern urban European society, would be the right audience for his valedictory message of cultural salvation.

The intended agent for these plans was Wagner's one American acquaintance, Dr. Newell Sill Jenkins (1840–1919), a dentist from Bangor, Maine, who had set up practice in Dresden in the late 1860s. On Friday, September 21, 1877, a few days after Wagner began to sketch out some of the music for *Parsifal*, Cosima recorded in her diary: "The American dentist Mr. Jenkins arrives from Dresden at my request, to attend to R., and the very agreeable man starts his operation immediately during the afternoon." On Saturday, "Another operation, R. bears it patiently, says that yesterday, while it was going on, he was composing! Departure of Mr. Jenkins, who utterly declines to accept any money from R." Under the current, post-festival economic circumstances, this recommended him very highly. And this, as Jenkins notes, "was the beginning of a friendship which lasted until Wagner's death."

Apart from *Parsifal* (and two occasional songs for the children at Wahnfried), Wagner's last completed work was a *Grand Festival March for the Opening of the Centennial Commemorative of the Declaration of Independence of the United States of America*, commissioned for the 1876 celebrations in Philadelphia by the "Women's Centennial Committee" and the leading American conductor of the day, Theodore Thomas.[1] Wagner was less than inspired by his work, admitting that he could muster no mental image while composing it besides the $5,000 he had stipulated as a fee, along with the European publication rights.[2] The dedication to his American friend ("Es lebe Amerika!") entered by Wagner in a copy of Joseph Rubinstein's piano arrangement of the march, alludes, as Jenkins notes in the memoir that follows, "partly to a hope we both entertained that he might sometime visit America."[3] Jenkins tactfully suppressed the Master's more grandiose visions by gently dispelling them on several occasions.

During an extended sojourn in Naples in the winter and spring months of 1880, Wagner seriously considered a permanent emigration, beginning with a trip of some months' duration as early as the following September. At the beginning of February he was suffering from rashes, inflammation of the eyes, and general irritability. "He wants to move to America (Minnesota)," Cosima writes, "and there, for a subscription of one million dollars, build a drama school and a house." (The project of a school for Wagnerian music and drama in Bayreuth had recently occupied him for some time, to no avail, echoing earlier such plans for Munich under Ludwig's patronage.) "He would dedicate *Parsifal* to them [the Americans] and stage it there, for he can no longer tolerate the situation here in Germany. . . . Again and again he keeps coming back to America, says it is the only place on the map he can contemplate with any pleasure: 'What the Greeks were among the peoples of this earth, this continent is among its countries.'"[4] A week later he spelled out his plan in a letter to Jenkins, back in Dresden. An association of interested citizens would put up a million dollars, half of which would allow Wagner and his family "to settle in a climatically favorable part of the Union" (Minnesota?) while the remaining $500,000 "would be employed as capital, to be placed on deposit in a state bank at 5 percent. America would thereby have purchased me from Europe forever."[5] To King Ludwig, at the end of March, he confides another financial motive: by emigrating to America he would be able, he claims, to buy back the performing rights to his works currently assigned to European agents—including, notably, the Bavarian king. Meanwhile, Wagner's million-dollar scenario did not include funds for reestablishing the Wagner festival and its theater on American soil, which apparently also depended on the supposedly limitless enthusiasm of Americans for transplanting the Wagnerian music drama to the New World.

It is true, of course, that lucrative American tours were becoming a common undertaking for European artists amid the rapid industrial expansion of the American economy in the decades after the Civil War, and above all with the ubiquitous growth of the railway. Still, a touring virtuoso or conductor is one thing and a translated Bayreuth festival quite another. Except for that large savings account "at 5 percent" with always more where that came from, Wagner's dreams of a new start in the United States were vague and undefined. To him it was all tabula rasa, a place where he might yet be received as a great cultural savior and thus show up the ungrateful Germans back home. After hearing on one occasion from Jenkins "some very interesting things about the Negroes" ("whom R. can hardly visualize taking part in public affairs; he feels that what has made them significant is their touching submission to a cruel fate"), he also discussed the character of the émigrés: "Yes the emigrants," Wagner opined, "those are the good ones, just as the earlier wanderers were the heroes; the ones who stayed home were the Philistines."[6]

After the summer of 1880 Wagner's dreams of the American El Dorado quickly began to fade, in part with the evident decline in his health. A series of dental appointments with Jenkins at his Dresden practice in September 1881 were limited to friendly conversation on local topics (and somewhat more taxing dental procedures than before), with no more talk about moving. In the meantime he had also relinquished as impractical the idea of a six-month American cross-country concert tour to raise funds for the original festival in Bayreuth and to help secure performing rights for his works, above all *Parsifal*, at home. The thought of consecrating some distant, foreign stage became still less attractive once King Ludwig came forward with resources for Bayreuth, forgoing his own claims on the score and putting the personnel of the Munich court theater at the disposal of the festival. No doubt in the end Dr. Jenkins was better pleased to be left with his assorted Wagnerian mementos, as described in his *Reminiscences*, rather than the burden of assisting in the transplantation of the Wagner festival to the American Great Plains.

A graduate of the Baltimore College of Dental Surgery (class of 1863), Newell Jenkins realized the potential for exporting the latest developments in American dentistry to the European continent, a project he continued while resident in Germany. He experimented with various materials for fillings (tin and gold mixtures, glass) and pioneered the use of porcelain enamel crowns. By the 1880s his patients included the King of Saxony and the Grand Duchess of Mecklenburg, and later Mark Twain, who offered to promote his products in the United States. Jenkins remained resident in Europe through the period of the First World War, moving to Paris after retiring from his Dresden dental practice in 1909. Around that time he patented Kolynos toothpaste, a product that earned him and his heirs considerable sums, and he continued to publish extensively in journals of dentistry.[7] His memoirs, *Reminiscences of Newell Sill Jenkins*, were privately printed in 1924, five years after his death at Le Havre, France. What follows here is the complete text of chapter nine.[8]

NEWELL SILL JENKINS
Reminiscences, 1875–1883
(1924)

In the middle of the seventies I made my first acquaintance with Richard Wagner. Frau Cosima Wagner came first to me as a patient, with her children. I was much impressed by this remarkable woman. She was the embodiment of physical and mental energy. Her tall form, her strong features, her quick resolves, as firm as they were intelligent, her disdain of obstacles standing between her and her purpose, and the tact and resource with which she overcame them, revealed her at first sight as a woman of extraordinary character. My first impression was confirmed by further acquaintance.

In 1877 Frau Cosima asked me to go to Bayreuth to treat her husband. The previous year had witnessed the first representation at Bayreuth of the "Nibelungen Ring" and the world was still ringing with echoes of this great musical and national event. Wagner was unable to come to me and greatly needed certain treatment, to relieve sufferings intolerable to a man of his temperament, and accordingly, although I was myself tired and overwrought, I determined to go; and this was the beginning of a friendship which lasted until Wagner's death.

For the first time I had occasion to rejoice that I was so unmusical, for it might well have been that, had I been a musical enthusiast, he would have been as bored by my society as he appeared to be by many whom I have seen trying to express to him their admiration. As it was, he accepted me as a novelty and took to me at once. Upon this occasion, and upon other visits which I made him, he was with me as much as possible. We had long walks together, conversing upon all things human and divine, barring music, except that I told him something of the plaintive character of the music of the American negroes under slavery, a quality inherent also in the music of the Russian serfs; but we could not decide if this were due to temperament or circumstance.

To my great delight, I found that he had an extraordinary sense of humour and that he was very fond of amusing anecdotes, telling them in a dry manner which added much to their piquancy. We have sat up until late in the night upon more than one occasion exchanging stories, he finding the American jest especially racy; and, indeed, he had a wide interest in everything American, for he was in theory a redoubtable republican, as shown by his participation in the revolution of '48 and in his subsequent indifference to the blandishments of royalties.

One evening Frau Cosima was speaking of the previous summer, when Bayreuth was visited by so many royal and princely personages and all the world beside, and she told how the Emperor of Brazil, upon his arrival, sent to ask Wagner and Liszt to call upon him. They were both absent but Frau Cosima sent a verbal reply, saying: "I know positively that my father will go, but I also know as certainly that my husband will not."

Once at dinner Wagner asked me about Brigham Young, who had recently died, and wished to know the secret of his power. I told him of the worldly position of the people among whom the Mormons made their converts, how ignorant and poor many of them were, and instanced the Cornwall miners, many of whom were converted and found Utah, which their strong hands made to blossom like the rose, an earthly paradise compared to their former dismal home. Like the followers of Mahomet, they gained not only the assurance of heaven, but such blessings in this life as they were capable of appreciating.

After a little time, Wagner looked at me with a twinkle in his eye which I knew to presage a jest, and began to speak gravely of his intention to establish a new religion as soon as he finished "Parsifal," which he was then composing. After the first moment, he especially regarded another guest, a nephew by marriage and a professor of mathematics at Kiel, whom I had already suspected of being devoid of imagination, and began to explain the details of the new enterprise.

It was to be founded upon a materialistic view of Heaven, like that of Mahomet, but there were to be also different grades of heavenly bliss and the services were to be magnificently choral, for musical art should be the means of worship and the passport to Heaven should be by tickets bought for hard cash from the priests. These tickets, however, should have something of the form of Papal indulgences and thus secure abundant income to the church. They should be also like railroad tickets, which would not carry the holder beyond the place for which they were bought, so that the pious soul should aspire through sacrifice of gold in this life to attain to the highest heaven in the world to come and not be satisfied with a third-class ticket, which would merely give him admittance to standing room, as in a theatre. Then he went on more and more fantastically and slyly, noting the amazement of the good professor, who might well have thought the *Meister* mad, until Frau Cosima and I could no longer restrain our merriment and it began to dawn upon the other auditor that it was but an extravagant jest.

This side of Wagner's character, revealed only in the "Meistersinger" among all his works, may have been the source of the many surprising stories which were related of him. I have myself observed that the awestricken reverence with which some of his worshippers approached him seemed to him fit subject for raillery, and indeed it was sometimes so exaggerated that the temptation to turn it into ridicule must have been irresistible. I remember a reception at Wahnfried one evening in the days of the first public performance of "Parsifal." I had obtained an invitation for a minor American composer, who was, except upon the subject of music, a very sensible fellow. He came early and I presented him to Frau Cosima, who was receiving, Wagner himself coming in only late upon such occasions. My friend was tremulous with excitement. He said to me that this was the most important experience of his life, he was about to see the two greatest men in the world, Wagner and Liszt.

When he did see and was presented to the *Meister*, he was too agitated to speak and was so much moved that I took early occasion to shunt him into a corner, where he could slowly recover. The next day I found that the poor man was suffering from a deep disappointment. Being familiar with pictures which represented only Wagner's massive head, he had expected to find a man of commanding stature and was greatly distressed to find him somewhat less than average height. But I consoled him by reminding him of Napoleon's diminutive stature, as I knew the Corsican was another of his heroes.

Upon one of my visits, the brother of the famous pianist Rubinstein was at Wahnfried, engaged in arranging the "Nibelungen Ring" for the piano. He was an interesting man, in a way. I believe he met with a tragic fate before the work was finished and that it finally appeared in the name of Klindworth. During the visit it happened that the family would be obliged to go out somewhere now and then, something which Frau Cosima always regretted, because, she said, she was unwilling to leave her husband even for a few hours, since all the time she could expect to be with him was so precious to her. Upon these occasions I remained with the *Meister*, for I did not dance and disliked general society, and these evenings were among the most delightful I have ever known. I found Wagner, like all the truly distinguished men I have met, a most human character with a very wide range of interests and sympathies. To talk with an American, who knew nothing of music, was probably to him a rare experience. In any event, he kept me up, even after the family had returned, talking familiarly upon many topics and always impressing me with his great mental endowments. In October 1877, after the adaptation of the "Ring" to the piano was published, he sent me a splendidly bound copy with his autograph and a *Widmung* in his own handwriting on the flyleaf of the first volume.

> *Ich sage nichts vom Zahn der Zeit,*
> *Die Zeit des Zahnes naht heran,*
> *Ist dann Herr Jenkins nicht mehr weit,*
> *Trotz' ich die Zeit mit Ihrem Zahn.*[9]

He was unwilling to speak English, of which he had only a literary knowledge, and was accustomed to say: "I speak English, but only in the dialect of North Wales." One day he asked me the origin of my name, saying that it should have a meaning, as German names generally did. Then I told him there was once a great king in Wales, of whom the English "King Cole" was but a degenerate copy. This king, whose name was Jen, was a model of all a monarch should be, pious, learned, just, generous and, above all, jovial. In his court were assembled all the great artists of his time and they were more honoured than princes. His happy subjects basked in the light of his jolly countenance and lived so happily under his gentle and prosperous reign, that, when at last he died childless, they decided that no successor should bear that beloved name. Only when later a man appeared who in his person and character reminded them of their lamented monarch, they called him "of the kin of Jen," and so originated the name of Jen-kins.

The next morning he gave me a copy of Alfred Forman's alliterative English translation of the "Ring," which the author had sent to the *Meister* and with which we had all amused ourselves the previous evening. It bore (I quote from memory, for the book is now inaccessibly packed away) written in Wagner's hand, the following inscription: "Translated in the dialect of North Wales, in the time of King Jen, forefather of my noble friend, Jenkins."

There are many legends which seem to have an equally stable foundation.

I have various other mementoes of the great *Meister* which you children will prize. Among them is a copy of Joseph Rubinstein's arrangement for the piano of the great Festive March composed by Wagner for the opening of the celebration in America of the hundredth anniversary of the United States' Declaration of Independence. The flyleaf of the book bears these words:

Mein lieber Herr Jenkins!
In Umtausch unserer Hoffnungen rufe ich mit dieser
freundschaftlicher Widmung Ihnen zu. Es lebe Amerika![10]
Ihr, Richard Wagner.

This refers partly to a hope we both entertained that he might some-time visit America and partly his sympathy with my belief that Europe would eventually become republican and not Cossack. Of this composition he told me a characteristic anecdote. *Der Festfeierfrauenverein* (Woman's Committee of the Celebration) had asked him to compose a march for the occasion, offering him a handsome honorarium. He had consented but, burdened with other duties, had neglected this work. At last, rather late, he began to occupy himself with it and, as he worked and thought what a century of republican government in America meant to the world, the importance of the occasion grew upon him and he finished it in a state of exalted enthusiasm. He cabled to America that the work was ready but received no reply. After a time he thought that perhaps it might be too late for its purpose and was sorely disappointed. Being in Berlin one day, he therefore took the score to the American legation, but, as the Minister was absent, he was obliged to explain the situation to a secretary.

Wagner's speech was not always clear, for often the thoughts were too rapid for the tongue; but, in his tempestuous manner, he tried to make plain the history of the work and that he was so proud of the honour of composing the March for this occasion, that he was quite willing to renounce the fee which had been promised him, if only the March could quite cer-tainly be accepted and performed. He showed the secretary the motto, taken from Goethe, which prefaced the score.

Nur der verdient sich Freiheit wie das Leben
Der täglich sie erobern muss.[11]

Whereupon the secretary burst out: "Sir, do you mean to say that the American people intend to rob you!"

Poor Wagner gave up his explanation as hopeless, but upon returning home to Bayreuth found a communication from the Committee which was in every way satisfactory, as it provided that the March should be accepted and performed and, moreover, the fee he was so willing to renounce was paid by cable.

After Wagner's death another memento was given to your mother by Frau Cosima, with a letter dated June 20, 1888. She wrote: "I put also some engravings, French ones, which have now got so rare that they are no more to be bought and from which I would be very glad if Mrs. Jenkins would accept them from me. Perhaps the fact that they have been for many years in Wahnfried's library will be able to size their worth. . . . Mr. Latour belongs to the impressionists in France, and his great picture of the Wagnerians in Paris made a great noise there."[12]

We knew the value, actual and sentimental, of these engravings, for they had been presented to Wagner by the artist upon the first representation of the "Ring" at Bayreuth and I had often seen and admired them hanging in the great library.

We did not like to accept them, thinking they ought to remain in the Wagner family, but Frau Cosima was so persistent that it was impossible to refuse. You will all remember how they have hung in our library for a quarter of a century.

I was always greatly impressed by Frau Wagner's devotion to her husband. She cared for him with motherly tenderness and wifely tact. She stood between him and every annoyance. There were innumerable practical questions constantly demanding attention, visits from the mayor or some committee, or from aspiring artists, or from builders and architects, and with all of them she made every way smooth and sent them off contented, without a thought of troubling the *Meister* himself. All the while he would be in his study, working undisturbed, singing from time to time, or darting to the piano and striking the keys again and again, and then falling into silence while rapidly writing his score. He seemed to work with great concentration of thought, but when he had finished he was as light-hearted as a child. His wife was so familiar with his needs that she always chose just the right moment and exactly the right tone and the best form of words to present to him any question upon which his decision was necessary, with the result that everything seemed easily accomplished with the least possible friction or disturbance.

In 1878 I received from Wagner a remarkable letter. At that time he had become discouraged at not having the assurance of being able to carry out his plans for perpetuating his temple of art at Bayreuth and fancied he might be able to find the support he longed for by going with his works to settle permanently in America, and that I could help him to realize such a plan. It was, of course, wildly impractical, but it was a delicate matter to convince him that it would be unwise. We went to Constantinople by way of Naples expressly to talk with him and Frau Cosima and found they were so full of illusions as to the conditions in America that arguments against this plan had no force. During the next year, however, it was possible, through the aid of a few of the great *Meister*'s friends and enemies in America, to make it plain that the place for his great triumph was in his own country and among his own people, and I rejoiced that that end was attained without a cloud resting upon our friendship.

Your mother and I were invited to attend the first performance of "Parsifal" on July 26, 1882. It was, even to me, a very great event. By nature I have a love of poetry, as well as for colour and meaning in painting, but my profession has been so absorbing that, despite all my advantages, I have been unable to cultivate the fine arts to the extent of my limited capacity. But music has always been a sealed book to me. I had often said that I would rather have written any one of the world's great poems than all the music of all time. You children will remember what a trial I have been to you at the opera, because the music which you enjoyed so much became to me, after the first half hour, only unmeaning and almost unendurable noise. But the performance of "Parsifal" was not opera; it was a mystical musical drama, composed by a great genius and performed by famous artists inspired by religious enthusiasm. At this first representation there were present musical celebrities from all the world, as well as an immense number of Wagner's devoted disciples. The whole town had an aspect of solemnity, which was as impressive as it was genuine, for everyone felt himself participating in a great historical event; but the audience in the theatre was in the mood of a congregation in a cathedral engaged in celebrating High Mass upon some famous national occasion. Although the audience had been requested not to applaud, there was, after the first act, a spontaneous outburst of delight, but it was instantly suppressed when the *Meister*, leaning over from his box, entreated the audience not to disturb the illusion. I can recall nothing of the close, I do not remember if we applauded or not, for even like those who had the ability to understand the music, I was overwhelmed with the sublime effect of this magnificent drama.

Throughout all my acquaintance with Wagner I had been more and more impressed by his intellectual greatness. He was a man apart from all others in mind and purpose. I came to understand the passionate devotion he received from his true disciples, to whom any faults he may have had seemed of no account in a genius so lofty and with aims so noble and I rejoice to possess for myself a flawless memory of this remarkable man.

On the thirteenth of February, 1883, Wagner suddenly died at Venice. On the morning of that day his son, Siegfried, who had been under my treatment, wrote me a letter, enclosing some small article, and he sealed it five times, using his father's seal. This is probably the last time it was ever used. Four of these seals I have given as souvenirs to friends, but one has been still preserved.

NOTES

1. Also known as the "American Centennial March." In the original: *Großer Festmarsch zur Eröffnung der hundertjährigen Gedenkfeier der Unabhängigkeit der Vereinigten Staaten von Nordamerika*. See John Deathridge, Martin Geck, Egon Voss, *Wagner Werk-Verzeichnis: Verzeichnis der musikalischen Werke Richard Wagners und ihrer Quellen* (Mainz and New York, 1986), no. 110.

2. *Cosima Wagner's Diaries*, ed. and trans. Geoffrey Skelton (New York, 1978), entry of 14 February 1876 (henceforth *CWD*).

3. The Russian-Jewish pianist Joseph Rubinstein was one of a group of musical assistants and copyists in Bayreuth sometimes referred to as the "Nibelung Chancellory." Rubinstein often performed works from the Classical and Romantic canon for Richard and Cosima in the salon at Wahnfried. Jenkins incorrectly identifies Joseph Rubinstein as the brother of Anton and/or Nikolai Rubinstein (who were brothers) in his *Reminiscences*. He is correct, however, in alluding to Joseph Rubinstein's suicide a year after Wagner's death.

4. *CWD*, 1 February 1880.

5. Cited in Martin Gregor-Dellin, *Richard Wagner: His Life, His Work, His Century*, trans. J. Maxwell Brownjohn (New York, 1983), 482. The full text of this letter can be found in Curt von Westernhagen, *Wagner: A Biography*, trans. Mary Whittall (Cambridge, 1978), 551–52.

6. *CWD*, 24 January 1879.

7. Jenkins's grandson, also Newell (1915–96), became a notable advocate of lesser-known Baroque and Classical musical repertoire from the 1950s through the 1970s in the United States and abroad as founder and director of the "Clarion Concerts," thanks in part to the proceeds of his grandfather's toothpaste patent. Details of the elder Jenkins's professional contributions are given by John M. Hyson Jr., DDS, MS, MA, and Scott D. Swank, DDS, in "Dr. Newell Sill Jenkins: Progenitor of Cosmetic Dentistry," *Journal of the California Dental Association* 31/8 (August 2003): 626–29.

8. Newell Sill Jenkins, *Reminiscences of Newell Sill Jenkins* (Princeton, 1924), 191–204.

9. Wagner's dedication to Jenkins is built around punning allusions to his dental profession. In Jenkins's own translation: "I speak not of the tooth of time, / The tooth's own time is drawing nigh. / Is Jenkins then within this clime? / Time and its tooth I will defy."

10. The dedication reads: "My dear Mr. Jenkins! In exchange of our mutual hopes I address to you this friendly dedication. Long live America! — yours, Richard Wagner."

11. "He alone earns his freedom, and his life, who daily must re-conquer them" (Goethe, *Faust*, Part 2, Act 5, ll. 11575–76). These famous lines of Faust refer to his symbolic land-reclamation project near the end of Part 2, embodying the theme of constant moral striving at the heart of Goethe's philosophical dramatic epic.

12. The engraving of Fantin-Latour's 1885 painting *Autour du piano* is reproduced as Figure 2 in "The *Revue wagnérienne*," in Part IV of this volume.

PART III

TOWARD A MUSIC OF THE FUTURE
1840–1860

The Overture to *Tannhäuser*

FRANZ LISZT

INTRODUCED, EDITED, AND ANNOTATED
BY DAVID TRIPPETT
TRANSLATED BY JOHN SULLIVAN DWIGHT

> *"Tannhäuser* . . . a disease from which I have recovered."
> —Liszt to Carolyne von Sayn-Wittgenstein

Early in 1842, Wagner knew he had failed to conquer Paris. In April of that year, he crossed the Rhein with Minna, relieved to return to Saxony and turn his back on the erstwhile dream of an eye-watering success at the Opéra. "This is something I must now leave behind me forever," he admitted to his friend, the minor philologist Samuel Lehrs in 1843; "we opera composers cannot be European— so the question is—either *German* or *French!*"[1] Of course, this was something of a Hobson's choice for Wagner as he assumed his post as royal Kapellmeister at the court of Dresden that year. But the instability of the German states during the 1840s made Wagner's statement about musical allegiance more complex than it might seem at first. After the serious harvest failures between 1845 and 1847 gave way to rising food costs and bread riots, and a downturn in the business cycle led to crippling bankruptcies and growing social unrest, it was hardly surprising that at the beginning of 1848 the widespread demand for liberal democratic reform emerged as outright bloody revolution.[2]

Fourteen months after the barricades were first erected in the Prussian capital, Wagner's Dresden also erupted into violence; between May 3 and 9 of 1849 he aligned himself with the provisional government. Indeed, Ernest Newman presented persuasive evidence in 1937 that Wagner was a confidant among Dresden's republican agitators. In the May uprising he apparently acquired hand grenades and hunting rifles, assumed a role as lookout atop the Dresden *Kreuzkirche,* and printed inflammatory placards demanding "Are you with us against the foreign troops?"[3] Mere weeks after Wagner's arrest warrant had been issued and he had fled the relative sanctity of Liszt's Weimar, he disdainfully coupled the political status quo to the modern stage in Germany, lamenting that the one plays itself out on the other by materializing "the ruling spirit of our social life."[4] This assertion would become self-reflexive for *Tannhäuser* and *Lohengrin* when Wagner followed up his participation in the abortive political revolution in Dresden with a prescription for aesthetic revolution in opera, one that effectively relegated even *Lohengrin* to an aesthetically adolescent "snakeskin."[5]

However unsubtle Wagner's mapping of politics onto art may be, his ideas remained susceptible to dubious misreading, as the traditional rhetoric of physical presence and persuasion became reliant on more anonymous technologies of mass communication. The incremental, fractured dissemination of his works and essays ensured that his post-1848 revolutionary ambitions were all too easily read into the pre-1848 works. Thus, in the 1850s, *Lohengrin* (1848) and *Tannhäuser* (1845) were received proleptically as "music drama." Wagner tried to clear up the confused chronology in both *Opera and Drama* (1851) and *A Communication to My Friends* (1851). In the former, he excused himself: "I must make mention of myself here, admittedly only in order to disclaim the suspicion that has grown in the reader, that I had, with this portrayal of the complete drama, also attempted to explain my own artistic works in the sense undertaken, that I accomplished in my operas the demands made by me, thus, that this intended Drama had already been accomplished."[6] And in *A Communication*, he lamented that "views on the nature of Art that I have proclaimed from a standpoint it took me years of evolution step-by-step to gain, [critics] seize on for the standard of their verdict, and point them back to those very compositions from which I started on the natural path of evolution that led me to this standpoint."[7] It seems that Wagner regarded the proleptical reception of his works as one reason for their lack of widespread acceptance by critics in the early 1850s, a view he protested vigorously.

The majority of German critics, however, continued to judge his most recent operas as exemplifications of the tenets laid down in his Zürich essays (1849–51), adding to the "misunderstandings" that Wagner privately dubbed "the depths of the most utter mindlessness."[8] The composer, pianist, and writer Joachim Raff explained the problem most clearly in *The Wagner Question* (1854), a dialectical commentary on *Lohengrin*'s position within Wagner's aesthetics: "By chance, the public received the two books [*Artwork of the Future, Opera and Drama*] before hearing *Lohengrin* and *Tannhäuser*. . . . These operas were naturally appointed as 'operas of the future' and their music in particular 'music of the future.' The truth is, however, that the operas had appeared long before the essays and have little or nothing in common with them. . . . The press reviewing the operas found no time to look for their own position on the Wagner question; they drew their particular conclusions about the aforementioned operas from Wagner's theories, conclusions that Wagner himself explains as his future artistic activity."[9]

This situation resulted in crisp tensions between celebrations of Wagner's artistic progress and charges of his failure to adhere to the stated theories. His public image vacillated between the charlatan and savior of German opera, and many writers—following their uncomfortable first encounters with what Slavoj Žižek terms the Wagnerian Sublime[10]—simply recoiled at the hubris, rebuking his aesthetic direction and calling for him to reform not opera but himself: "Are we to believe that Wagner entirely suppressed the illusion or made it unnoticeable; that he has transferred the stirring truth of actual drama completely to the higher realm of music? Absolutely not."[11] With a few articulate exceptions, Wagner's aesthetic aspirations were roundly reviled in the German states as megalomaniacal.

Wagner recognized that being understood in a print-enabled discourse—whether on bloody revolution or cultural politics—was particularly difficult since the definitions of most things—especially "politics"—were at stake during the *Nachmärz*. He confessed to Frédéric Villot in 1860 that "when all is said and done [an artist's theories] can only expect to be understood by one who already shares his artistic standpoint."[12] Much ink was spilled over Wagner's aesthetic discourse during the 1850s since "understanding" in Wagner's sense required agreement among politicized factions that often had little appetite to see eye to eye.

With pen and baton, Liszt sought to address the difficulties arising from what he perceived to be misunderstandings of Wagner's operas and unjustified distortions of their aesthetic value. In this, he aspired to clarify what he felt had been obfuscated in the vortex of Wagner criticism following his escape to Paris, when he temporarily secured notoriety among Germany's literati as a revolutionary with hand grenades in one hand and manuscript paper in the other.

Liszt's Weimar performance of *Tannhäuser* on February 16, 1849, was the first since the Dresden premiere in 1845. If theaters had been uninterested in staging Wagner before the revolution, they were positively afraid of putting his name on the playbill for some time after it. Liszt's decision to stage *Tannhäuser* in Weimar thus came to involve political as well as artistic risk.[13] Accordingly, this opera would prove the occasion around which Liszt's lopsided relationship with Wagner first began to solidify. Wagner is profuse in his gratitude to Liszt, who responded with an outstretched hand: "I thank you with all my heart for the thanks you proffer me. Once and for all, number me in the future among your most zealous and devoted admirers; far or near, count on me and dispose of me." Wagner for his part responded in like fashion: "If the world belonged to us, I believe we should do something to give pleasure to the people living therein. I hope we two at least shall agree with each other . . . and thus be our alliance sealed!"[14] As is well known, Wagner's fiscal irresponsibility and Liszt's generosity characterized the early stages of this "alliance"; and though it was a unique meeting of musical minds, the extent to which it could ever be said to have been a balanced, reciprocal partnership remains doubtful.

In May 1849, Wagner secretly audited a rehearsal of *Tannhäuser* in Weimar and expressed delight at the proposed piano transcription of the overture and "Abendstern" scene before fleeing Germany.[15] While exiled in Paris some months later, Wagner read Liszt's 1849 *Tannhäuser* essay in the popular daily *Journal des débats* with mixed feelings.[16] His tactful response praised Liszt's innately performative nature, and was no doubt intended to foster a powerful ally (it was also the first letter to Liszt in which Wagner used the familiar "du" address):

> You wished to describe my opera to the people, and instead of that you have yourself produced a true work of art. Just as you conducted the opera, so have you written about it: new, entirely new, and from your inner self. When I put the article down, my first thoughts were these: This wonderful man can do or undertake nothing without producing his own self from his inner depth . . . everything in him tends to absolute, pure production, and yet he has never yet concentrated his whole willpower on the production of a great work. Is he . . . too little of an egoist? Is he too caring, and does he resemble Jesus on the Cross, Who helps everyone but Himself?[17]

If Wagner's ostensive praise veiled a certain resentment at again being reduced to an insolvent black sheep in Paris, and now a criminal in Germany to boot, he was more explicit in grumbling later that the coincidental appearance in Paris of Liszt's article and of himself "has given a distinct color to my position in Paris . . . as black as possible."[18] Others received the essay with more enthusiasm, however; the teenage Hans von Bülow regarded it as "written in a perfectly masterly, superb manner," and particularly admired Liszt's translation of Wagner's German poetry into a French aesthetic.[19]

Liszt conceived the *Tannhäuser* monograph as promotional material for Wagner in Paris (both men had hoped to help secure a performance of *Tannhäuser* there). The essay thus began as a mere poetic description of the plot for the *Journal des débats*. When Liszt decided to produce a brochure containing both his *Tannhäuser* and *Lohengrin* essays in 1851, as well as a report on the Herder and Goethe festival in Weimar, he expanded his original 1849 article into a full personal reflection, a narrative analysis revealing his own experience of the work, though still for the purposes of Wagner propaganda. This was drafted between April and June 1851, and the larger brochure, titled *Lohengrin et Tannhäuser de Richard Wagner par Franz Liszt*, was published (in French) later that same year by Brockhaus of Leipzig. A year later, this was translated into German by Ernst Weyden, and published by Franz Carl Eisen of Cologne as *Richard Wagner's Lohengrin und Tannhäuser. Von Franz Liszt. (Aus dem Französischen.) Mit Musik-Beilagen.*[20]

Unlike the post-performance article from 1849, aesthetic distance and a complex of influences affected this second stage of his writing about *Tannhäuser*. First, Theodor Uhlig's recent article on the *Tannhäuser* overture asserted that Wagner had rejected his earlier artistic directions on several occasions, that the overture's existence (though not its musical content) was his one and only concession to outmoded tradition, and that Wagner flatly disputed the possibility of expressing anything particular in "absolute" music.[21] Second, Liszt was keenly aware of Eduard Hanslick's review praising the opera but intentionally disregarding the overture in 1846 as "not satisfactory as [an] independent musical [composition]."[22] Liszt appears to have avoided direct engagement with this critique by addressing what Hanslick did not—namely literary-poetic analysis, mythical background, and the overture as an independent musical composition. Third, Liszt had now read *Art and Revolution* and *Artwork of the Future*.[23] This exposure to Wagner's new ideas unsettled—if not entirely reoriented—Liszt's understanding of Wagner's pre-1849 aesthetics (he confessed to Carolyne von Sayn-Wittgenstein in May 1851 that *Tannhäuser* was now "a disease from which I have recovered"), though he also admitted to a certain lack of comprehension.[24] Fourth, Liszt's correspondence suggests that, as with Marie d'Agoult, he permitted his long-term mistress Sayn-Wittgenstein to help him draft portions of the expanded essay. The extent of her involvement is difficult to ascertain in the absence of a holograph. At precisely this time, Liszt was encouraging the princess's literary ambitions, and she wrote to him of her intent to write about *Tannhäuser*, which Liszt appears to have ignored. Given the princess's lack of musical education, her fondness for literary allusion, and the existence of corroborating evidence from Peter Cornelius, Kleinerz and Winkler deduced in their edition for the new Liszt *Sämtliche Schriften* that only a brief analysis of character depiction in part 4 of Liszt's essay is likely to have been written by Sayn-Wittgenstein.[25]

Like the *Lohengrin* monograph on which it was modeled, Liszt's extended 1851 version of the earlier *Journal de débats* essay on *Tannhäuser* pioneers a new mode of opera criticism, blending discussion of poetry, music, dramaturgy, plot, and character type. But whereas the *Lohengrin* essay is more extensive in this respect, and was written only after Liszt had absorbed the aesthetic lessons of Wagner's *Artwork of the Future*, the first version of the *Tannhäuser* essay, as mentioned above, began as promotional material—

a historically informed retelling of the plot in French. In its final version, then, the *Tannhäuser* essay actually merged two different stages in Liszt's reception of Wagner's opera.

Liszt's *Tannhäuser* essay is written in four parts. The first renarrates Wagner's plot within its historical background, drawing extensively on the libretto (essentially taken from the 1849 publication); the second (included here) is a descriptive analysis of the overture viewed as a closed, independent symphonic form; the third presents a linear description of Wagner's drama in its musical setting; and the fourth section is an overall assessment of the score's significance as the beginning of a new era of dramatic art.

Liszt's poetic style and individualized descriptions signal the degree of his personal investment in the essay. Even in 1849, he confirmed what Wagner termed his "purely productive" act to the Grand Duke Carl Alexander, declaring: "This poetical analysis of Wagner's [*Tannhäuser*] libretto was for me only an opportunity to express something that I feel very deeply."[26] But in view of Liszt's aspiration toward a new genre of symphonic "poetry," his later characterization of the overture as a "symphonic whole by itself . . . an independent composition . . . in spite of [Wagner's] own theories,"[27] and his interpretation of Wagner's thematic motives as "so characteristic that they contain in themselves all the striking sense demanded by the musical thought . . . [requiring] no explanatory text"[28] may have struck the exiled composer as particularly self-serving. Liszt carefully emphasizes the overture's "classical form," though lets slip his propagandistic agenda through hyperbole, stating that one could not ask for "more perfect logic in the exposition, development and solution of its premises."[29] Although poetic premises are surely different from their formal, topical, or procedural equivalents, Liszt's interpretation of Wagner's instrumental music, in express contradiction of his stated theories, marks the beginning of an ideological rift between them. This would widen during Liszt's Weimar decade, when he solidified his commitment to a newly expressive symphonic genre and increasingly distanced himself from the Wagnerian "musical drama."

A little over a year after Liszt's essay was published as a German brochure by Eisen, the Boston-based American music critic John Sullivan Dwight translated parts of this German text for serialization in his own publication, *Dwight's Journal of Music,* during November and December 1853.[30] Only the first three sections of Liszt's four-part essay appeared in the journal at this time. The fourth section, concerning *Tannhäuser*'s historical significance, was omitted because "the article has already reached a greater length than we anticipated."[31] We present here what Dwight called the "minute and glowing" analysis of the overture. His translation of a short section from the beginning of the essay's third part was reprinted in the same journal a decade later, suggesting that Dwight felt Liszt's narrative description was more appealing, and of more practical use, to readers than the more propagandistic historical assessment of Wagner.[32]

Foreign terms such as *motive, tremolo,* and *thema* are not in italics in Liszt's French and Weyden's German text, but I have retained italics from Dwight's translation to remain as close as possible to his original expression. Nevertheless, I have modernized many of Dwight's nineteenth-century spellings throughout this reprinted translation (*syrens, Shakspear, coöperation,* etc.) In addition, minor modifications have been made to punctuation.

FRANZ LISZT
Wagner's *Tannhäuser*

II. The Overture
Translated by John Sullivan Dwight, *Dwight's Journal of Music,* 1853

The overture to this extraordinary opera is in itself a no less wonderful production.[33] It sums up the ideas of the opera in brief. The chant[34] of the pilgrims and the song of the sirens are introduced, like two members, which find their equation in the finale. The religious *motive* appears at first quiet, deep, with slow pulsations, like the instinct of the finest, the sublimest[35] of our feelings; but gradually it is overflooded by the insinuating modulations of the voices, full of enervating languor, full of soul-lulling, although feverish and excited pleasures: seductive mingling of pleasure and unrest! The voices of Tannhäuser and of Venus rise above this hissing, foaming yeast of waves, which swells continually higher. The voices of the sirens and bacchantes grow continually louder and more imperative. The enchantment[36] reaches its climax; it leaves no chord within us silent, but sets every fibre of our being in vibration. The quivering, spasmodic tones now groan, now command in lawless alternation, until the resistless yearning for the infinite, the religious *thema,* gradually comes in again, subdues to itself all these sounds, melts them together into a sublime harmony and unfolds the wings of a triumphal hymn to their fullest breadth.

This great overture forms a symphonic whole by itself, so that we may consider it as an independent composition, separate from the opera which precedes it. The two leading thoughts, which are developed in it, ere they blend in their tremendous confluence, clearly express their entire character, the one with fury, the other with an irresistible influence, absorbing all into itself. These motives are so characteristic that they contain in themselves all the striking sense demanded by the musical thoughts, entrusted purely to the instrumentation. So vividly do they depict the emotions, which they express, that one needs no explanatory text to recognize their nature; not once is it necessary to know the words which are adapted to them afterwards.[37] To maintain that these were necessary to the understanding of this symphony, would be to imitate those of whom Shakespeare says, they "paint the lily and adorn the rose,"[38] etc., or at least to imitate certain Chinese writers, who, to make the purport of their style clear to their readers, see fit to write in the margin of their books: "Deep Thought" —"Metaphor"— "Allusion," etc., whenever such occur in their writings. In Europe writers and composers may presume more on the understanding of their public, on the eloquence of their art and the clearness of their diction. It would be to torment oneself with scruples, like the learned scholars of the Celestial Empire, to be unwilling to separate the overture to "Tannhäuser" from its opera, out of the fear that it might not be understood or might not prove interesting. Its glowing coloring depicts the passions, which animate it, too intelligibly, to give any room for such precaution.

Rhythmical and harmonic figures, distributed amongst violas, shrill[39] violins (divided over several desks) and wind instruments (pianissimo), accented by slight drum beats, and cut off into broken periods; groups of notes, ascending in swift spirals, losing and finding themselves in inexplicable windings, detaching themselves from an almost unbroken web of tremolo and trills frequently and strikingly modulated, enable us, by an entirely novel effect of languishing and amorous euphony, to recognize the magic arts of the sirens. The rich repertory of the existing music of this kind offers, as it seems to us, no such bold image, no such striking reflex, no such exciting stimulus and entrainement of the senses, of their brain-whirling intoxication, their prismatic illusions. Now and then tones glide in, which pass before the ear, as certain phantoms glimmer before the eye . . . seductive, penetrating, unnerving—faithless! Under their artificial, silky softness one perceives despotic intonations, feels the quivering of rage. Here and there ring out sharp, cutting tones of the violins,[40] like phosphorescent sparks. The entrance of the drums makes us tremble, like the far off echo of an insane orgy. Chords occur of a deafening intoxication, which remind us that the Messalinas[41] found their festivities not unadorned with horrors; that they did not deny themselves the satisfaction of seeing the bloodiest spectacles combined with amorous dallyings; that they knew how to unite barbarous pleasures with the dangerous emotions that are inspired by beauty. The presence of the Maenads and their tumultuous dances in the Venus-grotto soon confirm this impression; this distinguishes this most original development of the very acme of voluptuousness above all the musical compositions which have so frequently attempted to describe the same thing. Once borne away by these wildly exciting, ravishing effects, one oversteps the sphere of ordinary temptations. Wagner has by no means contented himself with the free and easy motives, used by most of those whose inspiration answers to the taste and tendencies expressed in the scenes of a Rubens, or a Teniers, when they wanted to portray the fascination and tyrannical seductions of the mother and the queen of love. His mental ear knew how to detect the indescribable subtlety of those graceful tones, which resound at the court of Cytherea, but to which only a small number consecrated by the Graces ever penetrate, ushered in by a smiling crew who offer them the cup of joy, in which a strange, mysterious, fateful, but by no means a coarse and brutal intoxication is to be found. A German genius needed something of a Shakespeare's universal intuition, to become so penetrated as it were with the blood of antiquity, and inspired with an effervescence so entirely foreign to the gloomy fermentations of the North.

Sensual passion is here represented with the tumultuous delights of a refined voluptuousness, which dull, cold, heavy natures cannot at all conceive of, but which energetic natures, that demand more than every day impressions, dream of and pursue exclusively: lofty and at the same time tender organizations, who give their superabundance of vitality a ready prey to every accident, and who let their stormy passions overflow without restraint, so long as they can find a channel broad and deep enough to contain their roaring, raging, and ungovernable waves. One must marvel how, in Wagner's production, the power of treatment is never destructive of tenderness. It was not easy for him to secure both these characters.[42]

In the midst of this harmony, which overflowing, sparkling, looms forth like a more and more dazzling mirage, we are suddenly awakened by a dramatic interest, when the feeling, vague as it may be, becomes individualized in two melodic phrases, one of which sounds to us like a cry of triumph and delight, mingled with a challenging expression, while the other lulls us with seductive invitation.

To scale majestically these dazzling precipices of voluptuousness and pleasure, the composer had to raise himself to an unwonted pitch of exaltation. The religious *thema,* once already drowned by this multitudinous hum of tones, that brushed past the ear with glowing breath, tingling at the fingers' ends, bewildering the brain, exciting the nerves, like fabled promises and mystical enchantments;—the religious *thema,* emerging again from this wild delirium, from this voluptuous languor, ran great risk of seeming cold, dreary, dry and barren, a mere soulless denial of contentment. . . . But it is by no means so. This holy *motive* rises before us not at all like a stern master, silencing the shameless whispering that rustles through those caves of hidden joys. In their presence it stands not gloomy and apart. It flows clearly and softly, creeping over all the strings, that vibrated with such sweet allurements; it holds them down, one by one, although they struggle against it with a bitter desperation. But ever clear and tranquil, in spite of this resistance, it extends its empire, transforming and assimilating all the friendly elements. The masses of glowing tones crumble into fragments, which form more and more painful discords, till they grow positively repulsive, like essences just turning into staleness; and joyfully we see it rising into a grand spiritual song, and overflooding with its radiance all the tempting illusions that preceded, as it spreads along, like liquid sunshine, brighter and brighter, till it swells into a mighty stream, that bears our whole soul and being on with it to an ocean of glory![43]

If we express ourselves at great length about this new opera of Wagner, it is because we cherish the conviction that this work carries in itself a principle of vitality and of glory, which will one day be universally recognized. The innovations which it contains, are drawn from the true powers of Art, and will justify themselves as acquisitions of genius. Accordingly, in speaking of the overture, we may remark that one could not desire of a symphonic poem that it should be written more consistently with the rules of classical form, or that it should have a more perfect logic in the exposition, development and solution[44] of its premises. Its arrangement is just as precise,[45] at the same time that it is richer, than that of the best models in this kind.

The first sixteen bars lay the first half of the religious *thema* in E major (see Example 1) in the lowest register of the clarinets, horns and bassoons, making a cadence on the dominant. The second part is wonderfully modulated through the violoncello, to which the violins add themselves in the ninth measure (see Example 2). The whole *thema* is then repeated *fortissimo* by the brass instruments in the same key, to a much more lively rhythm in eighth-triplets, continually accompanied by a descending diatonic figure in sixteenth-triplets. During the sixteen following bars the second half of the *thema* is modulated by the wind instruments to the same rhythm of triplets,[46] *mezzo forte, diminuendo* and *piano*; but the figure in sixteenth-triplets, repeating itself only in every second measure, produces a decrease of the rhythm, corresponding to the decrease of power and fullness. The repetition of the whole, merely moderated in the first sixteen bars,[47] forms the end of this introduction upon an inversion of the diminished seventh chord.

Example 1.

Example 2.

The Allegro [Example 3] begins with an indication of the alluring and voluptuous motive (a), immediately followed by a member of a rhythmical phrase (b), which serves it for an appendix, then develops itself completely in the overture, and only disappears in the religious thema again resumed as the finale. The motive, indicated at first, fully develops itself only some thirty bars later [Example 4], with the figures which we have already mentioned, when we spoke of the character which Wagner has given to the temptation scene of the sirens.

Example 3.

Example 4.

It lasts through more than twenty bars and is crowned by an outburst of the little appendix phrase (b) gradually swelling up through three ascending chords,[48] whose bacchic dissonance stuns both ear and mind.[49] The foregoing figures are again resumed pianissimo until the appearance of a lovely melody[50] in G major (afterwards in the opera itself assigned to Venus):

Example 5.

which is first given to the clarinet, is continued by one violin in the register of the highest harmonic tones, carried still farther through a fantastic arabesque of the voluptuous motive (traced out by the violas and thrown into half shadow, as it were, by a tremolo of the violins), and then dies away in F sharp. It gives place to the transition phrase, which had introduced the melody in B, a plaintive scream, which, this time on the ground tone of F♯, ends, through a chromatic progression, with the return of the same melody upon the tonic.

The Coda recalls the leading features of the commencement of the Allegro, and swells to a furious climax by a chromatic descent upon the ground-tone of B, which brings out the last repetition of the appendix phrase (b). At this moment, on the same dissonant chord which we have had before on the first entrance of the livelier tempo in 4/4 measure (E, G, A♯, C♯; but this time on the ground-tone of B), returns the well-known[51] figure in sixteenths, with the religious theme again, which now with accelerating speed mounts through various inversions of this chord, without pause or intermission, and again descends *decrescendo* through a chromatic scale, making a cadence on the tone of E. Thereupon the religious theme appears again in all its completeness through an accompanying figure[52] (two 4/4 measures against one 3/4), and is borne along upon the tone-wave of this peculiarly impassioned figure, which rushes onward like a stream of fire.[53] After sixty measures of this rhythm the theme begins again anew, anew increased (*three*[54] 4/4 measures against one 3/4), with all the brass and other wind instruments setting in *fortissimo*. Thus the conclusion stands in perfect symmetrical relation with the introduction. This conclusion moreover centuples the effect of the introduction and reaches that sublime announcement of a thought and of the power of an art, by which masterpieces secure the admiration of centuries, by the rising of the theme in a form more gigantic than we have any example of in any analogous work, as well as by the altogether unusual hastening of the rhythm in the accompaniment.

Although we have already remarked that the composer of "Tannhäuser" has lent to the passions represented under the name of Venus a character in correspondence with that name so dear to the fair Grecian land, yet we repeat again that there is absolutely no necessity of knowing the opera, the adventures of the Ritter Tannhäuser and the myth of Dame Venus, so singularly transplanted into the Middle Ages, in order to apprehend the musical drama in this overture. It is not merely a sort of gigantic prelude, to prepare the mind[55] for the emotions of the play that is to follow; not a necessary introduction, a short and solemn prologue, limited to the office of enchaining the minds of the audience in the region of feelings, which are designed to occupy it. It is unlike those orchestral pieces, which, without containing a single motive of the opera, which they announce, or possibly repeating some few of them, always form a necessary complement to the whole, by transporting the feelings of the spectator into the scene and atmosphere of the play. . . .[56] This overture is a poem upon the same subject with its opera, and[57] quite as comprehensive as the opera. Out of the same thoughts Wagner has made two different works; and since each is intelligible, complete, and independent of the other, they may be taken separately without sacrificing any of the meaning of either. They are bound together by identity of feeling and expression, but for the very reason of this identity they do not need to be mutually explained. If we must quote fact and experience in confirmation of our assertion, we will only say, that we have had this overture brought out, and that it was received with the most enthusiastic admiration, without one of the musicians who performed, or of the public who applauded, having had the slightest knowledge either of the subject or the text[58] of the opera. We cannot fear, therefore, that so much time will have to pass, as was necessary until Mozart's Quartets were no longer torn up by the musicians as unperformable, or until Beethoven's masterpieces were no longer treated as grotesque and absurd innovations, before this overture will belong to the repertoire of standard pieces, which will be long and repeatedly brought out by the great musical establishments.

We find a confirmation of our opinion that Wagner, in spite of his own theories, felt more impelled to create a symphonic work, than anxious to put a prologue to his drama, in his violation of the rules of acoustical perspective (if we may be pardoned the expression) by such an extended development of the motive, which is to be immediately resumed as the curtain rolls up. The laws of climax, so indispensable to scenic effects, would be utterly violated, (for what *forzando*[59] is there left to be added to the *crescendo* already reached by the song of the sirens long before the play begins?) if the spectacle, the dance and the human voice did not conceal the difficulty; did not by their magic, their cooperation and their art lend a new stimulus to curiosity; did not enhance the stormy impetuosity of the orchestra; did not rescue the public from that need of repose—which those who are most excited feel the most and revive again the well nigh exhausted interest seeing that the last word of the tragedy, that is about to be represented, has already been so powerfully uttered.

NOTES

1. Wagner to Samuel Lehrs, 7 April 1843, Dresden, in *Selected Letters of Richard Wagner*, trans. and ed. Stewart Spencer and Barry Millington (New York and London, 1988), 107–8.

2. For more information on the social and economic unrest as well as the political conditions that prepared the ground for widespread revolution in 1848, see David Blackbourn's detailed history of the topic, *The Long Nineteenth Century* (New York, 1998), 138–74.

3. Newman pursued a "common sense" approach rather than a "judicial enquiry" into the available details to weigh the evidence of Wagner's active involvement in the Dresden uprisings of May 1849. He summarizes that "far from his being a mere curious spectator of events, [Wagner] was as active a participator in [the Dresden uprisings] as most." See Ernest Newman, *The Life of Richard Wagner: 1848–1860* (London, 1937), 2:24–102, here 87.

4. Richard Wagner, "Art and Revolution," in *The Artwork of the Future and Other Works*, trans. William Ashton Ellis, *Richard Wagner's Prose Works* (London, 1895; repr. 1993), 1:43.

5. Wagner to Adolf Stahr, 31 May 1851, in Richard Wagner, *Sämtliche Briefe* (henceforth *SB*) (Leipzig, 1967–2000; Wiesbaden, 1999–), 4:57–58.

6. In *Opera and Drama*, trans. William Ashton Ellis, *Richard Wagner's Prose Works* (London, 1893; repr. 1995), 2:211.

7. *A Communication to My Friends*, in Ellis, *Richard Wagner's Prose Works*, 1:284.

8. "in der absoluten gedankenlosigkeit," Wagner to Theodor Uhlig, 27 July 1850, Zürich, in *SB*, 3:363.

9. Raff, *Die Wagnerfrage* (Braunschweig, 1854), 5–6 (my translation).

10. Slavoj Žižek, "The Politics of Redemption, or, Why Richard Wagner Is Worth Saving," in *Lacan: The Silent Partners*, ed. Slavoj Žižek (London and New York, 2006), 231.

11. Quoted in August Hitzschold, "Zur Physiologie des musicalischen Dramas," *Niederrheinische Musik-Zeitung* 23 (3 December 1853): 177 (my translation).

12. Quoted in Klaus Kropfinger, *Wagner and Beethoven*, trans. Peter Palmer (Cambridge, 1991), 70.

13. His stated motivation was to "establish firm roots for these masterpieces in German soil," in La Mara, ed., *Franz Liszt's Briefe*, (Leipzig, 1893), 3:136.

14. Liszt's words from his letter of 26 February 1849; Wagner's from 1 March 1849. See *Correspondence of Wagner and Liszt*, trans. Francis Hueffer (New York, 1897; repr. 2005), 18–21.

15. Liszt first told Wagner of his plan for the two transcriptions on 26 February 1849, to which Wagner responded on 1 March: "I feel highly flattered by your proposal." See Hueffer, *Correspondence of Wagner and Liszt*, 21. The warrant for Wagner's arrest (*Steckbrief*) was printed in the *Dresden Anzeiger* on 19 May 1849, one day before the scheduled performance of *Tannhäuser*.

16. The article "Le Tannhaeuser" appeared in the *feuilleton* section of the *Journal des Débats* on 18 May 1849, which had a sizable circulation of 10,600 in 1849. The same article appeared again two days later in *La Musique. Gazette de la France Musicale*. This double publication is unusual and may have been an attempt to hold Meyerbeer's continued ascendency in check; that is, to counter the enormous success of *Le prophète*, which had premiered in Paris on 16 April of that year. The Tannhäuser essay subsequently appeared with musical examples in Brockhaus's pamphlet *Lohengrin et Tannhäuser de Richard Wagner par Franz Liszt* (1851) and was translated into German by Ernst Weyden (*Richard Wagner's Lohengrin und Tannhäuser,* 1852). For full details, see Franz Liszt, *Sämtliche Schriften*, ed. Rainer Kleinertz and Gerhard Winkler (Wiesbaden, 1989), 4:211–39 (henceforth *SS*).

17. Wagner to Liszt, 5 June 1849, Paris, in *SB*, 3:72.

18. Ibid., 3:73.

19. "Liszt reproduces the opera's content almost with Wagner's words, transferring German poetry to French in a way that one would hardly have thought possible." Bülow

to his mother, 21 June 1849, Leipzig, in Hans von Bülow, *Briefe und Schriften,* ed. Marie von Bülow (Leipzig, 1896, 1908), 1:179 (my translation).

20. Full details of the genesis, revisions, and translations of these two essays are given in the excellent commentary by Gerhard Winkler and Rainer Kleinertz to volume 4 of Liszt's complete writings. See Liszt, *SS,* 4:211–33. For details of the editions and translations published during the nineteenth century, see *SS,* 4:234–39.

21. Theodor Uhlig, "Die Overtüre zu Wagner's Tannhäuser," *Neue Zeitschrift für Musik* 34 (11/18 April 1851): 153–56, 165–68, here 154. Wagner's own brief program to the overture for performance in Zurich posited specific objects and images as the elements of the music's expression. This appeared in the same journal in 1853, along with an extract from his instructions on the performance of the opera. See Wagner, "Über Inhalt und Vortrag der Ouvertüre zu Wagner's Tannhäuser," *Neue Zeitschrift für Musik* 3 (14 January 1853): 23–25.

22. Eduard Hanslick, "Richard Wagner, und seine neueste oper *Tannhaeuser*" in *Sämtliche Schriften,* ed. Dietmar Strauss (Vienna, 1993), 1/1:65. English translation from *Hanslick's Music Criticism,* trans. and ed. Henry Pleasants (New York, 1988), 37. Liszt almost certainly read Hanslick's review, for the twenty-two-year-old law student had borrowed Liszt's personal score to write it.

23. "I am looking forward to your book [*Oper und Drama*]. Perhaps I may try on this occasion to comprehend your ideas a little better, which in your book *Kunst und Revolution* I could not manage very well." Liszt to Wagner, 1 March 1851, in *Correspondence,* 85.

24. "le *Tannhäuser* étant pour moi une malade dont je suis guéri." Liszt to Carolyne von Sayn-Wittgenstein, 8 May 1851, in *Franz Liszt's Briefe* 4:112.

25. Full details of correspondence and manuscript evidence relating to the thorny question of Liszt's authorship are discussed by Kleinertz and Winkler in Liszt, *SS,* 4:225–56.

26. Liszt to Grand Duke Carl Alexander, 23 May 1849, Weimar, in *Franz Liszt Selected Letters,* trans. and ed. Adrian Williams (Oxford, 1998), 272.

27. Franz Liszt,"Wagner's Tannhäuser," trans. John Sullivan Dwight, *Dwight's Journal of Music* 4 (26 November, 3 December 1853): 27, 66.

28. Ibid., 13.

29. Ibid., 15.

30. Ibid., 49–50, 57–58, 65–66, 73–75, 81–82.

31. The fourth section concerning *Tannhäuser*'s historical significance was omitted because "the article has already reached a greater length than we anticipated." See *Dwight's Journal of Music* 4 (17 December 1853): 82.

32. See *Dwight's Journal of Music* 24 (12 November 1864): 339.

33. Liszt's term *oeuvre* is more typically translated as "work."

34. Dwight's synonym for song, *chant,* is misleading in a modern context. Liszt's term *chant* and Weyden's *Gesang* connote both song and singing, and both terms are repeated in their respective texts rather than being replaced by a synonym. See *SS,* 4:108–9.

35. Dwight's invocation of the sublime is perhaps overly casual, for Liszt's French reads *grand* and Weyden's German *höchsten.*

36. Dwight's term "enchantment" does not convey the sense of motion implied by Liszt's *l'agitation* or Weyden's *Bewegung.*

37. "Not once" slightly exaggerates Liszt's text, which simply says "il est inutile de connaître les paroles," and which Weyden translated as "es ist überflüssig, die Worte zu kennen." *SS,* 4:108–9.

38. See Shakespeare, *King John,* 4.2.12–13: "To gild refined gold, to paint the lily,/To throw a perfume on the violet."

39. Liszt refers neutrally to the higher register, "les violins à l'aigu," and Weyden to "Violinen in hoher Lage" so the modern connotation of a piercing high sound in Dwight's translation *shrill* is misleading.

40. Liszt refers specifically to "mordantes de violin." *SS,* 4:110.

41. Liszt refers specifically to "les Cléopâtras" (and Weyden to "eine Kleopatra"). Valeria

Messalina and Statilia Messalina were both Roman empresses who became the third wives of Emperors Claudius and Nero, respectively.

42. Dwight did not include Liszt's continuation: "And only their coming together, however, could bring transports of violent and languorous desire—the secret of which each man wishes to discover—to desire without tenderness [i.e. lust]. / And all this is in the middle of this harmony which numbs you by the quantity of its fine flowing sounds, the fact that it is sustained, incomprehensibly intoxicating and impassioned, all-enveloping like lakes of desire." *SS,* 4:110 (my translation).

43. Dwight omits twenty-nine lines of Liszt's text, in which he expounds on the public's inability to judge new works of art that are not easily classified, even though such works may offer more depth to an understanding of art than superficial norms. Liszt also explains that a thorough knowledge of past and present musical forms is a prerequisite for an understanding of new works, for a lively imagination can easily distort (*dénaturer/entstellen*) unfamiliar music, and the veracity of views resulting from this distortion becomes dependent on mere chance. See *SS,* 4:112–15.

44. Liszt's term *dénouement* connotes more the theatrical outcome of a symphonic process than a "solution" to an equation, though Weyden's translation was *Lösung,* which served as Dwight's original. *Dénouement* is typically translated in modern German as *Auflösung* (resolution) or *Entwirrung* (disentanglement), though neither would ordinarily be used to describe symphonic form. In this instance, *resolution* or simply the anglicized French original are perhaps the most appropriate English translations for Liszt's *dénouement.*

45. Dwight omits Liszt's phrase "just as clear" (*aussi claire / ebenso klar*). See *SS,* 4:114–15.

46. This should read: "During the following sixteen measures the woodwinds allow the second half of the theme to die away with the same triplet rhythm, mezzoforte, diminuendo, and piano." See *SS,* 4:116.

47. Dwight mistakenly corrects Liszt's text and appears to assume incorrectly that Wagner repeated the full opening sixteenth measures of the overture at the end of the maestoso section. Liszt writes correctly that Wagner repeated only eleven measures. *SS,* 4:116.

48. Dwight omits the musical illustration printed in Liszt's original pamphlet (overture mm. 113–22), meaning that Liszt's sixth and final illustration is given by Dwight as his fifth.

49. Dwight's translation "mind" is misleading. Liszt's word *sens* and Weyden's *Sinne* connote more a physical sense than disembodied or ideal mental perception, more typically referred to as *l'esprit* or *Geist.*

50. Liszt uses a French term from Aristides Quintilianus, *mélopée* (Weyden: *Melopöie*), as opposed to *mélodie.*

51. Dwight's adjective "well-known" is not quite the same as Liszt's *déjà entendue.*

52. Liszt does not mention the accompaniment here, only the augmentation.

53. Dwight omits Liszt's *incessamment* or Weyden's *ohne Unterlaß.*

54. Italics not used in Liszt's text.

55. Liszt's term *l'âme* means soul rather than mind.

56. Dwight omits five lines, in which Liszt further substantiates his point about transporting the listener's mind into the musico-dramatic world of the opera to come.

57. Liszt uses the subordinating conjunction *mais* (Weyden: *aber*) rather than Dwight's *and,* illustrating that Liszt felt there was an implicit contradiction of orthodoxy in the idea that an overture can be quite as complete and essentially aesthetically equal to the opera itself.

58. Dwight's *text* should not be interpreted here only as the libretto, for Liszt refers specifically to the *partition de l'opéra* (in Weyden: *Partitur der Oper*).

59. *Rinforzando* in Liszt's text.

Letters to a Young Composer About Wagner

JOHANN CHRISTIAN LOBE
INTRODUCED, EDITED, AND TRANSLATED
BY DAVID TRIPPETT

The flautist, music theorist, composer, and writer Johann Christian Lobe (1797–1881) embarked on a career in music criticism as early as 1826 as co-editor of the *Musikalische Eilpost*, and would work as correspondent, columnist, reviewer, and independent writer for a host of the most respected music journals and newspapers in Germany before editing the *Allgemeine musikalische Zeitung* in its final years (1846–48) and the music section from the *Leipzig Illustrirte Zeitung* (1861–63). By the mid-1840s, needless to say, he was intimately enmeshed in the debates about the purpose of music criticism, as well as acting as one of the profession's central voices.

The fourteen *Letters to a Young Composer About Wagner* were published between 1854 and 1855 as part of Lobe's self-authored music journal, the *Fliegende Blätter für Musik: Wahrheit über Tonkunst und Tonkünstler* (Loose leaves on music: Truth about musical art and musical artists), 1853–57.[1] This consisted of quarterly installments of about sixty pages containing essays and letters as well as smaller entries of anecdotal significance; it was written entirely in the first person—acknowledging the author's subjectivity—and had the purpose of making music accessible to as wide an audience as possible, though aside from connecting with the midcentury *Bildungsbürgertum* (an embryonic form of the bourgeoisie proper), the journal likely had very limited effect on the business class within the middle strata of society, and probably had no impact whatsoever on the rural population, which by 1848—following the steady growth of the small peasantry and a landless "underclass"—still constituted three-quarters of the people within the German states.[2] Thus, Lobe's altruistic outreach effectively applied to non-music specialists within a small, educated class. On the other hand, J. S. Dwight estimated in 1855 that as many as one in two people between the ages of ten and forty in Germany "has undergone some sort of musical training," and "at least" nine out of ten take "some interest" in musical matters.[3] The relatively small circulation of the major music journals—projected at under three thousand subscribers by Dwight—was a result of their impractical content, he surmised, which disregarded what the public wanted. Lobe's intention, at least, was thus to reach this wider, musically inclined demographic.

With this in mind, Lobe first expressed a sympathetic view of Wagner's music in 1850 when he favorably reviewed Liszt's Weimar premiere of *Lohengrin* in Heinrich Laube's *Signale für die musikalische Welt,* eliciting an uncharacteristically friendly response from Wagner.[4] In 1853, Lobe further defended *Lohengrin* and *Opera and Drama* against chronologically confused criticism from Julius Schaeffer, a Wagner supporter whose serialized, analytically dense monograph measures the essay against the opera with unwitting sophistry.[5] A year earlier, Lobe had half-cynically characterized the relationship of Wagner's operas to *Opera and Drama* as that between heavily laden sailing ships stuck at port (in windless weather) and a bellowing breeze; Wagner's essay whipped up such a "wind" that his fleet of dramatic works now "float with full sail on the sea of his fame."[6] Yet on the whole, Lobe disapproved of Wagner's polemical writing about music, assuming an aesthetic stance fundamentally opposed to increasingly jaded notions of "progress," a common cry he likened dismissively to the squawking of parrots.[7] Indeed, it was even argued at the time that the *Fliegende Blätter* were conceived entirely "in opposition to the extravagances of [Franz Brendel's] Wagner organ," the *Neue Zeitschrift für Musik.*[8] Although Lobe's biting satire of 1857, "A New Prophet of the Future," is not a direct attack on Liszt, Wagner, or Berlioz, it nevertheless takes aim at those composers whom he felt wrote incomprehensible music under the protective banner of *Zukunftsmusik.*[9] The main reason for the poor quality (and rapid disappearance) of many newly composed German operas, he argued in 1852, was that composers forgot to write "for their contemporaries," and instead sought out their fame by anticipating the future.[10]

Accordingly, Lobe admires conservative elements in *Tannhäuser* and *Lohengrin,* which he analyzes in terms of symmetrical, periodic melody, and formal structure. In the second letter he even rewrites Wagner's theory of a synthesis of the arts to justify it, in organicist terms, as the natural corollary of working from a single, poetic idea (*Idee*). Parroting "progress" was leading inexperienced composers astray, he feared. A response to this situation is Lobe's detailed analysis of the *Tannhäuser* overture, prompted specifically by Wagner's poetic program written for concerts in Zurich (1853), which Lobe systematically picks apart in his fourth letter.[11] Foreshadowing the corrective approach to Wagner, Lobe had analyzed the "progress" that Niels Wilhelm Gade had made in his celebrated third symphony (1847), and deduced that Gade had not in fact progressed beyond Beethoven. In that earlier essay, Lobe concluded that trends in criticism toward the "future" and "progress" were tempting young composers to innovate at the expense of appropriate study of older masters.[12] Hence, the Wagner letters are addressed specifically to such young composers.

Untangling the discourse of critics and mediating partisan views is Lobe's initial concern. He opens his letters by contrasting newspaper snippets that praise and censure Wagner's Romantic operas with equal ferocity. Writers are too one-sided, he begins diplomatically. The reader should look first at what Wagner has achieved as a composer, not what has been written about him (or what he himself has written). Practical considerations—such as the impossibility for smaller theaters to perform Wagner's operas, and the corresponding difficulty for people to actually hear and see them—also influence Lobe's didactic tone. The striking means by which he shepherds his readers through Wagner's unfamiliar scores is extensive musical illustration (including harmonic reduction), with all the "see for yourself," hands-aloft innocence such an approach projects. The tacit assumption is that musical notation that represents or *in*-scribes the works themselves (however philosophically problematic this equation may be) will trump the polemically biased and personally motivated arguments that *de*-scribe or *de*-cipher the operas' content into a critical muddle. In Franz Liszt's discussions of *Tannhäuser* and *Lohengrin*, the musical illustrations are offered as a means of sharing his listening experience with the reader. In Lobe's paradoxical view, on the other hand, music is posited as visually self-evident; against a wash of dirty phrases in the Wagner discourse, the notation functions as a cleansing agent, apparently offering a way out of the vortex of disagreements. Throughout his career, Lobe's view was that aesthetic criteria were not determined by philosophical systems, but by the musical works "themselves." As late as 1869, he continued to be respected for the salutary, "refreshing" impact his approach could offer.[13]

The *Fliegende Blätter* exemplify this perspective and enjoyed international circulation, as a New York reviewer put it, "in consequence of the practical knowledge and experience in musical matters exhibited in them."[14] Since a variety of serialized articles and letters extended through the various journal issues, Lobe anticipated that his readership would follow not only one series, but read his other articles as well, and he occasionally cross-references his work with this in mind. The *Fliegende Blätter* were even considered "a continuation of [Lobe's Musical] Letters,"[15] that is, of his *Musikalischen Briefe*—published in 1852 under the pseudonym "Briefe eines Wohlbekannten"—which also bore the subtitle: "Truth About Music and Musicians."

A particularly relevant series contemporary with and reinforcing the aesthetic stance of the Wagner letters was Lobe's "Aesthetische Briefe" (Aesthetic letters), in which he isolates music-analytical parameters for interrogation, including rhythm, harmony, melody, tone, dynamics, as well as modulation, modality, and key. The background for Lobe's skepticism about Wagner's rejection of most prior music, indeed about Wagner's aesthetic "system" *tout court*, is further grounded, for instance, in his very first "Aesthetic Letter":

> *There is no musical work that will give pleasure (or appear beautiful) to all men in every era.* For that reason there can be *no single, eternally valid aesthetics* . . . [He] who gathers and assembles the rules according to which . . . [paradigmatic] works are created will at any rate provide the best musical aesthetic relative to his own time.[16]

Since *Tannhäuser* is predominantly the lens through which Lobe focuses his critique of Wagner, the letters selected for translation here focus exclusively on Lobe's analysis of the *Tannhäuser* overture to aid comparison with Liszt's text about the same, also included in the present volume.

JOHANN CHRISTIAN LOBE
Letters to a Young Composer About Wagner
From *Fliegende Blätter für Musik: Wahrheit über Tonkunst und Tonkünstler*
Leipzig, 1854–55

Fourth Letter

A few think in this way, and many appear to want to do so; they shout and set the tone; the great mass remains silent and behaves indifferently, and sometimes agrees and sometimes disagrees. (Lessing)[17]

You have read it often enough and can still read it daily (for one side never tires of repeating things): a principal merit of Wagner is that he demands in his writings—and strives to apply in his works—an entirely new, indeed the only right-minded artistic direction in both operatic poetry and composition.

With this, the art lover is quite naturally directed toward the main vantage point from which he should observe, examine, and judge Wagner's music. This cannot happen, however, should one want to reach no more than a fairly plausible conclusion, with general propositions and gushing phrases; rather one must turn to the facts and ask oneself whether what is attributed to them is really there to be perceived.

Tannhäuser and *Lohengrin* constitute such facts.

Admittedly, Wagner does not yet want to acknowledge either work as a completed expression of his new system, but allows them to be performed where one wants to perform them. His friends raise them as felicitous proof of the new direction above all else that has been achieved before him by musical minds[18] of greatest genius in this field, and we cannot know what more he will achieve in them. We must therefore adhere to that which we have before us.

The first question for every artwork one wants to treat fairly must be: What did the artist intend with it? The second: Is the intention artistically reasonable? The third: Did he achieve this entirely, or only partially, or not at all?

Nobody will have any objections to these questions. I did not invent them, they lie in the nature of things, and have long been recognized as safe guiding criteria. Let us attempt to answer them in turn with good intentions and according to our best knowledge and conscience.

Wagner rejects all absolute music in his writings, i.e., all music that aims to describe something definite without recourse to words, as something for which its indefinite means are insufficient.[19] To begin with, this is nothing new, but rather a time-honored view. Wagner's overtures and introductions, his marches, preludes, interludes, and postludes in his operas prove that he does not count as absolute music that music whose content is to be intimated through a program, or is to be inferred from a given plot.

The Adagio from the *Don Giovanni* overture anticipates the entrance of the petrified guest in the last finale; the introduction to *Lohengrin* anticipates Lohengrin's entrance in the opera. The overture to *Freischütz* prefigures a series of moments from the plot, the overture to *Tannhäuser* does the same.

Let us take a close look specifically at the latter work, and direct our first question to it: what did the artist *intend* with it? The answer can only be: absolutely nothing different from what Weigel before him intended in his overture to *Schweizerfamilie*, or Weber in his overtures to *Freischütz*, *Oberon*, to *Euryanthe*, or Beethoven in his three overtures to *Leonore*, etc. The second question therefore takes care of itself. What all of these masters accomplished, including Wagner, will probably be artistically reasonable.

The question remains for Wagner: did he achieve his intentions entirely, or only partially, or not at all?

But this question would be blasphemous in the eyes of the converted, for Wagner's principal merit is of course the new direction that so markedly surpasses all precursors.

Thus we know to look for it in this overture nowhere more than in an increasingly powerful artistic treatment. Wagner will have expected his *Tannhäuser* overture to express something more specific, and he will have accomplished this in a far more excellent, truer, more apparent and more influential way than was ever possible for an earlier master.

This, my young friend, is what I want to examine as uninhibitedly and as precisely as possible after having become acquainted with the music through multiple listenings, score in hand.

That our composer was absolutely conscious of what he wanted to describe in the overture lies beyond all doubt.

Through his accompanying written program Wagner has documented irrefutably that he meant to express more in this overture than any other master before him, the most daring and genial not excepted.[20]

I want to set out for you the view on this of an unknown writer from the *Augsburg Allgemeine Zeitung* who discusses the performance of the overture in Vienna, first because of the apposite expression of some thoughts, and further to refute some matters in favor of Wagner, since it seems to be his tragic fate that his judges are unable to keep in balance either the "for" or "against."

The anonymous author writes:

Wagner proved that he still bears a secret love in his heart for these "dated viewpoints," for he still wrote a clarifying program for the *Tannhäuser* overture at the last music festival in Zürich.[21] This program—it lies before us—turned out strangely enough. We should really see with the ears, also smell at times, e.g., a "slim, youthful man"—Tannhäuser—"rosy mists"—"delightful scents," an "unspeakably enticing female form"—Frau Venus and such. In the end this even amounts to the musical solution of a philosophical problem: "the two sundered elements of spirit and senses, God and Nature, embrace one another in the sacred unifying kiss of love." The essence of this music, even a naïve reader must admit, lies in *not* being music; it is only fed to the imagination as a means of generating figures, in the process of which one never enjoys the freedom to imagine what one wants. The glorified nonsense that surrounds the Wagnerian interpretation of his overture fades somewhat, however, if we remember that this piece of music is put together from separate components which, individually, have their attendant meaning for the corresponding places in the opera. The overture, precisely because it is no introduction but a compressed summary of the whole, requires an acquaintance with the complete opera to be understood.

The final verdict of this Viennese judge of art reads: "It is a sorry effort pieced together without inner development, without organic execution that—one understands not why—breaks off suddenly!"

You know Wagner's complete program from an earlier issue of the *Fliegende Blätter für Musik* where I compared it with one by Berlioz to show that Wagner criticizes others in the harshest terms for the very things he allows himself to a far more exaggerated degree.[22] According to him, Berlioz demands that music express what music absolutely can never express, whereas Wagner, as you have just read, requires his music to paint.

Now this would certainly be a new direction of intent, but since it demands something that is quite simply impossible, it is an absolutely false one.

In this peculiar case, to avoid exploiting with hostile spirit the strengths of Wagner the composer against the weakness of Wagner the writer of programs, one comes to defend the weakness of the former to the detriment of the latter.

His intention is not nearly so bad in this overture as it might seem in light of his program. The music is comprised of discrete sections from the opera, and in the opera Wagner, of all composers, surely wants nothing more than that which all good masters have wanted and done before him. He expresses a character's feelings and, in doing so, symbolizes with his tones as far as is possible and productive the inner and outer ideas that those feelings induce and provoke. In the Pilgrim's Chorus he paints the sentiment of the penitents; of course, it does not enter his mind additionally to depict their figures, physiognomies, clothing, etc. Tannhäuser's song in praise of Venus expresses his drunken love for her. Wagner would have refrained from painting Tannhäuser's slender figure—even if tones were capable of depicting a person externally—because in the different possible Tannhäusers on stage he could not have counted on having only *slender* tenors, and could have run the risk of being proven a liar by a theatrical squirt. A rosy scent settling over the stage is not merely smelled, but also *seen*, and a composer can try hard to symbolize secondarily the appearance of color in nature, and has famously done so often enough, with and without success. Should the tone poet tasked with depicting a scene that takes place in darkest night not be able and allowed to awaken the idea of darkness in the listener's imagination with a dark instrumental color? Has Haydn not already in his famous passage managed to sensualize the entry of *light* through a tone picture, so that one believes one is really seeing light with one's ears (to use the Viennese expression)?[23]

So, to defend Wagner against himself concerning the relationship of his program to his music goes like this: if, like Berlioz, he had simply cared to write: Procession of Pilgrims; —magical apparitions at nightfall, lustful cries of joy; Tannhäuser's proudly celebratory love song; uniting of the Pilgrims' song with the cheers about the release from the Venusberg, etc. —well, in that case nobody—the Viennese critic included—would have had any objections, and all would have considered the matter quite natural and long customary.

Admittedly, Wagner and his friends want to talk us into believing that he does nothing like other artists, rather he does everything entirely differently, entirely new and more beautiful, deeper, more sublime, more art-worthy.

And here, my young friend, I come to the most dangerous point in the *literary* wheelings and dealings of Wagner and his largely or seemingly unconditional admirers. With unmistakable art and political savvy, Wagner and his acolytes use the same methods that have given rise to and continue to preserve the immense power of *hierarchy*: the power of resolutely persuasive, holy, awe-inspiring language, in the garb of infallibility, now apparently humble, now striking down with excommunication and sentence of hell, threatening and thundering against non-believers, even slight doubters. If you read papal allocutions, archiepiscopal pastoral letters, and compare these with most of Wagner's writings and those of his priests, it will immediately become clear to you what I mean.

This manner of representation with its purpose of letting a higher glory shine around Wagner's head than that allotted any earlier master (in the eyes of the great, undiscriminating mass) dictated through the phrases of his "program" by the very quill of the composer, can well be called, as has the Viennese critic, "glorified nonsense."

We then read: "This is the seductive magic of the 'Venusberg,' which can be heard at nighttime by those in whose breast there burns a brazen, sensual longing."

One strains the ear in vain, however, to hear this "seductive magic" during performances of the work. For me at least, with the best intention and passable aural skills, it was not possible to hear anything of the sort.

One reads: "A slim, youthful man appears, drawn by these seductive apparitions: this is Tannhäuser, the singer of love."

This is pure swaggering, intended for all-believing, unmusical readers. No composer in the world can depict such things with tones. Only the poet can awaken them in the imagination with words, only the painter and sculptor can bring them before our eyes' sensory impression through colors and stone.

"He sounds his proud, triumphant love song as a kind of joyful challenge to that sensual magic, bidding it approach him."

The tone poet can express the first part of this instruction, and he can do it in such a way that the mind is gratified by the fitting veracity of tones, the imagination by the novelty of the figures, and the ear by the magical sonority of the tones.

Just how far the music for this passage fulfills all of the expectations aroused by Wagner the author, thereby hugely outstripping all earlier composers of genius, I will leave to your own judgment in a later letter where I provide musical notation for your eyes and inner hearing.

"He is answered with wild cries."

Good. The composer may want to depict that. He does not merely sensualize wild rejoicing for us, but also lets us hear comfortable, pleasing music alongside. The description of what one ought to hear reads as follows:

"The rosy mists close about him more densely, delightful scents surround him and intoxicate his senses. In the seductive twilight atmosphere there materializes before his wonder-struck gaze an unspeakably enticing female form"—and a further number of similar promises (which you yourself may read in the program booklet) belong to such exuberances, which the poet can stimulate with words as a vague play of premonition in the imagination of the reader, but which the *composer*—no more than Schiller's "Power of Song" with its audible music can bring to satisfactory, confirmative, and effective expression. In his work, Wagner can never have intended for music to express such things as are absolutely inaccessible to it; he can have intended this all the less, since he reproaches Beethoven and, to a greater extent, Berlioz for precisely this. Nor can Wagner, *after* his work, have believed that these things had been instinctively created within it through his own genius and without conscious intention;[24] he now recognizes this plainly and thus wants to make it clear to the public after the fact, through the program. No, neither the one nor the other dictated those deceptive phrases in his program. It was, rather, either conscious intention or at least instinctive feeling, the deep poetry of his soul, the most ardent and highest artistic intentions, and the power and truth of musical expression (far surpassing all before him) which he wants to possess or perhaps imagines he does possess and which he at least struggles to awaken and fasten upon the credulous world with a fervent longing, energy, and stamina that cannot be praised enough.

Does that sound rather hostile and far from impartial? Patience. In case you should *think* so now, you will change your views in the next installment. I want to attribute the exaggerated excellence one imputes to him to quantity, which in my opinion and knowledge of the present *facts* must be reduced for the sake of truth. I will attempt to defend him on the same grounds against the exaggerations of the other side, against much unjustified censure, and thereby attempt in the end to gain and establish a conclusion that, if not completely *covering* the topic, as one likes to say of late, at least might lead to greater consensus than hitherto.

Fifth Letter

It is granted to any individual that he may have his own taste; and it is laudable to try to account for his own taste. But to grant a generality to the reasons through which one wants to account would have to make his the only true taste (if it were to be valid), and means leaving the bounds of the inquisitive amateur, and appointing oneself as an obstinate law maker.

The true judge of art deduces no rules from his taste, rather he has formed his taste according to the rules that the nature of things demands. (Lessing)[25]

In my previous letter, I tried to indicate *a priori* that—and why—Wagner's program promises more than any music is in a position to achieve. Now my task is to prove it to you.

"The glorified nonsense," professes the Viennese critic, "that surrounds the Wagnerian interpretation of his overture *fades somewhat, however,* if one remembers that this piece is put together from separate components, which, individually, take their *attendant meaning* from the corresponding places in the opera. Precisely because it is no introduction, but a compressed summary of the whole, the overture assumes an acquaintance with the complete opera to be understood."

Now then, if that is so, one does not have the right to say: "It is a *sorry effort* pieced together without inner development, without organic execution that—one understands not why—breaks off suddenly!"

But similar judgments have been made about very many overtures by those without familiarity with the opera and on hearing them completely for the first time; among others, namely the great overture to *Leonore*; in Vienna the great master even had to banish it because of the same reproaches now being leveled from that city at the *Tannhäuser* overture.[26] The *Tannhäuser* overture is not without inner development, not without organic execution, and besides it does not break off suddenly, but concludes because its life has been completed naturally, and one sees very *well* why it is completed.

First I want to prove this to you and thereby dismiss those complaints made about the overture wherever it has been heard without the opera. Only then will I allow myself to make some remarks and substantiate them through examples that situate the work in question in a canon of effective overtures, but in no way raises it above all precursors as the very best.[27]

The Overture is not without inner development, if with this term one means the reflection of the action. The *Tannhäuser* overture lives up to these demands as well as any other I know. You can see that if you read the program and track the tone pictures in accordance to them.

The Overture does not break off suddenly. It concludes in the same way the opera closes, with the Pilgrims' return from their penitential journey to Rome, and the rejoicing at Tannhäuser's atonement and the redemption of his spirit as it drifts away from the earth. One knows perfectly well why it ends; namely, because the action that it reflects has reached its end.

The Overture is not without organic execution, if by this we mean its technical form. Some principal ideas are set up and repeated often in order to achieve referentiality and roundedness, quite in the same way and form that other earlier composers crafted them.

You can convince yourself of all this by attentively observing the piano score, and it will arise by the by from my future letters.

Wagner therefore does not deserve the reproaches that have been made everywhere about his overture, when one could only hear it without knowing the opera; but at the same time you see that, with respect to the *Tannhäuser* overture's setting and expressive purpose, he has not followed a new direction, not opened up a new path; rather, he went the way of all good earlier masters.

If, then, not excepting this overture, the effusive assurances of Wagner's tremendous genius should be based on truth, as is still repeated sedulously by many, so can this genius be found only in a novelty and peculiarity of musical thought that far surpasses all prior achievements in its portrayal, instrumental coloring, harmonic and modulatory properties, in magically charming melodies, in hitherto unattained expressions of truth and hitherto unattained expressions of effect.

But let us leave these assurances aside and bring some facts before our eyes and eavesdrop on what *our own senses* feel and judge about it.

The Adagio is *quite a popular melody,* absolutely simple and flowing in its design. It belongs to the Pilgrims' song. It is a good melody, expressive, harmonically and instrumentally interesting. It must please anyone who opens his ear and heart to it without prejudice. Yet I neither want nor am able to explain it to you as the best, most original, pleasing, and most deeply moving of all melodies that have appeared up to now. Judge for yourself.

Example 1.

What follows is a repetition of the preceding material with a different accompaniment, which we can talk about later.

You see in passing that Wagner can certainly form clear and symmetrically structured periods and melodies, where he wants to. As mentioned above, Wagnerian melodies are not the *best* among all that exist. There are many that are equal to his melodies in value and effect, and some could be cited that surpass him in both respects. Listen to *this* melody, then listen to *Weber's* played by the horns in the Adagio of the *Freischütz* overture, and ask your ear and heart which makes a more pleasing impression. The answer, I think, will turn out decisively in favor of the second.

One can still doubt the *constant* originality of Wagnerian melody. Glance over at the final four measures. Do you not think of a composer who Wagner treats in the most contemptuous way in his writings? I mean Meyerbeer; I mean his "Mercy" aria.[28] See for yourself:

Example 2.

Do not think I want to indict Wagner as a deliberate plagiarist. That would be more than ridiculous, it would be slanderous. Less injustice would be done were one to think: Meyerbeer's phrase emerged from Wagner's quill unconsciously through memory while he worked, and he regarded it as his own invention. One may accept this all the more easily since Wagner appears to be congenitally blessed in the highest degree with the belief that he is absolutely original, that he creates everything purely from his spirit, and his apostles do what is possible to sustain and secure him in this belief.

If this assumption should prove warranted, one might suspect that the contempt Wagner supposedly feels toward Meyerbeer's works is not really all that intense, for musical thoughts that appear contemptuous to a great tone genius do not usually nest themselves in his head in order to dart out later in his own scores as reminiscences.

Nevertheless, I want to let this thought go as well. I want to suppose more in favor of Wagner than even his absolute admirers; namely, that Wagner has never heard a note of Meyerbeer.[29]

The irrefutable fact, however, remains: Wagner wrote down *four* meas-ures whose novelty does not surpass everything previously achieved in music. Rather, he wrote down four measures that had already been born identically in the head of a composer (*before* him) whom he deeply despises.

Only four measures of preexisting music, to be sure!

But we encounter these four measures right in the first part of the first opera that should have forged the *new* direction: the Adagio of the *Tannhäuser* overture.[30]

This discovery will mean nothing at all for those to whom *Tannhäuser* is recommended as the opera of a highly talented composer. Similar things happened to the greatest musical geniuses of every age. But if one extols Wagner as the composer who leaves far behind him all that has previously been achieved in music, if Wagner himself tells us that all prior masters strolled about in error, went along entirely false paths, and that he first dis-covered and entered along the only right one, so he who follows him attentively may become somewhat suspicious when right at the entrance to the new route he catches sight of a little spot already seen in almost exactly the same form on earlier walks along well-trodden paths. So comes to mind spontaneously the old saying: "Nothing new under the sun!"

There are individual passages in music that make very particular impres-sions on individuals and elicit quite opposed opinions. The long violin passage in the Adagio of the *Tannhäuser* overture must belong to these, for it has been praised by one side just as warmly as it has been rebuked angrily by the other.[31] There is nothing in this configuration that sins against any legitimate rule of art. It is clear in design and instrumentation. Wagner discloses its idea in his program: "It is the rejoicing of the Venusberg itself redeemed from the curses of unholiness, which we hear as Divine song. All pulses of life surge and bound to the song of redemption." Reproachful judgments of this passage can only flow from individual perceptions precisely because it cannot be proved that the passage con-travenes any essential rule of art. Of course, one cannot argue about the worth or shame of this passage with people who perceive differently. If you want to know my thoughts about it, I say to you that I like the idea as well as its musical symbolization very much indeed; the passage makes the same agreeable impression on me at every performance. Of all Wagner's inventions, I regard this as one of his most characteristic, and concern-ing the fitting expression of the object, one of his most excellent.

On all technical points, the whole Adagio is absolutely perfect, and it is therefore absolutely perfect because it does not want to develop any new-fantasized rule of art, rather it follows in its whole structure the best of the old rules exactly. As mentioned earlier, its spiritual content is signifi-cant, and very agreeable poetically, musically, and formally.

If it were really Wagner's innermost conviction that all previous musical forms are now defunct, and for that reason a new and living content can no longer be revealed in them, then in this Adagio our composer overturned his dictum through the facts of his own musical pen, for it presents precisely a *new Content in traditional Form,* as mentioned already.

And if Wagner's admirers were really inwardly transfigured to such an extent that they could not accept any piece of music that appears in a traditional form, then this Adagio should arouse in them no pleasure at all, but merely revulsion.

Nevertheless, Wagner allows this introduction in his overture, and his friends will surely regard it not as a bad passage, rather as a very good one, or indeed, as the very best that has ever opened an overture, since in their eyes Wagner is the greatest composer.

I too regard it as one of the best, and so I agree, as do certainly all uninhibited musicians and connoisseurs not prejudiced against Wagner; even the public at large agrees with the most absolute of Wagner's admirers.

Whoever can create such an Adagio, I would argue, must be a highly talented musical mind, and the despicable phrases that his opponents disseminate lock, stock, and barrel are no more justified than the effusive phrases of many of his most enraged defenders.

One can recognize and feel much—a great deal—in his works that contravenes the real rules of art, but he still is and remains a first-rate musical mind. It is only that he is not the greatest composer of all previous ages. I am afraid that I will be able to prove the latter remark to you through detailed analysis of just the Allegro of the *Tannhäuser* overture.

But that comes in the next letter.

Sixth Letter

One does not become acquainted with artworks when they are finished, one must grasp them in their process of becoming in order to comprehend them to some degree. (Goethe)[32]

Do not be shocked when I tell you that today's letters deal with little more than an analysis of the first sixty-one measures of the Allegro from the *Tannhäuser* overture, of which every detail will be subjected to such analytical precision and microscopic exactitude, in a way that perhaps no other comparatively small piece of a composition has ever been observed. The advantage of this approach will be clear to you in the next volume, where we can already bring to a close our considerations of Wagner's two main works that have appeared so far.

First look at the underlying material of the thoughts, the motives that form the basis of these sixty-one measures (Example 3).

You will not be able to say of any single musical figure viewed on its own that a similar or the same figure has never existed before; no single measure is absolutely new, indeed we and our forefathers have heard many of them very often.

You will object that this does not matter; that one arrives at the same result with the most genial works if one plucks and unravels them in such a way; that the genius may create the most original and noble composition from the same material with which a beginner or a dull-witted talent assembles only a trivial whole.

I will gladly tolerate this objection. I only wanted to leave nothing unexamined in a composer who accuses all his forebears of wandering down false paths, whom his devout supporters extol as the first and only true tone poet, so that I might uncover the point where the historically unprecedented begins.

Certainly Wagner cannot complain about unfairness if the material of his thoughts is declared no better and no worse than that of a Beethoven, C. M. v. Weber, and Schumann, among others.

Example 3.

Let's see what sketch or design he made from this for his [musical] painting (Example 4).

Example 4.

Example 4 continued

From a technical aspect this design is new through its deviation from the previous way of constructing an overture. The sixty-one measures take up the space in which our best masters executed the main theme and transition. In place of this appears first an expanded section of three measures in which two ideas are telescoped together (1); two four-measure phrases follow from this (2 and 3); after which follow two sections (4 and 5). None of these five miniature pictures has anything in common with the others; each is of an entirely different nature from the others in shape and meaning.

If one wanted to start a speech in this way, it would go something like: "I went walking yesterday. The church was well attended today. It looks like rain. I'm happy. The green tree." Here you have five short, consecutively stimulated ideas following each other; each is comprehensible in itself, but taken together they allow for no unity of thought.

The six musical thoughts following these five miniature pictures can be described as periods, but with these too, the feeling of being aphoristic remains, and so in these sixty-one measures eleven ideas flit over each other to us, which—however true you want each to be—do not combine into a clear organism, and must inevitably produce an impression of confusion.[33]

The result of such deviations from other masters' methods of composition should not be to obscure constructions, but rather to progress genially toward the music of the future.[34]

"Every deviation from the norm has confused and repulsed the old hats,[35] though it eventually was found pleasing and appealing to a later, riper time. The genius who opens new pathways has always failed to be recognized initially."

This is the argument of those who attribute a higher artistic wisdom to themselves, and take a brighter view of the future than all those who cannot believe in Wagner's absolute perfection as a composer.

It is a weighty argument, for it is backed up by many indisputable experiences. Therefore we want to get at it more sharply than others have hitherto, in order to see if what has been proved in some instances can be proved consistently. Truthfully, I am not writing these letters to encroach on Wagner's actual merit, but always and only to defend the laws of art without whose preservation art cannot exist.

It is true, many artists' innovations have only later emerged as successful innovations. But it is just as true that many innovations were and always remained unsuccessful.

I could give examples of the latter experience from all the arts; but I will cite only one from dramatic literature: *Grabbe*.[36] This poet was greeted by some of the critics almost as a new Shakespeare. And truly, he did not lack for genial tendencies and flashes, or in strength and daringness, nor was he unwilling to disregard many hitherto effective laws of dramatic art.

Those who denied he was a reforming genius, striding forth on a new path, were proved right. He did not achieve the goal that he might have been able to achieve if he had sought only to apply his ingenuity not in transgressing but in following the essential rules of art.

This argument is therefore not infallible. It has been proved, but also disproved.

But is this the case with Wagner? Does the present thrust him away apathetically? On the whole his works are received with approval wherever they are performed. He only recently reached the age at which a man is strongest and is already a celebrated figure as few earlier masters were at his age.

Those who oppose him do not deny his great talent and considerable success in some elements of his works; but they find weaknesses there as well, and cannot recognize in him the perfect composer against which all other masters sink into deep shadows.

There are details in Wagner's compositions that at this moment do not please us and which we believe can never become beautiful. Among these displeasing constructions I count the part of the overture that I am discussing here, thus I want to produce some further supporting evidence for this opinion.

Seventh Letter

In his seventh letter, Lobe poses the question of whether artistic "innovation" must always exceed the "boundaries" of art. To illustrate his skepticism, Lobe likens arias by Mozart and Handel to the orderly construction of a house, and implies that Wagner's imaginative freedom would fare less well in this particular simile:

If one scrutinizes a house according to the laws of natural consequence, and notices an irregularity in the parts and their relationships to each other, if e.g. in a row of eight windows one were only half the size of the other seven, this deviation from symmetry would incur one's displeasure. How this would only increase if every window were of a different size and form, the first forms a regular square, for instance, the second an oblong, the third a circle, the fourth a triangle etc.!

The builder could produce such a house full of irregularities. He could install a chimney above the door, could craft a row of windows of the kind just described, and instead of being level, he could let this row be askew. His imagination could indulge in quite different shapes if he did not want to take into account the real needs of human nature, and wanted to carry out a capricious construction! Would one credit such a builder with having opened new paths with his art and having effected artistic progress?"

Eighth Letter

I do not mean to say that—in a technical respect—the beginning of the Allegro of the *Tannhäuser* Overture is just as confusingly constructed as the house of capricious design mentioned in the previous letter; without doing injustice to the highly talented composer, however, I do believe that Wagner takes excessive leave of symmetry, of easily clear and comprehensible forms and division of thoughts.

One might reply: the idea takes precedence over technique, and the idea of the *Tannhäuser* Overture calls for a form different from the usual; it calls for exactly the form used here; the form must always conform to the idea, not the idea to the form.

Understood correctly, this dictum is true; misconceived and misapplied, it leads to the absurd; under the pretext that it *had* to be *this* way, it could easily excuse the most shapeless piece of hackwork as only able to emerge from the idea in this form.

Let us follow the new aestheticians behind even this barricade; do we see the ideas that Wagner expresses in these sixty-one measures?

His program specifies them:

a) At nightfall magical apparitions appear
b) a rosy scent of twilight swirls around
c) sensual sounds of joy reach our ear
d) the mad motions of a harrowingly voluptuous dance become faintly visible

The verbal expression of these four moments already lacks natural order; (b) would have to be first, (a) second. The spirit conjuror first lets incense rise up, and out of this the ghostly figures then emerge.

The program would therefore have to run:

a) At nightfall a rosy scent of twilight swirls around
b) magical apparitions appear

Aside from this, we now want to ask: Why did Wagner express these four ideas with words in normal language? Why does he comply as a writer to the recognized grammatical and rhetorical laws in the same way as every other sensible writer?

What would one say, for instance, if Wagner had expressed these four ideas in the following new way:

a) Fall at night around a scent
b) rosy of twilight swirls; appear apparitions
c) magical; sounds of joy etc.[37]

Would one be allowed to explain this way of connecting words as "the language of the future"?

Look again at numbers 1 to 5 in the sketch provided in our sixth letter, and tell me whether these short and heterogeneous mini-phrases do not produce an effect on your feelings not so very different from the effect of those rearranged verbal fragments above?

The thoughts are taken from the [composer's] introduction. Look at this—you surely have the piano score—and compare it with the overture. Instead of finding some genial innovation in the latter, which we musicians are still simply unable to grasp, it makes much more sense to declare that the composer failed in transforming the introductory form into overture form. For we have already encountered many composers who wrote only operas and did not have any practice in submitting their thoughts to the stricter forms of the symphony or quartet, etc., while still maintaining some semblance of creative freedom. Wagner generally preaches with conspicuous zeal about freedom of form, and recently he proposed that the opera overture . . . should be eliminated, as he does himself. It might well be for this reason that he senses quite well the genus of a specific given form and wants to liberate himself from it through a new postulate. Goethe says: "Recent German artists declare any branch of art they do not possess as harmful and something to be beaten into submission."[38]

And one more thing. Many people do not *feel* the lack of form. If they regard the expression as *true*, they are happy, and fail to see how others could wish for something more. We'll let it pass. Appreciation for graceful musical forms is not just innate, it must also be cultivated through study. If this appreciation is sometimes lacking even in artists, its total absence in some contemporary critics need not surprise us. We might be more justly surprised, though, when the latter kind of inconsequential people declare everything they are unfamiliar with to be chimerical, and dub everyone a "pettifogger" who knows and has learned more than they.

And what contradictions the despisers of form get caught in! By their assurance, art up to now has closed itself off like an aristocracy, existing only for a small chosen few; progress must consist in making music into a *general good for the people*. Do they believe they are reaching this purpose by construing form ever more artistically and intricately, on the one hand, while on the other sometimes dissolving it entirely? Formations of such an incomprehensible kind as these sixty-one measures of the *Tannhäuser* overture will hardly ever become a general good for the people.

"Among the men of letters from the north"—Mme. Staël says—"exists a peculiarity that depends more, so to speak, on party spirit than on judgment.[39] They are anxious about the defects of their writing almost as much as of their beauty; while they themselves should say, like a woman of wit, while talking about the weaknesses of a hero: *he is great in spite, and not because of them.*"

Up to this point, I have observed the material of this part of the Allegro and the design formed from it, and I have not been able to discover a perfected composition therein.

Let's look further to see whether this perfection is perhaps produced by the addition of the other musical elements.

The last aesthetic letter attempted to outline the laws of modulation with respect to what is pleasing.[40]

Wagner declares these laws to be narrow-minded.

Observe his freer modulation.

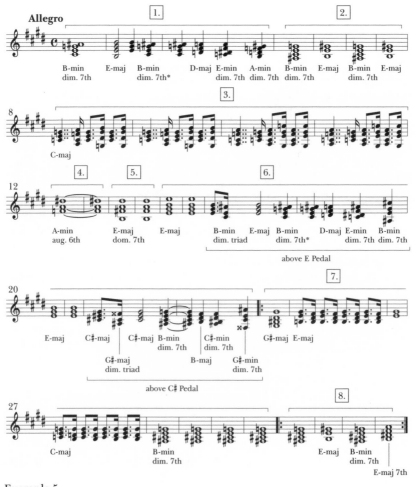

Example 5

* D-min resolution

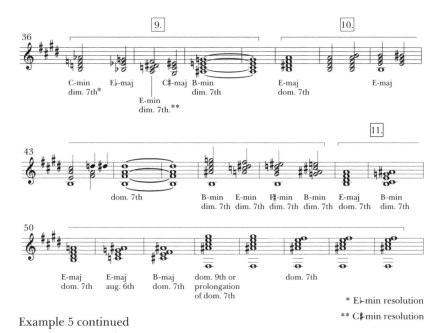

Example 5 continued

In the first three measures the music already passes through *five* different keys. What a number of dissonant chords here! *Forty-two* in *sixty-one* measures! Among them, *twenty-five* diminished seventh chords, and *fifteen* based on B minor.

Consider that a diminished seventh chord belongs simultaneously to four different minor keys, and resolves equally legitimately to four different major keys; consider furthermore that if these customary resolutions are passed over, that is to say, the diminished sevenths progress to other diminished sevenths, the feeling of a particular key cannot arise in us at all: so it is easy to understand that on hearing these first sixty-one measures, one has almost no clue as to the principal key. Here we have diversity in excess, while unity is lacking altogether.

We already encounter this manner of modulating in the first sixty-one measures of the Allegro. Follow the dissonant chords through the whole overture, or through the whole opera (as I did), and you will feel that this utterly lavish use of dissonances becomes irritating for the ear, and must sap the expression of all meaning. Here too one speaks of what is desired by the "Idea."

The demonic activities of the Venusberg, the whirring and straying about of magic apparitions, the mentally disorienting songs and dances, should all of this have been expressed in just one key?

In reply to this, we must say that eliminating one extreme does not entail summoning the other. Nobody can deny the dreadful truth of the devils' chorus in Don Juan; the modulatory element is also employed there, but the feeling for the principal key, D minor, remains. Keys and modalities arose from the mind's need to bring diversity into unity. The eradication of this achievement—the transition back from the fixed and particular into the wavering and indefinite—can never herald an improved system.

There is no doubt that the unclear design here is made no clearer through the use of modulation; rather it is obfuscated further. Thus the only remaining question is whether the instrumentation might allay this lack of clarity.

Tenth Letter

No expert will want to dispute Wagner's knowledge of the laws of instrumentation; his operas contain many interesting and effectively colored sections; the impartial listener cannot concede, however, that he portrays through the orchestra the outline of his thoughts in the most perfect way throughout, i.e., true for feeling and for mind, while equally clear and pleasant for the ear. The sixty-one measures offer as much evidence for one truth as for the other.

The most exquisite passage in these measures seems to me to be the following (Example 6).

One really does seem to see though one's ear the rosy scent of twilight, and though truth of expression is undeniably present, the ear is equally won over by the pleasing sonority and clarity of the music.

That the *divisi* effect of the violins is no invention of Wagner's, but has already been used by C. M. v. Weber, Mendelssohn, and Berlioz to most marvelous effect, I repeat not in order to diminish Wagner's achievement, but rather to put it in a proper perspective.

On the other hand, you can judge the following passage through a mere observation of the score (Example 7).

In itself, the figure in the flutes and oboes is ineffective, worn-out, and fails to conjoin with the figures of the other instruments either with respect to rhythm or sound quality to produce an agreeable overall picture. Observe the melody in the third and fourth measures, which the oboe and clarinet play in unison. This unison becomes unpalatable for the ear in the fourth measure at the clarinet's upward-shrieking notes and the oboe's spiky sharpness. I know perfectly well that the composer wanted to characterize the wild bacchanal-like singing, but we must regard it as an eternally fundamental principle that under no pretext should a composition offer unpleasant sounds to the ear.

Example 6.

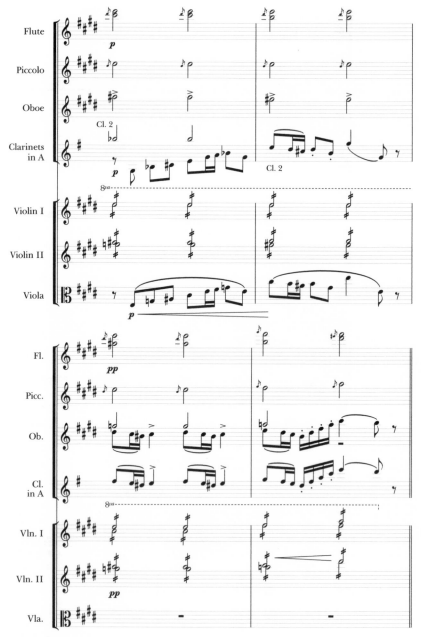

Example 7.

Above all things, one expects from the instrumental composer a precise knowledge of that which each instrument is able to achieve according to its nature. If he writes an unplayable passage for any instrument, he proves thereby that he is not well acquainted with its technique.

Take a look at the cello figures in the following passage, and think about the tempo at which they ought to be performed.

Example 8.

Example 8 continued

The greatest cello virtuoso cannot hope to play such figures (with their mixed succession of diatonic and chromatic intervals) purely and clearly at such a fast tempo. You can well imagine what a tonal mishmash results when this is played by three or four cellists in the orchestra at the same time, and anyone with a musically educated ear can hear this in performance. To be sure, this blending together of notes will be less noticeable to the unschooled ear, as a thick veil is thrown over it by the sustained notes of the four horns, two bassoons, and double bass, as well as the sixteenth tremolo of the triple-stopped viola notes; and the violin melody also draws the ear's attention away from it. Precisely from this, however, composite sound pictures [*Gesammtklangbilder*] arise, whose labeling as "muddled din" is not unjustified.

Incidentally, compare this cello figure with the following from Weber's *Euryanthe*.[41]

Example 9.

I set no great store by such similarities. Whoever is familiar with older music knows that hardly any composer featured more conspicuous reminiscences than—Mozart. This remark should only be further evidence of the truth that no artist can tear himself away entirely from his precursors, and be new through and through. In a later letter, I will bring more persuasive proof for this proposition when applied to Wagner. For the time being, it is enough to admit that even Weber's figure, cited here, is hard to perform. However, it does not pose nearly the difficulties that Wagner's figure does.

Purification of art is the great word by which Wagner denotes his mission. At times, however, his actions stand in direct contradiction to it. Whoever thinks he can find more purity in such passages as the two adduced above than in the artistic creations of our noblest masters is someone with whom we no longer wish to argue.

Purification of art! But surely of orchestration as well?! And then such pictures as these, in just one small section of the overture! —But consider the scores of *Tannhäuser* and *Lohengrin* from the point of view in which this new "art purification system" is meant to be revealed ! Truly, we hear things asserted whose direct opposite is plainly apparent for those with eyes to see and ears to hear—as if all true musical knowledge had been lost.

Eleventh Letter

The sixty-one measures have led me to speak at length. I will be able to be all the more concise about the remaining part of the overture. Ideas that are somewhat insufficient at the beginning of a piece of music can in the course of the work perhaps be enhanced through recurrence and further development. This remains for us to investigate in the *Tannhäuser* overture.

After the sixty-one measures, Wagner stops deviating from the customary form. He delivers a clearly constructed second group, a *Gesangsgruppe* based on Tannhäuser's love song, and—like other masters—in the dominant key. Our composer has been accused of wanting to eliminate melody in his artwork of the future because he is unable to compose any. I will show you later some of his melodies that belong to the most deeply stirring and simplest that have ever been sung by a tone poet.[42]

One would not deny the name melody, for instance, to Tannhäuser's song (Example 10).
I can, however, adjudge this melody as neither more charming nor more extraordinarily original than several of those by earlier masters. Consider Adolar's song of praise to his Euryanthe (Example 11).[43]

The spiritual similarity of both melodies jumps right off the page at you. The creator of this melody could just as well be Wagner as Weber, or Weber

Example 10.

Example 11.

as well as Marschner. But compare the measures marked "a" with those marked "b" in both melodies, and you also find something certainly technically akin. Every impartial listener must admit that here one is again concerned with an extended musical thought that exceeds the good structures of earlier masters in neither form nor content.

Thereafter, Wagner repeats and develops the material thematically.

To be sure, after attentive and frequently repeated study, one arrives at the same defense I proclaimed in contradiction of the Viennese critic in the fifth letter—namely that the *Tannhäuser* overture lacks neither inner development nor organic execution; nonetheless I must insist that it is in all respects more contrived and complicated than the best of other masters, and therefore cannot and never will be regarded as the most perfect of all overtures.

This is the only way in which the many brusque judgments rendered about this overture explain themselves. I have already shared the one from Vienna with you. One from London is still more terrible; there the overture is called a downright noise that confuses the senses.

Here again one might refer to other, similar cases, e.g., to the three *Leonore* overtures by Beethoven, that likewise first found only disapproval, but now please universally.

The comparison, though, is not completely correct. The *Leonore* overtures—when also heard without the opera, and for the first time—were never disliked by connoisseurs; on the contrary, they aroused the applause of all competent judges immediately. That could not have been otherwise, for there resides in the individual ideas of the overtures a graceful breath of melody alongside deep expressions of truth; my feeling is that the *Tannhäuser* overture lacks this component.

But let us at last illuminate this favorite objection—that "things were just the same with the works of other geniuses at the beginning!"—from a new point of view.

If it did turn out this way for several geniuses with one or another of their works—for we cannot claim that it is so for all geniuses with all of their works—should we not then ask at least once whether a genius absolutely *must fare like this*? Whether a real musical artwork can be produced under any other condition than that of total *lack of initial recognition*? Or whether this in fact documents a weakness of the artist, that he can form a product in no other way than that which on first appearance more likely repels the public rather than attracts them?

Works such as Goethe's *Egmont*, Schiller's *Maria Stuart*, and many other dramatic poems did not need the future; they pleased at once. The statues of Canova and Thorwaldsen found immediate recognition.[44] And how do the great actors fare with such absolute maxims about the future? If the roles portrayed by a Garrick, Iffland, Devrient, Schröder-Devrient had repulsed their contemporaries, in what way would they have ever pleased and been recognized by posterity?[45]

It remains an established truth, then, that artworks can be created whose worth and effect are apparent on their first appearance.

Through frequent *contact* and *habit*, an initially rejected entity can become likable, and through clever *commentary* many things become comprehensible. Just because this happens now and then, must it therefore be a necessary attribute of real artworks? I ought to say that creations which one must first become used to and which require commentaries in journals before they ever get a foot in the door (or as now happens more often, enormous encomiums), do not at least earn a preference above those artworks that are just as valuable, and immediately find recognition and give pleasure without such assistance.

Instead of excusing the umbrage aroused by what is complicated and hard to understand with the phrase: "Other geniuses fared no better!" it would be much better to say: this artist has surpassed his predecessors by understanding how to sensualize the deepest truth in the simplest, purest, most graceful forms, so that the whole world can instantly understand and completely enjoy them.

That would be real progress in my opinion; it would be the composer's most beautiful and most sublime task. Wagner did not set *this* task for himself, or at least he has not yet solved it. There are passages to be found in his works that are formed more artificially, confusedly, and incomprehensibly than everything that has been written so far in a similar way. And continuing to explain this as the effusions of a higher artistic spirit (as has happened up to now) and attempting thereby to entice talented young people on the same path can surely lead to *no* refinement, *no* purification, rather only to the decay of art.

"In every type of spiritual development," says Friedrich v. Schlegel, "there is, as in the graduated progression of nature, a moment of bloom and a highest point of completion that manifests itself in *a beautiful perfection of form and of language*."[46]

Fourteenth Letter

No composer has attracted such an exclusive and immoderately ennobling party as Wagner. It is not enough for them to compare and put him on the same level with other, perhaps even the most highly recognized geniuses; no, he is treated as incomparable, as though his like had never existed before.

Likewise it is also not enough to praise Wagner's striving after proper musical characterization (up till now his weakest side in my view); no, he is to have achieved this with a formerly unimaginable perfection. If one but opens the score or the piano arrangement to a passage like this one, or listens to it in the theater:

Example 12.

Example 12 continued

Example 12 continued

one must confess first that it is music, good music that cannot be mistaken for anything but a significant talent; but to insist that such music arises from such an ineffable, incomprehensibly effusive nature that nothing similar could ever have occurred to the mind of the greatest geniuses of earlier times—this can be called nothing but sheer apotheosis. The natures of a *goddess* and an *earthly* woman are certainly far apart from each other.

The enchanting, seductive *Venus* might have all the feelings and passions of the earthly woman; the characteristic difference between both, however—the same fit of temper over a renegade lover in terms of melody, harmony, instrumentation, etc.—would certainly have a different appearance for the *Goddess* and for the mortal beauty.

Look at the beginning of the duet between Tannhäuser and Venus in the example above.

You only see the vocal part and the accompaniment in the piano score, but even this will be enough to prove that the melodic and rhythmic accents of neither the singer Venus nor the accompaniment show any features that would particularly differentiate the *Goddess*'s anger characteristically from that of any single earthly female.

It is true, in *Lohengrin* Elsa is different from Ortrud and Lohengrin is different from Telramund when they appear in moments of calm emotion. At the apex of passion, however, they all declaim similar melodic phrases without characteristic difference; and Elsa has the same accompanimental figures, the same strong orchestration as Ortrud, Lohengrin the same as Telramund.

Look at Elsa's part in the following section (Example 13).

Example 13.

Example 13 continued

That is the same high pitch of passion as voiced by Venus, Ortrud, Tannhäuser, Lohengrin, and Telramund during agitated moments.

And, quite apart from these particular examples, I would ask if all of Wagner's characters are more sharply portrayed than Mozart's Sarastro, Moor, Papageno, Tamino, the Priests, the three women, the three boys, Pamina, the queen of the night; than Don Juan, Leporello, Zerlina, Elvira, Masetto, Ottavio; than Belmonte, Constanze, Pedrillo, Blonde, Osmin; than C. M. v. Weber's Max, Caspar, Agathe, Aennchen; Euryanthe, Eglantine, Adolar, Lysiart; than Méhul's characters in *Joseph in Egypt*; Cherubini's characters in *Les deux journées*, etc.?

Conclusion

But enough!

With an artist as highly talented as Wagner it is no pleasant business to have to emphasize not his many strengths but to draw attention instead to his weaknesses. Whoever truly loves art and artists, however, can do no other. Wagner *provokes* the comparison of his music with his doctrines by the way he indicts all previous masters for their misconceptions.

He possesses a great characteristic—*energy*. It is rare in our time, very appreciable in itself, and it wields an almost irresistible power over the majority of people. If he always knew how to hold this energy in the necessary bounds, where it remains energy without being driven into *Schwärmerei* or even fanaticism, he would be all the better for it.

Admittedly, the controversy that he aroused skillfully enough through his writings—like the clamor that his followers have raised around him—has awoken an extraordinary degree of curiosity about his operas.

Everyone simply must hear and see them, and it is entirely natural that they appeal everywhere through their real poetic and musical worth.

But the huge torrent of enthusiasm that has been aroused partly artificially will drain away. When curiosity is sufficiently satisfied, and through frequent enjoyment of the opera, the public does not merely catch several beautiful aspects, but is also able impartially to sense the weaknesses. Wagner's works will join the ranks of the better works, but will no longer be vaunted as the *highest* blossoming of our art. The real works of earlier masters will be vindicated, and the future? —will create its own works.

Certainly, Wagner has written no drama of the future—rather, he has written dramatically and musically effective operas, the understanding and enjoyment of which require no future generation. The *present* understands and grasps their merits, which are often of the best kind; it also recognizes and grasps the weaknesses, however, which at times are of a very *present* kind. On the whole, this will have to be the final assessment. It has already become such for everybody not exclusively caught up in the pro or the contra, in one-sided ways of viewing or willing or feeling, but who has and wants to have ears open to both.

I regard Wagner as one of the most significant, most powerful, and most energetic artistic natures of *our* time, not as the *only* one. Robert Schumann is completely equal to him musically, superior in technique and more universal in his creativity, even if he lags behind Wagner in the field of opera.

I cannot, however, hold back something in conclusion:

"*Geniuses alone ruin taste because taste does not exist without them, and geniuses can only ruin taste if they misuse their powers. There are two ways in which this is possible, through false ends and through false means. If a vessel is* already full, and one pours in more, it overflows. If the mind full of power has already achieved its aim and wishes to go still further, it progresses beyond the goal, into an unnatural land of false taste *as an end*. If it chooses a will-o'-the-wisp as a purpose, or wants to fly to the sun with Icarus's wings, so its name will signal swamp and sea, for it has chosen false ends and will succumb on the way. Or a genius has a noble, true goal before him, only he *has no guide*. In the initial heat of inspiration he takes the wrong path, realizes too late he has strayed. As a genius, he has achieved some good on the false path; he looks back and does not have enough great-ness to give up everything and come around to a better pathway. Perhaps irresistible false objects tantalized him along the way. With his powers he believed himself capable—on this wrong path—of going where no other had gone before him. He strode onward and with his noble powers became an archetype for false taste, a *seductive, negative greatness*. That is the sad *theory of corrupt taste of all ages, seen from the genius's point of view*."

It is not me saying this; it was written many years ago—by Herder in his "Causes of the Decline in Taste."[47]

NOTES

1. Lobe published his *Fliegende Blätter* in three volumes: 1 (494 pp.) in 1853–54; 2 (509 pp.), 1855–57; 3 (112 pp.), 1857. The *Briefe über Wagner* appeared in the first two volumes: 1:411–29, 444–65; 2:27–48. A complete itinerary of these volumes and indeed every-thing Lobe published is given in the bibliographic appendix of Torsten Brandt, *Johann Christian Lobe (1797–1881): Studien zu Biographie und musikschriftstellerischem Werk* (Göttingen, 2002), 317–31.

2. See David Blackbourn, *The Long Nineteenth Century: A History of Germany, 1780–1918* (New York and Oxford, 1998), 106–20.

3. J. S. Dwight, "Music Journalism in Germany," *Dwight's Journal of Music* 6 (13 January 1855): 115.

4. "Please also give Lobe my warmest thanks," he wrote to Liszt, "his judgment both surprised and pleased me very much." Wagner to Liszt, 24 December 1850, Zurich, in *Sämtliche Briefe* (Leipzig, 1867–2008), 3:486. Lobe's review, "Das Herderfest in Weimar," appeared in the *Signale für die musikalische Welt* 37 (11 September 1850): 345–50.

5. Lobe, "Ein Verteidiger Richard Wagner's," *Fliegende Blätter für Musik* 1 (1853): 54–56. Schaeffer's review sets out from the entirely incorrect assertion that "Wagner dedicated a special work—*Opera and Drama*—to precisely this [music and poetry], and within it, declared their relation to one another as their only possible position in the 'Drama of the Future.' But he did not stop at that, rather he simultaneously aspired to the realiza-tion of his principles in original composition, particularly in *Lohengrin* and *Tannhäuser*." See Julius Schaeffer, "Über Richard Wagner's *Lohengrin*, mit Bezug auf seine Schrift: 'Oper und Drama,'" *Neue Berliner Musikzeitung* 20 (12 May 1852): 153.

6. Lobe, *Musikalische Briefe: Wahrheit über Tonkunst und Tonkünstler, von einem Wohlbekannten* (Leipzig, 1852; 2nd ed., 1860), 277.

7. J. C. Lobe, "Fortschritt," *Allgemeine musikalische Zeitung* 50 (1848); "Erster Artikel," 49–51; "Zweiter Artikel," 65–69; "Dritter Artikel," 169–73; "Vierter Artikel," 337–41; "Fünfter Artikel," 581–87, 598–601, 615–28, 641–46, 673–78; here, "Dritter Artikel," 169.

8. J. S. Dwight, "Music Journalism in Germany," *Dwight's Journal of Music* 6 (1855): 115.

9. Lobe, "Ein neuer Prophet der Zukunft," *Fliegende Blätter* 2 (1856): 314–19.

10. Lobe, *Musikalische Briefe*, 33–34.

11. Wagner, "Ueber Inhalt und Vortrag der Ouvertüre zu Wagner's *Tannhäuser*," *Neue Zeitschrift für Musik* 3 (14 January 1853): 23–25.

12. Lobe, "Fortschritt. Vierter Artikel," 341.

13. See Eduard Bernsdorf's warm review of a reissue of several of Lobe's essays as "Consonanzen und Dissonanzen: Gesammelte Schriften aus älterer und neuerer Zeit" and his specific description of Lobe's approach as a "Neueinführung," in *Signale für die Musikalische Welt* 67 (6 December 1869): 1057–58, here 1058.

14. "Letters About Richard Wagner, to a Young Composer," *New York Musical Review and Gazette* (25 August 1855): 284.

15. J. S. Dwight, "Music Journalism in Germany," *Dwight's Journal of Music* 6 (1855): 115.

16. In Lobe, "Aesthetische Briefe: Erster Brief," *Fliegende Blätter* 1 (1853): 188.

17. "Einige Wenige haben diese Art zu denken, und Viele wollen sie zu haben scheinen; diese machen das Geschrei und geben den Ton; der größte Haufe schweigt und verhält sich gleichgültig, und denkt bald so, bald anders." Gotthold Ephraim Lessing, *Gesammelte Werke* VI, *Hamburgische Dramaturgie*, no. 11, (Berlin, 1767; repr. 1954), 63.

18. The untranslatable term "Tongeister" implies the lofty minds of great composers.

19. For detailed discussion of the term "absolute music" and its historical usage, see "The History of the Term and Its Vicissitudes," in Carl Dahlhaus *The Idea of Absolute Music*, trans. Roger Lustig (Chicago, 1989), 18–41.

20. Wagner's program for the *Tannhäuser* overture, "Ueber Inhalt und Vortrag der Ouvertüre zu Wagner's *Tannhäuser*," was written for his three-day festival in Zurich on May 18, 20, and 22, 1853. The festival featured concert performances of excerpts from all three of Wagner's Romantic operas, and is given in his letter to Liszt of 3 March 1853. See the translation of Wagner's program to the *Tannhäuser* Overture included in Part VI of this volume.

21. Franz Brendel alluded to the Viennese critic's phrase "überwundenen Standpunkte" (dated or outmoded standpoints) in his 1859 address to the Leipzig "Musicians' Assembly" (a translation of which can be found below in this section), by which time it had become closely associated with Brendel's advocacy of the "modern school" and his ideological dismissal of musical conventions and received styles.

22. Lobe, "Hektor Berlioz," *Fliegende Blätter* 1 (1853): 86–105.

23. Lobe refers to the opening dramatic effect in Haydn's *Creation*.

24. Wagner had no sympathy with the poetic notion of unconscious creation. Writing to Eduard Hanslick, he explained: "Do not underestimate the power of reflection: the unconsciously created work of art belongs to periods which lie far away from our own: the work of art of the most advanced period of culture can be produced only by a process of conscious creation." Wagner to Hanslick, 1 January 1847, Dresden, in *Selected Letters of Richard Wagner*, trans. and ed. Barry Millington and Stewart Spencer (New York, 1988), 134.

25. "Es ist einem jeden vergönnt, seinen eigenen Geschmack zu haben; und es ist rühmlich, sich von seinem eigenen Geschmacke Rechenschaft zu geben suchen. Aber den Gründen, durch die man ihn rechtferrtigen will, eine Allgemeinheit ertheilen, die, wenn es seine Richtigkeit damit hätte, ihn zu dem einzigen wahren Geschmacke machen müßte, heißt aus den Grenzen des forschenden Liebhabers herausgehen und sich zu einem eigensinnigen Gesetzgeber aufwerfen. / Der wahre Kunstrichter folgert keine Regeln aus seinem Geschmacke, sondern hat seinen Geschmack nach den Regeln gebildet, welche die Natur der Sache erfordert." Lessing, *Hamburgische Dramaturgie* (No. 19), in *Gesammelte Werke* (Berlin, 1954), 6:100–101.

26. A reference to Beethoven's *Leonore* Overture no. 3, which was eventually replaced with the simpler, less dramatically freighted *Fidelio* Overture, when Beethoven's opera was revived under the latter title in 1814.

27. Lobe's term *Reihe* (canon) does not imply canon formation as the notion is understood in modern criticism, but merely a series of related overtures. His concern is to insert Wagner's composition into a music tradition that the composer himself vehemently rejected.

28. Isabelle's cavatina "Robert, Robert, toi que j'aime" (mm. 15–18), the refrain of which runs "Grâce, grâce pour toi-même." From Act 4 of Meyerbeer's *Robert le Diable*.

29. Lobe was of course well aware of Wagner's contempt for Meyerbeer, and so rather than making a patently incorrect statement here, he is posing a hypothetical scenario: let's imagine, for the sake of argument and neutral criticism that Wagner had *not* heard a note of Meyerbeer.

30. Wagner's latest works, *Tannhäuser* and *Lohengrin*, were commonly received and assessed by German critics as exemplifications of Wagner's theory for *Worttonsprache*, *Versmelodie*, orchestral dialogue, and for his aspirations toward drama as laid out in *Opera and Drama*. They were by far the two most commonly performed of Wagner's operas in Germany during the 1850s, yet Wagner is at pains to point out in private correspondence that they antedate his theories (most notably a letter to Adolph Stahr on 31 May 1851), and he publicly distanced himself from them in the preface to the French translation of *Tristan, Der fliegende Holländer, Tannhäuser* and *Lohengrin* of September 1860: "[I wish] to draw your attention to the great mistake which people make, when they think needful to suppose that [*Holländer, Tannhäuser, Lohengrin*] were written with conscious purpose after abstract rules imposed upon myself . . . my system proper, if so you choose to call it, finds in those first three poems but a most conditional application." See "*Zukunftsmusik,*" in *Judaism in Music and Other Essays,* trans. and ed. William Ashton Ellis (Lincoln, Neb. and London, 1995), 295, 326.

31. Lobe alludes to the persistent figuration in the violins that decorates the Pilgrims' Chorus theme in the introduction and coda to the overture—an effect that struck listeners from the beginning, and created a similar sensation in Franz Liszt's difficult piano transcription of the work.

32. "Kunstwerke lernt man nicht kennen, wenn sie fertig sind, man muß sie im Entstehen aufhaschen, um sie einigermaßen zu begreifen." Goethe to Zelter, Weimar, 4 August 1803, in *Der Briefwechsel zwischen Goethe und Zelter,* 1799–1818, ed. Max Hecker (Frankfurt am Main, 1987), 1:44.

33. Lobe's use of the term *Perioden* (periods) in this sentence is idiosyncratic, perhaps indicating that he wants to mirror Wagner's use of old forms in new ways through his use of analytical terms.

34. Lobe's reference here to "die Musik der Zukunft" is among the earlier instances of this quasi-Wagnerian term which, as "*Zukunftsmusik,*" would become a standard weapon in the arsenal of anti-Wagnerian criticism by the end of the decade

35. Lobe's *Zopf* refers to the aristocratic, old fashioned stereotype of "alte Zopf" which is the German phrase for a pre-French Revolution aristocratic wig for men. In Lobe's usage, it connotes artistic and political outdatedness and conservatism in people, or an antiquated custom. In his essay on conducting from 1869, Wagner used the term to refer to a typical German Kapellmeister—"sure of his business, strict, despotic, and by no means polite"— who displayed an "old-fashioned" attitude toward modern music. See *Wagner on Conducting,* trans. Edward Dannreuther (New York, 1989), 2.

36. Christian Dietrich Grabbe (1801–36), a paradigmatically Romantic dramatist: eccentric, ambitious, rebellious, and short-lived. He himself wrote an essay "Über die Shakespeare-Manie" in the 1820s, and Heine—an admirer of Grabbe's poetry—likened him to a "drunken Shakespeare" because of his "tastelessness, cynicism, and exuberance." See Heinrich Heine, *Werke und Briefe,* ed. H. Kaufmann (Berlin, 1962), 7:194.

37. "(a) Beim der Nacht Einbruch auf ein Duft
   (b) rosig erdämmernder wirbelt; sich Erscheinungen
   (c) zauberische zeigen; Jubelklänge u. s. w.
   See Lobe, *Fliegende Blätter* 1 (1854): 451.

38. "Den Zweig der Kunst, den die neueren deutschen Künstler nicht besitzen, erklären sie für schädlich und daher wegzuhauen." Goethe, "Sprüche in Prosa," *Sämmtliche Werke: Vollständige Ausgabe in zehn Bänden* (Stuttgart, 1885), 1:768.

39. Anne-Louise-Germaine Necker, Mme. de Staël (1766–1817), novelist and essayist who was best known for her cultural profile of German Romantic thought, "De L'Allemagne," a work which caused her to be exiled from Napoleonic France upon its publication in 1807.

40. Lobe, "Aesthetische Briefe. Vierter Brief. Harmonie. Modulation. Tongeschlechter und Tonarten," *Fliegender Blätter für Musik* 1 (1854): 369–85.

41. This occurs in the Act 2 finale of *Euryanthe*, immediately after the chorus words "wir All' sind dein mit Gut und Blut," and coincides with the basses' phrase "Ha! die Verrätherin!"

42. Lobe's twelfth letter about Wagner, not included here, addresses Wagner's approach to melody and text-setting in *Lohengrin*.

43. Adolar's song occurs (with mild discrepancies) in *Euryanthe*, Act 1, no. 4 "scene and choir." It is set to the words "Ich bau' auf Gott und meine Euryanth'."

44. Antonio Canova (1757–1822) and Bertel Thorwaldsen (1770–1844) were both renowned sculptors.

45. The actors mentioned are, respectively: David Garrick (1717–79), August Wilhelm Iffland (1759–1814), Eduard Devrient (1801–77), and his sister-in-law, the singer-actor Wilhelmine Schröder-Devrient (1804–60).

46. "In jeder Art der Geistesentwickelung gibt es, wie in dem Stufengange der Natur, einen Moment der Blüthe und einen höchsten Punkt der Vollendung, der sich dann auch *durch eine schöne Vollkommenheit der Form und der Sprache kund gibt.*" See Friedrich von Schlegel, *Geschichte der alten und neuen Literatur*, ed. Hans Eichner (Paderborn, 1842; repr. 1961), 35.

47. "Ursachen des gesunkenen Geschmacks bei den verschiedenen Völkern, da er geblüht" [1775]. See Johann Gottfried Herder, *Schriften zu Philosophie, Literatur, Kunst und Altertum, 1774–1787*, in *Werke*, ed. Jürgen Brummack and Martin Bollacher (Frankfurt, 1994), 6:109–48, here 116. An English translation of this essay is available as "The Causes of Sunken Taste Among the Different Peoples in Whom It Once Blossomed," in Herder, *Selected Writings on Aesthetics*, ed. and trans. Gregory Moore (Princeton, 2006), 308–34.

Franz Brendel's Reconciliation Address

FRANZ BRENDEL

INTRODUCED AND ANNOTATED BY JAMES DEAVILLE

TRANSLATED BY JAMES DEAVILLE AND MARY A. CICORA

Franz Brendel (1811–68) took over the editorship of the *Neue Zeitschrift für Musik* from Robert Schumann at the end of 1845—Schumann had founded the journal in Leipzig in 1834, to provide an alternative to the conservative *Allgemeine musikalische Zeitung* (1798–1848). The twenty-fifth anniversary of the journal's founding was the occasion for the Leipzig Tonkünstler-Versammlung (musicians' assembly) of June 1859, at which Brendel delivered the opening address: "Advancing an Understanding."[1] The talk's historical importance resides in Brendel's coinage of the designation "New German School" for the music of Wagner, Liszt, and Berlioz, to replace the term "Zukunftsmusik" (music of the future) that the opposition had imposed upon the compositions and aesthetic writings of the progressive party.

It made sense that Brendel should open the assembly, since he had been responsible for the Leipzig Tonkünstler-Versammlungen of the late 1840s; moreover, he had dedicated the *Neue Zeitschrift* to the new movement in the early 1850s, tirelessly writing and publishing on behalf of Wagner and Liszt.[2] In other words, Brendel and his journal had become recognized respectively as the spokesman and the organ for the progressive cause in music. However, this central position also meant that the opposition—in large part music critics and musicians from northern Germany, the Rhine and Vienna—would focus their attacks on the editor. A vehement polemic battle between "progressive" and "conservative" forces had indeed raged in the press of Central Europe since at least 1853—this is the point of departure for "Advancing an Understanding," which recent scholarship on the one hand has dismissed as "drivel," and on the other uses as the platform for developing elaborate aesthetic systems for the New German School.[3] However, beyond the important neologism coined here, the address is also a reasoned argument aimed at both supporters and opponents of the new direction in music, a structured discourse that presents the editor's construction of music history and the essential role of the written word therein, recapitulating the nature of the aesthetic dispute and laying out the groundwork for a reconciliation. Its value resides in the articulation of Brendel's historical and polemic perspective on the positions of the "New Germans" and their opposition. That Brendel appeared to be working toward a reconciliation without making any real concessions to the opposition was not lost on them, for the well-known riposte (or "manifesto") in May of 1860 was specifically leveled against the direction of Brendel and his journal. The manifesto appeared on 6 May 1860, in the *Berliner Musik-Zeitung Echo* and was signed by Brahms, Joseph Joachim, Julius Otto Grimm, and Bernhard Scholz. However, the New Germans somehow came into possession of a pre-publication copy of the manifesto and published a parody of it in the *Neue Zeitschrift* two days earlier.[4]

Several aspects of "Advancing an Understanding" merit special consideration. In the opening paragraphs, Brendel clearly valorizes "the printed word" in his apology for the newest movement in music, noting how Schumann importantly pioneered the calling of composer-critic yet remained mired in subjectivity and caprice in his writings. Brendel takes credit for having introduced a more objective, "scientific" approach to the critical and aesthetic side of writing about music—the desire to bring about uniformity on that basis led to the first Tonkünstler-Versammlung, in 1847. For Brendel, this was the age of informed writing on music, when composers articulated their principles in print and critics relied upon reason in their judgments. It might seem strange that Brendel mentions only one composition (*Lohengrin*) in the entire address, but one must bear in mind that in 1859 relatively few recent works of Wagner and Liszt were known, the opposition was not championing any composer of its own (Brahms had yet to make a significant appearance), and—most important for Brendel—both Wagner and Liszt had significantly committed their aesthetic ideas to print.

Brendel presents a four-step plan to realize the reconciliation. The first phase involves "working toward the elimination of countless misunderstandings" (on the part of the opposition). Then he turns to the need to replace "naturalism" (Romanticism) and its world of "instinct" and "sensoriality" with "rationalism," "a thinking comprehension of art," which includes the practical reorganization of musical life. Once that basis of principles is achieved, it will be possible to determine whether the music itself conforms to them (he mentions no works in this short third section). Finally, he talks of the need to purge the field of things that remind us of the old battle. Here he proposes replacing the designation "Zukunftsmusik" with New German School. Brendel's final major argument regards the suitability of that term to collectively represent the three leading composers of the new direction (Wagner, and the unnamed composers Liszt and Berlioz), which he justifies on the basis of what he calls the "universal German." This category enables artists of foreign birth to adopt the German spirit and intellect, whereby they become just as German as the "specifically German."[5]

Brendel is not particularly helpful regarding the neologism New German School. After establishing the indebtedness of the movement's three coryphaei to Beethoven, he defines the term as "the entire [German musical] development after Beethoven," the German North having taken the lead from Beethoven after the "Italianate" Classical era of the Viennese masters. If we take him at his word here, Brendel would have to include Schumann and even Mendelssohn among the New Germans, at least as transitional figures.[6] He may have replaced "Zukunftsmusik" with another name for the progressive movement, yet when one investigates more closely, the new designation raises as many questions as the opposition's term. Indeed, Brendel seems to distance himself from any deeper interpretation when he wrote in the 1860 edition of his *Geschichte der Musik*, "As is generally known, . . . the Wagner-Liszt school . . . has now adopted the name of the 'New German [School],' for no other reason than to dispel invidious memories attached to the distasteful word 'Zukunftsmusik.'"[7] Elsewhere, Brendel does not appear to have used his own neologism, whether in the *Geschichte der Musik* or in the opening address to the next Tonkünstler-Versammlung, in Weimar in 1861.[8] By that time, he had turned his attention to the new organization called the Allgemeine Deutsche Musikverein, which was supposed to put the principles of the progressive party into practice and realize Brendel's own vision for the gathering of musicians. Certain progressive apologists like August Wilhelm Ambros and Louis Köhler did write prominently about the New German School in the 1860s, yet it was a later generation of music historians and aestheticians—arguably beginning with Hugo Riemann in 1901—that would consistently apply the designation to the three composers and their followers.[9]

That Brendel concludes the address with a complaint about the tone of debate in the musical press rather than a panegyric to the just-named New German School reflects his priorities in "Approaching an Understanding." He was primarily concerned with establishing a framework for discussing—even debating—the "music of the future." Elsewhere he had already presented the aesthetic agenda for the progressive movement—here Brendel needed to establish his credentials and to muster support as prophetic spokesman for the party (after all, he had assumed the power to name it), to show himself to be a reasonable, logical participant in the debates, and to cast whatever aspersions possible at the opposition, even while maintaining a surface position of evenhanded neutrality. In the final analysis the address served musico-political purposes, as the opposition perceived and as they reinforced in their 1860 manifesto. It also provides valuable insights into how Brendel—leading apologist for the "New

Germans"—perceived the movement around Liszt and Wagner to have taken shape and defended itself.

The programming of the concerts that accompanied the Tonkünstler-Versammlung was intended to underline the official message of reconciliation between old and new; between canonic "old masters" like Bach, early traditionalist Romantics like Schubert and Mendelssohn, and modern "New Germans" like Liszt and Wagner. Schumann, the founder of the *Neue Zeitschrift für Musik,* figured prominently. The programs for these concerts are reproduced below.

Neue

Zeitschrift für Musik.

Franz Brendel, Berantwortlicher Redacteur. — Verleger: C. F. Kahnt in Leipzig.

Sunfzigster Band. Nr. 22. Den 27. Mai 1859.

Allgemeines Programm der Tonkünstler-Versammlung in Leipzig.
Vom 1. bis 4. Juni 1859.

Dienstag den 31. Mai.

Zur Vorfeier der Versammlung: Festvorstellung im Stadttheater; „Genoveva." Oper in 4 Acten von Robert Schumann.

Casseneröffnung 1/26 Uhr. Anfang 1/27 Uhr. Ende gegen 10 Uhr.

Erster Tag, Mittwoch den 1. Juni, Abends.

Zur Eröffnung der Versammlung: Concert im Stadttheater unter Leitung des Hrn. Hofcapell-M. Dr. Franz Liszt und des Hrn. Capell-M. A. F. Riccius.

Erster Theil.

1) Ouverture, „Meeresstille und glückliche Fahrt" von Mendelssohn.
2) Prolog. Gesprochen von Frau Franziska Ritter, geb. Wagner.
3) Duo von F. Schubert, vorgetragen von den HH. v. Bülow und Concert-M. David.
4) Arie aus „Benvenuto Cellini" von Berlioz, gesungen von Frau v. Milde.
5) Ouverture zu „Manfred" von R. Schumann.

Zweiter Theil.

1) „Tristan und Isolde." Instrumental-Einleitung (Manuscript) von R. Wagner.
2) „Der Haideknabe", Ballade von Hebbel, comp. von R. Schumann. Gesprochen von Frau Ritter.
3) Duett aus „Der fliegende Holländer" von R. Wagner, gesungen von Herrn und Frau v. Milde.
4) Zwei Clavierstücke von Chopin und Liszt, vorgetragen von H. v. Bülow.
5) Lieder von R. Franz, gesungen von Hrn. v. Milde.
6) „Tasso, lamento e trionfo", symphonische Dichtung von Liszt.

Cassenöffnung 1/26 Uhr. Anfang 1/27 Uhr.

Nach dem Concert Zusammenkunft im Parterresaale des Schützenhauses, zur Vermittlung gegenseitiger Bekanntschaft.

Zweiter Tag, Donnerstag 2. Juni, Vormittags 1/211 Uhr.

Musikalische Vorträge im obern Saale des Schützenhauses für die Theilnehmer und deren Gäste — ohne Zutritt des Publicums.

Mittagessen (à la carte) im unteren Saale des Schützenhauses.

Concert program for the Leipzig Tonkünstler-Versammlung, June 1–4, 1859.

Nachmittags in der Thomaskirche: **Graner Festmesse von Franz Liszt**, unter Leitung des Componisten. Eröffnung ¼4 Uhr. Anfang 4 Uhr. Ende ½6 Uhr. Abends ½8 Uhr: Festmahl im oberen Saale des Schützenhauses.

Dritter Tag, Freitag den 3. Juni, Vormittags im oberen Saale des Schützenhauses: **Mündliche Vorträge.** Anfang 9 Uhr. Ende ½1 Uhr. Mittagessen (à la carte) im unteren Saale des Schützenhauses. Nachmittag: Wahl eines Vorsitzenden und des Stellvertreters, Besprechungen über Anträge. Abends in der Thomaskirche: **Hohe Messe von Seb. Bach.** Unter Leitung des Hrn. Musik-Dir. Carl Riedel. Eröffnung 6 Uhr. Anfang ½7 Uhr. Ende gegen 10 Uhr. Hierauf Zusammenkunft im Schützenhause.

Vierter Tag, Sonnabend den 4. Juni, Vormittags im Saale des Gewandhauses: **Concert für Kammermusik.**

1) Quartett in vier fugirten Sätzen (Manuscript) von **Carl Müller**; vorgetragen vom Meininger Hofquartett der HH. Gebrüder Müller.
2) Lieder von **Lassen** (Manuscript), gesungen von Hrn. v. d. Osten.
3) „Italienisches Concert" von **S. Bach**, vorgetragen von H. v. Bülow.
4) Psalm von **Ferd. Hiller**, gesungen von Frau Dr. Reclam.
5) Sonate von **Tartini**, vorgetragen von Hrn. Concert-M. David.
6) „Lenore", Ballade von **Bürger**, comp. von Liszt (Manuscript). Gesprochen von Frau Ritter.
7) Trio von **Franz Schubert**, vorgetragen von den HH. v. Bülow, Concert-M. David und Fr. Grützmacher.

Anfang 10 Uhr. Ende nach 12 Uhr. Mittagessen (à la carte) im unteren Saale des Schützenhauses. Nachmittag: Mündliche Vorträge und Besprechungen über Anträge. Anfang 3 Uhr. Ende 7 Uhr. Nacher: Geselliges Zusammensein in den Parterrelocalitäten. Hiermit Schluß der Versammlung.

Sonntag den 5. Juni: **Gemeinschaftliche Fahrt nach Merseburg.** Auf der thüringischen Eisenbahn, Vormittags. Nachmittags: **Orgelconcert im Dome zu Merseburg.** Veranstaltet von Hrn. Musik-Dir. D. H. Engel daselbst. Rückfahrt nach dem Schlusse des Concertes.

Besondere Bestimmungen.

1) Die Billets für die Festvorstellung von **Schumann's „Genoveva"** sind an der Theatercasse zu kaufen. Für das Concert im Stadttheater (Mittwoch) stehen uns nur eine bestimmte Zahl von Freibillets zu Gebote. Sollte dieselbe nicht ausreichen, so müssen wir die zuletzt sich meldenden Theilnehmer ersuchen, an der Theatercasse die erforderlichen Billets zu kaufen. Zum Entrée für alle übrigen Aufführungen und Vorträge berechtigt die allgemeine Eintrittskarte. Zum Festmahl erhalten die ankommenden Fremden bei der Anmeldung im Bureau Tischmarken, die daselbst mit 20 Ngr. zu bezahlen sind.

2) Das Anmeldungsbureau befindet sich im Haupteingange des Gewandhauses (von der Universitätsstraße aus, parterre) und ist Mittwoch den 1. Juni von 10 bis 12 und Nachmittags von 3 bis 7 Uhr geöffnet, sowie Donnerstag Nachmittags von 2 bis ½4 Uhr.

3) Behufs gegenseitiger Vorstellung werden die uns nicht persönlich bekannten Fremden, resp. Gäste ersucht, sich an diejenigen zu wenden, welche sie im Bureau empfangen und kennen gelernt haben.

4) Es liegt im Interesse des ganzen Unternehmens und wir erlauben uns daher den Wunsch auszusprechen, daß alle Theilnehmer der Versammlung bis zum letzten derselben (Sonnabend Abend) Antheil nehmen.

5) Alle Toaste sind bis vor Beginn des Festmahles bei Hrn. Dr. Richard Pohl anzumelden. Derselbe ist während der unter 2) angegebenen Stunden im Bureau der Tonkünstler-Versammlung anwesend.

Die russische Jagdmusik.

Nach J. C. Hinrich's historischen Quellen (1786) von **Theodor Rode.**

Johann Anton Maresch ist der Erfinder der russischen Jagdmusik, bei welcher bekanntlich jeder Spieler nur über einen einzigen Ton zu verfügen hatte. Dieses Curiosum ist so einzig in seiner Art, daß es sich wol lohnt, die Leser d. Bl. mit der Geschichte derselben näher bekannt zu machen.

Maresch wurde im Jahre 1719 zu Chotiborz, einer im Tschaslauer Kreise in Böhmen gelegenen Stadt geboren, wo sein Vater Inspector über die Schleusen war. Schon in frühester Jugend zeigte er große Lust

Concert program for the Leipzig Tonkünstler-Versammlung, June 1–4, 1859.

FRANZ BRENDEL

Advancing an Understanding
Address to the Opening of the Tonkünstler-Versammlung
Delivered in Leipzig on June 1, 1859

Esteemed Assembly!

A significant stage in the history of the *Neue Zeitschrift für Musik* provided the initial, ostensible occasion for this assembly: the twenty-fifth anniversary of its founding. You have come here to celebrate that anniversary together with us.

Since I am the one most directly involved in this event, as the person who initiated the celebration, it is incumbent on me to present you with its concept and intention. It is my task to lay out the inner significance of the activities of the assembly and to demonstrate how I consider it to be a beneficial and appropriate means for engaging with the musical conditions of the present.

Before I turn to this, my main topic, however, it is my agreeable first task to welcome you most heartily. I hope that you will like it here and that we will be in the position to meet your expectations to some extent. It is also my pleasure to thank you for the interest you have shown by attending this event, all the more so because of the heightened difficulties of the general conditions that prevail at the moment and that nevertheless did not deter you from coming.[10]

As regards more particularly the task just identified, this must inwardly result from the journal's development, even as it is externally determined by a stage in the history of this organ.

To this end we hardly require a detailed consideration of that which came before. I will only recall what is generally known when I direct your attention to the stages through which the journal has passed up to this point.

You know the circumstances under which Schumann began, how it was a matter of regenerating music criticism and at the same time pioneering a new direction in the art of the time. A general flagging of effort had taken hold both in the realm of musical production and that of criticism, the latter especially here in Leipzig. Concerning production, one held to the traditions of Mozart, while the implications of late Beethoven remained a closed book. For this reason it became crucial at the time to allow for a further development of art based on Beethoven, a direction that would take the intellectual as a point of departure, as opposed to the excess of sensuality in the prior school. You also know how Schumann carried out this task. It is significant that he initiated the period when artists undertook to represent their art through writing, that this now started to become the rule, while heretofore it had only been the exception. Schumann's work as critic distinguished itself through his deeply penetrating artistic perspective, even though it also relied primarily upon subjective foundations and the mood of the moment was often too decisive a factor. Needless to say, such a change could not advance without some *Sturm und Drang*, and at times what seemed to be acceptable limits were somewhat exceeded. Schumann nevertheless deserves much credit for having brought to life the new epoch of music.

While I later made these principles of my predecessor my own, above all emphasizing the present and demanding the advancement of our age and our art, I attempted at the same time to push for greater clarity of critical perception [*Auffassung*], that is to say, to work out the side of objective, empirical knowledge. It became necessary to conceptualize in its inner cohesion that which up to then had appeared merely as coincidental and arbitrary, especially to comprehend the present in its inner link with the past, which was not really Schumann's concern. It was a matter of attaining firmer principles than were possible up to that time, indeed, to attain principles at all. Musicians earlier only felt, or knew, themselves to be united through the technical side of art. In matters of aesthetic comprehension the most extreme arbitrariness prevailed, and the realm of opinion was a chaos of the greatest contradictions.

It was for this reason that now a number of years ago, I gave the first impetus for a *musicians' assembly*,[11] which was likewise held here in Leipzig, as you know.[12] The memory of that first undertaking is fresh, now that I see you all gathered here again, and if I were to make a comparison between then and now, it would not merely be one of externals and chance. No, a glimpse at that which we attained earlier will bring us closer to comprehending our current task.

It was remarked that that gathering had only slight results. This is admittedly true, if you have in mind that which directly impacts life, immediately visible and tangible; but it is very untrue if we are willing to think about less obvious results. At that time it was a matter of giving expression to the desire of musicians for mutual convergence, of drawing art and artists out of isolation, out of a state of fragmentation into as many atoms as there are artists—in other words, of working toward a community of knowledge and of endeavor through inclusion of individuals. This was actually attained, and the ground was laid for that which developed later; the efforts of the journal were considerably advanced and supported through it.

Now those earlier developments are undergoing a reprise. In the meantime, however, conditions have significantly altered. That greater clarity of critical perception initiated, then, the maintaining of specific principles, understandably led to renewed division—this time, however, not to a chaotic disarray but rather to a conscious separation, to the formation of special groups, and ultimately to the creation of parties. The *Neue Zeitschrift für Musik* thereby entered into a party position, although really against its will, in a certain sense. This occurred intentionally and consciously, if you see such partisanship as the desire to maintain specific principles in opposition to a worthless chaos of opinion, such as was the norm up to that time; it occurred against the will of the journal, however, if you confuse such partisanship with exclusiveness and one-sidedness.

How the newer partisan battles have developed as a result of such a position is so well known that I only need remind you of it here in passing. An unbroken organic development does reveal itself from that time up to the present. Even before debates over the newest endeavors, I had already represented the same principles, in part, as a glance through the early volumes of the journal will show you—it was only a fulfillment of that to which I had aspired when the masters of most recent times appeared and gave practical evidence through their artistic creations. This also explains, incidentally, the close affiliation of the journal with two of these, an affiliation that is thoroughly objective, a matter of principle.[13] Arriving independently from different points of departure, it was inevitable that we should come together. I admit that earlier I often doubted and asked myself whether I was not in the process of dictating to music an inappropriately heterogeneous, pluralistic agenda. The artistic activity of the latest masters has freed me from my doubts and provided me with the proof I was not mistaken.

It was in this way that the party battles of recent years originated—they have unfortunately increased to a degree that in terms of animosity they really could bring to mind the religious fanaticism from earlier centuries of our history, as one opponent recently observed.

Anxious dispositions have asked whether such partisanship is necessary for the well-being of the art, and they have lamented it from the start. I answer the question unhesitatingly in the opposing, affirmative sense, and see progress in such battle. Nothing really influential or lasting can be attained without some *Sturm und Drang*, without passions being spurred on, and if Schumann, in his time, had not also sometimes gone overboard in his enthusiasm, we would never have emerged from our earlier lethargy. Thus significant things have already been accomplished, in truth, and we can look back on them now as real achievements. A new epoch of heightened intellectual life has come about in the realm of music, with a rich literature of writings about music. Musicians have woken up, have been freed from immersion in their moribund, subjective emotional lives. Now almost all of them have had significant success as writers in representing their art and aims, while earlier, as mentioned, they hardly ventured to pick up the pen for the sake of making their critical views known. Through this activity, elevated interest has been stimulated in the furthest circles, also with the public. Such general engagement with the world of art puts musicians back in the position to accomplish infinitely more for their own discipline than would have otherwise been possible. Out of many potential examples one may suffice for you to infer the great difference between then and now. At the beginning of my journalistic activity I strove long and fruitlessly to promote a German translation of Ulibischeff's Mozart book before, eventually, I succeeded in this.[14] Now, every month brings more substantial works about music than once had appeared over a matter of years. It should be obvious, too, that much of this has also made possible the ambitious ventures in the realm of practical composition we now enjoy.

Certainly none of this could have been achieved without some detrimental consequences, too. I have already recalled the vehemence with which the battles have been waged. However, it is not just this vehemence we have to lament: there have also arisen boundless misunderstandings, and misrepresentations to such a degree that one hardly recognizes the original core; a prejudice has set in that does not and will not see or hear; a Babylonian confusion of tongues, amid which the different parties hardly understand each other; much unexampled animosity, even vulgarity, has become the order of the day in the field of music.

If we weigh these conditions, the question arises whether it is not high time to bring about some change, whether it is not time to hold on to our gains, to continue positive developments, and to expunge the more unfortunate ones, in a word: *to take steps toward the reconciliation of the parties*. Party positions are not abiding or final, but rather moments of transition— they have their significant uses, but are also likely to be discarded over time in order to make way for a mediating, more universal outlook.

I consider that this moment has arrived, a moment desired by all sensible, right-minded people. That is the cause I am presenting to you here and for which I request your participation. That is what I designate as our task, *as the idea behind our festival: this is something that can be attained to a lesser degree through the press, but fully only through such an assembly*. One might ask why such an assembly is needed, since the lectures are published, and time is too short for discussions that could go into more detail. The answer is the same as that given to individuals who think that university lectures are superfluous, since what is taught can already be found in a thousand books. One can agree with this straightaway, yet still decisively be of the opinion that those lectures cannot be replaced through any other means. The essence of our assembly does not consist of attaining immediately practical, palpable results in a few hours—for that we would need many days; rather, the internal stimulation, the direct observation are to be gained. A more personal approach, a personal familiarity with all of the conditions and relationships is the main thing—and it is a great deficiency of our opponents that they neglect this. Do not imagine, moreover, that I suppose I am speaking here to some assembly of dissenters with the aim of bringing them around. I know that the opposite is the case. I hope to find among you a *consensus,* and thus the moral force with which you are able to support such principles. An assembly of artists like the present one, consisting of men of quite differing perspectives (despite all their agreement on the main issue), must result in a more general understanding if the group is to endorse my principles, as I hope. As before, at the first of our gatherings, the further working out of that which has been established at this meeting remains a matter of the press—of [our] journal. Now it is a matter of having you disseminate within your circles the change, the progress that we hope to accomplish here, and to bear witness to your opinions.

If we are that far, if we have come to that point, it becomes necessary for me *to express my opinion more precisely about how I desire such an understanding to be taken,* to formulate the decisive propositions.

I do not mean an immediate amalgamation, a complete elimination of all differences of opinion, which would be an impossibility as well as an absurdity. Thus I do not intend a leveling, which rests only on the blurring and blending of differences. It also would not mean a cessation of battle where that is required by irrefutable necessity. I desire an understanding through the elimination of misunderstandings in those extraordinarily many cases where the differences really only arise from misunderstandings. I desire understanding, agreement with sensible opponents through becoming mutually clearer, through agreeing for the sake of art in all of those equally numerous cases where no differences of opinion can really exist. I desire moreover the elimination of the fully useless animosities in the press, the removal of those rude battles, even with a genuine and irremovable difference of opinion. I insist that, if argument is necessary, it be aboveboard and conducted with decency. For that purpose we sincerely extend our hand, so that the press can work itself out from the confusion of the present and make a step forward. Also, since to a certain extent we gave first initiative to action (while we are not responsible for the animosities, which are solely the work of the opposition), I think it is appropriate that steps toward conciliation should now be made from our side. However, should that not succeed, should my good word find no solid foothold, then I will consider myself sufficiently justified before you in ceasing to show that due respect we have maintained so far to those who would remain incorrigible, who close their eyes and ears to the clearest and simplest instruction, who cast about themselves armed only with prejudices pulled out of thin air, which they then lay at our own feet as if these represented our own opinion; I think, then, we will also be justified in quite freely pointing out to them how their opposition is unfounded, their argumentation mere empty chatter. We are not calling for reconciliation at any price, for understanding is only possible with those who understand. Moreover, no external coercion of any sort can determine this step for us. If need be, let the battle continue in the current manner.

If the latter, however, we do not fear. There is too large a majority of the well meaning, so that the few incorrigibles must soon be dispatched.

I. The first matter of concern in reaching an understanding is to work toward the elimination of the countless misunderstandings, simply by setting out what is true and accurate. We must recognize that many things have been and continue to be fought over to no purpose—in many cases we must realize that this has been much ado about nothing. The better informed have known this for some time, however much the opposition still misuses the situation, so that what began as honest misunderstanding continues to be exploited as a convenient tool to generate bad feeling.

To illustrate the point, let me recall in passing several examples of such drastic misunderstanding.

When Wagner appeared with his doctrine of the artwork of the future, many traditional, specialized musicians [*Sonderkünstler*] believed that they were to be immediately eradicated, and thus saw no more pressing need than to save their skin in the best possible way. Granted, Wagner cut a rather brusque figure, and some of what he published appeared rather hyperbolic. People did not sufficiently consider, however, that none of us fully agreed with Wagner in every detail, or that, in fact, we quickly endeavored to soften the brusqueness, to strip away the exaggerations. Time and again, nevertheless, these exaggerations were turned into the object of attacks, without subsequent mitigating efforts ever being taken into account. This has continued up to today: with this year's first *Lohengrin* performance in Berlin, the local papers have yet again trotted out familiar talk, oblivious of any later developments.[15] They still held on to the husk, failing to discover the great kernel of Wagner's teaching.

Moreover, the term I coined of a "superseded viewpoint" [*überwundener Standpunkt*] has given occasion for conflict, evoking more of the same attacks from the broadest public circles, even those where the views and tendencies of the new direction in music have not become known.[16] Misunderstandings have been the basis for this, however, and the confusion of opponents alone bears responsibility when a simple sentence is assigned an importance not intended for it. Accordingly, this type of confusion must finally cease—whoever cannot extricate himself from such confusion should just be told to learn more about the case before speaking on it. There have been exaggerations [on our part] now and then, exaggerations that seem to have granted the opponents greater justification on this count. Here as well, however, misunderstandings are the cause: the perspective of young hotheads has been mistaken for the general principles of our party. It is equally inadmissible—even in cases where mature individuals may express themselves disparagingly—to pass off subjective views as those of the school. One has to differentiate between the individual and the general. Exaggerations crop up everywhere there is life and activity, and if opponents are right to a certain extent in taking offense, they should not forget that during Mendelssohn's time such was exactly the case here in Leipzig, and no one would think of putting the blame on him.

Were we to pursue the origins of such misunderstandings, we would indeed have to lay the blame almost exclusively at the door of the oppositional party. This group failed to notice that a major new intellectual movement was afoot, that it had developed while they slept. Suddenly awakened, our opponents are now disoriented, in too much of a hurry, having read one thing not at all, and another only partially; they are unable to access the spirit of the times. They speak like the blind would of a color, about things whose development they have not followed at all, and then fail to notice how they are struggling really only against their own misunderstandings. If our opinions were truly represented by the absurdities so frequently attributed to us from the Rhineland, for example, I would be the first to concede to our opponents.[17] For this reason I must describe the necessity of the opposition to us as fundamentally pointless, unfounded and mistaken. Our principles are so embracing, and always so objectively supported, that the supposedly justifiable opposition has really nothing more to fall back on than those weaknesses that adhere to any human undertaking. Meanwhile they ignore any positive results of our efforts. This is a miserable, comfortless business; one might well suppose they pursue it merely in order to say something different, and so to preserve some form of existence. They want to maintain Classical principles, but their notion of the "Classical" resides not only in the true attributes of the idea but as much in its characteristic deficiencies. They seek to maintain these deficiencies because, simply, they have not advanced enough in insight to recognize them as such. If we agree with our opponents to a certain extent that the old days must provide the foundation and starting point of music education, they nonetheless err in defining the "Classical" too exclusively according to historical period, while neglecting undeniable good things produced in modern times. They believe it a matter of egoism and arrogant domination when we express ourselves brusquely in the interest of art and out of a sense of duty. They look for bad motives because, as a result of insufficient understanding, they cannot instinctively explain the matter to themselves. In all of this we encounter yet again—in those rarer cases, of course, where truly pure motives are decisive—the strange conceptual confusion; namely the belief that some are called to be the gatekeepers for art. Meanwhile they cannot comprehend or will not concede that we are led by a similar sense of duty: the endeavor to protect art from that stagnation and decay into which it would inevitably descend were they in fact correct.

But enough of this. It was necessary to provide several proofs, and in doing so I have not even considered the equally numerous cases where they believed they were able to press their own case best by simply opposing us. It has also occurred often enough that the others found their expectations disappointed; that they were not so represented in the journal as they would have liked to be, and as we would have gladly done were it possible—for that reason, they went off and wrote invective. Here I envision, as said earlier, the kind of understanding that is easy to achieve with good intentions, even without concessions from either side, since it is only a matter of mutual enlightenment.

As the situation now stands, I emphasize most the necessity of a personal exchange of opinions, the necessity of presenting one's own position on the spot. At this moment many who still incline toward the opposition would be quickly convinced, if they met the conditions I have just expressed here—as, in fact, duty obliges.

At any rate we, and the journal, are also to blame, up to a point, and I would be the last one to want to hide this. I spoke openly about the faults of the opposition, and the other side of the matter should be treated no less openly. I already indicated how, before Schumann started writing music criticism, the most lamentable half-measures and cautiousness had become the norm. Schumann took the path of greater open-mindedness, and thereby restored the state of musical life to vigor and health. It was only natural, then, that I took up this legacy, extending it further in many directions, and what for Schumann had still only been accidental and subjective, I elevated to a lasting foundation. In addition, to give you just one example, Schumann had not yet dared to debate with contributors to this journal in the journal itself. I immediately introduced this practice, and now it has become customary everywhere. That proper moderation could not always be observed in this has to do with the very nature of a development that had not yet reached its conclusion. Open-minded as I like to think myself, I have not always been so particular or apprehensive as to reject those perhaps all-too-decisive pronouncements of my esteemed colleagues, and for this reason some isolated excesses have certainly occurred that would have been better avoided.[18] Now, with a long and rich experience behind me, I have gained some perspective, I know exactly what I need to do, and how it must be done; thus my motto is: "*Mutual understanding among all who are impartial*, without of course doing damage to conviction; *a more decisive stand* against those who simply refuse to hear another's viewpoint and who continue to spread suspicious rumors and untruths—even now, when a conciliatory hand has been extended toward them.

II. While we clear up misunderstandings this way, we start to approach the core of the matter, getting closer to the *positive* side of things, to that which forms the true focus of our endeavors. That is *my second important point*, and we need to grasp this with full determination. Of course, here we see a wide, immense field; I cannot go into particulars here, any more than previously, I can only establish the *principle*.

This is, to summarize: *rationalism* versus the previous *naturalism*; self-consciousness versus instinct; the spiritual side versus the sensual; the characteristic versus the beauty of the merely formal. In our age the foremost thing is to cultivate a thinking appreciation of art. This does not altogether exclude the instinctive side; the unconscious aspect is the abiding foundation of all artistic production. But a theoretical, aesthetic consciousness should now accompany it, purifying and clarifying it; artistic production should maintain an equilibrium between both sides, whereas before the naturalistic side was given distinctly more weight. Furthermore, the great masters of the past were by no means just thoughtless naturalists; the greater the natural forces, the unconscious side, the more elevated and powerful the intellect has shown itself, in all ages and in all epochs. But the historical progression in the development of art nevertheless consists particularly in this, that the conscious side struggles more and more to emerge, so that earlier creations, when considered from the perspective of a later stage, always seem naïve. This can be seen, to give a few examples, in the much more correct handling of the voice in vocal music, a matter of extraordinary importance; and in purely instrumental music in the elimination of conventional schemata and in the greater dependence of form on content. As concerns harmony, this was originally a matter of discovering the *laws of euphony* over and against a raw simplicity. Thus the many restrictions and prohibitions [of theory]. We have now come to a point, long after this has been achieved, where we can consciously place the main emphasis upon the Ideal, though of course always still selectively recognizing earlier foundations. Thus every epoch may be viewed, relatively speaking, as correct in its own way.

Another product of this principle are the practical consequences. It is our task to see that the accidental, the fragmented, the naturalistic should all make way for conditions organized accordingly; we have to work toward establishing an *organization of musical life* upon artistic principles that will replace what has heretofore come about more arbitrarily. Though much of this is not in our power, much depends entirely on us. Among these latter things is the issue of improving the structure of concert programs, accepting the new without doing away with the old, but in some arrangement that manifests a guiding idea, in contrast to the old, slapdash routine. Equally important is the matter of theatrical reform, the improvement of musical instruction, developing institutions of musical education—the conservatories—according to modern principles; such an extraordinary number of things might be mentioned here that simply listing them would take too long. But much more is also happening these days that is not in our power to change. There has hardly been a time when the rulers of Germany were so inclined to sponsor and fund music as they are right now. Here I have occasion to recognize gratefully our esteemed patron, that German prince, whose support has made possible the present celebration; as you know, His Majesty the King of Hanover has, moreover, donated an annual subsidy of 1,000 thalers to the Handel Society, in a similarly generous act of musical patronage. The liberality with which the Weimar Court has for a long time now provided a haven for contemporary art, helping to provide a firm footing for this so that, as in the time of Goethe and Schiller, a new ideal of art might flourish throughout all of Germany—this has long been recognized and lauded. Through the support of His Majesty the Duke of Coburg the German Handel Society has been enabled to make use of manuscripts in the private possession of the Queen of England; the collaboration of two German princes has enabled Germany to achieve for Handel what England could not. And the same is true in many other cases. Now it is up to us not to remain behind, but to step forward with mature, practical suggestions worthy of such a generous promotion of art.

III. Granting all this, as I believe anyone must do, the question may then be posed whether the works themselves, those in which we see our principles realized, are really in accordance with the values and suited to serve as practical proofs of these principles. We can agree on the recognition of the fundamental principles and still harbor doubts regarding their concrete application. Even less than on previous points can I afford to elaborate on this question. Everything we have committed to print in recent years has some bearing on this, and we could point to all that by way of answers. Right now the most important thing for us is the following: the difference in opinions about [new] works has its cause primarily in their still deficient familiarity, in the lack of opportunity to make their acquaintance in performance. I have chosen the works to be performed here with this in mind.[19] Many can only be judged, as is right and natural, by being heard. Thus was created this opportunity; thus was performance enabled to take the place of argument and rhetoric. That is indeed all we ask for with regard to new works, and insofar as I bring it up, I have another opportunity to set right an absurd distortion. It is our quite harmless wish that room be made for contemporary works, without in any way detracting from the works of the past; indeed we have no intention of shunning these older works. So at the moment there is no talk of battle. Only when others deprive us of light and air, refuting our fully justified demands, will the flames of battle be kindled, and then it should hardly be wondered at if, in the face of persistent opposition, restraint should finally no longer prevail.

IV. Having come this far, we need then to remove anything else that recalls the old quarrels. This is a fourth point I would like to set before you.

In this respect what might seem at first a minor matter is of some importance: the name "Zukunftsmusik." In itself this name might appear rather neutral, but it assumes importance by virtue of its having been made a *party slogan. I would therefore like to suggest doing away with this name, and offer a step toward doing so.* You already know that the words in themselves are nonsensical, as I have already explained in the journal. Wagner has called the union of the arts the "artwork of the future." By this he means a synthesis of the arts, in which each one loses some of its independence to be absorbed into the whole. Accordingly, each separate art in this sense becomes no longer self-sufficient. Therefore by speaking of "Zukunfts*musik*" we single out one art—music—as a separate art, in contradiction to the whole initial intent. "Zukunftsmusik" is at one and the same time a music that is dependent and independent, something at once music and not music—a *contradictio in adjecto*. Of course, we cannot make any authoritative pronouncement about setting new standards right now, and so we must wait and see whether our suggestion will be accepted. But we can agree among ourselves to avoid this designation in the future, and through our example perhaps inspire others to follow; if this happens, I truly believe that the wishes I have outlined here may soon be attained.

What I have just said encompasses only half of my proposal. The other side is to employ a new phrase in place of the one to be discarded; and that is certainly the more difficult task. At any rate, the question might well arise whether any of this is necessary at all; at first glance, opinions might differ on this. Upon closer inspection, nevertheless, you will find that some new designation cannot be avoided, if not for the sake of musical practice then at least for the sake of writing about it—which is becoming more and more significant.

Therefore I will allow myself to propose a new name for you to consider and, if it meets with your approval, to adopt. My proposal is the designation "New German School"(*neudeutsche Schule* or *neue deutsche Schule*). If this new name surprises you, given that the said "school" includes two non-German masters, then allow me a few comments toward mitigating the alienating effect.[20] The correctness of my suggested name needs no proof as regards at least one member of the triumvirate representing the "music of the future": Richard Wagner. He was the first one who gloriously realized the ideal of a purely German opera, following the example of Beethoven, Weber, and a few others, and in contrast to the Italian-French-German direction represented by Gluck, Mozart, et al. The matter becomes more difficult, though, when we try to include two other, non-German masters under this rubric. Of course, it has long been recognized that these two took their point of departure from Beethoven, and thus they are fundamentally German in their roots. But both of them also exhibit undeniably foreign elements, such as might at first seem to call into question the aptness of my designation; the one betrays the intellectual-reasoning aspect of the French; the other one betrays a characteristic southern fire, the flaring up of passion, the glow and the ardor of the South, all in contrast to the unadorned inwardness and stark, compact power of the German. Burdened as they are with such qualities, the question might well be put whether both masters are to be regarded as German artists—the decisive matter here.

In my "History of Music" I have proven how two developmental paths coexist in Germany, one specifically German and one universal, the latter based on an amalgamation of German, Italian, and French styles. On the one hand we have Seb. Bach, Beethoven, et al.; on the other we have Handel, Gluck, Mozart et al. In our poetry we have the very same phenomenon: beside the specifically German of the Romantic school in Tieck, Kleist, etc. there stand the universal artistic creations of Goethe and Schiller, or Wieland's affinity for the French character next to the purely German tendency of Klopstock. Of these artists who occupy a universal standpoint, all possess foreign elements in abundance: Greek in Schiller and Goethe, the latter embracing oriental influences as well; yet no one would think of calling them non-German. On the contrary, the nation has recognized itself glorified in them, with the result that we do not narrowly limit the truly "national" to the specifically German; the decisive thing is the authentically Germanic foundation, regardless of whether that which is built upon it is primarily German or more universal. This universal disposition of the nation has the result, on the other hand, that highly talented foreigners who reach out beyond the boundaries of their nationality have attached themselves to us—these have sought and found a spiritual homeland in Germany. Cherubini, Spontini, Méhul, and many others belong to this category, just to mention musical figures. Of course, all of them retain foreign elements. Yet no one doubts that their spiritual center is really to be found in Germany—we have no misgivings about imparting them citizenship. This applies above all to Cherubini, who has become what he is thanks to Germany and whom we consider a German master. The birthplace cannot be decisive in matters of the mind, no more than exact chronology in other cases; for it often occurs that someone living and working in one era can really better be assigned, spiritually, to an earlier style, and vice versa. In this sense, the case at hand is fully analogous. Neither artist would have become what he is if at an early point he had not been nourished and strengthened by the German spirit. As a result, Germany eventually had to become the locus of their career, and in this sense I have recommended the designation *New German School* for the entire post-Beethovenian development. Through this we gain both clarity of arrangement and a simpler, more consistent nomenclature. Protestant sacred music up to and including Bach and Handel has already long borne the name *altdeutsche Schule* (Old German School). The Italian-influenced epoch of the Viennese masters is the age of Classicism, the perfectly balanced interpenetration of the ideal and the real. Beethoven extends his hand to the specifically Germanic North and so establishes the New German School.

Of course, I cannot exhaust my theme with these remarks, having only just touched on the main point. Perhaps, however, one of the honored participants here will soon undertake a further development of this theme.

My reflections are near an end. There remains only one topic that I would like to mention on this occasion, as briefly as possible, since I believe it may be more effectively treated here than elsewhere. *It is the tone that has become customary in the musical press*, the manner in which artists and artistic creations are handled. I must confess that I deeply lament this widespread lack of consideration, and I would urge all of the participants here to help bring an end to it. Any opinion deserves a modicum of respect if it rests in conviction and is open to proof; we grant it the right to exist just as we demand the same of ourselves, with the qualification, of course, that in the process some struggle is not to be ruled out. However, it is time for an end to the arrogance of thinking that one alone is right, and of making reckless pronouncements in a tone of infallibility—all artists must work as a solid majority toward this end. After such abundant advances in the arts and sciences as we have seen, it is great folly to believe that one single person can in and of himself bring about that which belongs to all of humanity; to think, that is, that one's own individuality is so all-encompassing as to contain within it every other individual. Admittedly, everyone tends to believe that his opinion is the only true, all-inclusive one, for without such an attitude it is impossible to achieve a complete honesty of conviction. Still, in our age each person should also be aware that there exist insights external to himself, which his own individuality will prevent him from ever truly assimilating. It is a matter of uniting *firmness* and *determination* with modesty, the certainty of truth with the self-restraint that is the source of true humanity, the result of all-embracing intelligence. Our philosophers once believed that each of them alone had solved the mystery of the world. Now we know that each person has at best contributed just *one* stone to the grand edifice of humanity: a teaching of the greatest importance for all of us.

With that I reach the end. I believe I have presented you with a picture of what we all have to strive for, and I hope that my words have been such as to find general agreement among you.

Thus I wish that this meeting may constitute a turning point, and at the same time fix the beginning of a historically significant stage.

The main thing is that we, who profess these principles, act on the basis of this collective awareness, maintaining our differences of opinion where this must be so, but in doing so not lose sight of the total picture. Musicians must stand together and represent their art, whichever party they may choose to belong to. They must recognize that reckless enmity will only serve to shake the foundations on which they stand. The opposition itself will suffer when they resist the cause of progress: without acknowledging our principles they cannot practically advance even in their own sphere. Moreover, the efforts of the opposition are rooted in the foundations we ourselves laid down, and only enabled by conditions we ourselves have worked for.

It was my wish that our assembly would be perceived in this sense. If the immediately evident results are modest, as must be the case, we may still cherish the hope that the further consequences will turn out to be all the more significant. If we should succeed in achieving this goal, the present moment will have been for us uplifting, inspiring, and these days will remain for me and for all of you who share my feelings one of our fondest memories.

NOTES

1. Assemblies took place in 1847, 1848, and 1849, the latter two truncated because of the revolutionary events of those years.

2. The first to promote the music of Wagner in the *Neue Zeitschrift* was the Dresden musician and critic Theodor Uhlig (1822–53), in 1850; Franz Brendel himself openly advocated the progressive movement beginning with his New Year's article of 1852, "Zum neuen Jahr," *Neue Zeitschrift für Musik* 36 (1852): 1–4. Above and beyond these numerous contributions to the *Neue Zeitschrift* (see the complete listing in Peter Ramroth, *Robert Schumann und Richard Wagner im geschichtsphilosophischen Urteil von Franz Brendel* [Bern, 1991]), Brendel also promoted Wagner and Liszt in his monograph *Geschichte der Musik in Italien, Deutschland und Frankreich* (Leipzig, 1852, with four later editions through 1867) and the journal *Anregungen für Kunst, Leben und Wissenschaft* (1856–61), devoted even more exclusively than the *Neue Zeitschrift* to the "New German" cause.

3. The dismissive evaluation can be found in Piero Weiss and Richard Taruskin, *Music in the Western World* (New York, 1984), 384; for attempts to support aesthetic systems through Brendel's article, see, for example, Detlef Altenburg, "Die Neudeutsche Schule—eine Fiktion der Musikgeschichtsschreibung?" in *Liszt und die Neudeutsche Schule*, ed. Detlef Altenburg (Laaber, 2006), 9–22; and Rainer Kleinertz, "Zum Begriff 'Neudeutsche Schule,'" ibid., 23–31.

4. The "manifesto" appeared on 6 May 1860 in *Berliner Musik-Zeitung Echo* and was signed by Brahms, Joseph Joachim, Julius Otto Grimm, and Bernhard Scholz. However, the New Germans somehow came into possession of a pre-publication copy of the manifesto, publishing a parody of it in the *Neue Zeitschrift* on 4 May. David Brodbeck reprints and translates both documents in "Brahms and the New German School," in *Brahms and His World*, ed. Walter Frisch and Kevin Karnes (Princeton, 1990; rev. ed. 2009), 111–12.

5. The text reproduced below is Brendel's address as printed in the *Neue Zeitschrift für Musik* 50/24 (10 June 1859): 265–73.

6. Indeed, Schumann figures more prominently in "Advancing an Understanding" than either Wagner or Liszt.

7. "Die bekanntlich jetzt den Namen der *neudeutschen* angenommen hat, aus keinem anderen Grunde, als um gehässige Erinnerungen, die an das abgeschmackte Wort '*Zukunftsmusik*' sich knüpfen, zu beseitigen." Franz Brendel, *Geschichte der* Musik, 3rd ed. (Leipzig, 1860), 612.

8. The one other post-1859 edition of Brendel's *Geschichte* that appeared during his lifetime (1867) reprints the same sentence about terminology, with no further use of the designation *neudeutsche Schule*. The 1861 address can be found in Franz Brendel, "Zur Eröffnung der zweiten Tonkünstler-Versammlung zu Weimar am 5. August 1861," *Neue Zeitschrift für Musik* 55 (1861): 61–64.

9. Specific published examples by the "progressives" include August Wilhelm Ambros, *Culturhistorische Bilder aus dem Musikleben der Gegenwart* (Leipzig, 1860); and Louis Köhler, *Die neue Richtung in der Musik* (Leipzig, 1864). For the twentieth-century perspective, see Hugo Riemann's *Geschichte der Musik seit Beethoven (1800–1900)* (Stuttgart and Berlin, 1901).

10. Brendel is referring to the political unrest resulting from the Austro-Sardinian War, or Second Italian War of Independence of 1859, which pitted Austria against France and Piedmont-Sardinia. At the time of the festival, the initial clash at Montebello had just taken place (May 20).

11. In the original published version of Brendel's address this italicized phrase and others we have italicized here were given in *Sperrschrift*, the German practice of spacing out letters for special emphasis. Brendel also used *Sperrschrift* for almost all instances of composers' names, a convention we have not followed in this translation.

12. The first Tonkünstler-Versammlung took place in Leipzig in mid-August 1847, and represented the first attempt to gather German musicians for the purpose of having a dialogue about the current state music.

13. The "two" masters alluded to here are, of course, Wagner and Liszt.

14. Russian author Aleksandr Dmitryevich Ulïbïshev (Ulybyshev, Oulibicheff, Ulibischeff; 1794–1858) published his life and works study of Mozart in French, as *Nouvelle biographie de Mozart, suivie d'un aperçu sur l'histoire générale de la musique et de l'analyse des principales oeuvres de Mozart* (Moscow, 1843); the German translation mentioned appeared as Alexander Ulibischeff, *Mozarts Leben, nebst einer Uebersicht der allgemeinen Geschichte der Musik und einer Analyse der Hauptwerke Mozarts* (Stuttgart, 1847). Brendel perhaps mentions this particular title as an instance of his intent to mediate between parties: on the one hand, Ulïbïshev's Mozart book subjects the composer's oeuvre to numerous Romantic literary-critical exegeses, though on the other hand Ulïbïshev went on to become an outspoken critic of "modern" tendencies in his subsequent Beethoven study, *Beethoven, ses critiques et ses glossateurs* (Leipzig, 1857).

15. The first Berlin production of *Lohengrin* took place at the Königliches Opernhaus (Royal Opera House) on January 23, 1859. The Viennese production a year earlier (opening August 19, 1858) had been an important milestone in the reception of the work, as one of the first performances in a major urban center and featuring a strong cast and orchestra.

16. Brendel had been repeatedly taken to task for his references to a "superseded" or "obsolete standpoint," being that of conservatives who used the Viennese Classical style as a point of reference in aesthetic debates. He was accused by the "opposition" of dismissing thereby the whole classical canon as no longer valid. This term (*überwundener Standpunkt*) arose in the late 1830s within the Hegelian sphere of influence, to which Brendel belonged. In the writings of German progressive thinkers of the 1840s (for example, David Friedrich Strauss), it became an expression of disdain for conservative positions in philosophy and the arts.

17. Brendel alludes, presumably, to the Cologne-based critic Ludwig Bischoff and the journal he edited (from 1853 to 1867), the *Niederrheinische Musik-Zeitung*. Bischoff and his journal played a major role in disseminating the term "Zukunftsmusik" as a skeptical and pejorative designation for the modern school of Liszt and Wagner. It was Bischoff, incidentally, who published the German translation of Ulïbïshev's Beethoven study (see note 13) in 1859, with its provocative criticism of the late period and, by implication, of the modern school that claimed to be the inheritors of that style and to have realized the implications for the "future."

18. One example Brendel might have had in mind here was the publication of Wagner's essay "Das Judentum in der Musik" ("Judaism in Music") in the *Neue Zeitschrift* in September 1850. Since the article was published under what was understood to be a pseudonym (K. Freigedank), Brendel had to assume even more responsibility for the piece, as editor.

19. The opening concert of the Tonkünstler-Versammlung, conducted by Franz Liszt, included Liszt's symphonic poem *Tasso* and the Prelude to Wagner's *Tristan und Isolde*, only the second time the Prelude had been heard in public (Hans von Bülow conducted the first performance in Prague on March 12, 1859; both the Prague and Leipzig performances used the concert ending Bülow had composed for it). To honor the *Neue Zeitschrift* founder Robert Schumann, his opera *Genoveva* had been performed the day before the Assembly (May 31). On June 2, Liszt conducted his Gran Festival Mass in St. Thomas Church, where Carl Riedel then directed a performance of Bach's B-Minor Mass on June 3. Subsequent concerts included Schubert's B-flat Piano Trio (with violinist Ferdinand David, cellist Friedrich Grützmacher, and Bülow), and an organ recital in the Merseburg cathedral. See Alan Walker, *Franz Liszt* (New York, 1989), 2:511–13. The New German critic

Richard Pohl published an extended account of the Assembly and concerts as a brochure, *Die Tonkünstler-Versammlung zu Leipzig, am 1. bis 4. Juni 1859* (Leipzig, 1859). See the printed program for the inaugural concert of June 1, 1859 reproduced as Figure 1.

20. Brendel assumes his audience's familiarity with the linking of the names Berlioz, Liszt, and Wagner as the principal representatives of "modern tendencies" in the 1850s. The fact that neither the names of Berlioz or Liszt are actually mentioned in the address (nor any work by them) suggests that Brendel felt some compunction about the term he coins here, hence also his attempt to defend it in this passage.

PART IV

WAGNER AND PARIS

Wagner Admires Meyerbeer (*Les Huguenots*)

RICHARD WAGNER

TRANSLATED, INTRODUCED, AND ANNOTATED

BY THOMAS S. GREY

The vituperation heaped upon the German-Jewish composer of French grand opera, Giacomo Meyerbeer, by Richard Wagner in such writings as "Judaism in Music" (1850) or *Opera and Drama* (1852) knew no bounds. Professional envy mixed with an element of persecution mania, exaggerated aesthetic convictions, and racial bigotry all contributed to this astounding flow of invective. In the notorious "Judaism in Music," Wagner does not even deign to speak the name of Meyerbeer, but merely refers to "a widely renowned Jewish musician of our time" who has made a business of catering to the boredom and confused musical tastes of the contemporary public. This unnamed composer is called a master of "deception," even self-deception, who foists on his bored audience a musical equivalent of Yiddish speech (*Jargon*), persuading them to accept it as a "smart and modern way of pronouncing all those trivialities" they had already become accustomed to hearing in their natural and undisguised banality.[1] In the critique of contemporary opera that forms the basis of Part 1 of *Opera and Drama*, Wagner famously castigates Meyerbeer's grand operas as the quintessence of the spectacular but superficial "effects" that constitute the core principle of the genre: "effect without cause."[2] To illustrate the depravity into which opera has fallen in recent times he has been obliged, so he says, to characterize the faults and excesses of Meyerbeer's works with absolute candor: "In Meyerbeer's music there is shown so appalling an emptiness, shallowness, and artistic nothingness, that—especially when compared with by far the larger number of his musical contemporaries —we are tempted to set down his specific musical capacity at zero."[3]

If this is indeed what Wagner thought of his elder operatic colleague in 1851, how to explain the encomium to Meyerbeer and *Les Huguenots* presented below, which he appears to have written sometime between 1837 and 1841? Here Meyerbeer's *Huguenots* is celebrated as the pinnacle of modern operatic achievement, the analogue in its own genre to Beethoven's

Ninth Symphony: "Just as the greatest genius would come to naught if he sought to perpetuate Beethoven's development, given that his last symphony cannot possibly be outdone, so too it seems impossible to progress beyond what Meyerbeer has taken here to the utmost point."[4] Granted, Wagner seems to be making room for some new phase in the history of opera, to be led by a worthy (German) successor to Meyerbeer.[5] Even so, the unstinting praise here for Meyerbeer as the most recent example of a great, specifically German tradition of synthesizing and "universalizing" the best traits of diverse national traditions is so diametrically opposed to the nearly libelous denunciation of the composer in *Opera and Drama* that— barring a diagnosis of critical schizophrenia or merely hypocritical mendacity—it is difficult to believe they were written by the same person.

The diagnosis of hypocrisy is easily surmised if we recall that, at the time this text must have been written, Wagner was planning a strategic assault on Paris and its Opéra, the most prestigious operatic institution of the day, and that with his second Parisian grand opera, *Les Huguenots* (1836), Meyerbeer had consolidated his claim to being the most prestigious composer connected with that institution. We also need to take into account that this essay was not actually published at the time it was written. Had it been calculated primarily as a piece of shameless, sycophantic flattery of the influential older composer, Wagner would certainly have realized by around 1841 that such tactics would never suffice to get his own work (the grand opera *Rienzi*) staged at the Opéra. The story of Meyerbeer's sincere if cautious advocacy of the young Wagner and Wagner's mounting suspicions of his benefactor is well known.[6] Wagner's letters to Meyerbeer between 1837 and 1841, starting when he introduced himself and his Parisian plans, display no lack of sycophancy—quite the opposite. (This abject deference to his successful colleague is at least one major factor in the vehemence of Wagner's subsequent rancor.)

At the same time there is ample evidence—not least of all *Rienzi* itself—that in his twenties Wagner looked to the most successful examples of French grand opera by Auber, Halévy, and Meyerbeer as models for his own work. From the time of his first published essay, "On German Opera" (*Zeitung für die elegante Welt*, 10 June 1834) up to the end of his early Paris sojourn (an extended appreciation of "Halévy and the French Opera" published in the *Revue et gazette musicale* in 1842) Wagner repeatedly articulated an ideal of cosmopolitan stylistic synthesis as an answer to the identity crisis of German Romantic opera.[7] In an article explicating the nature of *la musique allemande* to Parisian readers in 1840, Wagner concludes with sentiments very similar to those expressed in the Meyerbeer essay, presumably written about the same time. Germans have not yet developed "dramatic music on a grand scale," but their native musicality and capacity for cultural syn-

thesis now positions them to take the lead in opera. The German, he writes—
obviously reflecting wishfully on his own present circumstances—"possesses
the power to go to another country, develop its art to its highest peak, and
raise it to the plane of universal validity." Originally he went on to assert,
in a passage that was omitted from the publication of his own German
text in the first volume of his collected writings: "Handel and Gluck proved
this abundantly, and in our time another German, Meyerbeer, has provided
a fresh example." The Germans—first Meyerbeer, and now Wagner—were
uniquely poised to take French grand opera to the next level. Expressing
his high hopes for his own bid to become the new Meyerbeer, and at the same
time closing his essay on a note of *entente cordiale* toward his French hosts,
he writes: "At any rate, so far as dramatic music is concerned, one can assume
that at present the French and the German are identical. . . . That the two
nations are joining hands and reinforcing each other means that the foundations of one of the greatest artistic epochs are being laid. May this splendid
alliance never be dissolved, for one can conceive of no brotherhood of nations
likelier to lead to greater and more perfect results for art than between
Germans and Frenchmen, since the genius of each supplements what is
lacking in the other."[8] With the failure of his hope for launching an international career in Paris, Wagner's attitude toward his "German" colleague
Meyerbeer—no less than toward the French themselves—became markedly
and rapidly less charitable.

By February 1843, a month after his decidedly German opera *Der
fliegende Holländer* had been produced in Dresden, Wagner was already
chiding Robert Schumann for claiming to hear Meyerbeer's influence in
his work. "I do not know what in the whole wide world is meant by the
word 'Meyerbeerian,' except perhaps a sophisticated striving after superficial popularity." Shortly before, in the *Huguenots* essay, the aspiring
composer of a new breed of German grand opera had been able to sing
the praises of Meyerbeer's "German" virtues, his "naïveté and modesty
of feeling," his "chastely virginal features of a deep soul" and his "spotless"
aesthetic conscience. In these admirable traits he could discern the "deep
spring" whence issued the imposing waves of a vast, Meyerbeerian operatic ocean upon which he thought to chart his future. Back in Germany
and increasingly convinced of Meyerbeer's "treachery" toward his own
career aspirations, Wagner's earlier metaphor turned rancid: "I confess
that it would have required a wonderful freak of nature for me to have
drawn my inspiration from *that* particular source, the merest smell of which,
wafting in from afar, is sufficient to turn my stomach."[9] A more far-reaching
irony is to be found in another, later inversion of a passage from the essay.
"Meyerbeer wrote world history," enthuses the young Wagner over the
exciting, engaging qualities of grand opera as historical drama; "he

destroyed the shackles of national prejudice and the constraining boundaries of linguistic idioms; he wrote deeds of music." When, decades later, Wagner famously entertained the grandiose notion of classifying his great music dramas as "deeds of music made visible," he surely had long forgotten this early, discarded tribute to the man subsequently demonized as the veritable Antichrist of modern music.[10]

The early textual history of this short essay remains obscure. Wagner's autograph first surfaced in a catalog of the Berlin antiquarian dealer Leo Liepmannssohn in December 1886. The music scholar Max Kalbeck published extracts in the *Neue Wiener Tagblatt* (1902) and in the journal *Die Musik* (1911), but a complete text only appeared in one of the supplementary volumes of the expanded edition of Wagner's writings.[11] The editor of that edition, Richard Sternfeld, surmised that the piece was written as early as 1837, noting resemblances to the letter Wagner wrote introducing himself (from Königsberg) to Meyerbeer on 4 February 1837.[12] Considering there is no evidence Wagner had any chance to see *Les Huguenots* before he arrived in Paris in September 1839 (or for that matter, a score of the opera), it seems most likely that the essay was written sometime between 1840 and 1841, while he continued to nourish hopes of a Parisian success. Heinz Becker, in his edition of Meyerbeer's letters and diaries, has suggested that the essay may have been written as late as the winter of 1841–42, in appreciation of Meyerbeer's assistance to him in Paris, "but that Meyerbeer refused to allow it to be published on the grounds that its obsequious tone showed neither party in a favorable light."[13]

RICHARD WAGNER
On Meyerbeer's *Les Huguenots*
(1840?)

The phenomenon of Meyerbeer's music, especially in his latest work, *Les Huguenots*, has acquired such a distinct, well-rounded consistency that the time is come to locate the position of this oeuvre in the larger history of music. Thus the present attempt to place something still fresh and living in a historical perspective. If we observe the phenomenon of Meyerbeer we will be instinctively reminded—by general tendencies as well as by some specific external features—of Handel and Gluck; even some significant aspects of Mozart's training and musical direction seem to be replicated in this case. Above all one should never lose sight of the fact that those two earlier figures were Germans, like the composer in question here. For in that wretched, de-nationalized condition of Germany can also be found the basis of the external destinies, relationships, and artistic traits of these artistic phenomena, whose inner significance is so intimately connected.

We must in particular attribute to Germany's decided *non*-existence as a nation the fact that geniuses raised on German mothers' milk exhibit so few distinctive traits of their place of birth. So often we see them develop far away from their homeland; their music seeks our hearts while clothed in words of other, foreign tongues, and it is only recognition abroad that succeeds in drawing the attention of their own countrymen to them. We see how quickly they assimilate the various national characteristics native among their neighbors; and having done so, the Germans are able to find a firm standpoint from which their own inborn creative genius can freely take wing and soar above any limiting national boundaries. In this way it almost seems the ordained lot of German genius to search among its neighbors for that which it cannot find at home, and in the process to free what it has borrowed from its original, narrow limitations, so as to make of it something general and accessible to the whole world. Many have been inspired by such an impulse and have followed similar lines of study, only to remain stuck in place just where they are poised to begin in earnest; that is, they have wormed their way into a foreign nationality that cannot, in and of itself, provide the basis for something genuine on their part, so long as they have sacrificed the truest legacy of their mother country: the chaste modesty of feeling that constitutes their most valuable dowry and one they should never squander, for this alone will allow them to traverse all manner of cultural itineraries and still emerge pure and genuine. This naïve candor of which the German is capable (and it is the general quality that most compensates for the lack of specific nationality) is what places him above the circumscribed limitations that represent the disadvantage of national identity. The quiet seriousness and scholarly bent of his upbringing eventually puts him in a position to handle the technical aspects of his art like a true master. Yet he soon discovers, to his dismay, that he lacks a foundation, some broadly fraternalistic feature whose cultivation might establish a rapport with his own countrymen, that is, with the millions who speak the German language. Say that as a Prussian, for example, he has managed to strike some native provincial note; he knows all too well, alas, that this will only make him all the more alien to the Austrians. Soon enough he realizes that the cultivation of those natural tools necessary to his art is not likely to prosper at home: there he lacks that ideal of singing which he must either borrow from the Italians or else do without. The majority are destroyed by this sorry situation, or at least it prevents them from reaching the heights of which the German genius ought to be capable. It is a lucky one who does succeed in cultivating that which essentially eludes his native land—and such a lucky one is that great hero, Meyerbeer.

The victories that have made the name of Meyerbeer one of the most brilliant in the musical firmament are still new and fresh, but nonetheless they have already conquered most of the civilized world. Even where they found no civilized terrain, they have been able to level the ground in order to erect the temples where these happy victories of the art might be fitly celebrated.

Thanks to his excellent musical training, as well as a general education in the arts and sciences, Meyerbeer found himself early on in a position to master all the technical demands of his art; so, too, was he able to see, earlier and more clearly than most others, what was not available to him at home and what he must therefore seek to master elsewhere if he were to enjoy a perfect command of that art. Thus still in his earliest youth he saw Italy, and *heard* it; his well-favored mind understood exactly the beauty of those forms which, even if they have taken on a rather too coarsely sensual character among the more recent Italians, are nonetheless nowhere to be so well appreciated even by a truly artistic sensibility as in that happy land.

We may plausibly assume that Meyerbeer, so early warmed by the ardor of these forms, soon found himself subject to a bitter inward conflict. The majority of German artists feel a marvelous sense of artistic patriotism, but one whose external manifestations are generally founded on a serious misapprehension. Indeed, this sentiment reveals a most peculiar contradiction. The same Germans who are so ready to absorb every foreign influence, who are so willing to remain quietly in the background when foreign guests are received, or even to be altogether forgotten—we can hear these same Germans inveighing with great rigor against the tendencies of foreign art, even against the decided advantages of these, and rehearsing their arguments in the strangest phraseologies to the point where they feel themselves quite convinced of them. The point of pride to which these arguments refer is a perfectly honorable one, if misunderstood: namely the fact that so many great heroes of music have been German—and here they cite their Handel, Gluck, or Mozart. Oddly enough, however, they choose not to notice how Handel exhaled in England the cantabile he had inhaled in Italy; how Gluck fought for the cause of French dramatic music in Paris, and how even Mozart must be regarded as the most refined product of the Italian school.

Even Meyerbeer has felt the burden of the Germans' peculiar traits; his genius, too, was fettered by the struggles they occasion, and we can imagine that he was likewise close to foundering just where he saw the hopes of many others dashed. Meyerbeer was so much a German, however, as to follow in the footsteps of his old German forebears; they had journeyed across the Alps with all their northern vigor and conquered for themselves the beauties of Italy. And was not this course justified? Does not the beautiful belong to him who has the strength to win it?

So Meyerbeer traveled to Italy, and soon he had even the hedonistic sons of the South reveling in his music—this was his first victory. Must it not fill one with pride to succeed not only in making foreign beauty one's own, but even to compel those from whom it has been wrested to admire how this beauty has been ennobled in the process? Yet the German genius does not even rest satisfied with this; this victory is only one piece of his education. The hazy, indistinct mists of spirituality have formed themselves into a figure of warm, beautiful flesh, but one with pure, modest German blood flowing in its veins; the figure of the man is now complete and flawless; now he is ready to work, to bring about deeds worthy of posterity.

That Meyerbeer should not stop here, stretching himself out comfortably to lie in the shade of his own reputation—this then remained to make him perfect.

Just at this time the French school had reached is finest heights.[14] The masters of this era achieved things—independently, but also in full sympathy with their nation—as great as we might find in the history of art in any country. Their works embodied both the virtues and the character of the nation. The endearing chivalry of old France still inspired a work like Boieldieu's splendid *Jean de Paris*; the native vivacity, spirit, wit, and grace of the Frenchwoman all flourish in that typically, exclusively French genre of the *opéra comique*.[15] French dramatic music reached its absolute apex in Auber's incomparable *Muette de Portici*: any country would be lucky to boast even one national artwork of this caliber.[16] This tumultuous power of action, this ocean of feeling, of passions painted in the most vibrant colors, suffused with its own characteristic tone and melodic style, this admixture of delicacy and force, grace and heroism—is this not all a perfect embodiment of modern French history? Could such an astounding artwork have been created by anyone but a French artist? There is no other way to put it but to say that the new French school reached its very highest point here, achieving simultaneously hegemony over all the civilized world. How amazing, then, that Meyerbeer dared to compete on this terrain! Who but he would have had the courage and the power to do so? For what a terrain this is: the most attractive, but the most fearful! Attractive, because it was the most glamorous and brilliant; fearful, because of the danger of burning oneself on the very brilliance of it. Yet Meyerbeer needed just such a terrain for his artistic manhood to develop into a true universality.

Here Meyerbeer found what is needed to accomplish great things: a nation capable of the enthusiasm to achieve the greatest—but, we must also realize, a nation such that aimed to encompass the whole world, a nation whose deeds, under Napoleon, served as the measure of world history. If a simple Corsican might come along to provide the momentum to such deeds, why not a German as well? Armed with German solidity and Italian beauty, Meyerbeer plunged into French enthusiasm. There exist terribly prosaic expressions for all things; should we care to employ one of the plainest among these, one much favored by a certain party, we might say: he learned German, he worked through Italian, and now he started on French.[17] Who could deny that Meyerbeer now went about appropriating the forms of French opera? The French manner had reached its full flower; it had reached an attractive maturity and, more than any other style, it was capable of universal deployment. But have we not also witnessed how, in the hands of its creator[s], the style has gradually succumbed to the drawbacks of any manner, which is to say, it has become mannered? These French masters[18] became complacent in their conquests; their compositional style became flat by relying on external conventions, manners, exposing over time the disadvantages of any purely national style. Soon it seemed confined to a repertoire of hackneyed phrases and clichés, losing sight of its noble intentions.

So it was left to Meyerbeer to further develop the French manner, indeed, to elevate it to a generally valid classical idiom. He led this modern idiom beyond certain conventional and popular rhythmic and decorative gestures toward a style of grandiose simplicity, but one with the great advantage of having a strong basis in the heart and the ear of the people—not merely the refined invention of some innovation-happy speculator, some vague castle in the air without any real, solid foundations.

Meyerbeer also staked out his new terrain in an exceptionally strategic way, through his choice of subjects: in one case a folktale, disseminated by the voice of the people; in the other case, a moving episode of that people's history.[19] If we accept that some lively national interest is essential for any work in a grand style, Meyerbeer was in the position of drawing such an impulse from the national identity of a people who, at this period, enjoyed the widest international sympathy. But what Meyerbeer constructed on this foundation was not propagandistic praise to flatter national vanity; rather, he succeeded in elevating such feelings to a universal level.[20]

Meyerbeer wrote world history, a history of hearts and feelings; he destroyed the shackles of national prejudice and the constraining boundaries of linguistic idioms; he wrote deeds of music—music such as Handel, Gluck, and Mozart wrote before him. They were Germans, and Meyerbeer is a German. We may ask how it was possible for this German not to be limited by the emotional perspectives of one or another of the national manners he adopted, not to lose his way between these, after perhaps a brief moment of brilliance, and how he avoided becoming a mere slave to foreign influences?

He preserved his German legacy: naïveté and modesty of feeling. These chastely virginal features of a deep soul are the poetry and the genius of Meyerbeer. This genius has preserved a spotless conscience, a lovable consciousness; even within products of vast scope and highly refined invention the chaste rays of this consciousness still shine forth demurely, recognizable as the deep spring from which arise all these imposing waves of a majestic ocean.

Is not the strong impulse for religious expression in Meyerbeer's works a striking manifestation of the master's deep, inward intentions? Is not this feature precisely one that reminds us movingly of his German origins? In Germany one finds less ostentation in the divine service than in other Christian countries, and there is more division among different creeds; perhaps in an outward sense there is as little, or less, religion than elsewhere, for the German is a rationalist and a philosopher. But whether a German holds with the saints, with Luther, with Calvin, or with Kant, there lives in every German heart a wonderfully moving, simple, childlike strain of religiosity, such that the mere sound of the organ can coax tears from his eyes, even if he has not set foot in a church since the age of fourteen.

There is no longer any need to compose grand, learned, liturgically correct masses and oratorios; we have learned from this son of Germany that religion can just as well be preached from the stage—when amid all this splendor and passion such a noble, simple, virginal sense can be preserved, the source from which Meyerbeer draws for all his thrilling creations.

Let us assume it is the task of all universal genius, not so much to provide the first impulse to a whole new artistic period, but rather to develop such impulses into the most perfect possible ideal of the period. As such, the first impulses arise of their own accord over time, guided by the particular tendency of a people and its character, and even by the individual vagaries brought about by the changing historical times. In Handel we have seen an artistic culmination of the clear, powerful tendencies of Protestantism; in Gluck we have seen the antique classical tendency of French tragedy reach its highest, most dignified phase, here in the realm of dramatic music. Mozart raised the Italian school, strictly speaking, to an ideal point. And so each of these musical heroes marked the outermost boundary of an artistic period. Dramatic music could not reach any further heights in the same direction after Gluck and Mozart—on the contrary, we see it flatten into mannerism and then disappear altogether in a lack of talent and application. In Germany, Beethoven remained almost entirely aloof from dramatic music, throwing nearly the whole weight of his immense genius into the field of instrumental music, such that he quickly brought this important branch of music to dizzying, indisputable heights, while from the stage Weber's lyrical Romanticism won the hearts of all Germans and the ears of all the world; and during this there developed in other quarters a whole new epoch of dramatic music that would become, in fact, one of the most brilliant ones. —

We would have to identify the beginning of this period with Rossini; with genial frivolity (which alone could enable this) he tore down whatever remained of the old school, whose forms had indeed shriveled to a mere skin and bones. His joyful song fluttered forth into the world, and his best features—forms of lightness, freshness, and sensuous appeal—were systematically adopted everywhere, above all by the French.

The French lent character to the Rossinian style, which also gained a more dignified appearance thanks to the steadiness of their national bearing.

Any further progress on this terrain, where the national tendency of an art has already reached such a complete, insuperable phase of development, can only be effected by means of a universalizing turn (as we suggested above); this is also the direction by which any artistic period will achieve its highest potential.

All the external features of Meyerbeer's music confirm this to be so. A style that first struggled to absorb the influence of diverse schools has raised itself to a noble, ideal level of independence, free from any of the weaknesses of the individual manners it drew upon, while at the same time uniting all their best aspects. A gigantic, almost oppressive extension of forms has achieved a pure, pleasing sense of proportion. This is the area in which Meyerbeer's mastery is perhaps most strikingly manifest: this clarity, even cold-blooded calculation in matters of structural disposition characterizes him above all other things, raising him from the outset to an objective standpoint—indeed the only correct point from which his works, in all their massive abundance, can be clearly and perceptibly organized. To best support this claim I would cite here above all the greatest thing that has been achieved along these lines: the famous conspiracy scene in Act 4 of *Les Huguenots*.[21] Who can fail to be amazed at the disposition and development of this tremendous piece, at how the composer has been able to maintain a continuous intensification throughout the astonishing length of this number, never once letting up, but reaching, only after a tumult of raging passions, the highest fever pitch—the very ideal of religious fanaticism.

And then, having plumbed the depths of such repellent fanaticism, he fulfills the highest task of art: he idealizes this tumult of passions and—if such an expression might be permitted in this context—he dignifies it with the stamp of beauty! For who can hear the last, intensified repetition of the main theme at the close of this scene without feeling his soul fill not simply with horror, but exaltation?

Here we see the simplicity of means that Meyerbeer applies to achieve his ends. How clear and simple, how noble and sustained is this main theme that begins and ends the number; how carefully and thoughtfully the master commences the flow, which does not lose itself in confused rapids but issues, instead, in a grand, imposing sea! — It is difficult to see how anyone could achieve anything greater in this line; we sense that truly a culmination has been reached; just as the greatest genius would come to naught if he sought to perpetuate Beethoven's development, given that his last symphony cannot possibly be outdone, so, too, it seems impossible to progress beyond what Meyerbeer has taken here to the utmost point.

Thus we must stand by our view that the most recent great epoch in dramatic music has been brought to a close by Meyerbeer, that with him, as with Handel, Gluck, Mozart, and Beethoven before him, a perfected ideal has been achieved that marks the end of an artistic period. Now we must expect that the restless creative spirit of time will usher in a new artistic era, one in which there will be as much to accomplish as those earlier heroes have accomplished in their own epochs. And yet he is still alive among us, and at the height of his powers,— so let us not get ahead of ourselves, but rather wait and see what new things his genius will yet produce!

NOTES

1. Richard Wagner, "Das Judentum in der Musik," *Gesammelte Schriften und Dichtungen* (Leipzig, 1887–1911) (henceforth *GSD*), 5:82; see also "Judaism in Music," in *Richard Wagner: Stories and Essays*, trans. and ed. Charles Osborne (New York, 1972), 37.

2. Wagner, *Opera und Drama*, *GSD*, 3:301; see also *Richard Wagner's Prose Works*, trans. William Ashton Ellis (London, 1893–99; repr. Lincoln, Neb. and London, 1993–95), 2:95.

3. *Opera and Drama* in *Richard Wagner's Prose Works*, 2:100; see also *GSD*, 3:306.

4. Richard Wagner, *Sämtliche Schriften und Dichtungen* (Leipzig, 1911–16) (henceforth *SSD*), 12:30.

5. See the last paragraph of this essay: "Thus we must stand by our view that the most recent great epoch in dramatic music has been brought to a close by Meyerbeer. . . . Now we must expect . . . a new artistic era. . . ."

.6. See, for example, Helmuth Weinland, "Wagner und Meyerbeer," in *Richard Wagner zwischen Beethoven und Schönberg*, Musik-Konzepte 59 (Munich, 1988), 31–72, which also discusses possible influences of *Les Huguenots* on the later acts of *Rienzi* (those composed after Wagner arrived in Paris). Stewart Spencer notes that "Meyerbeer's diaries for the months between October 1839 and December 1840 contain no fewer than thirty-four references to Wagner, whom he introduced to members of the French musical establishment and whose cause he championed in innumerable letters to colleagues." Spencer, *Wagner Remembered* (London and New York, 2000), 31.

7. See Thomas Grey, "Wagner and the Legacy of French Grand Opera," in *The Cambridge Companion to Grand Opera*, ed. David Charlton (Cambridge, 2003), 321–43, particularly 322–38.

8. "German Music," in *Wagner Writes From Paris . . .*, ed. and trans. Robert Jacobs and Geoffrey Skelton (London, 1973), 50. The published German version can be found in *GSD*, 1:166. The sentence beginning "Handel and Gluck" is omitted, as is the rest of that paragraph. The subsequent homage to a French-German musical alliance, however, was retained.

9. Richard Wagner to Robert Schumann, 25 February 1843. In *Selected Letters of Richard Wagner*, trans. and ed. Stewart Spencer and Barry Millington (New York, 1988), 105.

10. The phrase comes from the 1872 essay "Über die Benennung 'Musikdrama'" (On the name "Music drama"), *GSD*, 9:302–8 (here, 306). See also the essay by Lydia Goehr in this volume.

11. *SSD*, 12:22–30.

12. The letter was a follow-up, in part, to an earlier missive to Meyerbeer's collaborator, the librettist and playwright Eugène Scribe, in which Wagner proposed that Scribe versify in French a scenario Wagner had drafted on the subject of Heinrich Koenig's historical novel *Die hohe Braut* (The high-born bride).

13. Spencer, *Wagner Remembered*, 30, quoting Giacomo Meyerbeer, *Briefwechsel und Tagebücher*, ed. Heinz and Gudrun Becker, with Sabine Henze-Döhring (Berlin, 1960–99), 3:396.

14. Wagner is speaking of the period around 1825, when Meyerbeer arrived in Paris from his period of Italian operatic apprenticeship to oversee a production of his *Il crociato in Egitto* at the Théâtre-Italien, and 1831, when his first French opera, *Robert le diable*, premiered. During this period the productions of the Opéra, the Opéra-Comique, and the Théâtre-Italien were setting standards for genre, style, and performance throughout Europe.

15. *Jean de Paris*, an *opéra comique* in two acts by Adrien Boieldieu (1775–1834), premiered in Paris, April 4, 1812. Along with *La dame blanche* (1825) it was a popular piece in the repertoire of smaller German theaters up through the time of Wagner's youth.

16. *La muette de Portici* was the first five-act grand opera by Daniel-François-Esprit Auber (1782–1871), first performed at the Paris Opéra on February 29, 1828. Famous for its semi-legendary role in propagating the Belgian Revolution of 1830, it was also a formative work in the operatic education of the young Wagner. He recalled the tremendous impact the work had made on him as a youth when writing an obituary essay on the composer (who died at age eighty-nine amid the chaos of the last days of the Paris Commune, on May 12, 1871): "Erinnerungen an Auber," *GSD*, 9:42–60 (on *La muette* in particular, 45–48); and see *Richard Wagner's Prose Works*, 5:37–55, esp. 38–43.

17. In the original: "er hatte Deutsch gelernt, hat das Italienische durchgemacht, und fing nun Französisch an." The allusions to "a certain party" and to a favorite expression of the same are both obscure.

18. Wagner speaks first of "the creator" of French opera, then of its "masters" (in the plural). Presumably he means both Boieldieu and Auber; Rossini would have a claim to the title as well, with *Guillaume Tell* (1829), but since he wrote no more operas, French or otherwise after that, he cannot be included in this critique. In some of his other writings from the early Paris time (and later) Wagner issued a similar critique of Fromental Halévy regarding his works after *La juive* (1835). The 1871 essay on Auber (see note 16) laments the rapid decline of his inspiration after the early years, around 1830—and Wagner was hardly alone in that opinion.

19. The reference is to *Robert le diable* (1831) and *Les Huguenots* (1836), the only two grand operas Meyerbeer had composed at the time Wagner was writing. Wagner's phrase describing the *Robert* material—"eine Volkssage, die in dem Munde des Volkes lebte"— makes for an ironic pre-echo of the later musical-dramatic ideology *Opera and Drama*, in which of course Meyerbeer has become a veritable Antichrist. The libretto by Eugène Scribe and Germain Delavigne, as Steven Huebner points out, actually "had very little to do with a widely disseminated medieval mystery play in which Robert leads a life of debauchery and crime but then, Tannhäuser-like, journeys to Rome to seek papal absolution and subsequently heads an important assault of the forces of Christendom against the Infidel." Huebner, "Robert le diable," *New Grove Dictionary of Opera* (London and New York, 1992), 3:1357.

20. It is unclear if Wagner means to say that Meyerbeer specifically elevated "national vanity" or its praise to a higher level; grammatically, it is the praise his text talks about.

21. That is, the "Conjuration et bénédiction des poignards" (Conspiracy and benediction of the daggers), the central number among the three that make up Act 4.

Debacle at the Paris Opéra

Tannhäuser and the French Critics, 1861

OSCAR COMETTANT, PAUL SCUDO

TRANSLATED BY THOMAS S. GREY

INTRODUCED BY ANNEGRET FAUSER

ANNOTATED BY ANNEGRET FAUSER AND

THOMAS S. GREY

By the time the curtain rose on the Paris production of Richard Wagner's *Tannhäuser* on March 13, 1861, French artists and critics had been discussing the German composer and his aesthetic ideas for almost a year. As the overture started in the pit of the splendid opera house in the rue Le Peletier, audiences and critics alike knew that they were attending a historic event in a theater that had seen the premieres of such stalwarts of French opera as Fromental Halévy's *La juive* and Giacomo Meyerbeer's *Les Huguenots*. Here was a mid-career German composer—who had had some success in German theaters with his operas *Tannhäuser* and *Lohengrin*—with a claim to be changing the face of opera forever with his new concepts of the music drama. Now the social and intellectual elite of the cultural capital of the Western world had gathered to see, hear, and judge for themselves.[1] The outcome turned into one of the biggest art scandals in modern times, and Wagner withdrew his work after only three increasingly riotous performances, leaving Paris never to return.

It has become one of the enduring myths of music history that the frivolous Parisian establishment wronged the great German visionary through their supercilious bigotry, mundane superficiality, and glib self-interest, dealing to true art a deadly blow that was to haunt France for the rest of the nineteenth century and beyond. Scholars and Wagnerian hagiographers alike quote contemporary writings of Charles Baudelaire and Jules Champfleury as proof of the artistic incompetence of Parisian audiences and critics on the grounds that at least some enlightened contemporaries were able to discern Wagner's genius even in this brouhaha of negative spin.[2] Yet this is a modernist story that reinterprets the events from the perspective of Wagner himself (who contributed significantly to its narrative) and celebrates artistic progress as the *ne plus ultra* of aesthetic value.

A return to the documents of the time shows that things were much more complex. Taking Wagner's critics seriously instead of disregarding them as incompetent, spiteful, or reactionary reveals that theirs was not simply an unreflected hostility toward Wagner and his new musical language; rather, their reviews mirrored deep concerns about the future of opera, the primary genre of French cultural life in terms of its institutional context and its musical and poetic language.[3] The two representative reviews included in this volume address some of the key issues of the Parisian *Tannhäuser* reception in terms not only of the performance itself but also of Wagner's ideas and their relevance for contemporary musical theater.

The first is by Oscar Comettant (1819–98), a successful music critic and writer who was trained as a composer at the Conservatoire. His articles were always informed and well written, and he rarely shied away from polemics.[4] A key member of the musical establishment in Paris, he wrote for a number of newspapers and journals, including *L'art musical*, the house magazine of the French music publisher Léon Escudier.[5] As Katharine Ellis has pointed out, *L'art musical* was "virulently and polemically anti-Wagnerian," and Comettant's musical aesthetics were strongly influenced by the formalist ideas of Victor Cousin and François-Joseph Fétis.[6]

Cousin also had some influence over the author of the second review presented here, Paul Scudo (1806–64).[7] At the time of the *Tannhäuser* scandal, Scudo was one of the city's most influential music critics. His monthly column in the prestigious and widely read *Revue des deux mondes* was a fixture in French aesthetic discussion. Less concerned with the nuts and bolts of either the music or the production, Scudo's reviews often engaged with aesthetic issues and musical politics. He was perhaps the most conservative among the Parisian critics, with his aesthetic firmly grounded in idealist notions of the transcendental and beautiful: indeed, in his review of Wagner's 1860 concerts, he quotes Cousin explicitly in his critique of Wagner's so-called artistic materialism.[8] These concepts are worked out in even greater depth in his *Tannhäuser* review, where he addresses the genre's aesthetic foundation and the history of opera on the one hand, and on the other, broader questions of musical beauty and compositional inspiration.

For Comettant, Scudo, and their contemporaries, the battle over *Tannhäuser* was a vital moment in the history of French music. What was at stake was no less than the future of opera, and this awareness shaped the rhetoric in significant ways. In contrast to the usual opera reviews that were addressed first and foremost to the Parisian opera-going public and focused on the plot, the music, and the performance (in descending order of importance), the criticism about Wagner's *Tannhäuser* had a different purpose and audience. The critics knew that their words would be scrutinized not only by contemporary Wagnerians in the Western world, but that they were also writing for posterity. Indeed, because the reviews of *Tannhäuser* imply a readership different from the usual *tout Paris*, the critical discourse in spring 1861 changed into something quite remarkable and exceptional in its scope.

Taken as a whole, the reviews of the 1861 *Tannhäuser* offer a number of fascinating insights.[9] Among the most striking is the near total absence of positive reviews of either *Tannhäuser* itself or Wagner's ideas more generally. Normally, journalists and music critics would be more divided in their judgment, especially concerning so high profile an event.[10] But in the case of *Tannhäuser*, Parisian critics were nearly united in their rejection. Although some were less negative—as, for example, Franck-Marie and Arthur Pougin, both of whom sought some measure of balance—the majority condemned wholesale the man, the theory, and the opera.[11] Underlying all this was a severe nationalist anxiety that France had lost her artistic vitality and now was going to be hostage to Germanic fortunes.

Comettant and Scudo both contrasted Wagner's more unwieldy epic concepts with those which—in Aristotelian terms—made for good theater and characterized the French tragedy as represented by Corneille and Racine: a unified dramatic action that progressed to a proper emotional catharsis. Wagner was reproached for his "lifeless" figures, a plot without development, and a lack of the kind of dramatic variety that would engage the audience in emotional terms. As Comettant put it: "What one wants to find in the theater is a gripping drama, one with a lucid exposition, a well-managed plot, a forceful denouement, and one that all the while allows the musician to take wing freely—not to indulge in idiosyncratic reveries, however, that can affect no one but himself, but to express genuine, well characterized emotions." As a consequence of this fundamental flaw, Wagner's poetry and music were viewed as monotonous and formless. Without form—so Scudo reminds his readers—there was no beauty, which was, after all, "the first aim of art." By linking such criticism with Wagner's "system"—as French reviewers termed his theories—they called into question the aesthetic value not only of *Tannhäuser* but also of any future work following these principles, whether by Wagner or anyone else.

After addressing these overall defects of structure and concept, the role and character of Wagner's music then took center stage. Reviewers linked

specific criticism (for example, of the Rome narration and the song contest in the Wartburg) with broader issues concerning music's role in opera:
if the action and poem were subordinate to musical form, then the result
would be an "endless" symphonic stream of sound, at best obeying rules
of purely instrumental music that were antithetical to the demands of
real drama. Here the French critics took Wagner's own arguments about
music and drama and turned them on their head, supported by choice
quotations from the composer's *Letter About Music*. (This *Lettre sur la musique*,
published in 1860 as a preface to French prose translations of the librettos to *Der fliegende Holländer, Tannhäuser, Lohengrin*, and *Tristan und Isolde*,
aimed to summarize the theories of a new musical-dramatic *Gesamtkunstwerk*
developed in Wagner's various treatises from a decade earlier.) For Scudo,
in particular, Wagner had committed the crime of arrogance by openly dis-
daining the grand tradition of Western art music embodied in the names
of, for example, Mozart, Beethoven, and Rossini. These composers "were
able to be original while respecting the eternal laws of their art," and
they were "all innovators who did not need to break away from the great
chain of tradition." Wagner's refusal to follow established convention was
a quixotic battle based on a fundamental misconception about the nature
of opera. According to Franck-Marie, "The form that Wagner gives to his
airs only serves to increase the tedium that results from the absence of
any dramatic element in his subject. Enemy of all convention, the master
does not want that singers set themselves apart to perform a cavatina, an
aria, a duet. The action stops during that time, he thinks, and it is not at
all natural that a person should step aside in that manner from those
who surround her in order to repeat a long *a parte*." But, he continues,
"opera is founded solely on conventions of all kinds; why not admit, among
so many others, one more when it can offer so much variety and interest
to singing?"[12]

If the critics could demonstrate convincingly, by using Wagner's *Tannhäuser*
as an object lesson, that true art reflected timeless concepts enshrined in
the great tradition of France's past, on the one hand, and of operatic
masterworks on the other, then they could establish universal and enduring principles of artistic production and consumption that would resist the
invasion of an upstart German composer. Beyond the chauvinism lay some
fundamental aesthetic issues. And even if our French critics were in the
end fighting a losing battle, their position deserves the respect and understanding we now conventionally grant to cultural insiders: the time has
come to hear voices that, for over a century, have been drowned out by the
Wagnerian master narrative of musical progress.

Tannhäuser at the Paris Opéra, March 1861

After six months of rehearsals, including many with full orchestra, the opera *Tannhäuser* has finally made its appearance on our leading lyric stage.[13] Never in the memory of opera enthusiasts has the curiosity of the public been excited to such a pitch; apart from the recognition by the Italian parliament of the Kingdom of Italy and of Victor Emanuel as its king, I can identify no other recent event of such general importance in Europe as the premiere of this work by M. Richard Wagner at the Académie imperiale de musique.[14]

For three months now there has been no more burning question than this weighty trial that is to decide the fate of the "music of the future," and thereby, the future of music itself.

A great number of foreign music lovers have descended on Paris in the last week to judge for themselves what effect this *Tannhäuser* will have on the constitution of its French audience. We are told that special chartered trains were to be organized, at the most advantageous prices, to bring to Paris the crowds of Prussian, Austrian, and Belgian devotees who have been rendered sleepless with excitement over *Tannhäuser*. To help identify these special trains, a thoughtfully attentive railway employee had proposed to come up with names for the various locomotives to be pressed into service, based on characteristics of M. Wagner's music. Thus, there was to be a locomotive named *Discord*, followed by another called *Tremolo*, then the *Enharmonic*, the *Chromatic*, the *Endless Melody*, and so on. Only considerations touching on the most serious interests of all the European governments finally prevented the realization of this genial project. That's too bad, and most of those jolly *Tannhäuser* tourists will now be reduced to reading secondhand accounts of the premiere, which (like the second performance) unfolded among whistling, laughing, and loud pleasantries exchanged among the spectators in all corners of the house, vying in spirit and commotion with a formidable claque, all in front of a distracted orchestra and an uneasy cast.

Of course, if M. Wagner had not publicized his scorn for the works of the great masters of the past and of the present in numerous writings printed in both Germany and in France; if he had not maintained, with incredible vanity, his own system of lyric composition as the *ne plus ultra* of beauty; had he not put forward his own operas as the only ones worthy to be listened to by serious minds—then the Parisian public, normally well intentioned and courteous, might have been willing to greet the deformed, somber, and false product of this unfortunate composer with a polite silence. But against such unchecked and unjustified pretensions some kind of example needed to be set; so, by protesting against the invasion of the preening Germanic muse among us perhaps the public also hoped to give satisfaction to our native composers—so often maligned in France, where one shows toward certain foreigners a ridiculous and quite unmerited degree of hospitality.

We shall not attempt to analyze the individual musical numbers here.— Are there in fact *any* musical numbers within this huge sonorous sandwich, so overly familiar today under the name *Tannhäuser?* To find them would be an impossible task. Suffice it to say that, apart from a few things like the overture, whose second part seems to portray a group suffering from convulsions (not a very agreeable thing to listen to), but whose first part is truly a noble inspiration; the very appealing march, sumptuously orchestrated but which suffers from being an imitation of the style of Weber and Rossini (one finds here those masterful triplet ornamentations so ridiculed by Wagner himself and his acolytes); a poetic *romance* for the baritone; a few winning phrases, a few nice orchestral effects, and a few melodic fragments dispersed throughout the score with desperate if not exactly systematic parsimony—apart from these things, this whole score by the apostle of the new school is composed of nothing but confusion, antithetical sonorities, pretentious and baroque combinations, dissonance, metaphysics, obscurity, and chaos.

Naturally, no one would compose in this way who was truly endowed with musical faculties. Now, M. Wagner has proven to us on the basis of some sufficiently rhythmic and melodic items that, with some independence of mind, he, like anyone else, is capable of writing good music should he choose to do so. Yet it seems that M. Wagner is in such a horror of appearing banal, or perhaps despairing of ever achieving celebrity by following the same path traversed triumphantly by the great masters of the past, that he has come up with a system of his own by which he has composed his operas. I am aware that M. Wagner himself insists to the contrary: he only determined the laws of this system *after* having written his scores. For my part, I believe he deceives himself. However that may be, after the striking failure of *Tannhäuser,* the only thing left to interest us about the oeuvre of M. Wagner is precisely his system of the lyric drama [*drame lyrique*], of which *Tannhäuser*, by the way, gives us only an incomplete notion, the true lyric drama, according to its inventor, needing to last from three to six days, and be purified of anything one might call melody, that is, of any sense of rhythm, any balance of design, any cadential or half-cadential points of respite, any logically considered articulation of phrases, etc. It is easy to see how mad this idea is and, consequently, how far from being realizable. Perhaps that is just one more reason for attempting it; it is, at any rate, a means for attracting universal attention to the inventor of such a system and for making a great fracas over his name.

It may be that, even after all this, M. Wagner remains convinced of the excellence of his method, and that he considers himself a martyr to ignorance and bad taste. Everything is possible among mortals, and the strangeness of the human spirit knows no limits when it is no longer kept in touch with truth by means of good sense—that supreme quality of genius and indispensable corollary of all creative faculties, without which the imagination amounts to nothing more than a mental fever.

But to understand the system on which the operas of M. Wagner are based is no easy thing, it demands sustained attention on the part of the reader. I will presume to demand such attention, at least in this one instance (once does not make it a habit).

After all I've heard, seen, read, played, and sung of M. Wagner (who, as we know, also writes his own opera librettos), here's what I take from him.

According to the celebrated innovator, all melodies known up to our time, including the theme of the funeral march from Beethoven's *Eroica* Symphony, are dance tunes solely by virtue of being rhythmically conceived, logically constructed, accentuated according to the laws of musical punctuation and divided into phrase structures in which some serve as *antecedents* and others as *outcomes*.

Behind the marvelous developments of Beethoven's symphonies M. Wagner sees nothing more than this ideal of dance melody, and whole sections of these immortal symphonic works are, for the author of *Tannhäuser*, nothing more than dance tunes in the primitive form of *airs de ballet*. It's quite true that the music of *Tannhäuser* does not make one want to dance—nor, for that matter, sing. Let me cite M. Wagner himself, as I shall have to do more than once here to support my explanation of his ideas, and to deflect any suspicion of malicious distortion as well.

"The symphonies of Beethoven retain, in those movements designated as *scherzo* or *menuetto*, actual dance music in its primitive form, to the accompaniment of which one could perfectly well dance."[15] (It had never occurred to me that the Scherzo of the Symphony in C Minor, to cite just one scherzo, could inspire such caprioles.) "One might say," adds M. Wagner, "that a powerful instinct compelled the composer to touch directly at least once, at the center of his work, on the principle that subtends the whole, rather as one tests the water with one's foot before leaping in."[16] One can well imagine the rather different sort of bathtub M. Wagner immerses himself in when taking *his* harmonic baths—he who didn't scruple to write that all operas by the familiar masters are, compared to his own, like an ape is to man.

The dance! There, in effect, is the root of all evil. Without the dance there would have been no composers, and if there had been no composers, M. Wagner might be the greatest of musicians. *Ah, la danse, la danse!* This is what ruined sacred music; this is what gives to Beethoven's symphonies that bouncing, frisky character you're familiar with; this, too, is what has fettered in its flowery chains all the opera librettos—which are, to tell the truth, nothing but spoken dance. "The original popular dance, deriving from the most concrete material relations, if then conceived in its richest possible development and applied even to manifestations of the most intimate motions of the soul, would be none other than a dramatic action."[17] *Diavolo!* So then love, the great motive behind every dramatic plot, is no more than a dance. . . . The dance of feelings, no doubt, in which two hearts standing face-to-face execute a series of *entrechats* and *chassé-croisées*! Yes, but then how could we make sense of these celebrated lines from *Richard Coeur-de-Lion*:[18]

Ce n'est pas la danse que j'aime,	It is not the dance I love,
Mais c'est la fille à Nicolas.	but the daughter of Nicolas.

But I digress! . . .

Be that as it may, M. Wagner tells us this with the disdain of a nonbeliever who will forever show himself unresponsive to the dance. "The ballet is the very worthy brother of the opera, of about the same age and born of the same defective principles. And so we see them proceed together step by step, as if to mutually conceal their respective weaknesses."[19] *Step by step* is good. M. Wagner likes to have a laugh. But then, why does he not care to *sing* like the rest of us?

"But really," you may ask me, "what does the poetry of a lyrical work need to express if it is to conform to the ideas of M. Wagner?"

"What does it need to express?"

"Yes."

"Nothing."

"What do you mean, nothing?"

"Nothing, I tell you. For (as M. Wagner tells us), 'the greatness of the poet is measured above all by what he *refrains* from saying so that we can say to ourselves, in silence, the inexpressible.'"[20]

In English, a *pantalon* and a *chemise* are inexpressible, but that can hardly have been what the author was thinking of. What *was* he thinking of, then?

Well, I must ask you. In any case, if it were really sufficient to prove one-self a great poet by simply saying nothing, then we would have plenty of great poets, since most of them (alas) mostly talk without saying anything.

We have now seen the role the poem is meant to play in operas based on the theories of M. Wagner. Now let's see about the music. "It is music that must make audible that which is not spoken, and the infallible form of this RESOUNDING SILENCE is the *endless melody*."[21]

This much is clear, and it is quite as true that clarity is one of the great qualities of music as it is of the theories of the new anti-dancing school of thought. Who could not understand that? — this melody that speaks for the poet, who remains silent for his part, thereby helping to shape an infinite melody into the infallible form of "resounding silence." . . . [22]

According to M. Wagner, music is really nothing more than the ideal of spoken poetry, and in the lyric drama it is necessary that words and music be fused to the point of becoming one and the same thing. But to achieve this result, which smacks more of chemistry than of art, an ideal expressivity must predominate in the text and actions of the characters, who must be human in form only, presenting themselves to the audience merely as abstractions.

The purpose of characters in this drama, we see, is much less that of representing an interesting plot, as in other kinds of theater, and much more that of furnishing attentive listeners, congregated here as if in a forest glade, the necessary explications for an understanding of the various epiphanies of the musical legend unfurling in the orchestra like a musical painting. Hence these interminable ritornellos intended to awaken in the mind of the listener those feelings the poetry is incapable of expressing, but which only succeed in lengthening the performance and straining our nerves, and in filling the auditorium with a sense of tedium that is too much for a French public to stand. This M. Wagner calls "infinite melody"; it would make more sense to call it "indefinite."

That a man alone in the forest might abandon himself to his dreams, listen to the rustling of the leaves, the soughing of the wind, and so let himself be gently lulled into a state of semi-ecstasy—all that I can quite well imagine. But a theatrical auditorium, where all sorts of things are calling for his attention, is hardly a good place to withdraw into oneself to prepare the soul for the fleeting and confused impressions of a music without form or fixed design, full of good intentions, perhaps, but intentions mostly without effects.

Everything has its place. Men being what they are, one cannot expect them to rush through their dinner, put on their white tie and suit to go off to their box at the opera and meditate, head in hands, upon the subtleties of a musical poetics that addresses the listener with something like sounding puzzles.

What one wants to find in the theater is a gripping drama, with a lucid exposition, a well-managed plot, a forceful denouement, one that allows the musician to take wing freely—not to indulge idiosyncratic reveries that can affect no one but himself, but to express genuine, well-characterized emotions. And since variety is one of the chief virtues of music for the theater we need, in addition to grand exhibitions of feeling, some assortment of graceful numbers of diverse character that charm the ear and hold our attention. To try to reduce the singing characters to a state of abstraction in line with the feelings they represent poetically—to a condition rather like that of walking and speaking clarinets, flutes, and bassoons as far as their role in the overall conception of the musical ensemble is concerned— is simply to destroy the genre of opera, not to renew it, and to transform artists into machines or living program notes.

Now, M. Wagner's inspiration consists of making the opera into an instrumental symphony with the obbligato accompaniment of singers. Yet will not any singer upon the stage always interest us more than some instrument in the orchestra? And if, by virtue of his living, intelligent, and animated being, the singer is of greater interest to the audience than a clarinet or a bassoon in the pit, should he not be given some distinctive role of his own? Or can one reasonably condemn him to function like an old telegraph, gesticulating without a word while the instruments speak for him? In truth, it's hard to believe such a system would find any sympathy from the good sense of our public, at least not for the present.

But I will go further and insist that opera as envisioned by M. Wagner is not only practically impossible but also fails to offer any serious resources even from a purely musical point of view.

What, in effect, does M. Wagner want? To expand the compass of melody by giving dramatic music something of the amplitude and interest of the symphony. The symphonist, M. Wagner tells us, still clings timidly to primitive forms of the dance; he never risks, even in the interests of expressivity, losing sight of the familiar routes that keep him aligned with those forms. But now the poet cries out to him: "Plunge boldly into the sea of music; with my hand in yours you can never lose contact with the things all men understand. For with my help you are in constant touch with the firm ground of a dramatic action, and the scenic representation of such an action is the most immediately understandable poem of all. Frame your melody boldly so that it pours through the whole work like an uninterrupted stream; in it you will be voicing what I leave unsaid, for only you can say it; while I in my silence will be saying it all [as well], because it is your hand I am guiding."[23]

How can a musician of the caliber of M. Wagner speak in this fashion? (For after all, he is truly a man of great talent.) Has M. Wagner forgotten that the principal interest, if not the only interest, of the symphony resides in the development of a given theme that serves, in some sense, as the thesis upon which the composer offers a commentary? Could one imagine a symphony without unity of thought, without that ingenious working of individual parts that generates a kind of piquant and often inspired conversation among the various instruments upon the given subject of the conversation, that is, the theme? Certainly not—about this there can be no doubt whatever. Well, such development of a principal theme or motive is simply out of the question when music is supposed to follow a dramatic and scenic action. In fact, as the plot advances and the characters express diverse sentiments in accordance with it, the music that expresses these sentiments must also necessarily vary in character. The result: no more unity of feeling nor development of a single leading musical idea.

The system of lyrical drama imagined by M. Wagner is thus to be rejected both from a dramatic and a musical point of view; and, as bad causes issue in bad effects, the music of M. Wagner is deplorable, despite the fact that he is really (again, I admit it) a very gifted artist.

M. Wagner has been convicted before the tribunal of logic as well as that of the ear. He can now only expect to find support among those few fanatics who always cling to one cause or another, and among those impotent musicians who, failing in the composition of *"constrained" melody* find it more convenient to practice *infinite melody*, that is to say, no sort of melody at all, while passing for deep minds and sublime composers.

M. Wagner hoped to create a revolution at the Opéra, but he has only succeeded in creating a riot.

What do I have to say about the performers? That which Napoleon said to his vanquished enemies: "All honor to ill-starred courage!"[24] They all did their best, and it is quite possible that M. Niémann [*sic*] has a good voice and sings well.[25] Though one can't say for sure.

As for the orchestra, it has proven that, in addition to military and civic courage, there is yet a third variety: musical courage.

PAUL SCUDO
Tannhäuser by M. Richard Wagner

The most remarkable musical event of the season has just taken place on the stage of the Opéra. *Tannhäuser* by M. Richard Wagner was performed there on March 13 before a vast public and in the presence of the head of state.[26] Now at last Paris has been afforded the opportunity to judge, based on primary evidence, the merits of a work that has been vigorously discussed in Germany for some fifteen years; moreover, Parisians may now also appraise the system on the basis of which the author defends this product of his imagination. For we must not forget that M. Wagner is at one and the same time a poet, a composer, and the philosopher of a new form of lyric drama that has occasioned endless debate across the Rhine. The appearance of *Tannhäuser* on the grand stage of the Paris Opéra should at least have this one good result, that it might help put an end to idle controversy.

The subject of the piece is drawn from a German legend of the thirteenth century, alluding to a national institution of that epoch, the *Minnesänger*: those poets of the Middle Ages who preceded this first phase of the literary Renaissance in the fourteenth century. This pious legend carries the stamp of that epoch in which it was conceived, and of the people whose naïve beliefs it expresses. The foundation of it is the conflict always present in our nature between paganism and Christianity, between the love inspired by Venus and the love that emanates from the soul, contenting itself with the divine feelings produced in us by a sense of the ideal. This is the same question that was so often treated by the singers of courtly love and the troubadors of the *langue d'oc*. . . . [27]

It should be readily apparent that the Tannhäuser legend, as treated by M. Wagner, does not contain the material for a lyric drama. No character is adequately drawn, no passion is strongly highlighted; the figures presented to us seem to be less real human beings, subject like us to the ordinary vicissitudes of life, than metaphysical symbols—more appropriate to a Platonic dialogue than to a dramatic action. M. Wagner's poetic diction is of an obscurity and density, if I may so express it, that seems rather suited to transmitting the equivocal intuitions of an oracle. To express the finite feelings and determinate passions of the human heart, however, such as music is asked to clothe with its magical colors, one needs a language that outlines its objects in a clear and supple manner without unduly constraining them. Those *stars*, that *blue sky*, those *celestial harps* and *great vaults of heaven* and *divine phalanxes*—the whole gibberish of lyric poetry of an inferior order that so hobbles the imagination of M. Wagner, will

not take in a French audience that wants to understand things, even those that are sung. In a word, *Tannhäuser* is a fairy tale ill-suited to the stage, lacking in action, lacking in characters and interest, based on a banal and puerile theme: one of those precious questions of sentimental metaphysics so eagerly pursued in the courts of the Middle Ages, in the Renaissance academies, or at the Hôtel de Rambouillet.[28]
. . . [29]

Berlioz, Berlioz, give up, you've been outdone; even in your most droll and eccentric articles you never asserted anything so far-fetched. Long live the future and the great melody of the virgin forest![30] There is a great deal of this sort of melody in the score of *Tannhäuser*, which we will now proceed to analyze.

The overture to this symbolic drama is well known, having been performed last year at the three concerts given by M. Wagner at the Théâtre-Italien.[31] It consists of a large, poorly built body, notable for an interminable phrase outlined in the violins for more than a hundred measures. This persistent feature seems to have some deep significance, since the author recalls it several times in the course of his legend;[32] against it the winds and brass and above all the trombones intone a kind of accentuated clamor that constitutes the peroration of this mysterious preface. The overture as such is not a good one: the coloration is drab, the joinery defective. The overtures to *Der Freischütz*, to *Oberon* and *Euryanthe*, those to *Don Juan* and *The Magic Flute*, the one to *Guillaume Tell*, Cherubini's overture to *Médée*, or Méhul's familiar overture to *Le jeune Henri*—these are instrumental works whose signification is self-contained, they represent vigorous and striking summaries, intelligible to anyone even without recourse to a psychological commentary. One senses immediately that M. Wagner is a confused mind with a tendency to overreach himself.

When the curtain rises we see a vast grotto where Venus is indolently reclining, Tannhäuser sighing with satiation at her feet, dreaming of some form of happiness that might prove more salutary to his enervated soul, while nymphs, fauns, bacchantes—in short, the entire populace of old Olympus—disport themselves about the loving couple. Venus is troubled by Tannhäuser's bewildered, taciturn behavior, and asks him, "What are you dreaming of, my beloved?" — "A dream I have had," responds Tannhäuser, "which has recalled to me the days of my youth and the *joyful chiming of the morning bells.*"[33] It's hard to imagine in what sort of music Wagner has wrapped this voluptuous scene, one of the most familiar, often repeated clichés in the poetics of opera. Neither the dancing of the nymphs nor the interminable dialogue of the two lovers—who quarrel without understanding each other or letting their voices join in any sort of reasonable ensemble—has inspired the composer with a single rhythmic, harmonic, or other sort of musical idea able to distinguish itself over the vast rumblings that leave the listener's wandering ear quite adrift. I do not exaggerate here, and I would beg the listener to believe that I speak the truth when I say that this whole first scene of *Tannhäuser*, written here in Paris in the composer's most recent manner, can really not be compared to any sort of music now extant.[34] This is chaos, a void—but a scientific chaos and void. It is that *great forest melody* that has nothing more in common with the melody of Italian opera, the kind that can only be appreciated in the company of the *setting sun*.[35] Perhaps you think I am joking? Just listen to these pretty verses sung by Tannhäuser to Venus

. . . *Malgré ce vif délire,*	*[Doch ich aus diesen ros'gen Düften*
Les doux parfums qu'ici j'aspire,	*verlange nach des Waldes Lüften,*
Tout me rappelle avec regret	*nach unsres Himmels klaren Blau,*
L'air frais et pur de la forêt	*nach unsrem frischen Grün der Au]*

Despite this strong delirium,
The sweet perfumes that I breathe here,
Everything recalls to me, regretfully,
The pure air of the forest[36]

The setting of the next scene transports us to a great sunlit valley from which one can see the feudal castle of the Wartburg. Seated upon an outcropping, a young shepherd sings a strange sort of unaccompanied melody, the refrain of which he repeats on his pipe:

Du ravin sortait dame Holda	*[Frau Holda kam aus dem Berg hervor]*

Lady Holda emerged from the mountain

This vague and monotonous song that verges on the archaic style of an old minstrel song excited a Gallic smile among the audience—one that turned into general hilarity at the piped refrain. Tannhäuser's arrival, his meeting with the Landgrave and his comrades Walther, Bitterolf, and Wolfram (poet-singers like himself), the whole scene of recognition in which the hero of this mystical legend recounts his sojourn in the Venusberg, his wayward transgressions and remorse—all of this fails to issue in any sort of definable, classifiable musical number. Instead we have interminable recitatives, a chanting[37] of one, two, three, or four voices that never coalesce into any fixed design, a melange of vocal and instrumental sounds that fail to awaken in the listener that general, vague, confused yet profound impression Wagner the theoretician speaks about and which, as poet and composer joined in one person, he intends to create. Whether Wagner deceives himself as a critic or is unable as poet and composer to realize the ideal *great melody of the forest* he has prescribed as the way of the future, it is certain the first act of *Tannhäuser* failed to excite anything in the audience at the Opéra besides bursts of Rabelaisian laughter.

The second act takes place entirely in the great hall of the Wartburg, where the poet-singers hold their competitions. The Landgrave's niece Elisabeth is secretly in love with Tannhäuser; she arrives and recalls impressions of her youth —

Salue à toi, noble demeure!   *[Dich, teure Halle, grüss ich wieder]*

Greetings to you, noble Hal!

in a sort of recitative that once again defies classification. It is not an aria, nor one of those beautiful, tragic recitatives such as we find in *Don Juan*, in *Fidelio*, in *Der Freischütz*, in *La vestale*, or in the masterpieces of Gluck (who largely created this intermediate form between pure, developed song and the musically notated declamation of Lully and Rameau). Elisabeth's kind of song has no name, nor ever will. Now Tannhäuser shows up, led by Wolfram (who plays a rather strange role in this affair). Tannhäuser throws himself at the feet of Elisabeth. The interview of the two lovers gives way to a dialogue scene in which the two voices do not unite until near the end, where they finally create what in the old style was called a duet, not lacking in animation. The Landgrave comes to announce to his niece the festival of song he has arranged, the competition among the poet-singers over which she and he together are to preside. The Thuringian lords and ladies proceed into the great hall of the Wartburg and it is during this entry that the march with chorus is performed, the most notable piece in the score of *Tannhäuser*. This march is beautiful, if not very original. It is broadly designed and succeeds in producing the effect intended by the poet-composer. With this page of honest, true music—warmly applauded by the public—the composer refutes the miserable sophistries of the reformer. Which of the two is right? If it is M. Wagner the theoretician and initiator of a new kind of music, then he has been unfaithful to those same doctrines in the march with chorus just cited, a number conceived and executed entirely according to the accepted canons of musical composition. But let us not be duped by the ruses of impotent vanity. The Landgrave rises from his sovereign seat to declare—in a pompous, declamatory, and not especially musical recitative—that the one to have most satisfactorily plumbed the mysteries of love shall be compensated with the hand of Elisabeth. And now begins an interminable psalmody on a series of burlesque verses, in which it is impossible to detect the trace of an idea or a character's feeling. The three-part mystical hodge-podge spouted by the three singers (Wolfram, Bitterolf, and Tannhäuser, one after the other), with the support of the chorus, who intervene in the debate with short interjections doubtless meant to recall the chorus of antique tragedy—this scene was much abridged in the performance. There is little to recommend here, apart from a few isolated phrases in Wolfram's hymn in honor of ideal love. These songs are followed by a prayer from Elisabeth, addressed to Tannhäuser's rivals, a mostly dry, declamatory piece that does, however, give way to a rather fine choral ensemble:

Un ange nous vient apparaître	*[Ein Engel stieg aus lichtem Äther,*
Pour proclamer l'arrêt des cieux.	*zu künden Gottes heil'gen Rat.]*

An angel has appeared to us
To proclaim God's holy decree.

But alas, this brief moment of respite, in which the composer, true to the laws of his art, refutes the errors of the theoretician, is succeeded by a dreadful outburst of discordant sounds constituting the finale of the second act, in which the critical innovator takes his revenge upon the artist and the musician. Thus we find throughout this peculiar work the sound instincts of a talented man succumbing to sophistry, the ill-conceived ideals of the reformer triumphing over the poet and musician.

The third act transports us back to the valley of the Wartburg. It is night [*sic*], and Wolfram, who for some reason or other has wandered to this spot, encounters Elisabeth kneeling before a devotional image of the Virgin. He laments the fate of this noble maiden as she anxiously awaits the return of the band of pilgrims from Rome, among whom she hopes to find Tannhäuser. And lo, a troupe of pilgrims does now traverse the stage singing a choral prayer:

Salut à vous, ô beau ciel! ô patrie!	*[Beglückt darf nun dich,*
	O Heimat, ich schauen]

Greetings to you, fair skies of my homeland!

The main motive of this prayer develops and expands in a *crescendo* to quite beautiful effect. Admirably accompanied by a phrase drawn from the overture, this chorus was warmly—and deservedly—applauded, proving that the public does not bear any prejudicial grudge against M. Wagner as a person or as an artistic talent. The prayer of Elisabeth that follows the Pilgrims' chorus

O Vierge sainte! que ta grâce   *[Allmächt'ge Jungfrau, hör mein Flehen!*
Enfin m'élève jusqu'à toi!   *Zu dir, Gepriesene, rufe ich!]*

O holy Virgin! Let your mercy
Raise me at last to be with you!

constitutes another of those vague, inarticulate songs, a sort of liturgical prose that seems not to belong to any precise tonality, although its general coloration and semi-religious character are not displeasing. I would even say as much of the symphonic passage that accompanies Elisabeth's exit, continuing up to the point where she disappears up the hill of the Wartburg. In this scene and in the evening hymn sung by Wolfram soon afterward

O douce étoile, feu du soir,   *[O du, mein holder Abendstern*
Toi que j'aimai toujours revoir!   *wohl grüß' ich immer dich so gern!]*

Oh sweet star, light of the evening,
You whom I always greet so fondly!

I believe that M. Wagner has best succeeded in creating that kind of floating melody that gradually extricates itself from its musical surroundings and envelops one like a poetic cloud, transmitting a calm yet elevated and noble feeling. Whenever a work of art is able to produce this desirable effect, dilating the soul and elevating the feeling to the heights of a poetic situation, we must acknowledge our gratitude to the artist and not worry him overmuch with questions about the means he has used to achieve such a fine result. Apart from these pieces, the third act includes only a long declamation in which Tannhäuser recounts to Wolfram his journey to Rome; one might detect here a few inspired flights amid what is generally a formless chanting—of somber and deadening effect, and during which we are mainly overcome by a mortal tedium.

Such is the effect of this strange work which we have now subjected ourselves to hear four times through, with a sense of self-denial that truly ought to earn us some measure of indulgence. We have attempted here, as before, to plead the cause of M. Wagner, to stay close to his point of view and to judge the result of his work according to his own doctrines. Inwardly, we continue to tell ourselves: it is not enough for a critic to understand and love only beautiful things; one must also be able to confront ugliness with a calm resolve. Where is the honor in admiring Mozart, the most divine and exquisite of musicians, or of admiring to a fitting degree Haydn, Beethoven, Weber, Mendelssohn, Schubert, and the great Sebastian Bach, that last of the scholastics? Where is the honor in appreciating the value of masterpieces by Gluck, Handel, Palestrina, Jomelli, Cimarosa, Rossini, Meyerbeer, Spontini, Méhul, and M. Auber? These are all true musicians, creative artists—all as different as the times and the countries that produced them, but all able to be original while respecting the eternal laws of their art, all innovators who did not need to break away from the great chain of tradition. The whole world appreciates the works of these admirable men, who may have been challenged at one time or another without ever having been entirely misunderstood. To say quite simply that Corneille and Racine are great poets and that *Athalie* is the most perfect masterpiece in any language is not to set oneself apart from the great majority of cultivated minds. —Well, prove the contrary, raise yourself above these commonplaces, I cry out to myself in an access of lyric enthusiasm! Maintain, along with M. Wagner, that Mozart is good for nothing more than *facilitating the digestion* of guests at an aristocratic table;[38] treat Rossini as a little boy who has not studied his counterpoint as M. Wagner has; speak scornfully and condescendingly of the French masters and of the Italian school with its "small melodies"; plunge yourself, at the *setting of the sun*, into the *great melody of the forest* invented by M. Wagner; extend your hands to MM. Liszt, Brendel, Hans von Bülow, and affirm that the *plain chant* delivered by Elisabeth in the third act of *Tannhäuser* is quite as beautiful as the trio of *Guillame Tell*![39] Prove yourself worthy to the occasion, confuse your *subjectivity* with M. Wagner's *objectivity*, elevate yourself to that high synthesis described by the philsophy of the absolute, such as has been so edifyingly discussed of late in the *Revue*[40]—and once you have achieved the summit of this ideal void, *in cima del campanile*,[41] you'll no longer be distracted by the small details. And you will understand at last how black and white, night and day, hot and cold, truth and falsehood, justice and injustice, the beautiful and the ugly, *Guillame Tell* and *Tannhäuser*—all of these are but one and the same. Then you will be regarded as a great mind, you will pass for the very phoenix among the critics of the future!

Despite all the advantages to our *amour-propre* in pursuing this ambitious dream, we find ourselves forced to concede that *Tannhäuser* has been quite fairly judged by the Parisian public, and that the failure of this poor piece of work seems to us to have been inevitable. We feel that we have earned the right to rejoice in an event that we both foresaw and ardently desired. It has been ten years now that we have been opposing the fatal doctrines propagated by M. Wagner and his partisans, the latter consisting for the most part of mediocre writers, painters, and sculptors without talent, quasi-poets, lawyers, democrats, people of suspect republican sympathies, false spirits, women without taste—dreamers of the void who judge artistic beauty by sentiment, as something that should strike the ear more than touch the heart through some hollow, unintelligible symbolism. Within the score of *Tannhäuser* are three numbers composed according to the ordinary canons of musical art, pieces immediately understood by the public, and applauded more than they really deserved to be: the overture, an ill-drawn symphonic design in which there's nothing more to grasp than a vast whirring of the violins the composer keeps bringing back in the course of his legend; the march of the second act; and the Pilgrims' chorus of the third act. We will be more generous than the audience, by also giving M. Wagner credit for the above-mentioned choral ensemble in the second act, "Un ange nous vient apparaître" or the religious coloration of Elisabeth's prayer, for the symphonic movement accompanying her exit, and for the evening hymn sung by Wolfram, as executed by the well-trained voice of M. Morelli. These fragments of a vague, chantlike character or of orchestral recitative, difficult to classify more precisely, are nonetheless not to be dismissed outright, since they do manage to awaken a certain broad emotional response and to communicate to the imagination a kind of poetic excitement. When M. Wagner does have musical ideas, which is rare enough, he is far from being original; when he has no ideas to speak of he is unique, and impossible.

The performance of *Tannhäuser* was about what one might expect. M. Niemann, of the court theater in Hanover, was chosen by M. Wagner himself as the artist best able to interpret the role of the knight and singer: a large, young blond German who possesses a strong, high tenor voice, though one that has not yet been subjected to good vocal discipline.[42] M. Niemann does not lack for dramatic feeling; in this department he is well schooled, being married to Mlle. Seebach, the leading tragedienne of the German stage.[43] He rose to the difficult task assigned him, keeping his cool in the face of an audience that made no efforts to conceal its discontent. All the same, he might profit from this experience by learning to better control a vigorous vocal organ that is still not without its faults. Mme. Tedesco in the role of Venus and Mlle. Sax in that of Elisabeth did their best to make their fine voices heard, but it was only M. Morelli in the role of Wolfram who was wholly able to save himself from the overall fiasco, lending as he did to the metaphysical chanting of M. Wagner's score a sense of musicality it does not itself possess.[44] As for the orchestra, it produced miracles under the direction of M. Dietsch.[45] Resisting the incredible presumption of M. Wagner, who had wanted to take up the conductor's baton himself, quite against all traditional protocol, M. Dietsch proved that he has both a sense of the dignity of his position as well as the talent required to carry out the job entrusted to him.

It was high time the Parisian public gave a firm check to the pretensions of the author of *Tannhäuser*. While never having doubted the futility of his attempts to alter the taste and good sense of the French, we had not expected to see M. Wagner, his system, and his oeuvre so quickly judged and placed beyond the pale of further debate. This turn of events will have good results, even in Germany, where in fact the followers of this vain reformer are not nearly so numerous as some would have us believe. In this decisive battle M. Wagner will have lost much, including his reputation as a man of system, intrepid and very sure about the rightness of his cause, for he has in fact agreed to all the cuts, all the mutilations of his work that had been proposed to him. It was scarcely worthwhile to have made such a fuss, to put on airs of a Galileo who suffers but refuses to give way, to organize a propaganda society, to launch programs and insulting prefaces, disseminate mendacious biographies and portraits in which M. Wagner is represented with pen in hand, meditating upon his masterpieces—just to run aground miserably upon gales of laughter from a merry audience. Better to win the day or else retreat with dignity, score intact, admonishing the Parisians: "You are not yet worthy of understanding the philosophical depths of this music, which I address to future generations!"

Let there be no mistake, however: M. Wagner is no ordinary musician. An ambitious spirit with an overactive imagination, glimpsing but dimly and confusedly the ideal to which it aspires, a strong but nervous disposition in which the will outweighs grace or feeling—the author of *Tannhäuser* and *Lohengrin* represents an exaggerated type of certain shortcomings characteristic of the country and the era that have produced him. A little bit of a poet, a little bit of a writer, a democrat and a great sophist, M. Wagner has aimed to derive from music something that it cannot be made to encompass without altering its very essence: pure ideas and symbols. Instead of aiming for beauty, the true goal of all the arts, and for form, without which nothing can be grasped by the human mind (since nothing exists for it outside the limits of some form), M. Wagner, gifted with talent but not with the power of invention, has thrown himself body and soul into various metaphysical reveries, has tried to create philosophy out of sounds—not being able to create expressive song accessible to all mortals who have ears and a heart. Perhaps bad Italian composers do resort to banal formulas, flat-footed cadences, vulgar *cabalettas*, fioratura and guitar-style accompaniments; and perhaps bad German composers intoxicate themselves with insoluble harmonic combinations, aimless modulations and symphonic divagations. Still, M. Wagner fails to recognize the genuine creative power of the Italian genius—a healthy and generous one that has managed to unite order with the highest level of inspiration, even in such fields as the mathematical sciences and the law; and he quite fails to apprehend the gifts of this privileged race that has civilized all of Europe and has even taught the art of music to Germany! Played up by a little cabal of mad Germans who would regard certain unhealthy features of the late works of Beethoven as the secret to a whole new evolution in the art of music, M. Wagner has severed all ties with common sense and with the great tradition of the German school, putting himself forward instead as the obscure prophet of an impossible future. The lesson he has just had to learn in Paris was rough, but it was also a just and salutary one! As the expression goes, *when the sky falls, there will be plenty of birds for the taking!*[46] We can be sure that the failure of *Tannhäuser* has nipped in the bud a large number of would-be Wagnerian imitators, people who would gladly have disguised their impotence by professing his dubious principles. I can think of at least three already inclined to tip their hats to the "great forest melody," as is apparent by certain traces in their own works. Now they'll change their tune and cry shame upon this impostor since, after all, they are agile politicians.

As for us, humble admirers of beautiful things, let us be allowed to rejoice for a moment in another event that confirms the truth of the doctrines we've been professing here for a decade and half. These doctrines are not of our invention, but are deduced from history and masterpieces of genius; and it is a good thing to be able to apply these beautiful words of the evangelist: "He that speaketh of himself seeketh his own glory: but he that seeketh the glory of him that sent him, he is true and there is no injustice in him."*

At the fifth Conservatoire concert, one of the most interesting this season, we saw performed among other pieces some excerpts from both the French and the Italian versions of Gluck's *Alceste*. The solos were sung by M. Cazaux of the Opéra and by Mme. Viardot.[47] This prodigious music by a master who has been neither surpassed nor equalled in the pathetic expression of grand, royal passions (if I may put it so) produced an extraordinary effect upon the audience. Mme. Viardot was outstanding, in

---

* John 7:18. "Qui a semetipso loquitur gloriam propriam quaerit; qui autem quaerit gloriam ejus qui misit eum, hic verax est, et injustitia in illo non est." (St. John)

particular; she brought to the various pieces she sang an intelligence and a style fully worthy of the works she was performing. Never, perhaps, has this great artist raised herself to such heights by means of penetrating emotional insight and taste; her success was brilliant and unanimous. The orchestra matched its efforts to those of the other performers, and Mme. Viardot may rightly consider the ovation she received at this recital one of the great triumphs of her career. Ah, what a consolation it is to see how true genius remains forever young, while the Titans find crashing about them the scaffolding by means of which they presumed to storm the heavens!

NOTES

All endnotes that follow are the editors'; the single footnote in the body of Scudo's article is his.

1. Walter Benjamin famously dubbed Paris the "capital of the nineteenth century" in his 1935 essay "Paris, die Hauptstadt des XIX. Jahrhunderts" ("Paris, capitale du XIXe siècle"), in which he outlines the issues to be discussed in his "arcades" project. See Walter Benjamin, *Das Passagenwerk*, ed. Rolf Tiedemann, 2 vols. (Frankfurt/Main, 1983), 1:45–77. See also Albert Wolff, *Le Figaro*, 24 March 1861: "Paris n'est pas seulement la capitale de la France, c'est le centre du monde artiste."

2. See Charles Baudelaire, *Richard Wagner et Tannhäuser* (Paris, 1861); this was first published as "Richard Wagner et *Tannhäuser* à Paris" in *La Revue européenne*. For Jules Champfleury, see his *Grandes figures d'hier et d'aujourd'hui: Balzac, Gérard de Nerval, Wagner, Courbet* (Paris, 1861).

3. See James Ross, "Crisis and Transformation: French Opera, Politics and the Press, 1897–1903" (PhD diss., Oxford University, 1998), 187.

4. For a concise and informative biography, see Gustave Chouquet and David Charlton, "Comettant, Oscar," in *Grove Music Online*, http://www.oxfordmusiconline.com/subscriber/article/grove/music/06182 (accessed January 24, 2009).

5. Richard Macnutt, "Escudier," in *Grove Music Online*, http://www.oxfordmusiconline.com/subscriber/article/grove/music/08980 (accessed January 24, 2009).

6. Katharine Ellis, "Wagnerism and Anti-Wagnerism in the Paris Periodical Press," in *Von Wagner zum Wagnérisme: Musik, Literatur, Kunst, Politik*, ed. Annegret Fauser and Manuela Schwartz (Leipzig, 1999), 51–83.

7. See Jeffrey Cooper, "Scudo, P.," in *Grove Music Online*.

8. Paul Scudo, "Revue musicale," *Revue des deux mondes* 2/26 (1 March 1860): 227–38. See also Ellis, "Wagnerism and Anti-Wagnerism," 59.

9. A significant collection of reviews is presented in the online database of "Francophone Music Criticism, 1789–1914," sponsored by the Arts and Humanities Research Council in the U.K.; see http://music.sas.ac.uk/fmc/fmc-home.html.

10. Apart from Baudelaire and Champfleury—both outsiders to Parisian music criticism—Wagner's supporters included Auguste de Gasperini, Adolphe Giacomelli, and Louis Laloy. For a representative collection of reviews that date from two years before the Parisian

Tannhäuser, see *Giacomo Meyerbeer, Le pardon de Ploërmel: Dossier de presse parisienne (1859)*, ed. Marie-Hélène Coudroy-Saghai (Bietigheim, 1992).

11. The more balanced reviews mentioned are Franck-Marie (pseud. Franco-Maria Pedorlini), "Revue musicale," *La Patrie*, 24 March 1861; and Arthur Pougin, "Chronologie musicale," *La jeune France*, 31 March 1861. For an in-depth discussion of all the reviews, see Annegret Fauser, "'Cette musique sans tradition': Wagner's *Tannhäuser* and Its French Critics," in *Stage Music and Cultural Transfer: Paris, 1830–1914*, ed. Annegret Fauser and Mark Everist (Chicago, 2009).

12. Franck-Marie, "Revue musicale."

13. Comettant's review appeared in *L'art musical*, 21 March 1861, 121–24.

14. The formal name, during the Second Empire, of the Paris Opéra (informally, the Opéra).

15. For the orginal text, see Wagner, *Gesammelte Schriften und Dichtungen* (Leipzig, 1887–1911), 7:128 (henceforth *GSD*). See also "Music of the Future," trans. Robert L. Jacobs, *Three Wagner Essays* (London, 1979), 39.

16. Comettant does in fact "distort" his source here. Wagner's original text reads "wie um mit den Füßen nach dem Boden zu fassen, der ihn tragen soll" (as if testing with one's feet the ground that's supposed to be one's support). *GSD*, 7:128.

17. This is a somewhat free paraphrase of Wagner's text (*GSD*, 7:128); Jacobs's translation of the passage in question reads: "Even folk-dancing in its original form conveyed a dramatic action, usually the wooing of a pair of lovers; when that simple representation of a sensual experience is developed into a revelation of its psychic impulses then you have a dramatic action." *Three Wagner Essays*, 39.

18. *Opéra comique* of 1784 by the Belgian composer André Grétry.

19. See Wagner, *GSD*, 7:128–29; and Jacobs, *Three Wagner Essays*, 39. Comettant seems to take the phrase in the French text of Wagner's essay, "du même pas" (literally, "in step" with one another), as a pun on the term *pas* (for a balletic number or solo).

20. Comettant is alluding here to the next passage in Wagner's essay where the famous idea of the orchestral "endless melody" of the music drama is construed in terms of how the composer's music (melody) provides a kind of transcendental supplement to what can be expressed in words (in the poem or libretto): "In truth, the measure of a poet's greatness is that which he does not say in order to let what is inexpressible speak to us for itself. It is the musician who brings this great Unsaid to sounding life, and the unmistakable form of his resounding silence is *endless melody*." Jacobs, *Three Wagner Essays*, 40.

21. See Wagner, *GSD*, 7:130, and Jacobs, *Three Wagner Essays*, 40.

22. Comettant quotes a long paragraph (omitted here) from "Music of the Future" (*GSD*, 7:131–32; Jacobs, *Three Wagner Essays*, 40–41), beginning: "To give you a final idea of this great melody which I visualize spanning the whole compass of a music drama I shall again employ a metaphor." This is Wagner's metaphorical "forest melody," also cited and satirized at length by Paul Scudo in the other review translated here. Wagner seeks to compare the overall musical impression of his dramatically motivated, motivically saturated score (thinking of the recently completed *Tristan* rather than of *Tannhäuser*) to the subtle sounds and textures of a forest setting at sunset. A further paragraph from the review, following the Wagner quotation, is also omitted, referring to Louis Jullien, founder of various concert series of dance and other light music in Paris and London who had died in an asylum (1860) shortly before the Paris *Tannhäuser* production. In addition to composing several grandiose, bombastic works such as a "Hymn of Universal Harmony," he is described by Comettant as having been prone to mystical aural "visions" reminiscent of ancient *musica mundana* or, to Comettant, Wagner's "forest melody."

23. "Music of the Future," Jacobs, *Three Wagner Essays*, 39–40; see also Wagner, *GSD*, 7:129.

24. "Honneur au courage malheureux!"

25. Albert Niemann, the German tenor who sang the role of Tannhäuser in Paris. See also annotations to the review by P. Scudo, who mentions more of the cast.

26. Napoleon III, and his wife, the Empress Eugénie, attended the first and second performances on 13 and 18 March 1861. Scudo's review appeared in *La revue des deux mondes,* 1 April 1861, 759–70.

27. An extended synopsis of the libretto is omitted here.

28. The Hôtel de Rambouillet was the original model for the French literary salon under the guidance of educated female nobility, founded in a specially designed suite of rooms in the vicinity of the Louvre by the Marquise de Rambouillet (Catherine de Vivonne de Savelli) in the early decades of the seventeenth century.

29. Two paragraphs, omitted here, address Wagner's ideas on the history of opera in relation to his own theorizing about a musical-dramatic *Gesamtkunstwerk* of the future, as summarized in the *Lettre sur la musique,* an open letter to Frédéric Villot published in 1860 as the preface to prose translations of his collected librettos: *Quatre poèmes d'opéra traduits en prose français précédés d'une Lettre sur la musique par Richard Wagner;* the essay was reprinted in German as *"Zukunftsmusik" "Music of the Future"* in 1861. Like many early critics of Wagner's theories, Scudo objects to the grounds of Wagner's criticism of traditional operatic melody and form, questioning what appears to him a regressive program to restore the declamatory tedium and melodic poverty of pre-1700 opera. With regard to the positive, creative side of Wagner's reform theories, Scudo invokes (skeptically) the claims that the new musical drama will cultivate *la grande mélodie symphonique,* which Wagner invokes by means of his metaphor of the "melody of the forest," an aesthetic impression he hopes to convey in the "endless melody" of his newest works, especially *Tristan und Isolde.*

30. An allusion to Wagner's metaphor of the "forest melody" meant to illustrate his idea of a new notion of "endless melody," proposed in the essay *"Music of the Future"* (the *Lettre sur la musique,* see preceding note). In the latter part of this essay Wagner tried to reply to his critics—who claimed that his music was devoid of identifiable "melody"—by outlining a broader conception of the term as an ongoing melodic discourse conditioned by the demands of text and voice, in opposition to more or less autonomous or "absolute" melody of conventional operatic practice. Both Scudo and his fellow critic Comettant make frequent reference to these ideas from the revised, synoptic account of his notorious theories of a new *Gesamtkunstwerk,* as published in Paris at the time of this production.

31. To familiarize Paris audiences with his works prior to the production of *Tannhäuser* at the Opéra, Wagner conducted three concerts of excerpts from *Der fliegende Holländer, Tannhäuser, Lohengrin,* and *Tristan und Isolde* (the Prelude) at the Théâtre-Italien on January 25, February 1, and February 8, 1860.

32. In this review Scudo suggests that the *Tannhäuser* Overture represents in itself a kind of orchestral musical "legend," perhaps influenced by recent debates in Germany over the idea of the new Lisztian "symphonic poem," itself conceived in some part under the impress of Wagner's overture. See Liszt's account of the *Tannhäuser* Overture, included in Part III of this volume.

33. The text in italics—"Les tintements joyeux des cloches lointaines"—as elsewhere in the review, is that quoted from the French libretto of *Tannhäuser* prepared in consultation with Wagner by Charles Nuitter (the pen name of librettist and Opéra archivist Charles-Louis-Étienne Truinet, 1828–99); these passages are given in italics in the text of Scudo's original review as well.

34. Wagner did revise for Paris much of the scene of Tannhäuser and Venus (Act 1, scene 2), in addition to the wholly recomposed and extended "Venusberg" music of Act 1, scene 1, into which the overture now segued directly, from the reprise of the theme of

"Tannhäuser's Song to Venus." Scudo is responding to the *Tristan*-influenced chromatic prolongations and sensuous reorchestrations of the scene.

35. Allusions, again, to the arguments about a new kind of "endless melody" proposed in Wagner's 1860 *Lettre sur la musique* and the metaphor of the "melody of the forest."

36. The lines are from the second strophe of Tannhäuser's "Song to Venus" in Act 1, scene 2. Scudo quotes from Charles Nuitter's French verse translation of the libretto, as performed and published in Paris. The original German text is included here for reference, as well as an English translation reflecting primarily Nuitter's French version.

37. Here and throughout Scudo uses the word *mélopée* to refer to declamatory, "reformed," or pseudo-archaic idioms in Wagner's musical setting of the text.

38. In "*Music of the Future*" Wagner had invidiously compared Haydn's motivically derived transitions to the more conventional "Italian" formulas generally encountered in Mozartian symphonic transitions, "stereotyped phrases giving his movements the character of . . . an attractive noise to accompany conversations between attractive melodies . . . it is as though the music were expressing the rattle and clatter of a princely dinner." Jacobs, *Three Wagner Essays*, 38; see also *GSD*, 7:126.

39. Probably referring to the florid, lyrical trio for treble voices (Mathilde, Jemmy, and Hedwiga) in Act 4, "Je rends à votre amour un fils digne de vous," although there is a more extended heroic trio for male voices in Act 2 ("Quand l'Helvétie est un champs de supplices").

40. Edmund Scherer, "Hegel et l'Hégélianisme," *Revue des deux mondes*, 31/2 (1861): 812–56.

41. "at the top of the belfry"

42. Albert Niemann (1831–1917) remained one of the best-known exponents of the Wagnerian Heldentenor roles during the rest of the composer's lifetime and beyond, particularly that of Siegmund (which he created at Bayreuth in 1876).

43. German actress Marie Seebach (1829–97) had married Niemann in Hannover in 1859, but was divorced from him shortly after they moved to Berlin in 1866.

44. Fortunata Tedesco (1826–after 1866), Italian soprano. After singing roles in America during the 1840s, she appeared regularly at the Paris Opéra from 1851 to 1862. Marie Sax (originally Sass, later Saxe) was born in 1838 and, after starting out as a café entertainer, turned to operatic roles at age twenty-one, undertaking Susanna in the *Marriage of Figaro* a year before being cast as Elisabeth. Ferdinand Morelli, a baritone of Italian origin active in Paris at the time, was chosen in preference to a French baritone for the sake of a fuller, more cantabile style that Wagner felt more suited the lyrical demands of Wolfram's part.

45. Pierre-Louis Dietsch (1808–65) famously received the commission to compose an opera for Paris based on Wagner's original scenario on the "Flying Dutchman" theme, which appeared in 1842. Having served as chorus director of the Opéra since 1840, he had just been appointed conductor there in 1860, shortly before the decision to produce *Tannhäuser*.

46. "Si le ciel tombait, il y aurait beaucoup d'alouettes de prises!"

47. Cazaux also sang the role of Landgraf Hermann in the Paris production of *Tannhäuser*. Mezzo-soprano Pauline Viardot-Garcia (1821–1910), one of the most notable musical personalities of mid-nineteenth-century Paris, was the sister of the equally notable but short-lived operatic soprano Maria Malibran (1808–36). Among Viardot's celebrated parts of the 1850s was the title role of Gluck's *Orfée*, in a version revised expressly for her by Hector Berlioz. Scudo is invoking the classical simplicity and perfection associated with her Gluck interpretations as a foil to the excesses of Wagner.

The *Revue wagnérienne*:

Symbolism, Aestheticism, and Germanophilia

J. K. HUYSMANS, TEODOR DE WYZEWA,
EDOUARD DUJARDIN
INTRODUCED BY STEVEN HUEBNER
SELECTIONS TRANSLATED BY BRENDAN KING
AND CHARLOTTE MANDELL

"I felt as if released from gravity, with rekindled memories of voluptuous pleasures that circulate in lofty places."[1] Thus wrote Charles Baudelaire on March 18, 1861, recalling the dream state triggered by the *Lohengrin* Overture performed at one of Wagner's Parisian concerts the previous year. Although Baudelaire's advocacy for Wagner's music did nothing to resuscitate *Tannhäuser* from its inglorious demise at the Paris Opéra that very week, his essay remained a touchstone for French Wagnerians until the end of the century. And thus, it also initiated a remarkably resilient double-track in the ensuing French reception of Wagner. Official and institutional obstacles faced by his operas (not least fostered by nationalist sentiment following the French defeat in the Franco-Prussian War of 1870) and pragmatic attempts to overcome these coexisted with the growing, and almost cultlike, adulation of artists, writers, musicians, and their high-society patrons. Wagner's works remained off-limits to Parisian stages for decades, while from the late 1870s onward concert societies led by progressive conductors such as Edouard Colonne and Charles Lamoureux picked up the slack with myriad performances of operatic excerpts. Even when an official endorsement finally occurred in the form of a production of *Lohengrin* at the Opéra in 1891, it was nearly derailed by popular protests fueled by strident rhetoric about the supposedly xenophobic tenor of Wagner's art and ideology. But with the political will now in place to overcome that hurdle, Wagner became the most popular composer at the Opéra in the 1890s, an irrefutable index of pent-up demand.

Before this breakthrough, *wagnéristes* had other options: *pèlerinages à Bayreuth* or other foreign centers where the operas were produced. It was on one such pilgrimage to hear the 1884 Munich *Ring* that the twenty-three year old writer Edouard Dujardin (1861–1949) conceived of the *Revue wagnérienne,* with encouragement from the young English Germanophile—and later proponent of Aryan-German supremacy in the Bayreuth circle—Houston Stewart Chamberlain.[2] Often seen sporting a waistcoat embroidered with Wagnerian musical motives, Dujardin conspicuously played the ultra-refined dandy and esthete. Somewhat paradoxically, he also had a good head for business and managed to secure funding from two wealthy industrialists, Alfred Bovet and Agénor Boissier, to launch the journal in 1885. Around the same time, Dujardin struck up a close friendship with Teodor de Wyzewa (1862–1917), whom he promptly brought on board to work on the *Revue.*[3] Wyzewa, a Polish expatriate from early childhood, came to *wagnérisme* from university studies in philosophy and languages in the provinces, and, according to the later account of his daughter, became the intellectual backbone of the journal.[4] Certainly his command of German, in contrast to Dujardin's halting efforts, proved valuable. Frail and introspective, it is not difficult to imagine him as a kind of *éminence grise* behind his flamboyant friend. Not long after the demise of the *Revue* in 1888 they parted company. Wyzewa moved on to the mainstream press and scholarly writing, and Dujardin to a checkered literary career.

Despite claims for Wyzewa's authority, any single intellectual perspective, or for that matter, purpose, is difficult to discern in the three-year run of the *Revue wagnérienne.* Part chronicle of domestic and international Wagner performances, it also functioned as a vehicle to translate Wagner's writings, a venue for critical essays on his work, and a forum for creative writing and lithography inspired by Wagner. Thus the *Revue* provided varied fare for its readers. The main Wagnerian critics in the daily press—Louis de Fourcaud, Victor Wilder, and Alfred Ernst—lent their pens. In the lead editorial of the first issue, Fourcaud, wary of the nationalist tinderbox, claimed the main purpose of the journal was to explain Wagnerian aesthetics to French composers and listeners so that the lessons might be applied to a rejuvenation of the French operatic tradition. The next year Hans von Wolzogen treaded a more incendiary path: in an essay titled "L'art Aryan" he enjoined acceptance of Wagner's Germanic art because it resonated with a shared Christian ethos and primeval tribal past. (Dujardin would remain committed to racial essentialism and a supporter of Chamberlain's thought until the end of his life, thereby earning opprobrium from the Resistance and an old age spent in relative isolation.) Wyzewa contributed studies of Schopenhauer's thought and, wearing his Russophile hat, the congruence between the spiritual worlds of Wagner and Tolstoy.

Chamberlain provided summaries of articles that had appeared in the *Bayreuther Blätter*. The critics Albert Soubies and Charles Malherbe offered a thumbnail account of Wagner's place in the history of harmony.

Despite such diversity, the legacy of the *Revue wagnérienne* has come to be understood largely as a mouthpiece for the emergent Symbolist movement in literature and the arts.[5] Near its midpoint, the brief run of the journal coincided with the 1886 Symbolist manifesto published in *Le Figaro* by the poet Jean Moréas, an effort to acquaint a wide public with avant-garde trends in literature that was met with some suspicion by the writers themselves, who were instinctually reluctant to be categorized. Symbolism has remained notoriously difficult to conceptualize, being variously taken as celebration of the art of suggestion; evacuation of the author's voice in the free contrapuntal play of phonetics and analogical language; rejection of evocative description as an end in itself; retreat from urban society; cultivation of an interchangeability of the senses; and self-conscious production of difficult literature in which the act of decoding and interpretation is meant to provide spiritual fulfillment. Although Symbolist-influenced contributions were the minority in the *Revue*, writing by Stéphane Mallarmé and Paul Verlaine—obscure figures at the time, but now of course bright stars in the French literary firmament—has helped in retrospect to tip the balance of attention to the journal's Symbolist content. So, too, have lithographs by artists Henri Fantin-Latour and Odilon Redon. Both Dujardin and Wyzewa were known to be sympathizers with, and to a certain extent practitioners of, avant-garde literary trends. And Wagner was almost unanimously cited as an influence by Symbolists, a connection that can be traced back to Baudelaire's famous essay. It also appears that the outright Symbolist pieces, though in the minority, were the ones that attracted the most attention, largely for their impenetrability and moral license. The financial backers Boissier and Bovet raised their eyebrows, and were eventually seconded by the conductor Charles Lamoureux, who had allowed the *Revue* to be sold at his concerts and had initially been a strong supporter. When he condemned the decadent style of the journal in 1887, Dujardin protested that this was a gross exaggeration. But he went on to attack Lamoureux for repeatedly programming unchallenging excerpts in order to assuage middlebrow taste and shore up his box office.[6] The two tracks in French Wagner reception emerged with particular clarity in Dujardin's positioning of *wagnérisme Parisien officiel* against the literary refinement of a *wagnérisme militant*. But musicians and sponsors sided with Lamoureux. The journal's days were numbered. And *wagnérisme militant* soon became outflanked by new challenges that issued from the avant-garde.

The three articles from the *Revue wagnérienne* translated here, by Huysmans, Wyzewa, and Dujardin give ample witness to its Symbolist side. Joris-Karl Huysmans (1848–1907) began his literary career as an art critic and novelist much taken with Emile Zola's naturalism. An aesthetic *volte-face* in the early 1880s crystallized in one of the great blockbusters of the fin de siècle and beacon of decadence for younger Symbolist writers, the novel *A rebours* (*Against the Grain*, 1884). Protagonist Jean Floressas des Esseintes modulates fluidly between the salacious sounds of bordellos and the sacred songs of chant, all the while passing in review many of the most prominent French artists and writers of his time. His house brims with rich fabrics and thick carpets, a *paradis artificiel* hermetically sealed from the quotidian so as to enshrine his self-indulgent synesthesic experiences and fantasies of the macabre. As a stimulus to reflect on the idea of a *paradis artificiel,* Huysmans could not have improved upon the Venusberg, and his gloss on the *Tannhäuser* Overture included here reads like a page out of *A rebours.* Synesthesic images communicate the sensory overload, the huge cymbals of "blinding purples and sumptuous golds" followed by "adorably blue and airily pink sounds." For Baudelaire in his famous essay, it had been "the ardor and whiteness" of the *Lohengrin* Prelude; for des Esseintes a bizarre mouth organ where the tastes of various fine liqueurs were activated by stops labeled flute, horn, and *voix céleste.* Somewhere in Wagner's *Gesamtkunstwerk* theory lay support for such analogical thinking, as claims for a unified artistic vision gave rise to ready erasures of sensory boundaries. The Huysmans Venus is a formidable creature, and a measure of the fin-de-siècle *femme fatale* is readily seen in a comparison with Baudelaire's description of the same music. Baudelaire's "the true, the terrible, the universal Venus" who incites "furious palpitations of the heart and all the senses" and "the entire dictionary of onomatopoeia attached to love"[7] becomes for Huysmans the "image of the irresistible and magnificent She-Satan" and the huntress who crushes her victims "under the force of enervating flowers . . . Sodimita Libido." Now, it is not entirely clear why Tannhäuser should quake before the lust of the sodomite in Wagner's scene, but the passage does seem redolent of des Esseintes' gender-bending infatuation with the acrobat Miss Urania, whom with repeated viewing he comes to think of as a man, all the while imagining himself feminized. In bed, however, Miss Urania proves decidedly lackluster, and after his seduction of her des Esseintes hastens to his one homosexual affair in the novel. Dujardin claimed that Huysmans understood little of music and jotted much of his text in the program during the concert at which he heard the *Tannhäuser* Overture.[8] It had little to do with Wagner, he said, but was worth a smile anyway on account of its extravagance. Except that it was precisely this kind of contribution that assumed inordinate prominence in the eyes of the journal's supporters—and detractors.

Wyzewa begins his report on the Salon of 1885 in "Wagnerian Painting" with a plea for the union of the arts as tied to a fundamental life force. In a more extended Schopenhauer-tinged disquisition on the salon of the following year in the *Revue*, he posited the primacy of inchoate sensations that blended in "a confused whirl of colors, sounds, and thoughts" to produce "the life of the soul."[9] Concomitantly, he attacked descriptive academic painting, just as in an earlier issue he had taken to task the program music of Camille Saint-Saëns for being *merely* descriptive.[10] That Wagner also wrote copious amounts of descriptive music could not be denied, but entwined as it was with the requirements of the *Gesamtkunstwerk*, it existed on a higher plane. What emerges with particular clarity in Wyzewa's writing is his folding of synesthesia into an impulse toward greater abstraction at the behest of greater emotional truth. The painter Gustave Moreau (also much praised in *A rebours*) is a "symphonist of refined emotions." James Whistler paints a "symphony of refined emotions," with Wyzewa perhaps recalling here the British-American painter's extensive use of musical terms in his previous titles (for example, the *Symphony in White* portrait series). In short, musical metaphors serve the cause of painting that does not care about "real forms" and combines "contours and nuances in pure fantasy." It was a mere five years later that Maurice Denis would publish his famous rallying cry for avant-garde artists: "Remember that a painting—before existing as a battlefield horse, a nude woman, or any sort of anecdote—is essentially a flat surface covered with colors and assembled into a certain order."[11] Denis did not mean to do away with representation altogether, and certainly neither did Fantin-Latour, whose lithographs of Wagnerian subjects Wyzewa singles out for their emotional resonance. Indeed, the work on which he lavishes the most attention, Fantin-Latour's oil painting *Autour du piano* (which Wyzewa calls *Homage to the Musician*; see Figure 2) is less noteworthy for its technical audacity (*pace* Wyzewa) than as an icon of French Wagnerism because of its size and depiction of the wide professional reach of enthusiasm for his music. The composer Chabrier sits at the piano surrounded by the likes of Vincent d'Indy, translator Camille Benoît, critics Adolphe Jullien and Amédée Pigeon, civil servant Edmond Maître, and patron and judge Antoine Lascoux. For all the brouhaha around the symbolist sympathies of the *Revue*, none of these figures was strongly associated with that movement.

Nevertheless, Wyzewa also draws an explicit connection between greater freedom in painting and more liberal approaches to poetry that were one of the hallmarks of Symbolism, "neglecting the conventional meanings of words" to evoke the "intense life of emotion."

Free verse and prose poetry sometimes (though not necessarily) formed a corollary to the liberation of diction. Syntactical discontinuity might challenge coherent narrative. In the dying days of the *Revue wagnérienne*, Edouard Dujardin marshaled discontinuity for particularly striking effect by inventing a *monologue intérieur* for his novel *Les lauriers sont coupés* (1888), a major influence on James Joyce's later stream-of-consciousness technique. Whereas the syntax of his short sentences in the novel is perfectly direct and unambiguous, "impulses of the soul" (as Wyzewa might put it) produce a chain of disparate thoughts and impressions.[12] Dujardin later compared this to perceived musical discontinuities in Wagnerian leitmotivic technique caused by their semantic role in response to different images in the text.[13] His "Amfortas: Paraphrase Moderne," included here, seems to occupy an interstice between prose poem and *monologue intérieur*, or perhaps a kind of bridge to the latter that extends right out of a specific Wagnerian passage, Amfortas's great monologue in the first act of *Parsifal*. The syntax is much more convoluted than in *Les lauriers sont coupés*, but common ground between them lies in the breathless succession of images and jagged course of the narrative shaped by a strong identification with the hysteria of Wagner's character. Perhaps the most Wagnerian aspect of Dujardin's piece is its play on memory. A German-language preface unfolds a succession of verbal fragments from the episode, evanescent sparks from a past experience in the theater. The French text gets spun around these as the speaker imagines himself transplanted into the scene, and indeed comes to assume Amfortas's subject position. "The flash of a diabolical kiss" hearkens back to Huysmans' satanic Venus, one of the many verbal details in Dujardin's paraphrase that stems not from Wagner's verbal text but from the music. The cumulative impact of this "impulse of the soul" is of overbearing psychological torment, almost expressionism *avant l'heure*—to hint at yet another of the many artistic directions spawned by Wagner's art.

J. K. HUYSMANS
The Overture to *Tannhäuser*
Revue wagnérienne (April 1885)
Translated by Brendan King

From a landscape such as nature wouldn't know how to create, from a landscape in which the sun pales to the most exquisite and utmost dilution of golden yellow, from a sublime landscape in which, under a sickly luminous sky, the crystallized whiteness of mountaintops opalesce above bluish valleys; from a landscape inaccessible to painters because it is composed solely of visual chimeras, of the silent shimmering and humid throbbing of the air, a chant ascends, a chant singularly majestic, an august canticle springing from the souls of tired pilgrims advancing in a group.[14]

And this chant, with none of that female effusiveness, none of those wheedling prayers trying to obtain through the perilous phonyness of modern worship that encounter with God reserved for the few, swells with that certitude of pardon and a conviction of redemption that was borne in upon the humble souls of the Middle Ages. Reverential and proud, manly and honest, it tells of the appalling fatigue of the sinner who has descended to the depths of his conscience, the unfailing disgust of the spiritual seer confronting the iniquities and accumulated errors in these strongholds, and it also affirms, after a profession of faith in the redemption, the super-human happiness of a new life, the inexpressible gladness of a reborn heart enlightened, as at Mount Thabor, by the rays of a mystic Superessence.

Then this chant grows weaker and little by little fades away; the pilgrims fan out, the sky darkens, the luminous light of day grows dim and shortly afterward the orchestra floods this authentic and unreal scene with crepus-cular gleams. It is a dissipation of colors, a fine spray of nuances, a crystalline haze of sounds that expire with the last echo of the canticle fading in the distance; and night falls on this immaterial nature, now withdrawn into itself in uneasy anticipation, created by the genius of man.

Then a cloud, irradiated with the colors of a rare flora, the expiring purples, the death-agony pinks and the moribund whites of the anemone, disperses, scattering fleecy vapors, whose ascending shades grow darker, exhaling unknown perfumes in which are mixed the biblical scent of myrrh and the voluptuously complex perfumes of modern essences.

Suddenly, in the middle of this musical scene, in this fluid and fantas-tical scene, the orchestra bursts out, portraying the advancing Tannhäuser in a few decisive traits, sketching him from head to foot with the outline of a heraldic melody: and the darkness is shot through with gleams; spi-rals of clouds take on the arched forms of haunches and palpitate with the pneumatic swelling of breasts; the blue avalanches of the heavens throng with naked forms; screams of desire, cries of lust, impulses of yearning for a carnal Beyond leap from the orchestra, and above the undulating espalier of fainting, swooning nymphs, Venus rises, but no longer the antique Venus, the old Aphrodite, whose impeccable contours inspired lechery in gods and men during the lustful festivals of paganism, but a more profound, more terrifying Venus, a Christian Venus, if the sin against nature of coupling these two words were possible!

Indeed, this is not the unfading Beauty appointed only to earthly joys, to artistic and sensual excitations as the salacious sculptures of Greece understood it; this is the incarnation of the spirit of Evil, an effigy of omnipo-tent Lust, an image of the irresistible and magnificent She-Satan who is unceasingly on the lookout for Christian souls, at whom she aims her delight-ful and malevolent weapons.

Such has Wagner created her, this Venus, an emblem of the physical nature of the individual, an allegory of Evil struggling against Good, a symbol of our internal hell opposed to our inner heaven, leading us back in a bound through the centuries, to the impenetrable grandeur of the symbolic poem by Prudentius, that living Tannhäuser who, after years dedicated to debauchery, tore himself from the arms of the victorious She-Devil to seek refuge in the penitential adoration of the Virgin.

In fact it seems that the Venus of the musician is the descendant of the poet's Luxuria, of that pure huntress who, steeped in perfumes, crushed her victims under the force of enervating flowers; it seems that the Wagnerian Venus attracts and captivates men like the most deadly of Prudentius' deities, her whose name the poet writes with a trembling hand: Sodomita Libido.

But even though the idea of her recalls the allegorical entities of the Middle Ages, she brings an additional spice of modernity, insinuating an intellectual current of refinement into this molten mass of savage delights; and to the naïve canvas of ancient times she adds a kind of provocative excitement, assuring more certainly through this overstimulation of a nervous acuity the ultimate defeat of the hero, who is suddenly initiated into the lascivious cerebral complexities of the worn-out epoch in which we live today.

And the soul of Tannhäuser buckles, his body succumbs. Deluged by ineffable promises and passionate murmurs, he falls, delirious, into the arms of the perverting clouds that embrace him; his melodic personality is obliterated by the triumphal hymn of Evil. Then the tempest of roaring flesh, the lightning flashes and electric blasts that are rumbling in the orchestra subside; the incomparable clash of those huge cymbals, which seems to be a transposition of blinding purples and sumptuous golds, fades away; and a gentle, deliciously tenuous susurration, an almost divine rustling of adorably blue and airily pink sounds, trembles in the nocturnal ether, which is already beginning to brighten. Then dawn breaks, the hesitant sky begins to whiten, as if painted with the white sounds of the harp, and is tinged with tentative colours which little by little become more definite and resplendent amid a magnificent alleluia, amid the crashing splendor of kettledrums and brass. The sun rises, flaring out fanlike, splitting the thickening line of the horizon, climbs as if from the bottom of a lake whose watery surface seethes with her reflected rays. In the distance, the intercessionary canticle hovers, the faithful canticle of the pilgrims, cleansing the last wounds of a spirit exhausted by this diabolical struggle; and, in an apotheosis of light, in a gloriole of Redemption, Matter and Spirit soar upward, Evil and Good are reconciled, Lust and Purity are bound together by the two musical motives that are snaking round each other, blending the rapid, exhausting kisses of the violins, the dazzling and mournful caresses of taut, nervous strings with the calm, majestic chorus that unfurls itself, with that mediatory melody, that canticle of the now kneeling soul celebrating its final immersion, its unshakable constancy in the bosom of God.

And, trembling and enraptured, you come out of the vulgar hall where the miracle of this essential music has been performed, carrying with you the indelible memory of this overture to *Tannhäuser*, this prodigious and initial summary of the overwhelming grandeur of its three acts.

TEODOR DE WYZEWA
Wagnerian Painting: The Salon of 1885
Revue wagnérienne (June 1885)
Translated by Charlotte Mandell

Richard Wagner's work, beyond its incomparable worth as a philosophical Revelation, still has, for us, the force—clear and precious—of an aesthetic doctrine.[15] It signifies the natural, necessary alliance of the three forms of Art—plastic, literary, musical—in the communion of a single, unique aim: to create life, to incite our souls to create life.

Thus Wagnerists should not shut themselves up in the narrow confines of pure music; they should study all works, in all the arts; and for this study, again, the Master provides them with a sure criterion, giving Wagnerian Painting, as well as Poetry and Music, this aim: the creation of life.

But what, in the vast field of life, is the special share that Painting should manifest? Should it give us only simple sensations of material bodies, through an exact representation of their forms? Or should it rather give us finer, more intimate emotions, and so to speak, portray the soul, as well as bodies? It can and must, certainly, do both these things. Just as the writer can, by the single method of the stable words of a language, immediately communicate to us the succession of his thoughts—and that in Prose or even in Poetry— almost neglecting the conventional meaning of words, using just the ordering of rhythms and sounds, and evoke in us, more exactly, the intense life of emotion; so, too, can painters, solely by the method of plastic procedures, translate, immediately, their vision of the objective world—or else, too, neglecting, almost, the usual meaning of figures, and by using only the ordering of lines and colors, evoke in us real and precise emotions that no poetry, no music, could express. There are two kinds of painting: one, immediate, the so-called realist painting, giving the exact image of things, as seen by the special vision of the painter; the other, mediate, like a Poetry of painting, not caring about real forms, but combining contours and nuances in pure fantasy, producing for our souls not the direct vision of things, but—a consequence of secular associations between images and feelings—a world of living, blissful emotion; there are two kinds of painting both equally legitimate and sacred, the different forms of a superior Realism, both of which the Wagnerist finds along the way outlined in Art by the revered Master.

A new pastel by Monsieur Degas, the prodigious ruler of plastic life; a painting by Monsieur G. Moreau, the symphonist of refined emotions, or some terrifying drawing by Monsieur Redon, or that exhibition of Old Masters opened recently at the Louvre, are all Wagnerian deeds; but not, alas, that yearly Market of Paintings, which is a Painting Salon the way wigmakers' or bootmakers' shops are Coiffure or Shoe Salons. This is because Wagnerism is, above all, the exclusion of Beckmesserisms, of academic exercises, of works of art made without the least divine hunger for speculative Creation. Thus we have sought in vain this year, among the miles of painted canvas, a few serious works capable of serving as examples for an exposition of Wagnerian theory. We were barely able, aside from the admirable Wagnerian master Fantin-Latour, to contemplate two such things—splendid, it is true: a symphony in somber colors (the catalog says: a Portrait), by Whistler; and a wonderful scene from daily life, young girls playing in a courtyard, by Bartholomé. Then, nothing aside from the recurring wretchedness of compromises, academicisms, dishonest visions.

Fantin-Latour consoled us for this wretchedness: he, first of all, is a conscious Wagnerist and knows, admires, celebrates the Master. But above all, his is the utter glory that he alone today resolutely understands the twofold task possible for the painter: he has, in his great paintings, each of which shows a new victory, reproduced, more precisely than anyone else and more completely, the objective, real, total life of forms: and he has, in lovely drawings, written the poem of plastic emotion, communicating to our souls emotions that are strangely sweet and warm, through a combination of lines and colors.

In this Exhibition, again, he has given us two remarkable models of these two arts. First of all, there is a lithograph: *The Rhine Maidens*, I think. From Wagner he has taken as subject the excited mockery of the river nymphs as Siegfried journeys off, toward his Death. But what does it matter here— the subject, the exactitude of location, the resemblance of this painting to the Bayreuth staging? Monsieur Fantin-Latour wanted to give us, in plastic language, the emotion of the scene, and he has given it to us. These pale maidens with their contours curving softly in light, and this darkened horizon, where the hero advances, sounding his horn: it all conveys a gaiety in which something like fear lurks; Monsieur Fantin has rendered the profound meaning of the scene, and of this entire drama, the GÖTTERDÄMMERUNG, where the young Siegfried, along with the joy of his strength, conveys to us something too much like the anguish of the cruel deed so close.

And, near this adorable fantasy, what a superb work of real, powerful life: the *Homage to the Musician*! In a room where air grows feeble, around a piano, piously stand six men. Real and alive is the room, real, alive, these

Figure 1. Henri Fantin-Latour, *Siegfried and the Rhine Maidens* (Salon of 1885), lithograph, 46.5 x 37.5 cm (Ottawa, National Gallery of Canada).

men, without one line of their faces having been changed; and yet, such is the psychological vision of the Master, that all these men, variously, with different expressions, bear witness to the private emotion given to all of them by the extraordinary music they hear. By design, to achieve an exact rendering, M. Fantin has turned these faces toward him; understanding, again, how stupid this so-called realism is, which forces the painter to show men in their habitual poses, and forces them to perceive, thus, inexactly, their features, deformed by the necessity of feigning a false task, inevitably.

A theoretician and an artist, and profoundly sincere, of an incomparable artistic honesty: such is the painter these two works have surprisingly revealed to us. It is not that they are perfect already; at least, they make painters see the only way that is suitable to them, the Wagnerian way of frankness, of fidelity to theories, of a continuous effort to feel life, and to express it. They are thus for everyone, a teaching, and for the rare initiates into Art, a joy; and, if he had known them, Richard Wagner, our divine Master, would have found them an homage worthy of his great soul.

Figure 2. Henri Fantin-Latour, *Around the Piano* (or *Homage to the Musician,* Salon of 1885), oil on canvas, 63 x 87 cm (Paris, Musée du Jeu de Paume).

EDOUARD DUJARDIN
Amfortas
A Modern Paraphrase
Revue wagnérienne (December 1885)
Translated by Charlotte Mandell

PROGRAM

The Temple of the Holy Grail; choir of knights: "*der Labung darf er nahn
. . .* "; choir of young men: "*den sündigen Welten . . .* "; choir of children:
"*die Glaube lebt . . .* " — Entrance of Amfortas; — Amfortas recumbent.
    Titurel; — Amfortas: "*Wehe! Wehe mir! . . .*" — Titurel.
    Amfortas: "*Nein! . . .*" — "*wehvolles Erbe . . .*" — "*nach ihm . . .*" — "*die Stunde
naht . . .*" — "*des eignen sündigen Blutes Gewell . . .*" — "*der dort dem Erlöser . . .*"
— "*und aus der nun mir . . .*" — "*aus der Sehnen's Quelle, das ach! keine Büssung
je mir stellt!...*" — "*Erbarmen! . . . dass heilig ich sterbe.*"

(Parsifal, I, 3)[16]

The church is lofty and filled with light; groups of people praying wan-
der here and there; people kneeling form indistinct rows of bowed heads;
the confused murmuring of litanies fades into grave silences. And, near
the huge, massive pillars, there are men, male voices, souls praising,
waiting for the divine Coming: "Let us come toward God! . . ." the voices
of young men chime in, moved by life, and who are not so much adoring, alas! as lamenting to the son of the Woman: "For this sinful world
Christ has given his body . . ." and, from time to time, voices come down
from invisible summits, childlike and angelic, virginal: "Faith lives, the Spirit
soars . . ." so pious songs of glorification and lamentation are intermingled
with heavenly virginities. And among the songs are grave silences, solemn
appeals to the Most Holy in the silences of human voices . . . silences and
songs intermingle, pious murmurings, under the high arches of the lumi-
nously expansive church.
    He, the Wounded, is motionless on his couch, prostrate, while there
flows around him a crowd of faithful; he remains still, and his body leans
back, his hands hang at his sides, his head is thrown back, and his face,
face-to-face with the heaven of the dome, his eyes staring into the upper
air; and his lips, half-opened by his feeble breath, preserve the rigid tor-
por of exhaustion . . .
    In the vast naves swarms the human crowd . . . Soar up, sounds of
prayers, wings of devout confessions! . . . the voices that thunder and the
silences that powerfully resound, the voices and silences in the soul that hears

them are murmurs. — Let us come to God! . . . sinful world! . . . Faith lives, the Spirit soars! . . . Hymns that go on and on, scattering in the soul of one gripped by the deathly anguish of the coming crucifixion; in his soul he hears them murmuring; and the words of these silences, as well as of these songs, drone all around his soul. Sing, voices! He remains trapped in perception of you; time is blurred, space is misted over in a chaos of vegetation; and he dreams of he knows not what pieties, what sufferings; he dreams obscurely of pious practices and penances; a mental sleep is in the rigidity of flesh; the soul is drowsy; it hears like one who sleeps; and there is, in that soul, a very distant echo of the circumfusing canticles mixed with silences, canticles intermingled, pious, lamenting, and virginal.

— Fulfill the Office, awaken, live, act — he must! The time has come to officiate, and to live: banish sleep! and speak the imperious and melancholic word that commands action. With a sudden start, the Wounded trembles; his senses return to him; he half lifts himself, and, on his couch, he sounds disturbed, with vague thoughts, vague gestures: "Ah! Ah me! . . ." the memory comes back, alas! the memory of sufferings, and of anguishes, and of lamentations, and of misdeeds, as well as of punishments, and of cries of Desire: "O Christ, your lamentation already resounds in me . . . No! let me sleep away my oblivion, my lethargic doze of pain: Do not awaken the Wounded! Oh! let me die! . . ." He must awaken, live: and the Holy One calls him, again, gravely, to his deed: "The Deed! Carry out the Deed! . . ." so he lives; he lives, and he rises, in a rage of tormenting thought.

Infernal Lust, laughter of the carnal Curse, fury of female Concupiscence: suddenly there shines a lustful eye, a swooning glimpse of throat, the flash of a diabolical kiss — while he shouts: "No!" and this evocation of laughing and concupiscent lust is the eternal motif that rises up from ancient Herodias, from Gundryggia, and from the Unnamed, Pre-Devil, the Rose of Hell, O original Downfall, Kundry!

It is sin — For he has sinned against the Grace of the Lord; the chosen one of the pure has become the only sinner among the pure: O punishment from the offended rich in Grace . . .

. . . Holy of Holies, oh memory of the Holy! Solemnly he rose in the soul, the Holy One today outraged! O memory of the salvation of benediction! memory of the Divine! Aspiration that from the very bottom of the soul steams toward exalted penances, penances to the lamenting Lord so wretchedly insulted! . . .

Song of the Most Holy, sing! Shine, light of the Pure! Open wide, veil of Mystery! Words, speak, all, in welcoming the Lord who comes! Open up, sad sky, so the rite of the eternal Sacrifice may be renewed! — here is the body of bread, here is the blood of drink; the mystic vase will shine, here is the food; God's blood, here is the wine; take, take, take; sinners, here is the wine and the bread; approach, most melancholy; for the wine will flow in your blood, the bread will become your flesh, and the sacred blood will flow from your heart . . .

The sacred blood flows, O Wounded, from his heart; the blood of the Suffering One flows in his veins; and it is his own blood, which boils up, and flows, terrifyingly! — once there was a perverse charm, a spell-like attraction, a pagan enchantment; once, a terribly beautiful lust; now this memory haunts him; now he believes the promise of the Master, he moans under Concupiscence, hurls infinite lamentations, always vibrating, from the Crucified who throbs in his flesh. For the sinful world Christ suffered, because he felt yearning pity for our Yearning . . . O pity of the Lord, see your agonizing son, throbbing, crucified: he was the Holy, and the Pure, and the Good; he sang your name, he who is crying today: pleasant he was to you, this outcast; he was your guard, your servant, your strength, your splendor, your joy, he who almost blasphemes, and who is lost, driven mad by sensual memories, and who whirls in the madness of his flesh, and curses himself, knowing your speech no longer . . . your divine speech under the effort of desires turns strange, it is altered, it is corrupted, now it becomes frighteningly other, and it turns into magical sounds: the prayer to God becomes a suggestion of hell: harsh, the charm brings back the Evil One; and it is she . . . O thought always quick with guilty delights, unforgettable, unforgettable thought! The Wounded sees again the damnable visions, and in his jaded eyes lewd things pass by: Sinning eyes! Sinning senses! Sinning sensations! He feels the great gardens full of smoking fragrances and hot colors; the softness of warmth was soft, when before his body she rose up, the animal female, mad with her body . . . she had that laughter and that voice, yes, that gaze that so restlessly caressed him, those lips, yes, so trembling on him, that hair cascading over him, yes, those flattering curls, and around his neck those arms, so tender those cheeks, so new that mouth that, in the communion of all sufferings, kissed away the salvation of his soul . . . monstrous kiss! A woman was there, shameless flowering of sensualities, a woman that he, the chaste one, had.

Pity, Lord! On illusory delight, pity! Lord! On joys, and on absolutely desirable joys, pity! Pity, for in this kiss I have known all that my flesh irrevocably thirsts for! — and I implore the grace of the Merciful One, — his unique grace on my misery, yes, redemption, peace, oblivion, death.

O suffering of Desire, of double Desire, the Mystical and the Carnal, suffering of the mysterious aspirations of the Angel and the Beast, o suffering of Concupiscence and Religion, carnal and mystical man, Amfortas, thus you lament, and we, with you, we live the great endless Desire of multiple lives.

NOTES

1. Charles Baudelaire, "Richard Wagner et *Tannhäuser* à Paris" (1861), in *Oeuvres completes*, ed. Claude Pichois (Paris, 1976), 2:784. For a translation of Baudelaire's essay, see Charles Baudelaire, *The Painter of Modern Life and Other Essays*, trans. and ed. Jonathan Mayne (London, 1964; repr. New York, 1986), 111–46.

2. Dujardin gives an account in "La revue wagnérienne," *La revue musicale* 4/11 (1923): 141–60.

3. For an account of their meeting, see Paul Delsemme, *Teodor de Wyzewa et le cosmopolitisme littéraire en France à l'époque du symbolisme* (Bruxelles, 1967), 20–21.

4. See Isabelle de Wyzewa, *La revue wagnérienne: Essai sur l'interprétation esthétique de Wagner en France* (Paris, 1934).

5. For further context, see Pamela A. Genova, *Symbolist Journals: A Culture of Correspondence* (Aldershot, 2002), 266–90.

6. Dujardin vented his side in "Question wagnérienne et question personnelle," *Revue wagnérienne* 3/5 (15 June 1887): 129–34.

7. Baudelaire, "Richard Wagner," 2:794.

8. Dujardin, "La revue wagnérienne," 151–52.

9. Teodor de Wyzewa, "Notes sur la peinture wagnérienne et le salon de 1886," *Revue wagnérienne* 2/4 (8 May 1886): 100–13.

10. Teodor de Wyzewa, "La musique descriptive," *Revue wagnérienne* 1/3 (8 April 1885): 74–77.

11. Quoted in Jean-Paul Bouillon, *Maurice Denis* (Geneva, 1993), 20.

12. Edouard Dujardin, *Le monologue intérieur*, trans. Anthony Suter (London, 1991), 111.

13. Ibid., 110–11.

14. Huysmans' article appeared in the *Revue wagnérienne* 1/3 (8 April 1885): 59–62. The translation given here is taken from *Parisian Sketches* (Sawtry, Cambridgeshire, U.K., 2004), 155–59.

15. Wyzewa's article appeared in the *Revue wagnérienne* 1/5 (8 June 1885): 154–56.

16. Dujardin's article appeared in the *Revue wagnérienne* 1/11 (8 December 1885): 310–13.

PART V

THE BAYREUTH ERA

Press Releases from the Bayreuth Festival, 1876:

An Early Attempt at Spin Control

J. ZIMMERMANN

INTRODUCED, TRANSLATED, AND ANNOTATED

BY NICHOLAS VAZSONYI

As final preparations for the first launch of the Bayreuth festival got under way, J. Zimmermann, editor of the local paper, the *Bayreuther Tageblatt*, began a series of what ended up as twenty-three press releases to report on the events. Every fourteen days between May and August 1876, these articles, under the heading "Bayreuther autographische Korrespondenz," were distributed by the festival board to approximately 180 press outlets throughout Germany.[1] The releases covered a wide variety of topics: the arrival of the performers, preparations by the town for the anticipated massive influx of visitors, the progress of the final rehearsals, listings of the dignitaries in attendance, and the various honors they bestowed on the performers. The press releases were capped by a description of the performances and an account of the audience response. Approximately halfway through the series, as the full stage rehearsals began, the musician and critic Heinrich Porges, an integral member of Wagner's rehearsal team, also began contributing to the reports, offering authoritatively written "behind-the-scenes" glimpses of the coming attractions.

It is difficult to determine the success of this venture. The *Neue Zeitschrift für Musik* published the Korrespondenz in its entirety, without additional commentary, as "Extra Beilagen" (special supplements) to their regular issues, as did the *Musikalisches Wochenblatt*— both journals based in Leipzig and decidedly in the pro-Wagner camp.[2] Some newspapers and journals ignored the press releases completely, while others published extracts both with and without their own commentary. Today, such a mixed reaction would be normal, but back in 1876 there was real novelty in this particular effort at public relations. As Susanna Großmann-Vendrey points out, Meyerbeer had already used the press effectively to promote his works and

391

influence public opinion prior to the premieres of his operas. Nevertheless, this effort by Zimmermann and Porges was different in several respects. First, the regularity and the consistency of the press releases, stretching over a four-month period, was unprecedented. Second, in addition to the basic "reporting" of events, both Zimmermann and Porges—from their different vantage points as "local correspondent" and "expert witness"— amplified their reports by commenting tirelessly on the historic significance of Wagner's work and the event itself. This was a rather bold attempt at a public relations technique which in our own time has come to be called "spin control," defined as the portrayal of an event or situation heavily biased in one's own favor. Public relations (PR) is a generic term, also of more recent vintage, which refers to the attempt by individuals, companies, or other groups to present a carefully crafted image or convey a favorable message to a larger public, usually relying on a creative presentation of the facts. "Spin" constitutes an intensified form of this process, usually limited to the news media and most often associated with politics, with an emphasis on aggressive and highly manipulative rhetorical tactics designed to promote an agenda and sway opinion. The goal of spin is to influence public discourse by supplying the vocabulary and the phraseology used in the discussion.

It is a testament to the breathtaking modernity of the entire Bayreuth venture that Zimmermann and Porges engaged in techniques that can best be described using a vocabulary developed much later. As with any PR campaign, they ignore the real organizational problems associated with the first festival and actively deny negative "rumors" circulating in the German-speaking press. In addition, they engage in spin by making grandiose claims that Wagner's *Ring* represents the rebirth of Greek tragedy, likening its greatness to Aeschylus and Shakespeare, and declaring the Bayreuth festival to be an event of German national significance. In this respect the Bayreuther autographische Korrespondenz transcends previous promotional efforts by the likes of Meyerbeer, Liszt, Paganini, and other artistic figures of the nineteenth century with a knack for publicity.

It is unclear just how much Wagner knew about, or had a hand in, this initiative. There is no mention of it in his published letters, nor in any of his numerous published writings and declarations accompanying the launch of the festival, nor does Cosima mention them in her diaries. However, the Korrespondenz borrows heavily from Wagner's own stylization of his work as the world-historical culmination of German musical-cultural development and as an antidote to the ills of modernity, modeled on an idealized vision of ancient Greece. Moreover, Wagner, fully aware of the "importance for the future" of any chronicle of the festival's first days, had written to Porges as early as 1872 asking him to take "intimate" notes during the rehearsals of the *Ring* in order "to create a fixed tradition" of its per-formance.[3] Thus, Porges's insider look at the rehearsals for the Bayreuther autographische Korrespondenz was fully authorized, so that the effort can legitimately be described as an in-house media and public relations under-taking and a forerunner of the *Bayreuther Blätter*, founded in 1878 with Hans von Wolzogen as editor and with Wagner's active participation.

The tactic of using the available media to disseminate a carefully crafted message was one Wagner had already begun to use in the 1840s. As such, the Korrespondenz is just one—arguably significant, though under-reported—aspect of the prescient, comprehensive, and innovative project of self-promotion that accompanied Wagner's creative work, a project I study elsewhere in greater detail.[4]

Wagner made no secret of his aim to get rich and famous.[5] In part to secure this goal (in part to escape creditors), he had journeyed to Paris in 1839 intending to break into the world's leading operatic scene. His fail-ure to do so has been well documented, in the first place by Wagner himself. In one of the most amazing personal transformations, Wagner made his self-styled inability to succeed within the profit-centered opera establishment the leading hallmark of the persona he began to construct as a response. This response was a comprehensive struggle—creative, rhetorical, theo-retical, and ideological—to establish for himself a self-contained niche in the opera market that he alone would control. His exclusion from the opera world became the basis of his claim to aesthetic exclusivity. Starting in 1840, he appropriated an initially German line of argumentation, already in exis-tence since the late eighteenth century, which critiqued modernity in general and specifically the commercialized artworld, manifested first and fore-most in the book trade. Thinkers and writers like Karl Phillip Moritz and Friedrich Schiller argued for an artwork created not in the hope of profit but for purely aesthetic reasons—an early articulation of the "l'art pour l'art" movement. "True" art was deemed an expression of quasi-religious significance, and its creator a divinely inspired genius. Wagner fused this with an increasingly assertive self-identification with Germanness, a national-ist identity he rediscovered even though, or perhaps especially because, he was still in Paris. These two basic components—Germanness and an anti-modern notion of pure art—became the foundation of the public per-sona he began to form during this early period.

Wagner's activities go well beyond the types of "self-fashioning" already common in his day. His theoretical works written in the early 1850s were as much an effort to articulate a coherent aesthetic agenda as they were a means to separate himself and his works from the mainstream. He even wrote that he was no longer writing "operas."[6] So successful was his effort that today, over a century later, we use a distinctive vocabulary to identify and describe his works: music drama, *Gesamtkunstwerk*, leitmotif, *Festspiel*. These terms—some introduced by Wagner, some not—refer in the first place to his own work. I argue that Wagner did nothing less than create a "brand," well before branding became standard among commercial companies in the later nineteenth century.

The crowning achievement of this forty-year effort was the construction of a theater exclusively dedicated to his artwork. "Wagner invented the modern music festival,"[7] Frederick Spotts quite rightly claims, even though the music festival as an institution predates Bayreuth by a century.[8] But more than just the first modern music festival, Bayreuth has become something like a company town, synonymous with the Wagner name, and hub of a complex "institutional network," which comprises a production plant (*Festspielhaus*), Wagner's home base of operations (Wahnfried), and the headquarters of the Wagner Society with its 136 chapters located in every continent except the Antarctic.[9] Wagner's effort to separate himself from the world of commerce, to create "genuine" works of art, has resulted in an industry nevertheless.

Though he protested vehemently against accusations of commercialization in his own lifetime, Wagner never hesitated to publicize his activities and encouraged others to do so. One example is Wagner's 1873 letter to Emil Heckel (founder of the original Wagner Society in Mannheim) in which he asks his most "energetic" friend to put together promotional materials informing the general public about the planned world premiere of the complete *Ring* cycle at the first Bayreuth festival. Once Wagner had approved the text, Heckel was then to "bring the matter to the public, and indeed with awesome publicity, so that no one can say 'I haven't heard anything about it.'"[10] In this sense, the Bayreuther autographische Korrespondenz was integral to Wagner's own initiative and continued a project that, by 1876, had been under way for over three decades.

The Korrespondenz also broke new ground as an in-house media outlet that tried to shape the image of an event, indeed to *create* an event, before it took place.[11] As a public gesture it also served to project the unique and exclusive nature of the Bayreuth festival, fashioning it as an event that represented and thus belonged to the German nation.[12] This image of Bayreuth has remained constant since its inception, and is a testament to the PR talents of Wagner, his team, and the consortium that continues to maintain a media presence. (Given this, it is short-sighted of Großmann-Vendrey to describe the Bayreuther autographische Korrespondenz as a PR "disaster.")

The following is a sampling of the releases. Since Heinrich Porges eventually published his own much more detailed essays on the rehearsals, serialized in the *Bayreuther Blätter* between 1880 and 1896,[13] the sampling here is limited to those written by J. Zimmermann.[14] All endnotes are mine.

The releases presented here include the first and last notices that frame the project, as well as a brief but characteristic one from the middle, chronicling the arrival of Wagner's patron, King Ludwig II of Bavaria. Ludwig is a recurring motif in the releases, representing as he does not only royal patronage but also a stamp of approval with both regional and national significance. It is also interesting to note in the first release how Bayreuth is presented as a tourist destination. This as yet underresearched aspect of the Bayreuth festival was a factor from the start and included the marketing of the town, the composer, and the work in the form of souvenirs, guest services, noteworthy sights, not to mention the "unique," "genuine," and "authentic" experience itself.

J. ZIMMERMANN
Richard Wagner's Stage Festival in Bayreuth

I
(2 June 1876)

The moment draws ever closer for the performance of Richard Wagner's *Ring of the Nibelung* in our "forgotten town"—as the Frenchman Victor Tissot calls it. Until recently, even friends of the poet-composer doubted the possibility of a performance. And, indeed, there were so many difficulties to overcome that it required Richard Wagner's unshakable faith in his own genius, and his steadfast willpower during the most uncertain and critical periods, to persevere until the goal was reached. And now that— thanks to the tireless activities of the Master and his friends—the goal soon approaches, now that the dates of the performance are set,* the ideological struggle has been unleashed: friends cheer the Master on and wish him well, that he may soon achieve his ideal to give German drama a vital and living basis, infinitely enriched through its union with music's unquenchable depths. Meanwhile, enemies compare this with the appearance of a meteor in the artistic firmament, not destined to stay illuminated for long. But everyone can agree that before us lies an event of the greatest significance for the arts. This is already clear from the interest that has been shown in the work from the loftiest circles all the way down to the average people. Registrations for the performances have been pouring in at a rate one could hardly have hoped for. The German Emperor (Kaiser)

---

* As is well known, the dress rehearsals will take place on August 6th, 7th, 8th, and 9th; the first performance on August 13th, 14th, 15th, and 16th; the second on August 20th, 21st, 22nd, and 23rd; the third on August 27th, 28th, 29th, and 30th.

and King Ludwig II of Bavaria, the magnanimous patron of the arts and Wagner's benefactor, have already officially announced their attendance. Twelve princes from home and abroad, whose names will be published later, have also made known that they will attend. The total number of visitors who will come here during the three months of the festival has already been estimated with reasonable certainty at 10,000. Given these numbers, why did Wagner select the tiny town of Bayreuth for the performance of his work? In his *Reise durch Bayern* (Journey through Bavaria), the Frenchman Victor Tissot criticizes the Master (even though he doesn't know him), he belittles and derides Bayreuth (without ever having seen it), and offers the cursory answer: "Because he didn't want to go to Munich." But there would still have been Berlin, Vienna, Stuttgart, Dresden, etc. The reason for selecting Bayreuth as the festival location is a different one. First of all, Wagner wanted to be in Bavaria. In gratitude to the magnanimous Prince and art connoisseur from the House of Wittelsbach, so intimately bound to the history of art, it was clear that Bavaria should have the honor of the first performance. Moreover, the Master—who has a loftier goal than just a one-time performance—wanted to erect his edifice of the future and have his work performed on *neutral* ground, where neither his supporters nor his enemies would be present in decisive numbers. He is motivated by the thought that here, on neutral ground, he would erect a permanent site for art, and each year have a selection of his works performed, to give the disciples of art an opportunity to gain momentum as they strive toward the ideal. Out of this practical art academy, if I may call it that, the longed-for dream shared by all Germans to create a *German national theater* would become a physical reality, the progeny of that holy union between drama and music that lives in the Master's soul as an ideal.

After this introduction, I now come to my actual topic: a brief description of the festival town Bayreuth, which is so little known elsewhere that a Berlin connoisseur recently dared to say that the one and only flaw of Richard Wagner's new work is that it was being performed in Bayreuth. This *Cicero pro domo* seems to form his judgments only from a bird's-eye perspective, just like the Frenchman Victor Tissot. I would like to offer a corrective to these prejudices.

Bayreuth, the capital of the Bavarian district called Oberfranken or Upper Franconia, lies at the foot of the Fichtelgebirge in an area that is as charming as it is healthy, purified by the air of the nearby mountains. For three generations there has been no plague or epidemic illness, and the town has been spared even sporadic appearances of the Asiatic disease, cholera. Bayreuth has about 20,000 inhabitants and is—for all who have seen it—without question one of those provincial towns that makes a most pleasant impression; it even has something of a metropolitan flair. Level, broad streets, with substantial houses throughout, intermingled with monumental structures give an inviting and agreeable stamp to the place. This exterior also characterizes the inner life of the bustling town, which also has a cozy, friendly charm. The fascinating history of the place is closely connected to that of the Margraves of Brandenburg, reaching back to its documented beginnings in the twelfth century. Bayreuth owes its current appearance to Margrave Christian of Brandenburg (d. 1655), to Georg Wilhelm (d. 1726), especially to the opulent tastes of Friedrich (d. 1763), husband of the Margravine Fredericke Sophie Wilhelmine, the witty sister of Frederick the Great of Prussia.[15] The Bayreuth line died out with Christian (d. 1769), and fell to the Ansbach line. On December 22, 1791, Margrave Alexander turned over the governance and territory to Prussia in exchange for an annual pension. Between 1806 and 1810, it was under French control and, on June 30, 1810, fell to the Crown of Bavaria. Bayreuth, as we have said, owes to the Margraves of Brandenburg its current attractive appearance, the beautification of the surroundings, and the wealth of avenues and amusements which make it a match for any other town under the Crown of Bavaria.

Let us take a look now at the town's sights. First up is Jean Paul's house in the Friedrichstrasse, which is marked with a gold-embossed plaque.[16] Jean Paul passed away here on November 14, 1825. The statue raised by King Ludwig I in honor of the poet—a masterpiece by Schwanthaler[17]— stands in the same street across from the Gymnasium. Devotees of the poet will find Jean Paul's grave, a huge block of granite, at the cemetery adjacent to the Erlanger Gate.

The Old and the New Palaces are both former residences of the Margraves of Brandenburg; the former is now furnished as offices and apartments, the latter belongs to the Bavarian Civil List,[18] and both are extremely interesting in terms of history and architecture. In front of the Old Palace, the Town of Bayreuth erected a statue of Maximilian II of Bavaria in memory of that beloved king. Behind the New Palace, the publicly accessible Palace Gardens stretch out their shady pathways and broad avenues, a beloved recreation spot for residents and visitors.

Among the city's seven churches, the Ordenskirche in the suburb of St. Georgen commands special historical interest. It is called the Knights' Chapel or Ordenskirche because the Knights of the Order "de la sincerité," founded on November 16, 1712, first assembled their chapter here. There are ceiling frescos and the coat of arms of eighty-six Knights of the Order of the Red Eagle from the years 1705 to 1768.

One must also not forget the opera house: a colossal building, completed in 1748 by Babima [recte: Giuseppe Galli-Bibiena][19] under Margrave Friedrich. The interior has three tiers of richly gilded boxes. The stage is the largest of any standing theater: 42 feet deep and 34 feet wide. The portico is supported by four columns and above it are giant stone figures of the muses. . . . [20]

So much, then, by way of a brief description of the major touristic attractions of Bayreuth and its surroundings, bestowed upon the town by its art-loving princes from the house of Brandenburg as well as by its current regent. May all our readers who have read these modestly written descriptions decide for themselves whether the fibbing Frenchman Victor Tissot was justified in calling Bayreuth a "forgotten town."

I will describe the town's major attraction—the Richard Wagner Theater—in the next article. I will also describe in detail what Bayreuth and its residents have been doing to suitably prepare for the arrival of their guests.

XII
(28 July 1876)

The pace of the past week has been brisk. Already during the general rehearsals, a large contingent of devotees and friends of art has arrived. This influx has increased substantially, now that the final dress rehearsals are under way, including the arrival of King Ludwig II of Bavaria. King Ludwig, accompanied by his Crown Equerry Graf Holnstein and his aide-de-camp, arrived here in the greatest secrecy during the night between last Saturday and Sunday. His Majesty ordered his special train to stop on open tracks near the famous Rollwenzelhaus (Jean Paul's favorite place) at 1:00 a.m., and then drove on to the Eremitage Palace (about one hour from the city) in a carriage that had been kept in readiness for him, accompanied by Master Wagner, who had been awaiting the King's arrival. The final dress rehearsal of *Rheingold* was set to commence on Sunday at 7:00 p.m. Thousands of residents of the festively adorned city, as well as visitors and local peasants, were gathered shortly before the departure to the theater to see the King. Only a few had the chance, however, because His Majesty, riding in a covered coupe, used a remote byway for his drive to the theater and so arrived unexpectedly. Master Wagner was seated beside the King in the coupe. The *Rheingold* dress rehearsal began as soon as the King took his seat in the royal box. The execution of both the musical and scenic elements was magnificent and extremely successful. It hardly needs stating that all the participants were inspired to produce their utmost because of King Ludwig's presence—the benefactor and patron of this massive work, whose royal support is chiefly responsible for the success of the venture. In the course of the rehearsal, which lasted until 9:30, a special lighting of the town was begun. The illuminated church towers and elevated sections of the town offered an indescribably beautiful vista upon emerging from the theater. In the low-lying areas of the city, the Palace of His Excellency, Duke Alexander of Württemberg, Richard Wagner's House, the Town Hall, the old opera house, and the Hospital Church are all marked by brilliant illumination. In the streets where a packed and highly spirited—though orderly—crowd awaited the King's return from the theater, it was almost like daylight. Around 10:00 p.m., His Majesty—in the same coupe he had used on his earlier ride—drove down from the theater through the Jägerstrasse, the Opernstrasse, along the Marktplatz, returning to the Eremitage via the Schlossplatz, the Ludwigs-strasse, and the Rennweg. Wherever His Majesty's carriage appeared, enthusiastic cheers resounded from the crowd that I imagine was at least eight thousand strong, including two thousand from out of town (conservatively estimated). The influx of visitors will only increase in the coming days, because yesterday we received official notice from Gastein that His Majesty, the Emperor of Germany will be arriving here next Saturday the 12th [of August] at 5:15 p.m. with an entourage of about sixty persons, and will be residing in the Royal Palace. Along with the Emperor, their Royal and Imperial Majesties the Grand Duke and Duchess of Baden, and Prince Georg of Prussia will also be arriving.

XXII
The Third Cycle of the Stage Festivals
(25 August 1876)

Today I report for the last time on the end of the great work that, with tomorrow's presentation of *Götterdämmerung*, will conclude the current performances. I will refrain from any declarations concerning the significance of this moment. Much has been written in the last days both for and against the work and its author. The disagreements are stark, but even opponents concede the monumentality of the work and its significance for the development of art. When the waves of excitement have calmed, when the storms of these days have abated, the divergent opinions will become clearer, and the evaluation of what occurred during the month of August in Bayreuth will be reserved for an impartial and just critique. After these opening thoughts, let me summarize the third cycle.

His Majesty King Ludwig II of Bavaria—the tireless and generous patron and benefactor of Master Wagner's intentions, without whose benevolent munificence the performances of the *Ring of the Nibelung* could never have been completed in this superb manner—arrived Sunday night at 12:30 a.m. on a special train, and once again disembarked at the Rollwenzelhaus in order to get to the Eremitage by the shortest possible route. The town was again festooned to honor its King; but the King gratefully declined any and all gestures of acclaim for the duration of this visit, so that he might devote himself fully and undisturbed to the pleasure of the artwork. At 7 o'clock on Sunday evening, the King drove through the town to the theater, and the performance of *Rheingold* began immediately thereafter to a sold-out house. Since I already gave the performers their due for the first and second cycles, I will limit myself today, and simply confirm that the third cycle was in every aspect a brilliant success. It seemed to me that the temperature in the house, which this time was rather cool, served to stimulate the performers, because their voices sounded so fresh and pure. Their amazing efforts really served to shame those naysayers who, out of jealousy and maliciousness, predicted that the singers would succumb even before the third cycle from the stress resulting from their colossal task. The task certainly was colossal for everyone, but the elite artists assembled by the Master for his work were immensely talented. Through to the very end, everyone's commitment to the goal whose achievement they all have subscribed to has been enormous, and every participant, both on stage and in the orchestra has understood that they are here to make an idea in honor of all German artists come true. It was this knowledge that gave them the strength to keep on until the glorious objective had been reached.

The performance of *Rheingold* ended at 9:45 p.m., whereupon the King drove through the illuminated streets of the town back to the Eremitage. Prince Georg of Prussia and the Duke of Leuchtenberg—who also took up residence at the Royal Palace —were also present for *Rheingold*.

The King was also present for the entirety of yesterday's performance of *Walküre*, along with Prince George of Prussia and the Duke of Leuchtenberg. This totally and resoundingly successful performance included renewed triumphs for Herr Niemann (Siegmund), Herr Niering (Hunding), Madame Scheffzky (Sieglinde), and then Herr Betz (Wotan) and Frau Materna (Brünnhilde). Between the second and third acts, the King had his aide-de-camp Freiherr von Neuffenberg bestow the Knight's Cross 1st Class of the Order of Merit of St. Michael on Herr Niemann, the performer of Siegmund.[21] I have heard that further decorations await the other performers of the leading roles.

Tomorrow evening, the King's immediate departure after the conclusion of *Götterdämmerung* will be marked by a torchlight procession from the Eremitage to the point of departure, an expression of the town's thanks to and respect for the beloved Monarch. A report on this will follow.

These are the contemporary circumstances that give the Bayreuth undertaking a national significance. Wagner was propelled to musically and dramatically shape a *national epic of the German peoples*, the *Nibelungenlied*, by ideas that were clear to him before they became so for the rest of us. Already in 1843, 1846, and 1848, Wagner conceived the work that was crowned in 1876.[22] Today, no one would object to the political ideas that guided him back then. Even the non-conservative view—that art was not especially beneficial to the civil life of an unfree people, bereft of rights, as it emerged out of feudal conditions—was not so hard to understand. Germans should hold their art in high esteem as did the ancient Greeks, who loved and honored their art; they should know the *Nibelungen* epic as well as the Greeks knew the *Iliad*. A lot of verbiage has accompanied such claims, but the basic principle was correct and has been proven. Even if Wagner's critics are correct that the festival which just concluded here was not entirely successful, and needs improving—nevertheless, *the idea can no longer be undone*. With ten Princes leading the way, thousands from north and south, east and west journeyed to Bayreuth with the greatest of sacrifice (in view of the current conditions) to become acquainted with the German artwork of a single man.

Consider briefly the following: in the seventeenth and eighteenth centuries, there was still no German art for the German courts to sustain. First Lessing swept our drama clean of foreign influences. Our poetry hails from the Court of Weimar starting 1759.[23] Our new music begins with the birth of W. A. Mozart whose education was entirely Italian. In painting, the Italians and Dutch set the tone. Speaking French and singing Italian was the "fashion" in the courts until now, spread by their easily influenced servants from the bourgeoisie to their families and thence into the public sphere—hardly a surprise when even C. M. von Weber's reconstruction of German opera met with boredom and indifference. Should we not honor this series of famous Germans who shook off the foreign yoke? Even if Wagner's Germanness is perhaps a bit chauvinistic, even if his alliterations sometimes seem like a comic exaggeration, all this is incidental. Let us not forget that this stubbornly persevering German composer—standing on the shoulders of Gluck, Beethoven, and Weber—has dedicated his life to the independence of German art. So let him benefit from the fact that his festival has taken place at a time of reawakened national pride, a renaissance of the German *Volk* together with its arts and crafts.

I close with the words of V. K. Schembera in the *Wiener Tageblatt*:

"This work no longer deserves to be met with petty hostility—the entire world knows now what sort of victory the new art has achieved at this festival in Bayreuth. A new era has dawned in the history of art!"

And that will remain so, despite Paul Lindau's bad jokes and despite the opposing doctrines of Dr. Eduard Hanslick![24]

I still need to report on the two concluding days of the third cycle of the stage festival. King Ludwig II was present from start to finish of the *Siegfried* performance and, likewise, that of *Götterdämmerung*. Before Act 1 of *Siegfried* started, but after the auditorium had been darkened and the orchestra had already begun playing the opening measures, the banker Herr Feustel, as member of the executive board, stepped before the curtain. The auditorium was immediately lit, and Herr Feustel called for a cheer to His Majesty the King of Bavaria, the patron and protector of art. Everyone present enthusiastically joined his call and the orchestra accompanied with a mighty flourish. The King proceeded to the edge of his box and graciously thanked everyone. The performance of *Siegfried* then proceeded brilliantly: all the participants executing their tasks at the highest level. At the conclusion of the performance, the fully packed house broke out into thunderous applause. —During the performance of *Siegfried*, the three lovely performers of the Rhine Maidens were awarded royal recognition. King Ludwig had his aide-de-camp Major von Stauffenberg present the ladies Marie and Lilly Lehman, and [Minna] Lammert with precious diamond rings along with the most flattering recognition of their efforts.

In just a few hours, we will be at the end of the festival and, with that, will have concluded an occurrence that deserves a few parting words. Let us cast our eyes back to the three months that lie behind us, from the beginning of the rehearsals to today's final performance. Let us praise the good fortune that allowed everything to go so well to the very end. — On June 1st, on behalf of the citizenry, we greeted the artists who were then arriving for the rehearsals: that select group, gathered around the Master to help glorify his work, deserves the warmest salutation as they depart. I don't need to repeat the artistic merit these musical luminaries have earned for performing this work. The daily press of both hemispheres has emphasized unanimously how such a massive undertaking could only have been achieved this successfully with assembled forces like these. Moreover, the fame of this noble band of artists will not be extinguished by time and daily life. No, it will remain eternally recorded with golden letters in the annals of art. And whenever Master Wagner and the *Ring of the Nibelung* are mentioned in the art history of the future, there must also be grateful acknowledgment of his friends and comrades, the performers and the orchestral players, who helped to raise this magnificent creation to the pinnacle of fame. Richard Wagner has repeatedly recognized this without reservation, and history will be no less fair than the Master himself. And that seems to us to constitute the truest laurels—*aere perennius*.[25]

May they all return to their accustomed lives happy and content, secure in the knowledge that the citizens and residents of Bayreuth, who learned to love and respect every one of them during this time together, will always remember in grateful friendship the beautiful days during which they came to regard them as family. Our town had very little to offer our beloved guests, but that very little was offered with open heart. We are certain that those who are departing will judge their Bayreuth hosts like noble souls, who measure the intent and not the deed itself, and will remember them fondly, ignoring the occasional and momentary shortcomings caused by the limited means at our disposal. This is the genuine hope I would like to express most fervently on behalf of the whole town.

Now that we have given hospitality its due, let us not forget, departing friends, as well as you citizens of Bayreuth, the most important thing: our gratitude to the glorious protector of the artwork that has just been realized here, His Majesty King Ludwig II. Unflinchingly faithful to the illustrious House of Wittelsbach's tradition of support for the arts, he was the first among all the German princes to recognize the importance of the Master—whose genius we thank for the grand work—and made it possible for him to achieve his lofty goal. Under his protective and generous hand, a Temple of Art was erected on the hill (Hohenwart). When the Master and his fellow artists, and all of us who were lucky enough to experience this celebration of art, look back on the course of epoch-making work with pride and joy, it is he (Ludwig) who is above all to be thanked. He honored both the Master and the performers by attending two complete cycles. He was responsible for securing the attention to and participation in the Bayreuth festival on the part of his illustrious relative His Majesty Emperor Wilhelm. All this royal favor and munificence bestowed on the arts may count as little in the book of history when compared to the political actions of our German King of Bavaria and the support he gave to the restoration of the German imperial crown.[26] Now, as then, we look up to our illustrious Monarch with pride and faith, he who has always known how to conduct himself regally, making the right decision in momentous political moments, or—like a true patron of culture—committing himself to the support and elevation of the arts, regardless of whether this also serves his own needs and the ideal nature of his own being. The city of Bayreuth especially, steadfast in its devotion, will not forget the lofty virtues of their beloved Monarch, and how His Majesty's support made the festival possible in the first place while also emphasizing its significance, all of which has increased the town's prosperity and the common welfare of its citizens.

May these few words find echo in the hearts of all our departing guests as well as the residents and citizens of Bayreuth! —And so let our joint parting gesture be a heartfelt "Hail" to His Majesty, the German King Ludwig II of Bavaria!!

On the closing day of the festival, thousands once again undertook the long walk to the theater. The crowd was as vast as had gathered on opening night. The last performance thus turned into a farewell celebration full of earnest devotion and enthusiasm. Before King Ludwig entered the theater, Herr M. Rothenstein from Hamburg stood up and celebrated with impassioned words the accomplishments of Richard Wagner, and ended by encouraging the assembled crowd to cheer King Ludwig of Bavaria, the illustrious patron of the Master. Following this, the performance began. It was as brilliant as everything that had come before. It was as if all the participants desired once again to give their all in honor of the great enterprise. In particular, Frau Materna sang with such captivating verve, with such freshness, that surely all were amazed that such a feat was still possible after all the exertions of the preceding days.[27] As evident once again yesterday, Frau Materna is a phenomenal presence in the artistic firmament. Herr Unger also gave his all for Siegfried to the huge acclaim of all present, even though one could discern something like exhaustion.[28] This artist has also deserved the greatest praise for completing this immense task with unfailing endurance. The awesome final scene of *Götterdämmerung* went off perfectly, and when the curtain fell, a thunderous applause spontaneously filled the hall once more, as we had experienced after every performance. Never-ending cheers for the King mixed with demands for Wagner to appear. King Ludwig appeared at the edge of his box and applauded continuously. At this, Master Wagner appeared from behind the curtain and, with emotion in his voice, said a few words of thanks and farewell—the Stage Festival (*Bühnenfestspiel*) was over, and he did not know whether it would be repeated. He had proudly called the performances "Stage Festivals," a name the approbation of those present seems to justify; this work so long in the making he titled *The Ring of the Nibelung, a Stage Festival,* and this day proves that it has truly been a festival. He had conceived this work, trusting in the German people, and had completed it to the glory of his magnificent benefactor, His Majesty King Ludwig II of Bavaria. The speaker then enthusiastically acknowledged the debt owed to the King for realization of the project, and thanked his lofty patron for all the palpable royal favor and grace. And then he again spoke about the confusion caused by the words he had spoken at the close of the first cycle.[29] He hoped he would not again be accused of arrogance, if he said that this festival represented a step in the direction of a self-sufficient German art. Only the future would determine whether this step had been successful. Even if the performances have only been a trial, they will perhaps nevertheless not have been entirely in vain for German art. With impassioned words, the speaker then thanked his fellow artists who helped him to complete the work. As he said these words, Master Wagner turned toward the stage and announced that he wanted to see everyone again at this hour of farewell. Thereupon, the curtain parted and all participants stood there in a beautiful arrangement, with the conductor Hans Richter in the center, ready to receive the thanks of the Master. It was a sacred and moving sight to see the creator of this work and his comrades once more exchanging sentiments of respect and love. King Ludwig remained present in the theater for the entirety of this farewell scene.

In the course of the day, and also partly in the evening during the performance, the King had the following decorations awarded: Mayor Munker received the Commander's Cross of the Order of St. Michael; the executive councilors Banker Gross and Attorney Käfferlein as well as Emil Heckel of Mannheim received the Knight's Cross 1st Class of the same order; in addition the Court Opera singer Betz, Kapellmeister Richter, Professor Wilhelmij, and the Director of the Stage Hands, Herr Brandt, also received the Order of St. Michael 1st Class. Frau Materna and the Court Opera singer Hill were decorated with the golden Ludwig Medal for arts and sciences. In addition, Wilhelmij received the Knight's Cross 1st Class of the Ernestine House Order from the Duke of Meiningen.[30]

Following the performance, the King traveled to the Eremitage and, after a short stopover, journeyed on to the embarkation point at Rollwenzel House, accompanied by the Town Mayor and Richard Wagner. To honor the King, a torchlight procession was set up along the entire Eremitage avenue up to the railway. The rows of torch bearers were for the most part composed of ordinary citizens and firemen from those communities in the vicinity of the Eremitage who had hurried over in large numbers before his departure to pay homage once again to their beloved Monarch— he who had stayed so happily in their midst— and to offer him joyously their heartfelt wishes for a safe journey home. The director of the district exchange, Councilor Kellein, together with representatives of the town council, accompanied His Royal Majesty to the departure point. To the sounds of the Bavarian anthem played by the musicians of the Seventh Infantry Regiment, His Majesty's special train departed at twelve o'clock midnight.

NOTES

1. In the following I rely heavily on Susanna Großmann-Vendrey, *Bayreuth in der deutschen Presse: Beiträge zur Rezeptionsgeschichte Richard Wagners und seiner Festspiele*, Dokumentband 1: *Die Grundsteinlegung und die ersten Festspiele (1872–1876)* (Regensburg, 1977), esp. 44–46.

2. The *Neue Zeitschrift* published the twenty-three reports in thirteen *Beilagen* between June and September 1876.

3. Letter to Heinrich Porges, 6 November 1872: "Noch ehe Sie mir schrieben, hatte ich Ihnen für mein Unternehmen ein für die Zukunft allerwichtigstes Amt bestimmt. Ich wollte Sie nämlich dazu berufen, daß Sie allen meinen Proben in derselben Weise, wie Sie es bei der 9ten Symphonie gethan, genau folgten, um alle meine, noch so intimen Bemerkungen in Betreff der Auffassung und Ausführung unseres Werkes, aufzunehmen und aufzuzeichnen, somit eine fixirte Tradition hierfür zu redigiren." (Even before you wrote to me, I had decided on an assignment for you that would have a most important role for the future of my undertaking. I would like to call upon you to keep close track of all my rehearsals in exactly the same manner as you did with the 9th Symphony, in order to record and note all my intimate remarks concerning the conception and execution of our work, and thus to edit a fixed tradition for it.)

The detailed notes on the rehearsals Porges produced in response to Wagner's suggestion have been published in English as *Wagner Rehearsing the Ring: An Eye-Witness Account of the First Bayreuth Festival*, trans. Robert L. Jacobs (Cambridge, 1983).

4. See my forthcoming book *Richard Wagner: Self-Promotion and the Making of a Brand* (Cambridge: projected 2010).

5. Richard Wagner, letter to Theodor Apel, 27 October 1834, in *Sämtliche Briefe*, ed. Gertrud Strobel and Werner Wolf (Leipzig, 1967–), 1:167–68. See also Wagner's "Autobiographische Skizze," in *Gesammelte Schriften und Dichtungen* (Leipzig, 1887–1911) (hereafter *GSD*), 7:128; 1:4–19; and Thomas Grey, trans. ("Autobiographical Sketch") in *Wagner Journal* 2/1 (March 2008): 42–58, here 52–55.

6. "Ich schreibe keine Opern mehr," *Eine Mittheilung an meine Freunde*, *GSD*, 4:345.

7. Frederic Spotts, *Bayreuth: A History of the Wagner Festival* (New Haven, 1994), 5.

8. London boasted a commemorative Handel festival in 1784 and, in the same year, Birmingham launched its Triennial Musical Festival, which would become one of the longest-running such events. By the first decades of the nineteenth century, music festivals like the Lower Rhine Music Festival (launched in 1818) also became established in Germany.

9. I borrow the term "institutional network" (*institutionelles Netz*) from Boris Voigt, *Richard Wagners Autoritäre Inszenierungen: Versuch über die Ästhetik charismatischer Herrschaft* (Hamburg, 2003), 208.

10. Richard Wagner, letter to Emil Heckel, 19 September 1873, in *Bayreuther Briefe (1871–1883)*, *Richard Wagners Briefe in Originalausgaben* (Leipzig, 1912), 15:195.

11. "Die Festspiele wurden damit zum ersten künstlerischen Unternehmen in Deutschland, das einen solchen Informationsdienst unterhielt" (The festival thus became the first artistic enterprise in Germany to be maintained by such an information service), Großmann-Vendrey, *Bayreuth in der deutschen Presse*, 45.

12. Ibid., 45.

13. Serialization published in Porges, *Wagner Rehearsing the Ring*.

14. The releases included here are numbers I, XII, XXII, and XXIII. They were all published as "Special Supplements" to the *Neue Zeitschrift für Musik*, June – September 1876.

15. Originally Princess Wilhelmine of Prussia, the Margravine (1709–58), together with her husband, Friedrich, undertook major building plans in and around the town, including the celebrated opera house (Markgräfliches Opernhaus) described in this article.

16. Jean Paul, born Johann Paul Friedrich Richter (1763–1825) was a German writer of highly experimental—some would say eccentric—novels. He resided for a while in Weimar, but was never accepted by Goethe and Schiller. In 1804, he moved to Bayreuth where he spent the remainder of his life.

17. Ludwig Michael Schwanthaler (1802–48), Munich-born sculptor, was involved for most of his life in the civic building and decorative projects of Ludwig I of Bavaria.

18. Civil List denotes the list of individuals receiving pay from the government. It is unclear what is meant in this case, though it might refer to a form of government housing or housing for government employees.

19. Giuseppe-Galli-Bibiena (1696–1757), Italian designer and member of the Galli-Bibiena family which, over three generations during the seventeenth and eighteenth centuries, produced buildings, theatrical sets, and interior design that epitomized the Baroque style.

20. Three paragraphs describing further tourist sights in and around Bayreuth are omitted here.

21. Albert Niemann (1831–1917) was a tenor who came to Wagnerian prominence singing the role of Tannhäuser in the 1861 production in Paris. He created the role of Siegmund in *Die Walküre* at Bayreuth.

22. The first two dates seem to refer to Wagner's preliminary readings; no material was committed to paper before the prose scenario/outline of October 1848, "Der Nibelungen-Mythus: Als Entwurf zu einem Drama" (The Nibelung myth: As the sketch of a drama).

23. In 1759 Anna Amalia, Duchess of Saxe-Weimar and Saxe-Eisenach, became regent for her son Carl August and began to establish Weimar as a center for the arts and culture. It also happens to be the birth year of Friedrich Schiller, who eventually moved to Weimar and became, along with Johann Wolfgang von Goethe, one of the principal exponents of Weimar Classicism.

24. Paul Lindau (1839–1919) was a German critic, dramatist, and novelist who wrote for the popular magazine *Die Gartenlaube*, including humorous reports on the first Bayreuth festival. He also published additional reports on the first festival titled *Nüchterne Briefe aus Bayreuth* (1876). See also Hanslick's feuilleton essay on contemporary *Parsifal* literature included below, which cites Lindau's reports on both the 1876 and 1882 Bayreuth Festivals.

25. "more lasting than bronze."

26. The agreement of Bavaria to the unification of Germany under the aegis of Prussia, thus elevating the King of Prussia to Emperor of Germany, was a key factor in the momentous events of January 1871.

27. Amalia Materna (1844–1918) was the Viennese soprano who created the role of Brünnhilde.

28. Georg Unger (1837–87) was the first Siegfried.

29. Immediately following the final curtain of the first ever complete performance of the *Ring of the Nibelung*, the audience demanded that Wagner appear to receive their applause. Wagner said a few words and ended with something like: "Sie haben jetzt gesehen, was wir können; nun ist es an Ihnen, zu wollen. Und wenn Sie wollen, so haben wir eine Kunst!" (You have now seen what we can do; now it's up to you to want. And if you want, we will then have an art!). This is the official version, published thirty years after his death in 1883 (*GSD*, 16:161). Since Wagner's speech was improvised, there is no actual record. As there was a lot of noise in the theater, there is disagreement about just what he said. Some thought they had heard "deutsche Kunst" (German art), emphasizing the national dimension of the Bayreuth project that was soon to become such a potent political and ideological symbol. Others heard no adjective before "Kunst," but instead thought Wagner had made the preposterous claim that before him there had been no art. Scandal and outrage ensued. The next evening, Wagner gave another improvised speech at the festival banquet, in which

he vainly tried to clarify his point and repair the damage. For more on this episode, see Großmann-Vendrey, *Bayreuth in der deutschen Presse*, 230ff.

30. Among the honorees listed in this paragraph, Adolf Gross and Emil Heckel were instrumental in managing the funding of the festival; Franz Betz and Karl Hill sang the roles of Wotan and Alberich, respectively; August Wilhelmij was the concertmaster of the festival orchestra; Hans Richter the conductor; and Emil Brandt, the machinist or technical director, also consulted in the construction of the theater.

Hanslick *contra* Wagner:

"The *Ring* Cycle Comes to Vienna" and "*Parsifal* Literature"

EDUARD HANSLICK

TRANSLATED, INTRODUCED, AND ANNOTATED
BY THOMAS S. GREY

"Actually, Wagner had no foes in the sense of absolute, one-sided enmity"—
thus wrote Eduard Hanslick in a short obituary piece commemorating the
composer's passing on February 13, 1883. "I have never met a musician
so obtuse, or so violently partisan, as to overlook his brilliant endowment
and his astonishing art, or underestimate his enormous influence, or to
deny the greatness and genius of his works, even granting personal antipathy. Wagner has been fought, but he has never been denied."[1] It is only
natural that Wagner's death might elicit a sympathetic note of appreciation from his celebrated nemesis. But by the 1880s the Viennese critic
had also become tired of being cast as Wagner's archenemy, an aesthetic
reactionary intent on turning back the clock on musical progress as proclaimed by believers in the Wagnerian musical-dramatic *Gesamtkunstwerk*.
"We lift our hats to its boldness and consistency," he concedes, "without,
however, giving it our allegiance. . . . Today I wish only to set right the
frequently misinterpreted conception of 'opposition,' and to state, for once
and for all, that there is no exasperated partisanship against Wagner, but
only against the Wagnerites."[2]

Nonetheless, Hanslick had undoubtedly developed both a good deal
of personal antipathy to Wagner and a principled, "objective" dislike of
the mature Wagnerian musical idiom. To the very end he continued to
oppose Wagner's "post-operatic" conception of dramatic composition that
eschewed conventional melodic and harmonic syntax, coherently shaped
musical-dramatic numbers, and elaborate ensemble singing—the last of

which was, for Hanslick, one of the glories of modern opera in more traditional styles.

Hanslick's personal antipathy to the composer goes back to the time Wagner spent in Vienna in the 1860s, when he pointedly rebuffed the critic's well-intentioned overtures in several public gatherings (probably because of Hanslick's less than favorable review of the Viennese productions of *Lohengrin*) and, most notoriously, read aloud the first draft of the *Meistersinger* libretto in Hanslick's presence, possibly with the critic-caricature Beckmesser identified as "Veit Hanslich."[3] Some years later, in 1869, Wagner reprinted his essay "Judaism in Music" as a brochure, with a new afterword largely devoted to attacking the "Jewish press" for an alleged conspiracy to destroy his reputation. Hanslick (a Catholic by upbringing but of Jewish descent on his mother's side) was denounced here as the ringleader of this alleged anti-Wagnerian Jewish conspiracy.

The professional or aesthetic antipathy developed more gradually. As an aspiring young critic in the 1840s, Hanslick had enthusiastically championed the composer of *Tannhäuser* as the great hope of a new school of German Romantic opera.[4] By the time Hanslick took time out from his nascent career as critic to write what would become the best-known treatise of the nineteenth century on musical aesthetics, *Vom Musikalisch-Schönen* (*On the Beautiful in Music*), 1854, Wagner had recently made a name for himself as a political and aesthetic radical with his extensively formulated theories of operatic and cultural reform: principally, *The Artwork of the Future* (1849) and *Opera and Drama* (1852). Hanslick was temperamentally averse to the intemperate polemical grandstanding in Wagner's writings. His attempt at a clear-headed account of the aesthetics and even the mechanics of musical form and expression in *On the Beautiful in Music* was certainly meant as a riposte, in part, to Wagner's overblown theorizing of the "dramatic-musical total artwork of the future," even if it is only cited in passing there. The legacy of this Wagnerian theory in the excessive posturing of "Wagnerites" and "Wagnerism" is a particular target of Hanslick's ire in his later criticism, including the two articles translated here, although he cannot disguise the ambivalence he feels toward Wagner the composer as well. A postscript to his later reviews of the Bayreuth festival, dissecting the phenomenon of the modern "Wagner cult," reinforces this opposition to the theory and ideology of Wagnerism above and beyond that to the works as such.[5] Hanslick is willing to evaluate these works as operas, like any one else's, but refuses to grant them special critical dispensation as some special genre above and beyond the reach of practical criticism.

The essays translated here are pendants, of a sort, to Hanslick's principal reviews of the two Bayreuth festivals held during Wagner's lifetime, the premieres of the *Ring* cycle in 1876 and of *Parsifal* in 1882.[6] The first of them brings together his reviews of the first productions of the four operas of the *Ring of the Nibelung* seen at the Vienna court opera (Hofoper) between 1877 and 1879. Together with Munich and Leipzig, Vienna was one of the first cities to see the *Ring* after its complete premiere at Bayreuth, and Hanslick is particularly concerned with proving that these supposedly *sui generis* musical dramas could be just as well served, if not better, by the resources of a leading modern-day opera house. Hanslick also feels that critics and audiences have a better chance of establishing the true musical, as well as theatrical merits and failings alike of these works, outside the "temple" of Bayreuth. The roundup review of *Parsifal* (and other Wagner) "literature" appearing in the wake of the second Bayreuth festival aims to deflate some of the overweening ideological pretenses of the "Wagnerites." (In this regard it is also a companion piece to the exposé of the "Wagner cult" mentioned above.) Hanslick diagnoses as symptomatic the extent to which this literature, like that published in Hans von Wolzogen's party organ, the *Bayreuther Blätter*, seeks out the higher significance of its idol and high priest, Richard Wagner, in almost every sphere of human activity besides music. "For a later age, which will be able to look back at the Wagner epidemic of our days in a spirit of calm evaluation, if also one of incredulous astonishment, the *Bayreuther Blätter* may yet prove to be of no little cultural-historical significance. . . . The future cultural historian of Germany will be able to give authentic testimony, on the basis of the first five volumes of this journal, how strongly the *delirium tremens* of the Wagnerian intoxication raged among us, and what sort of abnormalities of thought and feeling it occasioned in the 'cultured' people of the time."[7] In this regard, too, it is instructive to compare Hans von Wolzogen's own essay on *Parsifal* criticism included in this section, in which he denounces "unauthorized" interpretations of the drama by scholars or critics outside the anointed Bayreuth circle—an exclusionary tendency not unrelated to Wagner's intention of reserving the performance rights to the sacral "stage-consecration festival play" for Bayreuth alone.

All footnotes at the bottom of the page are Hanslick's; all endnotes are the translator's.

EDUARD HANSLICK
Richard Wagner's *Ring of the Nibelung* at the Vienna Hofoper
(1879)

The Vienna Hofoper [court theater] staged *Die Walküre* in March 1877, followed by *Rheingold* in January 1878, *Siegfried* in November 1878, and finally, in February 1879, *Götterdämmerung*.[8] Our much disputed prediction was thus quickly enough fulfilled: Mohammed will come to the mountain, and Bayreuth, after having hosted visitors from throughout Europe, now goes on tour across Europe.[9] These Viennese productions have conclusively invalidated the grounds on which the Wagner theater in Bayreuth was built at such expense: the claim that only there could *The Ring of the Nibelung* receive a viable performance.

Not everything that glittered in Bayreuth was pure gold. Like his own music, Wagner's deeply pondered stage reforms suffered from exaggeration and lack of proportion. Ideas that seemed intelligent and sound enough in themselves turned out to lose something of their intended effect through stubborn excesses in the course of their execution. It was more beneficial than detrimental to the resulting production in Vienna that these ideas were subjected here to reasonable limits. Consider these factors. First, the orchestra. In Bayreuth Wagner introduced the entirely invisible orchestra; sunken into cellar-like depths, this was covered at the top by a roof of tin. The modification of the sound thus achieved did create a poetically mysterious impression, but a musically weakened one. Orchestral brilliance was sacrificed, a dark pall cast over the jubilant sounds of the strings or the blaring horns. In Vienna, the recent lowering of the orchestra pit (following the example of Munich) was retained, but that was all; and as a result the orchestral timbres had more volume and brilliance here than in Bayreuth. Louder and more brilliant, too, despite the smaller instrumental contingent; while in Bayreuth the deliberate muting of the orchestra meant that one seemed to hear a group of only about half the size of the one actually performing.*

Another of Wagner's reforms that sounded wise in theory but proved to be distressing in its draconian application was the complete darkening of the auditorium, so that one's neighbors disappeared from sight, while the brightly lit stage with its panoply of changing colors had a blinding effect. Here at the Hofoper both of these situations were mitigated—the lighting

---

* In Bayreuth there were 16 first and 16 second violins, 12 violas, 12 cellos and 6 harps. Woodwinds and brass [*Harmonie*] were the same in Bayreuth as in Vienna. Hans Richter's new arrangement of the players in Vienna proved wonderfully effective, placing all of the violins in one compact group to the left-hand side of the orchestra, reserving the right-hand side for woodwinds [*Bläser*] and percussion.

above and the darkness below—with distinctly beneficial results. At Bayreuth the performance began at four o'clock; in Vienna, thankfully, not until six. Even so, the first performances of *Die Walküre* here lasted until ten-thirty! Every face registered complete exhaustion; musical enthusiasts sitting on either side of us who had delightedly applauded the first act were afterward heard to complain that their pleasure was turning to pain.

In comparing the Viennese productions with those at Bayreuth we certainly cannot overlook the fact that the construction of the Wagner theater (no boxes, no central chandelier, a higher and more distant stage, etc.) allows for a more perfect stage illusion, and one more equally available to all parts of the audience; even smaller things contribute to this, such as the removal of the prompter's box. All the same, we do think it worthwhile to retain the latter form of *aide-memoire*, since we cannot help but sympathize with the needs of ordinary mortals. We would no more want to withhold the prompter's assistance from the singers of the *Nibelungen*, who have to memorize hundreds of lines of the most hair-raising poetry, than we would wish to banish our musicians to the subterranean slave galleys of Bayreuth. Such measures, reminiscent of that imperial tone-poet Nero, hardly seem worth emulating, even if it means sacrificing a small bit of theatrical illusion. No amount of aesthetic despotism will ever make the audience completely forget that it is in a theater, after all, nor is it in the least necessary that they should do so. It has now been proven in Vienna that a modicum of intelligence and ability can suffice to realize the *Nibelungen*, even on the "operatic" stage so passionately denounced by Wagner.

The Vienna *Rheingold* was subject to an irregularity in that, contrary to the poetic structure of the cycle, it was performed *after* the *Walküre*. Thus the audience had already been exposed to the brave new world of Wagner's *Nibelung* style. Significant mainly as the prologue to the *Nibelungen* trilogy proper (*Die Walküre, Siegfried, Götterdämmerung*), *Das Rheingold* is by itself quite the least satisfying of the four pieces.[10] *Rheingold* does have one advantage over *Die Walküre*, however, in being significantly shorter. The listener does not leave the theater in that state of utmost exhaustion to which he is reduced by *Die Walküre*, spoiling the recollection of the individual beauties that work does contain. Granted, in Bayreuth the audience found their nerves fatally strained even after *Das Rheingold*; this was even more so the case earlier, in Munich, where they were not yet inured to the "stage festival play" manner and hence their sensibilities had not yet been hardened.[11] In Vienna the situation was considerably alleviated, thanks to a willingness to ignore the composer's imperious demand that *Rheingold* must be performed continuously, with no intermission, not even a short pause such as one gets between the movements of a symphony or the break that normally accompanies a change of scenery in the opera. In Munich and in Bayreuth the whole opera was played as Wagner wrote it, nonstop from beginning to end, for over two and a half hours. An opera of that length would be one thing, but a single act would be unimaginable. In Vienna one simply seized the reins of Wagner's restlessly galloping orchestra by means of a cadential chord at the end of the first Valhalla scene, and thus granted us a short intermission of ten minutes. In the future people will no doubt continue to emancipate themselves—for instance from the decree that no single measure may be cut. A theater is not a galley manned by slaves, and musicians—no less than listeners—are, after all, human beings.

By far the best impression was made here, as has been the case elsewhere, by the opening scene of the Rhine Maidens, a dazzling synthesis of poetic, scenic, and musical attractions. Otherwise one heard here in Vienna (just as in Munich, Bayreuth, etc.) much more talk about the wonders of the stage production than about the music. The technology of stage production has no doubt gained much in trying to meet the great challenges Wagner poses for it; indeed, the scenic arts of the theater already have his ambitious imagination to thank for some notable advances. It is just a pity that all of this spectacle is being expended on serious opera rather than on the ballet, where it would be more appropriate. In the opera, this sort of thing rather detracts from the music and from the dramatic content: it is a luxury that, when held up to scrutiny, only serves to mask poverty. There is no other opera whose success, indeed whose very existence, is so dependent on the role of stage design as is the case with *Rheingold*. In such scenic marvels and surprises Wagner has found himself a Nibelung's Ring that will only bring ruin to the entire field of opera.

At the Vienna Hofoper the musical performance succeeded splendidly; the scenery and the stage machinery achieved (within the limits of the possible) their intended effects. What I do *not* consider possible is a realistic representation of the Rainbow Bridge at the conclusion of the opera; this was ludicrous in Munich, and again in Bayreuth—and in Vienna. If one builds the Rainbow Bridge massively enough and positions it low enough to the stage so that half a dozen real-life "gods and goddesses" can promenade upon it, there is no way that it will resemble an actual rainbow, rather than, say, a painted bridge in a park, if not a seven-colored liverwurst. Were it truly to resemble a rainbow, there is no way that human beings, right in front of our eyes, could walk upon it. Wouldn't the best solution be to manage this troublesome Rainbow Bridge by means of *dissolving views* or in the manner of the Wild Hunt in the Wolf's Glen scene of *Der Freischütz*: that is, by means of projections on the back of the stage?[12]

Rheingold was received at its first performance in the Hofoper with enthusiastic applause, but already by the second performance the house was only half full.

Incomparably greater and more lasting was the effect of *Die Walküre*, as was to be expected, and which, as I have mentioned, was produced before *Rheingold* as a sort of *captatio benevolentiae*. Indeed, *Die Walküre* has no real need for the preceding *Rheingold* or the following *Siegfried*. It is quite intelligible by itself, insofar as these Wagnerian mythologies, so alien to our modern culture, can ever be wholly understood by a modern public. Of the Rhine Gold and the curse on the Ring, ostensibly the principal theme of the entire cycle, there is not a word in *Walküre*, and whatever will happen twenty years later to Siegmund's and Sieglinde's still unborn son (Siegfried) has no bearing on the self-contained narrative of the conjugal sibling pair of *Die Walküre*.

That demon of excess to which Wagner is subject (to an extent that recalls Faust's remark: "Reason becomes nonsense, good deeds turn into torments")[13] is most of all evident in the extreme length of Wagner's scores. In the second act of *Walküre* Wotan conducts two long dialogues, consecutively—first with Fricka, then with Brunhilde [*sic*]—which, in their exhaustive prosiness and their incredibly tedious music, tax the patience of the listener in the extreme. The fearful prolixity of this dim-witted, henpecked husband who passes for a "god" (alas, Nestroy died too young to do him satiric justice),[14] this endless beating around the bush about things that could easily be said in far fewer words caused some dismay even for many true believers in Bayreuth. There, of course, no word could be cut; in Vienna cuts were made, to the distinct advantage of the work. Wotan's narration[s] were subjected to two cuts amounting to fifteen pages of the vocal score (p. 107 to p. 119 and p. 247 to p. 248)—a sizable amputation, but even so, the scene was still too long with respect to its limited dramatic interest.[15]

The great success of *Walküre* in Vienna was due as much to the scrupulous casting—of which the roles of Sieglinde (Frau Ehnn) and Brünnhilde (Frau Materna) were especially outstanding—as to the virtuosic achievement of the orchestra under Hans Richter and the splendid staging.[16] The very important episode of the combat in the second act, which had been quite unintelligible in Bayreuth, was both clear and effective here.[17] The Valkyries leaping across the stage on their rapid coursers made for a wild and picturesque tableau, whereas the Bayreuth shield-maidens, unsaddled, merely boasted about their steeds. Even the ram-drawn chariot of the "noble" Fricka, an object of sardonic mirth in Bayreuth, suggested the dignified carriage appropriate to this Frau Privy Counselor of the gods.

Siegfried did not succeed in making the impression here that was being predicted for it after the Bayreuth festival. In Vienna it did not remotely approach the effect of *Walküre*, and before long it was playing to a very reduced audience. Even so, the performance could be called exemplary in musical as well as scenic terms. The tenor Jäger was sought out exclusively for the role of Siegfried at Wagner's own request.[18] Seemingly made for the role with his tall, powerful figure, Jäger is also vocally effective in the energy of his delivery and the clarity of his diction. The voice is not an appealing one, already somewhat worn (probably from singing too much Siegfried). It is characteristic of this "Wagner singer *par excellence*" that he is scarcely adequate in any other roles, and indeed as Joseph in Méhul's opera he was nearly a disaster.[19]

On February 14, 1879, the Hofoper produced the fourth and mightiest course of the musical banquet from Bayreuth: *Götterdämmerung*.

To the extent that *Götterdämmerung* exceeds the preceding three dramas of the *Ring of the Nibelung* in dramatic vitality, so it commanded a livelier, more consistent attention on the part of the audience. The opening scene of the three Norns (whose tossing about of the rope made a somewhat ludicrous impression in Bayreuth) was omitted entirely in Vienna; in view of the intolerable length of the first act, this seems quite justified. I would recommend the same course of action for another, equally superfluous scene similarly taxing of the public's patience: Waltraute's scene. This valkyrie shows up quite unexpectedly in *Götterdämmerung* when she visits Brunhilde in order to give her a most moving description of the poor condition in which the great Wotan finds himself. We suspect that by the fourth evening of the cycle the greater part of the public wishes, whether openly or secretly, that they might finally be altogether rid of this Wotan, and therefore they would be very happy to forgo any extended sentimental representation of his melancholy and loss of appetite. Similarly unexpected is the quite episodic appearance of the dwarf Alberich, who pops up from a trap in order to tell Hagen some long-familiar information in a scene rife with painful dissonances. Both Waltraute's and Alberich's scenes were cut (in addition to the Norns' scene), starting with the second Viennese performance of *Götterdämmerung*.

The most dubious part was, again, the ending: the unmotivated and unintelligible precipitation of the "twilight of the gods," which has really nothing to do with the fate of Siegfried and Brunhilde (the only thing that *does* command our interest here). The whole catastrophe is a very hasty affair. Most of the time Wagner is a master at drawing out situations to the most incredible lengths, yet he rushes headlong into the concluding scene of *Götterdämmerung*. The murder of Gunther by Hagen, Brünnhilde's sacrificial death, Hagen's *salto mortale* into the river, the reappearance of the Rhine Maidens, the flood below and the twilight of the gods up in Valhalla—all of this comes at us with such material haste, such balletic alacrity, that the audience scarcely has an opportunity to make sense of it. Wagner seems to have been unsure, for his own part, on just how to stage the concluding tableau of the gods' downfall. In Bayreuth it was confusing, unattractive, and misconceived—as it was in Vienna, even though it had been prepared according to Wagner's updated specifications and in collaboration with officially certified experts, as well as secret agents in the Master's service. This final tableau has been attempted in different ways by other German theaters, but with scarcely any better results. The root cause of the problem is undoubtedly to be found in the libretto: Wagner's demands here transcend the bounds of what is possible, at any rate of what can be reasonably executed. Two small changes could do much to mitigate the confusion of this fourth drama: the title *Götterdämmerung* (Twilight of the Gods) might be dropped in favor of the original title, *Siegfrieds Tod* (Siegfried's Death), and along with it, the cloud picture meant to represent that "twilight of the gods."

Initially, *Götterdämmerung* has enjoyed a loud and enthusiastic reception in Vienna. Whether this success will prove to be a lasting one, only the future can tell. *Die Meistersinger* was greeted even more enthusiastically, though soon its appeal began to diminish, and performances became fewer until now it has (unfairly) disappeared altogether from the repertoire.[20] And yet, at least in my estimation, *Die Meistersinger* stands far above the entire *Ring of the Nibelung*, musically as well as dramatically. There the poet's natural feeling and the composer's creative powers appear in all the glorious freshness and health of youth, quite unlike *Götterdämmerung*.

In May 1879 the Vienna Hofoper produced the four Nibelung dramas consecutively, as a complete cycle, thereby fulfilling the demands of the powerful musical party so prettily designated by Hans Hopfen as the "elegant conspiracy."[21]

And so we find that, quite contrary to Wagner's original assurances that the cycle could only be produced in his festival theater at Bayreuth, it has for some time been crisscrossing all of Germany like a huge wandering spider covering everything with its white web. Everywhere the first performances draw immense crowds and enthusiasm, but it seems both of these quickly dwindle. A considerable portion of the public finds that, after its initial curiosity has been sated, the rather demanding, indeed grueling pleasure afforded by the cycle is one they would rather not sample too often. A smaller portion admits outright that the overall impact of one Nibelung drama, let alone several in a row, is really more of a torment than a pleasure. To this unhappy minority I myself belong. I should like to convey this impression honestly to my readers, as a personal experience, leaving aside any critical pretense.

The critic cannot hope to deliver any definitive judgment of an artistic phenomenon so unusual, so divisive of public opinion; in such a case it can only be a matter of an individual judgment for whose truthfulness, not actual

correctness, the critic is responsible to his readers. As we know, critical judgment of Wagner's music dramas is very divided, rather resembling the relation
of the prosecution to the defense in a trial. In such cases only time can provide the court of justice that is to decide in favor of one side or the other,
and often a relatively long period of time is required for this. Under the immediate demands of the present moment the critic can hardly do more (and
certainly nothing more beneficial) than, after conscientious preparation,
observe his own responses to a work and give an honest account of these.
Although it is usually the first impression that is decisive and correct, I have
not spared myself the effort or the self-denial demanded by a subsequent justification of my feelings; and so I have continued to pursue my *Nibelungen*
education. The critic hears a first performance in a certain state of agitation: the need to focus his whole attention on the work, together with the
unwelcome thought that tomorrow he must write about it, is likely to render him a little testy. If then further impediments are added to the mix, as
in the case of the Bayreuth festival, that irritability will increase and thus diminish his receptivity, like a photographic plate slightly clouded by one's breath.
In such cases I never absolve myself of the responsibility of considering whether
the failure, the reason for displeasure, does not perhaps rest with me. One
might easily be misled by the heaven-storming jubilation of thousands of
Wagner enthusiasts and its propagation in countless brochures idolizing their
god. And then there is the ready retort of the enthusiasts: "It's always easy
to criticize!" No, my good sirs, it is *not* easy to criticize, least of all amid a
delighted throng, whose delight one would only be too glad to share. And
in this spirit I made a point in recent years, after Bayreuth, of repeatedly
attending the splendid productions of *Rheingold* and *Walküre* at the Vienna
opera. I wanted to hear them at my own leisure, without constraints, simply
for my own edification and, if possible, pleasure. And yet—edification and
pleasure would not align. It was already a significant (and fatal) indication
that, every time, I had to force myself to listen to these works again. Do not
all true musical artworks, even those we find at first puzzling or off-putting,
still leave us with a desire to hear them again? Not to mention the musical
creations [*Tondichtungen*] of pure, classical beauty—can one ever hear them
often enough? In this case I simply had to admit that I might live long and
very happily without ever again seeing one of these Bayreuth music dramas. However often I have heard one of the *Nibelung* operas at one theater
or another since that first *Rheingold* production in Munich (that is, over nine
years), however honest my intention of appreciating and taking note of anything beautiful in them, my experiences have always produced the contrary
result: the most brilliant passages, involving as they mostly do sudden and
surprising orchestral effects, lose their appeal upon repeated hearing; and all
the rest only affects me more unpleasantly than ever.

This, I must repeat, is the confession of only one individual; I do not begrudge or misconstrue anyone else's delight in this music, nor do I mean to convert anyone to my position. Rather, I myself would have gladly converted—gladly pronounced my newly won conviction, gladly published the obituary of my former error, if indeed it had died within me. Only fools can suppose themselves infallible (and besides them, one other).[22] But it was no good. Despite all the brilliant and clever details, Wagner's *Nibelung* operas have seemed to me upon each rehearing only less true, less natural, less beautiful. Each time I am further convinced, I see more clearly and feel more deeply that in Wagner we see a case of an unusual talent that has stubbornly committed itself to a false system—one that will not reform opera, but simply kill it. For the sake of this new system of the "music drama," and perhaps due also to a sense of diminishing melodic invention, the same tone poet who was able to marry genuine dramatic expression to musical beauty in the best pieces of his earlier operas will now only furnish us with "dramatic truth"—a stale, unappealing truth whose only effect is boredom. "A scandalous boredom" was the well-chosen phrase that hurtled from Speidel's latest critique and crashed like a meteor amid the Wagnerian camp.[23] Though not unreceptive to the individual beauties of the *Nibelung* dramas, still I found myself leaving each of the four performances with the unshakable feeling that my experience had been less one of pleasure than of martyrdom. It is indeed a torture to sit through five hours of a laboriously unfolding drama ranging from thin to preposterous in quality—as in *Siegfried* or *Rheingold*—declaimed in atrocious German by abdicated gods, ugly dwarfs, and ludicrous magical animals. It is a torture to have to listen to music that lurches from inebriation to barrenness, gnawing at our nerves in painfully restless modulations, in continually overstimulated chromaticism and enharmonicism, and in the yammering monotony of piercing ninth and eleventh chords. It is a torture to listen to a long opera without chorus, without ensembles, without finales, and in the case of *Siegfried* without even female voices until close to the end—an opera in which the singers do not so much sing as declaim to the most unnatural intervallic leaps, while we cannot understand *what* they are declaiming without constantly resorting to a printed libretto. And finally, my dear readers, it is a torture to have to write about all this for the umpteenth time.

Parsifal Literature
(October 1882)

Wagner's literary armada had already done so much work—preparatory, elucidatory, adulatory—on *Parsifal*, all *before* the first production, that it would seem there is nothing further left for them to do.[24] Granted, the brochures about this "stage-consecration festival play" [*Bühnenweihfestspiel*] have not flowed quite as liberally as one might have expected; in number and volume they remain at the moment significantly below the flood level reached in the *Nibelung* year 1876. At any rate, there is much among all this, whether serious or just amusing, that might interest our readers. Let's begin with the amusing. The leader of this pack is a treatise by Edmund von Hagen on "The Significance of the Morning Reveille in R. Wagner's *Parsifal*."[25] The "significance" of this first, introductory scene (in which the sleeping knights and pages are woken up) seemed so immeasurably deep and immense to Herr von Hagen that he has filled 62 pages (octavo) with its explication—surely enough to put back to sleep those the scene set out to wake up. In view of this prolixity we cannot help but smile when the author says in his foreword that "the condensed form of his essay" is "to be excused in view of the abundant spiritual and intellectual content." The quality of this intellectual superabundance may be gauged from the following sentences:

> With the first *Parsifal* performance we feel that we are on the eve of a new day of national-popular culture [*Völkerkultur*], as it was in Paris 52 years ago today. With *Parsifal* we feel that the path of mankind has been newly charted, new paths of illumination have been discovered. We sense, too, the illumination of the night of humanity, the approach of a light that will bring the end of human suffering and the eternal joy of the spirit, even now as in the pure delight of the morning of resurrection.*

Anyone who does not recognize the sanctimonious oracular tone of the true Wagnerian priest here, as this is to be found especially in the

---

* Thoroughly characteristic of the vaunted "intellectual compression" of this treatise are the following remarkable chapter headings: I. On the significance of the morning. II. On the awakening. 1. On sleep. (a) The aesthetic side of sleep. (b) The ethical side of sleep. (c) The metaphysical side of sleep. (d) The symbolic side of sleep. (e) The historical side of sleep. 2. On the action of awakening. 3. On waking and wakefulness. (a) Awareness of world history. (b) Awareness of life's symbolism. (c) Awareness of the intellectuality of one's own personality. (d) Awareness of the morality of one's own personality. (e) Awareness of corporeality. III. On the lesson of the calling.

earlier writings of von Hagen, might easily take this treatise on the "Morning Call to Awakening" for a parodistic jest. In truth, however, it is in bitter earnest. "A sorry business," one of our more courageous younger music critics, Gustav Doempke, calls it: "A sorry business, this incredible counterfeiting of philosophical ideas in the glow of the aesthetic frenzy of inspiration—something to be pitied, ridiculed, but also feared and hated if one considers that a direction capable of cultivating such apostles also dares to strive for spiritual dominion, and indeed already holds a spiritual sway over many weak minds and empty heads."

Herr von Hagen is also the author of a book devoted to *The Poetry of the First Scene of "Das Rheingold"*[26] and with that work he gave the signal for this new school of specialized critical studies which—considering the entirety of a Wagner opera as something beyond mortal compass, a world quite transcending the perspective of any individual person—immerse themselves in a microscopic investigation of just one small segment. There is something touching in the modesty of this younger generation of Wagner enthusiasts who, while driven by a tormenting need to write, feel that the better part of the field has already been grazed by those who have come before. Their solution is to select one individual scene or a secondary character whose "significance" has so far not been sufficiently scrutinized and to place this scene or character under the admiring gaze of their magnifying glass. What more could there be still to say about the characters of Tristan and Isolde, for example? But King Marke! He has yet to be placed on a worthy altar. Of course, even genuine admirers of Wagner's *Tristan und Isolde* have had to admit that this old king plays a rather sorry, minor part—indeed a tragicomic one; like every cuckold who finds himself entirely ignored by his wife and her lover he is condemned to accept his lot with humble composure. This view, however, has been attacked by Herr Moritz Wirth in his brochure on the subject of King Marke in which he proves that "Marke is by no means a secondary character in Wagner's drama; rather, in a certain sense, the central figure," and that in his calm resignation he provides an example of the highest human capacity in the moral realm.[27] This King Marke, we learn, is "in spiritual terms to be ranked far above the King of Thule and King Lear." But onstage he ought to be presented as a seventy-year-old with white hair and beard. That is decisive, since the leading trait of his character is "passion calmed by insight." Why not give the good king another ten years, say we: with an eighty-year-old the passions are calmer still, and the insight into that "highest human capacity in the moral realm" still greater. Plenty of ink has flowed even about Senta and her Dutchman, but until now we have been lacking a treatise on "Erik and his relationship to the Dutchman and to Senta." Now that lacuna has been filled. The similarly pressing need for a monograph on the "character of Eva Pogner" has likewise been met by a Viennese musical writer, who illuminates even the tiniest verbal nooks and crannies of that character—naturally discovered to be the "ideal of German maidenhood." A French-language brochure by the Wagnerian writer E. van der Straaten boasts the classic title *Lohengrin: Instrumentation and Philosophy*. What next? Perhaps a treatise titled *Parsifal: Religion and Chromaticism*?

Among the more serious and objective critiques that have been published on the "stage-consecration festival play" those by Kalbeck and Max Goldstein deserve special mention.[28]

By far the lightest, most readable of the many brochures on *Parsifal* is Paul Lindau's *Bayreuth Letters from a Pure Fool*; it should also certainly be the best-selling of them.[29] It remains to be seen whether people find it as entertaining as Lindau's *Sober Letters* from the Nibelung year of 1876.[30] The latter, though not of much significance as musical criticism, at least did manage to convey, in the guise of a harmless joke, some bitter truths about the Wagner tetralogy. The same irresistible spirit of persiflage does not inform these *Parsifal* letters. Either Lindau has deliberately refrained from such witty aperçus this time, or else they have withheld themselves from him. There is no lack, of course, of individual intelligent and witty observations (for example, on those bothersome leitmotifs). However our expectation that Lindau would take aim at the most egregiously weak and foolish aspects of the libretto remains largely unfulfilled. As a prolific dramatic author and critic who is wont to take on every modern boob of a playwright and give him a good skewering, Lindau for some reason exhibits an unusually gentle tolerance toward all the false and repellent aspects of *Parsifal*. How can he truly believe that Wagner has "deepened" the element of moral and ethical conflict in Wolfram's epic? And that this has been done, moreover, by having Parsifal chosen "to win back the holy spear from its heathen robber," and to have him go forth heroically "first to struggle against Kundry, and then against Klingsor"? Could Lindau really be blind to the fact that quite the opposite is true? That Parsifal in fact does not make the slightest effort to "win back" the spear, nor does he actively risk any kind of "struggle" with Klingsor? Here indeed is one of the most evident failings of the Wagner drama. Once he is rendered "knowing" by the kiss of Kundry—that is, when he has learned that only the spear now guarded by Klingsor will serve to heal Amfortas's suffering—then Parsifal ought at once to assail Klingsor and wrest the spear from him by force. And yet he does nothing of the kind; rather he sings some long monologues, and listens to a yet longer one by Kundry, and if Klingsor himself did not finally have the bright idea of hurling the spear right *at* Parsifal, then poor Amfortas would still be yammering away just as helplessly as he was back in Act 1. For the sake of a cheap operatic effect—the spear hanging in midair above Parsifal at the end of the act—Wagner missed the one opportunity he had to let Parsifal win our sympathy by showing a little courage. Instead, his "pure fool" remains here, as he does throughout, an untalented and simply lazy fool.

In his recently published historical study of *The Aesthetics of Music* (a very stimulating book to which we would like at some point to give the fuller attention it deserves) Heinrich Ehrlich of Berlin has very aptly demonstrated R. Wagner's reliance on the views of the Romantic school (Schlegel, Tieck, Adam Müller). *Parsifal* confirms this once again.[31] In this work Ehrlich, like so many critics, takes strong objection to its representation of Christian mysteries. "Is it really possible," he exclaims, "that any artist who truly honors the spirit of Christianity should allow the holy mysteries of his religion played out in such luxurious trappings before a mixed audience? Does this not rather bespeak a kind of aesthetic refinement [*Raffinement*] quite removed from true Christian feeling?"

Indeed. But precisely because this refinement takes on such an unapologetically theatrical form, it does not strike me as such a great danger. I would not want to think that these decriers of profanation underestimate the power and significance of true religion; yet I *would* say that they are overestimating the power and significance of the theatrical-religious games played in *Parsifal*. As an audience member watching the semi-biblical scenes of *Parsifal* I may have felt put off by their affectation and inner hollowness, but I felt no reason to take offense at their religious garb. At no moment did I suppose myself in church, but only in the theater. The controversial scenes of the foot-washing, the anointment, and the communion feast all made on me a thoroughly operatic impression—"operatic" not in a derogatory sense, but in a strictly technical-generic one. I cannot see this "stage-consecration festival play" as anything different from an opera, and there is no reason to see it otherwise if we want to do the work proper justice. Whatever Wagner supposes him to be, the white-clad fool with his youthful locks is no Christ, the screeching hermaphrodite [*Zwitter*] Kundry is no Magdalen, the hocus-pocus of the Grail and its Bengal-fire illumination is no sacrament at the altar. For this reason I was able to share in Bayreuth neither the religious indignation of the one party nor the religious ecstasies of the other. The latter least of all. For my part, I find myself much more moved to devout, religious feelings by the simple prayer of Agathe in *Der Freischütz* or the chorus of prisoners in *Fidelio* than by the whole of *Parsifal*. The holy spirit of this work impresses me only very slightly, while I am more greatly impressed, finally, by the secular artistic spirit of Wagner: that is what reveals itself here in many new and powerful features.

NOTES

1. Eduard Hanslick, "February 13, 1883," given as postscript to "*Parsifal* (Letters from Bayreuth, July 1882)," in *Vienna's Golden Years of Music, 1850–1900: Eduard Hanslick*, trans. and ed. Henry Pleasants III, (New York, 1950), 239. See also Hanslick, "Zum 13. Februar 1883," in *Aus dem Opernleben der Gegenwart* (Berlin, 1884), 353–55.

2. Pleasants, ed., *Vienna's Golden Years of Music*, 239.

3. For details on this event and a brief overview of the relationship between Hanslick and Wagner, see Thomas Grey, "Masters and Their Critics: Wagner, Hanslick, and Beckmesser," in *Wagner's "Meistersinger": Performance, History, Interpretation*, ed. Nicholas Vazsonyi (Rochester, N.Y., 2003), 162–89, esp. 168–73.

4. The complete text of Hanslick's extensive early review of Wagner's *Tannhäuser* can be found in the first volume of the new collected edition of his writings, Eduard Hanslick, *Sämtliche Schriften*, ed. Dietmar Strauss (*Aufsätze und Rezensionen* 1844–48; Cologne, Weimar, and Vienna, 1993), 57–93. See also the translated excerpts in Pleasants, ed., *Vienna's Golden Years of Music*, 21–36.

5. Hanslick, "Wagner-Kultus" (September 1882), in *Aus dem Opernleben der Gegenwart*, 338–49.

6. These reviews, originally published in a series of installments in Hanslick's hometown paper, Vienna's *Neue freie Presse*, are translated in Pleasants, ed., *Vienna's Golden Years of Music*, 139–74 and 212–38.

7. Hanslick, "Wagner-Kultus," 339. Hanslick mainly voices skepticism regarding Wagner's preaching of vegetarianism and his opposition to the use of animals for medical experimentation, as well as the related discourse of "regeneration." He mentions Wagner's anti-Semitic agenda once or twice, only in passing.

8. The text of this essay is taken from *Musikalische Stationen*, vol. 2, *Die moderne Oper* (Berlin, 1885), 277–89.

9. Hanslick seems to allude to Angelo Neumann's touring *Ring* production, which took the principal singers and a simplified version of the sets from the Bayreuth production to London and across much of continental Europe beginning in 1882. The Vienna productions under discussion here, however, predate Neumann's enterprise.

10. The *Ring* cycle was officially designated by Wagner as a "trilogy in three evenings" to which *Das Rheingold* served as a prologue (*Vorabend*, or "pre-evening").

11. Hanslick refers to the very first performance of *Das Rheingold* at the command of King Ludwig II (against the wishes of Wagner), which took place at the court theater in Munich in September 1869.

12. In Hanslick's reviews of the original Munich production of *Das Rheingold* he likened the orchestrally accompanied scene changes to the technology of "dissolving views," there as here using the English phrase for a particular kind of "magic lantern" projection developed in the early nineteenth century whereby one projected image is gradually replaced by a second, with no visual gap between. In describing the effect of Bayreuth's brightly lit stage space, in contrast to the darkened auditorium, he also likened the effect to "transparencies or dioramas." On the Munich production, see Hanslick, *Die moderne Oper* (Berlin, 1875), 308; on the Bayreuth theater, see *Musikalische Stationen*, 2:228, and Pleasants, ed., *Vienna's Golden Years of Music*, 151–52. Hanslick makes the same complaint, however, about the inadequacy of the Rainbow Bridge (*Musikalische Stationen*, 2:250; Pleasants, ed., *Vienna's Golden Years of Music*, 172). The optical technologies originally explored by Weber and his producers for the Wolf's Glen scene in *Der Freischütz* are investigated by Anthony Newcomb in "New Light(s) on Weber's Wolf's Glen Scene," in *Opera and the Enlightenment*, ed. Thomas Bauman and Marita McClymonds (Cambridge, 1995), 61–91. The difficulty of achieving a properly realistic Rainbow Bridge in *Das Rheingold* continued to be a vexing problem in the era of elaborate stage illusion. Moritz Wirth (mentioned in Hanslick's review of writings on *Parsifal*) devoted a three-part article to

the subject in 1888, including technical specifications: "Walhall und Regenbogen," *Musikalisches Wochenblatt* 19/10–12 (1–15 March 1888): 113–15, 129–31, 141–43.

13. "Vernunft wird Unsinn, Wohltat Plage." Goethe, *Faust*, Part 1, "Faust's Study," l. 1976.

14. Johann Nepomuk Nestroy (1801–62), Viennese satirical actor and author of numerous highly popular comedies and farces, began his career as an operatic bass.

15. The principal cut described here corresponds to the passage from Wotan's line "Ein Andres ist's: achte es wohl" (Act 2, measure 779) to "Fromm streite für Fricka" (Act 2, measure 996). Possibly the cut dovetailed Brünnhilde's question "Was macht dir nun Sorge, da nie wir gesäumt"? with the later, "O sag, künde, was soll nun dein Kind?" (each of these questions immediately precedes, respectively, the lines of Wotan just cited).

16. Bertha Ehnn and Amalie Materna (1844–1918): the latter was the first Bayreuth Brünnhilde. The two singers performed the roles of Elisabeth and Venus, respectively, in a *Tannhäuser* production admired by Wagner in Vienna in November 1875.

17. Hanslick is referring to the fight between Siegmund and Hunding (Act 2, scene 5).

18. Ferdinand Jäger (1839–1902), German tenor who had been coached by Wagner as a potential Siegfried for the first Bayreuth festival, although his first performances of the role were in Vienna and in private productions for Ludwig II in Munich. He sang the role in Berlin in 1881 and was one of Wagner's Parsifals in 1882.

19. Etienne-Nicolas Méhul's oratorio-like *opéra comique* of 1807, *Joseph*, remained popular in German theaters throughout much of the nineteenth century. The simple, lyrical style of the vocal writing is far removed from the style of Wagner's Siegfried, hence Hanslick's comment on Jäger's unsuitability.

20. *Die Meistersinger* was first produced at the Vienna Hofoper in March 1870. At that time (and earlier, at the 1868 Munich premiere) Hanslick reviewed it quite negatively. Afterward, and despite his own notorious implication in the failings of the master/critic Beckmesser, Hanslick came to admire the work as the most successful—in part because the most "operatic" and least pretentious—of Wagner's mature music dramas.

21. Hans Demetrius (Ritter von) Hopfen (1835–1904) was a Bavarian novelist and playwright.

22. By "one other" Hanslick presumably alludes to Wagner and his own widely advertised sense of infallibility.

23. Ludwig Speidel (1830–1906) was a fellow anti-Wagnerian critic who, like Hanslick, also wrote for the *Neue freie Presse*. Though he wrote on music and opera, he was primarily a theater critic.

24. This review was originally published in *Neue freie Presse* (Vienna), October 1882. The text is taken from *Aus dem Opernleben der Gegenwart*, vol. 3, *Die moderne Oper* (Berlin, 1884), 331–37.

25. Edmund von Hagen (1850–1907), *Die Bedeutung des Morgenweckrufes in Richard Wagners Bühenweihfestspiel "Parsifal" erörtert* (Berlin, 1882), 62 pages.

26. Edmund von Hagen, *Über die Dichtung der ersten Scene des "Rheingold" von Richard Wagner: Ein Beitrag zur Beurtheilung des Dichters* (Munich, 1876), 170 pages.

27. Moritz Wirth (1849–1917), *König Marke: Aesthetisch-kritische Streifzüge durch Wagners "Tristan und Isolde"* (Leipzig, 1882), 94 pages.

28. Max Kalbeck (1850–1921), *Richard Wagner's "Parsifal": Erste Aufführung am 26. Juli 1882 zu Bayreuth* (Breslau, 1883), 94 pp.; Max Goldstein, *Richard Wagners "Parsifal": Briefe aus Bayreuth von Max Goldstein* (Berlin, 1882), 57 pages.

29. Paul Lindau (1839–1919), *"Bayreuther Briefe vom reinen Thoren: "Parsifal" von Richard Wagner* (Breslau, 1883), 60 pages.

30. Paul Lindau, *Nüchterne Briefe aus Bayreuth: Vergeblicher Versuch im Jahre 1876, Zeit und Geister Richard Wagners zu bannen* (Breslau, 1876); ed. with introduction by Hellmut Kotschenreuther (Berlin, 1989), 95 pages.

31. Heinrich Ehrlich (1822–99), *Die Musik-Ästhetik in ihrer Entwickelung von Kant bis auf die Gegenwart: Ein Grundriss* (Leipzig, 1881), 186 pages.

Hans von Wolzogen's *Parsifal* (1887)

HANS VON WOLZOGEN
TRANSLATED, INTRODUCED, AND EDITED
BY MARY A. CICORA

With the foundation of the Bayreuth theater in 1872 and the first Bayreuth Festival in 1876, there began to form around Wagner in Bayreuth a group of followers known as the "Bayreuth circle." The publication organ of the Bayreuth circle was the *Bayreuther Blätter*, which was published from 1878 to 1938. With this periodical the members of the Wagner circle intended to discuss and spread Wagner's views on art and society. The composer, however, never fully identified himself with what was published in the journal, which remained the pet project of Hans von Wolzogen (he remained the sole editor up to the time of his death in 1938). Over the years the connection between the journal and Wagner's writings became more and more tenuous.

Wagner's *Parsifal*, the "stage-consecration festival-play" (*Bühnenweih-festspiel*) of Bayreuth, assumed special significance for the members of the early Bayreuth circle, as it embodied Wagner's late views on art and the regeneration of modern society. Wagner's Schopenhauerian interpretation of the Christian religion theorized how redemption would reside in the renunciation of the Will and by acquiring compassion with all living things, as in Parsifal's compassion with Amfortas and resultant regeneration of the Grail Realm. Through experiencing this final drama, the audience was to become, like Parsifal, wise through compassion. Of all of the music dramas, *Parsifal* was most closely associated with Bayreuth as the Master's last work and ultimate dramatic statement, and through its religious subject matter *Parsifal* led the Bayreuth circle to resemble a sacred cult.

In the following excerpts from an article that originally appeared in the *Bayreuther Blätter*, Hans von Wolzogen assumes the role of spokesperson for the Bayreuth circle, speaking *ex cathedra* to propound a correctly orthodox interpretation of *Parsifal*.[1] He is replying to another critic, Paulus Cassel, and sets him straight on various points of the drama, defending Wagner against what he perceives as irresponsible, uninformed misinterpretations of the drama on the part of Cassel and others. In his discussion of *Parsifal*, Wolzogen emphasizes the symbolic and ethical significance of the drama in his analysis of the two central symbols, the Grail and the Spear. In both cases, Wolzogen argues for the higher moral and ethical significance of Wagner's drama.

The first excerpt concerns the Grail, the central symbol of the drama. Wolzogen attributes Cassel's lack of understanding to his failure to grasp the correct religious significance of the dramatic features. Accordingly, Wolzogen stresses the symbolic, and with it, the higher moral and ethical significance of the Grail, and to substantiate this he traces the representations of the Grail through archaic folklore, the Christian versions, and the medieval romances, among others. Wolzogen carefully distinguishes the different forms that the Grail has assumed throughout the transmission of the legend: the *Kelch* (chalice), the *Schüssel* (bowl or serving dish), the *Schale* (basin, larger than a cup), and the stone of Wolfram von Eschenbach's version.

Wolzogen grasps the opportunity for a pseudo-scholarly folkloric exegesis that encompasses etymological derivations, following the Grail through Celtic, Nordic, Egyptian, Chinese, Mexican, Greek, Jewish, Indian, and Persian rites, demonstrating the regressive interest of nineteenth-century thinkers in primal materials. Regardless of the validity of Wolzogen's analyses when evaluated by modern critical standards, the importance of his thought lies in his assertion of the higher, ethical significance of the Grail and its universality. Wolzogen (sharing Wagner's disdain for traditional *Wissenschaft*) scoffs at the scholar for proposing the wrong (a historical) prototype of the Grail. The mention of the bloodless meal is also a reference to Wagner's concern, in the later writings, that pious care for all living things should be practiced through vegetarianism.

The next excerpt concerns a common topic of Wagner scholarship, the changes that the composer made to Wolfram's version of the Parzival legend. The medieval romance *Parzival* of Wolfram von Eschenbach provided the main source material for Wagner's drama, though Wagner felt that Wolfram had gotten the legend all wrong and thus warranted correction (as a result, Wagner has frequently been charged with distortion of his medieval sources). The case in point is the use of the Spear, which, Cassel had claimed, renders Parsifal's character development unnecessary, arguing that the two stipulations for Parsifal's healing of Amfortas—his character progression and the recovery of the Spear—render each other superfluous. Wolzogen takes care to justify Wagner's changes with reference to dramatic necessity. Wolzogen appeals to the strict dramatic determination of the course of events, following Wagner's theoretical premise of tightly knit dramatic causality. As in the excerpts on the Grail,

Wolzogen argues here, too, for the higher ethical significance of Wagner's work as compared to his archaic or medieval sources. His references to the importance of the "deed" echo Wagner's revision of dogmatic religion, appealing to a more active kind of Christianity. *Parsifal* symbolized the regeneration of modern society through a Schopenhauerian kind of compassion with all living beings.

HANS VON WOLZOGEN
Parsifal Criticism
From the pages of the *Bayreuther Blätter* (1887)

Three years after the text of *Parsifal* appeared, the professor and preacher Paulus Cassel, known to be an especially well-read expert and syncretist of mythological subject matter, published a fairly lengthy study of the legends of Tannhäuser, Lohengrin, the Grail, and Parsifal in a newly founded Berlin periodical, *Musikwelt* (Fall 1881, nos. 1–9), under the title "Aus dem Königreiche des Gral." When in this article he finally got around to discussing Wagner's treatment of the material, he could have been expected to deliver a really solid presentation of the musical-dramatic use of the legends that many would find enlightening, and on the same interesting and informative basis as his preceding articles. At any rate, we did not know how far the abilities of this scholar, so well versed in matters relating to the understanding of our German music, would extend. On the other hand, one could hope that he would of course understand and appreciate the religious aspect of the work, which can be fully comprehended by the emotions only through the music.

Let us first examine his interpretation of the Grail, which differs from all of the usual ones.

If we trace the Grail through the older variations of the legends that allude to it or relate to it, then we find among others its mythological prototype in the Gaelic North as the purification vessel of the maternal goddess Ceridven, to whose cult later the order of the Druidic bards of the "Cauldron of Ceridven" was consecrated. In this cauldron the juice of particular herbs was brewed. This vessel refers back to various related phenomena in the myths of many peoples. We know the legend from the Edda about how Odin cleverly steals the magic mead of poetry (*Begeisterungstrank*), the *Odhroerir* (that is, a "sensation-stirrer" or stimulant) of Kvasis's blood from the care of Gunnlödh in the lair of Riesenheim. The Egyptian Odin-Hermes, Thot, passes the cup of grace in the Realm of the Dead. He is the dog-god, whose star, Sirius, is thought to be the harbinger of the deluge and the star of rain. Hu, the husband of Ceridven, the Gaelic "lord of the deep"—who, like Hermes and Odhin, was also a rain- and water-god—corresponds to Thot-Hermes as a god of death. The fertilization of the earth by water for revival (rejuvenation, rebirth) is the initial idea for the worship of a sacred vessel. In our Nordic mythology the guardian at the rainbow bridge, Heimdallr, is supposed to be a son of nine mothers. A bardic song "Quarry of the Deep" says: "I fight for the glory of the teaching, the first word of which was revealed by the cauldron that was warmed by the breath of the nine maidens. Is it not the cauldron of the lord of the deep?" The realm of water is at the same time the realm of the deep, of death, as all life is thought to have evolved from there. It was the true home of all belief in mysteries; and even more it offered significant points of contact for the secret cult, as the realm of water became a realm of wine, beverages that have been prepared by humans, and thereby the mystery of nature further developed into a celebration of culture, human ability, and knowledge, the superiority of spirit over nature.

The union of people who work together for the welfare of the whole, as in the practices of agriculture and viniculture, also leads to a worshipping community, which gradually assumes the character of mysteries through the celebratory connection with the mysterious life of nature itself. The simple form of production and the enjoyment of the products of nature already acquired a spiritual significance. In China the sacred meal with bread and wine is celebrated in remembrance of Confucius. The Mexicans believed that in the consecrated bread they were eating the god himself and named it Tuokualo (god-meal). Soma and Hom of the Indians and Persians were also divine beings that were partaken of with intoxicating drink. At first the mysteries of Eleusis celebrated only the drink "Kykeon" (in the holy bowl) and "Sesam" (bread in the holy chest), that is, the gifts of Dionysos and Demeter; afterward these gods themselves were celebrated, enjoyed through their gifts. Through this communal enjoyment each felt himself initiated into the sacred essence of nature, sworn into a higher spiritual brotherhood, and now celebrated the god as Dionysos Isodaites, the god of the same love-feast. Pythagoras and Plato, the greatest philosophers of Greece, joined into these mysteries, with their schools. As opposed to the bloody sacrifices of battle advocated by the cult of heroism, the bloodless meal was introduced there. In it was established the union of man with his fellow human beings through pious protection of all that is living. This ancient vegetarianism recurs as a moral precept among the Pythagoreans and later Platonists. The Jewish Essenes adopted the same idea in their secret society, and the teaching of Christ was more than symbolically sealed with the bloodless meal, instead of the sacrificial Easter lamb of the Jews. While in this manner the ancient service of the holy vessel achieved higher and higher ethical significance, the festive celebratory meals of the first

human community came to the Christians as sacred feasts of brotherly love
(Agapai) and formed in their legends the symbol of the Grail. This is what
we see now in the Grail Castle of our *Parsifal*, radiating its light over
the bread and wine of the love-feast to spread sustenance and blessings: the
heathen cauldron has been transformed into the bowl of the Christian
Eucharist.

In the story of the magician Merlin from the chronicle of Geoffrey of
Monmouth (twelfth century) we already find Joseph of Arimathea in the
desert ordained by Christ to guard the Eucharistic meal with the golden
chalice. This Eucharistic vessel—which is also the basin into which Christ's
blood is said to have flowed from the cross—surfaces for the first time after
that under the name *Grail* in the Old French romance *Joseph d'Arimathie*,
by Robert de Boron.[2] Then Chrétien de Troyes, Wolfram's predecessor
in the Parzival literature, has the Grail of Joseph of Arimathea, to which
he adds the bloody lance.[3] In Wolfram, by contrast, the Grail is a stone, a
glowing *Lapis erilis*, which nevertheless, just like the ancient bowl of myth,
also gives food and drink, grants health and youth; its power is renewed
every year on Good Friday through the host placed on it by heaven.[4]
This stone comes from the southern sources of the Grail legend, where
evidently Oriental star- and stone-worship had been influential. Wolfram
names Kiot as his authority, who in turn had relied on the Spanish-Arabian
half-Jew Flegetanis (*Felek-daneh*, that is, astronomer). Flegetanis is said to
have read the name of the Grail in the stars. When the author of the *Jüngeren
Titurel* came along, this precious stone evolved into the basin, in which
Christ performed the Last Supper, and which was brought by angels to
Titurel.[5] If the knighthood of the *Templeisen*, with its kings from Titurel's
family called to guard the Grail, is for the medieval world a depiction of
the Oriental Templar order, one can point to the fact that for the cult of
the Templars not the Oriental stone but rather the Christian chalice plays
a sacred role. The chalice with two torches, just like the glowing Grail,
was the main feature of the Templar building in Syria.[6] The Templars were
also accused of worshipping a bloody head in a bowl (the head of John
the Baptist)—a symbol that recurs in the Gaelic form of the legend, as
shown to us by the far newer collection called the *Mabinogion*.[7] In this
way the sacred vessel also comes from the South as from the North, for the
two to combine to form the basin of the Grail. The word *Grail* is, accordingly, traced back to the Old French *graal*, *greal*, *gradal*; in Old Spanish,
grial; Provencal, *grazal*; Old Catalonian, *grasal*, that is, vessel, dish, basin.
Uhland cites a *Testamentum comitis Everardi* from the year 873, in which
the plate is designated with *garalis*. The roots of these words have been
identified with the Greek *gra·o*, that is, *graso* (gnaw, eat), the same word
that is to be found in Slavic *kros* and in our colloquial speech *krasen*

(*schmausen*). The main root would thus be *gar*, with the original meaning: *schlingen, schlucken*; from which also *gara, garos, giré*, that is, drink, derives directly; and the Greek *gras*, Old Roman *gras, graz*, and *grad*, are further permutations.

By contrast, Professor Cassel (without any evidence relating to the legend) presents his own unique and striking discovery: that according to a Roman custom introduced by the emperor Aurelius and transmitted by Constantine to Byzantium, bread by the name of *panes gradiles* was distributed to the populace from the steps of the palace. This Byzantine *panes gradiles* is supposed to have been the prototype of the Grail by virtue of its significance and name. He considers that fact so sound that wherever he does not find this view shared and the Grail is portrayed instead as a vessel or bowl, he automatically feels the foundation of the legend or literature has been shaken. Thus he takes great exception to Wagner's Grail, which is designated "an ancient crystal basin." As far as he is concerned, this serves as proof that Wagner's *Parsifal* is untrue to the genuine spirit of the Christian legend. To the discoverer of the *panes gradiles,* any gentle swaying of the vessel in Wagner's drama rocks the very foundation of the Grail Castle. He finds that thereby "a magic game is played" which so confuses him that in the sublime scene of the love-feast he can only glimpse unmotivated glaring light. He can explain this in no other way than by saying it is an operatic craving for decorative and machinistic stage effects. Isn't it lamentable that even such experienced and gifted men as our clerical mythologist can be so taken in by preconceived notions as to view a great work of art from the outset with a half-closed look of doubt and distrust?
. . .

The learned scholar also failed to grasp Parsifal's folly, because Wagner's version lacks the question that is talked about so much in Wolfram. Immediately the whole work again enters that shady and evil realm of opera, so that he complains loudly about "the distortion of the hero, the most beautiful character of the Middle Ages." "There is not a trace of the thought that encompasses Parcival's question;[8] the most important thing is to have fancy scenery, spectacles, 'gloomy lighting,' and above all, that lastly 'the Grail glows'!" He sees no further and knows nothing else, but he is learned in folklore research and believes that as such he is allowed to pronounce his critical verdict about our stage consecration festival play even before it has been performed. In what kind of light he wishes to thereby be regarded is illuminated by a later postscript that especially needs to be taken into consideration as he explains: "I have spoken not so much as a critic of Wagner's work as an apologist of Wolfram—or, to express myself more precisely, as a rescuer of the 'simplicity' of Parcival himself." And as this rescuer of simplicity he then continues:

> I cannot believe that if Richard Wagner had known the sublime idea
> of simplicity represented by Parcival—to which alone the signifi-
> cance of the question can be reduced—he would have concerned
> himself with the mythological story about the lance that wounds and
> heals, and which belongs to a totally different complex of ideas. For
> does the question have any meaning whatsoever in his *Parsifal* any-
> more, if it can't have any effect and needs to wait until the recovery
> of the lance? And then why is Parsifal's not asking so severely repri-
> manded?! Nothing would have been gained if he had asked, and
> nothing lost if he didn't ask. If Wagner had correctly grasped the
> power and significance of the "simplex"—and it is as morally as it is
> poetically glorious—then he would have just let Klinschor [Klingsor]
> keep the lance. It has absolutely no dramatic justification.

If the scholar could not find "any trace" of the "thought" that "encompasses Parcival's question"—and even less because in Wagner's *Parsifal* it
is not a matter of this "question," because this question is not even an issue—
then we must think of what this question really means in order to arrive
at some "dramatic justification" for the lance. For the epic poet, the question contains the formulaic symbol of something silent; it is not a question
posed to find out something not previously known. For when Wolfram's
Parcival, on his final return to the Grail Castle, asks Anfortas:[9] "Uncle, what
is ailing you?" he already knows what ails Anfortas; but to fulfill the
prophecy—that by his question the uncle will be cured—he must ask, despite
his knowledge.

What else could the question signify but compassion? But just the feeling of compassion alone cannot redeem the suffering of Amfortas. For the
epic poet the compassion, according to the symbolism of legends, must be
clothed in the form of the question, which has taken up a specific expression; and indeed, an expression from the mouth of the one human being,
who out of childlike simplicity through error and struggles, just as the promise predicts, achieves the fulfillment of his healing mission: Parcival. For the
dramatist the mere expression does not suffice; for him the compassion
must become a deed. The question, the symbolic word, becomes the recovery of the stolen Spear, an actual symbol. It is not the compassion alone or
its expression, but rather the deed of compassion that heals and redeems.
This is what the scholar has not understood, if he can ask in astonishment
what the foolish Parsifal is supposed to do at his first visit to the Grail Castle;
because then—even if he were no fool, but already "wise through compassion"—he could not have cured Amfortas, for this can be accomplished

only by the Holy Spear. For him the two stipulations of the cure—the "pure fool" and the touching of the wound with the Spear—comprise two separate issues, so that one renders the other superfluous. This is how he "understands" the content of the great despairing lament of Amfortas, which seems to him full of misunderstanding, and he paraphrases it with the following nice words: "Amfortas loses himself in the thoughts that Wagner added, and that were borrowed from mythology, that the spear that wounds should also heal, and thereby Parcival's healing is lost. For in Wagner's version it depends on the spear, not on the person."

In Wolfram's version, the saying inscribed on the Grail promises only who will come and ask the question, but not the nature of this person ("wise through compassion"). The question is, as mentioned, the symbol of the nature of the compassionate pure one. When the promised helper, the young Parcival, arrives at Monsalvat, but does not ask the question, he is reproached for being hardhearted; since everyone knows that he is the helper, and they see that he does not help. In Wagner's version it is different. Here Parsifal is not promised by name, but rather just as one "made wise through compassion, a pure fool." Gurnemanz is the only one who, since he has recognized in Parsifal a pure fool, believes that he has found in him the one whose compassion with Amfortas, when he sees him, will make him wise, and thus the helper. But he is disappointed when Parsifal, even after seeing Amfortas, remains the unwise fool. This is where the privilege of the dramatist comes in. He must have Parsifal undergo a character development to become the helper and healer through suffering and deeds. The pure fool must fight to win the wisdom from compassion. Only in this way does he also acquire the power to regain the Holy Spear. On his first visit to the Grail Castle, Parsifal is not yet the helper. He becomes this through the course of the drama, to then return with the symbol of the healing (the Spear), and carry out the redeeming deed of compassion. If he had become wise on his first visit he would nevertheless, even with this knowledge, have sought to alleviate the cause of this suffering by regaining the Spear from Klingsor. The helper must act in order to be able to help. That he delayed the redeeming deed through his folly, that he had to remain so deeply ensnared in his faulty and idle lack of compassion—that drives him to despair even after he has recovered the Spear; and then the others feel compassion for him, whereas in Wolfram's version they curse him.

In this way everything in Wagner's dramatic depiction in *Parsifal* changes through the vital deepening of the ethical significance of the legendary transmission, and thereby the necessary transformation of question into deed. But one learned authority [Cassel] says to this that the lance, the symbol and means of the deed, "has absolutely no dramatic justification"!

NOTES

In his early prose sketches for *Parsifal*, Wagner used Wolfram von Eschenbach's spelling of the hero's name, "Parzival"; in 1877 he switched to "Parsifal" for the verse text. In the quarrel over philological accuracy between Wolzogen and Paulus Cassel the two critics use another, cognate spelling of the name, "Parcival." In this excerpt I have retained their inconsistencies.

    1. The article was reprinted in *Wagneriana: Gesammelte Aufsätze über R. Wagners Werke vom Ring bis zum Gral* (Leipzig, 1888), 133–62. The excerpts presented here are taken from pages 133–38 and 147–50.

    2. Robert de Boron: French poet of the late twelfth and early thirteenth century; author of *Joseph d'Arimathie* and *Merlin*.

    3. Chrétien de Troyes: medieval French poet whose romance of Perceval in *Li Contes del Graal* served as the source for Wolfram's *Parzival*.

    4. Wolfram von Eschenbach (ca. 1170–1220), the German knight and poet (probably Bavarian), was the author of *Parzival*, Wagner's main source for *Parsifal*.

    5. *Der jüngere Titurel* (The younger Titurel): poem by Albrecht von Scharfenberg (written ca. 1260–75) in which the poet speaks through the persona of Wolfram; based on Wolfram's *Titurel* fragment and on his *Parzival*.

    6. Knights Templar: military order of the Middle Ages, founded after the First Crusade of 1096 to ensure the safety of Europeans who made the pilgrimage to the Holy Land after it was conquered.

    7. *Mabinogion*: a collection of medieval Welsh folktales.

    8. "Anfortas" is the Grail King in Wolfram's version; Wagner changed the name to "Amfortas," in 1877, at the same time he switched from "Parzival" to "Parsifal."

Cosima Wagner's Bayreuth

RICHARD POHL, ARTHUR SEIDL, EUGEN GURA, ARNOLD
SCHERING, HEINRICH CHEVALLEY
TRANSLATED BY MARY A. CICORA
INTRODUCED AND ANNOTATED BY DAVID BRECKBILL

"Der grosse Todte lebt!" (The great dead man lives!) With this slogan—the conclusion of his lengthy essay-review for the *Musikalisches Wochenblatt* of the 1886 Bayreuth Festival, a portion of which appears below—Arthur Seidl deftly captures the meaning of Bayreuth for a significant swath of Wagnerians in the years just following Wagner's death. Seidl himself spelled out the matter more specifically in another, slightly later review. After listing and criticizing numerous shortcomings in Munich's *Ring* production of August 23–29, 1886, Seidl was moved to claim:

> It will always seem to me that Wagner is still not sufficiently understood and valued as a genius of stage direction and of theater. People seem completely to forget that he also set us problems in the technique of staging and of decorative apparatus that still need to be solved, because in these realms too he rushed ahead of his time and left to us the task of reflecting and working out the details, just as we once needed to assimilate his music, his poetry, and his music-dramatic style in general.[1]

In the early twenty-first century, producing Wagner's works in ways that help audiences to grapple afresh with the implications of his dramatic themes or his problematic legacy to Western culture often means overriding his specific staging instructions. In such a context, Seidl's perspective seems to come from another world. Nevertheless, instead of seeing Wagner's operas as dramas requiring modifications and glosses to retain relevance, in the late nineteenth century the technical difficulties that needed to be surmounted were part of what made it seem that Wagner's works and legacy remained unfinished and thus alive, striving toward an ideal embodiment that had not yet been attained. And Bayreuth was in many ways the laboratory in which work toward this end was most concentrated.

Bayreuth during its two decades (1886–1906) under the direction of Cosima Wagner has—despite its undoubted achievements—customarily been characterized as overly reactionary, excessively pious, and impossibly rigid.[2] Thus thinking of it as an institution that was productively addressing issues Wagner had left unfinished requires an alteration of perspective. To do so, we must dig deeper than to accept unquestioningly Bayreuth's inconsistencies and sanctimoniousness as reported (and reveled in) by such disgruntled or irreverent commentators as Lilli Lehmann, Felix Weingartner, Mark Twain, and George Bernard Shaw, who have too often been allowed to shape our perception of this period. Collections of writings like those assembled by Robert Hartford or Susanna Großmann-Vendrey tend to emphasize what might be called the "tourist experience" or larger issues concerning Bayreuth's place in society, culture, and politics.[3] The present selection of documents, however, attempts to take Bayreuth on its own terms by focusing on detailed accounts and evaluations of actual performances given there. Each of these excerpts, all of them by German writers, usually explicitly and always at least implicitly stresses particular ways in which Bayreuth performances compared to those of the past (including those supervised by Wagner himself) or those on other German stages. Although none of them are entirely uncritical, these excerpts help modern readers to learn the modes of thinking and perception employed by earlier Wagner audiences, and thereby to understand why those observers valued what they did in Bayreuth performances of the years immediately after Wagner's death.

The extent to which the present documents focus on the work of singers contrasts significantly with evaluations of present-day Wagner productions, in which the critic's chief responsibility is to explain the premise and nature of the production. In early Bayreuth, by contrast, since the framework of the production did not stray far from Wagner's actual instructions for staging and scenery, the singers' abilities to embody and portray character were a primary dimension in the way the works were perceived. The artistry of the singers in question can no longer be experienced, but the descriptions of their work by these authors usually manage to relay the fundamental impression they made on at least one observer.

News of the Day: Musical Letters from Bayreuth
(1886)

The editor of the Musikalisches Wochenblatt, *Ernst Wilhelm Fritzsch (1840–1902), was a staunch supporter of Wagner and of the Bayreuth enterprise, and the festival of 1886, the first in which Cosima Wagner was publicly recognized as the festival director, was an especially crucial one in the attempt to set the festival on firm artistic and financial footing. Fritzsch therefore commissioned two critics to cover the revival of* Parsifal *and the first Bayreuth production of* Tristan und Isolde— *Richard Pohl (1826–96), a longtime associate of Richard Wagner, was to discuss the opening performances (*Parsifal *on July 23 and* Tristan *on July 25), and Martin Krause (1853–1918) was assigned the performances of August 1 (third* Tristan *performance) and August 2 (fourth* Parsifal *performance). In the event, Krause, a pupil of Franz Liszt, was called upon to look after matters arising from the death of his Master in Bayreuth on July 31, and so the young Arthur Seidl (1863–1928) substituted for Krause in commenting on the second set of performances.*[4] *Fritzsch allowed his writers plenty of rein; both reviews were extended essays in several sections and were spread over six issues of the magazine (with the last section of Pohl's review and the first section of Seidl's appearing in the same issue).*

Although both of these writers were enthusiastic champions of the Wagnerian cause, the contrast between them reflects both temperamental and generational differences. Pohl emerges as a kindly commentator whose idealization of Wagner leads him to formulate appreciative but often bland and generalized observations. (For example, his discussion of the individual singers in Parsifal *is so unspecific, tactful, and complacently considerate that it has been omitted here.) One recalls that Wagner, though thankful for Pohl's devotion to him, was not overly impressed by his acuity (see letter to Erwin Rohde of 28 October 1872).*[5] *Seidl, by contrast, demonstrates the idealism of youth (he was still early in his career and a student in Munich when this review was written), and digs into performance details with great relish, seizing on spontaneous moments, specific failings, and his own perceptions of particular performances as if they possessed life-or-death significance. Although his experience with Wagner's work was not yet as long as Pohl's, for the purposes of this festival he possessed valuable background, since he attended some performances before the ones he stepped in to review, and was thus able to provide a sense of ways in which, and the degree to which, standards varied from one performance to another. Unlike Pohl, he seems strongly opinionated and not especially diplomatic, so much so that (for example) his initial sentence disapproving of Heinrich Gudehus as Tristan earns a question mark from the editor (omitted below). (Regional differences may be at play here—Seidl, then studying in Munich, seems devoted to the artistry of Heinrich Vogl, the Munich-based tenor whose attributes were clearly quite different from those of Gudehus, engaged in Dresden and thus not far from the Leipzig-based Fritzsch.) At the same time, he is if anything even more enthusi-astic than Pohl about the Bayreuth enterprise (he was ultimately to become an extremely prolific writer about Wagner, and a member of what Winfried Schüler has designated the "middle generation" of the Bayreuth circle).*[6] *For him, Bayreuth represented a model toward which all other theaters should strive, a place where all admirers of Wagner should come to study, learn from, and experience multiple performances of each work (he is dismissive of the tourists who breeze in for a performance as "the thing to do"). When read beside Pohl, the intensity and detail with which Seidl experiences and evaluates performances demonstrates a new stage in the criticism of Wagner productions.*

RICHARD POHL

Bayreuth, 24 July 1886.

Here we are again, in the one and only Bayreuth—yes, indeed, the one and only, for where else can one see and hear anything like what is offered to us here?[7] This is surely the cause of much partly hidden, partly obvi-ous rancor on the part of all those who either could not come here or do not want to come, "because they have it much better at home"—and by that they mean it's more comfortable to stay home. Others, even if they will never admit it, are jealous at the thought that things are really more beautiful in the tiny Bayreuth than where they live, in the larger cities.

As though this were surprising! The best talents of the foremost thea-ters of Germany are invited here for a small number of performances, and they prepare them for months in advance. And that is not all. Where else does one find the pious devotion, the sacred dedication with which every-thing here is conceived and executed? Where else does one find the inspiring harmony of *all* elements that instantly elevates us to the desirable, indeed necessary, mood for complete enjoyment, and that holds us fast from begin-ning to end?

All this has been clearly stated and proven by our eternal Master in the most convincing way. But we are struck anew with the full force of this truth as we return here. If one has gone for several years without seeing this festival theater, so sublime in its simplicity, if one has not heard for some time the incomparably beautiful sound of this invisible orches-tra, nor felt the magic of these scenic images, then all of this seems once more new and powerful, like something from another, more beautiful world. It's a constant battle to bear up under the force of these impressions and then afterward to free oneself from them, to return again to every-day life.

My friendly readers know that I do not speak of these impressions as a novice. I am now in Bayreuth for the tenth time,* but the tenth time feels exactly like the first. One can't judge this if one hasn't experienced it oneself. Whoever can blithely let these impressions pass right by him without being moved, in spite of having been here, whoever is lukewarm to this and takes a critical stance toward this—I truly do not envy this person! There must be some odd fellows like that, as there are those who are not moved by Saint Peter's in Rome, just because they are not Catholic.

This year the festival is especially significant. We are celebrating the tenth anniversary of the consecration of the Festspielhaus, an event that was such a milestone in the history of art. But this time there are no joyful banners and flags flying from the festival hill, as then; the outside of the building is solemn and plain. For the supreme protector of this festival, the sublime friend of the Master, is no longer.[8] As of a few weeks ago he rests in the royal crypt in Munich. But we are also celebrating a resurrection this year. The deceased Master's noble widow, who has mourned for years in total seclusion, has returned to the realm of art and has taken the leadership of the festival in her hands. Nobody knows the intentions of the Master the way she does; nobody has ever understood him as she does. All that she endeavors is done to his honor alone. The participants, foremost among them the conductors Levi and Mottl, cannot praise highly enough what she has accomplished, how she has delved into everything, and how she has thoroughly grasped the spirit of his works.[9] Levi told me himself that he has learned much from this wonderful woman; he said that totally new insights had been given to him concerning musical and scenic details, which he thought he had thoroughly comprehended long ago. Frau Cosima lives only for these works; since the start of the rehearsals she resides in the Festspielhaus, so she can be ever right at hand.

One can sense her influence: a spirit of sacred devotion enlivens everything and penetrates every detail. I am not the only one who has this impression; all competent voices I have heard agree that the performances this year are the most perfectly realized, the most cohesive, the most sublime since the death of the Master. Everything is in harmony down to the smallest detail; the participants from the earlier years feel that their skills have improved, they are freer, clearer, more precise in expression, and the

---

* For the skeptics, I shall enumerate these visits: 1872 for the laying of the foundation stone and the Ninth Symphony; 1876 for the first and third *Nibelungen* cycles; 1878 for the general meeting of the patrons; 1879 for the founding of the *Bayreuther Blätter*; 1881 for a conference on the means for producing the "Bühnenweihfestspiel"; 1882 for *Parsifal*; 1883 for the funeral of the Master and for *Parsifal*; and now once more for *Parsifal* and *Tristan und Isolde*.

new personnel demonstrate a noble eagerness to follow in their footsteps, not to lag behind.

Everyone I have talked to has confirmed my own impression that the first performance of *Parsifal*, with which the festival opened on 23 July, was among the best we've ever had—a truly exemplary performance that did honor to the Master. Everything sounds and feels more beautiful, more transcendent in this theater than anywhere else; if one hasn't heard it for several years, one forgets the supernatural beauty of the sound of the invisible orchestra in this ambience. . . .

The Prelude begins—it seems so different here than in the concert hall. One knows every note of it by heart, but here it emerges as though in a transfigured light; here it becomes a "Bearer of the Grail," ideal "Passion music," and it creates such a powerful mood that it's difficult to control one's emotion. We are transported out from the external world, we are right there in the realm of "Montsalvat." Then the curtain parts, and from the dark house we behold this ideal landscape and hear the trombones of the guardians of the Grail.

We have experienced all of this often, we know this impression well, but each time it seems new: "Hört Ihr den Ruf? Nun danket Gott, / Dass Ihr berufen, ihn zu hören!" (Do you hear the summons? Now thank God that you have been called to hear it!) [*Parsifal*, Act 1].

It is impossible to follow the work step by step here. Suffice it to say that the newly assembled orchestra (as we know, the Munich court orchestra no longer plays here) has proven itself in every way exemplary, indeed incomparable; and that Kapellmeister Levi leads it in exemplary fashion. All of the nuances were as clearly wrought as they were carefully gradated; nothing was too strong, nothing too soft, everything shaded magnificently. Also the choruses, which were also newly assembled—not only those of the Grail Knights and those from above, but also that of the Flower Maidens— all had been coached brilliantly, thanks to our dear friend Porges, and have attained a purity and perfection leaving nothing at all to be desired.[10] The choruses behind the scenes meshed rhythmically with the performance onstage better than they ever have before.*

The scenery is, granted, mainly the same as before, but the lighting effects are more energetic and brighter due to the electric lighting that has just been installed—particularly in the forest in the first act, where the huge tree in the middle of the stage stands out majestically against the

---

* Just one criticism: the bells still aren't tuned right. That this should be so hard to achieve, here, where so much is accomplished that had once been considered impossible! In the matter of the bells, one should not let piety for the past prevail but should rather have new ones made. The tamtams now being used *cannot* be tuned properly because they have *no specific* pitch. Steel bars would be the only reliable option here.

background, and also in the third act where the flowering meadow looked even more pleasant than before, all decked out in the glory of springtime.

What is there left to say about the applause issue? Deeply moved, silently withdrawn into ourselves, we left the house as though exiting a temple. A few newcomers—this time there were many who were attending for the first time, in particular Russians, English, and Americans—did in fact try to express their enthusiasm by applauding as usual, but they were silenced. At the end, though, this torrent could not be contained. Then the applause burst forth, and all the singers appeared onstage. They had all earned it. In Wagnerian drama each singer gives his best and uses all his talents. Whether the role be large or small, it makes no difference—each is part of the whole.

If only we did not have to tear ourselves away from these performances so soon. Here, where the world with its everyday cares lies beneath us "as though an immaterial appearance"!

Bayreuth, 27 July 1886.
. . . After having seen *Parsifal* here, I did not think it possible that anything else would impress me more strongly; but this was indeed the case with *Tristan und Isolde*.[11] Many expected just the opposite. It seemed doubtful that *Tristan*, compared with *Parsifal* (two completely different emotional worlds), could still have its full effect; also, everybody said they had already heard *Tristan* so often, and in excellent performances, in such places as Munich, Weimar, Berlin, Hamburg, Dresden, Leipzig, and Karlsruhe, and that this work, with the same singers, wouldn't be that much different in Bayreuth. One doesn't travel to Bayreuth to hear *Tristan*, one goes there because of *Parsifal*.

They were mistaken, as they were often mistaken about the works of the Master. It was precisely with *Tristan* that the difference between Bayreuth and "everywhere else" became perfectly clear. Where else does one hear, *can* one hear, *this* orchestra? This ideal balance of sound? This truly intoxicating effect in all gradations of softness and extra softness, to loud and very loud? In some places in *Tristan* the instrumentation is very strong; there are spots in the first and third acts that in *no* theater, other than Bayreuth, *can possibly* have the same effect, because no other theater has the perfect acoustics of this house, and nowhere else is the orchestra covered. Elsewhere, if the sound is dampened it doesn't carry the audience away with the same force; but if it isn't muted, then it drowns out the voices or else the singers will involuntarily overexert themselves to be heard above it. That doesn't happen in Bayreuth. The singers are quite free to use their voices without fear of being drowned out; but also the orchestra can be freely unleashed without hindering the effect of the singers' voices.

Wagner wrote *Tristan und Isolde*, no less than the *Ring*, or *Parsifal*, or *Meistersinger*, for his ideal, covered orchestra, and for that reason *Tristan* was being performed for the first time in the correct place in Bayreuth, just as *Die Meistersinger*, whose performance is planned for a future festival, will finally achieve its full effect here, in the theater the Master intended it to be performed in.

But also the singers accomplish greater things at Bayreuth than they do anywhere else. This is partly because they are carried and elevated by the waves of this ideal orchestra; and partly because here they are totally transported out of everyday life and devote themselves to their lofty tasks in an unconditional way. They know that the eyes and ears of the most educated audiences rest upon them, and they are being listened to by the most discriminating musicians; they know how much depends on giving their best when they are here and consequently they attempt to bring both the work and their artistry to the highest point of perfection. Finally, the most careful preparation, the most thoroughly spiritual supervision of those in charge here—on the stage, as in the orchestra—brings its influence to bear in all things.[12] The sacred aura of the Festspielhaus leaves its mark on every motion, every musical phrase.

Foremost and above all should be mentioned Frau Sucher-Hasselbeck as Isolde.[13] We have already heard her highly praised in just this role, but she far surpassed our expectations. Frau Sucher draws on her own personality to interpret Isolde differently from anyone else we know; that is, she is more *lyrical*, girlish, feminine, inward. The greatest Isoldes we are used to hearing place the main emphasis on the supreme emotional passion, on the most tragic moments. Because of this they seem more moving, more powerful, in the first and third acts—but then the transition to the second act becomes problematic.[14] It is in the great love scene with Tristan that none has fully sufficed as far as I am concerned, for here the tragic heroism just does not and cannot fit with the self-effacing love of a woman. In contrast, Frau Sucher places the main emphasis on the *second act*. It is here that she is simply *ideal*, and she develops the characterization of the entire role from this great scene. For this reason her portrayal in the first act is already more of a loving woman than a heroine striving for retribution, for redemption; and also in the last act, the final scene is more ethereal, more visionary. She is, through and through, the yearning, loving, self-sacrificing woman who wants nothing, seeks nothing, except to forget herself in the union with the only one she loves. And I believe that that is the Isolde the Master intended.

Since the death of Schnorr, who created the role, Vogl is considered the greatest interpreter of Tristan, along with Niemann. Heinrich and Therese Vogl had a monopoly on the roles of Tristan and Isolde for nearly a decade, for nobody besides them dared attempt these tremendous roles.[15] Thus not only in Munich were they the only Tristan and Isolde, they were invited by other opera houses (Weimar, Frankfurt, Bremen, Königsberg), for only with their participation was it possible to perform the work at all. There is thus nothing new for me to say anymore about Vogl's Tristan—it is a recognized masterpiece. His whole vocal and dramatic conception of the role—with a knightly, noble, yet also gentle tone—is so exceptional, that immediately in his first scene of the first act the characterization of Vogl's Tristan is totally comprehensible to us. In the second act it had never occurred to me before to desire a still warmer, more passionate performance from Vogl until I heard him alongside *this* Isolde in Bayreuth, who is all love and perfect devotion. In the third act, Vogl is remarkable, also in his acting, which is startling in its realistic truth. But he spared his voice excessively here, as neither Schnorr nor Niemann did. He saves himself for those few moments of the most intense expressivity and uses much *mezza voce*, even lapsing into a speaking voice, which might be dramatically justified but musically is less effective. Yet we must not forget that this entire huge scene was being given here *without cuts*, and that never happens anywhere else. The only one who could get through this with full voice was the unforgettable Schnorr.

The Brangäne of Frau Staudigl-Koppmeyer from Karlsruhe is an exceptional achievement.[16] The freshness, warmth, and beauty of her voice are very impressive, most of all in the second act. Nowhere else have we so fully understood what was going on in the duet of Isolde and Brangäne in the second act; her warning in the second act floats down from the heights of the watchtower in perfect clarity and beauty. It is no mistake to have Frau Staudigl, who looks so young and full of life, playing Brangäne. There is no reason Brangäne should appear old. Rather the opposite: her empathy with Isolde's overpowering longing and passionate love is far more natural if Brangäne, herself still young, experiences and sympathizes with it at the same time.

King Marke—even in Bayreuth he is the weak point. Herr Wiegand from Hamburg is of course a skilled singer with much warmth of feeling, but for him this becomes almost a liability for it misleads him into a certain whiny tone that detracts from the nobility and majesty of the king.[17] Also, his appearance is not regal enough. I know only *one* Marke who can meet all of the demands: Kindermann in Munich; but unfortunately he does not sing in Bayreuth.[18] When Richard Wagner heard Kindermann in Munich in 1881, he expressed his unqualified admiration. Scaria must also have been just as exemplary as Marke. But he will also never be back![19]

. . .

The scenery is wonderful. It is modeled after that of the first performance (1865) in Munich, but now boasts numerous improvements. The image of the ship, when Brangäne opens the curtain in the first act, is unforgettably beautiful, rich, and lively; that of the park lit by the moon of the second act enchanting, everything is tangible and distinct. The arched walkway [*Bogengang*] in front of Isolde's quarters, the staircase, and the watchtower are realized in a very practical way for the staging; I also think it is a great improvement that the bench in the bushes, where Tristan and Isolde seat themselves, is arched in a half circle and placed in a niche: this way the positions of the lovers are more natural and more picturesque. The castle Kareol in the third act is also exceptional. The courtyard is narrower than one usually sees it, and the watchtower is therefore moved nearer the front of the stage; the gate lies more centrally, so that one can follow the fighting closely, and Tristan is lying not in the center of the scene, as though on a litter, but rather sideways: this way we get a freer perspective of the sea and Tristan's resting place under the tree seems more natural.[20]

And now—*last not least*[21]—this orchestra. It always comes back to this, because of its unparalleled beauty, the way it carries and binds everything, as becomes fully evident in every detail. Mottl leads the orchestra with a freedom and certainty that shows us how completely he rules it. That mastery allows him to risk the most extreme tempi and intensifications [*Steigerungen*], but it all works. In short—the more often one has heard *Tristan und Isolde*, the better acquainted one is with this unique work, the greater the enjoyment of hearing it in Bayreuth. Therefore: "Off to Bayreuth!" Whoever has not been here should make haste to do so—and whoever *has* been here will most dearly wish to return as soon as possible! The magic of the place is irresistible.

Bayreuth, 29 July 1886.
It is an established fact—the travel agencies confirm this, as well as the housing agency in Bayreuth, and the box office sales quite definitively— that this year the festival drew more visitors to Bayreuth than in 1883 and 1884.[22]

Why is this so?

First of all, because of the growing recognition of the greatness of the Wagnerian work of art and the impact of the impressions that are created in the Festspielhaus in Bayreuth. It may also have become partly the fashion. One needs to have been in Bayreuth, in order to participate in the conversation—it has become a "great art-sport," as one of the "upper ten thousand" put it to me, who came to Bayreuth with his wife and daughter and was more moved by the impressions he had in Bayreuth than he would admit either to himself or to me. But in the last analysis the motivations for going to Bayreuth are irrelevant; the main thing is that people do feel drawn there. Every one of them thereby helps to promote the great cause, and many unbelievers change their minds, doubters are converted, and many who wavered are here strengthened in their beliefs. The great Wagnerian community is visibly growing, not only in Germany, but also in other countries as well.

A further reason for the increased attendance in this festival year is that, besides *Parsifal*, *Tristan und Isolde* was also performed [for the first time]. Through this expansion of the Bayreuth repertory we have in a decisive way approached the ideal of the deceased Master to found a school of performance style here, and the more works we adopt into the repertory, the more perfectly the intentions of Richard Wagner will be fulfilled. Therefore it is with joyful satisfaction we note that it is now decided that *Die Meistersinger* will be produced next year for the first time in Bayreuth.

Then the time will come for a revival of the *Nibelungen* cycle in Bayreuth. All due respect to the ambition and the accomplishments of those theaters that have made it a point of honor to put the *Nibelungen* cycle in their repertory. But of course to want something and to make it happen are two different things. We know the obstacles that all theater managements, even the best ones, inevitably face in casting these roles; we know the hair-raising cuts that are made, the necessary reductions in the size of the orchestra, —for how many orchestras have thirty-two violins at their disposal, for instance, or how many can muster enough brass players without relying on ringers with poor intonation, and whose tone production [*Tonansatz*] is either coarse or insecure? Even in the exceptional event that a great outlay of expense can avoid some of these problems, where is the theater that can match the acoustic of the Bayreuth Festspielhaus and the incomparable sound of the covered orchestra? Who advises the conductors on tempo? Who does the staging? Who coaches the style of the dramatic presentation? When such a massive work is forced into the Procrustean bed of the "weekly repertory" it will inevitably succumb to operatic routine, that universal destroyer of art which will ultimately make the best of them into mere workmen. Another result of this routine is that they want to perform the *Nibelungen* work piecemeal. Their guiding principle is that of the Theater Director in the Prologue to Goethe's *Faust*: "Gebt Ihr ein Stück, so gebt es nur in Stücken!" (If you're going to play a piece, then do it piece by piece!) Goethe knew these people. They did no better by him with his *Faust*, or by Schiller with *Wallenstein*!

This ruination of art will never cease completely, because there are no legal protections that can prevent it. But we can and should work to oppose it— *and that is the reason why the Bayreuth Festival was founded and must be maintained.*

We know that Wagner went even further in his original plan to found a school of performance style: he also wanted to rescue the works of Gluck,

Mozart, Beethoven, and Weber from their enslavement to the stages of these other theaters and transfer them to Bayreuth, to establish finally a *standard* or model performance for these masterpieces. But the time was not yet ripe for this ideal—his plans did not receive sufficient support, and now he has been forever taken from us, the only one who could have accomplished this.

Let us therefore rescue what can still be rescued, and let us maintain the tradition of the Master, as long as there are still people around who know it thoroughly and will work piously to preserve it.

There is one other thing to consider: *how often* should the Bayreuth Festival take place? We hear that the management, encouraged by the success of this year's festival, plans to repeat the festival as soon as next year. That seems too early to me. One reason I can find for the decline in visitors to Bayreuth in 1883 and 1884 is precisely that there was no break in between; whereas the increase in attendance this year strengthens my opinion, because in 1885 no festival took place. Richard Wagner had at first intended to have the successive festivals at intervals of an "Olympiad" (four years). This may be too long for our quick-moving and pleasure-loving age, but a half-Olympiad (two years) seems correct, and it will also prevent the attraction of the festival from being dulled by too frequent repetition, as well as providing the necessary time to prepare and rehearse the works that are being taken up into the repertory for the first time.[23]

The Wagner societies may also be inspired by this year's festival to accomplish even more than they have in the past, particularly to acquire more members and raise more money to ensure the continuation of the festival. Each year the festival leads new worshippers to our great cause, and we can hardly doubt their willingness to sacrifice for it. It is a matter of seizing the right moment and taking the appropriate measures. More on this, however, once the official report of this year's general meeting (on July 24) is made available—a meeting that was not well attended and became so tiresome (it lasted all day), that only the most patient stayed until the very end. There was much that had to be discussed, to be sure, by-laws revised, etc., but we did not find the unanimity of views that we had hoped for. That is, of course, the fate of all general meetings.

That *Bayreuth is our modern Olympia and must be preserved as such*, this has been demonstrated more clearly than ever before. Those who bode disaster, who prophesied the decline and imminent cessation of the festival after Wagner's death, have been gloriously proven wrong, contradicted by the *facts*. When it comes to Wagner's art, this is truly nothing new. We have already experienced this so often we must wonder that these false augurs of art still insist on being heard!

ARTHUR SEIDL
The Bayreuth Festival

When former anti-Wagnerians, with whom I have had to contend for years, write to me in Leipzig from Bayreuth about the enthusiastic greeting of the express train from Vienna, which they can only describe as "elevating";[24] when these people begin their postcards to me with the heading "Bayreuth in the Year of Salvation 1886"; when someone who saw *Parsifal* in Bayreuth two years ago and is now passing by Bayreuth on his way from Thuringia, and cannot help but stop and buy a ticket to see another performance of the work, even though he didn't really intend to do so this year; when finally—I shouldn't conceal this, either—my own mother, a calm and reasonable woman of fifty years, who visited Bayreuth for the first time this year and learned about *Tristan* for the first time, tells me of the truly "earth-shattering" impact [*weltentrückenden Wirkung*] the work had on her—these are not mere *effects*, but rather in fact they are matters of genuine impact [*Wirkung*], the result of real, deep, and significant causes.[25] It's no wonder, then, that I was overcome, even before leaving Leipzig for Bayreuth, by a feeling of receptive enthusiasm and an elevated joyful mood, which became more powerful and more lively, taking hold of my entire being more and more as I approached the sacred "culture spot" itself. How completely different from the *Mikado* and *Fledermaus* or even *Drei Paar Schuhe* at the Staegemanner Hoftheater, or even from Herr Staegemann's recent endeavors to stage uncut performances of *Tannhäuser* and *Lohengrin*. . . .

Of course, we also unfortunately had some first, sad obligations to fulfill that we had not expected. Not only did the Festspielhaus lack this year the joyful adornment of banners, whose absence reminded us that this year's festival has also to serve as the obsequies of its sublime protector, and not only did we learn to our sorrow, at the beginning of the festival, of the deaths of Scaria and Degele (two outstanding exponents of the Bayreuth style) during the night of July 31 to August 1, in the midst of the jubilation; right here in Bayreuth we suffered the loss of the maestro Franz Liszt, whose vigor and spiritual vitality we had marveled at only a few weeks previously in Sondershausen and whose personal appearance we all were so delighted with when he was honored in Leipzig —Wagner's noble, great friend, his "second self." Weimar has its Goethe and Schiller, and so Bayreuth its Wagner and Liszt! . . . On Monday joyful blue-white and black-white-red flags to celebrate the presence of the German Crown Prince; on Tuesday funereal black flags and mourning crepes hanging from lampposts! . . .

There is one point I would especially like to expand upon here: the concept of "model performance." Although this was once defined for me in Bayreuth as meaning "an excellent performance of ideal perfection," this would seem to me an error of principle. Performances of "ideal perfection," of absolute beauty, just don't exist. The expression "model performances" can only mean: performances that, by means of the relative ideality they achieve, become *models* for all other German theaters, providing an example to the other theaters of how one should progress from *fashion* [*Mode*] to *style*, to show the Germans that they possess a unique, supremely original style, and that they *can* accomplish something in this area, if they truly *want* to! And in this sense certainly *Parsifal* remains a model production, and now we have one for *Tristan* as well. . . . There is a unique spirit and a special atmosphere in Bayreuth that scarcely allows one to remain sober and reasonable; we are caught up in a great philosophical updraft, as it were, carried away far above all philological hair-splitting. That is precisely the great advantage of Bayreuth, that we can all once again experience something fresh and immediate, we can devote ourselves entirely to such a great cause, that we can at the same time once again believe in ourselves and in the power of the human spirit. The core of the human being resides not in the *head*, but rather in the *heart*— Schopenhauer already told us this.

(To be continued.)

"*Parsifal* remains a model production, and now we have one for *Tristan* as well."[26] This statement can be properly understood only when one remembers that this year a number of artists were, for Bayreuth—as the Latin saying goes—*homines novi*; that the orchestra was almost completely new, assembled piecemeal; that the choruses of Flower Maidens and Knights needed to be made up in part from totally different forces; and finally when one also recalls the fact that *Tristan* was newly produced, with no Bayreuth performance that could serve as a model—only the first Munich performance of 1865 had been overseen by the Master. What I can offer as the most important and decisive argument for my judgment is the nearly perfect directing. Everything in *Parsifal* according to the tradition and the spirit of the Master, and the perfection of the scenic images retained; likewise in the newly produced *Tristan* the spirit of the Master spreads its wings with an agreeable sense of security: in the performance on August 1, the third act, for example, proceeded so perfectly, from the first note of the Prelude to the words "Die alte Weise" etc., that even the strictest critic would not have found *one* iota to quibble about. This year, moreover, some things not yet achieved in Wagner's time were now given their due.* Just to single out one example, this time Klingsor wasn't anxiously watching the conductor's baton while he described the battle being waged outside his castle between his knights and the "pure fool," as he did in 1883. And Kurwenal didn't make that mistake either, when, from the watchtower, he described to the ailing Tristan the landing of the ship below. How splendidly the shepherd's song in the third act was done, both the acting and the music! What stylish scenery in the first act! In the second and third acts, what truly ideal sets, everything was so vivid and clearly wrought—such a perfect illusion as we have never experienced before in any opera house! We might suggest there be a *society* to provide the directors of *all* German theaters with funds and free tickets, and to send them all to Bayreuth, *nolentes volentes*. Leipzig, for example, ought to have a closer look at how the ship is supposed to approach land. (Frau Stahmer-Andriessen has already learned which costume, which pose, and what kind of rendition fits the role of Brangäne!)[27] Also accomplished in the way the Master intended are the subtle indications of dawn and dusk, as opposed to the familiar, shallow operatic routine that makes such "effects" an end in themselves, and which sees in the Magic Fire music mainly an opportunity to feed the public's appetite for spectacle. In order to achieve a *unified* scenic image for a landscape one needs to cover the floor of the theater with grass; a Grail Temple can't have boards on the floor but ought to have a mosaic-like stone floor— these are things that are done in Bayreuth, while unfortunately one rarely, if ever, sees them done correctly in other opera houses. I ought to make a little display concerning the Bayreuth performances which would have the motto: "Wenn schon, denn schon!" (While we're at it, let's do it right!) requesting, for example, that the artists not step *off* the grass carpet onto the wooden floor, which is worse than having *no* lawn or mosaic floor to begin with. Finally, one should note in particular what fantastic unity and coherence is achieved throughout between the movements of the individual actors and the rhythmic and dynamic moments of the musical accompaniment; the facial expressions and gestures of all the Grail Knights, especially the Bearer of the Grail (Frau [Pauline] Cramer) and the Squires who accompanied her, had a noble clarity. . . .

Of course, there were still many problems one might mention, some rather small, some larger: but compared to what was done right these are

---

* A change was even made to the 1882 performance that proved appropriate and sensible: in the third act, Parsifal does not come with Gurnemanz and Kundry (as he did in the first act) from the right side, but rather from the left side to the right side, in the transition from one scene to another, and thus he moves, as the transformation scenery also does, in the opposite direction from what occurred in the first act!

minor things, incidental imperfections [*reale Unvollkommenheiten*] affecting only a *single* performance. At any rate, we can apply to them what Plüddemann stated: "If in the scenic presentation not everything was perfect (and nothing else can be expected in so immensely difficult a work) . . . then this is *one more reason for us to insist that we do it again.*"[28] We Wagnerians should all agree to talk among ourselves about any possible shortcomings of what we saw, so we can know what needs to be improved next year. Among these I would like to think it possible to make *less* noise in assembling the Grail Temple backstage during the transformation scene. I admit that there are insurmountable difficulties here; but the director backstage cannot really gauge how much noise the audience hears, and I don't remember in earlier years that the noise was quite so obtrusive, especially during the *piano* passages. Likewise in the performance of August 2, Herr Reichmann was rather careless with the glowing Grail (or was it negligence on the part of the lighting crew?) such that the vessel just did not seem to glow quite enough.[29] In Act 3 of *Tristan* Kurwenal and the shepherd looked too far over to the right for the approaching ship: if the ship had come in from that direction, it would have had to pass by in front of the audience on the horizon before it could land and before those on board could enter through the gate on the left. Similarly, the fight between Kurwenal and Melot was not made a significant stage event and remained totally incomprehensible for the audience. Finally, in the performance of July 29 the performers of Tristan and Isolde did not express the idea of the *death potion*—also the cause for their declaration of their love (as this is represented and argued in all *official* Wagner essays and brochures)—but only the physical effects of the *love potion*, a portrayal that should be carefully avoided, above all in Bayreuth, where the main thing is to rid the audience of a false way of thinking so deeply ingrained from regular opera productions, and to accustom them instead to the psychologically far deeper idea: that only the *belief that they have drunk the death potion* can break through their mutual defiance and *finally* allow them to admit their love, a love that is *a priori* "not of this world," totally removed from common sensuality.[30] . . .

And now . . . finally I will discuss the musical aspects of the performances, strictly limiting my comments to the performances of August 1 and 2, for which I am charged with reporting. In keeping with "tradition" I should first of all mention that not only is Levi beginning to take his tempi significantly slower (a fact that several competent people have noticed), but also that the prelude to *Tristan* has become distinctly too slow as Mottl is playing it. This is the opposite extreme to the performances in Leipzig under Nikisch, who as far as I am concerned took it mostly too fast, or rather: not slowly *enough*.[31] Of course this objection has nothing to do with our unconditional esteem and admiration for the talent, ability, and supreme artistry of the orchestra, and both of its brilliant leaders. This year the lion's share of admiration and honor is due without a doubt to the excellent Mottl in view of the new production of *Tristan*. But also the two excellent concert-masters, Halir from Weimar and Fleischhauer from Meiningen, deserve our special recognition, as well as all others who, with such touching dedication and amazing eagerness for this cause, have returned every year since 1876.[32] It is incomparably beautiful, this Bayreuth orchestra with its ideal sound, its marvelous acoustic, its unified playing: no matter how many people are there, they all sound as *one*; no matter how many instruments are playing the Kundry motive, it rushes downward into the depths in *one* motion; no matter how many voices go their separate ways in the great sound-tapestry of the *Tristan* Prelude, not one of them strays egoistically from his connection to the whole, all join in *one* thought—the ideal model of the most noble communism; not virtuosity, but rather "the violins in the plural," as Wagner once expressed it, citing a phrase of Mephistopheles. Among the singers in *Tristan*, Frau Sucher as Isolde and Frau Staudigl as Brangäne particularly capture our interest. The former is the best Isolde I have ever seen. In her looks, her bearing, and her inward, spiritual portrayal she strongly recalls Frau Vogl, and has the great advantage of more adequate and fresher vocal abilities. The first act—with the exception of the scream at the end, which was a little too realistic and lacking in dignity—was exceptional in every way; the second act was as a whole totally majestic; and at the conclusion of the third act, in Isolde's great swan song, Frau Sucher sang with the heroic plasticity, antique dignity, and grandeur we remember from Frau Vogl.

About the Brangäne of Frau Staudigl there was a unanimous verdict of joy and enthusiasm. Not only was she vocally irreproachable (for the first time I heard the difficult entrances of the watch song in the second act sung correctly and with pure intonation), she knew how to lend real meaning to the character, who for the first time was placed in the proper light as "Isolde's confidante." . . .

The portrayal of Tristan by Herr Gudehus was in my opinion unsatisfactory.[33] Above all his singing had a kind of diction that too often seemed ignoble, in particular the vowel sounds, and in many places he also just could not act well. The only time he was impressive was in the third act. His voice is certainly extraordinarily powerful and metallic; maybe this leads him *to want to sing too much*. Herr Wiegand did not portray King Marke very well. Vocally he was generally adequate (the notoriously difficult unaccompanied vocal entrances at the start of his long speech I have never heard sung really well—not even by Herr Gura!), but his acting lacked a certain dramatic depth.[34] And of course this is an important character who needs to be given dramatic significance—this is a necessary demand for all opera houses, one that Leipzig totally disregarded by implementing three large cuts in this scene. The Kurwenal of Herr Plank was just magnificent; he sounded like a harsh, coarse soldier in the first act, then in the third act he had more the tone of the faithful, sacrificing servant. But nobody is perfect here on earth, and so this critic feels compelled to add one small but urgent plea: the artist could use a vacation at a spa! Special mention is due the shepherd of the third act (Hr. [Wilhelm] Guggenbühler), whose portrayal magnificently maintained the spirit of desolation and sorrow that spreads across the entire scene. Every detail of his declamation was impeccable. The short, vigorous sailors' choruses were also excellently done; it was fascinating to watch the lively, knowing manner of a few isolated chorus members at the start of the folksong Kurwenal sings about Tristan; then how one after another caught on and joined in, and how they all finally took up the refrain together. (Taking all of these details together, you begin to recognize yet again what constitutes the Bayreuth "style"!) I would have liked to hear the song of the young sailor from the mast above sung a little more softly, more languishing—but this is a purely subjective matter.[35]

And now we arrive at the August 2 performance of *Parsifal* (at which the German Crown Prince was present), above all the portrayal of the hero by Herr Vogl.[36] He is indisputably the best Parsifal who has ever walked upon the Bayreuth stage,[37] and this judgment holds, despite the fact that in part of the second act and through the third act he was indisposed and struggled with impaired vocal abilities, something that is said to have happened more than once to this excellent artist in Munich recently.* His exclamation in Act 3 "Und ich—ich bin's, der all dies Elend schuf!" was unquestionably inadequate; it was not strong, emphatic, and grievous enough. I must also admit that the painful, terrible cry in Act 2 "Amfortas—die Wunde!" so important to the entire drama, was more gripping when Gudehus sang it this year than when sung on this occasion by Vogl, who evidently needed to spare his voice. What raises Vogl's Parsifal far above that of both his colleagues is the marvelous, pithy way in which he brings out the religious dimension. The individual traits comprising the figure, and certain episodes in the plot, gained a depth and religious solemnity that I have long thought I could only imagine. In his religiosity he had a grandeur, a moral gravitas and noble dignity that raise this character above

---

* I have heard, by the way, that later performances did not suffer from this indisposition anymore. It could be that the artist just needed to get reaccustomed to Bayreuth and reacclimated to the place.

all other Wagner heroes! The various little acting and singing mannerisms this artist has unfortunately relied on too much of late (though the Munich critics seem to have overlooked them) were all at once—if I may use a common expression—"blown away" [*wie weggeblasen*]: nothing of that kind disrupted the general impression, and a unified, grand, and ideal effect was created. How true to life he was, for example, as the *lad* Parsifal, his childlike naïveté and vitality! How eloquent his silence during the Grail ceremony! (The clutching at his heart during the most agonized of Amfortas's cries—a detail so significant for the later development of the character—could have been made more noticeable and hence clearer to the audience, however.) He found the most proper coordination of the acting and the music. How he brightened with joyful recognition when he saw the Spear in Klingsor's hand; how dignified and solemn he was, as he *slowly* strode away with the Spear! He gave such meaning to the whole scene with Kundry in the second act! How beautiful, noble, and innocent was his tender voice in the Good Friday scene! There was just one thing I didn't understand about his character portrayal, something I pondered with considerable perplexity in the meantime. Vogl played Parsifal as totally unreflective, led by his own momentary volition, as one who seems to react quickly and instinctively to everything that provokes him. This character trait was carried out consistently through the entire first act; it came across as charming naïveté in the scene with the Flower Maidens; and then it continued into the seduction scene with Kundry, where it was particularly interesting to follow how the boy totally forgot himself, at one moment finding himself at first physically attracted by Kundry's words, the next moment repulsed by what she is saying, and this manner of instinctive, quickly changing response continued even *after* he resolved to resist her. I admit that this character portrayal was more true to life and more vivid, also more interesting, but we might ask if it was really right—at any rate there's a concern that in a character like this, it all becomes a question of which urge is stronger, more attractive at any given moment: good or evil. One *could* then attribute Parsifal's mission as redeemer of Amfortas and the Grail Knights purely to accident! I freely admit that I'm not sure how this contradiction of Vogl's portrayal could be resolved.

Frl. Malten's Kundry is known as a major achievement.[38] Although in 1882 she gave us little reason to rave about her portrayal in the third act (where as we know it depends mainly on the acting—"a thankless role" as the modern audience calls it!) in subsequent years she has grown with each festival, so that by now her performance in the third act is quite spiritual and leaves nothing to be desired;* her great struggle of wills with Parsifal

---

* She will certainly also with the years perfect the role of Isolde (which I did not think she could fully do justice to this year) as she did Kundry.

in the second act is a pinnacle of artistry. Her portrayal is supported by an unusually beautiful, noble voice that is supple in all registers (by contrast, that of Frau Materna has a touch of the soubrette in it!) and by a radiant presence, if one that has somewhat taken on harsher edges of late.[39]

Herr Gura has shown us, as Herr Fuchs did back in 1884, that from the standpoint of acting there's more to be done with the role of Amfortas than Herr Reichmann does.[40] Of course, Reichmann has the great advantage of an unusually soft, pleasant voice that is equally fresh and responsive in all registers; but unfortunately this doesn't prevent it from exploding here and there in a rather disturbing way. The Gurnemanz of Scaria has yet to be surpassed by any of his successors. Siehr has at least assumed *one* quality of Scaria, his unusually clear and correct diction; otherwise he gives us his best and we are thankful for that.[41] But he cannot erase Scaria from our memories; his voice is a bit brittle [*spröde*]; we noticed, too, that many people spoke this year of how boring the long narratives of Gurnemanz seemed (even the Good Friday scene!) Isn't that the fault of the singer? Herr Plank delighted us immensely, as he did in 1884, through the characteristic weight and dramatic grandeur he gave to Klingsor's satanic nature; his sonorous, forceful, and full voice allowed him to do this, and especially gripping this time was the passage "Furchtbare Noth! So lacht nun der Teufel mein!" (Dreadful misery! The devil is mocking me!).[42] And the Titurel of Herr Schneider (this is not an insignificant character, as one leading critic has assured me it is!)[43] the Knights, and the Squires all contributed perfectly to a unified success of the entire performance. The "Voice from Above" that speaks the promise of the pure fool at the end of the first act, as if enunciating a prophetic revelation, deserves special mention.[44] One cannot describe what an incomparably pleasing effect it can have on the audience when an attractive alto voice sings this line beautifully and inwardly: this can be the decisive factor, regardless of whether the audience laughs at the line of Gurnemanz "Suche dir, Gänser, die Gans" (Just bother geese from now on!) or is able to subsume it into a higher conciliatory idea.

As for the choruses, without a doubt the Knights, Squires, and Pages were better than they were in the previous *Parsifal* performance of July 30; but there were still signs of disturbing fluctuations of intonation, also with the orchestra. The Flower Maidens—enchanting and flawless in their round dance and teasing play—were still not secure and perfect enough in the admittedly difficult entrances at the start of the act. At any rate I have heard this chorus sung much differently. It must be said explicitly, however, that neither in the whole marvelous play of the Flower Maidens, nor in the wonderfully artistic choreography of the two Grail Temple scenes, was a single letter of the law (that is, of the tradition of the Master) violated.

As for the bells—which even in Wagner's time sounded uneven—I am convinced that the entire apparatus is such a difficult one that even with the best of intentions it seems impossible to guarantee a correct, proper effect in every instance. It belongs among those "incidental imperfections" of which I have already listed many in this report. In the performance of August 2 the bells sounded very good, except for one cursory passage.[45]

All in all the general impression was: *Parsifal* "works," whereas *Tristan* must still gradually be worked up into a truly living, organic creation. But that is not surprising when we learn that *Tristan* had to be rehearsed in just three weeks, alongside *Parsifal*, and that there was not even a chance to hold a proper dress rehearsal of the entire work, just for the first and second acts; and that the third act had to be squeezed in only after the festival had already begun.

EUGEN GURA

Impressions of Bayreuth (1901)

Münchener Neueste Nachrichten, 26 August 1907

The renowned bass-baritone Eugen Gura (1842–1906), whose primary professional engagements were in Hamburg (1876–82) and Munich (1882–96), appeared in the first Bayreuth Ring *of 1876 as Donner and Gunther, and returned to sing King Marke in 1886, 1889, and 1892, as well as Amfortas in 1886 and Hans Sachs in 1889. In 1901, after his career had ended, Cosima Wagner invited him and other veterans of 1876 to the dress rehearsals for the twenty-fifth anniversary festival, and his letters to his wife during that visit fit appropriately here. Mixed in among lively and appreciative observations about the personalities in the Bayreuth circle at the turn of the twentieth century and descriptions of the anniversary festivities are comments about the productions themselves. They offer a perspective on Bayreuth performers of the time that stands in contrast to the far better-known verdicts of another 1876 participant, Lilli Lehmann, who believed that both her performances and authority were too little appreciated when she sang Brünnhilde in Bayreuth's 1896 revival of the* Ring.[46] *One result of her unhappiness was a tendency to compare the 1896 performances unfavorably with those of twenty years earlier. Gura, on the other hand, who felt that he gave some of the best performances of his life as Hans Sachs and King Marke at Bayreuth in 1889, had no axe to grind where Cosima was concerned, and thus, given his vast experience, his view that certain performers in 1901 surpassed the achievements of their famous predecessors cannot be dismissed, in part because he also regards certain performances from the earlier period as unmatched (for example, Scaria's Gurnemanz and Vogl's Loge).[47]*

Many of the leading performers Gura observed on this visit were shortly to begin making recordings, a new technology at the time. In theory such recordings—when coupled with comparisons to singers of the past like Gura's—have the potential to help historians of performance style re-create profiles of singers who left no recordings. There are limits to this possibility, however. For example, Gura's verdict on the singing of Anton van Rooy, coupled with his observations on the sheer size of van Rooy's voice, suggest that early recording techniques were unable to cope with so voluminous a sound, and that this may explain in part why certain decisive features of van Rooy's artistry are either distorted or not captured by the recordings he made.[48]

It is to be expected that Gura, as a singer himself, would be predisposed to comment on performance dimensions directly related to his own area of endeavor and expertise, so it comes as something of a surprise to read his comments on the overall impression produced by certain moments in Das Rheingold *and* Der fliegende Holländer, *although he freely admits that he may sense certain impressions more forcibly as an audience member than he did as a participant. As such, his observations serve as a poignant reminder of potential differences between the evaluations by performers and those by other observers.*

Bayreuth, 13 July 1901, afternoon. I arrived yesterday after a pleasant if somewhat hot journey. Here at the Hotel zur Sonne I have the nicest and largest room on the second floor. After a quick midday meal I drove to the Festspielhaus. There I learned that the dress rehearsals (as indeed Frau Wagner's telegram had informed me) do in fact begin today, the 13th. After wandering around a bit I waited for Frau Wagner at the Festspielhaus, where she had arranged a piano rehearsal. At 3:15 she arrived with her daughters. I was greeted with much jubilation. After a short walk around the grounds I took my leave of her at 4:45, after she had invited me this evening at 7:30 for a friendly gathering in the familiar restaurant establishment next to the theater. From here I walked back to my hotel, drank some tea, dressed, and arrived precisely at 7:15 back up on the festival hill. The whole family was assembled there. On the corner of the terrace stood Siegfried, who greeted me warmly.[49] The back of the terrace, facing the town, was covered. I was to take my seat immediately next to Frau Wagner. On her other, left-hand side there sat van Dyck, on the other side Frau Professor Thode and Eva, and immediately across from me the poetic-painter, Professor Hans Thoma.[50] To my right there sat Professor Klindworth, one of the oldest friends of the Wagner household (who made the piano-vocal arrangements of the *Ring*), whose company was most entertaining.[51] On the way home (10:30) I had some animated conversation with Prof. Hans Thoma, who is normally *not* a very loquacious type. Today again I am invited to lunch with Frau Wagner at 12:30.

This afternoon at 5:00 the dress rehearsals begin with *Rheingold*, and they will conclude on the 19th of this month with *Der fliegende Holländer*.

Bayreuth, 14 July 1901. . . . In the afternoon I slowly walked up the hill to the dress rehearsal of *Rheingold*; I had a reserved seat in the middle of the fourth row. Hans Richter is conducting the *Ring*.[52] The impression that I had was overwhelming. Now I am convinced that no other opera house can attain such all-encompassing, masterly effects.

The first scene, in the depths of the Rhine. The Rhine Maidens really seemed to be fishlike creatures out of folklore when they moved around the reef, and I am sure this illusion has never been portrayed so well onstage before. The three Rhine Maidens (Frl. Artner, David, and Metzger, from Cologne) were excellent.[53] Friedrichs, who is known for his portrayal of Beckmesser, was Alberich: admirable! Not even Karl Hill has sung and acted Alberich with such terrible, horrible demonic force. Unique, splendid! And how gloriously powerful and magnificent his voice sounded! I was totally astonished. Even after producing elemental, uncultivated sounds in his laughter after stealing the gold, his voice still has the richest supply of tones at its disposal. The curse scene succeeded masterfully. After the rehearsal I just had to thank him with an enthusiastic embrace.[54]

By the way: All of my acquaintances and friends were happy to see me. Elmblad, the giant from Stockholm (if I am not mistaken, he is the Intendant there), the one who portrayed Fafner, greeted me with tears in his eyes and even kissed my hand.[55]

Bertram is an imposing Wotan; his voice is a little too bright, but it has a granitic weight and steely sound.[56] In a few places where he had to make the transition from very loud to very soft, for example, "Den Reif verlang ich, mit dem Leben mach, was Du willst!" (I demand the ring, I don't care about your life!)—where he went from violent anger to contemptuous mockery—he did very well.[57]

Unfortunately van Rooy is sick. Bertram, who recently sang all rehearsals of *Holländer* and the *Ring*, demanded three days' vacation. Today Schütz from Leipzig, who is singing Donner, is stepping in as Wotan in *Walküre*.[58] Burgstaller, who sang Froh's cantilenas with a pleasant and full [*rund*] voice, was very good.[59] Dr. Otto Briesemeister (Breslau) was a skilled Loge: a good actor, always in motion, and he knows how to use all vocal colors imaginable. There has been nobody better since Vogl.[60] As Mime, Breuer from Vienna was very good.[61] The giants, Elmblad and Kehler [*sic*] (Karlsruhe), were a little too uncouth and loutish, particularly the latter.[62] Fricka, Reuss-Belce (Dresden), good, looks glorious in the costumes by Thoma.[63] As Erda, Frau Schumann-Heink was splendid with her sonorous voice.[64]

Of the many finely wrought scenes I would like to single out one in particular. When the giants demand from Wotan the ring he had stolen from Alberich, Wotan hesitates, and Erda appears with her sinister grandiose warning, an unspeakable mood of impending disaster such as I have never felt before weighed on the scene (at any rate I could never actually feel it before, because I was always participating in the drama); and then the way this mood was dispelled through Wotan's resolve ("Ihr Riesen, nehmt euren Ring") (Giants, take your ring!) and the rejoicing of the gods, embracing one another, cannot be described in words.

Never before has *Rheingold* seemed so captivating to me. . . .

Bayreuth, 18 July 1901 . . . At three o'clock Friedrichs picked me up. He had rented an open omnibus in which we, the Ritters, and the two Fräulein Spicharzes from Frankfurt drove out to a farmstead near Konnersreuth called "Kamerun" (Cameroon). There we drank coffee out of doors, ate bread and butter with honey, and took a walk in the woods. On the way home we stopped by the Ermitage, near the stone theater, and beneath the great oak tree there we had *Pfannkuchen* with ham and sat for a long while outdoors. The evening was wonderfully mild, the air warm and very still. Toward 10 o'clock we drove down the darkening Lindenallee toward Bayreuth. I went home, the others continued on to the tavern. I sat up reading until about 11:30 when I heard the group pass by on its way home, singing raucously: "Laß Dir zu Füßen wonnesam mich liegen!" (Let me blissfully lie at your feet!) "O Margiana!"[65] I bellowed out, in tempo, quickly sticking my head out of the open window. Tremendous laughter! During the afternoon Fräulein Spicharz had given me her album, and in the meantime I had made an entry for her. I threw it to her out of the window. By the light of the electric lantern of the hotel she read it over, made some glosses to it, and soon peace was restored.

Van Rooy has recovered and is definitely going to sing the dress rehearsal of *Der fliegende Holländer* tomorrow, July 19. He drives his own coach here, with his servants sitting in the back. I have ridden with him a few times. He has accomplished more in the last few years than I have in my entire lifetime. His father and one of his brothers came here, too. When I remarked to his father (a real Dutchman) how much he resembled his sons, he said: "I still have four more *dawters* and eight *sawns*."[66]

Bayreuth, 19 July 1901 . . . Yesterday *Parsifal* once more gave us great sublime enjoyment, and it would be petty to nitpick and carp in the face of such grand offerings. Nevertheless, such a sublime performance as Scaria's Gurnemanz in 1882, sung with such moving simplicity and clarity, is not likely to be achieved again.

Bayreuth, 20 July 1901 . . . Yesterday the dress rehearsal of *Holländer* was utterly unique, glorious, such as has never before been heard and seen.

Playing the work through in one act, without an intermission, according to Wagner's original idea and intention, had in itself a notable impact. I am convinced that the title role has never before been done with such grandeur and power, with such fascinating, quite overwhelming force, and with such vocal majesty, as by van Rooy. What an enviable voice! Not even old Kindermann's throat could produce such huge sounds. And how tenderly he sang lines such as: "Was frommt der Schatz, ich habe weder Weib noch Kind, und meine Heimat find' ich nie." (What good is the treasure, I have neither a wife nor a child, and I will never find my homeland again.) With what a broad sense of line and what breath control he sang, in the great opening monologue, "Dich frage ich gepriesener Engel Gottes." He generated a *piano* of enchanting tenderness at the beginning of the duet in the second act ("Wie aus der Ferne").

Yes, he is a God-gifted singer! I was often so deeply moved that I could not hold back the tears, and now I am getting emotional just thinking about it. He sang with titanic force in the final scene, without doing violence to the beauty of the tone. Frau Wagner really shouldn't have anybody else sing this role.[67]

It was a charming sight when the curtain parted again and Senta's beamed room became visible. From where the audience was seated, Senta was at the right side of the stage, in her armchair in front of a wide window, with the other women grouped *closely* around her, almost all in profile and looking at her. In their midst in the *center*, almost in the background, was Mary (not parading in *front* of them as soloist and first alto); she was portrayed by Frau Schumann-Heink with exquisite, almost drastic precision. Her scolding remarks stood out with a light, humorous effect because at the main points her large bonnet rose up from among the maidens.[68] A broad beam of sunlight fell through the large window upon the colorful group. Frl. Destinn (Berlin), a Czech singer from Bohemia, plays Senta simply, with a youthful delicacy, and her bright silvery (not large) voice has an indescribable effect.[69] She doesn't sing the ballad like a prima donna; no, she sings it rather the way I myself would sing a ballad. Her Senta is touching. Burgstaller was very good as Erik, and he sings many passages with urgent force.[70] Heidkamp was a capable Daland.[71] The choruses of the last scenes of the sailors, the men on the Dutchman's ship, and the women, will never again be heard so perfectly on any stage in the world. Here in Bayreuth one becomes aware for the first time of the powerful ingenuity, the captivating beauty of this youthful work. All previous performances have been only weak approximations or unintentional parodies. The atmosphere of ghostly magic is unique. Before the crew of the Dutchman's ship comes to life, the ship itself is shrouded with eerie fog (steam) and veils of cloud, from which ghostlike sparks flash down the rigging. When, after the horrible laughter of the Dutchman's crew, the whole ghostly apparition sinks with a crash, the two ships stand there motionless while the skies have become suddenly calm and friendly, with little scudding clouds: it is like waking up from a terrible dream. Our chilled blood starts to circulate again when Senta rushes out of the house, followed by Erik.

ARNOLD SCHERING

Review of *Das Rheingold*, Bayreuth Festival 1904
Leipziger Neueste Nachrichten, 27 July 1904

The musicologist Arnold Schering (1877–1941), whose reviews of Das Rheingold *and* Die Walküre *from the 1904 festival are offered below, is more generally associated with Bach, Beethoven, and the oratorio than with Wagner. In the years 1903–5, however, he edited the* Neue Zeitschrift für Musik *and in that role was responsible for covering the concert and operatic life of the time. He wrote an overview of the first six performances of the 1904 Bayreuth festival for the NZfM,[72] but that essay drew selectively on his more detailed reviews for the* Leipziger Neueste Nachrichten. *Whereas the overview is undoubtedly the more thoughtful and considered piece of work—and in fact addresses larger issues that are not always apparent in the daily reviews—these detailed accounts of the specific performances have considerable value (and they are entertaining, since Schering sees fit to tweak the pretensions of Wagnerian art, for example by referring to the orchestral transition between the first two scenes of* Das Rheingold *as "Zwischenaktsmusik," that is, an entr'acte!) In these two reviews, Schering's strategy was to provide a blow-by-blow account of the performances from first to last. This tactic is often derided as of little imaginative or intellectual interest, but for the historian of performance history such reviews are treasure troves that reveal the sorts of considerations that registered with the critic, and how the observations about the nature and quality of the performance intersect with or relate to the perceptions of the work itself.*

In three respects Schering's observations merit some attention. First, his conception of Wagnerian drama seems sometimes to betray what might be called a leitmotivic way of listening: in particular, he finds it unfortunate that the singers involved fail to highlight the actual words of Alberich's curse and, in Die Walküre, *Wotan's final words (which he attributes to immature conception and insufficient stamina or volume, respectively), because these moments are, in Schering's view, decisive determinants of the future course of the drama and thus demand the utmost vocal emphasis. Second, it is intriguing to see how thoroughly Schering's concern with precise coordination between the action on the stage and illustrative music in the orchestra is ingrained in his assessments. Third, although Schering nowhere overtly refers to a specifically Bayreuthian style of singing, his appreciation of clear enunciation and dislike for singing that does not possess it possibly show the extent to which Cosima Wagner's ideals in this regard had become part of the German understanding of "correct" Wagnerian style.*

During the festival of 1904 the Gramophone and Typewriter Company, Ltd., sent a recording team to Bayreuth to record festival participants. Thus Schering's reviews are further interesting for offering often detailed accounts of various singers who recorded excerpts from their roles within days of the performances described here: Josephine von Artner (Woglinde) and Maria Knüpfer-Egli (Wellgunde), Theodor Bertram (Wotan), Otto Briesemeister (Loge), Hans Breuer (Mime), and Alfred von Bary (Siegmund).[73] The reader is encouraged to hear these recordings, which in some instances enhance Schering's descriptions and evaluations, and in others demonstrate ways in which performance expectations and styles have changed in the intervening century.

Bayreuth, 25 July. After a break of one day, which gave the performers, orchestra, and audience the opportunity to get some fresh air and recover from the phenomenal heat that lasted for the first two performances of the festival, *Das Rheingold*, the prelude to the *Ring* trilogy, was performed. The Donner motive, sounded as a fanfare, invites us to enter. Quickly the house fills with an expectant international audience eager to hear what is to come—half of them standing and directing their opera glasses at the loges where Frau Cosima with her family and various royalty have taken their places, and half of them sitting and preparing themselves for the two-and-a-half-hour seance. The lights go down. A few minutes of silence. The deep E-flat of the basses is tremblingly released from the depths of the orchestra, and with an elemental intensification, flowing this way and that, the orchestra begins to sketch the waves in the depths of the Rhine River. When this has grown to a *forte*, the curtain opens. It is as though one is looking into an aquarium, dark green, blurry, becoming brighter toward the top. The waters of the Rhine lie before us. In the middle is an enormous reef, around which the three Rhine Maidens immediately begin their cheerful play. *Josephine von Artner* (Woglinde) sings her teasing call to her sisters. She does not seem to be in best form; at least in the beginning her voice seems markedly unsettled. *Maria Knüpfer-Egli* (Wellgunde) answers her clearly and distinctly, gliding around the slippery reef and joining her and Flosshilde, the excellent *Adrienne von Kraus-Osborne* who has just floated over, to form a delightful trio.[74] Wheezing, Alberich the Nibelung approaches. Even in the first measures Herr *Eduard Nawiasky* indicates his lewd aspirations with mastery.[75] His distinct enunciation and lively acting are delightful. His thrice-rejected courtship of the three Rhine Maidens takes place in an exquisitely humorous fashion. The dialogue between these four characters proceeds effortlessly, unconstrained and uninfluenced by the contingencies [of the staging] such that the listener quite forgets about the perfectly effected illusion of swimming, although now and again he might still be put in mind of the paradox of speaking underwater. By the way, some twelve conductors behind the scenes take care that the unprecedentedly complicated swimming apparatus and the movements of the Rhine Maidens are in harmony with the rhythms of the orchestra—no easy task, considering that the entire scene takes place in partial darkness. One can well imagine how at the time when *Rheingold* was new and the production technology was not as advanced as it is now, some superficial clumsiness in this scene would have provided the mockers with ample material for persiflage. Today, when years of assiduous work have reduced such problems to a minimum, only those who are fundamentally opposed to Wagner could mount such objections.[76] The illumination of the Rhine Gold takes place in an extremely logical way. It doesn't start to shine all of a sudden, as in provincial theaters; rather, the small bar of gold gradually begins to glow, starting with a faint illumination of the reef, as though the sun were shining through the waves. The illusion would of course have been more true to nature if the natural flickering had been imitated by having the lump become alternately brighter and darker. In any case the scene in Bayreuth offers a real feast for the eyes.

Meanwhile Alberich, trembling with rage, has turned away from the coy nixies, climbed the reef, and stolen the gold: he wants to renounce love and gain power with the ring, which the magic runes tell him to forge. Shrieking, the Rhine Maidens flee in different directions. Clouds veil the scene. In the meantime *Hans Richter* leads the well-coordinated orchestra off through the exquisite entr'acte with an inimitable understanding of how to motivate the transition into the realm of Wotan through marvelous shading of the motives, from which that of Valhalla finally and triumphantly emerges. One really senses the divine breath of Wotan and Fricka when the curtain rises. Both are still resting. It seems no later than three o'clock in the morning here, not twelve o'clock noon, as in other theaters where the scene opens fully lit. Frau *Reuss-Belce* is a natural-born Fricka, dignified, majestic, and gifted with a voice that in fullness and clarity leaves nothing to be desired; it never lapses into the shrillness we hear from most Frickas. Overall this Fricka was an especially pleasant character; her reproaches did not at all smack of scolding. One was even more ready to sympathize with her, as the performer had taken the care to have appropriately dignified clothing—gathered up in a medieval fashion, with wide sleeves and no robe [*Talar*], just as one imagines "Frau Holle."[77]

Theodor Bertram as Wotan warmed up gradually throughout the performance. At first he was not very interesting and was hard to understand.

Heroic power, mixed with gentleness and melancholy, was basically lacking from his figure. It is possible that he will fulfill this demand better as Wotan in *Walküre*. Freia the Fair, charmingly portrayed by *Emilie Feuge-Gleiss*, is carried away by the giants.[78] Froh (*Alois Hadwiger*)—this time really youthful, costumed in light green, a God of Spring—and Donner (*Robert vom Scheidt*), with his black beard, both rush in to protect their sister.[79] But Fafner (*Johannes Elmblad*) and Fasolt (*Hans Keller*) will not be intimidated; they rival one another in the rough tone of their voices and are quite terrifying in appearance, the one clothed in black skins, the other in white.[80] Fafner certainly outdoes his colleague in volume (with excellent declamation), while Fasolt, somewhat less brusque, brandishes his staff furiously. They finally reach their goal: as payment for building the gods' castle (which oddly enough is in Bayreuth vaulted to a dome without windows!) they demand the hoard of Alberich, their deadly enemy. Loge helps the desperate Wotan out of the fatal predicament and sets out with him on the journey to Nibelheim. The Loge of Dr. *Otto Briesemeister* is an agile, almost nervous, eerie figure. Everything about him is lively, from the facial expressions, arms, and hands down to the little finger. How he jumps around to and fro in time with his flickering motives, flings the saffron-yellow cloak in a hundred different ways around his red body, sizing up the situation with a clever look, inspiring neither confidence nor loathing but preserving a wholly neutral attitude—all of this suggests a finely calculated performance, naturally increased still further by his complete mastery of the music. The voice is clear, often piercing, and the performance richly interspersed with parlando effects in just the right places. Here and there, in fact, the theatrical artist in him seemed nevertheless to take the upper hand, approximating the tone of a comedian. Loge does, after all, belong among the gods (even if only a half-god himself), and he should not be seen to compromise himself, least of all in the presence of the other gods.

With the help of Mime—*Hans Breuer* counts the role of this dwarf among his best, as is well known—the outwitting of Alberich is accomplished. Wotan and Loge reappear in the upper regions and we witness the battle of the two giants over Alberich's ring, cursed by the Nibelung. Herr Nawiasky succeeds vocally in the powerful curse scene; in future performances he ought to give still more emphasis to the climax, namely the actual words of the curse. In spite of the necessary foregoing exertions, the singer's whole vocal strength must be saved up for this moment, the very climax of *Rheingold* and also the point that encapsulates the conflict of the trilogy to follow. Now Erda, the wise Mother of the Gods, rises up from the depths to warn Wotan of the sinister ring that will bring misfortune. Frau *Louise Geller-Wolter* filled in at the last minute for Frau *Metzger-Froitzheim*, which might explain why she did not fully realize the possibilities of the role.[81] Finally Fafner kills Fasolt (n.b.: with a *single* stroke, though the orchestra clearly enough said the opposite with several sets of drumrolls), takes off with the hoard, and leaves the rescued Freia in the company of the gods, who are delighted things have worked out so well. With a forceful call Donner summons clouds and lightning. In the orchestra triadic harmonies begin to spread in wider and wider arcs of melody, and onstage the clouds disperse and the rainbow to Valhalla becomes visible. Bayreuth can be proud of this rainbow. However, because it is created by means of reflected light, the front of the stage needs to remain somewhat darkened, which in my opinion rather detracts from the orchestral effect here, growing as it does to such a powerfully luminous intensity, and hence too from the effect of the end as a whole.[82] Even so, the coloristic shading of the final tableau was developed with such artistic sensitivity that it will long live in the memory of the audience, just as *Rheingold* on the whole, one of the most scenically demanding of dramas, appeals as strongly to the eye as to the ear. In Bayreuth neither one suffers—that was proven once again by this performance.

Review of *Die Walküre*, Bayreuth Festival 1904
Leipziger Neueste Nachrichten, 28 July 1904

Bayreuth, 26 July. The second day of the *Ring* has arrived. *Rheingold* presents, as it were, the exposition; with *Walküre* the tragedy sets in. A double tragedy takes place before our eyes. In one case Siegmund and Sieglinde are at the center, in the other Wotan and Brünnhilde; the two tragedies overlap and develop parallel to each other.

Stormy weather rages away wildly in the orchestra, terrible string crescendi mixing with roaring brass chords. The scene shows Hunding's spacious hut. Siegmund staggers in, exhausted: "Wess Herd dies auch sei, hier muss ich rasten" (No matter whose hearth this is, here I must rest). Herr Dr. *von Bary* thrusts the words out with overwhelming realism, not sung, but entirely spoken, and one quite believes that he is collapsing in exhaustion on the flickering hearth.[83] This is the way Sieglinde finds him. Frau *Wittich* possesses the right appearance and eyes for Sieglinde and, even more, she has a voice with captivatingly pleasing tone and metallic hue, completely suitable to revive the dwindling life spirits of the stranger.[84] She hands him the drinking horn, and while the cello spins out tones of longing, the stranger is refreshed. The drinking scene is done excellently and makes us expect that the whole act will progress in an exemplary way.

They are both roused from their contemplation by Hunding's motive. The powerful man appears and glares at the pair with sinister looks.

Herr *Paul Knüpfer* gives a strong voice to Hunding, but without strong accentuation.[85] Timidly Sieglinde announces what has transpired. "Rüst uns Männern das Mahl" (Give us men something to eat). This happens, and Siegmund reports to the inquisitive lady whence he comes. Herr von Bary proves here and in what follows that he is a singer of incomparable vocal means and superior artistic taste—we have already admired him for this in *Parsifal*—but as an actor he shows that he is not yet ready for the most exacting demands of Wagnerian drama. His narration, though it seemed finely thought out as a vocal accomplishment, suffered from his failure to get his whole person involved in it. Not only the audience, but Sieglinde wants to know his fate, this is what he forgot when he sang into the orchestra; and his account of the pursuit of the Wälsungs clearly proved how little he has grown beyond stylized theatrical heroics. Ah, but how the action should blaze with youthful bravado when he jumps up and pulls the sword out of the trunk of the ash tree! Herr von Bary has only recently made his debut and that excuses much of his stiffness in this scene. Even if the audience cannot find him believable, it can find Frau Wittich so, his faithful partner from Dresden. The "Love Song" is sung very beautifully, and both give their best. The act rushes to its conclusion, and out of that the rest of the directors can learn a valuable lesson: the sword should not *suddenly* start shining, for example thanks to a phosphorescent hilt, but rather gradually, as a result of a shaft of light that has fallen upon the tree from a fire that is blazing up in the hearth. If only they would finally stop playing around with the electric lighting in our theaters!

Siegmund has carried his sister off as his bride. Fricka, the goddess of mothers, wants to punish them and bombards Wotan with reproaches. Frau *Reuss-Belce*, the Fricka of *Rheingold*, hits more powerful notes than yesterday, but is not always able to avoid in expressing emotion a certain hard edge to the sound. The dramatic conception of her role is flawless. The Wotan of Herr *Theodor Bertram* was disappointing. The lack of clarity in his enunciation more than once made even someone who knew the text miss meaningful points, while the voice only seldom attained the nobility of tone that is so appealing in such a singer of Wotan as van Rooy or Perron.[86] Moreover the power of his voice was not sufficient for the last scene, Wotan's Farewell. The words "Wer meines Speeres Spitze fürchtet, durchschreite das Feuer nie" (He who fears the point of my spear shall never pass through this fire!) were lost in the rustling sounds of the orchestra, even though they are just the words that must by all means be comprehensible as the key for the development of the following Siegfried drama. I am by no means denying that many moments appeared in a favorable light— we didn't come to Bayreuth in vain. But on the whole, and measured against the highest standard, this accomplishment was in my opinion deficient. Frau *Ellen Gulbranson* is widely recognized for her interpretation of Brünnhilde at Bayreuth.[87] Imposing in appearance, gifted with a full, although not excessively strong voice, at her first entrance she hurls forth her Valkyrie call successfully. Later her energy wanes and one loses interest in her fate. On the other hand the action always becomes lively and attractive when Siegmund and Sieglinde appear. Siegmund's reaction to the annunciation of death is expressed in the heartfelt tones of his response. The battle with Hunding and Wotan's appearance leave nothing to be desired in sublimity, and here once again the Bayreuth weather machine works its best artifice.[88]

An extremely turbulent picture is produced by the scene on the Valkyrie rock. This cliff is in Bayreuth higher than it is elsewhere, so that the very climbing up and down of the figures is captivating in itself, as is the magnificent ensemble work here and the highly intelligent directing! The sword maidens shout with joy to each other, moving not like a herd of little lost sheep, but rather like real warrior maidens with a will of their own. Also their ride through the air, long considered unstageable, was here represented in a satisfying way by means of projections, which solution has surely been taken up in the meantime by other theaters.[89] A splendid "Magic Fire" closes the events of the first day of the *Ring*, one which we have reason to praise once again for the great artistic impressions it offered, to be sure not in every respect, but in its most important moments.

HEINRICH CHEVALLEY
Review of 1904 Bayreuth Festival
Breslauer Zeitung, 28 July 1904

Although in the brief excerpt we reproduce here Heinrich Chevalley (1870–1933), the famous and respected music critic from Hamburg, piously maintains that Bayreuth had no need for introducing novelties in order to gain attention, it seems clear that by 1904 the festival management was worried that Americans might not continue to venture across the Atlantic to Bayreuth once Parsifal *became a regular part of the Metropolitan Opera repertory—as it finally did when Heinrich Conried produced it there on December 25, 1903. (Cosima Wagner persisted throughout her life in thinking that* Parsifal *was Bayreuth's* raison d'être). *The decision to engage the innovative, iconoclastic American dancer Isadora Duncan (1877–1927) to stage and perform in the bacchanal in the 1904 Bayreuth revival of* Tannhäuser *was, therefore, partly a calculated attempt to retain the American contingent as part of the Bayreuth audience.*

Even more strikingly than in the reviews by Arnold Schering which precede it, this brief passage by Chevalley shows how well engrained the Bayreuth point of view had become in German critical consciousness by the first years of the twentieth century. For Chevalley, there is a self-evident way in which a bacchanal should be conceived and performed; he sees the task of a Bayreuth performance as that of realizing this obvious conception as perfectly as possible, and his negative verdict on Duncan's solo contribution causes him to spell out clearly some of what he regards as the essential features of the Bayreuth aesthetic. Ironically, his description of the staging of the bacchanal confirms that Duncan achieved her conception of the scene: she thought of the bacchanal proper as "only visions" in the mind of the slumbering Tannhäuser, and her own role as performer was to indicate passion through understatement.[90] *(According to her autobiography, during the festival she began an ecstatic but platonic relationship with Heinrich Thode, Cosima's son-in-law, which seems to have possessed something like the elevated, spiritualized character her movements on the Bayreuth stage were intended to embody.)*

In short, this scene in the 1904 Tannhäuser *production marks an early instance in which a production concept went beyond the attempt to realize the plain meaning of Wagner's instructions, and Chevalley's response shows how ill-prepared Bayreuth audiences were to appreciate or seek out the intention of such innovations.*[91] *As for her behavior, Duncan remained unrepentant—she accepted the invitation to perform at Bayreuth on the grounds that Bayreuth was willing to adapt to (or at least tolerate) her views, and she found the milieu to be genuinely in need of the fresh air she could provide: "In fact, I could not do anything without seeming extravagantly different from other people, and therefore shocking."*[92]

24 July 1904. . . . After the *Tannhäuser* performance the name of Isadora Duncan was on everybody's lips. When Frau Cosima decided to invite the renowned barefoot dancer to perform at Bayreuth, it was of course the furthest thing from her mind to provide the English and the Americans with a star attraction. Bayreuth is in the fortunate position of not needing attractions, sensations, and the star industry. Frau Cosima Wagner was correct in believing that she was acting in the spirit of the Master, who considered the union of the arts to be the end goal, when she summoned the world's most famous dancer to her side. Unfortunately, the endeavor was a complete failure. Even outside the Festival Theater Miss Isadora Duncan's behavior demonstrated that she had imperfectly understood the fundamental Bayreuth principle of selfless subordination to the greater artistic whole. In the last analysis it is perhaps besides the point that during intermissions the Miss strolled around barefoot in a classical outfit among the guests, trying to attract attention—she could be forgiven for this vanity and tastelessness. But she also quite misunderstood the essence of Wagner's music. Of course, she struck a few attractive, effective poses in the Bacchanal; but then she always broke up the dance—which is based on the fundamental law of motion—into a series of pictures, and what she danced had no relation to the spirit of the Bacchanal's music, nor did it have anything to do with the other dancers. In her insensitivity to the nature of the work she managed to make the notion of innocence the leading motive of the Venusberg Bacchanal; that the idea of a chaste Venusberg is a contradiction in terms should be self-evident. Her costume was not in keeping with the rest of the performance either; in this regard as well she did not learn any lesson in Bayreuth. On the other hand, the rest of the choreography in the Venusberg scene was done wonderfully: the sultry air of a most ardent sensuality wafted through the majestic, artistic groupings, and if, as we are told, the entire choreography is the work of Miss Duncan, then she has two souls living close to each other in her breast.[93]

But personally I would be inclined to say that Siegfried Wagner had a strong hand in this too, because to be honest, I wouldn't trust that the classical Miss Duncan could realize the ardor of this Bacchanal by means of her own talents alone.

NOTES

As noted in the introduction, descriptions of the performances of early Bayreuth singers are a primary characteristic of some of the documents presented here. It is intriguing to attempt to recapture something of these writers' impressions through photographs and recordings when they are available; for photographs, relevant resources include illustrated studies by Dietrich Mack, *Der Bayreuther Inszenierungsstil 1876–1976* (Munich, 1976); and Gisela Zeh, *Das Bayreuther Bühnenkostüm* (Munich, 1973); and for recordings, *100 Jahre Bayreuth auf Schallplatte: The Early Festival Singers 1876–1906* (Gebhardt JGCD0062-12, 12 CDs) is the most comprehensive collection of relevant material. Endnotes given here refer to specific photographs by illustration numbers ("Mack, 118," for example) and to specific recordings in the Gebhardt set in the following form: *100JB*, 6/7 refers to disc 6, track 7.

1. Arthur Seidl, "Der 'Nibelungen'-Cyklus am Münchener Hoftheater. (Aufführung vom 23.–29. Aug.)," *Musikalisches Wochenblatt* 27/38 (16 September 1886): 460.
2. Although it took her longer to do so than she originally had hoped—an undated document in her hand, probably from late in 1883, proposed a schedule in which all of Wagner's operas from *Der fliegende Holländer* onward would be performed at Bayreuth by 1889—Cosima expanded the festival's repertory from *Parsifal* (the only work in production at the time of Wagner's death) by adding *Tristan und Isolde* (1886), *Die Meistersinger von Nürnberg* (1888), *Tannhäuser* (1891), *Lohengrin* (1894), a new production of *Der Ring des Nibelungen* (1896), and *Der fliegende Holländer* (1901), with all of these save *Lohengrin* repeating in at least one subsequent festival during her tenure. Beginning in 1891 the number of performances per festival attained and held at twenty, and for the last five festivals

under Cosima's direction, the invariable pattern was to give seven performances of *Parsifal*, two of the *Ring*, and five of one of the other operas.

3. The two books discussed are Robert Hartford, ed., *Bayreuth: The Early Years* (Cambridge, 1980); and Susanna Großmann-Vendrey, *Bayreuth in der deutschen Presse*, 3 vols. (Regensburg, 1977–83).

4. Not to be confused with the sometime Bayreuth conductor Anton Seidl (1850–89), who subsequently carried the Wagnerian torch to New York, from 1885 to his death. Arthur Seidl published critical and aesthetic studies of the Wagner oeuvre in the *Musikalisches Wochenblatt* and later wrote about the musical dramatic works of his own contemporaries such as Richard Strauss and Hans Pfitzner. His Wagner essays were collected as *Wagneriana* (Berlin and Leipzig, 1902) and *Neue Wagneriana* (Regensburg, 1914). He also published a sort of Wagnerian riposte to Hanslick's "formalist" aesthetics of musical beauty under the title *Vom Musikalisch-Erhabenen: Ein Beitrag zur Ästhetik der Tonkunst* (Leipzig, 1907).

5. Stewart Spencer and Barry Millington, trans. and eds., *Selected Letters of Richard Wagner* (New York, 1987), 815.

6. Winfried Schüler, *Der Bayreuther Kreis von seiner Entstehung bis zum Ausgang der Wilhelminischen Ära: Wagnerkult und Kulturreform im Geiste völkischer Weltanschauung* (Münster, 1971), 149.

7. The letter of 30 July appeared in *Muzikalisches Wochenblätt* 17/31 (30 July 1886): 388–89.

8. King Ludwig II of Bavaria died under mysterious circumstances on June 13, 1886.

9. The conductors mentioned are Hermann Levi (1839–1900) and Felix Mottl (1856–1911). Levi was an important German conductor whose principal engagements were Karlsruhe (1864–72) and Munich (1872–96). Bayreuth career: led *Parsifal* 1882–94 (except 1888). Felix Mottl's association with Wagner began during preparations for the first Bayreuth *Ring* in 1876. Principal engagements: Karlsruhe (1881–1903) and Munich (1903–11), with many other significant international appearances. Bayreuth career: all but two of the thirteen festivals 1886–1906. Mottl remains the only conductor to have led all ten of the canonical Wagner operas at Bayreuth.

10. Heinrich Porges (1837–1900), an associate of Wagner's, was entrusted with writing down Wagner's comments and suggestions during rehearsals for the Bayreuth festivals the composer himself supervised.

11. The letter of 27 July appeared in *Musikalisches Wochenblatt* 17/32 (6 August 1886): 399–400.

12. But see Arthur Seidl's comments on the rehearsal schedule leading up to the opening performance at the end of his review below.

13. Rosa Sucher (1849–1927). Principal engagements: Leipzig (1877–82), Hamburg (1882–88), Berlin (1888–98); Britain's first Eva and Isolde (both in 1882). Bayreuth career: nine festivals (1886–99), as Isolde, Eva, Venus, Kundry, and Sieglinde.

14. The recording of the Liebestod by Pelagie Greef-Andriessen (*100JB*, 4/14), who was one of the Brangänes in this 1886 production, seems to reflect the heroic model Pohl identifies as the prevailing conception in the late nineteenth century.

15. Ludwig Schnorr von Carolsfeld (1836–65). Principal engagements: Karlsruhe (1854–60), Dresden (1860–65). Of all the singers with whom Wagner worked, Schnorr best embodied his artistic ideal. Heinrich Vogl (1845–1900). Principal engagement: Munich (1865–1900), with many prominent guest engagements. Bayreuth career: Loge (1876), then five festivals (1886–97) as Tristan, Parsifal, Loge, and Siegmund. Albert Niemann (1831–1917). Principal engagements: Hanover (1854–66), Berlin (1866–89). In 1861 sang the title role in the first Paris production of *Tannhäuser*, supervised by Wagner. Did not sing Tristan until the Berlin production of 1876. Bayreuth career: Siegmund (1876). Therese Vogl (1845–1921). Principal engagement: Munich (1866–92), with many prominent guest engagements. Did not sing at Bayreuth.

16. Gisela Staudigl, née Koppmeyer (1864–1929). Studied with Mathilde Marchesi. Principal engagements: Karlsruhe (1884–87), Berlin (1887–92), Dresden (1901–4). Bayreuth career: five festivals (1886–92) as Brangäne, Alto Solo (Parsifal), and Magdalena, then again as Magdalena in 1911–12.

17. Heinrich Wiegand (1842–99). Principal engagement: Hamburg (1884–94). Bayreuth career: four festivals (1886–91) as Marke, Gurnemanz, Pogner, and Landgraf Hermann.

18. August Kindermann (1817–91). Early in his career, at Leipzig (1839–46), he created important roles in operas by Albert Lortzing. Principal engagement thereafter was in Munich (1846–89), where he sang Wotan in the premiere performances of *Das Rheingold* (1869) and *Die Walküre* (1870). Pohl's assertion notwithstanding, he did sing at Bayreuth as Titurel in 1882.

19. Emil Scaria (1838–86) died on July 22, the day before the 1886 festival began; memories of his achievements were thus very much on critics' minds in the reviews generated by this festival. Principal engagements: Dresden (1865–73), Vienna (1873–86). First Wotan in Berlin (1881) and London (1882); also many other significant guest engagements and tours. At Bayreuth he appeared as Gurnemanz in 1882–84 and served as stage director in 1883.

20. The sets for each act of this production can be seen in Mack, 81–83; Vogl as Tristan appears in Mack, 84, and Sucher and Staudigl appear as Isolde and Brangäne in Mack, 85.

21. This phrase is in English in the original text.

22. Pohl's letter of 29 July appeared in *Musikalisches Wochenblatt* 17/33 (12 August 1886): 413.

23. During Cosima Wagner's tenure no more than two festivals took place in successive years; of the twenty-one summers in the span 1886–1906, festivals occurred in only thirteen.

24. This first section of Seidl's report on Bayreuth 1886 appeared in the same issue as Pohl's last letter, *Musikalisches Wochenblatt* 17/33 (12 August 1886): 413–14.

25. Seidl is alluding to Wagner's distinction between *Effekt* and *Wirkung* in Part 1 of *Opera and Drama*, the passage in which he coined the definition of Meyerbeerian operatic "*Effekten*" (effects) as "Wirkungen ohne Ursache" (effects without causes). Strictly speaking, the difference between the words is merely etymological, not semantic.

26. This second section of Seidl's report appeared in *Musikalisches Wochenblatt* 17/34–35 (26 August 1886): 425–27.

27. Pelagie Greef-Andriessen (1860–1937). Primary engagements: Leipzig (1884–90), Frankfurt (1893–1907). Sang at Bayreuth only as Brangäne in 1886. Recorded in 1903, *100JB*, 4/5 contains a snippet of Greef-Andriessen singing this role, the earliest Bayreuth impersonation to survive in aural form.

28. Martin Plüddemann, *Die Bühnenfestspiele in Bayreuth, ihre Gegner und ihre Zukunft* (Leipzig, 1876).

29. Theodor Reichmann (1849–1903). Principal engagements: Munich (1875–83), Vienna (1883–89, 1893–1903), with significant appearances in London and New York. Bayreuth career: 1882–91 as Amfortas, Hans Sachs, and Wolfram von Eschenbach, returning in 1902 as Amfortas.

30. Seidl forbears to identify Therese Malten and Heinrich Gudehus, both from Dresden.

31. Arthur Nikisch (1855–1922). The most magnetic conductor of his time, he held important posts in Leipzig (1878–89), Boston (1889–93), Berlin (Philharmonic) (1895–1922), Leipzig (Gewandhaus Orchestra) (1895–1922), and Hamburg (Philharmonic) (1897–1922).

32. Karl Halir (1859–1909), Czech violinist. A student of Joachim and later second violinist in Joachim's string quartet, he was concertmaster at Weimar beginning in 1883,

and eventually was concertmaster at the Berlin Hofoper (1893–1907). He gave the first performance in Germany of the violin concerto of Tchaikovsky, who greatly admired him. Friedhold Fleischhauer (1834–96) studied with Joachim, began his long tenure as concertmaster of the Meiningen Court Orchestra in 1864, and was a regular member of the Bayreuth Festival Orchestra (usually as co-concertmaster) from 1876 to 1892.

33. Heinrich Gudehus (1845–1909). Principal engagements: Dresden (1880–90), Berlin (1891–96), with additional appearances in London and New York. Bayreuth career: six festivals (1882–89) as Parsifal, Tristan, and Walther von Stolzing.

34. Eugen Gura (1842–1906), German bass-baritone, held important engagements in Leipzig (1870–76), Hamburg (1876–82), and Munich (1892–96), was involved in several important Wagner productions and premieres in London (1882), and sang at Bayreuth occasionally during the years 1876–92. See introduction to next document.

35. José Kellerer sang this role in the August 1 performance under review.

36. This third section of Seidl's report appeared in *Musikalisches Wochenblatt* 17/36–37 (9 September 1886): 440–42.

37. The singers Seidl dismisses with this statement are Hermann Winkelmann (1849–1912) and Gudehus, both of whom sang the role in all four festivals, 1882–86, as well as Ferdinand Jäger (1839–1902), who sang the role twice in 1882 and once in 1888. Despite Seidl's high opinion of him in this role, Vogl appeared in it only three times in this single festival.

38. Therese Malten (1855–1930). Primary engagement: Dresden (1873–1903), with important appearances in Munich, London, and Russia. Bayreuth career: Kundry in nine festivals (1882–94), plus Isolde (1886) and Eva (1888). Mack, 64 shows her as Kundry the seductress.

39. Frau Materna is Amalie Materna (1844–1918). Principal engagement: Vienna (1869–94), with important appearances in Berlin and New York. Bayreuth career: Brünnhilde (1876), Kundry (1882–91).

40. Seidl's claim that Anton [von] Fuchs (1849–1925) sang Amfortas in 1884 contradicts the standard cast lists by Neupert and Ellwanger, which indicate he sang the role only in 1883. Nevertheless, the review of the final performance of the 1884 festival in the *Bayreuther Tagblatt* confirms that Fuchs appeared as Amfortas in place of Reichmann, who had departed Bayreuth suddenly and unexpectedly. Fuchs's principal engagement: Munich (beginning in 1873 and extending for several decades). Bayreuth career: numerous roles in *Parsifal* in 1882–84 and 1889, including Klingsor, Amfortas, Titurel, and a solo Knight of the Grail, plus Kurwenal in 1889. He also served as stage director in 1884 and 1889–99.

41. Siehr is Gustav Siehr (1837–96). Principal engagement: Munich (1881–96). Bayreuth career: Hagen (1876), Gurnemanz (1882–86 and 1889). Although he was announced as one of the performers of King Marke in the promotional material for the 1886 festival, so that the standard cast lists (and thus reference works that rely on them) mention him in that connection, all performances of the role that summer were sung by either Heinrich Wiegand or Eugen Gura.

42. Fritz Plank (1848–1900). Principal engagements: Mannheim (1875–1884), Karlsruhe (1884–1900). Bayreuth career: Klingsor and/or Kurwenal in every festival involving *Parsifal* and/or *Tristan* in the years 1884–97, plus Hans Sachs (but not Pogner, as standard cast lists claim) in 1892.

43. Dr. Oskar Schneider from Munich. Bayreuth career: small roles 1886–88.

44. Some sources claim Gisela Staudigl sang this line in 1886.

45. In a letter of 1 April 1881 (Spencer and Millington, eds., *Selected Letters of Richard Wagner*, 912–13), Wagner instructs Eduard Dannreuther (then living in London) to find Chinese tamtams that would play the notes of the bells in the Act 1 Grail scene. Apparently these instruments were procured and used for the earliest performances of *Parsifal*, in 1882–84. Pohl seems to think that only tamtams are being used in 1886, whereas Seidl's

description (see his review included here) suggests a more complicated apparatus. In any case, the long-term solution to the problem of the bells in *Parsifal* was introduced by Felix Mottl (who conducted the work in 1888 and 1897). This bell-machine is discussed in Cecil Forsyth, *Orchestration*, 2nd ed. (New York, 1935), 54–55. In Forsyth's colorful words, "It is as if an amateur carpenter had been trying to convert a billiard-table into a grand pianoforte, and in the course of his experiments had left the works outside. There is a deep sounding-board over which are strung heavy pianoforte wires, six for each note required. In each of these sets of six three are tuned to the octave above. The strings are set in vibration by a broad flapper or hammer loosely covered with cotton wool."

This machine was apparently introduced as a supplement to the tamtams already on hand and was further supplemented by a tuba playing each note staccato and a constant roll on a fifth (unpitched) tamtam. How long this combination persisted is not clear, since only this bell-machine, without any further instruments, can be heard on the 1927 Columbia recording of the Act 1 transformation music conducted by Karl Muck (*100JB*, 9/3), probably recorded to sound more imposing than it did when played behind the scene in the theater. In 1935 Forsyth reports that this contraption had been superseded at Bayreuth by a set of tubes, but Friedrich Kranich (*Bühnentechnik der Gegenwart*, 2 vols. [Munich, 1929–33], 2:165) claims that in 1931 the sounds of the grail bells were produced by metal discs amplified through loudspeakers that hung on music stands placed between the stage and auditorium.

46. Lilli Lehmann tells the story of Bayreuth in 1896 from Lehmann's point of view. *My Path Through Life*, trans. Alice Benedict Seligman (1914; repr. New York, 1977), 415–36.

47. Eugen Gura's self-evaluation, which according to him was seconded by Hermann Levi, can be found in his *Erinnerungen aus meinem Leben* (Leipzig, 1905), 114.

48. Anton van Rooy (1870–1932). After studying with Julius Stockhausen, van Rooy's Wotan was a sensation of the 1897 Bayreuth festival and he returned in subsequent festivals through 1902 as Wotan, adding to that role Hans Sachs in 1899 and the Dutchman in 1901–2; meanwhile, he became the leading Wagnerian bass-baritone at both Covent Garden and the Metropolitan Opera. After singing Amfortas in the Met's 1903 production of *Parsifal*, he was banned from Bayreuth and never reappeared there, although his international career continued for another decade. His Dutchman, which is the role in which Gura observed him in 1901, can be sampled on *100JB*, 1/17.

49. Siegfried Wagner (1869–1930), composer, son of Richard and Cosima Wagner, conducted at the festival beginning in 1896, helped with production work beginning in 1901, and succeeded his mother as director after her physical collapse in December 1906.

50. Gura's dinner companions: Ernest van Dyck (1861–1923), Belgian tenor with an international career encompassing Paris, Vienna, London, and New York. Bayreuth career: Parsifal (1888–97, 1901, 1911–12) and Lohengrin (1894). Heinrich Thode (1857–1920), art historian, professor at Heidelberg (1884–1911), married to Cosima's daughter Daniela (1886–1914). Eva Wagner (1867–1942), daughter of Richard and Cosima Wagner, married Houston Stewart Chamberlain (1855–1927) in 1908. Hans Thoma (1839–1924), artist who sketched the costumes for the 1896 Bayreuth production of the *Ring*, still current in 1901.

51. Karl Klindworth (1830–1916), pianist; friend of Wagner from 1855 on and pupil of Franz Liszt; adopted Winifred Williams (1897–1980) in 1908. Winifred married Siegfried Wagner in 1915, was the mother of his children Wieland, Friedelind, Wolfgang, and Verena, and succeeded him as director of the festival upon his death in 1930.

52. Hans Richter (1843–1916). One of the leading conductors of his time, he became an assistant to and associate of Wagner as a young man, led the first Bayreuth *Ring* in 1876, and went on to become an immensely influential conductor in Vienna (at both the Hofoper and with the Vienna Philharmonic) until 1898 and thereafter in England. At Bayreuth he conducted *Die Meistersinger,* which he had helped to copy when Wagner was composing it, and the *Ring* regularly from 1888 to 1912.

53. The three Rhine Maidens: Josephine von Artner (1867–1932). Primary engagement: Hamburg (1893–1908). Bayreuth career: regular portrayer of minor roles in the *Ring* and *Parsifal* (1896–1906). Sophie Bischoff-David (1875–?). Active career throughout Europe and with the Henry Savage Opera Company in America. Bayreuth career: Rhine Maiden, Valkyrie, and Flower Maiden (1901, 1911–12). Ottilie Metzger (1878–1943). Primary engagement: Hamburg (1903–15). Bayreuth career: minor roles in the *Ring* (1901–4, 1912).

54. Fritz Friedrichs (1849–1918). Primary engagement: Bremen. Bayreuth career: Beckmesser (1888–89, 1899), Alberich (1896–1902), Klingsor (1902). Karl Hill (1831–93). Primary engagement: Schwerin (1868–90). Bayreuth career: Alberich (1876), Klingsor (1882).

55. Johannes Elmblad (1853–1910). International career, including engagements in Hanover, Prague, New York, Russia, and Breslau; as Gura claims, he was the director of the Royal Swedish Opera in Stockholm in 1897–1902. Bayreuth career: Fafner (1896–1904), as well as Hunding (1896). Incidentally, since he did not make his stage debut until 1880 in Dresden, he is *not* the "Elmblad" advertised as alternating as Donner with Eugen Gura in 1876, and in any case Gura sang all three performances.

56. Theodor Bertram (1869–1907). Primary engagement: Munich (1893–99), thereafter international guest engagements. Bayreuth career: minor Mastersinger (1892), Wotan, Amfortas, and Dutchman (1901–6).

57. Gura's description of Bertram's way of performing this line—even the fact that he draws attention to it at all—suggests the density of inflection and contrast in declamation that Bayreuth singers of the time were encouraged to cultivate. Certainly nothing so detailed emerges in recordings of this line by prominent Wotans since 1950, although the broadcast recording of April 3, 1937 by Friedrich Schorr (1888–1953) shows something of the split in character within the line that Gura describes.

58. Hans Schütz (1862–1917). Primary engagement: Leipzig (1898–1908). Bayreuth career: Donner, Amfortas, Klingsor (1899–1902).

59. Alois Burgstaller (1871–1945). Trained at the Bayreuth Stilbildungschule. Bayreuth career: minor roles in 1894, Siegfried, Froh, Siegmund, Parsifal, and Erik (1896–1902). After singing the title role in the Metropolitan Opera's 1903 *Parsifal* production he was banished from Bayreuth but returned to sing Siegfried in 1908 and Siegmund the following year. He is pictured as Froh in Zeh, 130.

60. Otto Briesemeister (1866–1910). Both a medical doctor and a tenor throughout his career, which was based in Breslau from 1895. The most celebrated Loge of his time, he was heard all over Europe in the part. His Bayreuth career spanned seven festivals (1899–1909), where other than his monopoly as Loge he sang only minor roles. Briesemeister is pictured as Loge in Zeh, 142.

61. Hans Breuer (1868–1929). Trained at Bayreuth. Primary engagement: Vienna (1900–29). Bayreuth career: sole performer of Mime in all twenty-six Bayreuth *Ring* cycles from 1896 to 1914, plus a page in *Parsifal* (1894–1909), David (1899), and occasional additional minor roles. See Zeh, 138 and Mack, 148 for photos of Breuer as Mime.

62. Gura is referring to Hans Keller (1865–1942). Primary engagement: Karlsruhe (1898–1911). Bayreuth career: Fasolt (1899–1901, 1904), minor Mastersinger (1899).

63. Luise Reuss-Belce (1862–1945). Primary engagements: Karlsruhe (1881–97), Wiesbaden (1897–1901), Dresden (1901–11), with appearances in London and New York. Bayreuth career: Flower Maiden (1882–86), Eva (1889), then Fricka and occasional other roles in the *Ring* (1899–1912); assistant stage director (1908–33). Her only surviving recording—a Mapleson cylinder from 1903 in which she sings Ortrud—can be heard on *100JB*, 3/14.

64. Ernestine Schumann-Heink (1861–1936). Primary engagements: Hamburg (1883–97), Covent Garden (debut in 1892), Metropolitan Opera (1899–1932). Bayreuth career: sang Erda, Waltraute, and First Norn at most festivals (1896–1914), plus Mary and Magdalena less frequently. Her Rheingold *Erda* can be heard on *100JB*, 11/13.

65. The lyrics are from Peter Cornelius's opera, *Der Barbier von Bagdad*, in which Margiana is the romantic heroine.

66. Gura renders the accent of van Rooy's Dutch father by writing "vier Dochtern und acht Sohne," rather than *Töchtern* and *Söhne*.

67. Nevertheless, of the ten Bayreuth performances of this work in 1901 and 1902, Bertram sang the title role on three occasions.

68. This bonnet can be seen in Zeh, 169.

69. Emmy Destinn (1878–1930). Primary engagements: Berlin (1898–1908), Metropolitan Opera (1908–16 and 1919–21), Covent Garden (1904–14, 1919). Bayreuth career: Senta (1901–2), Forest Bird (1902). The third of her recordings of Senta's Ballad— and the least characteristic—can be heard on *100JB*, 1/9. She is pictured as Senta in Zeh, 170 and (with van Rooy as the Dutchman) in Mack, 168.

70. A sample of Burgstaller as Erik can be heard on *100JB*, 1/19, and he is pictured in this role in Zeh, 168.

71. Peter Heidkamp (1864–1902). Primary engagement: Cologne (1897–1902). Bayreuth career: Hunding, Daland, and minor roles (1899–1901). Pictured as Daland in Zeh, 167.

72. *Neue Zeitschrift für Musik* 71/32 (3 August 1904): 565–67.

73. Josephine von Artner (Woglinde) and Maria Knüpfer-Egli (Wellgunde; *100JB*, 6/1), Theodor Bertram (Wotan; *100JB*, 6/9), Otto Briesemeister (Loge; *100JB*, 8/18 and 6/6), Hans Breuer (Mime; *100JB*, 6/6), and Alfred von Bary (Siegmund; *100JB*, 8/19–20).

74. The Bayreuth career of Maria Knüpfer-Egli (1872–1924) consisted of minor roles in the *Ring* and *Parsifal* (1901–8). Her primary engagement: Berlin (1895–1900), thereafter guest engagements only. As for Adrienne von Kraus-Osborne (1873–1951), her Bayreuth career is made up of minor roles in (primarily) the *Ring* (1899, 1904–9), the most substantial of which was Waltraute in *Götterdämmerung* (1908–9).

75. Eduard Nawiasky (1854–1925). Primary engagements: Frankfurt (1885–1902), Braunschweig thereafter. Nawiasky sang at Bayreuth only in 1904, replacing Fritz Friedrichs as Alberich on a few months' notice.

76. Evidence of the degree to which "years of assiduous work" eventually eliminated the problems associated with performing this scene according to Wagner's practice and instructions can be found in Fritz Kranich, *Bühnentechnik der Gegenwart*, vol. 1 (1929), where in Table 12 (an eight-page insert between pp. 184 and 185) the author diagrams the movements of the various pieces of machinery so specifically that the scene can be mastered by untrained stagehands in only three rehearsals.

77. Reuss-Belce is shown as Fricka (in *Die Walküre*) in Mack, 134.

78. Emilie Feuge-Gleiss (1863–1923). Primary engagement: Dessau (1890–1916). Bayreuth career: Forest Bird and Flower Maiden (1897–1901); same roles plus Freia (1904–6).

79. Alois Hadwiger (1879–1948) was trained at Bayreuth, where his career consisted of minor roles plus Froh (1904); Froh and Parsifal (1906–8). Principal engagement: Bremen (1910–18). Robert vom Scheidt (1881–1964) was known for his principal engagements in Cologne (1897–1903), Hamburg (1903–12), and Frankfurt (1912–40). Bayreuth career: Biterolf, Donner, Klingsor (1904). Note that he did not sing Alberich at Bayreuth as *100JB* claims, although he did record at least one excerpt from the role at the "Gramophone and Typewriter" recording sessions at Bayreuth in 1904.

80. Other singers wearing these Bayreuth costumes can be seen in Mack, 138 (1896) and Zeh, 128 (1909).

81. Luise Geller-Wolter (1859–1934). Principal engagement: Berlin (Theater des Westens) beginning in 1898. Bayreuth career: minor roles (1897–99, 1904), of which Erda was the most significant. Much confusion has arisen over the respective roles of Geller-Wolter and Ottilie Metzger during the 1904 festival, but reference to reliable reviews shows that Geller-Wolter sang Erda in both relevant operas (*Das Rheingold* and *Siegfried*) of both

cycles, and Metzger sang Waltraute in both performances of *Götterdämmerung*, whereas standard cast lists show the two singers sharing both roles. They did, however, apparently share the role of Waltraute in *Die Walküre*, with Geller-Wolter performing in the first cycle, Metzger in the second—and this splitting of duties is *not* reported by the cast lists!

82. The challenge of realizing the "Rainbow Bridge" effect at the end of *Das Rheingold* and some of the ingenious solutions devised for it at Bayreuth between 1876 and the early 1900s (above all by the local technician and inventor Hugo Bähr) are detailed by Carl-Friedrich Baumann in *Bühnentechnik im Festspielhaus Bayreuth*, vol. 9 of *100 Jahre Bayreuther Festspiele* (Munich, 1980): 227–31. One witness of the 1904 production, Eduard Reuss, remarked on the "remarkably realistic Rainbow reaching from the edge of the rocks [*Felsspitze*, i.e., where the gods are congregated] to the foot of the fortress, created in a new way by Fritz Kranich" (230). More precise details are not forthcoming, however.

83. Alfred von Bary (1873–1926). Primary engagements: Dresden (1903–12), Munich (1912–18). Bayreuth career: Siegmund, Parsifal, Tristan, Lohengrin (1904–9), Siegfried (1911–14). Von Bary was extremely near-sighted, which limited both the extent of his stage career (he never performed in England or America) and his naturalness of movement on stage, as some of Schering's comments suggest.

84. Marie Wittich (1868–1931). Primary engagement: Dresden (1889–1914). Bayreuth career: Kundry, Sieglinde, and Isolde in five festivals between 1901 and 1909. Created Salome in 1905.

85. Paul Knüpfer (1865–1920). Primary engagement: Berlin (1898–1920). Bayreuth career: Gurnemanz, Titurel, Landgraf, Daland, Hunding, Marke (1901–6); Hunding and Pogner (1912).

86. Carl Perron (1858–1928). Primary engagement: Dresden (1892–1913), where he created Jokanaan, Orestes, and Baron Ochs. Bayreuth career: five festivals between 1889 and 1904 as Amfortas, Wotan, and Gunther.

87. Ellen Gulbranson (1863–1947). Bayreuth was at the center of her career: she shared Brünnhilde with Lilli Lehmann in 1896, but thereafter was the only Bayreuth exponent of that role in the years 1897–1914, and also sang Kundry (1899–1906). Pictured as Brünnhilde (in 1899) in Mack, 144.

88. The register in which artists' salaries were recorded by the festival administration in 1904 casts interesting light on Schering's observation about Siegmund's battle scene. Paul Glitsch, a bass in the festival chorus, received 20 marks in special pay for portraying Siegmund in the battle scene in the two performances of *Die Walküre* given that summer. As already mentioned, Alfred von Bary, who performed Siegmund in 1904, was terribly near-sighted and later required a stunt man for the fight with the dragon when he appeared as the young Siegfried in 1911–12. The fact that Schering draws attention to the staging of this scene without publicly noting the substitution of one actor for another makes one wonder whether such a procedure was an assumed practice in non-Bayreuth productions as well. In any case, this is only one of several scenes in which stunt doubles or mannequins were common in early Bayreuth productions.

89. The basic set of the 1896 production appears in Mack, 125; doubles for the Valkyries (children on wooden horses) from the same year are pictured in Mack, 135; and the Valkyries (also from 1896) are pictured in 136. The relationship between the projections Schering mentions and these other dimensions remains somewhat obscure.

90. Isadora Duncan, *My Life* (1927; repr. New York, 1942), 144. Duncan's fascinating description of her summer in Bayreuth occurs over the course of chap. 15, 142–58.

91. Relevant photographs from the scene discussed by Chevalley can be found in Zeh, 88, 90, and 103; and in Mack, 102–3.

92. Duncan, *My Life*, 156.

93. The allusion is to Faust's line, "Zwei Seelen wohnen, ach, in meiner Brust" (Two souls, alas, live in my breast). Goethe, *Faust*, Part 1.

PART VI

THE COMPLETE
PROGRAM NOTES OF
RICHARD WAGNER

Wagner Introduces Wagner (and Beethoven)

Program Notes Written for Concert Performances by and of Richard Wagner 1846–1880

TRANSLATED, ANNOTATED, AND INTRODUCED
BY THOMAS S. GREY

A common denominator of Wagner's activities as a composer, a drama-tist, and a writer might be identified as "the urge to communicate," as James Treadwell has put it. "Addressing readers as urgently and powerfully as possible seems to be a habit he was born with," he remarks of Wagner the writer.[1] Such influential critics as Nietzsche and Adorno expressed simi-lar reactions to Wagner the composer. It would be fair to suggest that his central commitment to musical drama as a medium or a genre reflects this urge to speak to his audience at once articulately (through language), imme-diately (through dramatic representation), and passionately (through music).

The small but interesting corpus of program notes he devised for con-cert excerpts of his own works, along with several orchestral standards by Beethoven, can be seen as by-products of this same instinct. At a time when "program notes" were by no means the institutional fixture of the concert hall they have since become—indeed, when the genre still scarcely existed—Wagner felt a need to present his concert audiences with an imagi-native context for the music he programmed. In the case of overtures, preludes, or other excerpts from his operas, which had not yet become well known on stage, he was naturally concerned to provide an idea of the relevant dramatic content. Such content may necessarily be located in the librettos of the operas, but Wagner also sought to transmute it in "purely musical" terms within the orchestral pieces that introduced *Der fliegende Holländer*, *Tannhäuser*, *Lohengrin*, *Tristan und Isolde*, or *Parsifal*.

The role of the program note in mediating between musical and poetic or dramatic representation of that content situates Wagner on the margins, at least, of the debates over form and content in instrumental music central to the emergence of a "New German School." His championing of the "poetic content" of such Beethoven works as the *Eroica* and Ninth symphonies or the *Coriolan* Overture feeds even more directly into those debates, not to mention his larger theories about the evolution of musical composition altogether in the post-Beethovenian era. The notes he produced for Beethoven's works in Dresden (for the Ninth Symphony, in 1846), and subsequently during his political exile in Zurich, reflect a sense of missionary zeal characteristic of Wagner in the years around 1848, when he was responding to the socialist-utopian and revolutionary energies coursing through Europe and channeling these into his own theories of modern art and culture. He felt convinced that his intuitive understanding of Beethoven's major works contained vital truths about their expressive value as well as Beethoven's historical significance for the present and future of music. Naturally he felt the same way about his own music and what he had to say about it. But among the "explanatory notes" he devised for excerpts from his works, only those to the overtures and preludes resemble those for Beethoven's works in form and hermeneutic ambition. The texts designed to accompany other "numbers" or passages (with or without the vocal parts) are more pragmatic in nature, aiming mainly just to draw the listener's attention to the characters and situations involved.

Beethoven's Ninth Symphony
Palm Sunday Concert, Dresden, April 5, 1846

That the first and most extensive of Wagner's program notes was written for Beethoven's Ninth seems significant on several levels. Not long after the concerts for which the note was written (the 1846 installment of an annual "Palm Sunday" concert series he organized as Kapellmeister of the Dresden court theater) Wagner would be citing the Ninth Symphony as the end of symphonic history and the harbinger of the new musical-dramatic "total artwork" of the future in both The Artwork of the Future *(1849) and* Opera and Drama *(1852). Indeed, the very element of this challenging work that most clearly embodied its epochal status for Wagner was its own impassioned, transgressive "urge to communicate." Referring to both the striking introductory dissonances of the finale and its use of "instrumental recitative," Wagner points to the "more distinctly speaking character" assumed by Beethoven's music: "It leaves behind the character of pure instrumental music that had been maintained throughout the first three movements, the realm of infinite and indistinct expression." "We must admire," he continues, "how the master has prepared the entrance of language and the human voice as something both anticipated and necessary by means of that shattering recitative of the double basses when, nearly transgressing the boundaries of absolute music, it engages the other instruments with its powerfully emotional discourse."*

These *"boundaries of absolute music" were to become hotly contested in the coming decades, when a belief in the progressive role of programs, "poetic ideas," and drama in modern music was pitted against a view of pure or "absolute" music influentially articulated in Eduard Hanslick's* Vom Musikalisch-Schönen *(On* the Beautiful in Music, *1854). Ironically, Wagner's 1846 program note on the* Ninth *is generally accepted as the first instance of the term "absolute music," a term which he would go on to redefine negatively in the polemical context of* Opera and Drama, *prior to Hanslick's defense of "pure, absolute music" in his aesthetic treatise of 1854.*[2] *(Similar coinages can be identified in other sources from 1846 or as early as 1836, although it is not possible to claim originary status for any one of these.)*[3] *Wagner's program notes were not written with the aim of engaging this critical debate, but they offer an intriguing glimpse into its early stages.*

Program

In view of the great difficulties an understanding of this wonderfully significant musical work poses to novice listeners trying to achieve a true, inner familiarity with it (and this is surely a sizable proportion of the audience), we might be permitted to attempt in helping them reach, if not an absolute understanding of Beethoven's masterpiece (such as only direct personal experience could vouchsafe), at least some sense of its artistic conception.[4] Some indication of this could, at the very least, avoid the confusions or misperceptions that might otherwise afflict the less fully initiated listener confronted by the peculiar, utterly inimitable novelty of this piece. If we admit the nature of higher instrumental music to consist in the expression in tones of that which is inexpressible in words, then we can perhaps best hope to suggest an indirect solution to an impossible task by turning to a text by our great poet Goethe.[5] Although Goethe's verses bear no immediate connection to Beethoven's composition, hence in no wise can be thought to provide a comprehensive exegesis of the purely musical creation, they do nonetheless express so sublimely the higher human spiritual moods underlying the work that, if nothing else, the recollection of these verses might afford the listener a greater degree of emotional engagement with this composition than would otherwise be possible.

First Movement

At the basis of the first movement there seems to be a struggle, conceived in the grandest sense, between the soul striving for joy and the oppression of some inimical power interposing itself between us and earthly happiness. The great principal theme heard at the outset, naked and powerful as if emerging from behind some uncanny concealing veil, could perhaps be translated (in a sense apt also for the entire musical poem)[6] through Goethe's line:

Entbehren sollst du! Sollst entbehren![7]   Renounce you must, you must
                                                  renounce!

Opposing this mighty foe we discover a noble defiance, a virile energy of resistance that increases, in the center of the movement, to a state of open battle against its opponent: two powerful combatants who prove equally invincible, so that each finally desists from the struggle. During a few fleeting moments of light we can perceive a bittersweet smile of happiness, seeking us out (as it seems)—that very happiness toward which we have been struggling, but which our crafty, powerful antagonist has prevented us from finding; now his darksome wings eclipse the desired goal such that we sink back in brooding until roused again to defiance, to renewed struggle against that demon bent upon robbing us of all our joy. Thus the never-ending motion of this astounding musical work is composed of elements of force, resistance, surging combat, yearning, hope, near achievement, renewed loss, renewed searching, and renewed struggle. Throughout, the struggle is reduced now and again to a more sustained state of despondency such as Goethe evokes in these lines:

Nur mit Entsetzen wach' ich, morgens auf	In very terror I at morn awake,
Ich möchte bittre Tränen weinen,	Upon the verge of bitter weeping,
Den Tag zu sehn, der mir in seinem Lauf	To see the day of disappointment break,
Nicht einen Wunsch erfüllen wird, nicht einen,	To no one hope of mine—not one —its promise keeping:—
Der selbst die Ahnung jeder Lust	That even each joy's presentiment
Mit eigensinn'gem Krittel mindert,	With willful cavil would diminish,
Die Schöpfung meiner regen Brust	With grinning masks of life prevent
Mit tausend Lebensfratzen hindert.	My mind its fairest work to finish!
Auch muß ich, wenn die Nacht sich niedersenkt,	Then, too, when night descends how anxiously

Mich ängstlich auf das Lager strecken;	Upon my couch of sleep I lay me:
Auch da wird keine Rast geschenkt,	There, also, comes no rest to me,
Mich werden wilde Träume schrecken.[8]	But some wild dream is sent to fray me.[9]

At the end of the movement this somber, joyless mood swells to huge proportions, as if encompassing the whole world in its terrifying, sublime majesty: this world that God had created—for joy.

Second Movement

Upon hearing the first rhythms of this second movement we are instantly seized with wild abandon: we enter a new world, or rather, we are swept up in a delirium, a frenzy. As if driven by despair, fleeing from it, we seem to be constantly, unceasingly chasing after some new, unknown happiness—since the old one that had earlier radiated its distant smile is now quite thoroughly lost to us. Goethe expresses something like this impulse in these lines:

Von Freude sei nicht mehr die Rede,	But thou hast heard, 'tis not of joy we're talking.
Dem Taumel weih' ich mich,	I take the wildering whirl,
dem schmerzlichsten Genuß![10]	enjoyment's keenest pain[!]
Laß in den Tiefen der Sinnlichkeit	Let us the sensual deeps explore,
Uns glühende Leidenschaften stillen!	To quench the fervors of glowing passion!
In undurchdrungenen Zauberhüllen	Let every marvel take form and fashion
Sei jedes Wunder gleich bereit!	Through the impervious veil it wore!
Stürzen wir uns in das Rauschen der Zeit,	Plunge we in Time's tumultuous dance,
Ins Rollen der Begebenheit!	In the rush and roll of Circumstance!
Da mag denn Schmerz und Genuß,	Then may delight and distress,
Gelingen und Verdruß	And worry and success,
Miteinander wechseln, wie es kann,	Alternately follow, as best they can:
Nur rastlos betätigt sich der Mann!	Restless activity proves the man!

With the appearance of the Trio a scene of earthly pleasures, amusements, and contentment is suddenly disclosed to us: a certain coarse merriment is expressed in the simple, much repeated theme, a naïveté and self-satisfied cheerfulness which calls to mind Goethe's description of such simple cheer:

Dem Volke hier wird jeder Tag ein Fest.	Here, for the folk, each day's a holiday:
Mit wenig Witz und viel Behagen	With little wit, and ease to suit them,
Dreht jeder sich im engen Zirkeltanz	They whirl in narrow circling trails,
[Wie junge Katzen mit dem Schwanz.][11]	[Like kittens playing with their tails.]

Yet we are not inclined to regard such narrowly circumscribed pleasures as the true goal of our tireless pursuit of happiness and noble joy; our view of this scene becomes clouded, we turn away and yield once more to that unceasing drive that had chased us ever onward in hope of achieving a happiness that (alas!) is never truly to be found in this manner. And so, once again, at the end of the movement we are driven toward that scene of pleasurable contentment previously encountered,[12] and which, no sooner have we recognized it again, we thrust from us with hasty impatience.

Third Movement

How differently these tones speak to our heart! How pure, with what heavenly calm they resolve the defiance, the wild press of the soul driven by despair, into feelings of gentle resignation! It is as if a memory has been awakened of some pure happiness enjoyed long, long ago:

Sonst stürzte sich der Himmelsliebe Kuß	Once Heavenly Love sent down a burning kiss
Auf mich herab in ernster Sabbatstille,	Upon my brow, in Sabbath silence holy;
Da klang so ahnungsvoll des Glockentones Fülle,	And, filled with mystic presage, chimed the church bell slowly,
und ein Gebet war brünstiger Genuß.[13]	And prayer dissolved me in a fervent bliss.

With this memory we also experience a sweet yearning, so beautifully expressed in the second theme of this movement, to which these lines of Goethe might provide an appropriate caption:

Ein unbegreiflich holdes Sehnen	A sweet, uncomprehended yearning
Trieb mich, durch Wald und Wiesen hinzugehn,	Drove forth my feet through woods and meadows free,
Und unter tausend heißen Tränen	And while a thousand tears were burning,
Fühlt' ich mir eine Welt entstehn.[14]	I felt a world arise for me.

It appears as the yearning of love, answered by the hopeful, sweetly calming first theme, and now adorned with a more mobile expression. Thus when the second theme returns it is like the embrace of love and hope, their gentle powers now dispensed upon our tormented spirit.

Was sucht ihr, mächtig und gelind,	Why, here in dust, entice me with your spell,
Ihr Himmelstöne, mich am Staube?	Ye gentle, powerful sounds of Heaven?
Klingt dort umher, wo weiche Menschen sind.[15]	Peal rather there, where tender natures dwell.

Our still palpitating heart gently resists this balm, yet its calming power is greater than that of our now relenting defiance. Thus overcome, we throw ourselves into the arms of these fair messengers of purest happiness:

O tönet fort, ihr süßen Himmelslieder,	Sound on, ye hymns of Heaven, so sweet and mild!
Die Träne quillt, die Erde hat mich wieder![16]	My tears gush forth: the Earth takes back her child!

Yes, our wounded heart seems to convalesce, to recover strength and resolve;[17] this we can hear in the almost triumphal passage toward the end of the movement. This newly won resolve is not quite free from repercussions of the storms we have weathered; but each bout of renewed pain is immediately met by that fair, magical power before which, finally, the dissipating storms yield as with the last, faint flickering of lightning.

Fourth Movement

The transition from the third to the fourth movement, which begins with a kind of harsh outcry, we might suitably connect with Goethe's lines:

Aber ach! schon fühl' ich bei dem besten Willen	But ah! I feel, though will thereto be stronger,
Befriedigung noch nicht aus dem Busen quillen!	Contentment flows from out my breast no longer.
Welch holder Wahn,—doch ach, ein Wähnen nur!	How grand a show! but, ah! a show alone.[18]
Wo fass' ich dich, unendliche Natur?	Thee, boundless Nature, how make thee my own?
Euch Brüste wo? Ihr Quellen alles Lebens,	Where you, ye breasts? Founts of all Being, shining,
An denen Himmel sowie Erde hängt,	Whereon hang Heaven's and Earth's desire,
Dahin die welke Brust sich drängt. —	Whereto our withered hearts aspire,—
Ihr quellt, ihr tränkt, und schmacht' ich so vergebens?	Ye flow, ye feed: and am I vainly pining?

With the beginning of this finale Beethoven's music takes on a more distinctly speaking character: it leaves behind the character of pure instrumental music such as had been maintained throughout the first three movements, the realm of infinite and indistinct expression.* The further progress of this musical poem[19] strives toward a resolution, a resolution that can only be articulated by human speech. We must admire how the master has prepared the entrance of language and the human voice as something both anticipated and necessary by means of the shattering recitative of the double basses when, nearly transgressing the boundaries of absolute music, this recitative engages the other instruments with its powerfully emotional discourse, pressing for some resolution, and finally issuing

---

* Regarding the character of instrumental music from a similar point of view, [Ludwig] Tieck was moved to observe: "In these symphonies we perceive, as from out of the furthest depths, an insatiable yearning that wanders forth only to be turned back on itself, the inexpressible longing that nowhere finds fulfillment and so, in a consuming passion, casts itself into a current of madness, now struggling against all manner of notes, now overcome, now proclaiming its victory from amid the torrent, and now seeking rescue as it sinks deeper and deeper." —It almost seems to us that Beethoven was moved by a similar conception of the nature of instrumental music in the conception of this symphony. [Footnote by Wagner, *GSD*, 2:61.]

in a lyrical theme.[20] The lyrical theme progresses with simple, stately joy, carrying the rest of the instruments along with it and so swelling to great heights. This seems to be the last effort to express a securely circumscribed, unclouded, joyful happiness. But the unbridled element seems incapable of submitting to any constraint, rearing up like a storm-tossed ocean and sinking back, until the wild, chaotic outcry of unsatisfied passion again strikes our ear even more forcefully than before. Here a human voice and the clear, secure expression of language counter the raging of the instruments, and we scarcely know whether it is the master's bold inspiration we ought to admire, or rather his great naïveté, when he has this voice address the instruments:

O Freunde, nicht diese Töne!	Oh friends, not these tones!
Sondern laßt uns angenehmere und	Rather let us sound more pleas-
anstimmen freudenvollere!	ant and more joyful ones!

With these words a light shines upon the chaos; a surer, more determinate manner of expression is achieved; now, supported by the controlled element of instrumental music, we hear articulated clearly and distinctly that which must seem, in view of the earlier tormented striving for joy, like the greatest happiness finally within our grasp.

Freude, schöner Götterfunken,	Joy, fair spark of divinity,
Tochter aus Elysium,	daughter of Elysium,
Wir betreten feuertrunken,	we enter, drunk with fire,
Himmlische, dein Heiligtum.	thy sanctuary, O holy one.
Deine Zauber binden wieder,	Your magic binds again
Was die Mode streng geteilt,	that which fashion strictly sundered,
Alle Menschen werden Brüder,	every human is a brother,
Wo dein sanfter Flügel weilt.	where your gentle pinions wave.
Wem der große Wurf gelungen,	He who has achieved the luck
Eines Freundes Freund zu sein,	of being a true friend to friends,
Wer ein holdes Weib errungen,	he who has attained a fair wife,
Mische seinen Jubel ein!	let him join his cry to ours!
Ja, — wer auch nur eine Seele	Yes, — whoever calls but one soul
Sein nennt auf den Erdenrund!	his upon this earth!
Und wer's nie gekonnt, der stehle	And who never has been able,
Weinend sich aus diesem Bund!	let him steal away and weep.
Freude trinken alle Wesen	Every being drinks of joy
An den Brüsten der Natur;	at the breasts of nature;

Alle Guten, alle Bösen	Both the good as well as bad
Folgen ihre Rosenspur!	seek to trace its flowery path!
Küsse gab sie uns, und Reben,	Joy gave us kisses, gave us wine,
Einen Freund, geprüft im Tod!	and a friend true unto death!
Wollust ward dem Wurm gegeben,	The merest worm may know contentment,
Und der Cherub steht vor Gott! —	while the cherubim wait on God!

Stalwart military strains approach: we seem to hear a band of youths approaching whose joyous heroism is expressed in the lines:

Froh, wie seine Sonnen fliegen	Gladly, as his planets move
Durch des Himmels prächt'gen Plan,	through the splendid firmament,
Laufet, Brüdern, eure Bahn,	Run, my brothers, your own course,
Freudig, wie ein Held zum Siegen.	joyful, like a conquering hero.

This leads into a joyous combat, expressed by instruments alone: we see those youths courageously hurl themselves into a battle whose victorious issue will be *joy*. Here once more we are inclined to cite Goethe's verses:

Nur der verdient sich Freiheit wie das Leben,	He only earns his freedom and existence,
der täglich sie erobern muß.[21]	Who daily conquers them anew.

The victory, which we had never doubted, has been fought and won; the reward of all these exertions is the smile of joy as it breaks out triumphantly in the consciousness of newly *achieved* happiness:

Freude, schöner Götterfunken,	Joy, fair spark of divinity,
Tochter aus Elysium,	daughter of Elysium,
Wir betreten feuertrunken,	now we enter, drunk with fire,
Himmlische, dein Heiligtum.	thy sanctuary, O holy one.
Deine Zauber binden wieder,	Your magic binds again
Was die Mode streng geteilt,	that which fashion strictly sundered,
Alle Menschen werden Brüdern,	every human is a brother,
Wo dein sanfter Flügel weilt!	where your gentle pinions wave.

Now the proclamation of universal philanthropy bursts from the swelling breast as it experiences the fullest feelings of joy; in a state of sublime exaltation we turn from the embrace of the whole human race to the great creator of the natural world, acclaiming his beneficent being—whom, indeed, it seems we can see in a moment of sublime, trance-like clairvoyance through the parting folds of the blue empyrean:

Seid umschlungen, Millionen!	Be embracèd, all you millions,
Diesen Kuß der ganzen Welt!	in this kiss of the whole world!
Brüder, überm Sternenzelt	Brothers, above the firmament
Muß ein lieber Vater wohnen!	there must dwell a loving father!
Ihr stürzt nieder, Millionen?	Bow you down, O all you millions?
Ahnest du den Schöpfer, Welt?	Can you sense your creator, world?
Such ihn überm Sternenzelt!	Seek him beyond the firmament!
Über Sternen muß er wohnen!	Beyond the stars is where he lives!

It is as if some revelation has justified us in this most blessed belief: *every human being has been created for joy.* With the most powerful conviction we cry out to one another:

Seid umschlungen, Millionen!	Be embracèd, all you millions,
Diesen Kuß der ganzen Welt!	in this kiss of the whole world!

and:

Freude, schöner Götterfunken,	Joy, fair spark of divinity,
Tochter aus Elysium,	daughter of Elysium,
Wir betreten feuertrunken,	now we enter, drunk with fire,
Himmlische, dein Heiligtum.	thy sanctuary, O holy one.

For now we may experience the purest joy allied with this universal philanthropy, blessed of God. No longer merely in a shuddering of sublime ecstasy, but now by way of expressing a sweetly beneficent truth revealed to us we are able to reply to the question:

Ihr stürzt nieder, Millionen?	Bow you down, O all you millions?
Ahnest du den Schöpfer, Welt?	Can you sense your creator, world?

with the lines:

Such' ihn überm Sternenzelt!	Seek him beyond the firmament!
Brüder, überm Sternenzelt	Brothers, above the firmament
Muß ein lieber Vater wohnen!	there must dwell a loving father!

In the secure possession of the happiness thus bestowed on us, with a renewed sense of childlike joy, we deliver ourselves to the pleasure of it: we have recovered an innocence of heart, and the gentle wings of joy spread their blessings over us:

Freude, Tochter aus Elysium,	Joy, daughter of Elysium
Deine Zauber binden wieder,	Your magic binds again
Was die Mode streng geteilt,	that which fashion strictly sundered
Alle Menschen werden Brüder,	every human is a brother
Wo dein sanfter Flügel weilt.	where your gentle pinions wave.

Following the calm happiness of joy there ensues its celebration: —thus do we press the world to our breast, jubilation and cheer fill the air like the thunder of heaven, like the roaring of the sea—such things as animate the earth through constant motion and beneficent awe, preserving it thus for the joy of humankind as God gave it to be lived upon, happily.

Seid umschlungen, Millionen!	Be embracèd, O ye millions!
Diesen Kuß der ganzen Welt!	in this kiss of the whole world
Brüder, überm Sternenzelt	Brothers, above the firmament
Muß ein lieber Vater wohnen!	there must dwell a loving father
Freude! Freude schöner	Joy! Joy, fair spark of divinity!
Götterfunken!	

Beethoven's *Eroica* Symphony
Zurich Concert, February 26, 1851

At the beginning of Wagner's nearly nine years in Zurich as a political exile from Saxony, following his involvement with the revolutionary insurrection of May 1849 in Dresden, there was much local curiosity to hear the visiting celebrity conduct. Wagner, for his part, was developing an appetite to hear some live music, not least of all something from his last completed opera, Lohengrin *(1848). He fairly quickly abjured the idea of working with the severely limited resources of the Zurich theater. He was more willing to collaborate with the local Music Society (Allgemeine Musik-Gesellchaft) in a number of mixed instrumental and vocal programs, conducting as many as twenty-two concerts between January 1851 and February 1855 and featuring forty different works, apart from featured solo or chamber works.*[22] *For a few of the more substantial works he devised the "programmatic commentaries" translated here, later taken up in the fifth volume of the* Gesammelte Schriften: *Beethoven's* Eroica Symphony *and* Coriolan Overture, *the overtures to* Der fliegende Holländer *and* Tannhäuser, *and the first-act Prelude from*

Lohengrin.[23] *Here is the first, on Beethoven's* Eroica, *in which Wagner significantly steers clear of the traditional speculations about a Napoleonic program detailing battles, victories, defeats, a hero's funeral, and his apotheosis. Instead, he reads the symphony in generalized terms as expressing the heroic struggle of the individual human subject in dialogue with dynamic properties ("power") and affective ones ("love"), and the ultimate synthesis of these properties.*

This highly significant musical poem [*Tondichtung*]—the master's third symphony and the work with which he first set out upon his own distinctive path—is in many respects not so easy to understand as its name might lead us to suppose.[24] For the title "Heroic Symphony" would instinctively lead us to imagine a series of heroic situations in a more or less historical or dramatic sense, represented by means of musical illustrations [*Tonbildungen*]. Yet he who approaches an understanding of this work under such premises will find himself at first confused and ultimately disappointed, without having truly achieved any pleasure from the experience. If I therefore permit myself to communicate here as succinctly as possible my own perspective on the poetic content of this musical creation [*Tonschöpfung*], I do this in the sincere hope of helping many listeners of the upcoming performance of the *Eroica* Symphony to an understanding that they might otherwise only achieve after repeated hearings and in especially animated performances.

To begin with, the designation "heroic" is to be understood in the broadest sense, in no way limited to that of a specifically military hero. If we understand by "hero" rather the man in general, the complete man in full possession of the purely human feelings of love, suffering, and power in their highest, most powerful degrees, then we have grasped the true object that the artist has communicated to us in the compellingly articulate tones of his composition. The artistic space of this work is filled with all the manifold, powerfully felt sensations of a strong, perfected individuality to whom nothing human is alien—who rather encompasses all truly human attributes within him, and who manifests these in such a way that all the noblest passions are united, from the most tender sensibility to the most energetic force, into a perfect whole. The progress toward this synthesis defines the heroic conception in this artwork.

The first movement encompasses, as in one glowing focal point, all the feelings of a richly endowed human nature, seething with restless youthful activity. Delight and sorrow, pleasure and pain, grace and melancholy, brooding and longing, languishing and wallowing, boldness, defiance, and an unbounded self-confidence alternate and infiltrate one another so fully and immediately that, even though we are able to experience each one of these feelings, no one of them can be perceptibly isolated from any other; rather, our attention is at every moment directed to that one all-feeling persona that seems to address us here.[25] Yet all of these feelings emanate from one principal faculty, and that is *power* [*Kraft*].

Infinitely augmented through the expression of these diverse feelings and driven to articulate its own excessive nature, this power is the motivating force of the composition: it accrues a truly annihilating strength toward the center of the movement, where its defiant manifestation gives the impression of some world-destroying entity, some titan in combat with the gods.

This annihilating power that fills us with delight and terror at once has pressed toward a tragic catastrophe, one whose earnest significance is demonstrated to our feeling in the second movement of the symphony. The tone poet clothes this demonstration in the musical garb of mourning, as a funeral march. A sentiment chastened by deep sorrow and moved by solemn mourning is communicated to us in compelling musical speech. From out of the lament there emerges a serious, manly sorrow, proceeding through feelings of tender emotion, tears of love, inward exaltation, to the most animated acclamations. Out of sorrow a new power wells up, filling us with sublime warmth; and to nourish this power we instinctively look again to our sorrow, yielding ourselves thereunto, even to the point of collapsing in sighs, though at just this point we rally our full power yet once more: we submit not to defeat, merely to endurance. We do not resist mourning, which we are now able to support upon the strong surge of a courageous, virile heart. Who could possibly convey in words these infinitely various (and for that very reason inexpressible) feelings, ranging from pain to the greatest exaltation, from exaltation to the most tender sorrow, up to a final dissolution into an infinite remembrance? Only the tone poet could convey these, as he has done in this wondrous composition.

Power, whose destructive hubris has now been tamed, returns in the third movement in a spirit of bold cheerfulness. Where before we had wild, restless energy, we now have fresh, jolly activity; a lovable, merry person stands before us, striding with pleasure and high spirits through nature's fields, smiling at the flowery meadows as the hunting horns sound from the forest heights. What this person feels amid such scenes the composer tells us in this robust, cheerful tone picture—he tells us, finally, through those hunting horns themselves that give expression to the beautiful, cheerful, but also tenderly sentimental feelings of such a person. In this third movement the tone poet exhibits to us the feeling human being in opposition to what is represented in the second movement: there we encountered a deeply, powerfully suffering subject; here it is a merry, cheerful, active person.

These two sides are then combined by the master in the fourth, and last, movement, so as to show us finally the whole man, in harmony with himself and his feelings, in whom even the remembrance of suffering can become a motive toward noble action. With this finale we have arrived at the clear, defining counterpart to the first movement. Where in the first movement we witnessed the full array of human feelings in infinitely varied expression, sometimes penetrating and sometimes vehemently, diversely repelling one another, here in the finale this diverse array is unified into one whole, resolving that diversity into one harmonious conclusion that represents itself to us in a pleasing, well-formed shape. This shape is first of all manifested in a very simple theme, presenting itself securely and determinately, capable of infinite evolution, from the utmost delicacy to the greatest power. This theme, which we can regard as representative of firm masculine individuality, is from the very outset of the movement wreathed by all manner of soft and delicate feelings, evolving into a suggestion of a pure womanly element that reveals itself gradually and with increasing devotion as the overwhelming force of love in relation to the masculine main theme that strides energetically throughout the whole movement. At the conclusion of the movement this power clears a broad path to the heart. The restless motion pauses, and love speaks forth in noble, expressive calm— at first soft and gentle, then expanding to delightful breadth of feeling, and finally encompassing the entire virile heart, down to its deepest core. Here, too, that heart recalls life's sufferings: the love-filled breast swells, the breast whose rapture does not exclude sorrow, just as rapture and sorrow, as purely human feelings, are ultimately one and the same. The heart tugs once more, and profuse tears of noble humanity pour forth; yet from this delightful sorrow the triumphant power breaks forth, power allied to love, in which union the *whole, complete human being* affirms and celebrates his divinity.

But only the musical speech of the master can truly articulate that which words, all too aware of their limitations, have here merely attempted to suggest.

Beethoven's *Coriolan* Overture
Zurich Concert, February 17, 1852

Writing to Hans von Bülow two days before the Zurich concert of February 17, 1852, which featured the Coriolan Overture, *Wagner offered some interesting musical and critical glosses on his reading of the work: the importance of accenting an offbeat eighth note throughout the development section and a general emphasis on the significance of a "poetic" (but also gestural) understanding of the composition in realizing an adequate performance. "If you undertake a detailed comparison . . . of my own account of the graphic and poetic content of the* Coriolan Overture *with the composition itself, you will, I am sure, admit the justice of my view, and at the same time be bound to concede that all attempts to convey an understanding of such works, although hitherto regarded as the absolute preserve of the absolute musician, have so far met with total failure on the latter's part." "Only now," he adds, "have I been able to perform this work in such a way that what the poetic composer intended is conveyed clearly and intelligibly at all times: the effect this has on the purely musical execution of the work is unbelievable."*[26]

This relatively little known work of the great tone poet is nonetheless one of his most significant creations, and no one intimately familiar with the object it represents will fail to come away from a good performance deeply moved.[27] I therefore permit myself to describe here this object just as I hear it represented by the tone poet himself, so as to assist sympathetic listeners in enjoying the same sublime pleasure I do when hearing this piece.[28]

I may assume general knowledge of Coriolanus: a character of limitless power, incapable of cowardly hypocrisy. For that very reason he finds himself banished from his native city, and in league with its enemies in their attempt to destroy it, until he is moved by the pleas of mother, wife, and child to renounce this vengeance, only to be condemned to death for this betrayal of his erstwhile comrades. The poet could draw on a whole range of intricate relationships in creating a richly detailed political portrait; but this was not possible for the musician, who can express only moods, feelings, passions, and the conflicts of these—yet never political relations of any sort. For this reason Beethoven selected only one scene—albeit the single most decisive one—for his representation, so as to locate the true, purely human emotional content of the discursive historical narrative in one focal point, and thereby to communicate it as compellingly as possible to our purely human feelings. This is the scene between Coriolanus, his mother, and his wife at the enemy's encampment before the gates of his native city.[29] —We would not be far from the truth in supposing that nearly all of the master's symphonic works take as the plastic object of their expression the representation of scenes between man and woman, scenes whose prototype can be identified in the very idea of the dance, from which the symphony as a musical genre may indeed be understood to originate.[30] And here we have the most sublime and moving instance of just such a scene. The entire composition could easily be conceived as the musical accompaniment to a pantomimic representation of that scene, but only if we also suppose that this accompaniment simultaneously expresses, in a language intelligible to the hearing, the same object that the pantomime represents in visual terms.

The opening gestures of the composition first present to us the figure of the man himself: incredible power, limitless self-confidence, impassioned defiance, and an annihilating temperament are expressed through feelings of anger, hate, and vengeance. We need only hear the name "Coriolanus" spoken to call up, as with one magical stroke, this figure and to feel an instinctive sympathy for all the emotions of his impatient heart. Right next to him the feminine principle appears: mother, wife, and child in one. The defiant man is confronted by pleasantness, mildness, and gentle dignity; these impulses conspire to deter the proud one from his destructive bent, combining a child's pleas, a wife's beseeching, and a mother's admonition. —Coriolanus recognizes the threat to his defiant resolve: his homeland has sent to him the most dangerous of emissaries. He could with equanimity turn a cold shoulder to any of the clever and virtuous politicians of his homeland: their embassies have addressed only his political reason, his civic wisdom; one word of scorn from him regarding their cowardice sufficed to make him unapproachable. But by this alternative strategy the fatherland has addressed his heart, his purely human and instinctive feelings; against this attack he has no defense but—to protect his eyes and his ears from an irresistible apparition. — And so he does, at the first approach of the imploring group, quickly seek to avert his eyes and ears; we perceive the impatient gesture with which he interrupts the pleas of his wife, closing his eyes—only to hear the woeful lament whose sounds still echo in his averted head. — In the depths of his heart this gigantic figure feels the serpent of remorse begin to gnaw at his defiance. And yet this defiance defends itself mightily; roused by the first sting of that serpent, it breaks out in raging pain. Its forceful shouts, its dreadful convulsions betray the terrible majesty of this vengeful defiance along with the burning sensation of pain engendered by the tooth of remorse. We see the woman, deeply moved by this terrible display, break into despairing sobs; her pleas stick in her breast, tormented as she is by the wild suffering of the man. This battle of emotions pitches us fearfully from side to side: the woman had expected to meet only with stubborn pride, but she witnesses instead the most terrible suffering even within the strength of defiance. — Defiance has now become the only source of the man's strength: without his vengeance, without his destructive anger, Coriolanus would no longer be himself; and if his defiance yields, he must cease to live. This is the clasp that holds firm the very possibility of his life; once banned as a rebel, once allied to the enemies of his country, he can no longer return to what he had been before. To let go of his vengeance would be to let go of his existence; renouncing his vow to destroy his native city would be to destroy himself. He advances to meet the woman and inform her of this terrible, final choice he must make. He cries out to her: "Rome or myself! One of these must fall!" Here again he exhibits the full sublimity of his annihilating anger. And here, too, the woman regains the power to implore. "Pity! Conciliation! Peace!" she beseeches him. Ah, she does not understand him, she does not grasp the fact that a truce with Rome means—his downfall. But the woman's lament tugs at his heart; he turns away once more to fight the terrible battle between his defiance and the necessity of self-destruction. In tormenting indecision he pauses and then makes a forceful resolve: he seeks out the gaze of the dear woman, and with painful pleasure he reads his own death sentence in her beseeching gestures. That sight fills his breast with powerful emotion, all the hesitations and the uproar within him condense into one great resolve; his self-sacrifice is decided: Peace and Conciliation! — All the power the hero had heretofore concentrated toward the aim of destroying his homeland, all the thousand swords and arrows of his hate and vengeful ire he now grasps in a terrible, mighty fist, drawing them together into one single point, which—he plunges into his own heart. Thus struck by his own death-dealing blow the colossus falls: at the feet of the woman who had entreated him to peace he breathes his last, dying breath.

And thus did Beethoven write *Coriolan* in music!

Overture to *Tannhäuser*
Zurich Concert, March 16, 1852

Under the influence of his own "programmatic commentaries" to Beethoven's Eroica *Symphony and* Coriolan *Overture, Wagner decided that the orchestral movements he had composed to introduce his so-called Romantic operas* (Der fliegende Holländer, Tannhäuser, *and* Lohengrin) *would benefit from similar explications when performed in concert. In particular the* Tannhäuser *Overture (as suggested in the critical accounts by Liszt and Johann Christian Lobe in Part III of the present volume) became an influential model for the new genre of "symphonic poem" pioneered by Liszt, and the central genre of Romantic program music. As Ernest Newman noted, Wagner even came to believe that this overture belonged more to the concert genre, offering rather too much material to be digested before a performance of his opera in the theater.*[31] *As Wagner wrote to his friend Theodor Uhlig after rehearsing the overture with the Zurich Music Society (augmented for the occasion with players from throughout Switzerland), the orchestra had especially requested from him "an explanation of the overture on the model of the one he had written for the* Coriolan *Overture," which they said would help them play this new work better and with greater understanding.*[32] *When this note was printed for the concert of March 16 it actually bore the title "The Venusberg," as if to suggest an independent tone poem based on the opening scene of the opera. Players and audience alike were tremendously impressed by the force of Wagner's personality as a conductor and even, to their surprise, as a composer. "The effect was terrific," he reported to Uhlig; "the women in particular were turned inside out, and had to find relief for their emotion in sobs and weeping."*[33] *Like the programs to the* Holländer *Overture and the* Lohengrin *Prelude, this one was soon printed in the* Neue Zeitschrift für Musik *and thereby contributed not a little to the association of Wagner with the major exponents of Romantic program music, Berlioz and Liszt.*

At the beginning of the piece the orchestra plays for us the Pilgrims' song; this approaches from afar, increases to a mighty outpouring, and finally moves away again into the distance.[34] — Twilight: the dying strains of the song.[35]

—As night falls magical forms start to appear: a rosy evening mist swirls up, and ecstatic notes of pleasure reach our ear; the confused motions of a dreadful voluptuous dance can be heard. This is the seductive magic of the "Venusberg," which can be heard at nighttime by those in whose breast there burns a brazen, sensual longing. A slim, youthful man appears, drawn by these seductive apparitions: this is Tannhäuser, the singer of love. He sounds his proud, triumphant love song as a kind of joyful challenge to that sensual magic, bidding it approach him.

—He is answered by wild cries: the rosy mists close about him more densely, delightful scents surround him and intoxicate his senses. In the seductive twilight atmosphere there materializes before his wonder-struck gaze an unspeakably enticing female form. He hears a voice singing a siren song, tremulous and sweet, and promising the bold youth the satisfaction of his wildest desires. It is Venus herself who has appeared to him.

—Now he is all aflame, heart and soul; a glowing-hot, consuming desire warms the blood in his veins, an irresistible force draws him closer, and he advances before the goddess of love with his song in celebration of love, which now sounds forth ecstatically in her praise. This has the effect of a magical incantation, and all the wonders of the Venusberg suddenly appear to him in brilliant abundance. From all sides can be heard frantic cries of joy and wild rapture. The bacchantes rush at Tannhäuser in drunken revelry, drawing him into their furious dance and conducting him thence into the warm, loving arms of the goddess herself. She embraces him, drunk with rapture; with wild ardor she draws him far away, even to the realm of nonexistence. There is a terrible commotion, like the Wild Hunt, and soon a storm whips up. The air is still filled with humming, voluptuous lament—an eerie, sensual whisper passes like a breath of demonic sensual longing across this site upon which such unholy magical delights have descended, and over which night now spreads again.

—But already morning begins to dawn: from afar we can hear the returning song of the Pilgrims. As the song comes ever closer, as day continues to displace the night, the humming and whispering sounds that had first filled the air like a dreadful lament from the souls of the damned now swell into increasingly joyful waves. Now the sun rises in full splendor and the song of the Pilgrims animatedly proclaims a newly won salvation to all the world and everything that lives upon it, and this sounding wave finally becomes a rapturous roaring of sublime delight. This is the rejoicing of the Venusberg itself, redeemed from its unholy curse, singing out praises to God. Every pulse of life rushes and leaps to this song of redemption; the two sundered elements of spirit and senses, God and Nature, embrace each other in the sacred, unifying kiss of love.

Overture to *Der fliegende Holländer*
Prelude to *Lohengrin*
Zurich Concerts: May 18, 20, 22, 1853

The most extensive sampling of Wagner's own works offered to the inhabitants of Zurich during the composer's residence there occurred in the series of concerts produced on May 18, 20, and 22 (the latter date being Wagner's birthday, which he rarely failed to observe in high style). These included excerpts from Rienzi *(the "Messengers of Peace" chorus at the beginning of Act 2), "Senta's Ballad" and the Act 3 choral-ensemble scene from* Der fliegende Holländer, *the "Entry of the Guests" (or so-called March) and the orchestral introduction to Act 3 of* Tannhäuser, *"Elsa's Procession to the Minster" from Act 2 of* Lohengrin, *the Prelude and "Bridal Chorus" from Act 3, as well as the* Fliegende Holländer *Overture (billed as "The Dutchman's Voyage," in tune with the programmatic elucidation provided), and the* Lohengrin *Prelude, which Wagner now was able to hear for the first time in its essential orchestral guise.*

Overture to *Der fliegende Holländer*

The terrible ship of the "Flying Dutchman" is tossed about by storms; it approaches the coast and lands there, where its captain has been promised he might one day find happiness and salvation.[36] We perceive the sympathetic strains of this promise of redemption, which suggest the feelings of prayer and lament at once: the accursed man listens, somber and despondent; tired and longing only for death he steps ashore, while his crew silently battens down the ship, likewise exhausted and weary of living.[37]

—How many times the unfortunate man has gone through this routine! How many times has he steered his ship from the ocean's waves to the peopled shores, where once each seven years he is allowed to land. How many times has he imagined that his sufferings were at an end, and yet—how many times, bitterly disappointed, has he not had to set sail once again on his endless, senseless sea voyage! Hoping to bring about his own end, he steers madly toward the tempestuous swells: he plunges his ship into the ocean's gaping maw—and yet this maw will not swallow it; now he steers for the breakers crashing upon the rocks—and yet the rocks will not splinter it. All the terrifying dangers of the sea, at which he once laughed in the abandon of heroic hubris,[38] now mock him in turn, by refusing to harm him. For now he is immune to such dangers, condemned to chase forever across the vasty deep in search of treasures he can never enjoy, never to find that one thing that could save him!

—A spry and hearty ship sails by; the Dutchman harks to the merry, carefree singing of its crew, who are on their return voyage and elated by the thought of the imminent arrival at their homeland. Such jollity fills him with rage; he causes his ship to storm furiously past theirs, terrifying and intimidating that happy crew into silence and flight. In his distress the Dutchman utters a dreadful cry for salvation: he is surrounded by men and by the empty seas—but only a woman can achieve his redemption. Where is this savior, in what land does she reside? Where does a feeling heart beat in sympathy with his woes? Where is she who will not flee from him in horror, like these cowardly men who cross themselves in terror at the sight of him?

—Then a light breaks through the night: like a lightning bolt it strikes his tortured soul. For a moment it is extinguished, then it flares up again; the seafarer fastens his gaze on this beacon and steers for it with vigorous determination through wave and current. What draws him on so powerfully is the glance of a woman, radiating sublime pity and divine sympathy. One heart has fathomed the infinite depths of sorrow experienced by this accursed man, and that heart is breaking with sympathy, it is impelled to offer itself in sacrifice, to annihilate itself together with this man's suffering. The wretched man collapses before this divine apparition, just as his ship shatters into pieces; the ocean swallows up the wreck—but the Dutchman rises from the waves, safe and sound, the victorious redemptress leading him by the hand toward the rosy dawn of sublime love.

Prelude to *Lohengrin*

It seemed as if love had disappeared from a world now filled with hate and strife: in no human community was it any more present as the ruling spirit.[39] Yet amid the dreary concern for gain and possession directing all worldly traffic the inextinguishable longing for love that resides in every human heart still yearned to be satisfied. The more this need increased in intensity under the yoke of reality, the less it could hope to find satisfaction, so long as it remained subject to reality. So it was that the mystic imagination located the source of this intangible longing for love, and likewise its final destination, outside of the empirical world, ascribing to it a marvelous form (in the desire for a consoling physical representation of this metaphysical conception). This object was imagined as really existing, though infinitely far away: it was believed in, longed for, and sought for under the name of the "Holy Grail." This signified the precious goblet from which long ago the Savior drank farewell to his apostles, which afterward caught his blood as he suffered on the cross out of love for his brothers, and which was thought to have been lovingly preserved ever since as a source of imperishable love. This sacred vessel had been for some time removed from unworthy humanity when a host of angels from on high returned it to a band of devoted, loving men who lived withdrawn from the world. These pure ones were thus consecrated as its guardians, finding themselves marvelously strengthened and blessed by its presence, and so they became earthly champions of eternal love.

The tone poet of *Lohengrin* chose this episode of the miraculous descent of the Grail accompanied by the host of angels, and their entrusting of it to these happy mortals, as the object of the introduction to his drama concerning the Grail-knight (Lohengrin). It is the representation of this episode in tones that he wishes to elucidate for the imagination by describing it as an object visible to the human eye. —Our rapturous gaze toward the highest, divine yearning for love perceives the clear blue celestial vault; a wonderful, at first scarcely perceptible apparition begins to materialize, magically compelling our sight as it does so. The angelic host is depicted through infinitely delicate lines that gradually take on a more distinct contour; the host descends imperceptibly from the luminous heights, conveying in their midst the sacred vessel. As this apparition comes more fully into view, floating nearer to the terrestrial zone, it seems to emanate sweetly intoxicating scents. This delightful incense wells up like a golden cloud, captivating the senses of the astonished onlooker even to the innermost fibers of his thrilling heart, stirring in him wondrous, sacred feelings. The onlooker is now seized with a rapturous pain, now shudders with blissful pleasure; in his heart every latent kernel of love begins to germinate, irresistibly awakened to wondrous life and growth by the animating magic of this vision. The breast swells, even to the point of breaking, under this powerful longing; it experiences an impulse to surrender and to dissolve such as no human heart has felt before. This feeling is nourished by the greatest, most delightful rapture as the divine vision expands before the transfigured senses, coming into ever closer, more intimate contact with them. When at last the sacred vessel itself is exposed in its wondrous, naked reality to the sight of the privileged beholder, when the Grail radiates from its sacred contents rays of sublime love like the light of a celestial fire such that all hearts around it tremble in the flaming brilliance of this eternal glow—at that point the onlooker's senses fail him altogether, and he sinks down overwhelmed, devoutly prostrate. Still the Grail pours forth its blessing upon this subject lost in the raptures of sacred love, consecrating him as its knight: the radiant flames die down to a gentler glow, which spreads out over the earth like a breath of inexpressible delight and deep feeling; the breast of the devout servant is filled with an unimaginable serenity. The angelic host ascends toward heaven, looking back with a smile: that source of love that had previously withered on earth has here been restored, as the host leaves behind the Grail in the care of pure men into whose hearts its blessed contents have been tipped. And so the glorious host disappears back into the brightness of the celestial ether, from whence it had first approached.

Tannhäuser
Lohengrin
Zurich Concerts: May 18, 20, 22, 1853

In addition to the explanations of the Prelude to Lohengrin *and the* Holländer Overture, *Wagner provided short contextual glosses for the other* Tannhäuser *and* Lohengrin *excerpts included on the programs of the May 1853 concerts. Although these are primarily paraphrases of the dramatic scenes in question, some interest attaches to them for the way they reveal the composer's own scenic visualization of these central episodes from the operas. The description of the introduction to the third act of* Tannhäuser, *however, is a genuine "programmatic commentary" in the same sense as those to the overtures, in this case specifying the way this orchestral piece aims to narrate in musical terms the story of Tannhäuser's unsuccessful pilgrimage to Rome, which he himself narrates vocally later in the act. The "wedding music" from* Lohengrin *included both the lively orchestral prelude to Act 3 and the famous "Wedding Chorus" that opens the act, "Treulich geführt ziehet dahin." In the concert presentation, the orchestral prelude was repeated, da capo, after the gentle chorus and provided with a new conclusion.*[40]

Tannhäuser

Entry of the Guests at the Wartburg

Trumpets from the ramparts announce the arrival at the Wartburg gates of the first of the guests the Landgraf has invited to attend a grand tourney of song.[41] Noble pages jump up to alert the marshal that the guests are to be greeted; he duly appears at the head of a group of heralds and heads toward the door of the hall to receive the arrivals. These guests are dukes and nobles of Thuringia accompanied by their ladies and followed by their pages. They proceed into the hall, arrayed in splendid habiliments; they are led before the Landgraf and Elisabeth, who cordially greet them. The pages and heralds arrange the guests into a broad semicircle, from which position they, in turn, form an audience for the next group of arriving guests. As they observe the proceedings, in eager anticipation of the festive contest about to begin, the guests are moved to sing the praises of the chivalrous and art-loving lord:

Chorus

Freudig begrüßen wir die edle Halle,	Joyfully we greet the noble hall,
Wo Kunst und Frieden immer nur verweil',	Where art and peace forever reign,
Wo lange noch der frohe Ruf erschalle:	Where long shall sound the happy cry:
Thüringens Fürsten, Landgraf Hermann, Heil!	Lord of Thuringia, Landgrave Hermann, hail!

The trumpets have repeatedly greeted a great throng of festival guests: the hall is now resplendent with the flower of chivalry. A gracefully executed formation prepares the entrance of the singers themselves: with harps in hand, but also with swords at their side, these singers proceed into the hall in ceremonial costume. They bow to the assembled nobility with dignity and grace; the pages draw lots for them from a golden vessel to determine the rank and order of their seating, which they take now amid repeated greetings from the assembled onlookers. —In this picture is revealed to us the fairest, most appealing image of medieval Ghibelline manners. The following excerpt will show us a different, deep and inward feature of the same culture.

Tannhäuser's Journey to Rome

In the course of the song contest, Tannhäuser has revealed the secret that he has tarried in the Venusberg, in the arms of Venus herself. Elisabeth has interceded on his behalf, shielding him from the swords of the outraged nobles: she has pleaded for his salvation, she whose heart has been pierced by his reckless confession. Softened by her appeal, the men have allowed Tannhäuser to go free, so that he might journey to Rome to attend the ceremony of general pardon there and implore forgiveness for his terrible transgression. This chastened erstwhile knight of Venus has seized upon the sole path to salvation now pointed out to him, terribly aware of the outrage he committed against his good angel Elisabeth. He is stung with remorse and animated solely by the desire to perform the direst acts of penance for the deadly blow dealt to the pure heart of this loving maiden—not for the pleasure of his own redemption, but only so as to be able to return with a pardoned soul and thereby conciliate the angel who has wept for him the bitterest tears of her life.—

At the outset of this piece we perceive the pious song of the faithful band of pilgrims: Elisabeth's blessing follows the pilgrims as they depart from the homeland. Tannhäuser, however, does not join in that song: rather, bent low and silent, he walks to one side. While his comrades progress upon comfortable paths and strengthen themselves for the continued journey with rest and nourishment, he chooses a route of stones and thorns, hunger and thirst. In this way the flock arrives at its destination. The eternal city lies resplendent before their wondering eyes. In joyful devotion they all sink to their knees before the house of the Lord. From the great church, bathed in the first rays of dawn, sweet, celestial sounds waft upward to the praying pilgrims like the singing of angels, and in an ecstasy of devotion they softly repeat the sacred strains. At the full break of day the gates are opened. He through whom God speaks to His people, His powerful priest on earth, appears upon the steps of the church, amid unparalleled sacred splendor.[42] He proclaims forgiveness and salvation to all who have assembled at this holy site: the cheerful jubilation of the assembled masses rises up toward heaven. —

Then Tannhäuser approaches the priest. Humbly and deeply mortified he confesses his sin, begging for redemption from the fires of unholy passion that have been lit in him by Venus's magic. Yet no matter how woefully he prostrates himself in the dust, the priest shows him no mercy: instead, he cries anathema upon this sinner, thunders eternal damnation on this penitent, the most desperate of all for salvation. All Tannhäuser's senses go dark, and he sinks down. He can still hear the faint echoes of the hymn of salvation as he stares, unconscious, into the twilight. A gentle light appears above the lonely figure in the dark, like the glowing of the evening star; indeed, one eye still watches over the unhappy man, abandoned by all the rest of the world: mournful and alone, Elisabeth remains true to him. She cries tears of infinite sorrow and love for the fallen one; from her lament, impassioned and chaste, she lifts herself with gentle force to issue one last blessed greeting, calling her beloved to heaven.

The returning flock of pilgrims can be heard approaching the peaceful valley of their homeland, their song now piously and joyfully announcing their salvation, filling every breast, moving them to share this joy with every sinner, far and wide.

Lohengrin

Male Chorus and Bridal Procession

The young knight of the Holy Grail, Lohengrin, has gone forth into the world.[43] He rescues an unjustly accused maiden through divinely ordained victory in a trial by combat. Elsa's ecstatic love has won the heart of her champion: he will remain by her side, and the dawning day will see the two married in the minster. The present scene conveys to our sympathetic feeling the wonderfully beneficent, inspiring, and compelling impression made upon every heart by this hero sent at God's bidding.

Wedding Music and Bridal Song

Lively displays to mark the wedding festivities: exuberant praises of the hero ring out in celebration. Alternating with this hearty jubilation is more gentle praise of the lovely maid who has won him, and whose chaste, modest gaze fixes upon him alone amid all joyful tumult. The noisy celebration pauses, so that the happy pair may be led away from all this commotion to the singing of the Bridal Song.

(Bridal Song)

The guests now leave the loving pair to their quiet happiness; when the guests have returned to the brightly lit hall they break out once more in festive jubilation, honoring that high point of human existence: the happiness of a lovingly united pair—which happiness we should like to imagine (putting aside for now the further serious developments of the drama) as forever untroubled.

L. van Beethoven, String Quartet in C-sharp Minor, op. 131
Zurich Quartet Society Concert, December 12, 1854

In the autumn of the same year as the Zurich concerts of his own music, Wagner helped sponsor the formation of a "Quartet Society" drawing on the first-chair string players of the Zurich Music Society orchestra. During a brief stay in Paris around the same time he had the opportunity to hear the Maurin-Chevillard Quartet playing the late quartets of Beethoven, still rarely performed in public at the time. This inspired him to coach the Zurich players in the C-sharp Minor Quartet, op. 131, which they programmed in a concert on December 12, 1854. As with the difficult Ninth, Wagner thought it well to mediate this presentation of Beethoven's unaccustomed late style in print: the short notice translated here was published in the local Eidgenössische Zeitung *on 3 October 1853 and again at the time of the performance.*[44]

(Adagio). Melancholy morning thoughts of a deeply suffering mind: (Allegro) a pleasant vision awakens new desire for life.[45] — (Andante and variations). Attraction, pity, longing, love. — (Scherzo). Whimsical moods, humor, exuberance. (Finale). Transition to a mood of resignation. Painful renunciation.

———

At my special request the gentlemen performers [of the Zurich Quartet Society] have undertaken the very demanding study and rehearsal of this difficult quartet, which, as a work of Beethoven's late period, is still regarded by many musicians and amateurs as unintelligible—and no doubt, at any rate, it is most often performed quite unintelligibly. For these reasons it may seem audacious to present this work to a larger public, a public still generally unused to this genre as a whole, and inclined to prefer lighter works over more deeply felt ones. Nonetheless I was emboldened to give my sponsorship to a public performance of the work thanks to the success of the extended study of this piece undertaken by these players in collaboration with me. But at the same time I consider it my responsibility to call the audience's attention to the peculiar nature of this extraordinary work, such that those who are willing and able to do so might follow in this composition all the varied moods of the tone poet's rich inner life expressed therein: from the melancholy morning thoughts of a deeply suffering mind; through the pleasant visions that take us in and lift us up; through feelings of rapture, delight, desire, love and surrender; then even to a dawning cheerfulness, a playful contentment; until we arrive at the ultimate, painful renunciation of every earthly happiness.

Tristan und Isolde: Prelude to Act 1
Written for Paris Concerts of January 1860

Wagner's answer, in a sense, to the enigma of Beethoven's Opus 131 Quartet might be identified as Tristan und Isolde, *in particular its Prelude, long regarded as the most influential challenge to the limits of tonal composition in the entire nineteenth century. (At the same time he was coaching the Quartet Society in the Beethoven, Wagner was finishing his first reading of Schopenhauer's* World as Will and Representation, *another key moment in the prehistory of* Tristan*). Well before this most radical of Wagner's music dramas made its way to the stage, the Prelude had been floated a few times before generally bewildered audiences. It was the one* *recent composition Wagner included on his concerts in Paris at the beginning of 1860, concerts which themselves formed the prelude to the ill-fated French production of* Tannhäuser *the following year. Words alone were not likely to explain this wholly unfamiliar musical language to its first listeners (Wagner claimed he even had to guide the players laboriously from note to note). Still, he thought it advisable to provide some poetic gloss on his musical conception. The longer program translated here was sent to Mathilde Wesendonck in December 1859, along with an arrangement of his concert ending for the prelude; both were drafted for the Paris concerts. In the event, however, Wagner replaced the program note with a summary account of the Tristan story as represented in the opera.*[46]

An old, primeval tale of love—inextinguishable, retold and reshaped in all the languages of medieval Europe—tells us of Tristan and Isolde. The king's trusty vassal has wooed for his royal liege the very woman he himself would not admit to loving: Isolde. She followed him as his master's bride; she had no choice but to follow the suitor, helplessly. The goddess of love, jealous of her rights which she saw so disdainfully suppressed, took her revenge: she caused the young pair to be served (by means of a resourceful oversight) a love draught, one that the bride's mother had thoughtfully provided for her daughter, as was the custom in those times in the case of politically arranged marriages. Having tasted this draught the young pair was suddenly seized by a fervent ardor; they confessed that they loved each other, alone. But now there was no end to love's longing, yearning, rapture, and distress: the world, power, fame, honor, chivalry, loyalty, friendship—all were dispersed like an insubstantial dream. Only one thing remained alive to them: desire, insatiable desire, a longing ever renewed, ever thirsting and languishing. And from this, no salvation but death— annihilation, never again to awaken!

Having chosen this theme for the introduction to his drama of love, the musician had only to be concerned (since he was aware of working here in the peculiar, unbounded element of music) with how to set limits for himself, since it would be quite impossible to exhaust this subject. Therefore he let this insatiable longing well up just once, in one single process spanning several smaller segments:[47] from the most timid avowal of a delicate inclination; through fearful sighs, hope and trembling, lamentation and prayers, rapture and torment; up to the mightiest pressure, the most forceful efforts to find a breach that will open the way for the infinitely hungering heart to reach the ocean of love's unending delight. In vain! The heart sinks back unconscious, back into languishing desire, desire without fulfillment, since fulfillment can only initiate new desire. Exhausted, the fading gaze finally catches an anticipatory glimpse of ultimate rapture: the rapture of death, surcease, an ultimate redemption within that wondrous realm from which we stray the furthest when we most strenuously try to force our way into it. Should we call it death? Or is it the nocturnal world of wonder from out of which, as the tale tells us, an ivy plant and a vine grew up over the graves of Tristan and Isolde, to wind about each other in intimate embrace?

Tristan und Isolde: Prelude to Act 1 and Conclusion ("Transfiguration")
Vienna Concert, December 27, 1863

For a concert at the Redoutensaal in Vienna on December 27, 1863, undertaken together with the young piano virtuoso Karl Tausig, Wagner provided these short evocations of the Prelude (here subtitled Liebestod *or "love-death") and the conclusion of the opera (Isolde's "Transfiguration").*[48]

(a) Prelude (*Liebestod*)
Taking on the role of suitor for his uncle, the king, Tristan brings to him Isolde.[49] They love each other. From the most timid complaint of unquenchable longing, from the most delicate quivering, up through the most fearsome outburst confessing a hopeless love, the feeling here traces every phase of this hopeless struggle against inner passion—until, sinking back unconscious, that passion seems to be extinguished in death.

(b) Concluding Movement (Transfiguration)
And yet, what fate has kept apart in life now lives on, transfigured, in death: the gates to their union are open. Isolde, dying atop Tristan's body, perceives the blessed fulfillment of her burning desire: eternal union in measureless space, no bounds, no fetters, indivisible! —

Die Meistersinger von Nürnberg: Preludes to Acts 1 and 3
Prelude to Act 1, Concert of December 2, 1863
Prelude to Act 3 (Letter of Early July [?] 1868 to Judith Gautier)

Shortly before the Vienna concert with Karl Tausig featuring the short notes to the Tristan *Prelude and "Transfiguration," Wagner conducted the recently completed Prelude to Act 1 of* Die Meistersinger *in a concert with the private orchestra of Prince Friedrich Wilhelm Konstantin of Hohenzollern-Hechingen at his palace in Löwenberg, near Breslau in Silesia. The following program note to the Prelude was written for this event. The concert also included the two* Tristan *excerpts along with the* Lohengrin *Prelude, the* Tannhäuser *Overture, and the "Ride of the Valkyries." The first performance of the* Meistersinger *Prelude had occurred only about a year earlier (November 1, 1862) at a Leipzig Gewandhaus concert organized by the young New German acolyte, Wendelin Weissheimer. The score of the opera as a whole was still far from complete.*

The Sämtliche Schriften und Dichtungen *also includes among posthumously published program notes to Wagner's works a short description of the instrumental introduction to Act 3 of* Die Meistersinger, *taken from an undated letter to Judith Gautier, apparently written soon after the opera's Munich premiere in June 1868 (and thus a year before she and her husband, Catulle Mendès, visited Wagner at Tribschen: see the memoir by Mendès included in Part II of this volume). This is the first letter to be addressed by Wagner to Judith, who became an intimate friend of his later years, although their personal encounters were of limited duration. Gautier had sent Wagner a collection of her essays, the contents of which prompted him to observe that she was as yet unfamiliar with* Die Meistersinger.[50] *"The introduction to the third act," he writes, "made a particularly strong impact on our audiences; just recently my barber remarked to me that this piece moved him more than anything else, reminding me how difficult it is to appreciate properly the instincts of the people."*

Prelude to Act 1

The mastersingers process in full festival regalia before the people of Nuremberg; they carry with them the *Leges Tabulaturae*, the archaic poetic code whose laws they so carefully preserve, even while the true spirit has long been forgotten.[51] A banner bearing the image of King David playing the harp is held proudly aloft, followed by that singular figure of the people, Hans Sachs. His own songs greet him from the mouths of the populace.

From amid the crowd we hear a sigh of love. This sigh is addressed to the fair young daughter of one of the masters; she has been designated as the prize for a song contest. She too is decked out in festive finery, though she glances with timid longing toward her beloved: he has achieved the status of poet, but not yet that of mastersinger. He makes his way through the crowd; with glance and voice he conveys to the object of his desire that old love song of ever-renewed youth. —Eager young apprentices to the masters come between them, carrying out their orders with childish assiduity and interrupting the communion of the two lovers; noisy confusion ensues among the crowd. Hans Sachs, who has wisely perceived that song of love, jumps up to assist the young singer, yielding his place at the head of the procession of masters, close to the beloved daughter. The people greet the masters volubly. The love song rings out in the strains of genuine master song: poetry and pedantry are happily reconciled. All cry out vigorously: "Hail to Hans Sachs!"

Prelude to Act 3

The first motive of the string instruments here has already been antici-pated in the third strophe of the cobbler's song in Act 2. There it expressed the bitter lament of a resigned man, who nonetheless showed to the world a cheerful, energetic mien. Eva had understood this disguised lament, and it pierced her heart so deeply that she wished to flee the spot, merely in order to escape this seemingly so jolly song. Now, in the Prelude to the third act, the motive is isolated and newly evolved so as to die away with a feeling of resignation. Yet at the same moment the horns, as if from a dis-tance, intone a solemn chorale theme, the song with which Hans Sachs greeted Luther and the Reformation, and which won for him an incom-parable popularity. After the first strophe of that song the strings take up—very delicately, in hesitating motion—individual details of the actual cobbler's song, as if Sachs were turning away from his handiwork for a moment to look upward and lose himself in pleasant daydreams. The horns then recommence the master's hymn melody in greater amplitude, the same hymn with which the assembled population of Nuremberg will greet Hans Sachs upon his arrival at the festival in a great, thunderous unison acclamation. Now the opening string motive returns, with the feeling of a soul deeply moved; calm and settled, it achieves the exalted sense of good cheer that may follow from the achievement of a mild, beatific resignation.

Götterdämmerung
Vienna Concerts of March 1875

In the early 1870s Wagner was several times in Vienna again, hoping to raise funds for the Bayreuth Festival while at the same time scouting for vocal talent he might draw upon for that great enterprise. He had been cautious about releasing material from the Ring of the Nibelung *cycle prior to the festival that would constitute its official unveiling, where every detail was to be carefully supervised by the Master himself. He would not allow his publisher, Schott, to disseminate excerpts from the* Ring *dramas, for example, although he had been programming a few of these on his own concerts since the early 1860s, in Vienna and elsewhere. In the Vienna con-cert of March 1, 1875, the audience was granted a preview of the final* Ring *drama,* Götterdämmerung, *the full score of which had only been completed the previous November. The notes provided for these four excerpts consist mainly of the relevant stage directions and cues for the libretto text of the excerpts included (except for the Prologue, which was presented without text and continued through the "Rhine Journey" music that forms the transition to Act 1).*

I. Prologue

(For the purposes of presenting the orchestral-symphonic portion of this dramatic pro-logue it was necessary to implement some cuts in accordance with the suppression of the vocal parts, which would not make sense outside the context of an actual stage production.[52] Since the imagination of the listener must now be called upon to supplement the scenic directions which cannot otherwise be realized here, the fol-lowing description is offered by way of an explanatory program to the present excerpts; it is meant to suggest the action something in the manner of a pantomime.)

Nocturnal scene upon a rocky mountainside. The three Norns weave the rope of destiny and pass it among themselves: — it breaks; — the Norns wrap the broken ends of this rope about themselves and sink down. — Early dawn, and daybreak. — With the rising sun Siegfried and Brünnhilde appear, Siegfried bearing the arms of the Valkyrie, who also gives him her horse, since he is about to embark in search of new deeds. Ardent vows, oaths of fidelity: a hero's farewell. — Siegfried leads his horse down the mountain-side, Brünnhilde calls joyously after him until he suddenly disappears from view, as if behind an outcropping, and she can only follow him by the sound of his horn from the valley depths. But then she spies him again, as he boldly forges ahead into the distance; overcome, she waves once more to him. He passes through the fire protecting the mountain; the bright tones of his horn seem to set the flames dancing merrily about him as he proceeds on his way. Reaching the Rhine he is welcomed by the Rhine Maidens, who regard him as their champion and savior and who speed him safely on his way. They accompany him as far as the court of the Gibichungs, where he will meet his destiny through Hagen, the heir to the Nibelung's ring.

II. Hagen's Watch

(This excerpt from the first act begins with the departure of Siegfried and Gunther for Brünnhilde's rock. Gutrune gazes raptly after Siegfried as he hurries off, then she turns with high feelings to go to her chamber. Siegfried grasps the oars of the skiff and rows vigorously as he and Gunther make their way upstream, where soon they disappear from view. — Hagen, left to oversee the Hall of the Gibichungs, has sat down comfortably with spear and shield before him; during the following excerpt he leans, motionless, on a post of the entryway.)

HAGEN:

Hier sitz' ich zur Wacht,	Here I sit and keep watch,
wahre den Hof, . . . (bis)	guarding the hall, . . . (up to)

ihr dient ihm doch,	You serve him, though,
des Niblungen Sohn! —	the Nibelung's son! —

(A tapestry conceals the stage from the audience. An orchestral entr'acte provides a transition to the next scene, in which we see Brünnhilde at the entrance to her cave dwelling atop the mountain, gazing upon Siegfried's ring with sweetly melancholy remembrances—the ring that is the cause of all of the tragedy yet to come.)

III. Siegfried's Death

(This excerpt from the third act begins with the flight of Wotan's ravens at the end of Siegfried's narration concerning the adventure that brought him to Brünnhilde. The orchestra accompanies the events which are here to be imagined pantomimically in the listener's mind, according to the following stage directions.)

Two ravens fly up from the underbrush, circle over Siegfried, and fly off. Siegfried starts up and looks at the ravens, turning his back to Hagen. Hagen plunges his spear into Siegfried's back. With two hands Siegfried raises his shield high above him, intending to crush Hagen with it. However, his strength fails him, the shield falls from his hands. He himself crashes to the ground, upon the shield. Hagen points to the fallen hero, signifying that he has merely exacted the vengeance due him for Siegfried's perjury. With that, he calmly turns aside and strides slowly away up the neighboring hill. Gunther is passionately moved, and leans down to Siegfried's side. The vassals range themselves about the slain man, as Siegfried opens his bright eyes one last time, and utters in a solemn voice:

SIEGFRIED:

Brünnhilde —	Brünnhilde —
Heilige Braut — usw.	holiest bride — etc.

(He dies. — Long silence, all deeply moved. — The vassals lift the body upon the shield to accompany it slowly in solemn mourning over the mountain. This last action is accompanied by the orchestra in the manner of a tragic chorus,[53] at once celebrating and mourning the origins, the glory, and the sad fate of the hero, praised now as a figure of divinity.)

IV. Conclusion of the Final Act

(This excerpt likewise begins in the middle of an energetic action. In his struggle to gain the Nibelung's ring Hagen has slain Gunther and now reaches for the hand of the dead Siegfried while crying out: "That ring is for me!"—at which Siegfried's hand

clenches into a fist, threateningly raised aloft. General horror and outcries, during which Brünnhilde strides forward, with firm and solemn step, from the back of the stage.)

BRÜNNHILDE:

Schweigt eures Jammers	Quit all your noisy,
jauchzenden Schwall!	puling laments!
Das ihr alle verrietet,	She whom all have betrayed,
zur Rache schreitet sein Weib. —	his wife, comes to avenge him. —

She turns with solemn dignity toward the men and women standing about her.

Starke Scheite	Great timbers
schichtet mir dort	pile up for me there
am Rande des Rheins zu Hauf': usw.	on the banks of the Rhine: etc.

During the following passage the younger men erect a mighty funeral pyre close to the banks of the Rhine; the women adorn it with shrouds, which they then strew with herbs and flowers.

BRÜNNHILDE (lost in contemplation of the corpse, her features are gradually transfigured by calmer emotions):

Wie Sonne lauter	Pure as the sun
Strahlt sich sein Licht: (usw. bis)	his light shines forth: (etc., up to)
Ruhe, Ruhe du Gott! —	Rest now, rest, you god!

She gestures to the men that they should raise Siegfried's body and carry it to the pyre; at the same time she takes the ring from Siegfried's finger, regarding it during the next passage, and finally puts it on her own hand.

Mein Erbe nun	My inheritance
Nehm' ich zu eigen (usw.)	I claim as my own (etc.)

She turns toward the back of the stage, where Siegfried's body now lies outstretched upon the scaffolding; from one of the men she takes a burning torch.

Fliegt heim, ihr Raben!	Fly home, you ravens!
Raunt es eurem Herrn, (usw. bis)	Tell your master, (etc., up to)
So—werf' ich den Brand	So—I heave the torch

In Walhalls prangende Burg.	that will reach unto proud Valhalla.

She thrusts the torch into the pyre, which immediately ignites. Two ravens fly up from the riverbank and disappear toward the background. Two young men have led her horse onto the scene. Brünnhilde takes it, and quickly loosens its bridle.

Grane, mein Roß,	Grane, my steed,
Sei mir gegrüßt! (usw. bis)	well met! (etc., up to)
Siegfried! Siegfried!	Siegfried! Siegfried!
Selig gilt dir mein Gruß!	Receive now my blessing!

She has vigorously mounted the steed, and jumps it into the burning pyre. At that moment the flames rise up higher until the fire covers the whole area before the hall, and seems to begin engulfing that as well. Then suddenly the flames die down so that only a dark, smoldering cloud remains hovering over the site; this cloud rises and dissipates as the Rhine begins to overflow its bed, flooding the site of the fire and washing up to the edge of the hall. The three Rhine Maidens appear on the cresting flood. Upon seeing them Hagen is seized with a terrible fright and throws himself into the flooding waters as if crazed, crying out: "Stay back from the ring!" Woglinde and Wellgunde wrap their arms about his neck and, swimming back, they draw him into the depths, while Flosshilde, ahead of them, holds the ring aloft in jubilation. — In the sky a bright light breaks out at a great distance, something like the North Star; gradually one can perceive amid this light the hall of Valhalla, the gods ranged about it as if sitting in judgment. A mighty flame suddenly obscures the whole scene, and the curtain falls.

Die Walküre
Excerpts Performed for Ludwig II, December 11, 1869

The notes accompanying Siegmund's "Spring Song," the "Ride of the Valkyries," and "Wotan's Farewell and Magic Fire Music" from Die Walküre *programmed on a private "grand musical performance" (*große Musikaufführung*) for King Ludwig on December 11, 1869, in contrast to those for the later Vienna concerts presented above, omit the libretto text and offer more extended narrative paraphrases of the episodes in question. Details from both sets of notes can be instructively compared to the published librettos and scores.*

I. Siegmund's Love Song

Siegmund, pursued by overpowering foes and on the point of exhaustion, has found his way to Hunding's dwelling, where the young wife, Sieglinde, has refreshed and cared for him.[54] Soon the two begin to share mutual, unspoken intimations. Siegmund had a twin sister he was separated from in earliest childhood; throughout his wild and lonely youth he had never encountered anything or anyone who spoke to him with a sense of intimate, familiar kinship. Sieglinde was likewise torn from her home at a tender age; scarcely had she reached maturity than she was given in marriage to a dark and ill-tempered man. The encounter with Siegmund awakens in her the sense of inner kinship that she, too, has longed to feel. To confirm her intuition, she risks seeking out the guest during the night. He is overwhelmed to discover her by his side, and he draws her close. With a crash the door to the room bursts wide open; alarmed, Sieglinde pulls herself free and cries:

Ha, wer ging? wer kam herein? usw.   Ha, who goes there? Who
                                                    entered? etc.

II. The Ride of the Valkyries

The scene represents the peak of a rocky mountainside. Dark strips of cloud scud by the cliffs, as if chased by the storm, illuminated now and then by flashes of lightning. A Valkyrie on horseback comes into view; across her saddle hangs a slain warrior. More Valkyries appear on the scene in similar manner, greeting one another from near and far with wild, exuberant cries. At last they are all assembled on the peak of this place which the sagas later named Brünnnhilde's rock; they put their flying steeds to pasture and take mutual stock of their quarry. This quarry consists of the corpses of heroes slain in battle, those chosen by the Valkyries upon the field of battle [55] to be led, afterward, to Valhalla, where Wotan, the father of battles, will awaken them to new life and where the Valkyries, as wish-maidens, will wait upon them most cordially.

III. Wotan's Farewell and Magic Fire

The Valkyrie Brünnhilde, the wish-maiden dearest to Wotan, was initially charged by him, the god of battles, to grant victory to Siegmund over his foe, Hunding. Afterward, greater considerations forced him to sacrifice his favorite among heroes, and accordingly he retracted the orders he had given the Valkyrie. She, however, moved by sublime compassion, dared to protect her charge as she had first been told to do, and as she imagined still to be Wotan's true wish. Angered by this insubordination, Wotan pursues the Valkyrie with intent to punish her. She has sought refuge from the oncoming god of battles on the aforementioned Valkyrie's rock. He discovers her there and demands that the band of sister Valkyries desist from protecting her; she throws herself at his feet to receive her punishment. She is to be placed in a deep sleep, alone here upon the mountaintop, so that whichever man should first discover her may awaken her and take her as his wife. Incensed by the shame to which this would expose her, the Valkyrie seeks to wrest from the god a promise that she should never be won in this manner by just any boastful coward. He refuses to concern himself any further with her destiny. In desperation she falls to her knees, embracing his, and implores him with heartrending laments not to dishonor *himself* in this way, by thus exposing her to such depths of shame—she who was once so dear to him. At the least he might protect the defenseless sleeping maiden with some deterrent terror: let him bid a fire spring up, surrounding the rock with its flickering flames, let the burning tongue of these flames dismay the timid should they think to approach this dreadful cliff. These desperate pleas warm Wotan's heart to fulsome love for his dearest child; he draws her close to him and looks into her eyes, deeply moved. He kisses each of her eyes, which thereupon close in sleep; she sinks back into his arms in gentle quiescence. He leads her tenderly to a nearby mossy tuft. One last time he regards her features, then closes her helmet firmly over her face. His gaze lingers sadly upon her figure, which he finally covers with the Valkyrie's own tall steel shield. He strides away, but then turns again; approaching a rocky outcropping with noble resolution, he touches the rock with the point of his spear.

Parsifal: Prelude to Act 1
Private Performance for Ludwig II, November 12, 1880

The following paraphrase of the Parsifal *Prelude was written for a private performance of the Prelude for Ludwig II in Munich on November 12, 1880, when the composer had only recently embarked on the full orchestral score of the whole opera.*[56] *This note evokes the passages from the Act 1 Grail scene referenced in the music of the Prelude: the Eucharistic presentation of the Grail and Amfortas's tormented reaction to the ceremony. The latter is given a similar, but more extensive poetic gloss by Edouard Dujardin in the "modern paraphrase" of Wagner's character, published in the first volume of* Revue wagnérienne *(translated with two other articles from that journal in Part IV of this volume.) Wagner's note loosely suggests the thematic and structural design of the Prelude; the question mark after the word* Hope *at the head of the note perhaps reflects the harmonically open-ended nature of the music in its operatic context, where it evanescently floats into the upper reaches of the strings while outlining a dominant seventh sonority.*

"Love — Faith: — Hope?"[57]

First theme: "Love"

"Take this, my body; take this, my blood, for the sake of our love!" (Repeated by angelic voices, floating away.)

"Take this, my blood; take this, my body, in remembrance of me." (Likewise repeated, floating away.)[58]

Second theme: "Faith"

The prophecy of redemption through faith. Faith proclaims itself, strong and sound, willingly strengthened through suffering. — This prophecy is renewed and answered by faith, which descends from the delicate heights as on the wings of a white dove, drawing toward itself the hearts of humankind, ever wider and fuller, infusing all nature with a mighty power, and then regarding the celestial ether with soft serenity. There arises once more, from out of shuddering loneliness, the lament of loving sympathy: fear, the sacred perspiring anxiety of the Mount of Olives, the divine sufferings of Golgotha—the body is pale, the blood flows forth and glows with a blessed heavenly radiance in the chalice, showering the rapturous grace of salvation through love upon everything that lives and suffers. This prepares our view of Amfortas: with the sinner's terrible remorse in his heart, he must face the divinely admonishing sight of the Grail—he who is himself the sinning keeper of the Grail. Will the gnawing torments of his soul find redemption? Once more we hear the prophecy, and—we hope!

NOTES

1. James Treadwell, "The Urge to Communicate: The Prose Writings as Theory and Practice," in *The Cambridge Companion to Wagner*, ed. Thomas S. Grey (Cambridge, 2008), 181.

2. See, for example, Carl Dahlhaus, *The Idea of Absolute Music*, trans. Roger Lustig (Chicago and London, 1989), 18–19. Before Dahlhaus (original German edition 1978), Wagner's apparent coinage of the term had been pointed out by Klaus Kropfinger, *Wagner und Beethoven* (Regensburg, 1975), 33.

3. At almost the exact moment Wagner drafted his program notes for the Ninth, the music critic Julius Wend wrote of "pure instrumental music as the actual center of musical expression, as the absolute form of music as such, freed from any heterogeneous

elements" ("die *reine Instrumentalmusik* als das eigentliche *Centrum* der musikalischen Ausdrucksweise, als die *absolute Form* in der Tonkunst als solche—abgelöst von jedem heterogene Elemente") in an article on the aesthetics of modern music prompted by the example of Berlioz: "Berlioz und die moderne Symphonie: Ein Beitrag zu einer Philosophie der Musik," *Wiener allgemeine Musik-Zeitung* 6/40 (2 April 1846): 157. Ten years earlier the Berlin critic Ludwig Rellstab had written, in the unlikely context of a notice about a "characteristic rondo" by Charles Haslinger titled "Le voyage sur le Rhin," of "absolute musical" talent (". . . es muß auch eine Funke absoluten musikalischen Talents in ihm keimen") in *Iris im Gebiet der Tonkunst* 7 (1836): 55.

4. The text given here is from *Gesammelte Schriften und Dichtungen*, 10 vols. (Leipzig, 1887–1911) (henceforth *GSD*), 2:56–64; it has been excerpted from "Bericht über die Aufführung der neunten Symphonie von Beethoven im Jahre 1846 in Dresden, nebst Programm dazu," *GSD*, 2:50–64.

5. That is, Goethe's major work, the epic-dramatic poem *Faust*. The subsequent program is structured around quotations from *Faust* that Wagner finds illustrative or suggestive of the moods, feelings, and "poetic content" of the symphony, as he understands these.

6. Wagner's word *Tondichtung* (musical poem) anticipates the vocabulary of his later programmatic commentaries, particularly that to Beethoven's *Coriolan* Overture, as well as Hans von Bülow's commentary on Wagner's own *Faust* Overture.

7. Goethe, *Faust*, Part 1, l. 1549 ("Faust's Study").

8. Ibid., ll. 1554–65.

9. This and subsequent translations of the lines quoted from Goethe's *Faust* are taken from the 1870 verse translation by Bayard Taylor, as published in the Modern Library edition (New York, 1912). The translations of Schiller's ode "An die Freude" (To joy) are by the present translator and editor.

10. Wagner slightly reorders the lines quoted here. The first two are emended from three lines of Goethe's original: "Du hörest ja, von Freud' ist nicht mehr die Rede. / Dem Taumel weih' ich mich, dem schmerzlichsten Genuß, / Verliebtem Haß, erquickendem Verdruß" (*Faust*, Part 1, ll. 1765–67; "Faust's Study"). The following lines: "Laß in den Tiefen der Sinnlichkeit/ Uns glühende Leidenschaften stillen!" etc. occur just before that (*Faust*, Part I, ll. 1750–59).

11. Goethe, *Faust*, Part 1, ll. 2162–64; "Auerbach's Cellar." Wagner omits the fourth line that completes both the rhyme scheme, the poetic figure, and the sentence; it is inserted here.

12. That is, in the Trio, as described in this same section of the program.

13. Goethe, *Faust*, Part 1, ll. 771–74; "Night."

14. Ibid., ll. 775–78.

15. Ibid., ll. 762–64.

16. Ibid., ll. 783–84.

17. Wagner's word *Erhebung* might also be construed as "elevation" or "uplift."

18. Wagner again conflates lines from different places in the text: The first two, "Aber ach! . . . aus dem Busen quillen!" are lines 1210–11 from Part 1, "Faust's Study"; the following six are lines 454–59 ("Night"), though Wagner somewhat oddly paraphrases the first (well-known) of these, which reads in the original: "Welch Schauspiel! Aber ach, ein Schauspiel nur!"—Faust's response to the signs of the "Microcosmos" he has conjured from his books of magic. The translation given here reflects the original.

19. Here Wagner's original phrase is *musikalische Dichtung* (as compared to *Tondichtung* above). In either case, the terminology, especially as applied to Beethoven's Ninth, points toward the vocabulary of the New German School and Liszt's coinage "symphonic poem" for the characteristic instrumental genre of that school.

20. *Gesangsthema*, literally, "song theme." This term was often applied as a generic-formal rubric for the second theme of a sonata form, regarded by this time in the nineteenth century as typically lyrical, in contrast to the more forceful motivic-rhythmic character considered appropriate to first themes.

21. Goethe, *Faust*, Part 2, ll. 11575–76.

22. Ernest Newman, *The Life of Richard Wagner*, 4 vols. (New York, 1933–47; repr. Cambridge and New York, 1976), 2:178. Eventually Wagner did agree to productions of *Der fliegende Holländer* and *Tannhäuser* at the Aktientheater in Zurich, in April–May 1852 and February–March 1855, respectively. For more details on the Zurich concerts, see also Max Fehr, *Richard Wagners Schweizer Zeit*, 2 vols. (Aarau, 1934), 1:73–98, 129–51, 215–43; as well as the entries by Uri Fischer (on the Allgemeine Musik-Gesellschaft and the Aktientheater) and Eva Martina Hanke (on Wagner's orchestral programs with the Musik-Gesellschaft) in the exhibit catalog *Das Kunstwerk der Zukunft: Richard Wagner und Zürich, 1849–1858*, ed. Laurenz Lütteken and Eva Martina Hanke (Zurich, 2008), 53–61 and 63–65.

23. The Beethoven program notes were first printed by Brendel in the *Neue Zeitschrift für Musik* in the issues of 15 October 1852 (*Eroica*), 5 November 1852 (*Coriolan*); the note for *Tannhäuser* appeared in the issue of 14 January 1853.

24. This translation is based on the text as reprinted in *GSD*, 5:169–72.

25. The list of complementary and contrasting affects Wagner hears so fully commingled in this movement is, in the original German, audibly informed by the idea of alliterative verse or *Stabreim* that preoccupied him in Part 3 of *Opera and Drama*, completed around the same time as the first set of orchestral concerts in Zurich for which the *Eroica* program was drafted: "Wonne und Wehe, Lust und Leid, Anmut und Wehmut, Sinnen und Sehnen, Schmachten und Schwelgen, Kühnheit, Trotz und ein unbändiges Selbstgefühl" (*GSD*, 5:170). In particular, the first two pairs in this series recall the lines with which Wagner sought to illustrate the concept of a "poetic-musical period" in Part 3: "Die Liebe bringt Lust und Leid" and, subsequently, "Doch in ihr Weh auch webt sie Wonnen" (*GSD*, 4:152, 153). Wagner alludes to the same affective-verbal pairing again toward the end of the present note when he writes: "The love-filled breast swells out, the breast whose rapture [*Wonne*] does not exclude sorrow [*Weh*], just as rapture and sorrow, as purely human feelings, are ultimately one and the same."

26. Wagner to Hans von Bülow, letter of 15 February 1852, in *Selected Letters of Richard Wagner*, trans. and ed. Stewart Spencer and Barry Millington (New York, 1988), 245.

27. Text given here was first published in *Neue Zeitschrift für Musik*, 5 November 1852, and reprinted in *GSD*, 5:173–76.

28. Following this short introductory paragraph, Wagner divides his program note into two long paragraphs, the first outlining the subject of Coriolanus and his enforced conflict with fatherland and family, the second describing Beethoven's composition of the subject. These two paragraphs (particularly the second) are broken up by a series of dashes. The format is maintained in this translation, since it appears to be Wagner's purpose to represent in this way the continuity of the musical "narrative" within his text.

29. Wagner was perhaps aware that Beethoven's overture was written for the 1804 neoclassical tragedy *Coriolan* by the Viennese dramatist Heinrich Josef von Collin (1771–1811), yet the confrontation between Caius Martius Coriolanus and his family is most likely being recalled here with reference to Shakespeare's *Coriolanus* (Act 5, scene 3). His generalized account here could equally well be derived from the common source for both dramas in Plutarch's *Lives of the Noble Grecians and Romans*.

30. Throughout the program note Wagner continues to refer to the characters generically as *Mann* and *Weib*. The German terms allow him to suggest at one and the same time a generalized "male" and "female" principle (as in the foregoing characterization of the fundamental principles of "dance" and dance forms) and the specific roles of husband and wife. Since both Coriolanus's wife, Virgilia, and especially his mother, Volumnia, are implicated in the confrontation identified here as the subject of Beethoven's overture, Wagner makes use of the semantic fluidity of the German words *Mann* and *Weib*, meaning either "husband and wife" or "man and woman." To that end, he avoids the possessive forms *ihr Mann* or *sein Weib* that would point specifically to the meanings "husband" and "wife."

31. Newman, *Life of Richard Wagner*, 2:179.

32. Richard Wagner, letter of 26 February 1852, in *Sämtliche Briefe*, ed. Gertrud Strobel, Werner Wolf et al. (Leipzig, 1967–), 4:298.

33. Ibid., letter of 20 March 1852, 319. See also Newman, *Life of Richard Wagner,* 2:179. Wagner refers in this letter to the remarkable *Wirkungssymptome* or "effective symptoms" produced by his music, anticipating a significant trend of later critical discourse on his music dramas concerned with the psychic and even physical "pathology" of their effects. From the beginning, *Tannhäuser* played a central role in this discourse.

34. Text from *GSD*, 5:177–79.

35. The originally continuous text of this note has been broken into separate paragraphs according to the articulating dashes in the text corresponding to implied divisions of introduction—Allegro/exposition—development—recapitulation—coda.

36. Text from *GSD*, 5:176–77.

37. As with the program notes to Beethoven's *Coriolan* Overture and Wagner's own *Tannhäuser* Overture, Wagner gives his account of the musical "narrative" of the *Holländer* Overture in one continuous paragraph, articulated by dashes. Because the principal articulating dashes (following the introductory paragraph) clearly correspond to the principal musical divisions of exposition—development—coda in the overture, this text has been broken into three paragraphs.

38. Wagner's original phrase, "in wilder Männertaten-Gier," would mean more literally "in men's wild impulse toward deeds."

39. Text from *GSD*, 5:179–81.

40. See Wagner's letter to Franz Liszt of 30 May 1853. Wagner, *Sämtliche Briefe*, 5:304.

41. Text from *Sämtliche Schriften und Dichtungen*, 16 vols. (Leipzig, 1911–16), 16:167–69 (henceforth *SSD*).

42. As in the libretto, Wagner avoids specific references to the Pope (or St. Peter's), which would have created problems with the censors in much of 1840s Europe.

43. This translation is based on the text as given in *SSD*, 16:170.

44. See also Fehr, *Richard Wagners Schweizer Zeit*, 1:253–57.

45. Text from *SSD*, 12:350.

46. See Robert Bailey, ed., *Wagner: Prelude and Transfiguration from "Tristan und Isolde"* (New York, 1985), 28. The present translation is based on the text from *SSD*, 12:346–47.

47. Wagner's original phrase here "im lang gegliederten Zuge" has a singular predicate (*Zug*, a line or trajectory), while the adjectival phrase modifying it (literally, "broadly articulated") suggests the idea of multiple segments or subdivisions.

48. Liszt's piano arrangement of the "Transfiguration" transferred the name *Liebestod* to this concluding portion of the opera, by which name it has long since been known. On Liszt's arrangement, see Kenneth Hamilton's essay in this volume.

49. The translation here is based on the text as given in *SSD*, 12:347–48.

50. Richard Wagner, *Die Briefe Richard Wagners an Judith Gautier*, ed. Willi Schuh (Zurich and Leipzig, 1936), 103. The letter, like the rest of Wagner's correspondence with Gautier, was originally written in his "wretched French" (as he apologized to her), but is given in Schuh's edition in German translations by Paul Amann. It differs only in minor details from the translation of the letter excerpt in *SSD*, 12:348–49.

51. Text first printed in the *Bayreuther Blätter* 8 (1885): 291; and 25 (1902): 168; reprinted in *SSD*, 12:347–49.

52. This translation is based on the text as given in *SSD*, 16:173–75.

53. In the original, "in der Weise eines Trauerchores," which could be construed either as "in the manner of a mourning chorus" or "of a tragic chorus" (i.e., the chorus of ancient Greek tragedy).

54. This translation is based on the text as given in *SSD*, 16:171–72.

55. *Wallstatt*, a word whose prefix (signifying those slain in battle) relates it to *Walküre* as well as to *Walhalla*.

56. *König Ludwig II. und Richard Wagner: Briefwechsel*, ed. Otto Strobel, 4 vols. (Karlsruhe, 1936), 3:186–87.

57. Text first printed in the *Bayreuther Blätter* 8 (1885): 291; this translation is based on the text as given in *SSD,* 12:349.

58. The quoted lines are from the Grail scene of Act 1 of *Parsifal,* whose accompanying stage directions are included in somewhat altered, simplified form. In *Parsifal,* following Titurel's injunction to reveal the Grail ("Enthüllet den Gral!") a version of the Christian Eucharist is reenacted by the Grail knights.

INDEX

Index

Page numbers followed by n indicate notes; italicized page numbers indicate material in tables, figures, or musical examples.

Index to Wagner's Works

MUSICAL WORKS

Centennial March (Grand Festival March for the Opening of the Centennial Commemorative of the Declaration of Independence of the United States of America), 238, 243

Faust Overture, 32, 50–51, 62n46, n51, 517n6

Feen, Die, 23, 65, 75

Fliegende Holländer, Der, 3–7, 9, 12, 20, 23n2, 24n13, 25n23, 65, 66, 71, 75, 79, 204, 220, 221, 235n4, 309n30, 337, 350, 456–58, 468n2, 479, 501, 518n22, 519n37; Liszt's transcriptions of, 40–41; Overture to, 479, 490, 496, 501, 519n37; program notes on, 498–99, 519n37

Götterdämmerung, 8, 23, 29, 65, 76, 96, 158, 160, 161, 165, 189n24, 399, 400, 402, 404, 412, 413, 416–17, 474n74, 475n81; Heintz's transcription of, *140;* program notes on, 509–13; see also *Ring des Nibelungen*

Kaisermarsch, 115

Kapitulation, Eine (libretto), 88, 90–117, 119n16, 120n18, n23, 121n32, 235n7

Liebesverbot, Das, oder die Novize von Palermo, 65, 75, 121n35, 204

Lohengrin, 8, 9, 11, 34, 63n57, 65, 72, 84, 145, 193n66, 224n, 229n50, 252, 254, 270–73, 297, 304–5, 307n5, 309n30, 312, 321, 331n15, 347, 350, 366, 370n31, 410, 447, 468n2, 475n83; Liszt's transcriptions of, 35–36, 39, 40, 53, 61n23; Prelude to, 372, 375, 479, 490–91, 507; program notes on, 499–501, 504

Meistersinger von Nürnberg, Die, 11, 13, 21, 34, 41, 60n9, 65–66, 71–74, 76, 78–79, 124, 154, 155, 165, 184, 189n20, 193n66, 410, 417, 425n20, 442, 445, 468n2, 472n52; program notes on, 507–9

Parsifal, 4, 8, 14, 15, 20, 21, 42, 63n54, 65, 66, 71, 72, 76, 136, 146, 154, 170, 176, 179, 182, 188n17, 193n66, 194n79, 234, 237–39, 241, 242, 246, 377, 384, 411, 420–23, 426–34, 437, 439n, 440–42, 445, 447, 448, 452–55, 458–59, 465, 466, 468n2, 469n9, 471n40, n42, n45, 473n53, n59, n61, 474n74, 475n83, 520n58; Prelude to, 51–53, 479; program notes on, 515–16

Rheingold, Das, 13, 16, 17, 56, 65, 96, 143, 146, 149n4, 398, 400, 412–16, 418, 419, 424n12, 456–58, 460–65, 470n18, 473n64, 474n81, 475n82; see also *Ring des Nibelungen*

Rienzi, 3, 4, 8, 23n2, 65, 75, 79, 84, 144, 146–47, 186, 201, 204, 220, 221, 229n48, 336, 498; Liszt's transcriptions, 36, 40, 60n18

Ring des Nibelungen, Der, 4, 11, 13–22, *19, 34,* 63n54, 65, 71, 76, 90, 96, 133, *134,* 135–36, *137,* 139, 141, 144, 155, 156, 160, 161, 164, 170, 193n66, n68, 240, 242–43, 245, 373, 392–95, 399, 402, 404, 407n29, 411–20, 424n9, 435, 439n, 442, 445, 455–57, 461, 464, 466, 468n2, 469n9, 472n50, n52, 473n53, n61, n63, 474n74, 509; see also *Götterdämmerung; Rheingold; Siegfried; Walküre*

Siegfried, 8, 16, 45, 51, 58, 65, 72, 76, 79, 88, 165, 402, 412, 413, 415, 419, 474n81, 475n88; see also *Ring des Nibelungen*

Siegfried Idyll, 88, 105

Tannhäuser, 7–9, 11, 21, 25n24, 61n23, 65, 72, 73, 84, 88, 145, 167, 193n66, 204, 207, 221, 222–24, 229n50, 230, 231, 234, 236n12, n14, 271, 300–305, 307n5, 309n30, 347–72, 410, 447, 466–68, 468n2, 506, 518n22, n23, 519n33; Liszt's transcriptions of, 36–37, 39–40, 60n18; Overture to, 37, 377–80, 60n18, 166, 251–68, 270, 272–300, 309n31, 375, 379, 490, 507, 519n37; program notes on, 496–98, 501–3

• 523 •

NOTES ON THE CONTRIBUTORS

Notes on the Contributors

Karol Berger is the Osgood Hooker Professor in Fine Arts in the Department of Music, Stanford University. His most recent book, *Bach's Cycle, Mozart's Arrow: An Essay on the Origins of Musical Modernity* (2007; paperback 2008) received the 2008 Marjorie Weston Emerson Award of the Mozart Society of America. An earlier book, *A Theory of Art* (2000; paperback 2002), appeared recently in a Polish translation.

Leon Botstein is president and Leon Levy Professor in the Arts of Bard College. He is the author of *Judentum und Modernität* (1991) and *Jefferson's Children: Education and the Promise of American Culture* (1997). He is the editor of *The Compleat Brahms* (1999) and the *Musical Quarterly*, as well as the coeditor, with Werner Hanak, of *Vienna: Jews and the City of Music, 1870–1938* (2004). The music director of the American and the Jerusalem symphony orchestras, he has recorded works by, among others, Szymanowski, Hartmann, Bruch, Toch, Dohnányi, Bruckner, Chausson, Richard Strauss, Mendelssohn, Popov, Shostakovich, and Liszt for Telarc, CRI, Koch, Arabesque, and New World Records.

David Breckbill holds a PhD in musicology from the University of California, Berkeley and studies music making as preserved on and perceived through recordings. He has contributed to *Wagner in Performance* (1992), *The Wagner Compendium* (1992), and the Cambridge Opera Handbook *Richard Wagner: "Der fliegende Holländer"* (2000). His reviews of recordings have appeared in the *BBC Music Magazine*, the *Wagner Journal*, and the *ARSC Journal*. He has participated in panels and symposia on recording and performance sponsored by the IMS, the AMS, ARSC, CHARM, and Stanford University. In 1996 he was an Edison Fellow at the British Library. Based in Nebraska, he teaches music history at Doane College and is active as a collaborative pianist.

Mary A. Cicora holds a BA in literature from Yale University and an MA and PhD in German literature with a minor in musicology from Cornell University. Her research interest is literature and music, and in particular, Richard Wagner. She has published extensively in the scholarly journals on the interrelationship between Wagner's works and the German literary tradition as represented by such diverse writers as Thomas Mann, Günter Grass, Ingeborg Bachmann, and Friedrich Nietzsche. Her numerous book publications deal with such aspects of Wagner's works as interpretation, influence, and reception.

James Deaville is associate professor of music in the School for Studies in Art and Culture, Carleton University, Ottawa. He has lectured and published on Wagner, Mahler, Strauss, Reger, Liszt and his circle in Weimar, music criticism, music and gender, television and film music, and music and race. He is coeditor and cotranslator, with George Fricke, of *Wagner in Rehearsal, 1875–1876: The Diaries of Richard Fricke* (1998) and is author of the essay "Publishing Paraphrases and Creating Collectors: Friedrich Hofmeister, Franz Liszt, and the Technology of Popularity" in *Liszt and His World* (2006).

Annegret Fauser is professor of music at the University of North Carolina at Chapel Hill. Her publications include books on orchestral songs in France (1994), Wagner reception (1999), and Jules Massenet's opera *Esclarmonde* (2001). In 2005, she published the monograph *Musical Encounters at the 1889 Paris World's Fair*. Currently she is editing the correspondence between Nadia Boulanger and Aaron Copland and writing a monograph on music in the United States during World War II.

Lydia Goehr is professor of philosophy at Columbia University. She is the author of *The Imaginary Museum of Musical Works: An Essay in the Philosophy of Music*; *The Quest for Voice: Music, Politics, and the Limits of Philosophy* (essays on Richard Wagner); *Elective Affinities: Musical Essays on the History of Aesthetic Theory* (essays on Adorno and Arthur Danto); and coeditor with Daniel Herwitz of *The Don Giovanni Moment: Essays on the Legacy of an Opera*.

Thomas S. Grey is professor of music at Stanford University. He is the author of *Wagner's Musical Prose: Texts and Contexts* (1995), and editor of the Cambridge Opera Handbook *Richard Wagner: "Der fliegende Holländer"* (2000) and *The Cambridge Companion to Wagner* (2008). Other publications involve the music of Beethoven and Mendelssohn, Eduard Hanslick and the history of musical criticism, opera, and the intersections of music and visual culture in the nineteenth century.

Kenneth Hamilton is a member of the music department of Birmingham University, UK. He has performed worldwide as a concert-pianist, and has published extensively on nineteenth-century music. His latest book is *After the Golden Age: Romantic Pianism and Modern Performance* (2008).

Steven Huebner is James McGill Professor of Musicology at McGill University. He has written extensively on French and Italian music of the nineteenth and early twentieth centuries, including recent essays on the sources of *Madama Butterfly*, Ravel's operas, and Beethoven reception at the fin de siècle.

Brendan King is a freelance writer, reviewer, and translator with a special interest in late-nineteenth-century French fiction. His PhD dissertation investigates the life and work of Joris-Karl Huysmans, and his translations of Huysmans' writings (*Là-Bas, Croquis parisiens*) were published in 2001 and 2004. He lives on the Isle of Wight.

Charlotte Mandell has translated over thirty books from the French, including work by Blanchot, Genet, Proust, and Flaubert. Two recent music-related translations are *Listening* by Jean-Luc Nancy and *Listen: A History of Our Ears* by Peter Szendy, both published by Fordham University Press. Her most recent translation is *The Kindly Ones* by Jonathan Littell.

Katherine Syer is assistant professor of musicology at the University of Illinois at Urbana-Champaign. She is coeditor, together with William Kinderman, of *A Companion to Wagner's 'Parsifal'* (2005) and author of the volume's chapter on production history. She is a regular contributor to the *Wagner Journal* and is currently working on a book on the production history of Wagner's *Ring* with a focus on productions of the last thirty years.

Christian Thorau is professor of music theory at the Hochschule für Musik und Darstellende Kunst in Frankfurt, Germany. His research concerns the intersection of music theory, history of theory, semiotics, aesthetics, and cultural history. His 2003 monograph, *Semantisierte Sinnlichkeit,* investigates the reception of the Wagnerian "leitmotif" concept as a theory of musical signs and as evidence for the history of listening. In 2008–9 he was a fellow at the National Humanities Center in Raleigh-Durham, NC, with a project entitled "Guided Listening and the Touristic Gaze: The Emergence of 'Musical Baedekers.'"

David Trippett is completing his PhD dissertation, "Wagner's Melodies," at Harvard University, and will shortly take up a Junior Research Fellowship at Christ's College, Cambridge University. In addition to the music of Wagner, the range of his scholarly interests is reflected by research articles on Franz Liszt in *19th-Century Music,* on modernist media and temporality in *Journal of Musicology,* and on Rudolf Kolisch's theory of performance in *Musiktheorie.* He is also a collaborative pianist and conductor; recordings of his playing can be heard at his website, www.davidtrippett.com.

Nicholas Vazsonyi, associate professor of German and comparative literature at the University of South Carolina, has written extensively on issues of German identity and music in the eighteenth and nineteenth centuries. His book *Lukács Reads Goethe* (1997) was followed by two edited volumes,

Searching for Common Ground: Diskurse zur deutschen Identität 1750–1871 (2000) and *Wagner's "Meistersinger": Performance, History, Representation* (2003). His current book, *Richard Wagner: Self-Promotion and the Making of a Brand,* is forthcoming with Cambridge University Press.